Heaven and Earth
in the Gospel of Matthew

Heaven and Earth
in the Gospel of Matthew

Jonathan T. Pennington

a division of Baker Publishing Group
www.BakerAcademic.com

© 2007 by Koninklijke Brill NV, Leiden, The Netherlands

Published in 2009 by Baker Academic
a division of Baker Publishing Group
P.O. Box 6287, Grand Rapids, MI 49516-6287
www.bakeracademic.com

Originally published in 2007 in Leiden, The Netherlands, by Koninklijke Brill NV

Printed in the United States of America

All rights reserved. No part of this publication may be reproduced, stored in a retrieval system, or transmitted in any form or by any means—for example, electronic, photocopy, recording—without the prior written permission of the publisher. The only exception is brief quotations in printed reviews.

Library of Congress Cataloging-in-Publication Data is on file at the Library of Congress, Washington, DC

ISBN 978-0-8010-3728-3

I dedicate this work with much gratitude to the many family and friends who gave generously so that I might pursue an academic ministry, including the people of the Evangelical Free Church of Mount Morris, Illinois, and especially the Tom Shaw family.

CONTENTS

Preface ix
Acknowledgments xi
Abbreviations xiii

Introduction 1

Part One

Clearing Ground and Building Anew

Chapter One   Challenging the Circumlocution
  Assumption 13
Chapter Two   A Survey of Heaven in the Old Testament
  and Second Temple Literature 39
Chapter Three   A Survey of Heaven in Matthew 67
Chapter Four   Heaven and Earth in the Context of
  Matthean Studies and Theology 77

Part Two

Matthew's Idiolectic Use of Heaven Language and the Theme of Heaven and Earth

Chapter Five   Οὐρανός and Οὐρανοί in the Septuagint and
  Second Temple Literature 99
Chapter Six   Οὐρανός and Οὐρανοί in Matthew 125
Chapter Seven   Heaven and Earth in the Old Testament and
  Second Temple Literature 163
Chapter Eight   Heaven and Earth in Matthew 193
Chapter Nine   God as Father in the Old Testament and
  Second Temple Literature 217
Chapter Ten   The Father in Heaven in Matthew 231
Chapter Eleven   The Kingdom of God in the Old
  Testament and Second Temple Literature 253
Chapter Twelve   Matthew's "Kingdom of Heaven" 279

Conclusion Heaven and Earth in the Gospel of Matthew	331
Appendix Data from a Synoptic Comparison of Οὐρανός	349
Bibliography	353
Index of Texts	377
Index of Modern Authors	395

PREFACE

A much-overlooked aspect of the Gospel of Matthew is the theme of heaven and earth. A close examination of Matthew reveals that this theme is woven deeply and skillfully throughout the First Gospel and interacts with several other theological emphases there. The language of heaven and earth appears repeatedly throughout Matthew and is highlighted in crucial passages such as the Beatitudes, the Lord's Prayer, the ecclesiological passages (16:13–20; 18:18–20), and the Great Commission. Rather than being a reverential circumlocution for God as is typically assumed, "heaven" in Matthew is part of a highly developed discourse of heaven and earth language. Matthew has developed an idiolectic way of using heaven language that consists of four aspects: 1) an intentional distinction in meaning between the singular and plural forms of οὐρανός 2) the frequent use of the heaven and earth word pair as a theme; 3) regular reference to the Father in heaven/heavenly Father; and 4) the recurrent use of the uniquely Matthean expression, ἡ βασιλεία τῶν οὐρανῶν, "kingdom of heaven." After providing a detailed examination of the historical precedents for each of these elements as well as their outworking in Matthew, this book argues that Matthew's four-fold idiolect serves one overriding theological purpose: to highlight the tension that currently exists between heaven and earth or God and humanity, while looking forward to its eschatological resolution. Matthew's emphasis on the current tension between heaven and earth functions as one of the more important themes in the First Gospel, and it makes several theological, pastoral and polemical points in his first-century context.

ACKNOWLEDGMENTS

This book is a revised version of my PhD thesis submitted to and accepted by the faculty of St Mary's College at the University of St Andrews, Scotland, July 2005. I am grateful to the editors of the *Novum Testamentum Supplement Series* for accepting this volume into their series. Thanks are also due to George and Jill Carraway for their excellent work in proof-reading and preparation of the indexes. Any remaining errors are mine. A small portion of two different chapters here are revisions and rearrangements of arguments made earlier in my articles, "'Heaven' and 'Heavens' in the LXX: Exploring the Relationship Between שָׁמַיִם and Οὐρανός," *Bulletin of the International Organization for Septuagint and Cognate Studies* 36 (2003): 39–59, and "Dualism in OT Cosmology: *Weltbild* and *Weltanschauung*," *Scandinavian Journal of the Old Testament*, 18/2 (2004): 260–277. Permission has been obtained by the publishers for their use here.

The original idea that Matthew may have used singular and plural forms of "heaven" with different meanings first occurred to me while teaching Greek at Trinity Evangelical Divinity School in Deerfield, Illinois. Many years later it has now developed into this. I am very grateful for the excellent education and mentorship I received at Trinity, especially from Dr Robert W. Yarbrough and Professor D. A. Carson. I am also thankful for Professor Carson's original recommendation that I go to St Andrews to study with Richard Bauckham.

My time in St Andrews consisted of two very different kinds of education. On the one hand, the supervision of my PhD research was ably conducted at different times by both Professor Richard Bauckham and Professor Philip Esler. Professor Bauckham's insightful comments, especially in his final read of my completed thesis, helped patch up several potential leaks in the hull of the thesis. Professor Esler graciously took over my supervision from the middle period until the end, guiding me through the defense process. His encouragement, enthusiasm, and keen eye for structure and argument greatly shaped the form and flow of the entire project from beginning to end. His perceptive challenges always came at just the right time to improve my ongoing research. Rather than being a mere substitute supervisor in Professor Bauckham's absence, Professor Esler gave generously of his time and skills to my great benefit. To both of these academic mentors I say thank you.

My "other" education at St Andrews came from the countless hours of stimulating conversation and mental wrestling that occurred among our group of postgraduates that comprised the Scripture and Theology seminar led by Professor Christopher Seitz, as well as our own subgroup that we affectionately termed the CTRG. I cannot imagine a better assembly of colleagues and friends than these. These rich times in St Andrews will always be cherished as golden years.

I would be remiss if I did not conclude by acknowledging with love and affection my wife, Tracy, and our cornucopia of children. All of this would have been impossible and empty without them. The psalmist spoke truth when he sang: "Like arrows in the hand of a warrior are the sons of one's youth. Happy is the man who has his quiver full of them!...Blessed is every one who fears the LORD, who walks in his ways! You shall eat the fruit of the labor of your hands; you shall be happy, and it shall be well with you. Your wife will be like a fruitful vine within your house; your children will be like olive shoots around your table. Lo, thus shall the man be blessed who fears the LORD." (Psalm 127:4–128:4)

March 2007

ABBREVIATIONS

The works below on Matthew are cited regularly throughout this work and thus will be referenced only in the abbreviated form given here. Abbreviations for all other reference works as well as for the titles of journals follow the standards as found in *The SBL Handbook of Style*. For all other references, the first occurrence of the item anywhere in the work will be given in its full form. All subsequent references (including in later chapters) will be given only in abbreviated form.

ABBREVIATION	FULL CITATION
Albright and Mann, *Matthew*	Albright, W. F., and C. S. Mann. *Matthew: Introduction, Translation, and Notes*. The Anchor Bible. Garden City, New York: Doubleday & Company, 1971.
Allen, *Matthew*	Allen, W. C. *A Critical and Exegetical Commentary on the Gospel According to S. Matthew*. 3d ed, *International Critical Commentary*. Edinburgh: T&T Clark, 1912.
Beare, *Matthew*	Beare, Francis Wright. *The Gospel According to Matthew: A Commentary*. Oxford: Basil Blackwell, 1981.
Betz, *Sermon on the Mount*	Betz, Hans Dieter. *The Sermon on the Mount: A Commentary on the Sermon on the Mount, including the Sermon on the Plain (Matthew 5:3–7:27 and Luke 6:20–49)*. Hermeneia. Minneapolis: Augsburg Fortress, 1995.
Carson, *Matthew*	Carson, D. A. *Matthew. The Expositor's Bible Commentary, Vol. 8*. Grand Rapids: Zondervan, 1984.
Davies and Allison, *Matthew*	Davies, W. D., and Dale C. Allison. *A Critical and Exegetical Commentary on the Gospel According to St. Matthew. International Critical Commentary*. Edinburgh: T&T Clark. 3 vols.: Vol. 1, Matthew 1–7

	(1988); Vol. 2, Matthew 8–18 (1991); Vol. 3, Matthew 19–28 (1997).
France, *Matthew*	France, R. T. *The Gospel According to Matthew: An Introduction and Commentary.* The Tyndale New Testament Commentaries. Grand Rapids: Eerdmans, 1985.
France, *Matthew: Evangelist and Teacher*	France, R. T. *Matthew: Evangelist and Teacher.* Downers Grove, Ill.: InterVarsity Press, 1989.
Gundry, *Matthew*	Gundry, Robert H. *Matthew: A Commentary on His Literary and Theological Art.* Grand Rapids: Eerdmans, 1982.
Gundry, *Matthew*[2]	Gundry, Robert H. *Matthew: A Commentary on His Handbook for a Mixed Church under Persecution.* 2d ed. Grand Rapids: Eerdmans, 1994.
Hagner, *Matthew 1–13*	Hagner, Donald A. *Matthew 1–13.* Word Biblical Commentary 33a. Dallas: Word Books, 1993.
Hagner, *Matthew 14–28*	Hagner, Donald A. *Matthew 14–28.* Word Biblical Commentary 33b. Dallas: Word Books, 1995.
Hill, *Matthew*	Hill, David, *The Gospel of Matthew.* London: Oliphants, 1972.
Luz, *Matthew 1–7*	Luz, Ulrich. *Matthew 1–7: A Commentary.* Translated by Wilhelm C. Linss. Minneapolis: Augsburg, 1989.
Luz, *Matthew 8–20*	Luz, Ulrich. *Matthew 8–20: A Commentary.* Hermeneia. Translated by James E. Crouch. Minneapolis: Augsburg Fortress, 2001.
McNeile, *Matthew*	McNeile, Alan Hugh. *The Gospel According to St. Matthew.* London: MacMillan and Co., 1915.
Morris, *Matthew*	Morris, Leon. *The Gospel According to Matthew. The Pillar New Testament Commentary.* Grand Rapids: Eerdmans, 1992.

Nolland, *Matthew*	Nolland, John. *The Gospel of Matthew. The New International Greek Testament Commentary*. Grand Rapids: Eerdmans, 2005.
Plummer, *Matthew*	Plummer, Alfred. *An Exegetical Commentary on the Gospel According to S. Matthew*. London: Robert Scott, 1928.
Riches, *Matthew*	Riches, John. *Matthew. New Testament Guides*. Sheffield: Sheffield Academic Press, 1997.
Schnackenburg, *Matthew*	Schnackenburg, Rudolf. *The Gospel of Matthew*. Translated by Robert R. Barr. Grand Rapids: Eerdmans, 2002.
Stanton, *Gospel for a New People*	Stanton, Graham N. *A Gospel for a New People: Studies in Matthew*. Louisville, Ky.: Westminster/John Knox Press, 1993.

INTRODUCTION

The Gospel of Matthew has been the pride of the church throughout most of her history.¹ It was only in the wake of higher critical studies on the origins of the Gospels that Matthew began to have a rival for preeminence in Mark. But when reading the Gospels in their long-standing canonical order, it is easy to understand why Matthew has been so beloved and so important. Herein we sense a great fulcrum point of the epochs: flavors and scents of the Old Testament mingle with the new wine of the eschatological Messiah and his coming kingdom. From the mysterious Babylonian magi at the beginning to the memorable mountaintop commission at the end, Matthew presents a richly painted story, ripe with literary allusions (looking backwards) and bold teachings (looking forward). Additionally, some of the most important and succinct elements of the Christian faith and liturgy stem directly from Matthew: the Lord's Prayer, the Beatitudes, the Great Commission, and scores of parables about life in God's kingdom.

The Gospel of Matthew is such a rich literary and theological work that we should not be surprised that students of the New Testament continue to bring forth from Matthew "treasures old and new." A literary work of such a high caliber as Matthew can develop and maintain many important themes simultaneously.² Some of the more important theological emphases which have been identified include: the fulfillment of OT prophecy; the righteousness of God; the kingdom of God/heaven; discipleship; the Son of Man; and the relationship of Gentiles and Jews as the people of God in salvation-history. Yet no single theme can be said to encompass all the intentions, purposes, and nuances found in the First Gospel. There is another topic, hitherto only hinted at in

---

[1] See especially Édouard Massaux, *The Influence of the Gospel of Saint Matthew on Christian Literature before Saint Irenaeus* (ed. and trans. Norman J. Belval, Suzanne Hecht, and Arthur J. Bellinzoni; 3 vols.; Macon: Mercer University Press, 1990). The predominance of Matthew in the early church that Massaux demonstrates continues unabated in the subsequent centuries.

[2] In Dale Allison's insightful reflections on hermeneutics, he observes how odd it is to ask what *the* meaning of Matthew is because "works of literature are inevitably constituted by a complexity of meanings." Dale C. Allison, Jr., *The New Moses: A Matthean Typology* (Edinburgh: T&T Clark, 1993), 3.

Matthean scholarship, which deserves a full-length treatment, namely *the literary and theological motif of heaven and earth*. This theme constitutes one important thread in the Matthean fabric and can be analyzed by itself to shed light on Matthew's purpose and effects. Yet, like each of the many themes in Matthew, it does not stand alone, but interacts with and informs the rest of the theology of the book.

THE DATA

The language of heaven is peppered generously throughout Matthew. Matthew uses forms of οὐρανός a total of 82 times, making up over 30% of the total uses of οὐρανός in the NT. This is more frequent than any other NT work, including a full thirty more occurrences of heaven than in Revelation, a book whose contents are more apparently related to the subject. Matthew's recurrent use of the language of heaven is particularly striking when measured against the other Gospels. Matthew's 82 occurrences make it clear that the theme is far more important for the First Gospel than for Mark (18x), Luke (35x), or John (18x).

Heaven moves within a wide semantic domain in Matthew, even as it does in the OT and other Jewish literature. We learn in Matthew that God is the Father in heaven (5:16; 6:1; 16:17; 18:19; et al.) and his throne is there (5:34; 23:22). Heaven is whence the Spirit of God descends (3:16) and the voice of God speaks (3:17). It is also the place of promised rewards (5:12; 6:20; 19:21) and the realm of the existence of the angels (18:10; 22:30; 24:36; 28:2). In addition to these "spiritual" uses, οὐρανός can also refer to the created order of the sky and atmosphere. Jesus will appear on the clouds of heaven, i.e., the (eschatological) sky (24:30; 26:64), the color of the face of the heavens reveals the weather (16:2–3), and birds are regularly referred to as τὰ πετεινὰ τοῦ οὐρανοῦ (6:26; 8:20; 13:32).

In many ways, Matthew's use of heaven lines up with the Jewish literary tradition, both in the OT and Second Temple literature. However, there are many occurrences of heaven in Matthew that are unique to his Gospel or quite rare: 32 times we encounter the expression ἡ βασιλεία τῶν οὐρανῶν (kingdom of heaven), and an additional 20 times God is referred to as ὁ πατὴρ ὁ ἐν τοῖς οὐρανοῖς (Father in heaven, 13x) or the related ὁ πατὴρ ὁ οὐράνιος (heavenly Father, 7x). Kingdom of heaven is found nowhere else in the OT, NT or any preceding Second Temple literature. Similar phrases appear occasionally in the Apocrypha, but kingdom of heaven is found only in literature which postdates Matthew. And even these occurrences are quite infrequent (e.g., twice in the Mishnah and three times in the Gospel of Thomas).[3] References to a heavenly Father are not unique to Matthew, but his recurrent use of the term stands out, especially relative to the other NT documents. These two important uses of heaven language in Matthew highlight the centrality of the theme in his record of the life and teachings of Jesus.

There is another way that Matthew's employment of heaven language stands out: Matthew prefers the otherwise uncommon plural forms of οὐρανός over the singular by two to one (55 plural, 27 singular). While at first glance this may appear normal in light of the unvarying plurality of the Semitic words for heaven (Hebrew שָׁמַיִם, Aramaic שְׁמַיִן), in fact, plural οὐρανοί is quite exceptional, even in the Septuagint (less than 9% of the total occurrences of οὐρανός). In the predominance of the singular forms, the LXX aligns very closely with the Greek of antiquity. In fact, outside of the LXX, one is hard-pressed to find more than a handful of plural forms of οὐρανός in all of Classical or secular Hellenistic Greek well into the Christian era. It is not until the writings of the New Testament that plural forms of οὐρανός appear alongside the singular with any frequency. Yet, even there they remain in the minority. Only about one-third of the occurrences of οὐρανός in the NT are plural (90 of 273). But even this percentage is a little misleading. Fifty-five of these ninety occurrences are found in Matthew alone (61%). Thus, apart from Matthew, the NT is very much like the LXX: plural forms occur only about 13% of the time. This analysis highlights the uniqueness of Matthew in this regard. In sharp contrast to the LXX and the NT, Matthew shows a great inclination to use plural οὐρανοί.

The frequent use of heaven in Matthew finds focus in one particular usage: the theme of heaven and earth. In fact, each of the uses of heaven just described also overlaps with the heaven and earth motif. In the OT, the phrase "heaven and earth" occurs frequently, and as a merism, is the regular way of referring to the created, visible universe.

---

[3] In the Patristic literature kingdom of heaven can be found with some frequency, but this likely reflects the influence of Matthew on this generation of theologians.

"Heaven and earth" can also be used in a contrastive sense, demarcating heaven as the place of God's dwelling versus earth as the realm of humanity. In the whole of Scripture, the pairing of heaven and earth occurs well over 200 times, being found in various genres throughout. But in the NT, it is in Matthew particularly that this stock phrase occurs more often than anywhere else. There are more than a dozen explicit conjunctions of heaven and earth in the First Gospel, in addition to several pairings where the sense is the same though an alternative word is used for "earth." There are also many thematic "heavenly versus earthly" contrasts throughout Matthew. In comparison, Mark has only two instances of the heaven and earth pair and Luke four. Matthew is also the only Evangelist to use the expression, ἐν (τῷ) οὐρανῷ... ἐπὶ (τῆς) γῆς, which occurs in several very important contexts in Matthew. These recurrent and varied ways of combining heaven and earth in Matthew show in part how this motif serves as a key theme. Even more strongly, analysis reveals that some of the most important parts of Matthew's narrative (including the Sermon the Mount, the Lord's Prayer, the Olivet Discourse, and the Great Commission) are full of heaven language and the heaven and earth theme.

The Contemporary Consensus

Despite the data presented above, Matthean scholarship has paid very little attention to the language of heaven or the theme of heaven and earth. The only use of heaven that receives regular mention is the uniquely Matthean idiom, ἡ βασιλεία τῶν οὐρανῶν. But generally only brief comment is given. Almost without exception, kingdom of heaven is explained away as a mere circumlocution on the part of the Evangelist to avoid saying the name of God. This explanation is given by nearly every commentator, both erudite and popular. It is not surprising that reference works of all kinds follow the same line of thinking as the commentators. The argument in the case of Matthew is typically made in this way: A comparison of Matthew's "kingdom of heaven" with Mark and Luke's "kingdom of God" reveals that the two have the same referent. Therefore, the apparently "Jewish" Matthew must have inserted kingdom of heaven for the occurrences of kingdom of God found in his sources, being motivated by a shared Jewish aversion to the name of God. Therefore, heaven is simply a circumlocution to avoid the name of God. There have been a few scholars who also postulate some *additional* reason for the use of kingdom of heaven,[4] and an even smaller number who express disagreement with the explanation.[5] But overall, this understanding of kingdom of heaven as a reverential circumlocution stands as a widespread assumption.

Though less often than comments on kingdom of heaven, we do also find some scholarly discussion of why Matthew uses the plural forms of οὐρανός so often. Like the explanations of kingdom of heaven, there is a nearly-universal and simple account given: plural οὐρανοί reflects the Semitic words behind heaven (Hebrew שָׁמַיִם, Aramaic שְׁמַיִן) which always occur in the plural. One regularly finds comments that Matthew's frequent use of the plurals is "in accordance with the Semitic idiom."[6] Again, this understanding is found throughout the commentaries as well as in standard dictionary and grammar discussions of οὐρανός. Occasionally scholars will suggest that plural οὐρανοί reflects a belief in multiple heavens, but few follow this line.

In neither the case of kingdom of heaven nor plural οὐρανοί has Matthean scholarship observed that these are but two instances of the broader discourse of heaven language throughout the Gospel. Additionally, few have discerned that this discourse of heaven language is itself a part of the widespread theme of heaven and earth. Regarding this theme almost no one has made more than a passing mention. One exception is Gerhard Schneider's article, "'Im Himmel—auf Erden': eine Perspektive matthäischer Theologie."[7] In this seminal piece, Schneider catalogs the various uses of heaven in Matthew and observes the uniqueness of the heaven and earth theme to Matthew. He suggests that the "in heaven—on earth" scheme is a key idea. But this short article is *only* seminal and far from comprehensive. It focuses on compiling the raw data with a mere paragraph or two of comment on each usage, followed by a very brief synthesis at the end.

---

[4] For example, E. Schweizer, L. Morris, D. A. Carson, R. Gundry, J. Marcus and A. H. McNeile.

[5] Particularly, D. Garland, K. Clark, R. Foster, and R. Guelich, whose views will be examined in the next chapter.

[6] Beare, *Matthew*, 356. Almost verbatim is Davies and Allison, *Matthew*, 1:328.

[7] Gerhard Schneider, "'Im Himmel—auf Erden': eine Perspektive matthäischer Theologie," in *Studien zum Matthäusevangelium: Festschrift für Wilhelm Pesch* (ed. Ludger Schenke; Stuttgart: Katholisches Bibelwerk, 1998): 285–297. On the theme in the Rabbinic materials, treatment can be found in Beate Ego, *Im Himmel wie auf Erden. Studien zum Verhältnis von himmlischer und irdischer Welt im rabbinischen Judentum* (Tübingen: Mohr Siebeck, 1989).

Several issues are left untreated, and the impact of the article is suggestive more than conclusive. In a 1990 article, Kari Syreeni picked up Schneider's observation about heaven and earth as distinct realities in Matthew, and tried to trace the theme of polarization and mediation in Matthew and his community.[8] Syreeni's discussion focused on the construct of Matthew's "symbolic universe" and how this was communicated to the Matthean community. However, this article covers even less ground than Schneider's in exploring heaven and earth as a theological theme in Matthew.

Besides these treatments, only occasional observations about the recurrence of heaven and earth can be found in the commentaries,[9] but no one develops this idea. A full treatment of the language of heaven and the theme of heaven and earth in Matthew is needed for this important subject to become more than an occasional footnote or passing comment. And such it deserves.[10]

The Thesis

The thesis propounded in this work is that by focusing on the patterns of Matthew's use of heaven and the heaven and earth motif we will discover a key theme—woven skillfully into his Gospel throughout its entirety—that pays rich exegetical and theological dividends for our understanding of the First Gospel. Through the failure to recognize the centrality of heaven language and the heaven and earth theme, the interpretation of Matthew has been partially impoverished.

A detailed study of the Jewish literary context reveals that Matthew has drawn on semi-developed concepts in his heritage to create an idiolectic[11] way of using the language of heaven. This idiolectic usage

---

[8] Kari Syreeni, "Between Heaven and Earth: On the Structure of Matthew's Symbolic Universe," *JSNT* 40 (1990): 3–13.

[9] For example, Gundry, *Matthew*, 595; Schnackenburg, *Matthew*, 67.

[10] Robert Foster suggests that "the landscape of Matthean studies is thirsty for fresh inquiry into the rhetorical and sociological impact of the recurrent use of KH [kingdom of heaven] in this gospel." Foster offers a brief essay on this phrase, but much more can be said on this expression as well as how it fits into the broader heaven and earth theme. Robert Foster, "Why on Earth Use 'Kingdom of Heaven'?: Matthew's Terminology Revisited," *NTS* 48 (2002): 487–499, at 487.

[11] In *After Babel: Aspects of Language and Translation* (3d ed.; New York: Oxford University Press, 1998), 47, George Steiner observes that no two human beings ever use words and syntax in exactly the same way. Instead, "each living person draws, deliberately

consists of four aspects: 1) an intentional distinction in meaning between the singular and plural forms of οὐρανός; 2) the frequent use of the heaven and earth word-pair as a theme; 3) regular reference to the Father in heaven; and 4) the recurrent use of the uniquely Matthean expression, ἡ βασιλεία τῶν οὐρανῶν. Each of these uses of οὐρανός is developed by Matthew in such a way that they emphasize a very important theological point: the tension that currently exists between heaven and earth, between God's realm and ways and humanity's, especially as it relates to God's kingdom ("the kingdom of heaven") versus humanity's kingdoms. This tension will be resolved at the eschaton—in the new genesis (παλιγγενεσία, 19:28)—that has been inaugurated through the life, death, and resurrection of Jesus Christ. In fact, only by recognizing the intensity of the tension that currently exists between heaven and earth can we fully appreciate the significance of the eschaton in which the kingdom of heaven will come to earth (6:9–10).

My contention is not only that this theme of heaven and earth has been unduly overlooked in Matthew, but also that many of the standard explanations concerning heaven language in Matthew are wrong. In the case of heaven as a reverential circumlocution, I will argue that despite the widespread acceptance of this view, it rests on very thin historical evidence. This notion apparently stems from but a singular modern source (Gustaf Dalman) and is teeming with methodological flaws. A close analysis of the literature in question reveals that there is very little reason to believe that there was a clear pattern of using heaven to avoid the name of God in Jesus' day, nor that this was motivating Matthew's usage. Attention to the frequent and varied uses of heaven in Matthew reveals that there is much more at work in his usage than the circumlocution explanation would have us believe.

Dalman's influence on the scholarly understanding of βασιλεία likewise proves unfounded for Matthew. Dalman spearheaded the view that βασιλεία always means "rule" or "reign" and not a territorial kingdom. In Matthew, however, close attention to the phrase ἡ βασιλεία τῶν οὐρανῶν and other heaven language in Matthew reveals that the qualifying genitive reference to heaven indicates that a spatial understanding *is* central to Matthew's usage, even though this does not preclude a connotation of reign as well.

---

or in immediate habit, on two sources of linguistic supply: the current vulgate corresponding to his level of literacy, and a private thesaurus.... They form what linguists call an 'idiolect.'"

The typical scholarly explanation that plural οὐρανοί in Matthew is merely the result of the plurality of the Semitic words for heaven likewise proves quite mistaken. Examination of the use of οὐρανός throughout the Septuagint and other Second Temple Greek literature will show that plural οὐρανοί did not come about as a result of Semitic morphology. Moreover, Matthew develops a unique usage of the singular and plural forms of οὐρανός: the singular is used to refer to the visible realm (and in the heaven and earth pairs), and the plural refers to the invisible and divine. This special Matthean practice serves as part of his broader goal of presenting two separate and competing realms: heaven and earth.

Research into Matthew's Jewish literary context reveals that both the OT and the Second Temple literature pave the way for Matthew's more extended use of heaven. Along with the OT's rich and varied employment of heaven and heaven and earth, Daniel 2–7 in particular stands out as significant for Matthew's treatment. In this portion of Daniel (demarcated by its Aramaic form) the concepts of heaven versus earth and the kingdom of God are juxtaposed in the narrative. This juxtaposition is picked up and developed by Matthew and likely explains his use of the phrase ἡ βασιλεία τῶν οὐρανῶν. Both the OT and the non-canonical apocalyptic literature also prove important for Matthew: the dualistic worldview found in much of the OT as well as the dualistic substructure of books like *1 Enoch* is manifested in Matthew through the repeated refrain of heaven and earth. In this way, the worldview of Matthew could be described as apocalyptic,[12] though it should be noted that the later apocalyptic speculations about the multiple layers of heaven are not evidenced in Matthew. Instead, closer correspondence is found with the OT traditions (including Gen 1–2) and the earlier strand of apocalyptic thought which focuses on the heaven and earth contrast rather than the multi-layered inventory of the mystical vision traditions.

So, rather than ignoring the heaven language in Matthew or explaining it away as mere circumlocution or Semitic linguistic evidence, we

---

[12] I use this term here in the basic sense of referring to a worldview that emphasizes an otherworldly and transcendent reality revealed by God. See, for example, the definition of the apocalyptic genre in John J. Collins, ed., *Apocalypse: The Morphology of a Genre*, Semeia 14 (Missoula: Scholars Press, 1979), 9. A fuller discussion of what apocalyptic entails will be found in Chapter Four below.

must see the centrality and significance of the heaven and earth theme. Once we have done so, we can see that the use of this theme serves several theological and pastoral purposes for the Evangelist:

- to emphasize the universality of God's dominion (cf. allusions to Dan 3:31–4:34). In the same way that Second Temple Jews emphasized their God's superiority with the expression "God of heaven," Matthew uses heaven language in reference to God to highlight the universal reign of the God and Father of Jesus.
- to shade Matthew's entire discourse with an Old Testament flavor, especially that of creation (heaven and earth), highlighting the importance of Genesis and Daniel.
- to thematically lock together several of the most important theological emphases in Matthew, such as Christology, Kingdom, Fatherhood of God, Ecclesiology, and Eschatology.
- to legitimate Matthew's readers as the true people of God and encourage them with this reality. Jesus' disciples, according to Matthew, are a heavenly people in that they alone have a kingdom that is from heaven and a Father who is in heaven. The people of God are defined by Jesus as the ones who "do the will of my Father who is in heaven" (7:21; 12:50). There is also a profound connection between the creation of heaven and earth and the creation of the true people of God.
- to undergird the radical nature of Jesus' teachings by providing a symbolic universe based on the tension between the two poles of heaven and earth and encouraging Jesus' disciples to align themselves with the kingdom and Father in heaven while awaiting the eschaton.
- to critique all earthly/human empires, most notably the ever-present Roman Empire, as well as to critique Jewish expectations for a Davidic kingdom which was Israel-specific and failed to grasp the prophetic vision of universal Gentile inclusion. All the while, this critique of earthly kingdoms and ways looks forward to the eschaton when God's heavenly kingdom will come to earth through Jesus Christ (6:9–10; 28:18–20).

Outline of the Argument

This volume is broken into two major parts. Part One is titled "Clearing Ground and Building Anew." The first chapter is an extensive argument against the current prevailing understanding of heaven as a reverential circumlocution in both the Second Temple literature and in Matthew. Chapters Two and Three provide a general survey of the use of heaven in the OT, Second Temple literature, and Matthew. Chapter Four reviews some of the key issues in the scholarly interpretation of Matthew and shows how the heaven and earth theme informs and interacts with each of these. These four chapters provide a necessary introduction to the main argument in Part Two. Part Two is titled "Matthew's Idiolectic Use of Heaven Language and the Theme of Heaven and Earth," and is comprised of eight chapters. In these chapters I will examine the four elements of Matthew's idiolectic use of heaven: 1) an intentional distinction in meaning between the singular and plural forms of οὐρανός; 2) the frequent use of the heaven and earth word pair as a theme; 3) regular reference to the Father in heaven/heavenly Father; and 4) the recurrent use of the uniquely Matthean expression, ἡ βασιλεία τῶν οὐρανῶν, "kingdom of heaven." The chapters in Part Two are paired together such that each of the four elements is first traced through the preceding literature in a diachronic fashion, followed by an examination of this topic in Matthew specifically. Throughout this entire section, I will seek to show that these four aspects of his idiolectic usage of heaven language are developed to serve a consistent purpose: to emphasize the current tension or contrast between heaven and earth, or God and humanity. Finally, the concluding chapter will discuss the matters of dualism, Matthew's symbolic universe, and the reception-history of kingdom of heaven, in addition to summarizing the findings and offering several overall conclusions.

PART ONE

CLEARING GROUND AND BUILDING ANEW

CHAPTER ONE

CHALLENGING THE CIRCUMLOCUTION ASSUMPTION

Matthew's Heaven as a Reverential Circumlocution

As subsequent chapters will show, heaven in Matthew is both a frequently used term and part of a key literary and theological theme in the First Gospel. However, despite the striking frequency of οὐρανός in Matthew, the topic of heaven language is rarely discussed in Matthean scholarship. This is because when it does arise, heaven is almost universally explained away as a mere circumlocution employed by Matthew to avoid using the name of God. This account is given especially when explicating Matthew's anomalous expression, kingdom of heaven. For example, Albright and Mann describe heaven as a normal Jewish synonym for God, "to save the devout from using even the substitute word *Adonai*."[1] David Hill understands Matthew's kingdom of heaven as equivalent to kingdom of God, "indicating faithfulness to the Aramaic and avoiding the name of God."[2] Similarly, F. W. Beare writes off any difference between kingdom of heaven and kingdom of God by stating that heaven is "simply a circumlocution adopted in Jewish usage to avoid speaking directly of God."[3] T. W. Manson says heaven is a substitute for the divine name, "another touch of Jewish-Christian piety."[4]

These are but representative examples. This explanation is given by the vast majority of commentaries including Davies and Allison, Luz, France, Filson, Plummer, Schnackenburg, Hagner, Schlatter, and Nolland.[5] It is not surprising that reference works follow the same line

---

[1] Albright and Mann, *Matthew*, 49.
[2] Hill, *Matthew*, 90. Here we see the two most common explanations for heaven language in Matthew put together, that of reverence-circumlocution and Semitic influence. On the question of Semitic influence on Greek οὐρανός, see Chapter Four and my arguments in "'Heaven' and 'Heavens' in the LXX: Exploring the Relationship Between שָׁמַיִם and Οὐρανός," *BIOSCS* 36 (2003): 39–59.
[3] Beare, *Matthew*, 33.
[4] T. W. Manson, *The Sayings of Jesus* (Grand Rapids: Eerdmans, 1979), 152.
[5] Nolland's view is not entirely clear. When commenting on 4:17 (*Matthew*, 175–176) he does not speak of "circumlocution" or "avoidance of the divine name," but he does say that the "common" view is correct: that Matthew prefers the "standard Jewish

of thinking as the commentators. The explanation of οὐρανός as a reverential circumlocution is found in many standard dictionary entries under "Heaven," including *TDNT, DJG, NIDNTT, ISBE, New Dictionary of Biblical Theology*, and *The Jewish Encyclopedia*.⁶ In addition to these writings, more popular commentaries as well as a host of articles and books follow their lead, thus giving the impression that circumlocution is the universally accepted explanation.

The argument in the case of Matthew is typically made in this way: A comparison of Matthew's kingdom of heaven with the Synoptics' kingdom of God reveals that the two have the same referent. Therefore, Matthew must have inserted kingdom of heaven for the kingdom of God found in his sources. Why did he do this? In light of the apparent "Jewishness" of Matthew, he must have been motivated by a shared Jewish aversion to using the name of God. Therefore, heaven is simply a circumlocution to avoid the name of God.

While it is true that heaven in Matthew does often refer to God in a metonymic way (thus, kingdom of God and kingdom of heaven have the same referent),⁷ close examination reveals that the original circumlocution argument (from Gustaf Dalman) suffers from a faulty methodology and rationale. The historical arguments given for heaven as a reverential circumlocution in the first century rest on very slim evidence. Moreover, there is a better solution within Matthew's own usage. Nonetheless, as is often the case, the scholarly repetition of the same arguments has created a substantial edifice. This chapter will seek to show the structural weaknesses in this edifice and dismantle it by challenging the common assumption about heaven as a circumlocution. As a result, we will clear the ground for a comprehensive examination of Matthew's frequent use of heaven language.

---

expression 'kingdom of heaven'." It seems he means by this the common circumlocution view.

⁶ Surprisingly, the brief article on heaven in the *ABD* makes no mention of heaven as a circumlocution, but it focuses on OT usage, barely mentioning NT usage, and not Matthew's at all. *BDAG* is somewhat ambiguous: The final major heading is entitled "an indirect reference to God," but reverential circumlocution is not specifically mentioned. Instead, *BDAG* points out that heaven as a reference to God was both a Hebrew and Greek polytheistic practice.

⁷ A few scholars have tried to suggest that kingdom of God and kingdom of heaven in Matthew refer to two different realities. This view proves ill-founded and has not been adopted by many Matthean scholars. See Chapter Twelve below for a discussion and refutation of this idea.

Two Points of Prolegomena

1. *Definitions and the Problem of the Collapsing of Categories*

We must begin with a clarification of terms. "Circumlocution" or "periphrasis" refers to the mode of discourse in which one uses words "which move roundabout their subject rather than announcing it directly."[8] There are a number of reasons why one may speak in a circumlocutionary way: for euphemistic purposes, out of reverence, ironically, or even by mistake. A common circumlocution (of the euphemistic sort) is to speak of someone "passing away" rather than "dying."

Similarly, a speaker or writer may also use the related technique of "metonymy" in which he or she substitutes the name of a thing by the name of an attribute of it, or something closely associated with it.[9] Thus, one might hear that "both the White House and Downing Street criticized the action," with "White House" and "Downing Street" serving metonymically for the U.S. President and the British Prime Minister.

These are standard concepts. Unfortunately, however, when discussing heaven as a circumlocution, there is commonly a confusion or collapsing of categories. Scholars do not only argue that Matthew's use of οὐρανός is a circumlocution in the technical sense as defined above, but they add to it an important narrowing qualifier: that Matthew uses circumlocution *because of a Jewish aversion to speaking the name of God.* Thus, in scholarly discussion, "circumlocution" has been narrowed in meaning to refer only to one, specific kind of circumlocution—the Jewish avoidance of the name of God—a definition which is really only a subset or example of the meaning of the term. A more careful use of language might call this narrower definition, "reverential circumlocution," but in the literature no such distinction is made.[10]

The problem with this narrowing or collapsing of categories is that it disables us from being able to recognize circumlocution at work without

---

[8] Martin Gray, *A Dictionary of Literary Terms* (2d ed.; Essex: Pearson Education Limited, 1992), s.v. circumlocution. These terms are basically synonymous. Biblical scholars discussing Matthew tend to use circumlocution more than periphrasis but they employ them interchangeably.

[9] Gray, *A Dictionary of Literary Terms*, s.v. metonymy.

[10] In the following discussion I will use the fuller expression "reverential circumlocution" for greater clarification.

assuming it is being used particularly to avoid the name of God. In other words, if we have in our minds that "circumlocution" means "a roundabout way of saying something *to avoid the name of God*" (which is really only one kind of circumlocution) then when we see heaven being used instead of God (as in kingdom of heaven for kingdom of God in Matthew), *by definition* we unwittingly assume it to be a reverential circumlocution. But as I will argue below and in subsequent chapters, there are indeed other reasons why Matthew uses heaven rather than God in phrases such as kingdom of heaven. Therefore, we must be more circumspect when using the term circumlocution (such as qualifying it with "reverential") or not use the term at all.

2. *The Surprisingly Singular Source*

Before dealing in depth with the arguments for and against heaven as a reverential circumlocution, we may also note the interesting fact that this widespread view has a surprisingly singular source in the modern period. That source is the well-known late 19th-century scholar Gustaf Dalman. We have already seen that the vast majority of Matthean scholars explain heaven in the First Gospel as merely a reverential circumlocution. A glance at the footnotes in any commentary will reveal that this pervasive idea stems from Dalman's influential volume, *Worte Jesu* (ET: *The Words of Jesus*).[11] Not long after Dalman, the now-famous volumes by Strack and Billerbeck began to appear. These commentaries on the NT are based on rabbinic parallels which are supposed to shed light on our understanding of the meaning of NT expressions. The widespread influence these volumes had on a generation of scholars is matched only by the vehemence with which they were subsequently attacked as idiosyncratic and methodologically mistaken.[12]

Strack and Billerbeck use a very similar approach as did Dalman, and thus it is not surprising to find in their work the same explanation given

---

[11] Gustaf Dalman, *The Words of Jesus* (trans. D. M. Kay; Edinburgh: T&T Clark, 1902).
[12] See the discussion of methodology in Günter Stemberger, *Introduction to the Talmud and Midrash* (2d ed.; trans. Markus Bockmuehl; Edinburgh: T&T Clark, 1996), 45–55. A very helpful and straightforward illumination of the problems of using rabbinic materials in the way that Strack and Billerbeck suggested can be found in Philip Alexander, "Rabbinic Judaism and the New Testament," *ZNW* 74 (1983): 237–246.

for the use of heaven in Matthew, that of reverential circumlocution.[13] In fact, it turns out that this explanation is more than a coincidental occurrence—Dalman is the *only* secondary literature source listed in Strack and Billerbeck for this entire section! Thus, we find again that the fount of this argument is clearly Dalman, as even those Matthean commentators who also quote Strack and Billerbeck are leaning on Dalman's original argument.[14] Even more striking, modern Jewish encyclopedias also rely exclusively on Dalman: In both the *Universal Jewish Encyclopedia* and *The Jewish Encyclopedia* under "Heaven," Dalman is the only bibliographic source given for these articles.

I make these observations here because the assumption of reverential circumlocution in Matthew is so widespread that it seems somewhat suspicious that this theory is based primarily on one man's argument, especially when few contemporary scholars have likely actually read Dalman's work. Of course, Dalman could indeed be correct in his view. But there are sufficient grounds to now go back and revisit and evaluate Dalman's original argument.

Dalman's Argument Outlined

Dalman was rightly recognized in his day as a scholar of great skill and erudition. He produced many works dealing with first-century Palestine and Aramaic. But certainly his most influential book was the one which came into English in 1902 as *The Words of Jesus*. This volume stands in the late-nineteenth and early-twentieth century tradition of a philological and Aramaic approach to Gospel studies.[15] The subtitle of Dalman's work—"considered in the light of post-biblical Jewish writings and the Aramaic language"—reveals two key assumptions behind the work: 1) that discerning the Aramaic prototype of Jesus' words is

---

[13] See Str-B 1:172–185 on Matt 4:17 and 1:862–865 on Matt 21:25.

[14] The same can be said for Hans Bietenhard, whose volume on heaven was an important work in the last generation: *Der himmlische Welt im Urchristentum und Spätjudentum* (Tübingen: J. C. B. Mohr, 1951). In his section entitled "Das Wort 'Himmel' als Ersatzwort für Jahve" (pp. 80–82), Bietenhard depends primarily on Str-B. Note also that Bietenhard was the author of the NT section on οὐρανός in the influential *TDNT*, thus the widespread understanding of heaven as a reverential circumlocution boils down to a single line of thought: Dalman.

[15] See the helpful overview to this tradition in Craig Evans' introduction to the third edition of Matthew Black's *An Aramaic Approach to the Gospels and Acts* (Peabody, Mass.: Hendrickson, 1998), v–xxv.

essential to interpreting them;[16] and 2) that the rabbinic sources' use of words and phrases gives vital information for understanding the NT ideas. Although Dalman does not assume written Aramaic originals for the Gospels (as some would after him), he is convinced that Jesus' teachings were spoken in Aramaic. Therefore, his stated goal is to investigate "in what form the words of Jesus must have been uttered in their original language, and what meaning they had in this form for the Jewish hearers."[17]

Dalman proceeds by discussing fourteen "fundamental ideas" in Jewish literature, including the sovereignty of God, eternal life, son of man, son of God, and son of David. These "fundamental ideas," as found in the Second Temple literature and especially the Rabbinic material, are then used to explain the words of Jesus. Within this discussion, a significant part of the book (chapters V–VIII) deals with the issue of other names being substituted for the sacred name of God, the Tetragrammaton. Dalman observes how the Mishnaic tractates often (though not always) eliminated the divine name or substituted other words for it, such as heaven or "the Holy One."[18] Then working backwards, he argues that this same circumlocution was occurring in Esther, 1 Maccabees and Daniel as well, though he acknowledges this usage is not consistent in all of the literature. The NT references then, especially Matthew, are assumed to provide the connection between the Second Temple literature and the Rabbis.

Chapter VIII, "Evasive or Precautionary Modes of Referring to God," is devoted specifically to the issue at hand. Under this heading, Dalman gives fourteen words or phrases, which, according to him, reveal the development of the evasion of God's name by Jews. Seven of these are tied directly to the word heaven.[19] Under each of these, he lists NT examples followed by rabbinic examples, some of which parallel closely and others less so. He concludes this section by stating that Jesus followed the standard Jewish custom of avoidance of the

---

[16] Cf. the translator's prefatory remarks: "the Greek versions of the Synoptists cannot be finally interpreted without taking due account of the Aramaic prototype," vii.

[17] Dalman, *Words*, 72.

[18] Dalman, *Words*, 194.

[19] The fourteen phrases are: 1) The voice (from heaven); 2) Swearing by heaven; 3) Reward, treasures in heaven; 4) Names written in heaven; 5) Before the angels, before God; 6) Bound, loosed in heaven; 7) Heaven; 8) From heaven; 9) Hosanna in the highest; 10) From on high; 11) Use of the passive voice; 12) Amen; 13) The dwelling (Shechinah), the glory, the word; 14) The place.

name of God, although modifying it "by His marked preference for the appellation of God as Father."[20] He acknowledges that there were some superstitious elements in this practice, but most Jews including Jesus sought to avoid the name of God out of sincere reverence, based on the commandment of the Decalogue (Exodus 20:7).

Therefore, according to Dalman, Matthew's (and Jesus') regular employment of the phrase kingdom of heaven is clearly one of reverential circumlocution. As mentioned above, Strack and Billerbeck followed Dalman's conclusion in their own work, and nearly everyone has followed suit since.

A Four-Fold Response

However, a close examination of Dalman's argument reveals several flaws. What follows is a four-step argument against the assumption of first-century reverential circumlocution.

1. *The Chronology of Creeping Circumlocution*

The first point to make concerns what we might call the chronology of creeping circumlocution. Avoidance of uttering the divine name has a long history in Judaism. "Yahweh" (יהוה) was the special, revealed name of the God of the Jews, however, at some unknown point (but probably at least by the third century BCE), a sacred taboo was placed on pronouncing it as written. The Tetragrammaton occurs over 6800 times in the Hebrew Bible, though, as is well known, the tradition of reading "Adonai" or even "The Name" eventually replaced the pronunciation of the divine name.[21]

Eventually, this reverential attitude spread to scribal practices as well. At Qumran, a number of different techniques were used to avoid writing the Tetragrammaton.[22] We also find in the Septuagint that at

---

[20] Dalman, *Words*, 233.
[21] For a succinct discussion of this development, see Louis Jacobs, *A Jewish Theology* (London: Dartmon, Longman & Todd, 1973), 140–141. More fully explained and well-argued is Ephraim E. Urbach, *The Sages: Their Concepts and Beliefs* (trans. Israel Abrahams; 2 vols.; Jerusalem: Magnes Press, 1975), 1:66–79. An earlier discussion can also be found in Arthur Marmorstein, *The Old Rabbinic Doctrine of God* (London: Oxford University Press, 1927), 1:54–107.
[22] See Donald W. Parry, "Notes on Divine Name Avoidance in Scriptural Units of the Legal Texts of Qumran," in *Legal Texts and Legal Issues* (ed. M. Bernstein, F. Garcia

times κύριος replaced the Tetragrammaton,²³ and some traditions began to shy away from even the generic θεός. In the Rabbinic materials we find mixed rules on the pronunciation of the name. In the Mishnah we find several references to the fact that in the Temple the priests would pronounce the Name as it was written during the priestly blessing, but those in the provinces would not (*m. Soṭah* 7:6; *m. Tamid* 7:2). Similarly, we find that on the day of atonement the high priest would pronounce the "Expressed Name" (*m. Yoma* 6:2; *m. Tamid* 3:8). By the time of the Mishnah (ca. 200–220 CE), of course, the Temple was no longer standing and most Jews likely avoided pronouncing the divine name. Yet the data is somewhat inconsistent, as *m. Ber.* 9:5 states that in order for the faithful to recognize each other and in response to the corrupt teaching of some heretics, they should use the divine name as a greeting. Regarding the writing of the Tetragrammaton, we know that the Hebrew numbering system avoided the normal pattern for the number fifteen by substituting טו (9+6) for יה (10+5). Additionally, rabbinic literature gives seven names of God which can never be erased (*b. Shebu.* 35a).²⁴ We also find that a custom develops which prohibits the destruction of any biblical manuscripts in case the section contains the name of God.

Over the centuries, such reverential habits continued. By the 20th-century, many German and French Jews referred to God with the title, "The Eternal." And many Jews today are even reticent to write

---

Martinez, J. Kampen; Leiden: Brill, 1997), 437–449. Marianne Dacy, "The Divine Name in Qumran Benedictions," *Australian Journal of Jewish Studies* 15 (2001): 6–16. Dennis Green, "Divine Names: Rabbinic and Qumran Scribal Techniques," in *The Dead Sea Scrolls Fifty Years After Their Discovery* (ed. L. Schiffman, E. Tov, J. VanderKam; Jerusalem: Israel Exploration Society, 2000), 497–511. P. W. Skehan, "The Divine Name at Qumran, the Masada Scroll, and in the Septuagint," *BIOSCS* 13 (1990): 14–44.

²³ See Albert Pietersma, "Kyrios or Tetragram: A Renewed Quest for the Original LXX," in *De Septuaginta: Studies in Honour of John William Wevers* (ed. A. Pietersma, C. Cox; Mississauga, Ont., Canada: Benben Publications, 1984), 85–101. This replacement occurred at times, though not always, as was previously argued in scholarly discussion. More recently, Wevers responded in kind with his essay in honour of Pietersma: John William Wevers, "The Rendering of the Tetragram in the Psalter and Pentateuch: A Comparative Study," in *The Old Greek Psalter: Studies in Honour of Albert Pietersma* (ed. Robert J. V. Hiebert, Claude E. Cox, and Peter J. Gentry; Sheffield: Sheffield Academic Press, 2001): 21–35. Cf. also George Howard, "The Tetragram and the New Testament," *JBL* 96 (1977): 63–83; Sean M. McDonough, *YHWH at Patmos: Rev. 1:4 in its Hellenistic and Early Jewish Setting* (Tübingen: Mohr Siebeck, 1999), 98–116.

²⁴ Jacobs, *A Jewish Theology*, 141. Green, "Divine Names," 501, discusses which titles could be erased and which could not.

the generic "god," but instead use the form, "g*d" or "G*d."[25] This phenomenon could be called a "creeping (reverential) circumlocution"—an expanding development which included more practices over time by accretion.

As this creeping circumlocution continued, a plethora of other techniques arose which were designed to protect the sense of God's transcendence. One familiar to students of the NT is the "divine passive," in which a passive voice verb is used to refer in a roundabout way to God's actions. For example, the familiar phrase from the Sermon on the Mount reads ἐν ᾧ μέτρῳ μετρεῖτε μετρηθήσεται ὑμῖν ("by the measure you measure, it will be measured to you") (Matt 7:2). The allusive subject of the second phrase is certainly God, but the third person passive verb is used instead, thus making God's involvement more abstract.[26] Of course, for some authors this may be simply a familiar way of speaking and does not always indicate conscious avoidance of the divine name. Another related phenomenon which has been observed in the Targumic material is the tendency to remove anthropomorphic and anthropopathic references to God found in the Hebrew Bible. Thus, for example, instead of leaving God as the subject of verbs such as "do," "say," or "speak," the Targums often change the subject to "the Word of the Lord."[27]

At the same time that we find many of these circumlocutionary techniques developing, a wide assortment of epithets begin to be applied to God: names that emphasize some aspect of God's character, such as "King," "Master," and "Father." The use of "Heaven" begins to appear as one such epithet, along with several other words communicating

---

[25] Louis Jacobs comments that although some Orthodox Jews follow this practice, others consider this "pernickety, since there is no particular significance to the letter 'o' in English and G-d stands as much for God as the actual word God." Louis Jacobs, "Names of God" in *A Concise Companion to the Jewish Religion*, Oxford University Press, *Oxford Reference Online* <http://www.oxfordreference.com/views/>.

[26] Similarly, we find in Revelation a voice "coming out from the throne." Richard Bauckham in personal conversation suggests this avoids directly attributing the judgments to God's activity. Cf. also 2 Peter 1:17.

[27] Such tendencies have been discussed by many, including H. M. Orlinsky, "Introductory Essay: On Anthropomorphisms and Anthropopathisms in the Septuagint and Targum," in *The Septuagint Translation of the Hebrew Terms in the Relation to God in the Book of Jeremiah* (ed. B. M. Zlotowitz; New York: Ktav, 1987): xv–xxiv. Helpful discussions of these techniques can also be found in the introductions to most of the English translations of the Targums in the series edited by Martin McNamara: *The Aramaic Bible: The Targums* (Edinburgh: T&T Clark).

great height.²⁸ For example, we do find several instances in the Mishnah where heaven is used as an apparent reference to God,²⁹ and the typical explanation is that this is motivated by reverential circumlocution. It remains a question, however, whether this is simply another epithet for God rather than being a further example of the spread of creeping circumlocution. In light of the mixed traditions on the issue of divine name avoidance, the difficulty in dating such highly stratified documents, and the large number of other appellations used for God, we cannot merely assume reverential circumlocution is the function of heaven in these texts.

And this leads to the main point in this stage of the argument: There is no doubt that reverential circumlocution was a phenomenon in Jewish practice. *But the question remains as to the chronology, geography and exact form of such practices.* That is, avoidance of the divine name (YHWH) is one thing; avoiding other ways of referring to God is another (e.g., *Elohim* or θεός); substituting heaven is yet another development beyond these.³⁰ But *when* these practices occurred and how widespread reverential circumlocution crept at any given time is very difficult to determine. And almost certainly, due to the variegated nature of Judaism, no custom was consistent and universal chronologically and geographically. Each text or group of texts must be evaluated individually. For example, in Qumran we find quite a bit of variance in how the Tetragrammaton is treated. The practice was not consistent and may have varied by individual scribe. And further, there are no instances in this corpus where heaven is used to refer to God directly (see below). In the Mishnah, while heaven is at times used metonymically for God, we find that a much more direct name for God still appears throughout: forms of *Elohim* occur twenty-eight times in reference to the Jewish God,³¹

---

²⁸ Pages 54–107 of Marmorstein's *Old Rabbinic Doctrine of God* offers an extensive catalog of 91 epithets used for God in the older rabbinic materials. Interestingly, from the third century CE onward the use of heaven in this way and the corresponding term *māqôm* fell into disuse. Urbach, *The Sages*, 1:76–77, suggests this is due to a reaction against Gnostic dualism. Marmorstein, 106, speaks similarly.

²⁹ For example, "the kingdom of heaven" (*m. Ber.* 2:2; cf. *b Hag.* 5*b*), "the fear of heaven" (*m. 'Abot* 1:3; cf. *b. Ber* 33*b*), "the sake of heaven" (*m. 'Abot* 4:11), and "the name of heaven" (*m. 'Abot* 4:4; cf. *b. Hag.* 16*a*).

³⁰ Green, "Divine Names," 508–511, discusses the debates among Rabbis and includes a taxonomy of different tiers of prohibitions.

³¹ *Elohim* also occurs a few times with the meaning of false, pagan "gods."

across many different tractates.³² It may be granted that this practice is a minority, but the point stands that this name for God is not absent. The logic of creeping circumlocution suggests that *Elohim* would be consistently eliminated before the more abstract heaven would be substituted via divine reverence, yet this has not happened. Therefore, even in the third-century CE rabbinic literature (which has been consciously edited and codified), it is not at all clear that heaven is being used as a reverential circumlocution. And significantly, the Targums, like Qumran, do not contain any uses of heaven as a substitute for God (again, see below).

Referring specifically to Dalman again we can note that not only does he collapse the categories of circumlocution and reverential circumlocution, but he also lumps together all kinds of techniques and levels of divine name avoidance to make his case, thereby wrongly mixing earlier and later developments. He fails to distinguish between utterance of the Tetragrammaton and other techniques, and he neglects pointing out that when we move from Hebrew and Aramaic to Greek, the question of the actual four-letter divine name becomes moot. As Maurice Casey observes regarding Dalman's statements about the kingdom of God:

> in discussing this Dalman made an extraordinary and extraordinarily influential mistake: he attributed to Jesus the use of מלכותא דשמיא rather than מלכותא דאלהא on the ground that he was avoiding the divine name. But אלהא is not the divine name! It was the ordinary Aramaic term for 'God'.³³

Casey's point is strengthened by the arguments I have presented above that there is no clear evidence that the generic term "God" was being replaced in the first century either.

These inconsistencies at least cast doubt on whether we can assume this practice is up and running and widespread in the time of Jesus. Apart from the Gospel of Matthew, where this practice is typically assumed, there is indeed very little supporting evidence.³⁴

---

³² Other substitutionary names for God also appear in the Mishnah, such as *ha-Māqôm*, *ha-Shĕm*, and the abbreviation 'ה, translated as "the Lord."

³³ Maurice Casey, *Aramaic Sources of Mark's Gospel* (Cambridge: Cambridge University Press, 1998), 17.

³⁴ The prodigal son's words from Luke 15:18 and 21 are typically listed as the other primary NT example of reverential circumlocution ("I have sinned εἰς τὸν οὐρανὸν καὶ ἐνώπιόν σου"). The translation of "against heaven" is common but not certain.

2. *A Flawed Methodology*

A second significant weakness in Dalman's argument is the fundamental problem that his methodology is at many points flawed. In the first instance, many scholars now question Dalman's type of approach which organizes material around certain ideas (*Begriffe*) supposedly in Jesus' mind. For example, Casey dismisses this method by stating that these *Begriffe* are hardly something Jesus would have had: "They are culturally German, and barely at home in first-century Judaism."[35]

Even if this might be a bit overstated, Dalman's methodology for using the Rabbinic materials is problematic, even as it was quite commonly in his day. In vein with his collapsing of chronological categories, Dalman uncritically utilizes rabbinic sources in his reconstruction of Second Temple and NT practices. One hundred years ago, in the wave of excitement over applying the plethora of rabbinic literature to the interpretation of the NT, such basic methodological errors were rampant. Many scholars, including Dalman and Strack and Billerbeck, jumped in with both feet, as it were. However, due to the codified nature of the rabbinic materials and uncertainty concerning the dating of particular rabbis, it is simply impossible to definitively use the rabbinic literature as a direct window on to NT usage. As Michael Lattke observes about the works of Billerbeck, Dalman and G. F. Moore, "these compilations pose enormous methodological and hermeneutical problems for any critical researcher who is particularly interested in the provenance of the early traditions."[36] Similarly, John Meier, speaking specifically about understanding the Pharisees and Sadducees in the first century, sums up the scholarly evolution in this way:

> It was common among older Jewish scholars to rely heavily on the Mishna (ca. AD 200–220), the Tosefta (3rd century), the Palestinian (or Jerusalem) Talmud (5th century), and the Babylonian Talmud (6th century) as well as the rabbinic midrashim from various centuries to reconstruct the

---

Instead, the intended meaning may be that the sins are so great as to reach unto heaven (cp. LXX Jer 28:9; 2 Chron 28:9; Ezra 9:6). Interestingly, this is how Dalman understands this text (*Words*, 217–218). Alternatively, if "against heaven" is correct, then there is likely some other metonymic reason for this substitution. There does not appear to be any other evidence of Luke removing θεός out of a "Jewish avoidance of the name of God."

[35] Casey, *Aramaic Sources*, 17.

[36] Michael Lattke, "On the Jewish Background of the Synoptic Concept 'The Kingdom of God'," in *The Kingdom of God in the Teaching of Jesus* (ed. Bruce Chilton; London: SPCK, 1984), 86.

historical Pharisees and Sadducees. More recently, Jewish scholars like Jacob Neusner and Shaye Cohen, as well as Christian scholars like E. P. Sanders and Anthony Saldarini, have urged greater caution in the use of rabbinic literature to delineate the very different conditions of Judaism in pre-70 Palestine.[37]

One example of a balanced approach to the use of rabbinic materials comes from Philip Alexander. He offers several reasons why NT scholars must be very circumspect in handling the rabbinic material. These include the state and dating of the texts, the accuracy of the attributions, as well as various other considerations. While Alexander's goal is constructive, at the end, he is compelled to convey "some idea of the degree of doubt and uncertainty which must hang over any pronouncement" coming from the study of rabbinic literature.[38]

In the case of Dalman, such a needed note of "doubt and uncertainty" is missing. Instead, he jumps from NT phrases assumed to be reverential circumlocutions to a concatenation of rabbinic parallels, some of which seem close and others which are simply not. At best, his arguments illumine the *possibility* of early circumlocution; at worst, they are a classic example of Sandmel's "parallelomania" in which similar-looking texts are strung together and causal relationships are wrongly assumed.[39]

3. *The Rabbinic Materials are Mixed*

A third problem with the reverential circumlocution argument is that the Rabbinic materials are indeed mixed in their witness to this supposed phenomenon. Even if Dalman had been more careful in his appropriation of rabbinic literature, this would not have provided a strong enough case for reverential circumlocution there. As observed above, the rabbinic material is mixed in its prescriptions in this regard. While there was a general avoidance of the pronouncement of the Tetragrammaton—certainly the highest tier of reverence and clearest

---

[37] John P. Meier, *A Marginal Jew: Rethinking the Historical Jesus, Volume 3: Companions and Competitors* (New York: Doubleday, 2001), 305.
[38] Alexander, "Rabbinic Judaism," 238.
[39] Cf. Samuel Sandmel's well-known article by this name in *JBL* 81 (1962). In discussing dating of rabbinic materials by comparing similar texts, Stemberger reminds the reader that "one cannot automatically assume the continuity of an idea between two chronologically distant literary references." Stemberger, *Introduction*, 48.

form of circumlocution—this was not universally so.[40] Some Rabbis announce as cut-off anyone who pronounces the name with its vowels (*m. Sanh.* 11:1; *b. Sanh.* 90a), while another tradition ordains that Jews should use the name when greeting one another (*m. Ber.* 9:5). This applies to the highest level of circumlocution and the most sensitive issue related to the name of God. Certainly, on circumlocutions of less importance practices were likely mixed. Such inconsistencies should caution us against a flat reading of the materials that assumes heaven was used consistently in a circumlocutionary way, if at all.

Günter Stemberger criticizes this kind of unthoughtful approach to rabbinic literature because it results in

> a rather undifferentiated image of 'the' rabbinic theology. Because of its simplicity and homogeneity, this image is readily adopted in the comparative history of religion and especially in New Testament exegesis... Symptomatic of this situation is... the use of (H. L. Strack &) P. Billerbeck's *Kommentar zum Neuen Testament aus Talmud und Midrasch* as a quarry of useful quotations.[41]

This criticism of the misuse of Strack and Billerbeck can also be leveled against several of the assumptions in Dalman. The foundation of his argument is a reconstructed monolithic idea culled selectively from the rabbinic literature.

So even using the Mishnah, Dalman's arguments are inconclusive. But when we look beyond the Mishnah to other early Jewish literature such as the Targums we discover that the idea that heaven was used as a reverential circumlocution finds little support. Strikingly, the Targums do not use heaven in a reverential circumlocutionary way, nor even as a metonym for God. From my examination of all the occurrences of heaven in the Targums I have found that they align very closely with the usage in the Hebrew Bible, and that even the occasional instances where a reference to heaven is added in the Targums, these do not provide any novel uses of heaven and certainly not a development of heaven as a circumlocution.[42] Indeed, in discussing the phrase kingdom

---

[40] See Dacy, "Divine Name," 10–12. See especially the discussion in Urbach, *The Sages*, 1:126–134. A helpful discussion of the use of YHWH in the Rabbinic materials can also be found in McDonough, *YHWH at Patmos*, 98–116.

[41] Stemberger, *Introduction*, 45–46.

[42] This analysis stems from my own observations based on the recent series of concordances to the Targums produced by Brill: J. C. de Moor, W. F. Smelik, and B. Grossfeld, eds., *A Bilingual Concordance to the Targum of the Prophets* (Leiden: Brill, 1995–).

of heaven in the rabbinic literature, Bruce Chilton observes that a pious reticence of using heaven to avoid referring to God is *not* found in the Targums.[43]

4. *The Second Temple Evidence is Not Sufficient*

The fourth and final problem with Dalman's argument is that the Second Temple evidence is simply not sufficient to sustain his thesis. From the reconstructed idea of heaven as a reverential circumlocution in the Mishnah, Dalman works backwards, attempting to connect the dots of his argument by finding evidence of reverential circumlocution in the Second Temple literature. This move is crucial for him to place these practices as functional at the time of Jesus. His proffers three examples: the book of Esther, Daniel 4:23, and 1 Maccabees.

In the case of Esther, Dalman asserts that avoidance of the name of God is the explanation for the absence of "God" throughout the book. This argument is far from conclusive, especially when one considers that the various Septuagintal versions, which are ostensibly later, insert references to God. Moreover, the case of Esther proves irrelevant to the question of whether heaven is being used in this way. There are no instances of heaven in Esther at all and little evidence of other circumlocutionary terms.[44] Therefore, the text of Esther provides no data for the question of heaven as a reverential circumlocution. This kind of argument from silence gives no credence to the proposal.

An examination of Daniel 4:23 [4:26 in Septuagint and English] shows that it provides far from conclusive evidence as well. Here, in Daniel's interpretation of Nebuchadnezzar's dream, the prophet says that שַׁלִּטִן שְׁמַיָּא, which is usually translated as "Heaven rules." It is supposed that heaven is used here as a way to avoid the name of God (based on the Rabbinic practice read backwards). This serves for Dalman as the sole canonical example of a reverential circumlocution.

However, for several reasons this interpretation of שַׁלִּטִן שְׁמַיָּא is unlikely. First, the typical translation of "Heaven rules" is far from certain. The phrase דִּי שַׁלִּטִן שְׁמַיָּא could easily be understood to mean "that there is a heavenly power" or "who the heavenly power is."

---

[43] Bruce Chilton, *Pure Kingdom: Jesus' Vision of God* (Grand Rapids: Eerdmans, 1996), 19.
[44] Esther 4:14 is sometimes given as an example of the divine passive: "relief and deliverance will arise for the Jews from another place." Beyond this, examples are hard to find.

The word שָׁלִטִן is a plural adjective in agreement with שְׁמַיָּא, not the expected verb שְׁלַט. Further evidence of this interpretation is found in the Theodotion (θ) version of the LXX, a text which typically follows the MT of Daniel very closely. Theodotion 4:26 reads ἀφ' ἧς ἂν γνῷς τὴν ἐξουσίαν τὴν οὐράνιον ("from the time you that you know the heavenly power"), using the rare adjective οὐράνιος ("heavenly")—precisely the way I am suggesting we interpret the Aramaic phrase.

However, even if one wants to hold to the traditional "Heaven rules" translation, then on textual grounds, it is probable that the MT reading is a later edition. MT Daniel 2–7 is extant in Aramaic only and we have two different Greek versions as well (Theodotion and Old Greek). Although the OG and especially Theodotion typically follow the Aramaic rather closely, we have here the rare instance where all three differ from each other:

MT 4:23 מִן־דִּי תִנְדַּע דִּי שַׁלִּטִן שְׁמַיָּא
"from the time that you know that heaven rules"
θ 4:26 ἀφ' ἧς ἂν γνῷς τὴν ἐξουσίαν τὴν οὐράνιον
"from the time you that you know the heavenly power"
OG 4:26 εἰς καιρὸν καὶ ὥραν... [v.27] κύριος ζῇ ἐν οὐρανῷ καὶ ἡ ἐξουσία αὐτοῦ ἐπὶ πάσῃ τῇ γῇ
"until a time and a moment... the Lord lives in heaven and his authority is over all the earth"

In this reading, there is a progression in explicitness that runs from the OG to the Thedotion to the MT. The OG clearly refers to the Lord who is in heaven, the Theodotion is somewhat more vague, and the MT eliminates all but the ambiguous "heaven." In each case, it is clear from the context that the Jewish God is the subject. The preceding parallel in 4:17 [MT 4:14] shows a similar progression. The OG says that Nebuchadnezzar will come to know that "the Lord of heaven has authority over everything in heaven and on earth." The θ reads "the Lord is the Most High over the kingdoms of men"; and the MT, "the Most High rules over the kingdom of men."[45]

Determining which of the three readings in 4:26 [4:23] was original is ultimately impossible, but if in fact there is a trajectory toward using heaven as a substitution for God, this would argue that whatever *Vorlage*

---

[45] The OG also has a third expression of this sentiment in 4:31, which does not occur in the MT or θ: "so that you might know that the God of heaven has authority in the kingdom of men."

lies behind the OG is the oldest, followed by the θ tradition and finally, the Aramaic of the MT. In this reconstruction, the Aramaic reflects somewhat later sensibilities than either of the Greek versions, *sensibilities stemming from a time much later than Dalman assumed.* This progressive reconstruction finds at least partial support in the scholarly consensus that the OG is older than the Theodotion. Additionally, the fact that the Theodotion inexplicably varies from the MT here provides some evidence for a later revision of the Aramaic.[46] Moreover, there is strong scholarly support to argue that the OG in chapter 4 is translating an older, Aramaic *Vorlage* than is found in the MT tradition.[47] Therefore, the Aramaic of 4:23 may indeed reflect later notions and be a later reading.

Regardless, there is another reason why Daniel 4:23 is likely not a reverential circumlocution. Although heaven is certainly substituted as a metonym for God here, the context and language of Daniel cast doubt on whether explaining these words as a reverential circumlocution is justifiable. Just four verses earlier we read that Nebuchadnezzar's kingdom and dominion have extended to heaven and to the ends of the earth; his greatness seems insurmountable. But the true God is now about to humble him and show his utterly *earthly* nature by making him a beast of the *earth who* will lie down in the dew which comes from *heaven*. Thus, in this context, full of such word-plays, Yahweh is called by epithets such as the "God of heaven" (2:18, 19, 37, 44), the "Most High God" (3:26; 4:2; 5:18; 5:21), and more simply, "the Most High" (4:17, 24, 25; et al.). Likewise, in 4:23 we have another of these metonymic titles, "Heaven," which, like the others, serves a *rhetorical* purpose rather than a reverential one—to emphasize the universal greatness of the God of the Jews over all sovereigns, even the one who holds them in bondage. As Urbach explains, when Jonah (or Daniel or other Second Temple Jews) declare faith in the God of heaven, they are attesting faith "in the God who is God of the universe and not a

---

[46] Unfortunately, none of the extant Daniel manuscripts from Qumran contains 4:23. This might have solved the puzzle of the *Vorlage* here.

[47] R. H. Charles was the earliest scholar to argue this way. T. J. Meadowcroft and others have also argued that the *Vorlage* of OG Daniel likely predates the MT of Daniel 2–7. See T. J. Meadowcroft, *Aramaic Daniel and Greek Daniel: A Literary Comparison* (Sheffield: Sheffield Academic Press, 1995), 263. See also, A. A. Di Lella, "The Textual History of Septuagint Daniel and Theodotion Daniel," in *The Book of Daniel: Composition and Reception* (ed. J. J. Collins and Peter W. Flint; 2 vols.; Leiden: Brill, 2001), 2:586–607.

deity of a given country or temple."[48] Therefore, Daniel 4:23 cannot serve as an example of heaven as a reverential circumlocution in the Second Temple period.

The only remaining plank in Dalman's argument for an early pattern of reverential circumlocution is 1 Maccabees. A first reading indicates that here we will find the most evidence for Dalman's theory. There are fourteen occurrences of heaven in 1 Maccabees and none of "God" or "Lord" in reference to Yahweh. In all but two of the occurrences of "heaven," there is a clear metonymic reference to God. In several instances, the replacement of heaven for God is so abrupt that it renders the sentence sounding rather odd. For example, "On their return they sang hymns and praises to *Heaven*, for *he* is good, for *his* mercy endures for ever" (4:24). Thus, heaven is apparently functioning as an intentional circumlocution or metonymy for God. It is unclear, however, whether this metonymic substitution is for reverential reasons or not. This possibility cannot be dismissed out of hand, but neither is there clear evidence to support it. William Oesterley, commenting on heaven in 1 Maccabees, observes that its usage may stem from reverence for the divine name, but suggests that alternatively, it points to the first-century BCE emphasis on God's transcendence.[49] This seems quite reasonable in light of the frequent use of the Second Temple expression "God of heaven" for the same purpose.

Additionally, we may observe how strikingly 'secular' or devoid of traditional Jewish emphases that 1 Maccabees is. The Hasmoneans are depicted more like Greek military heroes, and in sharp contrast to 2 Maccabees, God is quite distant and his role in the actual historical events could almost be described as deistic. That is, we may suggest that the blatant use of 'Heaven' to refer to God in 1 Maccabees is a function of the consciously divinely-generic account that is 1 Maccabees. There is nothing else in the book to suggest the kind of pietistic attitude that would so scrupulously avoid the name of God out of reverence. It is difficult to say with certainty what the motive for the use of heaven in

---

[48] Urbach, *The Sages*, 1:70. Urbach concludes that Daniel 4:23, along with several other post-Exilic uses of heaven are simply a metonymy of place, where the name of a place is substituted for the people (or in this case, person) of that place (p. 69). Similarly he observes that "Heaven" by itself is a short-hand metonym for God of heaven (p. 72).

[49] William O. E. Oesterley, *An Introduction to the Books of the Apocrypha* (London: SPCK, 1953), 78.

1 Maccabees is, but reverential circumlocution does not seem likely. If it was reverential circumlocution, then this text is certainly the exception. As Dalman himself admits, this pattern "in other writings is not in every case so consistent."[50] This proves to be an understatement, as it is *only* in 1 Maccabees that such a consistent use of heaven to refer to God is evident at all.[51] The exceptional nature of 1 Maccabees stands out when one considers that of all the hundreds of references to heaven throughout the OT, Philo, Josephus, and the Pseudepigrapha, in no other text is θεός avoided and heaven substituted in its place as we find there.[52]

Finally, there is one other crucial corpus of Second Temple literature that argues strongly against Dalman's theory: the scrolls of Qumran. In this instance, no blame can be laid on him, as the first scrolls came to light only after his death (d. 1941). Nonetheless, the use of heaven in the Qumran documents provides strong counter-evidence to his theory that heaven was an early reverential circumlocution. Of the approximately 200 occurrences of heaven in the non-biblical documents, *not one functions in this way*. While this is admittedly an argument from silence, this is a case where the silence speaks volumes. In light of the scrupulous care taken with the divine name at Qumran, and the close chronological connection between Qumran and the NT, the lack of the use of heaven in this way is strong evidence against its usage before the later rabbinic period.

To sum up, the widespread adoption of Dalman's conclusion proves to be as precarious as an inverted pyramid. Although the breadth of the belief is large today, it rests on a singular and very weak point. The evidence for heaven as a reverential circumlocution in the time of Jesus is simply too slim to adhere to this theory. It may indeed be that the (later) rabbinic material reflects a real trend toward heaven as a reverential circumlocution, but this yet remains to be proven. Further, the variegated nature of first-century Judaism militates against postulating a definitive trend, even if it were rather widespread in the

---

[50] Dalman, *Words*, 195–196.

[51] One nearby contrary example is 2 Maccabees where there are twenty-one instances of "heaven," many of which are clearly *not* reverential circumlocution, in addition to forty-nine explicit references to God, including several in conjunction with heaven.

[52] Indeed, the exceptional nature of heaven usage in 1 Maccabees led one Jewish commentator to date the book in the late first-century CE: Solomon Zeitlin, *The First Book of Maccabees* (New York: Harper & Bros., 1950), 28.

literature.⁵³ Yet Dalman's assumption of reverential circumlocution has continued as the dominant view, although it has been largely unexamined. A fresh analysis of his argument reveals that it is too weak to support the weight that has been placed upon it.

CONTRARY EVIDENCE IN THE GOSPEL OF MATTHEW

But what about the Gospel of Matthew? Is this not the missing link that provides evidence for the practice in question? We can now turn to the final stage of the argument: *There is contrary evidence in Matthew that argues against the traditional reverential circumlocution interpretation of heaven in the First Gospel.*

Although the assumption of reverential circumlocution is so widespread that it functions as a consensus in Matthean studies, a close reading of Matthean scholars reveals that several scholars have indeed sounded a minor note of disagreement. E. Schweizer, Morris, Carson, Gundry, Marcus and McNeile each tips his hat to the circumlocution explanation, but goes on to suggest that there may be some *additional* factor at work in Matthew. Schweizer suggests that Matthew uses the ambiguous term heaven in kingdom of heaven so that both God the Father and Christ can be understood as king without conflict.⁵⁴ Morris vacillates somewhat on his explanation, but at one point states that "heaven" in kingdom of heaven is intended to communicate a

---

⁵³ There are also several examples in Hellenistic Greek where οὐρανός is used as a circumlocution which, by the nature of their source, are clearly not because of "a Jewish aversion to pronounce the name of God." Examples from various centuries include *Philippides Com.* 27; according to Clement of Alexandria: *Protr.* 5, 66, 4; Appian, *Hann.* 56; Herodotus I, 131; and the "Epigram for Apollonios of Tyana." Quoted in G. H. R. Horsley, *New Documents Illustrating Early Christianity: A Review of the Greek Inscriptions and Papyri Published in 1978* (North Ryde, Australia: Macquarie University; 1983), 49–50. Some have suggested that this secular usage was in fact the source of the later Jewish custom. Cf. Jacobs, *A Jewish Theology*, 143. The point is that using heaven as a metonym (or circumlocution in the technical sense) does not require the explanation that this came about *because* of the (later) Jewish habit of avoiding the name of God. As the *Dictionary of Biblical Imagery* points out, speaking of God in figurative and symbolic ways is in fact the normal way for humanity to converse about the divine, "since through this imagery we proceed from the known to the lesser known or unknown, making it an excellent way to talk about God." Leland Ryken et al., eds., *Dictionary of Biblical Imagery* (Downers Grove, Ill.: InterVarsity, 2000), s.v. God.

⁵⁴ E. Schweizer, *The Good News According to Matthew* (trans. D. Green; London: SPCK, 1976), 47.

kingdom that extends beyond the earthly realm.⁵⁵ D. A. Carson offers both suggestions,⁵⁶ while McNeile remarks that the use of heaven emphasizes a contrast between heaven and earth.⁵⁷ In an article on 16:18–19, Joel Marcus makes a passing comment about circumlocution while discussing the meaning of kingdom of heaven.⁵⁸ He argues that circumlocution is probably only a "partial truth" because, according to 6:10, the kingdom of heaven "is the projection of God's heavenly rule into the earthly sphere."⁵⁹ Among those in this group, Gundry offers the strongest challenge and states, "the Jewish practice only gave Matthew a means of stressing another of his favorite motifs, the majesty of God's universal dominion."⁶⁰ Nevertheless, each of these commentators still maintains that circumlocution is at least part of the explanation for Matthew's usage.

More strongly than these writers, a few scholars writing on Matthew have decidedly disagreed with the reverential circumlocution idea. The earliest example comes from the once-famous German scholar Hermann Cremer. Cremer's work actually predates Dalman, but his insights into the meaning of ἡ βασιλεία τῶν οὐρανῶν have been largely lost.⁶¹ He gives several reasons why heaven does *not* serve as a circumlocution in this phrase, most strongly because he sees an antithesis between the heavenly kingdom and earthly hopes.⁶² Also writing before Dalman, the famous early 18th-century commentator Matthew Henry comments that by 'kingdom of heaven' Matthew means it is a kingdom that is of heaven, "not of this world."⁶³ David Garland, in his commentary, states that kingdom of heaven is not a pious aversion, but is used to refer

---

⁵⁵ Morris, *Matthew*, 53.
⁵⁶ Carson, *Matthew*, s.v. 3:2.
⁵⁷ McNeile, *Matthew*, xxiii.
⁵⁸ Joel Marcus, "The Gates of Hades and the Keys of the Kingdom (Matt 16:18–19)" *CBQ* 50 (1998): 443–455.
⁵⁹ Marcus, "The Gates of Hades," 447.
⁶⁰ Gundry, *Matthew*², 43. Notice also the connection with the use of heaven language in Daniel.
⁶¹ This does show that at least some had considered the idea of heaven as a reverential circumlocution *before* Dalman, but this view does not appear to be widespread before Dalman and it certainly finds its full argumentation in Dalman's treatment.
⁶² Herman Cremer, *Biblico-Theological Lexicon of New Testament Greek* (trans. W. Urwick; 4th ed.; Edinburgh: T&T Clark, 1895), 662–663. Cremer's views, which I discovered after fully formulating the thesis in this work, have many similarities to my own, as subsequent chapters will show.
⁶³ Matthew Henry, *Commentary on the Whole Bible by Matthew Henry*, ed., L.F. Church, (Grand Rapids: Zondervan, 1961), s.v. 3:2.

to "God's transcendent work and lordship that is coming down from heaven," though he offers no argumentation for this rejection.[64] Similar is Gerhard Schneider who states that God and heaven are not synonyms in the phrase ἡ βασιλεία τῶν οὐρανῶν, but that this expression underlines the spatial, heavenly background to God's kingdom.[65] In an article arguing for Matthew as a Gentile author, Kenneth Clark also rejected the circumlocution explanation. His reasoning was that Matthew did often use the term θεός (including in his four occurrences of kingdom of God) and that evidence from other Jewish writers such as Paul and Mark shows that using θεός apparently did not violate the aversion to speaking the name of Yahweh.[66] More recently, Robert Foster has made similar arguments in rejecting circumlocution as the background of kingdom of heaven. Foster also observes that kingdom of heaven does not stand alone in Matthew but is part of a larger "heavenly language" discourse.[67] Most clearly argued is the position of Robert Guelich, who observes that Matthew "does not exhibit any predilection for avoiding the divine name" but that heaven "has a much broader function in his Gospel than simply as a metonym for God... [it refers to] God's realm where, enthroned, he rules over all the world."[68]

The uncertainty of Dalman's argument combined with the observations of these last two groups of scholars puts us well on our way toward a rejection of the reverential circumlocution argument in Matthew. I will add to these arguments a few additional observations. As we observed, often the circumlocution argument in Matthew stems from the recognition that Matthew's phrase kingdom of heaven corresponds to the other evangelists' kingdom of God. While I agree that these terms correspond and have the same referent, the implication is that Matthew must have not wanted to use θεός, thus following the supposed

---

[64] D. Garland, *Reading Matthew: A Literary and Theological Commentary on the First Gospel* (New York: Crossroad, 1993), 47.

[65] Gerhard Schneider, "'Im Himmel—auf Erden'," 287.

[66] Kenneth W. Clark, "The Gentile Bias in Matthew" *JBL* 66 (1947), 169. Davies and Allison, *Matthew* 1:21, dispute Clark's arguments but not convincingly. Their opposition to Clark stems from his insistence on Gentile authorship, which Davies and Allison (rightly) reject. However, a rejection or revision of the circumlocution argument in no way necessitates rejection of the Jewish flavoring, provenance or authorship of Matthew, especially if there is no strong evidence for reverential circumlocution as a Jewish practice in the time of Jesus.

[67] Robert Foster, "Why on Earth Use 'Kingdom of Heaven'?," 488–489.

[68] Robert Guelich, *The Sermon on the Mount: A Foundation for Understanding* (Dallas: Word, 1982), 77.

Jewish custom. However, as has been observed by others, Matthew shows no such aversion but in fact uses θεός 51 times, even more often than kingdom of heaven! Additionally, Matthew also employs the phrase kingdom of God on four occasions (12:28; 19:24; 21:31, 43).[69] As McNeile observes, it does not make much sense to say Matthew systematically avoided θεός in the instances of kingdom of heaven out of a scrupulous aversion to the name of God, while he continues to use θεός in other texts where Mark or Luke have "God."[70] There must be something going on other than reverential circumlocution.

Finally, and most importantly, there is simply a better solution with more explanatory power than reverential circumlocution: Matthew's frequent use of heaven is part of a rubric of heaven and earth language woven richly throughout his Gospel account. As the rest of this book will show, this heaven and earth theme is manifested by the frequent recurrence of this word-pair, an idiolectic use of singular and plural οὐρανός, the predominance of the uniquely Matthean kingdom of heaven, and the repeated reference to the Father in heaven. Rather than dismissing heaven in Matthew as a reverential circumlocution, we need to understand its great literary and theological significance in the First Gospel. It does not stand alone but must be interpreted in light of the whole narrative of Matthew.[71]

Conclusion: Metonymy not Circumlocution

To sum up the argument, the widespread reliance on Dalman to explain heaven in Matthew is an unfortunate mistake. This standard solution has in fact blinded our ability to see the much more elaborate scheme at work in Matthew's use of οὐρανός, one which the remainder

---

[69] The most insightful discussions of why both kingdom of heaven and kingdom of God are found in Matthew is Robert Mowery's article, "The Matthean References to the Kingdom: Different Terms for Different Audiences," *Ephemerides Theologicae Lovanienses* 70 (1994): 398–405. One of Mowery's concluding remarks is that clearly Matthew did not avoid kingdom of God "to piously avoid writing the noun 'God'."

[70] McNeile, *Matthew*, xxiii.

[71] The only scholar to observe something close to this idea is Robert Foster, "Why on Earth Use 'Kingdom of Heaven'?" who notices that kingdom of heaven and Father in heaven combine together to make up a heavenly language discourse. This observation is correct as far as it goes, but fails to see that indeed Father in heaven and kingdom of heaven are themselves only part of an even larger and more pervasive heaven and earth theme.

of this work will seek to explore. While some scholars have suggested the insufficiency of this standard explanation, the note has not been sounded loudly enough to call into question the widespread assumption. The history of the reverential circumlocution idea is an example of an unsubstantiated suggestion becoming an unquestioned assumption through the magic of publication, repetition, and elapsed time. Norman Perrin, in commenting on Dalman's explanation of kingdom of heaven, says "there can be no going back from his conclusions in regard to the meaning of this phrase."[72] On the contrary, our return *ad fontes* reveals the great deficiency of Dalman's original argument, an argument which has subsequently become a supposition for most Matthean scholars.

The way out of this self-inflicted conundrum is to attend anew to careful definitions of our literary categories. "Circumlocution" and "periphrasis" should not be limited to the narrower definition of *reverential* circumlocution that has come to dominate. This narrowing of the definition, or maybe better, this conflation of two different ideas—a roundabout way of saying something and avoidance of the divine name—has served to eliminate the possibility of clear thinking on the matter. It is often the case that the literary/rhetorical practice of circumlocution is used with no motive of avoidance of the divine name, but instead for other reasons: style, variety, literary allusions, word-play, or theological purpose. *There is no doubt that Matthew often uses heaven to refer indirectly to "God"—in the expression kingdom of heaven, and in texts such as Matt 21:25 ("Is the baptism of John from heaven or from humans?"). But these are clearly cases of metonymy, where heaven refers indirectly to God, not a direct substitution out of avoidance of the divine name, but for a rhetorical and theological purpose: to contrast heaven (God's realm) with earth (humanity's realm).*[73] Interestingly, E. E. Urbach makes the same observation about the use

---

[72] Norman Perrin, *The Kingdom of God in the Teaching of Jesus* (London: SCM, 1963), 24. While Perrin follows Dalman on the explanation of heaven and the "kingly rule" meaning of kingdom, he does critique Dalman for viewing the Jewish literature as a unity and not giving sufficient attention to the differences between the apocalyptic and prophetic writings compared to the rabbinic literature. This is certainly a valid critique of Dalman's methodology and applies also to his misunderstanding of heaven as a reverential circumlocution.

[73] Note that I am not suggesting that "circumlocution"/"periphrasis" and "metonymy" are entirely separate, hermetically-sealed concepts, but because "circumlocution" has come to have a much narrower meaning in its usage in biblical studies, it is helpful to use the less-loaded term "metonymy" to describe the function of heaven in the Second Temple literature and beyond.

of heaven in the Rabbinic literature. Rather than being used to avoid the name of God, he points out that heaven in "God of heaven" and in phrases such as "fear of Heaven," "kingdom of Heaven," etc., is an antithesis which "stressed the difference between God and human beings"[74]—that is, between heaven and earth. To speak of God as in heaven or heavenly (especially in the Second Temple period) also stresses his universal greatness over all other so-called gods. Thus, we can delineate at least two powerful rhetorical ways that heaven could be used metonymically and there are likely others. In fact, there are over 90 various names for God used in the Rabbinic literature.[75] The point of this rich variety of expressions is not to uniformly avoid all direct reference to God, but instead to highlight via metonymy some attribute of God or aspect of his care for his people (e.g., "Master of the Universe," "Father," "the Creator," "King"). So too, I contend, with heaven.

In sum, heaven as a reverential circumlocution should be jettisoned from our understanding of Matthew. Instead, heaven serves in Matthew as a potent metonym for God. It has a positive purpose (part of the larger theme of heaven and earth throughout the book) not a negative one (avoidance of the divine name). This language and theme of heaven and earth stands in a rich and full tradition of heaven language throughout the Jewish literature, commencing with the foundational statement of Genesis 1:1 and flowing abundantly into Matthew's usage. Rejecting the mistaken circumlocution assumption about heaven in Matthew opens the door for a clearer understanding of the literary and theological uses of the term.

This chapter has served a primarily deconstructive purpose: to clear away a common misconception about heaven in Matthew. In the following chapters we will begin the reconstructing of our understanding of the function of this concept, and the entire second part of this book will offer a positive alternative in the place of what has been rejected here.

---

[74] Urbach, *The Sages*, 1:70–71.
[75] Jacobs, *A Jewish Theology*, 142, following Marmorstein.

CHAPTER TWO

A SURVEY OF HEAVEN IN THE OLD TESTAMENT AND SECOND TEMPLE LITERATURE

The purpose of this chapter is to explore the general usage of heaven throughout the Hebrew Bible, the Septuagint, and the Second Temple Jewish literature so as to provide the literary and religious context for an examination of heaven in Matthew.

Hebrew Bible

Morphology

Heaven is an important and frequent word in the OT.[1] The Hebrew שָׁמַיִם and the Aramaic שְׁמַיִן, both translated as heaven, occur 458 times (420 Hebrew; 38 Aramaic)[2] in the MT. שָׁמַיִם plays an important role in many central OT texts including Genesis 1–2, and it occurs quite frequently in certain books: Gen (41x); Deut (44x); Isa (33x); Jer (33x); Ps (74x). It is absent from only a few OT books: Numbers, Obadiah, Micah, Ruth, Song of Songs, and Esther.

Cognates of שָׁמַיִם exist in many ANE languages including Phoenician, Ugaritic, and Akkadian. The Assyrians analyzed the etymology of this root to mean the place of the waters, though this explanation is uncertain.[3] There may indeed be a close connection in Hebrew between שָׁמַיִם and מַיִם (waters), both of which occur only in the plural. However, etymology is a tenuous affair, and the best sense we can get from such study of this ANE root is the notion of a hollow and high place.[4]

---

[1] For the use of heaven in the OT in general, comprehensive and exhaustive is Cornelis Houtman's *Der Himmel im Alten Testament: Israels Weltbild und Weltanschauung* (Leiden: Brill, 1993). Houtman's detailed work covers all the various uses of heaven in the OT, focusing particularly on the combination of heaven and earth. I will not attempt to recreate his tome, but highlight common and important uses.

[2] The Aramaic term occurs 8 times in Ezra, twice in Jer 10:11, and 28 times in Daniel.

[3] D. T. Tsumura, שָׁמַיִם," *NIDOTTE*, 4:160.

[4] Simon, *Heaven in the Christian Tradition* (London: Rockcliff, 1958), 39. Also, Luis I. J. Stadelmann, *The Hebrew Conception of the World: A Philological and Literary Study* (Rome: Pontifical Biblical Institute, 1970), 37.

The consistent plurality of שָׁמַיִם is one of its most curious features. There has been debate for over 100 years about the morphology of this word.[5] Due to its final root being weak, the dual and plural forms are indistinguishable.[6] Thus, several scholars formerly argued the word is actually a dual form, reflecting influence of Egyptian cosmology.[7] However, the consensus is now that שָׁמַיִם is in fact plural morphologically.[8] Yet, as with several other Hebrew words, the sense of the plural is not purely numeric, but functions as a *pluralis amplitudinis*, a plural which "points attention to the overwhelming concern: heaven is a giant territory with incalculable heights and unknown distances..."[9] Or as J. Edward Wright concludes, "the Israelites intended to stress the sweep or vastness of the heavenly realm from horizon to horizon."[10]

On the other hand, some assume that the plural form of שָׁמַיִם indicates a true plurality of heavens in number, relating to the concept of multiple heavens as found in the apocalyptic literature. This view has some merit in light of the cosmological structure of the Bible which does use שָׁמַיִם to refer to various levels or heights in the heavens (e.g., clouds, stars, dwelling of God). However, this understanding of a plurality of heavens is quite different from the multiple heavens found in later apocalyptic literature. It is important to note that the cosmological levels that are indicated in the biblical accounts are not clearly defined and are imprecise. As Stadelmann says:

> The few references to different kinds of heaven are either so generic in their scope or metaphorical in their significance that an exact determination of the stages of the heavenly dome is impossible...this space was not conceived as a structured complex of clearly distinguishable levels.[11]

---

[5] A survey of this debate can be found in Houtman, *Der Himmel im Alten Testament*, 5–7.

[6] Bruce K. Waltke and M. O'Connor, *An Introduction to Biblical Hebrew Syntax* (Winona Lake, Ind.: Eisenbrauns, 1990), 118.

[7] Stadelmann, *Hebrew Conception of the World*, 38–39, reviews this argument.

[8] GKC §88, 124b; Bernard Alfrink, "L'expression 'šamain or šᵉmei Haššmaim' dans l'Ancien Testament," in *Mélanges Eugène Tisserant* (ed. Paule Hennequin; Vatican City: Biblioteca Apostolica Vaticana, 1964): 1–7.

[9] Houtman, *Himmel*, 6–7 (my translation). Similar language is found in Rüdiger Bartelmus: "der Himmel in seiner ganzen ungeheueren Ausdehnung." Rüdiger Bartelmus, "šāmajim—Himmel: Semantische und traditionsgeschichtliche Aspekte," in *Das biblische Weltbild und seine altorientalischen Kontexte* (ed. Bernd Janowski and Beate Ego; Tübingen: Mohr Siebeck, 2001), 89.

[10] J. Edward Wright, *The Early History of Heaven* (Oxford: Oxford University Press, 2000), 55.

[11] Stadelmann, *Hebrew Conception of the World*, 41. Simon, Heaven *in the Christian*

Unlike the later apocalyptic and rabbinic literature, we find nothing in the Bible like the detailed speculations concerning multiple levels of heaven.[12] Therefore it is difficult to draw a direct line between the various uses of heaven and its plural form in the biblical literature as if a belief in multiple heavens resulted in the plural form of שָׁמַיִם. Instead, a sense of the innumerable heights above could reasonably result in a preference for the plural.

Semantics

The semantic domain of שָׁמַיִם is wide enough to accommodate rather varied meanings according to the context of the word.[13] Reference works have categorized the connotations of שָׁמַיִם in sundry ways, but two distinct poles of meaning are universally recognized: heaven as (1) the sky, atmosphere, and space of the created order; and (2) the dwelling place of God.[14]

1. *Heaven as the Space of the Created Order*

In the first instance, שָׁמַיִם is quite fluid and can refer to the place of meteorological phenomena such as rain, snow, frost, dew, hail, thunder, wind, and clouds (e.g. Gen 8:2; Isa 55:9–11; Job 38:29; Deut 33:13; Josh 10:11; 1 Sam 2:10; Zech 6:5; Ps 147:8), as well as to astronomical uses including the place of the stars, sun and moon (Gen 15:15; Deut 4:19; Job 9:8–9; Ps 8:3). It is also used very frequently in combination with earth to refer to the entire created world (heaven and earth) and to contrast God with humankind (heaven versus earth).[15]

Tradition, 39, agrees that we may be misled if we assume that the plurality of שָׁמַיִם relates specifically to multiple layers.

[12] Collins points out that discussion of the heavenly world is one of the major differences between the OT prophetic tradition and the apocalypses: "there is significant continuity between the apocalypses and the prophetic tradition...yet some major defining characteristics of apocalyptic thought are lacking in these oracles [i.e., the prophetic]. One is the interest in the heavenly world." J. J. Collins, *The Apocalyptic Imagination* (2d ed.; Grand Rapids: Eerdmans, 1998), 24.

[13] Of course, one must always be careful to avoid the linguistic fallacy of considering the meaning of words apart from specific contexts. Nevertheless, the following categories are helpful guides to the varied patterns within the semantic domain of heaven.

[14] Jürgen Moltmann refers to these two different senses of heaven as "direct meanings" and "symbolic meanings." *God in Creation: An Ecological Doctrine of Creation* (trans. Margaret Kohl; London: SCM Press, 1985), 158, 160.

[15] This will be discussed extensively in Chapter Eight below.

In the Genesis 1 creation account, heaven is the name given to the רָקִיעַ (firmament or expanse), a solid surface which separates the waters above from the waters below (Gen 1:7-9).[16] This firmament is often pictured as an inverted bowl or vault over the earth (Job 22:14; Prov 8:27) which has doors (Ps 78:23) or windows (Gen 7:11) which are opened at intervals and through which the meteorological waters pass. The heavenly ocean is situated above this luminous vault and casts its blue hue onto the firmament. Some biblical writers speak of Yahweh's royal palace as being built on pillars standing in the celestial sea, firmly grounded on this firmament. It appears that the רָקִיעַ was conceived of as a solid piece in which the stars were fixed, the רְקִיעַ הַשָּׁמַיִם (Gen 1:14). Later ancient exegetes were understandably confused by the identification of רָקִיעַ with שָׁמַיִם (Gen 1:8) in addition to its distinction from שָׁמַיִם (Gen 1:14).[17] It is best to understand that in the common use of heaven the term רָקִיעַ is hyponymous with שָׁמַיִם, i.e. what רָקִיעַ refers to is a subset of or included in the broader term שָׁמַיִם.[18] רָקִיעַ was a more technical cosmological term while שָׁמַיִם was used more widely and fluidly.[19] Additionally, it is helpful to acknowledge that at times in the biblical images of the heavenly realm the metaphors are mixed; we should not press the variety of images used into overly specific distinctions. "It is likely that the ancient Israelites held these and other images together as part of a large complex of ideas about the heavenly realms."[20]

שָׁמַיִם, which is usually translated as either heaven or sky, should also at times be understood as air. This is most obvious in the recurrent OT phrase, עוֹף הַשָּׁמַיִם (birds of the heavens/air), which occurs 38 times in the MT in addition to one occurrence of the Aramaic equivalent (Dan 2:38).[21] The birds occupy a place which is above the earth but

---

[16] רָקִיעַ and שָׁמַיִם are also put in parallel construction, such as in Ps 19:1. At other times we find the phrase, "the firmament/expanse of heaven" (e.g., Gen 1:14; Dan 3:56 Th).

[17] Étan Levine quotes Berešit Rabbah 6:13 in this regard: "We do not know whether [the heavenly bodies] fly through the air or glide on the firmament...The matter is very difficult, and mortals cannot solve it." Quoted in "Air in Biblical Thought" in *Heaven and Earth, Law and Love: Studies in Biblical Thought* (Berlin: de Gruyter, 2000), 8, n. 34.

[18] D. T. Tsumura, "רָקִיעַ," *NIDOTTE*, 3:1198. Tsumura discusses the meaning of hyponyms more fully in "A 'Hyponymous' Word Pair: *'rṣ* and *thm(t)* in Hebrew and Ugaritic," *Biblica* 69 (1988): 258-269.

[19] G. von Rad, *TDNT*, 5:503 (s.v. οὐρανός).

[20] Wright, *Early History of Heaven*, 56.

[21] There are three additional phrases which use heaven but a different word for bird,

below the (heavenly) firmament. This way of speaking is also found on occasion apart from reference to birds, as when Absalom's voluminous hair got caught in the branches of an oak, leaving him suspended "between heaven and earth" (בֵּין הַשָּׁמַיִם וּבֵין הָאָרֶץ) (2 Sam 18:9), which apparently means, "mid-air."

Another interesting use of שָׁמַיִם is in the intensive phrase, "heaven and the heaven of heavens." This occurs five times in the MT in the form of a nominative שָׁמַיִם followed by two more occurrences of שָׁמַיִם in construct: שְׁמֵי הַשָּׁמַיִם.[22] Psalm 148:4 contains a simpler "heaven of heavens" phrase using the construct chain (שְׁמֵי הַשָּׁמַיִם) without the preceding nominative, plus an additional occurrence of שָׁמַיִם at the end of the verse: הַלְלוּהוּ שְׁמֵי הַשָּׁמַיִם וְהַמַּיִם אֲשֶׁר מֵעַל הַשָּׁמָיִם, "Praise him, heaven of the heavens, and the waters that are above the heavens!" Finally, Ps 115:16 [LXX 113:24] combines two nominative forms together: הַשָּׁמַיִם שָׁמַיִם לַיהוָה, "The heavens are the heavens of YHWH." The LXX in each case follows suit with a comparable nominative + nominative + genitive phrase (ὁ οὐρανὸς καὶ ὁ οὐρανὸς τοῦ οὐρανοῦ), including in Ps 115:16 [113:24] where the translator apparently interpreted the two Hebrew nominatives as a construct (ὁ οὐρανὸς τοῦ οὐρανοῦ τῷ κυρίῳ).[23] The LXX also has another occurrence of the full three-fold phrase in Sir 16:18 and the simpler, "heaven of heaven" (οὐρανὸς τοῦ οὐρανοῦ) in 3 Macc 2:15.[24]

English translations usually render these phrases as "heaven and the highest heavens." This translation is reasonable in light of typical Hebrew expression for the superlative and the root idea of "heights" in שָׁמַיִם.[25] Yet what exactly the expression means is uncertain. It may be

---

one in Hebrew (Ps 8:9) and two in Aramaic (Dan 4:9, 18). The Septuagint translates all of the occurrences with the phrase τὰ πετεινὰ τοῦ οὐρανοῦ, and adds this phrase seven times where it is lacking in the MT.

[22] Deut 10:14; 1 Kgs 8:27; 2 Chron 2:5 [Engl 2:6]; 6:18; Neh 9:6.

[23] Alternatively, Katz argues that the Greek text is "greatly superior" to the confused Hebrew here and we should emend the Hebrew accordingly. Peter Katz, *Philo's Bible: The Aberrant Text of Bible Quotations in Some Philonic Writings and Its Place in the Textual History of the Greek Bible* (Cambridge: Cambridge University Press, 1950), 142 n. 2.

[24] 2 Chron 6:23 in Codex Vaticanus (B) also has an occurrence of οὐρανός τοῦ οὐρανοῦ in reference to God's dwelling place, adding the latter phrase (τοῦ οὐρανοῦ) to a request for God to hear *from* heaven.

[25] On two Hebrew substantives for the superlative, see Paul Joüon, *A Grammar of Biblical Hebrew* (trans. and rev. T. Muraoka; Rome: Pontifical Biblical Institute), §141 1. Wright, *Early History of Heaven*, 55, defines the superlative phrase "heaven and the

observed that in each occurrence, the phrase is directly connected to YHWH. Additionally, each occurs in sections of elevated and superlative style, which explains the intensification of language. This expression seems to be an all-inclusive way of speaking about the immeasurable spaces above the earth in all their glory.[26] Despite its later use as the basis for views of multiple heavens, the expression in the OT remains more vague and undefined; it is poetic language, not technical-cosmological nor apocalyptic.[27]

2. *Heaven as the Dwelling Place of God*

In addition to these varied uses of שָׁמַיִם which all relate to the created universe, the semantic domain of heaven in the OT also has another pole: as a reference to the dwelling place of God. From reflection on the majesty of the heights above and a belief in the connection of deity with the always-important phenomena of weather, it was an easy transition to understand this place above as the habitation of God. At the same time, the Israelites were commanded to keep an important distinction between the created heavens and the creator. Failure to maintain this distinction by worshipping the created heavenly bodies (sun, moon, and stars) instead of the invisible God above was strictly forbidden (Deut 4:19; 17:3; 2 Kgs 17:16). Instead, God dwells above these created bodies in heaven. He abides there, sees all things and reveals himself from there (Gen 21:17; 28:12, 17; Job 22:12; Ps 14:2). In heaven is the temple and throne of God (Ps 11:4; 103:19; Is 66:1). He is many times referred to as the "God of heaven," especially in the post-exilic literature (e.g., 2 Chron 36:23; Ezra 1:2; Tob 7:12).

Von Rad points out that the Bible actually speaks of God's dwelling place in a number of non-harmonized ways: on Mount Sinai, in the

---

heaven of heavens" as "vast heaven," or "the highest reaches of the sky." Related to this notion, in the post-exilic literature we begin to find God described as the "Most High" God, often put into an appositional relationship with heaven.

[26] Stadelmann, *Hebrew Conception of the World*, 42. After a lengthy discussion of the phrase, querying whether it is a way of referring to the dwelling of God, Houtman (*Der Himmel im Alten Testament*, 341) concludes in the negative. Instead, it should be understood as "der Himmel mit all seinen majestätischen Eigenschaften...der Himmel in all seiner himmlischen Herrlichkeit."

[27] Wright agrees: "there probably was no idea of multiple heavens in ancient Israel," *Early History of Heaven*, 55, contra Othmar Keel, *The Symbolism of the Biblical World: Ancient Near Eastern Iconography and the Book of Psalms* (trans. Timothy J. Hallet; London: SPCK, 1978), 34.

Ark, on Zion, and in heaven.[28] It is best to understand these as various theologically significant metaphors, with heaven being the supreme abode of God.[29] Speaking of God in heaven emphasizes God's separateness, transcendence and limitlessness.[30] At the same time, there is awareness that not even "heaven or the heaven of heaven" (i.e., the heights above the heavens) can contain God (1 Kgs 8:27).

Although the references are not as specific as those in the NT, the OT also reveals that God's angels (and "the angel of the Lord") abide with him in heaven (Ps 103:20–21; Isa 6:1–2; Gen 21:17; 22:11). There are several depictions of God in his heavenly court, surrounded by what is sometimes called "the host of heaven" (1 Kgs 22:19–22; Job 1 and 2).[31]

Because God's exalted dwelling place is in the heavens, it is the epitome of hubris for any creature to attempt to rise to the heights of God. This is the cause of the destruction of the Tower of Babel (Gen 11:4) as well as the debasing of the "star of the morning" in the Isaiah 14 oracle. Instead, humility is the required response because God is in heaven and humankind is merely on earth (Eccl 5:2). The use of heaven to refer to God's dwelling as well as to the created order separate from him again shows the semantic flexibility of שָׁמַיִם.

3. *A Semantic Ambiguity*

To conclude this discussion on the semantic range of שָׁמַיִם, we should note that the flexibility and theological weightiness of the word often creates an ambiguity of meaning, one which some authors likely exploit intentionally. The connection between heaven as the created "above" and God's dwelling place conceived as "above in the heavens" is not merely accidental. Often the two senses of meaning are quite distinct,

---

[28] Gerhard von Rad, *Old Testament Theology* (trans. D. M. G. Stalker; 2 vols.; Edinburgh: Oliver and Boyd, 1962–1965), 2:346.
[29] M. G. Reddish, "Heaven," *ABD* 3:90.
[30] Donald K. Innes, "Heaven and Sky in the Old Testament," *EvQ* 43 (1971), 148.
[31] At times, however, "host of heaven" apparently refers to the stars rather than heavenly beings, or alternatively, as pagan deities (e.g. Deut 4:19). As J. J. Collins points out, "the stars were the visible manifestation of the heavenly beings, but the precise relationship between them is elusive," *Daniel* (Hermeneia; Minneapolis: Fortress, 1993), 331. D. Tsumura likewise points out that "host of heaven" can refer to either the stars or to the angels in God's court, שָׁמַיִם," *NIDOTTE*, 4:163. Peter Katz discusses the various forms of the phrase in Hebrew and Greek in *Philo's Bible*, 146–149.

as in many of the heaven and earth pairs. At other times, however, there is a vagueness or overlap of meaning between the two semantic foci of heaven. As Meredith Kline observes, "So close is the association of God's dwelling and actions with the visible heaven that it may be difficult to determine in given cases whether 'heaven' refers to the visible or invisible heaven, or both at once."[32] John Goldingay, writing about heaven language in Daniel, describes it this way:

> שָׁמַיִם means "heaven" both in the physical sense of the sky and in the metaphysical sense of God's dwelling; the passage [Dan 4] makes use of the fact that the former is a symbol of the latter, lets one meaning hint at the other, and sometimes leaves unclear which is referred to.[33]

Such ambiguous uses which hint at both poles in the semantic range of heaven occur several times throughout the OT. For example, the promise of bread raining "from heaven" (Ex 16:4) or judgment coming in the form of Yahweh throwing stones "from heaven" (Josh 10:11) carry a double meaning: the use of heaven here indicates both the physical place of the material arriving (in the sky) *and* the divine source of that bread and stone (God in heaven). Such an ambiguity, while not the norm in the use of heaven throughout the OT, often is found there.

Heaven in Daniel

The use of heaven in Daniel deserves separate mention for a number of reasons. First, simply, heaven appears frequently in the book, especially in chapters 2–7. Second, the Daniel tradition played an important role in much of the later Second Temple period literature and the NT, including Matthew. Third, the book of Daniel shows development in how heaven was used and provides clues to later usage. And fourth, the use of heaven in Daniel will be very important to my argument concerning Matthew's expression ἡ βασιλεία τῶν οὐρανῶν in Chapter Twelve below.

Heaven appears thirty-three times in the MT of Daniel (five times in Hebrew and twenty-eight in the Aramaic portions). The occurrences

---

[32] Meredith G. Kline, "Space and Time in Genesis Cosmogony," *Perspectives on Science and Christian Faith* 48 (1996), 3. D. K. Innes, "Heaven and Sky in the Old Testament," 146, goes further and questions whether the Hebrews clearly distinguished between "figurative" and "literal" uses of heaven, observing that in many instances it is impossible to tell which use is intended. He gives Isa 64:1 [MT 63:19] as such a case: "O that thou wouldst rend the heavens and come down."

[33] John Goldingay, *Daniel* (Word Biblical Commentary; Dallas: 1989), 85.

in the Hebrew sections do not provide any great surprises relative to the rest of the OT; the usage is quite similar. We find two references to the "four winds of heaven" (8:8; 11:4); an angelic messenger lifts his hands toward heaven (12:7); all the earth is referred to as "under the whole heaven" (9:12; cf. Job 28:24); and the starry realm is described as the "host of heaven" (8:10), put into a contrasting conjunction with the earth.

In the Aramaic portions of Daniel, however, the use of שְׁמַיִן reveals both similarities to and some marked differences from the earlier portions of the MT. The similarities include the use of "the birds of heaven/sky" (2:38; 4:9, 18); a great height described as "reaching up into heaven" (4:8, 17, 19); use of the phrase "dew of heaven" (4:12, 20, 22, 30; 5:21; cf. Gen 27:28, 39); and an angel or voice coming down from heaven (4:10, 20, 28). Noteworthy is the fact that thirteen of the twenty-eight Aramaic references are joined in the context with a reference to the earth, thus forming a thematic pair as is quite common in the OT. These thematic pairs include all of the references to the birds of heaven, reaching unto heaven, and the dew of heaven, as well as two other occurrences (4:32; 6:28).

On the other hand, several of the occurrences of heaven in Daniel 2–7 reveal a later development in the use of heaven, specifically in the phrase, "the God of heaven" (2:18, 19, 37, 44) and the related, "God in heaven" (2:28), "Lord of heaven" (5:23), and "king of heaven" (4:34). This way of referring to the God of the Jews appears almost exclusively in the post-exilic literature,[34] and was used to emphasize God's universal authority.[35] It is worthwhile to note that a full quarter

---

[34] For example, "God of heaven" appears 13 times in Ezra and Nehemiah and once each in 2 Chronicles, Jonah, and the Psalms. Further, there are 13 more occurrences in the LXX Apocrypha and many more in the Greek Pseudepigrapha. By contrast, there are only two instances in Genesis. According to J. Montgomery, "the term was disowned in Israel's religion, but was revived after the Exile, when it became the title by which the Persian government recognized the Jewish God. It was generally used by the Jews only in external correspondence, and finally fell into disfavour again as too similar to Zeus Ouranios." Quoted in N. Porteous, *Daniel* (Old Testament Library; London: SCM Press, 1965), 41.

[35] As Cohen explains, God of heaven highlighted God's universal power: "God is the omnipotent, omniscient creator of the universe, exalted above all his creatures, ruling in majestic splendor, and ultimately beyond human ken." Shaye J. D. Cohen, *From the Maccabees to the Mishnah* (Philadelphia: Westminster, 1989), 80. For a helpful discussion of "God of heaven" and related exalted names for God, see Simon, *Heaven in the Christian Tradition*, 52–85.

of the Aramaic Daniel instances of heaven are in this epithet for God.[36] Additionally, Dan 4:23 [MT], as discussed in the previous chapter, has been understood by many as an example of heaven used independently as a reference to God himself. This metonymical usage does not occur elsewhere in the MT, but makes an appearance in 1 Maccabees and the Rabbinic traditions.

"Canonical" Septuagint[37]

Despite some differences in Greek and Hebrew cosmology, the Greek word οὐρανός was a good translation for שָׁמַיִם. In the parts of the LXX which correspond to the Hebrew Bible, οὐρανός is used almost exclusively to translate שָׁמַיִם, occurring as a translation equivalent nearly 450 times. Conversely, in only a few instances is שָׁמַיִם translated with another Greek word such as ἄστρον (Job 15:15?) or ἥλιος (Job 8:29). The semantic domain of οὐρανός was sufficiently flexible to communicate the varied senses of שָׁמַיִם. Thus we find οὐρανός functioning in reference to the created order, meteorological phenomena, in connection with earth, and as the place of God's dwelling. In these ways the LXX use of heaven is very close to that of the MT.

Septuagintal scholars use the term "plus" for a word or passage found in the Greek but not in the Hebrew, and "minus" for a word found in the Hebrew Bible that lacks a corresponding term in the LXX. In the portions of the LXX which are found in the MT, excluding Daniel, there are approximately 45 pluses of οὐρανός, depending on textual variants and inclusion of certain passages.[38] These pluses continue in the trajectory of the Hebrew Bible's usage of heaven, usually repeating typical OT phrases such as "birds of heaven" (e.g. Gen 40:17, 19; Isa 18:6), or in the case of Job, using the phrase ὑπ' οὐρανόν as a periphrasis for the earth. Also, the LXX translators often include a reference to heaven to make a heaven and earth pair more explicit. As

---

[36] The percentage is even higher for the OG Daniel where "God of heaven" occurs an additional seven times.
[37] I use "canonical" as a qualifier to Septuagint to refer to those books of the Septuagint which have a corresponding book in the Jewish canonical Hebrew Bible.
[38] This number excludes two instances in Esther and one in 1 Kings 8:53 which have no corresponding text in the MT. These can be considered pluses in the sense of passages not in the MT, but for our purposes here the question is where οὐρανός occurs as a plus in closely corresponding Hebrew passages.

will be discussed in Chapter Seven, the pairing of heaven and earth is very common and significant in the OT. This fact was apparently not missed by the LXX translators who at times substitute οὐρανός for some other Hebrew word so as to highlight this word pairing (e.g., Exod 10:13; Deut 32:43; Ps 113:11; Isa 8:21–22). The pluses in Greek Daniel are complicated due to the two different Greek versions extant (OG and θ).[39] OG Daniel particularly stands out in its extra uses of heaven, nearly all of which are used to describe God as a heavenly God with phrases such as "God of heaven" (7x a plus over the MT), "God in the heavens" (3:17), "Lord of heaven" (4:17), and the "Lord [who] lives in heaven" (4:27). This lord is said to have authority over all things "in heaven and on the earth" (4:17; cf. 4:27, 31). This regular pattern of pluses in the OG highlights a theological emphasis and way of speaking about God.[40]

Conversely, there are only seven minuses, or instances where the MT (excluding Daniel) has שָׁמַיִם but the LXX is lacking οὐρανός in corresponding texts—none of which have any theological significance. The assorted minuses in the versions of Daniel are the same.

In sum, the use of heaven in the Septuagint reveals the close semantic connection between οὐρανός and שָׁמַיִם. In these two words we have an example of a rather easy and good-fitting translational equivalent from biblical Hebrew to Hellenistic Greek. Moreover, the significance and frequent usage of heaven in the Hebrew Bible is in no way diminished in the LXX, but is instead even strengthened through numerous pluses.

"APOCRYPHAL" SEPTUAGINT[41]

In addition to its great frequency in the Hebrew books of the OT, the language of heaven also plays an important role in the books and

---

[39] On this issue and the tendencies of the two different versions, see Meadowcroft, *Aramaic Daniel and Greek Daniel*; Di Lella, "The Textual History of Greek Daniel," 586–607; Tim McLay, *The OG and Th Versions of Daniel* (Atlanta: Scholars Press, 1996).

[40] It must be acknowledged that the pattern is not entirely consistent, however, outside of chapter 4. In 2:18–19, as discussed above, there are two instances where the MT/Th "God of heaven" is lacking in the OG and instead we find, "the Lord Most High."

[41] The term "apocryphal" is notoriously unclear and the books included under this category vary significantly by church tradition as well as scholars' demarcations. Additionally, it is not always plain which books should be called "apocryphal" and which "pseudepigraphical." Here the term "apocryphal" will be used to refer to the

sections of the LXX which do not correspond to the Hebrew Bible. In these places οὐρανός occurs an additional 114 times (depending on variants). All of the Septuagintal apocryphal books or sections contain at least one reference to heaven and many books, several. Most prominent are 2 Maccabees (20x); Tobit (15x);[42] 1 Maccabees (14x); and Sirach (14x).[43]

It is difficult to make a great many generalizations across all of the writings of the LXX apocrypha. There are simply too many variances in dating, provenance, genre, and purpose. Nonetheless, we can see several similarities in how heaven is used in the apocryphal books relative to the other parts of the LXX. These include references to God as the maker and ruler of heaven and earth (6x), other heaven and earth pairs (21x), and the use of heaven in meteorological and astronomical ways (20x). Yet it must be acknowledged that the usage varies considerably by book. For example, some books use heaven and earth pairs several times (e.g., Wisdom of Solomon and Sirach), while others only rarely (e.g., Tobit; 1–3 Macc).

One difference between the apocryphal literature and the canonical books is the much more (relatively) frequent use of heaven in some sense as an indirect reference to God, particularly in 1, 2, and 3 Maccabees. The reasons for this probably vary by author. However, this change is likely related to the greatest difference in the usage of heaven in the Apocrypha: the considerable increase in phrases such as crying out to heaven, lifting hands and eyes to heaven, and receiving help from heaven. Expressions such as these occur some 22 times, especially in 1–3 Maccabees. These idioms play on the ambiguity we have noticed

---

books and sections found in Rahlf's edition of the Septuagint which are not found in the Hebrew canon, including books such as Psalms of Solomon and 3–4 Maccabees which are often considered OT Pseudepigrapha. The collection of Odes appended to the Psalms in Rahlf's edition will be excluded from this analysis with the exception of Ode 12, the Prayer of Manasseh, which is often reckoned with the LXX Apocrypha. The Odes in general, which are not found in codices B or S, are repetitions of prayers culled from the OT and NT (with the exception of numbers 12 and 14) and thus do not contain truly separate occurrences of heaven.

[42] There are two significantly different manuscript versions of Tobit: the shorter is witnessed by Vaticanus and Alexandrinus; the longer by Sinaiticus. The consensus today is that Sinaiticus is older, primarily because the Aramaic and Hebrew fragments found at Qumran support the longer text. In Sinaiticus there are 15 occurrences of heaven; in Vaticanus/Alexandrinus there are only 7.

[43] The remaining occurrences by book are as follows: 3 Macc—9x; 1 Esd—8x; Jdt—7x; Wis 6x; Pss Sol—6x; Bar—5x; Sg Three—5x(Th)/4x(OG); 4 Macc—4x; Pr Man—3x; Ep Jer—2x; Esth—2x; Sus—2x(Th)/1x(OG); Bel—1x; Pr Azar—1x.

before between the physical and metaphorical senses of heaven. People lift eyes, hands, and voices upward to the God who dwells above the heavens.[44]

In the apocryphal literature, there are also two words closely related to οὐρανός which begin to appear: οὐράνιος and ἐπουράνιος. The adjective οὐράνιος occurs only seven times in the apocryphal LXX books[45] and once in the Theodotion recension of Daniel (4:26; MT 4:23), but nowhere in the non-apocryphal LXX. Nearly half of the apocryphal occurrences (3 of 7) appear in 4 Maccabees, which is likely a first-century CE work. Οὐράνιος appears only thirteen times in the Greek Pseudepigrapha, most of the time in the *Sibylline Oracles*.[46] Outside of the Pseudepigrapha it occurs frequently only in Philo (81x). The relative infrequency of this word (outside of Philo) in Jewish Greek literature may explain why it was not significantly picked up in the NT, despite its widespread usage in non-Jewish Greek writings. The only exception in the NT is Matthew who uses it seven times in the phrase "heavenly Father." There are also two additional occurrences in Luke-Acts.

The compound adjective, ἐπουράνιος, occurs even less frequently in the apocryphal LXX (once in 2 Macc and twice in 3 Macc), and once in Ps 67:15.[47] However, this word is much more frequent in the NT and according to *NIDNTT*, eventually prevailed over οὐράνιος.[48] It occurs twelve times in the Pauline epistles, six times in Hebrews, and once in John.

Second Temple Literature

We may now continue our general survey of heaven by turning to Second Temple Jewish literature beyond the Septuagint. Here we will

---

[44] Significantly, the book which most frequently uses heaven as an epithet for God, 1 Maccabees, is almost completely lacking in its use of the traditional biblical categories of heaven, such as in meteorological references and the heaven and earth pair indicating the entire world. Instead, nearly every instance of heaven metonymically refers to God in some way, such as the crying out to heaven/lifting voices to heaven phrases.

[45] Only in 1 Esdras, 2 Macc, 3 Macc, and 4 Macc.

[46] We also find ten occurrences of the adverb οὐρανόθεν in the *Sibylline Oracles* (10 of 13 in the Greek Pseudepigrapha). This uncommon word is found but once in 4 Macc 4:10 and twice in Acts (14:17; 26:13).

[47] There are a few textual variants of both οὐράνιος and ἐπουράνιος, where the major codices A and S vary between which word is found in the text, specifically in Th Dan 4:26 and 4 Macc 4:11 and 11:3.

[48] Philo, however, prefers the simpler οὐράνιος (81x) and uses ἐπουράνιος only 3x.

examine five bodies of literature: the pseudepigraphal and apocalyptic materials, the Qumran documents, Philo and Josephus, the Mishnah, and the Targums.

Pseudepigraphal and Apocalyptic Materials

Although the term "Pseudepigrapha" is notoriously inadequate, it is used throughout scholarship for want of a better substitute. I will use the term here to refer generally to the body of literature typically defined as "the Early Jewish literature (largely in the 200 BCE to 200 CE period) that resembles the Apocrypha or deuterocanonical literature but is not included in the Jewish or Western Christian canons, or in rabbinic literature."⁴⁹ The focus of my examination of heaven in the Pseudepigrapha is on the Greek Pseudepigrapha and on those works which are, by their date, most likely to have potentially influenced the language and worldview of the NT, though the dating of many of the pseudepigraphal works is decidedly difficult.⁵⁰ What follows in this section are general comments about trends in the use of heaven, not a book by book survey. In subsequent chapters specific themes in the use of heaven will be highlighted through a closer look at particular pseudepigraphal texts.

Forms of οὐρανός are extant nearly 300 times in the Greek Pseudepigrapha.⁵¹ Additionally, a number of οὐρανός-related words begin to appear and multiply in this literature. These derivative lexemes include adjectives such as οὐράνιος (14x), ἐπουράνιος (12x) and οὐρανίων (1x)

---

⁴⁹ James A. Sanders, "Introduction: Why the Pseudepigrapha?" in *The Pseudepigrapha and Early Biblical Interpretation* (ed. J. H. Charlesworth and Craig A. Evans; Sheffield: Sheffield Academic Press, 1993), 13. Though this is as good a definition as any, Sanders rightly admits there are qualifications that must be made even to this, due to the fluidity of various canons.

⁵⁰ For the apocalypses, I will follow the decisions as expressed in Richard Bauckham's review of Charlesworth's *OTP* in "The Apocalypses in the New Pseudepigrapha," *JSNT* (1986), 97–117. Those which Bauckham judges to fall within the Second Temple period (until Bar Kokhba) are: 1 Enoch, 2 Enoch (?), Sib Or 3–5,11, Apocryphon of Ezekiel, Apocalypse of Elijah fragments, the "Apocalypse of Zepheniah," 4 Ezra, 2 Baruch, 3 Baruch, Apocalypse of Abraham, Ladder of Jacob. Since the publication of this list he would also cautiously add the Seven Heavens apocalypse.

⁵¹ According to the *Concordance Grecque des Pseudépigraphes D'Ancien Testament* (ed. Albert-Marie Denis; Louvain: Catholic University of Louvain, 1987) and my own examination, there are 241 occurences of οὐρανός in the pseudepigraphal works (with 8 further alternate readings) plus an additional 41 in the Greek fragments. There are also many other references to heaven in the non-Greek pseudepigraphal writings. For example, *2 Enoch* contains 80 occurrences in longer recension J and 45 in recension A.

and adverbs like οὐρανόθεν (13x) and οὐρανόθι (2x). Interestingly, most of these offshoot terms are found in the *Sibylline Oracles*,[52] whose late first century Alexandrian Greek shows greater affinity with broader Hellenistic Greek than with Septuagintal and NT vocabulary. Only in Matthew does the frequent Hellenistic adjective οὐράνιος appear with any frequency.[53] Additionally, the *Sibylline Oracles*, Books 3, 4 and 5, each use other heaven-related terms which are found almost exclusively in secular Greek literature, such as αἰθήρ ("ether, sky") and ἀέριος ("high in the air"), and πόλος ("heavenly vault").[54]

Regarding the semantic uses of heaven throughout the Pseudepigrapha, some definite trends can be noted. Some phrases quite common to the OT and/or the Apocrypha drop off in frequency in the Pseudepigrapha. For example, the recurrent phrase "birds of heaven" almost completely disappears in this literature. Only a few examples are found in *1 Enoch* and *2 Enoch*. Similarly, ascriptions to God using heaven, such as "God of heaven" and "Lord of heaven," quite common in the Apocrypha, are noticeably less frequent in the Pseudepigrapha. We do find occasional uses of these terms in *Jubilees, Joseph and Aseneth*, and the *Testament of the Twelve Patriarchs*, but rarely in *1 Enoch* or *2 Enoch* and other works. Use of heaven in meteorological and astronomical references is still quite common in many of the pseudepigraphal works (e.g. *1 Enoch; Joseph and Aseneth; Sibylline Oracles*), but relatively slightly less so than in the OT. Similar is the recurrence of the heaven and earth theme. Overall, the heaven and earth pair does not appear to occur relatively as often

---

[52] The Jewish *Sibylline Oracles* that fall under the purview of our survey are Books 3, 4, 5, and 11. These books consist of composite oracle collections of assorted dates, but the final form of each can be dated within the Second Temple period. For discussion, see J. J. Collins, *Sibylline Oracles* in *OTP* 1:317–472; idem, *Apocalyptic Imagination*, 116–126, 233–241; and idem, *Between Athens and Jerusalem* (2d ed.; Grand Rapids: Eerdmans, 2000), 83–96, 160–167.

[53] Οὐράνιος occurs only 1x in the canonical LXX (Th Dan 4:26) and 8x in the Apocrypha (1 Esd 6:14; 2 Macc 7:34; 9:10; 3 Macc 6:18; 4 Macc 4:11; 9:15; 11:3). It is found only 9 additional times in the NT, 7 of which are in Matthew and 2 in Luke-Acts (Lk 2:13; Acts 26:19). On the other hand, οὐράνιος is very common in secular Greek literature from the Classical period onward, including the non-literary papyri. Compare also the frequent use of οὐράνιος (81x) in the Alexandrian Greek of Philo versus its infrequency in the Palestian Josephus (6x).

[54] "Ether" occurs 12x in Books 3–5, and 2x in the Testament of Abraham. There is no clearly consistent pattern of its usage in the Sibylline books; at times it is synonymous with οὐρανός (4:133, 166; 5:531), while at others it appears to be used to refer to the immortal God's realm of existence in contrast with the lower cosmological heavens (3:11, 81; 5:298).

as in the OT and LXX, yet some pseudepigraphal texts maintain this as an important theme. Most outstanding are *1 Enoch* (where heaven and earth are combined over 90 times) and the *Testament of the Twelve Patriarchs*. On the other hand, some pseudepigraphal documents do not connect heaven and earth at all. This discrepancy in usage across the corpus reflects the varying provenance and style of the assorted books which make up the Pseudepigrapha. It is not surprising that books which closely follow the biblical texts in theme and content will also often mimic biblical phraseology more closely.

By far the most common use of heaven in the Pseudepigrapha is in reference to the divine realm, the dwelling place of God, up above in the heavens. While this usage is of course also found in the OT, it comes to hold a more dominant position in the Second Temple literature, especially the Pseudepigrapha. For example, in *1 Enoch* we find 25 references to the angels, watchers, and holy ones "of heaven," and more than 30 additional times heaven refers to the place of God or the angels' dwelling. In *Joseph and Aseneth*, the majority of its 25 occurrences of οὐρανός allude to the divine realm, referring to angels coming to and from heaven (14:3; 17:8–9; 19:5) as well as to the abode where personified Repentance lives (15:7) and the place of the name-filled Book of the Living (15:4). Likewise, most of the occurrences of οὐρανός in *Testament of Abraham* refer to ascending to the presence of God (4:5; 7:4; 8:1; 15:11) or angels or the divine voice coming down out of heaven (7:3b; 7:5; 7:8; 10:11–12; 14:13).

The most distinct use of heaven in the Pseudepigrapha comes from the apocalyptic innovation of journeys into the multiple heavens. It is not necessary for our survey to review all the details of this development and the scholarly discussion is widespread and well known.[55] For

---

[55] Standard discussions of apocalyptic include J. J. Collins, ed., *Apocalypse: The Morphology of a Genre*; D. Hellholm, ed., *Apocalypticism in the Mediterranean World and the Near East: Proceedings of the International Colloquium on Apocalypticism, Uppsala, August 12–17, 1979* (Tübingen: Mohr Siebeck, 1983); J. J. Collins, *The Apocalyptic Imagination*; and Christopher Rowland, *The Open Heaven: A Study of Apocalyptic in Judaism and Early Christianity* (London: SPCK, 1982). On heavenly journeys in particular, standard works include Alan F. Segal, "Heavenly Ascent in Hellenistic Judaism, Early Christianity and their Environment," *ANRW* II: 23:2: 1333–94; James D. Tabor, *Things Unutterable: Paul's Ascent to Paradise in Its Greco-Roman, Judaic, and Early Christian Contexts* (Lanham, Md.: University Press of America, 1986); Martha Himmelfarb, *Ascent to Heaven in Jewish and Christian Apocalypses* (Oxford: Oxford University Press, 1993); and James Davila, "Heavenly Ascents in the Dead Sea Scrolls," in *The Dead Sea Scrolls After Fifty Years: A Comprehensive Assessment* (ed. Peter W. Flint and James C. VanderKam; 2 vols; Leiden:

our purposes, we can comment on how this new usage pertains to a diachronic evolution of οὐρανός. Simply, within the heavenly journey apocalyptic texts the usage of heaven undergoes a narrowing in semantic meaning. Astronomical and meteorological references, as well as other traditional OT uses of heaven, fade to the background relative to a focus on the various levels explored by the traveling seers. While the astronomical and meteorological elements are often mentioned when the lower levels of heaven are passed, the use of heaven becomes intentionally constrained by the purpose of explicating its apocalyptic mysteries to the reader. A comparison of *1 Enoch* with *2 Enoch* is instructive at this point. Unlike *1 Enoch* where there are over 80 astronomical and meteorological uses of heaven and a limited heavenly journey theme, in *2 Enoch* astronomical and meteorological references to heaven are quite rare.[56] Instead, heaven is typically used in its highly developed apocalyptic sense, referring to specific levels, only the first of which contains the meteorological elements. This reflects a particular trend in the apocalyptic description of the cosmos, one which evinces a shift in the use of heaven. The same can be said for the *Martyrdom and Ascension of Isaiah*. Chapters 6–11 of this work contain a seven heavens journey, the oldest certainly Christian composition to make use of this motif.[57] Within this journey, heaven occurs an amazing 76 times. Most striking, each of these uses refers to the various levels of heaven in the journey ("the first heaven," "the seventh heaven," etc.) and the other typical uses of heaven (cosmological; astronomical; meteorological) are completely absent with the exception of but two places where heaven and earth are paired together thematically. As A. Y. Collins comments: "There is virtually no astronomical interest in this work."[58] This severely curtailed use of heaven is arresting in comparison with the variety and dexterity of heaven throughout the rest of the biblical and apocryphal corpus.

Brill, 1999), 2:461–485. See also A. Y. Collins, "The Seven Heavens in Jewish and Christian Apocalypses," in *Death, Ecstasy, and Other Worldly Journeys* (ed. J. J. Collins and Michael Fishbane; Albany: SUNY Press, 1995): 59–93.

[56] Granted, the various parts of *1 Enoch* have different dates and provenances, but compared to *2 Enoch*, the work as a whole is earlier and therefore a diachronic distinction can still be observed between *1 Enoch* and *2 Enoch*.

[57] A. Y. Collins, "The Seven Heavens," 77. For discussion of the composition of the book, see M. A. Knibb, *OTP* 2:143–150, and especially Richard J. Bauckham, "The Ascension of Isaiah: Genre, Unity and Date," in *The Fate of the Dead: Studies on the Jewish and Christian Apocalypses* (Leiden: Brill, 1998), 363–390. Against several of the other treatments, Bauckham does not see the two parts as a composite work.

[58] A. Y. Collins, "The Seven Heavens," 76.

However, it should be noted that such narrowly apocalyptic usage of heaven is not commonplace throughout the Pseudepigrapha. The amount of scholarly attention paid to the apocalyptic literature and its relevance often obscures the fact that there are in fact relatively few (if any) developed heavenly journey texts before the Christian era. As J. J. Collins states: "The familiar pattern of ascent through a numbered series of heavens, usually seven, is not attested in Judaism before the Christian era...for a Jewish writer who claims to have ascended to heaven (apart from 4QM), we must wait until St Paul."[59] Himmelfarb evaluates the data the same way:

> These apocalypses are by no means easy to date, but the works that contain seven heavens (the *Testament of Levi*, *2 Enoch*, the *Apocalypse of Abraham*, the *Ascension of Isaiah*, and, as I argue in chapter 4, *3 Baruch*, although it mentions only five) all seem to date from the first century CE or later. Those ascent apocalypses that hold on to a single heaven (the Similitudes of Enoch, the Apocalypse of Zephaniah) may well be earlier, perhaps from the first century BCE.[60]

Those texts which are clearly pre-Christian are undeveloped on this point and continue to use heaven in ways basically contiguous with the OT usage (e.g., portions of *1 Enoch*). In contrast, those works which contain heavenly journeys and thereby use heaven in a more particular and narrow way, are either post-Christian texts or composite works with Christian interpolations (e.g., *Test Levi* 2; Slavonic *Apocalypse of Abraham*; *3 Baruch*; *Apocalypse of Zephaniah*).

In sum, though the use of heaven in the Pseudepigrapha shifts a bit from the OT usage, it remains a flexible term with a wide semantic range. The usage of heaven in the heavenly journeys texts manifests a particular interest in describing the cosmos, and in these texts heaven is used in a more circumscribed and narrow way. This may have fed into a similarly narrower usage of the term in the Christian tradition, but from the perspective of the OT and Second Temple literature, it is a notable but minor exception.

---

[59] J. J. Collins, "A Throne in the Heavens: Apotheosis in Pre-Christian Judaism," in *Death, Ecstasy, and Other Worldly Journeys*, 46.
[60] M. Himmelfarb, *Ascent to Heaven*, 127, n. 14. Cf. also Richard J. Bauckham, "Early Jewish Visions of Hell," *JTS* (1990): 355–385, who dates many of the apocalypses from the same era.

Qumran

The people associated with Qumran and the Dead Sea Scrolls, who at times called themselves "the Community of the Renewed Covenant," were by and large religiously conservative, albeit with some apocalyptic and polemic elements in their worldview.[61] It is not surprising, then that the use of heaven in the Qumran literature accords in many ways with OT usage. There are approximately 53 occurrences of שְׁמַיִן in the Aramaic documents and 148 instances of Hebrew שָׁמַיִם in the non-biblical materials.[62] Like the OT, the Qumran documents often use heaven to refer to astronomical and meteorological phenomena and in heaven and earth combinations. These are the most frequent uses. We also find several instances of heaven used in the ambiguous sense of people looking up to heaven and objects falling from the heavens, as is common in the LXX Apocrypha and elsewhere.

On the other hand, the scrolls use heaven on several occasions in one distinct way, in the phrase, "sons of heaven." This expression is found 8 times, three of which are in the Thanksgiving Hymns (1QH^a)[63] with the promise that members of the sectarian community will enter communion with "the congregation of the sons of heaven," apparently referring to the angels.[64] The related expressions "holy ones of heaven" and "watchers of heaven" also occur several times, especially in the *1 Enoch* manuscripts.

---

[61] In general, see James VanderKam and Peter Flint, *The Meaning of the Dead Sea Scrolls* (San Francisco: HarperCollins, 2002) and S. Talmon, "The Community of the Renewed Covenant: Between Judaism and Christianity," in *The Community of the Renewed Covenant: The Notre Dame Symposium on the Dead Sea Scrolls* (ed. E. Ulrich and J. VanderKam; Notre Dame, IN: University of Notre Dame Press, 1994): 3–24. On the belief system of the Qumran community, see Helmer Ringgren, *The Faith of Qumran: Theology of the Dead Sea Scrolls* (expand. ed.; trans. Emilie T. Sander; New York: Crossroad, 1995), and J. J. Collins and Robert Kugler, eds., *Religion in the Dead Sea Scrolls* (Grand Rapids Eerdmans, 2000). On apocalyptic worldview at Qumran, see J. J. Collins, *Apocalypticism in the Dead Sea Scrolls* (London: Routledge, 1997).

[62] These figures are based on a search of the database in *The Dead Sea Scrolls Electronic Reference Library 2* (Leiden: Brill, 1999). Of course, there are many reconstructions from lacunae in the texts and these numbers are necessarily approximate. Moreover, not all of the non-biblical texts are included on this CD. There are also 4 occurrences of Greek οὐρανός in the scrolls, 3 of which are from the Nahal Hever Minor Prophets scroll in very traditional phrases: stars, birds, and four winds "of heaven."

[63] 1QH^a *Col.* XI, 22; *Col.* XXIII, bottom, 10; *Col.* XXVI, bottom, 11.

[64] James R. Davila, *Liturgical Works* (ECDSS; Grand Rapids: Eerdmans, 2000), 100.

Surprisingly, another difference between the Qumran use of heaven and other Jewish literature is that heaven as the dwelling place of God and the angels is not one of its dominant uses. While such references do occur occasionally, their frequency is small compared to the astronomical uses, and they are not widespread, but concentrated in a few texts (e.g. *1 Enoch*, 4Q Wisdom poems 416, 418, 298, 521).[65] This is unexpected in light of this common use of heaven in other bodies of literature and the particular interest at Qumran in angels.[66]

But the most striking aspect of heaven language usage at Qumran is how relatively *infrequently* the term is used. That is, to find only some 200 occurrences of heaven in fragments of approximately 670 nonbiblical scrolls[67] is surprising, especially in light of the supposed apocalyptic and dualistic worldview manifested in the sectarian documents.[68] Moreover, many of these occurrences (approximately 45) are found in the fragments of *1 Enoch*, which has a concentrated interest in the heavenly realm. Indeed, as Newsom has observed, apart from 1 Enoch, in the sectarian literature "references to heaven tend to be brief and nondescriptive" and "incidental."[69] Newsom states that the one partial exception to this rule is the *Songs of the Sabbath Sacrifice* (her area of expertise).[70] While this document is exclusively concerned with the heavenly realm and the heavenly tabernacle, unexpectedly, it only contains two instances of שָׁמַיִם. Similarly, in the Rule of the Community (1QS) there are only two references to heaven (both "sons of heaven") and

---

[65] Thus, Carol Newsom's comment that in the scrolls "heaven is, above all, the place of God's presence and rule," is difficult to understand. This seems to be an assumption based on the common usage of heaven elsewhere. Carol Newsom, "Heaven," in *Encyclopedia of the Dead Sea Scrolls* (ed. Lawrence Schiffman and James VanderKam; 2 vols.; Oxford: Oxford University Press, 2000), 1:339.

[66] On the topic of angels at Qumran, see *inter alia*, J. J. Collins, "Powers in Heaven: God, Gods, and Angels in the Dead Sea Scrolls," in *Religion in the Dead Sea Scrolls*, 9–28.

[67] This figure comes from VanderKam and Flint, *The Meaning of the Dead Sea Scrolls*, 103.

[68] On apocalypticism, see J. J. Collins, *Apocalypticism in the Dead Sea Scrolls*. On dualism, see Jörg Frey, "Different Patterns of Dualistic Thought in the Qumran Library: Reflections on their Background and History," in *Legal Texts and Legal Issues* (ed. M. Bernstein, F. Garcia Martinez, and J. Kampen; Leiden: Brill, 1997): 275–335.

[69] Newsom, "Heaven," 338.

[70] Carol Newsom, *Songs of the Sabbath Sacrifice: A Critical Edition* (Atlanta: Scholars Press, 1985). See also the commentary by James Davila in *Liturgical Works*, 83–167, and idem, "The Macrocosmic Temple, Scriptural Exegesis, and the Songs of the Sabbath Sacrifice," *DSD* 9.1 (2002): 1–19.

in the lengthy War Scroll, with its well-known dualism of the sons of light versus darkness, only a handful of occurrences are found.

Related to this lack is the interesting fact that the Qumran documents show relatively little interest in speculations about the content and composition of the heavens. As J. Edward Wright comments:

> In spite of the apocalyptic orientation of the Qumran sectarians' world view, one finds remarkably little speculation about the world beyond. This is especially significant since these people imagined themselves as a community of angels whose rigidly pious life was thought to imitate that of the angels in heaven.[71]

This is not to say that the people of Qumran had no interest in the cosmic realm, as there is ample evidence of concern about astrological signs and astronomical issues related to assorted calendars.[72] However, this interest is notably different from an apocalyptic interest in the heavens. There are no multiple-heavens speculations as we find in much of the apocalyptic material,[73] and the evidence for clear heavenly ascent journeys is minimal.[74] Moreover, the instances of heaven and earth combinations are generally merismatic, not contrastive. That is, the biblical stock phrase "heaven and earth" is primarily used in the scrolls to refer to all of creation, not to contrast the heavenly (divine) realm with the earthly, as is common in the full Ethiopic *1 Enoch* and other apocalyptic literature.

Thus, in light of the meager use of heaven language at Qumran and the particularly scanty evidence of apocalyptic heaven notions there, Collins seems to be overstating the case that "the interest in the heavenly world that we find in the scrolls is more intense than anything we

---

[71] Wright, *Early History of Heaven*, 128.
[72] Wright, *Early History of Heaven*, 128–130.
[73] Newsom, "Heaven," 339, indicates that any spatial hierarchy present in the *Songs of the Sabbath Sacrifice* is undeveloped. Wright, *Early History of Heaven*, 130, likewise concludes there is no evidence of a notion of multiple heavens in the Qumran literature. Wright's interpretation is that the people of Qumran did not expend much energy on such matters because "their eschatologically oriented sect was more concerned with defining and promoting holy living in the here and now," 129.
[74] James Davila mines the scrolls for all possible heavenly ascent texts in "Heavenly Ascents in the Dead Sea Scrolls." Several of the texts he cites are from the Enochic material and there is little evidence in the sectarian literature. Davila takes a more positive view of the attestation to heavenly ascents in the scrolls than I do, but regardless, it must be acknowledged that any such evidence is patchy and undeveloped compared to other apocalyptic literature.

find in the earlier apocalypses."⁷⁵ While an apocalyptic worldview may still have been fundamental to the sectarians' theology, for some reason this did not translate into a great amount of writing about heaven at Qumran, nor many of the typical uses of heaven language found in the apocalyptic literature or even the biblical materials.⁷⁶

Philo & Josephus

In Philo of Alexandria we find heaven to be a frequently used concept, with over 400 occurrences of οὐρανός in addition to 81 instances of the adjective οὐράνιος.⁷⁷ It should not be surprising that heaven occurs so often in Philo as such a large portion of his corpus is dedicated to a systematic exposition of Genesis. Indeed, one of the books in which οὐρανός occurs most often (approx. 30x) is *On the Creation of the World* which extrapolates upon the first six days of creation.

While heaven is occasionally used in reference to astronomical bodies (e.g., *On the Cherubim*, 21; *Who is the Heir of Divine Things?*, 221ff.), this usage is small in comparison with the overwhelmingly dominant use of heaven in Philo: in contrastive pairs of heaven and earth, used to distinguish the divine realm from the earthly. Fundamental to Philo's Platonism⁷⁸ is the superiority of heaven over earth. Heaven is Mind while Earth is merely Sense-perception.⁷⁹ For example, Philo begins his

---

⁷⁵ J. J. Collins, *Apocalypticism in the Dead Sea Scrolls*, 148.
⁷⁶ This fact may be related to the insight by Frey that dualism in the scrolls is not as prevalent nor consistent as formerly thought. As he states, contrary to typical assumptions, "only a limited portion of the material is characterized by explicit dualistic terminology and thought," and "even the texts and sections labeled 'dualistic' show notable differences in content and terminology." Frey, "Different Patterns of Dualistic Thought," 277–278.
⁷⁷ These figures are based on Günter Mayer's *Index Philoneus* (Berlin: de Gruyter, 1974). Beyond οὐρανός and οὐράνιος, Philo uses other related terms only rarely: ἐπουράνιος (3x), οὐρανομήκης (3x), and οὐρανόθεν (1x). The frequent use of οὐράνιος reflects his Greek parlance and provenance (cf. the recurrence of this term in the *Sibylline Oracles and* non-Jewish Greek literature).
⁷⁸ Craig Evans sums up Neo-Platonism (and really all of Platonism) as "the view that what the physical senses perceive on earth below is but an imperfect reflection of the true and perfect reality of heaven above." Craig A. Evans, *Noncanonical Writings and New Testament Interpretation* (Peabody, Mass: Hendrickson, 1992), 81. More technically correct, Philo's Platonism should be understood as a form of Middle Platonism rather than Neo-Platonism.
⁷⁹ As Colson and Whitaker write: "In 1–18 Philo deals with Gen. ii. 1–3, which tells first of the completion of Heaven and Earth. He takes these to mean the originals of Mind and Sense-perception, and bases on the Greek version a contrast between the numbers 6 and 7, making the former represent things earthly, and the latter things

discussion of the creation of the world by interpreting "in the beginning God created the heavens" as meaning that the first thing God created was the heavens because

> It is natural in reality that [the heavens] should have been the first object created, being both the best of all created things, and being also made of the purest substance, because it was destined to be the most holy abode of the visible Gods who are perceptible by the external senses. (*On the Creation of the World*, 27)

Similarly, he posits a sharp heaven-earth distinction by saying:

> And by the one which he calls truth he expresses figuratively that it is absolutely impossible for falsehood to enter any part of heaven, but that it is entirely banished to the parts around the earth, dwelling among the souls of impious men. (*The Special Laws, Book 1*, 89)

This theme of the heavenly realm as the pure and divine in contrast to the earth is woven throughout Philo. The frequent OT use of heaven and earth language, especially in the Pentateuch, provided ample ammunition for this kind of philosophical spin-off. Thus, we find in Philo a commandeering of heaven language and thereby a narrowing of its meaning for his own theological-philosophical purpose.

The writings of Flavius Josephus, however, reflect a different use of heaven. Writing some fifty years later, Josephus also retells many biblical stories but with a very different purpose than Philo. Unlike Philo's narrow and philosophical use of heaven, Josephus uses many standard biblical turns of phrase involving οὐρανός. For example, of his 40 occurrences of οὐρανός,[80] 15 times heaven is used with reference to the astronomical and meteorological phenomena and there are 12 heaven and earth pairs. Following astronomical uses, heaven is also frequently used in phrases referring to lifting one's hands or eyes to heaven or objects (such as manna) coming down from heaven. These types of usage were classified above as semantically ambiguous. They refer in the first instance to the physical skies above and more ambiguously to God as the source or object. Such usage is common in the Second Temple literature, especially the Maccabean writings.

---

heavenly." F. H. Colson and G. H. Whitaker, *Philo* (12 vols.; Cambridge: Harvard University Press, 1927), 1:140.

[80] This figure comes from Karl H. Rengstorf, *A Complete Concordance to Flavius Josephus* (Leiden: Brill, 1979). There are also 6 occurrences of οὐράνιος and none of ἐπουράνιος, οὐρανόθεν, or οὐρανομήκης.

But unlike the biblical materials or other Second Temple literature, Josephus infrequently uses heaven as a reference to the divine abode: only 5 or 6 times.

Rabbinic Literature—The Mishnah

With the examination of Philo and Josephus we move beyond strict predecessors to the time of Jesus and the Gospels into roughly contemporary literature. One step further in this direction is a survey of the earliest Rabbinic documents. Since my purpose is focused on the use of heaven language in Matthew and not more fully into the later Christian era, I will restrict my examination here to the Mishnah.[81]

Hebrew שָׁמַיִם does not occur with great frequency in the Mishnah, being found in various forms approximately 40 times.[82] Most tractates make no mention of heaven while in a couple, שָׁמַיִם occurs several times.[83] There are two uses of heaven which particularly stand out as interesting: מלכת שמים ("kingdom of heaven"), two times in *m. Ber.* (2:2, 5); and the compound prepositional form שבשמים ("which is in heaven"), usually combined with אב ("father"). The latter results in eight occurrences of "Father in heaven" referring to God and one "God in heaven."[84] Neither of these phrases is found in the preceding literature with the exception of Matthew. Also unlike other Jewish literature,

---

[81] The Mishnah itself certainly contains earlier traditions than the date of its compilation (ca. 200–220 CE), however, deciphering such layers (e.g., by Rabbis' names) is an uncertain business and must be done only cautiously. Moving beyond the Mishnah into the Talmud provides insights into the development of terms and ideas, but the historical dating for this moves well beyond the time of even the latest NT books. As Stemberger states in his *Introduction to the Talmud and Midrashim*, 47: the Mishnah and Tosefta "must be interpreted on their own and not by means of the Talmuds; the Talmuds already belong to the history of interpretation and are no more and no less useful in determining the original meaning of the Mishnah than patristic texts are for the interpretation of the New Testament." For a helpful evaluation of the state of Rabbinic studies regarding usefulness for the NT, see Philip S. Alexander, "Rabbinic Judaism and the New Testament," 237–246.

[82] This figure is based on my own calculations using C. Y. Kasovsky, *Thesaurus Mishnae: Concordantiae Verborum quae in Sex Mishnae Ordinibus Reperiuntur* (Jerusalem: Massadah Publishing, 1960). Variance in number is due in part to the fact that two references in the concordance are from *m. 'Abot* 6, a chapter which is a later gloss added to chapter 5 in the 11th-century CE or later. It is included in Danby's translation but not Neusner's.

[83] Most frequent are *m. Ned.* ("Vows")—11x and *m. Sanh.*—7x.

[84] "Father in heaven" is found in *m. Kil.* 9:8; *m. Yoma* 8:9; *m. Roš Haš.* 3:8 (2x); *m. Soṭah* 9:15 (3x); *and m. 'Abot* 5:20. "God in heaven" occurs in *m. Sanh.* 7:10.

surprisingly, the Mishnah rarely combines heaven with earth, either as a direct copulative pair or even thematically. Only in *m. Ta'an.* 4:3 (which is a direct quote from Gen 1) and in *m. Sebu.* 4:13 are heaven and earth directly combined.[85] Additionally, only once is heaven used to refer to the skies (*m. Yad.* 4:3), and once in reference to the heavenly realm (*m. Sanh.* 4:5). All of this is unexpected in light of the predominance of the heaven and earth word-pair throughout and the typical uses of heaven throughout the OT and Second Temple literature.

These differences are a function of the legal content of the document as well as the fact that the use of heaven in the Mishnah is focused more specifically on its use as a metonym for God. Apart from the Father in heaven references and the occasional other uses just mentioned, all the rest of the occurrences of שָׁמַיִם function as a substitution for God. Thus we find phrases such as "at the hands of heaven"; "by an act of heaven"; "acquired by heaven"; "belongs to heaven"; and "dedicated to heaven." There is no doubt that the reference in these cases is to God. In this way, the Mishnah is strikingly similar to 1 Maccabees which likewise, uniquely, restricts the use of heaven in this particular way.

The Targums

There is one final corpus of literature worthy of mentioning in this survey of heaven in the Jewish literature: the Targums, or Aramaic translations and paraphrases of the Hebrew Bible. Targums came into existence before the time of Christ because of the decline in understanding of classical Hebrew among many of the Jews, including those in Palestine. They likely reflect the understanding and exegetical traditions of many ordinary Aramaic-speaking Jews in the first few centuries.[86] The Targums in their present form came about through the same, long processes of preservation and revision that the other Rabbinic materials did. As Bruce Chilton points out, the use of the Targums as literary context for the New Testament must be pursued only very circumspectly. This is because the extant Targums are usually several centuries later than the New Testament and have gone through much revision. Nevertheless, a careful methodology can lead to insights into

---

[85] There are four heaven and earth combinations in the later-added chapter 6 of *m. 'Abot* (see note above). This vocabulary difference from the rest of the Mishnah is one of the ways in which this chapter stands out as non-original.

[86] See Geza Vermes, *IDB* Supplement, 441–443.

elements of the language and theology current in the time of Jesus.[87]

Despite the obvious paraphrasing and theologizing that occurs in the Targums, the use of heaven (שמיא) in these works aligns very closely with that of the Hebrew Bible. This is in noticeable contrast to the Mishnah, as just mentioned, where a more narrow use of heaven can be observed. In each of the Targums of the Prophets, for example, the Aramaic paraphrases follow the MT very closely in every occurrence of heaven.[88] In each book of the Prophets there are a handful of pluses in the Targums, i.e. places where heaven occurs in the Aramaic and not in the Hebrew, but in each case there are no surprising or strongly novel uses, despite the late dating of most of the extant Targums. Most importantly for the current project, as was mentioned in Chapter One, in no case do the Targums evidence the use of heaven as a stand-alone metonym for God, even though God's dwelling place in heaven is regularly emphasized (e.g., *Tg. 2 Sam* 22:13; *Tg. Mic* 6:6; *Tg. Jer* 17:12). Additionally, I have found no instances of the Rabbinic and Matthean phrase, "the kingdom of heaven." Regarding these last two statements, the fuller analysis of heaven throughout the Targums, the Mishnah, and other literature presented above serves to strengthen the conclusion of Chapter One that there is little evidence for heaven as a reverential circumlocution for God.

Conclusion

The preceding survey has sought to reproduce an accurate and representative setting in which to understand the language and conceptual milieu of heaven for the Gospel of Matthew. We have seen that heaven is a very important and variegated notion in the Hebrew Bible, Septuagint, and Second Temple literature. The assorted bodies of literature surveyed in this broad period reveal many consistent threads in the use of heaven, both as a cosmological term and in reference to the divine abode. Yet at the same time, there are noticeable streams of development as the semantic flexibility of heaven is appropriated

---

[87] Bruce D. Chilton, *Targumic Approaches to the Gospels: Essays in the Mutual Definition of Judaism and Christianity* (Lanham, Maryland: University Press of America, 1986), 100.

[88] This analysis stems from my own observations based on the recent series of concordances to the Targums produced by Brill: *A Bilingual Concordance to the Targum of the Prophets*.

in different ways at different times. Thus, for example, we can observe significant differences in the employment of heaven between the apocalyptic materials and the Mishnah. The different genres, authors, and purposes of the wide variety of literature in this period prevent us from making definitive statements of a diachronic nature, though we can observe some trends within the diversity. This rich variety of usage provides a multi-colored palette with which Matthew will paint his own distinctive picture of heaven.

CHAPTER THREE

A SURVEY OF HEAVEN IN MATTHEW

Having surveyed the usage of heaven in its Jewish literary context, we may turn to the NT and Matthew's use of heaven in particular. In light of the frequent recurrence and theological significance of heaven in the Old Testament and Second Temple literature, it is not surprising that all of the NT authors (except Jude) also regularly utilize this language. Forms of οὐρανός appear some 273 times in the NT in addition to several other related terms such as οὐρανόθεν, μεσουράνημα, οὐράνιος, and ἐπουράνιος (see Table 3.1 below).

Much as in the OT and Second Temple literature, heaven in the NT is used in a plethora of ways. God is said to be the creator of heaven and earth (Acts 4:24, 14:15, 17:24; Rev 10:6, 14:7) and to dwell there (Matt 5:34; Acts 7:49; Heb 8:1; Rev 4). There are angels in heaven as messengers and servants of God (Matt 18:10; Mark 12:25, 13:32; Eph 3:15; Rev 12:7, 19:1), and from heaven Jesus will return with his angels (Matt 24:31; 1 Thes 4:16; Rev 19:11f.). There is a heavenly tabernacle and heavenly Jerusalem (Gal 4:26; Heb 12:22; Rev 3:12, 11:19, 21:2–22). People lift their eyes to heaven (Mark 6:41; Luke 18:13; John 17:1; Acts 1:11; 7:55), and the Christian's citizenship is said to be in heaven (Phil 3:20), along with his or her treasures and rewards (Matt 5:12, 6:20; Luke 5:23; 1 Pet 1:4).

From these and other uses of οὐρανός, various categories of meaning have been proposed.[1] These can be summarized as follows:

1) οὐρανός in reference to portions of the visible creation distinguished from the earth, such as the firmament or sky above, the starry heaven, and the atmosphere where the birds fly.
2) οὐρανός combined with γῆ as a merism to refer to the whole world, heaven and earth.
3) οὐρανός in reference to the invisible, transcendent place(s) above where God dwells along with his angels and the righteous dead.

---

[1] See the helpful enumeration of categories in Louw and Nida's, *Greek-English Lexicon*, s.v. οὐρανός.

When we move from the NT in general to the Gospel of Matthew in particular, we find the language of heaven plays a very prominent role. In fact, it is interesting to find that of all the NT books, the Gospel of Matthew employs heaven language significantly more often than any other.

As can be observed from the chart, 30% (82 of 273) of the occurrences of οὐρανός in the NT are found in Matthew. This is a strikingly high number in comparison with the other synoptic Gospels (see Synoptic Analysis below). Matthew's frequent use of this term also stands out relative to the Revelation of John in that this latter work is concerned very much with the architecture, furniture and workings of heaven per se, while Matthew is evidently not.

Table 3.1 Occurrences of Οὐρανός and Related Terms in the NT[2]

	οὐρανός	ἐπουράνιος[a]	οὐράνιος[a]	μεσουράνημα	οὐρανόθεν	Total
Matthew	82	–	7	–	–	89
Mark	18	–	–	–	–	18
Luke	35	–	1	–	–	36
John	18	1	–	–	–	19
Acts	26	–	1	–	2	29
Pauline Epistles[b]	21	12	–	–	–	33
Hebrews	10	6	–	–	–	16
Catholic Epistles	11	–	–	–	–	11
Johannine Epistles	–	–	–	–	–	0
Revelation	52	–	–	3	–	55
Total	273	19	9	3	2	306

Notes
a – According to *NIDNTT*, s.v. "Heaven," ἐπουράνιος was the preferred adjective and eventually prevailed over οὐράνιος.
b – These include the so-called deutero-Pauline writings, though there are no occurrences of οὐρανός in the Pastorals, but only one instance of ἐπουράνιος (2 Tim 4:18).

---

[2] These statistics are based on the NA[27] text, including terms bracketed in the main text. Three such bracketed occurrences of οὐρανός in Matthew are in 16:2–3 which is uncertain textually. Metzger's discussion of the uncertainty of the evidence rightly leaves the decision open on this difficult text. Bruce M. Metzger, *A Textual Commentary on the Greek New Testament* (3d ed.; New York: United Bible Socities, 1971), 41.

The contexts in which heaven is used in Matthew are multifarious due to the flexibility of οὐρανός, even as they are in the rest of the NT.[3] We find that God is the Father in heaven (5:16; 6:1; 16:17; 18:19; et al.) and his throne is there (5:34; 23:22). Heaven is whence the Spirit of God descends (3:16) and the voice of God speaks (3:17). It is also the place of promised rewards (5:12; 6:20; 19:21) and the normal realm of existence of the angels (18:10; 22:30; 24:36; 28:2).

In addition to these "spiritual" uses, οὐρανός can also refer to the created order of the sky and atmosphere. Jesus will appear on the clouds of heaven, i.e., the sky (24:30; 26:64), the color of the face of heaven reveals the weather (16:2–3), and birds are regularly referred to as τὰ πετεινὰ τοῦ οὐρανοῦ (6:26; 8:20; 13:32). Such astronomical and meteorological uses, however, are not as prominent as they are in the preceding literature.

By far, the most common uses of οὐρανός in Matthew are in the phrases ἡ βασιλεία τῶν οὐρανῶν (kingdom of heaven), occurring 32 times, and ὁ πατὴρ ὁ ἐν τοῖς οὐρανοῖς (Father in heaven) and the related ὁ πατὴρ ὑμῶν ὁ οὐράνιος (heavenly Father), occurring 13 and 7 times, respectively. Kingdom of heaven is found nowhere else in the OT, NT or any preceding Second Temple literature. Similar phrases appear occasionally in the Apocrypha and rabbinic material and only infrequently in subsequent literature such as the Gospel of Thomas. These phrases are apparently very significant for Matthew.

When we examine Matthew's usage of οὐρανός at a more detailed level, some specific patterns emerge. Of the 82 instances of οὐρανός in Matthew, 35 occur in prepositional phrases. By far the most common is with the preposition ἐν (27x).[4] A distant second is οὐρανός used with ἐκ (5x). Only three other times does Matthew use οὐρανός with any other preposition: once each with ἕως, εἰς, and ἀπό. In percentage, this corresponds roughly with other NT usage,[5] although some other authors use ἐκ, ἀπό and εἰς far more frequently with οὐρανός.

Also very similar to general NT usage is Matthew's use of the article with οὐρανός. Both Matthew and the other NT authors use articular

---

[3] The following ordering is similar to Gerhard Schneider's categorization of uses of οὐρανός in Matthew in "'Im Himmel—auf Erden'."

[4] All four possible permutations of this phrase occur: ἐν οὐρανῷ (6x), ἐν οὐρανοῖς (7x), ἐν τῷ οὐρανῷ (3x), ἐν τοῖς οὐρανοῖς (11x).

[5] Matthew uses οὐρανός in prepositional phrases a little less frequently than the NT in general (43% and 68% respectively).

forms of οὐρανός just over 75% of the time.⁶ Like the rest of the NT (and preceding literature), there does not appear to be any particular pattern to Matthew's use or non-use of the article. Both the plural and singular occurrences of οὐρανός are most commonly articular. Within prepositional phrases, both articular and anarthrous instances occur. Moreover, the referent connected to οὐρανός seems to have no effect on whether the form is articular or anarthrous. For example, θησαυρός is the referent of οὐρανός on three occasions, each with a different form: ἐν τοῖς οὐρανοῖς (5:12), ἐν οὐρανῷ (6:20), and ἐν οὐρανοῖς (19:21).⁷

One of the most unusual things about Matthew's usage of οὐρανός is his uncommon employment of the plural. Plural οὐρανοί is not a common occurrence in the LXX or other Second Temple literature. In the NT, plural forms do occur more frequently than in the preceding literature, but still amount to only about a third of the instances. However, 55 of the 90 occurrences of plural forms of οὐρανός in the NT are found in Matthew. This accounts for a striking 61% of the plural forms in the NT, and it contrasts sharply with the usage throughout the LXX and Pseudepigrapha.

Synoptic Analysis[8]

An analysis of parallels in the Synoptic tradition sheds further light on Matthew's use of οὐρανός.⁹ Of his uses, ten appear in parallel in the triple-tradition (II), nine in Matthew and Luke only (V), and five in

---

⁶ According to the NA²⁷ text, Matthew has 64 articular forms and 18 anarthrous. However, there are six instances where the textual witnesses are quite difficult to sort out, thus leaving some degree of uncertainty (6:1; 10:32, 33; 16:17; 18:10; 18:18b,c).

⁷ In his massive *Johannine Grammar* (London: A&C Black, 1906), §1952–1958, Edwin Abbot argued that John made an intentional distinction between "heaven" and "the heaven." Whether this is accurate for John or not, it does not appear to be the case in Matthew or the other Synoptic Gospels.

⁸ For full verse listings, see the Appendix, "Data from a Synoptic Comparison on Οὐρανός."

⁹ For this analysis, the two-source theory of Marcan priority and Matthew and Luke's use of Mark and Q will be utilized as the working hypothesis, though with the acknowledgement that these hypotheses are not unassailable. The following conventions will be used: "Q" refers to material deemed to be in a written source used by both Matthew and Luke, as demarcated in J. Robinson, P. Hoffmann, and J. Kloppenborg, *The Critical Edition of Q* (Minneapolis: Fortress, 2000). Roman numerals refer to the classification of pericopae according to Eusebius' Canon Tables (see NA²⁷ 79, 84–89 for full details). Those used here are: II = 3 Gospels (Mt, Mk, Lk); III = 3 Gospels (Mt, Lk, Jn); V = 2 Gospels (Mt, Lk); VI = 2 Gospels (Mt, Mk); X = pericopae unique

Matthew and Mark only (VI). The remaining 58 occur only in Matthew (X). Of the 58 occurrences in canon X, nearly half (27) occur in what is considered "M", special Matthean material, while 13 appear in canon II material, and 18 occur in Q sections. In other words, Matthew not only has or creates instances of οὐρανός in his unique pericopae and sayings, but he also regularly inserts οὐρανός into both Q material and the Marcan source. Of the insertions of οὐρανός into both Q material and the Marcan sections, a strong majority of these (24 of 31) occur in the form of either kingdom of heaven (17) or Father in heaven (7). That is, the majority of οὐρανός-redactions to his received sources comes in the form of his two key phrases, kingdom of heaven and Father in heaven.

Matthew's unique phrase kingdom of heaven occurs 32 times, but contrary to the impression one usually gets from commentaries, in only 12 instances is it a Synoptic substitute for kingdom of God.[10] The other 20 occurrences of kingdom of heaven in Matthew appear without parallel in Mark or Luke, most of which are in M, but not all. Thus, while there are several instances of Matthew's kingdom of heaven in parallel to others' kingdom of God, the most common source of kingdom of heaven in Matthew comes from redactional insertion or from M material.[11]

Matthew's recurrent phrases Father in heaven and heavenly Father occur a total of 20 times (combined). With the exception of Mark 11:25, neither of these dominant Matthean expressions occurs anywhere else in the NT.[12] Many of these occurrences are in M material, but

---

to each evangelist. The use of both traditional source-critical designations and the much older Eusebius Canon Tables grants different angles of sight on to the synoptic comparison.

[10] My calculations differ on two counts from Robert Mowery's article, "The Matthean References to the Kingdom." Mowery includes 18:3 as an instance where Matthew substitutes kingdom of heaven for Mark's kingdom of God, but I find no parallel there. Conversely, I would add 22:2 to Mowery's list as another instance (albeit a rougher parallel) where Matthew changes Q's kingdom of God for kingdom of heaven. The net change results in the same number of occurrences: 12.

[11] Of the four instances where Matthew does have kingdom of God (12:28; 19:24; 21:31; 21:43) instead of kingdom of heaven, the first two find parallel in Luke (12:28) or both Mark and Luke (19:24), while the latter two are unique to Matthew. For discussion of the anomaly of the kingdom of God occurrences in Matthew and their relationship to kingdom of heaven, see Chapter Twelve.

[12] Though there is no textual evidence for conflation, I am somewhat suspicious of the originality of Mark 11:25 (from within the Marcan priority theory) for the following reasons: It is the only instance where Mark has any parallel to Matthew's ὁ πατὴρ

most have some parallel in Q, though the parallels are often not exact. Most commonly, Father in heaven or heavenly Father is substituted in Matthew for Q's πατήρ, θεός, or even, ἄγγελλοι τοῦ θεοῦ.¹³ The closest Lukan parallel is Luke 11:13 which reads, ὁ πατὴρ [ὁ] ἐξ οὐρανοῦ for Matthew's ὁ πατὴρ ὑμῶν ὁ ἐν τοῖς οὐρανοῖς.¹⁴

One of Matthew's other key uses of οὐρανός is in the pairing of heaven and earth. Along with kingdom of heaven and the Father passages, this pair also shows interesting redactional markings. The instances where Matthew uses this pair in a merismatic sense occur in either Q or the triple-tradition,¹⁵ while his uses of heaven and earth in a contrastive sense occur only in his Gospel.¹⁶

ὁ οὐράνιος; it is the only instance of these words together (in any form) in Mark; and it occurs in the exact *Matthean* form of Father in heaven which occurs nowhere else in the NT outside of Matthew. If on the basis of external textual criticism this verse in Mark is original, then this is an example where Matthean priority better explains the phenomenon than Marcan priority. Alternatively, Marcan manuscripts may have picked up this Matthean phrase at a very early stage. According to Birger Gerhardsson, following Stendahl, the reading in Mark 11:25 is indeed disputed. B. Gerhardsson, "The Matthaean Version of the Lord's Prayer (Matt 6:9b–13): Some Observations," in *The New Testament Age: Essays in Honor of Bo Reicke* (ed. W. C. Weinrich; 2 vols.; Macon, Georgia: Mercer Universty Press, 1984), 1:218, n. 26.

¹³ Theoretically, Matthew's phrases could have been in Q and Luke made the modifications. However, there are several factors that make Matthew's modification of Q most reasonable: the phrasing in Matthew is quite consistent; this phrasing is not found elsewhere in the NT (except Mark 11:25); it corresponds with Matthew's other οὐρανός language; and Luke's usage reveals no particular idiolect or interest regarding οὐρανός language.

¹⁴ Most English translations dubiously render Luke's wording here as "heavenly Father." The originality of the attributive position ὁ (in brackets) is very difficult to ascertain. Without this article, the expression is better translated, "the Father will give *from* heaven" with the prepositional phrase modifying the verb, δώσει. If the article is retained, then the construction is quite odd and it is difficult to understand what is meant by this phrase. In all the other Gospel occurrences of ἐξ οὐρανοῦ including the other five in Luke, this phrase has an ablative sense, "from heaven." If this is the sense here, it is unclear why Luke would speak of the Father (as opposed to the Son) as the one "from heaven." All of this raises questions about the originality of the full expression. Notably, P⁴⁵ reads οὐράνιος for ἐξ οὐρανοῦ.

¹⁵ The merismatic pairs are: 5:18—Q; 11:25—Q; 24:35—Triple-tradition. For a full explanation and argumentation regarding merismatic and antithetic uses of heaven and earth, see Chapter Eight.

¹⁶ The contrastive pairs are: 5:34–35; 6:10, 19–20; 16:19b,c; 18:18b,c; 18:19; 23:9; 28:18. All of these come from M material with the exception of 6:10 and 6:19–20. However, in 6:10, the heaven and earth phrase is completely missing from the Lukan parallel (11:2), and likewise, no heaven and earth pairing is in view in the Lukan parallel (12:33) to Matt 6:19–20. Thus, all of the heaven and earth contrast pairs in Matthew are unique to his Gospel.

When one examines the synoptic comparison in the opposite direction—i.e., instances where Mark and/or Luke have οὐρανός when Matthew does not—the results confirm the dominance of the οὐρανός theme in Matthew. There are only two instances in Mark where οὐρανός occurs that are not paralleled in Matthew: Mark 7:34 and 16:19, the second of which is from the textually-dubious longer ending of Mark. The material in these instances is unique to Mark and there is no parallel pericope found in either Matthew or Luke.[17] The instance in Mark 7:34 is a reference to Jesus looking up εἰς τὸν οὐρανόν, but it does not seem to have much theological significance there. Regardless, in all instances but one, Matthew has subsumed Mark's uses of οὐρανός and added to them significantly. In contrast, there are seven instances where Mark has οὐρανός and Luke has *not* retained the parallel. If the Marcan-priority two-source theory is correct, then apparently Luke was not as concerned to maintain the references to οὐρανός found in Mark.

On the other hand, there are 14 instances when Luke does have οὐρανός where Matthew does not.[18] An examination of these instances reveals that 11 of the 14 occur in uniquely Lukan material (L).[19] The other three are Lukan redactions to triple-tradition material in which he adds a unique phrase, all cases in which Matthew and Mark agree against Luke. At the same time, in every Lukan occurrence of οὐρανός from Q, Matthew also has retained οὐρανός (albeit sometimes in a different form). Therefore, we can summarize the findings in this way: In both the Marcan material and Q, Matthew has retained the occurrences of οὐρανός available in his sources and has added to them. The only instances of οὐρανός in Mark or Luke where Matthew does not have the word are from blocks of material unique to each evangelist or sentences which are inserted by the evangelists. Thus, again working from the two-source hypothesis, there is only one instance in either Mark or Q (Mark 7:34) where Matthew has dropped a reference to οὐρανός in the sources available to him. He not only employs the instances of οὐρανός in his sources, but he expands on them in number and meaning.

---

[17] Mark 16:19, which is unlikely original, is paralleled in Luke 24:51, but the Lukan verse is likely the source of the reading in Mark, thus it is not a true parallel.

[18] Or thirteen if the textually-uncertain Luke 22:43 is excluded.

[19] These are: 2:15; 4:25; 9:54; 10:18, 20; 15:18, 21; 17:29; 18:13; 22:43; 24:51.

Hints from the Hot Spots

Thermal mapping is a technique used by scientists to identify "hot-spots" or points of greater heat across a geographical area. If one were to make a thermal map of the Gospel of Matthew, it would be clear that the hottest spots in the Gospel—i.e., those places with the greatest theological heat—all contain heaven language. Or analyzed from a different vantage: those places which show a concentration of heaven language prove to be hot-spots in Matthew. Thus, in addition to the sheer frequency of heaven language in Matthew, there is a weightiness of value where it appears.

For example, the entire Sermon on the Mount is rife with the language of heaven—heaven and earth pairs, kingdom of heaven, and the Father in heaven—especially when lined up side by side with Luke's version.[20] Even more specifically, the highest peaks of the Sermon are particularly concentrated in heaven language. The Beatitudes begin and end with an *inclusio* of kingdom of heaven references (5:3, 10). Within the poem, earth (5:5) appears in thematic connection with the two kingdom of heaven references. And the addendum to the Beatitudes (5:11–12) promises reward *in heaven*. Similarly, Matthew's Lord's Prayer leans heavily on heaven language: God is addressed as the Father in heaven and petitioned for his kingdom and will to come on earth as it is in heaven. As in the Beatitudes, the addendum to the Lord's Prayer speaks of the heavenly Father (6:14–15).[21]

Similarly, a great number of Jesus' parables in Matthew are prefaced with reference to the kingdom of heaven. This serves as a repeated refrain in the parables discourse of chapter 13 (cf. 13:11, 24, 31, 33, 44, 45, 47, 52), as well as in the introduction to other parabolic teachings (e.g. 20:1).

---

[20] In a unique and insightful article, B. B. Scott and M. E. Dean present a "sound map" of the Sermon on the Mount. Their study shows that references to heaven in the Sermon are not only frequent, but serve key functions throughout, such as the beginnings and endings of inclusios, chiastic centers, and repeated epithets. This strengthens my point here. Bernard Brandon Scott and Margaret E. Dean, "A Sound Map of the Sermon on the Mount," in *Treasures Old and New: Recent Contributions to Matthean Studies* (ed. David R. Bauer and Mark Allan Powell; Atlanta: Scholars Press, 1996): 311–378.

[21] Robert Foster, "Why on Earth Use 'Kingdom of Heaven'?," 499, similarly observes that heavenly language forms an *inclusio* at several points in the Sermon. He concludes, "Thus, rhetorically the heavenly language guides the whole structure of the sermon, beginning major sections (5.3, 20; 6.1, 20) and bracketing off major sections (5.10, 48; 7.11, 21)."

Even more striking, Matthew's unique and important ecclesiological passages have at their center various forms of heaven language. In 16:17-19 the Father in heaven, the kingdom of heaven, and two heaven and earth pairs are all crowded together in one short saying of Jesus. Likewise, in 18:18-20 the church is promised binding and loosing power on earth that corresponds with that in heaven, sanctioned by the Father in heaven.

Another hot-spot in Matthew is the Olivet Discourse. One section in particular has a high concentration of references to heaven. In speaking of the coming of the Son of Man, Jesus, leaning heavily on OT and apocalyptic imagery, speaks of the stars of heaven, the powers of heaven, the clouds of heaven, and the four winds of heaven (24:29-31). In the midst of his coming *from heaven*, all the tribes *of the earth* will mourn (24:30). Jesus promises that his words are true, that *heaven and earth* will pass away rather than his words (24:35), although neither he nor the angels *of heaven* know the hour of fulfillment (24:36).

A final example of a theologically-heated pericope in Matthew is in the conclusion to the book, the Great Commission (28:16-20). In this "red-lettered" climax to the Gospel, Jesus sums up his authority (cf. the crowds' response to the Sermon on the Mount in 7:28-29) as encompassing heaven and earth. This bold claim forms the basis of the church's entire subsequent mission: Trinitarian baptism and discipleship even to the end of the age. This post-resurrection universal authority consummates the authority that the Son of Man had *on earth* previously (9:6). It is more than coincidence that Matthew ends his Gospel with this weighty word pair of heaven and earth to describe the risen Lord's ongoing presence and authority—the very word pair that also begins the ancient Jewish Scriptures in Genesis 1:1 and ends them at 2 Chronicles 36:23, thus consummating God's work from the beginning of time, and forming an inclusio with the OT witness.

From these examples, it is not difficult to see that the language of heaven and particularly the theme of heaven and earth are very important in Matthew. From a survey of the preceding and contemporary literature, it is clear that no book has such a concentration of heaven language nor a focus on it as a theme as does Matthew.

Conclusion

Matthew's specific usage of heaven has only been sketched so far. This chapter serves to highlight its basic continuity with much of the preceding

Jewish literature as well as its predominance as a theme in Matthew. Along the way I have mentioned four particularly unusual elements of Matthew's usage of heaven language. These can be summarized as follows: (1) a preference for the plural οὐρανοί; (2) frequent use of the heaven and earth pair; (3) use of the phrases, Father in heaven and heavenly Father; and (4) the repeated expression, kingdom of heaven. Subsequent chapters (Part Two) will explore these four elements in detail and show how each of them contributes to Matthew's literary and theological theme of the contrast between heaven and earth. Before proceeding to this analysis, we will situate the theme of heaven and earth in the context of Matthean theology.

CHAPTER FOUR

HEAVEN AND EARTH IN THE CONTEXT OF MATTHEAN STUDIES AND THEOLOGY

In the previous chapter we observed how heaven language and the theme of heaven and earth correspond closely with the weightiest or "hottest" passages throughout the First Gospel. In a similar vein, this chapter serves to show how the theme of heaven and earth interacts with several key theological emphases that scholars have observed in Matthew. The point is to establish firmly the *importance* of the major thesis of this work: that heaven and earth is a key theological theme in Matthew. The second part of this work will provide full analysis of heaven and heaven and earth in Matthew and thus full argumentation of this point. For the present, this concluding chapter to Part One seeks to found the rest of the project on a solid basis of relevance by showing how this theme relates to other key theological themes in Matthew.

Of course, it is impossible to offer a comprehensive review of even one of the many crucial and debated issues in Matthean scholarship, the study of which has been famously called "a new storm centre in contemporary scholarship."[1] In the twenty years since this statement, scholarly output on the First Gospel has only increased. Nor can I claim that the heaven and earth idea touches on every theme or emphasis in Matthew, but it does on most of them. In this chapter I will briefly survey the state of the question on a number of current topics which arise in the study of Matthew and then demonstrate how a recognition of Matthew's emphasis on the heaven and earth theme informs our understanding of each of these matters.

A survey of a large number of commentaries and other works on Matthew reveals many topics that are identified repeatedly as particular emphases in Matthew. Each scholar presents a slightly different list of "distinctive characteristics," "prominent themes," or "central theological emphases" in the First Gospel. The variations in the lists

---

[1] Graham Stanton, "Introduction: Matthew's Gospel A New Storm Centre," in *The Interpretation of Matthew* (ed. G. Stanton; London: SPCK, 1983), 1.

are due primarily to the fact that the themes inevitably overlap with each other at many points and are thus categorized differently by different scholars. For example, one cannot talk about the theme of *OT Fulfillment* without also speaking of *Christology*—how Jesus fulfills messianic expectations—and the *Kingdom*—the consummation of OT expectations with Christ as its king. Similarly, the matters of *Discipleship*, *Righteousness*, and *Law* all overlap and interact with each other, as do *Matthew's Jewish Setting* and issues of *Ecclesiology* and *OT Fulfillment*. Here I have identified seven key topics in Matthean studies which can be reviewed in light of the heaven and earth theme: (1) Matthew's *Sitz im Leben*; (2) Christology; (3) Kingdom; (4) The Fatherhood of God; (5) Fulfillment of the Old Testament/Old Covenant; (6) The New People of God and Ecclesiology; (7) Eschatology and Apocalyptic.[2]

Matthew's *Sitz im Leben*

Certainly the hottest topic of discussion in Matthean studies, as well as the most complicated, is the inquiry into Matthew's setting and community in light of early Jewish-Christian relations. John Riches, writing in 1996, observes a shift in focus within Matthean studies between the 60s–70s and the 90s. The concern of scholars in the earlier period was using redaction criticism to "to chart as fully as possible the evangelist's own theological stance" on particular theological questions such as salvation history, the OT, the Law, Christology, and ecclesiology. In contrast, scholarship in the 90s focused much more on the social setting of the Matthean community and how the first readers might have received the Gospel of Matthew.[3] Accordingly, a third of Riches' guide to Matthew is dedicated to Matthew's community and the reception of the Gospel within it.

---

[2] The only other major category typically discussed in Matthew but not dealt with here is *Soteriology*, often discussed under the headings of *Righteousness* and *Discipleship*, though certainly the theme of heaven and earth could be tangentially related to these as well.

[3] John Riches, *Matthew* (New Testament Guides; Sheffield: Sheffield Academic, 1996), 7–8. The other, accompanying shift Riches observes is the change in methodological approaches: redaction criticism is no longer the favored son, but one of a plethora of critical methodologies employed by Gospels scholars. On this shift, see also Graham Stanton, *A Gospel for a New People: Studies in Matthew* (Louisville: Westminster/John Knox, 1993), 23–84; David R. Bauer and Mark Allan Powell, "Introduction," in *Treasures New and Old*, 1–25.

Such an emphasis is common in commentaries and has spawned a host of works dedicated specifically to this question.[4] One of the first major books to stimulate this discussion was W. D. Davies' *The Setting of the Sermon on the Mount*,[5] and in the intervening decades, the question of how to understand Matthew's community and its relation to Judaism has been the focus of many Matthean scholars' efforts. For example, Graham Stanton prefaces his well-respected volume of essays on Matthew by stating that the primary concern woven through the book is with "the relationship of the Christian communities for whom Matthew writes to contemporary Judaism."[6] Interestingly, Robert Gundry changed the subtitle of the second edition of his commentary from "a commentary on his literary and theological art" to "a commentary on his handbook for a mixed church under persecution" to give prominence to what he sees as the purpose of Matthew.[7] And in accord with such trends, Bauer and Powell call the situation of Matthew's church in relation to Judaism and to Gentile Christianity "the most central and perduring issue facing Matthean scholarship."[8]

Reconstructing Matthew's life setting is a difficult task because of the mixed messages found throughout the First Gospel. There are strong themes in Matthew which stand in tension with one another: Jewish particularism juxtaposed with Gentile-including universalism, and a stress on the continuing validity of the Law combined with a harsh critique of (Pharisaic) Judaism. Matthew is clearly the most "Jewish" of the Gospels, yet at the same time it provides the strongest condemnations of Judaism and the most straight-forward claims about mission to

---

[4] Examples include David L. Balch, ed., *Social History of the Matthean Community* (Minneapolis: Fortress, 1991); David E. Garland, *The Intention of Matthew 23* (Leiden: Brill, 1979); Douglas R. A. Hare, *The Theme of Jewish Persecution of Christians in the Gospel According to St. Matthew* (Cambridge: Cambridge University Press, 1967); J. Andrew Overman, *Matthew's Gospel and Formative Judaism* (Minneapolis: Fortress, 1990); idem *Church and Community in Crisis: The Gospel According to Matthew* (Valley Forge, Penn.: Trinity, 1996); Anthony J. Saldarini, *Matthew's Christian-Jewish Community* (Chicago: University of Chicago Press, 1994).

[5] W. D. Davies, *The Setting of the Sermon on the Mount* (Cambridge: Cambridge University Press, 1964). In this work Davies considers an assortment of settings in which to understand the Sermon on the Mount: its setting in the rest of Matthew, in Jewish Messianic expectation, in contemporary Judaism, in the early Church, and in the ministry of Jesus.

[6] Stanton, *A Gospel for a New People*, 1. Seven of Stanton's chapters in this volume are organized under the rubric of "The Parting of the Ways."

[7] Gundry, *Matthew*², xi.

[8] Bauer and Powell, "Introduction," 4.

the Gentiles. Not surprisingly, various scholars interpret these themes differently as they seek to understand Matthew's *Sitz im Leben*.[9]

As a result of these mixed messages, there have been several positions in the history of interpretation:[10] (1) Matthew was the earliest Gospel, written in Aramaic for a Jewish Christian community; (2) the Gospel was written between 70 and 85 CE (before Yavneh) coming from a Jewish Christian community closely related to Judaism (thus, an *intra muros* debate); (3) Matthew comes from a post-85 CE community which has experienced a definitive break with Judaism (thus, an *extra muros* debate); (4) the author and community were Gentile and reflect an era well after any discussion with Judaism has ended. In the more recent debate, several scholars such as Donald Hagner have opted for some type of mediating position. Hagner discerns several other versions of a mediating view in the writings of G. Stanton, K. Tagawa, S. Brown, B. T. Viviano, and S. H. Brooks.[11]

It is not the place here to arbitrate this large and contoured debate. The relevant issue is how a recognition of Matthew's heaven and earth theme relates to the life situation of his original hearers. *Simply stated, the strong contrast that Matthew crafts throughout his Gospel between heaven and earth serves as both a point of continuity with the OT/formative Judaism and part of a sharp "parting of the ways" polemic.* As will be shown in subsequent chapters, Matthew uses heaven language in a pattern designed to distinguish "insiders" and "outsiders," thus emphasizing a break with Judaism (at least non-Christian forms of Judaism in Matthew's time) and the separation of the Church from the synagogue.[12] In the same vein, Matthew depicts the heavenly realm and its values as those of the disciples versus those of the Pharisees (e.g., Matt 6:1–21)—again, emphasizing a polemical break with established Judaism.[13] Yet at the

---

[9] See especially, Donald A. Hagner, "The *Sitz im Leben* of the Gospel of Matthew," in *Treasures New and Old*: 27–68. Hagner provides an updated and more focused discussion of this issue in "Matthew: Christian Judaism or Jewish Christianity?" in *The Face of New Testament Studies: A Survey of Recent Research* (ed. Scot McKnight and Grant Osborne; Grand Rapids: Baker, 2004): 263–282.

[10] Based on Graham Stanton's essay, "The Origin and Purpose of Matthew's Gospel," 1910–1921.

[11] Hagner, "The *Sitz im Leben* of the Gospel of Matthew," 36–40.

[12] The terms "insider" and "outsider" language are borrowed from Robert Mowery's article, "The Matthean References to the Kingdom." On the use of οὐρανός for this purpose, see Chapter Six below.

[13] One of the very few scholars to reflect at all on the purpose of Matthew's heaven language comes to a similar conclusion about the purpose of οὐρανός in the

same time, this heavenly versus earthly contrast reflects strong *continuity* with OT language (particularly Genesis and Daniel) and aligns particularly with the Israelite prophets' critique of their *own* people.¹⁴ Thus, the criticism is one "from within"—as only the most pointed critiques can be.

In light of this, Donald Hagner's mediating view of Matthew's life setting seems very astute. He argues that:

> The evangelist's community partook of two worlds, the Jewish and the Christian. Although they saw their Christianity as the true fulfillment of Judaism, they also were very conscious that they had broken with their unbelieving brothers and sisters. They were struggling to define and defend a Jewish Christianity to the Jews on the one hand and to realize their unity with Gentile Christians on the other.¹⁵

Hagner observes that continuity with the past is stressed, but at the same it is always transposed into a new, higher level because of the Christ¹⁶—"treasures old and new." The same could be said for the theme of heaven and earth. It reflects continuity and is very "Jewish," but it also serves as a dividing point: One must choose between the way of Christ (heaven) or the way of the Pharisees and scribes (earth).

Christology

On the more traditional inquiry into particular *theological* themes in Matthew, none stands so central as the topic of Christology. Matthean scholars commonly observe the vital role that the identity of Jesus plays in the First Gospel and how this drives and informs all the other theological categories. Such sentiments are widespread:

First Gospel. Robert Foster argues that Matthew's heavenly language was used "to demonstrate that Jesus was Messiah in ways the leaders of formative Judaism did not understand and to reaffirm to Jesus' disciples that their identity, affirmation, and goal were in heaven and not on earth" (p. 490). The phrase, kingdom of heaven, functions in Matthew "to legitimate the community of his readers and discredit the leaders of formative Judaism who clearly reject God and his reign" (p. 495). Robert Foster, "Why on Earth Use 'Kingdom of Heaven'?".

¹⁴ Cf. Matthew's unique emphasis on "the Law and the prophets." See Alexander Sand, *Das Gesetz und die Propheten: Untersuchungen zur Theologie des Evangeliums nach Matthäus* (Regensburg: Friederich Pustet, 1974).

¹⁵ Hagner, "The *Sitz im Leben* of the Gospel of Matthew," 49–50. Elsewhere Hagner gives the helpful analogy of a person who is the holder of passports from two different countries which are now at war.

¹⁶ Hagner, "The *Sitz im Leben* of the Gospel of Matthew," 53.

> "Every aspect of Matthew's theology is ultimately connected with his convictions about the identity and meaning of Jesus."[17]
>
> "Matthew's doctrine of Jesus as the Christ is fundamentally important to every theological emphasis in the Gospel, for it is the identity of Jesus that determines such things as fulfillment, authoritative exposition of the law, discipleship, ecclesiology, and eschatology."[18]
>
> "Christology, the explanation of *who Jesus is*, must be at the heart of Matthew's theological task. Virtually every aspect of the Gospel's theology could be subsumed under this heading."[19]

Many scholars have also observed that a lofty Christology is particularly focused in Matthew. Hagner states that Matthew has heightened the Christological theme from his Marcan material,[20] and Schnackenburg observes that Matthew underscores his Christology relative to the other Gospels in many ways, including Peter's confession and the reverence Jesus' disciples show him on several occasions.[21]

Thus, the study of Matthew's emphasis on Jesus as the Christ has been a constant feature of Matthean studies. What has changed, however, is a move away from a purely titular approach to observe other ways in which the Evangelist paints a picture of Jesus' messiahship. There is a growing awareness, due largely to the influence of literary critical methods, that we must attend to the structure and flow of the narrative, not just the verbal content, to discern the theology and intent of the text. Older studies typically delineated a number of titles used by Matthew such as Christ, Son of God, Son of Man, Son of David, King, and Emmanuel, and sought to show how these present Jesus as the Christ.[22] The last two decades have added to this approach the insights that the *allusions* and *actions* of Matthew's Jesus also communicate his messianic claims. In addition to the Christological titles, themes such

---

[17] Donald Senior, *What Are They Saying About Matthew?* (New York: Paulist Press, 1983), 56.

[18] Hagner, *Matthew 1–13*, lxi.

[19] France, *Matthew*, 41.

[20] Hagner, *Matthew 1–13*, lxi.

[21] Schnackenburg, *Matthew*, 9.

[22] One of the most comprehensive and debated studies of Matthew's titles is Jack Dean Kingsbury's *Matthew: Structure, Christology, and Kingdom* (Philadelphia: Fortress, 1975). Later, Kingsbury again made use of Christological titles but through employing a literary critical methodology rather than redaction critical in Kingsbury, *Matthew as Story* (2d ed.; Philadelphia: Fortress, 1988).

as Jesus as Wisdom,[23] Jesus as healer,[24] and Jesus as a New Moses,[25] fill out and enrich our Christological understanding in Matthew. As John Riches concludes, Matthew

> develops his views about Jesus' person and relationship to God by weaving titles *and* motifs from his tradition into a rich narrative. Focusing on the titles is one way to see what Matthew is attempting, but it needs at least to be supplemented by a consideration of the narrative setting of the titles and their interaction with other motifs.[26]

How does this relate to the theme of heaven and earth? This fuller, narrative-sensitive reading of Matthew's Christology enables us to see that the heaven and earth contrast theme likewise contributes to the high Christology of the First Gospel. That is, one of the functions of Matthew's distinction between the heavenly and the earthly realms is that Jesus is clearly aligned with the divine side of the equation as compared to the human and earthly. His identity is very much defined through his connection with heaven.[27] Jesus is the one about whom the *heavenly* voice speaks (3:17); He is the one who proclaims the kingdom *of heaven* (4:17); He is the one with the intimate relationship with the Father *in heaven*, such that he makes the audacious claim for himself that "no one knows the Son except the Father, and no one knows the Father except the Son and any one to whom the Son chooses to reveal him" (11:27). Clearly, through such a repeated refrain of heaven connections, Jesus is unmistakably associated with the divine. All of this stands in contrast to the earth, which repeatedly is identified with the human (6:19–21; 18:18–20; 21:25–26; 23:9). And most importantly, the Gospel climaxes with the Christological claim that this Jesus has authority not only in the human realm, but also in the divine—"in heaven and on earth" (28:18; cp. the Christological allusion to the

---

[23] Pioneering works in this area were M. Jack Suggs, *Wisdom, Christology and Law in Matthew's Gospel* (Cambridge: Harvard University, 1970) and Fred W. Burnett, *The Testament of Jesus-Sophia: A Redaction-Critical Study of the Eschatological Discourse in Matthew* (Washington: University Press of America, 1981).

[24] H. J. Held, "Matthew as Interpreter of the Miracle Stories," in *Tradition and Interpretation in Matthew* (ed. G. Bornkamm, G. Barth, and H. J. Held; Philadelphia: Westminster, 1963): 165–299.

[25] Allison, *The New Moses*.

[26] Riches, *Matthew*, 102–103. Emphasis mine.

[27] This corresponds with Richard Bauckham's arguments concerning how the NT includes Jesus in the unique divine identity of the monotheistic God, in Bauckham, *God Crucified: Monotheism and Christology in the New Testament* (Carlisle: Paternoster, 1998).

Son of Man in Dan 7). In Genesis 1:1 God has authority over the chaos of the heavens and the earth, and this authority is the basis of his redemptive purposes for all the world through Abraham (Gen 10–12). In 28:18–20 Matthew shows that Jesus now participates in this same uniquely divine prerogative of ruling over all creation, and this too forms the basis for his disciples' mission to all the nations (cf. also Abraham in Matt 1:1). Accordingly, Jesus is worshipped (28:17). This fascinating connection between Genesis and Matthew hinges upon the language of heaven and earth. Thus, again, an understanding of the heaven and earth theme in Matthew contributes to our understanding of his emphasis on Jesus as the Christ sent from God.

Kingdom

Alongside Christology, another key theme in each of the Gospels is the proclamation of the kingdom of God. Matthew is no exception and indeed, may be said to have the greatest emphasis on the theme of kingdom. βασιλεία occurs fifty-five times in Matthew in a wide variety of phrases, including kingdom of heaven (32x), kingdom of God (4x), and several other references such as "his" or "your" kingdom.[28] Moreover, many scholars understand the central emphasis of the First Gospel to be found in Matthew's unique phrase, "the gospel of the kingdom" which occurs at important structural seams (4:23; 9:35; 24:14).[29] The kingdom is what heads the preaching ministry of John the Baptist (3:2) and Jesus (4:17), and is what Jesus commissions his followers to say in turn (10:7). Matthew's Jesus gives an important series of teachings explicating the ways of this kingdom (esp. chapter 13), and the disciples are taught to pray for its coming (6:10). Of course, Matthew's emphasis on kingdom overlaps with several other key themes he develops including Christology, OT fulfillment, and eschatology. Indeed, Kingsbury understands the kingdom to be "the single most comprehensive concept" in Matthew, touching on "every major facet of the Gospel, whether it be theological, Christological, or ecclesiological in nature."[30]

---

[28] Cp. Mark (20x); Luke (46x); John (5x); rest of the NT combined (36x).
[29] See especially Jack Dean Kingsbury, *Matthew: Structure, Christology, and Kingdom*, 128-131. Cf. Hagner, *Matthew 1–13*, li ff.
[30] Kingsbury, *Matthew: Structure, Christology, and Kingdom*, 128.

The subject of kingdom in Matthew has provided grist for a number of scholarly debates and shifts, some of which are more significant than others. One matter of great interest in the 20th-century has been what concepts inform Jesus' understanding of the kingdom.[31] Was kingdom primarily an apocalyptic/eschatological idea (Weiss; Schweitzer), and if so, was this an imminent future for which Jesus mistakenly hoped, a "realized eschatology" (Dodd), or something that was "already but not yet" (Kümmel; Ladd). Or instead, was Norman Perrin correct that kingdom is not a concept at all, but a *symbol* which evokes a *myth* of God's kingship?[32] A related matter of discussion concerns how we are to understand and translate βασιλεία: as the locative "kingdom" or instead as "reign," "rule," or "sovereignty."[33] More recently, some Matthean scholars have been more interested in reading Matthew's kingdom language against the context of the Roman Empire.[34] There are also occasional flare-ups of debate about whether Matthew intends something different with his phrases, kingdom of heaven and kingdom of God.[35]

Most of these debates will be analyzed more closely in Chapter Twelve of the present study. The matter at hand here is how the emphasis on kingdom relates to the broader heaven and earth theme in Matthew. The connection is not difficult to see. Out of all the NT and preceding literature, Matthew alone uses the phrase ἡ βασιλεία

---

[31] A helpful overview of this large topic can be found in the volume of collected essays edited by Wendell Willis, *The Kingdom of God in 20th-Century Interpretation* (Peabody, Mass.: Hendrickson, 1987).

[32] Norman Perrin, *Jesus and the Language of the Kingdom* (Philadelphia: Fortress, 1976). See the discussion of this idea and how Amos Wilder influenced Perrin in W. Emory Elmore, "Linguistic Approaches to the Kingdom: Amos Wilder and Norman Perrin," in *The Kingdom of God in 20th-Century Interpretation*, 53–65.

[33] Gustaf Dalman was the pioneer in advocating that the Jewish notion of βασιλεία focused on God's sovereignty and kingly rule. Dalman, *Words of Jesus*, 91ff. See also the discussion in Sverre Aalen, "'Reign' and 'House' in the Kingdom of God in the Gospels," *NTS* 8 (1962): 215–240; Joel Marcus, "Entering into the Kingly Power of God," *JBL* 107/4 (1988): 663–675.

[34] One of the leaders in this trend is Warren Carter: *Matthew and Empire: Initial Explorations* (Harrisburg, Penn.: Trinity Press International, 2001). Carter was also involved in coordinating discussions for the SBL Matthew Group on this topic.

[35] Margaret Pamment's article, "The Kingdom of Heaven According to the First Gospel," *NTS* 27 (1981): 211–232, argued for a distinctive difference in referent between these two terms, but has met with little acceptance. Other surveys of this issue and attempts at understanding include John C. Thomas, "The Kingdom of God in the Gospel According to Matthew," *NTS* 39 (1993), 136–146, and Mowery, "The Matthean References to the Kingdom."

τῶν οὐρανῶν. Only in later Rabbinic writings and subsequent Christian literature dependent on Matthew do we occasionally find this unique expression. I have argued in Chapter One that the typical understanding of this phrase as a mere reverential circumlocution is gravely mistaken. Instead, kingdom of heaven must be understood as part of Matthew's broad and nuanced use of heaven language. As will be shown in Part Two, kingdom of heaven is one of the four elements of Matthew's idiolectic use of οὐρανός, all of which serve the same purpose: to contrast heaven (used metonymically for God) with earth (humanity). A close reading of Matthew as a narrative whole reveals that throughout the kingdom of heaven is contrasted with all earthly kingdoms and societies.

Fatherhood of God

The theme of the Fatherhood of God is not one usually demarcated by commentators as a particular emphasis in Matthew, though it should be. Matthew refers to God as πατήρ forty-four times compared to only four times in Mark and seventeen in Luke. Only John refers to God as Father more often than Matthew. Moreover, only Matthew among the Synoptics refers to God as Father nearly as often as he uses θεός for this purpose.[36]

Luz, commenting on key words in Matthew, states that together the words "righteousness" and "Father" indicate well the subject-matter of the whole Sermon on the Mount.[37] More wide-ranging, F. W. Burnett states: "The presentation of God as father is so comprehensive in Matthew that few would disagree with Gottlob Schrenk's conclusion that 'we certainly find a true father theology in Mt.'"[38] Burnett goes on to outline how crucial Jesus' special filial relationship with God is to the theology and Christology of Matthew, most clearly expressed in 11:25–27.[39] Similarly, H. F. D. Sparks concludes that Matthew "had a

---

[36] Robert L. Mowery, "God, Lord and Father: The Theology of the Gospel of Matthew," *BR* 23 (1988), 24. See also idem, "From Lord to Father in Matthew 1–7," *CBQ* 59 (1997), 642–656.

[37] Ulrich Luz, *The Theology of the Gospel of Matthew* (trans., J. Bradford Robinson; Cambridge: Cambridge University Press, 1995), 3.

[38] Fred W. Burnett, "Exposing the Anti-Jewish Ideology of Matthew's Implied Author: The Characterization of God as Father," *Semeia* 59 (1992), 164.

[39] Burnett, "Exposing the Anti-Jewish Ideology," 165–168.

special interest in the Divine Fatherhood,"[40] and Armin Wouters argues that "the will of the Father" is a central idea in the whole proclamation of Matthew.[41] It is surprising that most commentators do not mention this as one of Matthew's distinctive elements, despite such insights from scholarly study.

Not only does Matthew prefer to call God Father, but his usage also stands out by regularly connecting God as Father with the idea of heaven. Twenty times Matthew modifies Father with some form of heaven: thirteen times in the phrase ὁ πατὴρ ὁ ἐν (τοῖς) οὐρανοῖς ("Father in heaven"), and seven times with the adjectival ὁ πατὴρ ὁ οὐράνιος ("heavenly Father"). "Father in heaven" occurs elsewhere only in Mark 11:25, parallel with one of Matthew's occurrences of ὁ πατὴρ ὑμῶν ὁ οὐράνιος (6:14), in addition to the less exact parallel ὁ πατὴρ [ὁ] ἐξ οὐρανοῦ in Luke 11:13.[42] Notably, the first instance in which the reader of Matthew encounters God as Father ascribes to him his place ἐν τοῖς οὐρανοῖς (5:16).

These statistics lead directly into our interest in this chapter. Just as in the case of kingdom of heaven, Matthew interweaves his theology of God as Father with his particular use of heaven language. And as in the case of kingdom of heaven, the point is one of contrast between the heavenly and earthly realms. Matthew depicts the Father God as heavenly (and his kingdom) as a counterpoint to the earthly alternatives. Jesus and his disciples (by association with him) have the Father in heaven as their God (6:9; 7:21; 12:50), rather than merely earthly fathers or rabbis (23:8–9) with their earth-bound, perishable benefits (6:1–21).

Fulfillment of Old Testament/Old Covenant

As observed above, several of the topics treated thus far overlap greatly as they are worked out in Matthew. For example, Matthew's Christology is organically related to his emphasis on Jesus' relationship with God

---

[40] H. F. D. Sparks, "The Doctrine of Divine Fatherhood in the Gospels," in *Studies in the Gospels: Essays in Memory of R. H. Lightfoot* (ed. D. E. Nineham; Oxford: Basil Blackwell, 1967), 251.

[41] Armin Wouters, "... *wer den Willen meines Vaters Tut": Eine Untersuchung zum Verständnis vom Handeln in Matthäusevangelium* (Regensburg: Friedrich Pustet, 1992).

[42] On the originality and translation of the Mk 11:25 and Lk 11:13, see my Synoptic Analysis in Chapter Three.

as Father and Jesus as the King of God's kingdom. The theme of Old Testament/Covenant fulfillment in Jesus is no exception, and several commentators understand this as the rubric through which to interpret all the other theological themes. France, for instance, calls "the essential key to all Matthew's theology" the view that God's purposes have been fulfilled in Jesus.[43] This topic relates closely to the perennially-debated issue of the Law in the New Testament, as well as the concept of Salvation History.

Matthew's vigorous use of the OT is well-recognized and well-studied and does not need to be rehearsed here. In addition to the "on the surface" formula quotations, Matthew employs scores of implicit quotations and allusions to the OT.[44] Matthew very clearly breathes the air of the OT and repeatedly interprets Jesus' words and actions through a typological lens. Stanton describes the importance of the OT in Matthew this way: "The OT is woven into the warp and woof of this gospel; the evangelist uses Scripture to underline some of his most prominent and distinctive theological concerns."[45]

As the present work seeks to show, one overlooked literary and theological concern for Matthew is the heaven and earth distinction. Matthew's employment of this theme provides another example of the way in which the First Gospel is very apparently steeped in OT traditions, concepts, and phraseology. The progression of the chapters in Part Two below shows how Matthew took up OT language about heaven and crafted it for his own theological purposes; OT phrases and texts find their completion in the revelation of Jesus Christ. This is especially true for the phrase heaven and earth which Matthew uses to present Jesus' coming as a New Genesis, the beginning of a new creation (see Chapter Eight), while at the same time giving a prophetic call for all to align their loyalties with God (heaven) rather than humanity (earth).

It is clear that Jesus as the Christ and Emmanuel (1:23; 28:20) is the focal point of the Gospel, with its concomitant shifts in God's dealings

---

[43] France, *Matthew*, 38.

[44] The data can be found in numerous works and are surveyed by most commentators. Some of the early important works in the modern debates include Krister Stendahl, *The School of St Matthew and Its Use of the Old Testament* (Lund: Gleerup, 1968); Robert H. Gundry, *The Use of the Old Testament in St Matthew's Gospel: With Special Reference to the Messianic Hope* (Leiden: Brill, 1967); W. Rothfuchs, *Die Erfüllungszitate des Matthäusevangeliums* (Stuttgart: Kohlhammer, 1969).

[45] Stanton, *A Gospel for a New People*, 346.

with humanity (cp. 10:5–6 with 28:18–20). Yet at the same time, Matthew is at pains to show that the Christ-event is not an abrogation of the Law and the Prophets nor of God's promises, but in fact, just the opposite: it is the consummation and fulfillment (1:22; 2:5, 15; etc.; 5:17–18). The strong verbal connection of "heaven and earth" with Genesis and the rest of the OT (especially the Prophets) forges another link in the continuity and fulfillment chain through which Matthew binds the Old and New Covenants (cf. 13:52).

The New People of God and Ecclesiology

Matthew has been long recognized as "the Gospel of the Church," both for its famous ecclesiological passages and because of its central importance in the life of the Church throughout her history. Much of what has already been covered above informs our discussion of Matthew's ecclesiology. As with each of the topics in this chapter, one cannot understand ecclesiology apart from its connection to OT fulfillment and especially Christology. John Meier states that "the nexus between Christology and ecclesiology is one of the most typical characteristics of Matthew's gospel."[46]

Matthew alone of the Evangelists uses the term ἐκκλησία (16:18; 18:17 [2x]) and many scholars understand these references as reflecting a later, developed ecclesiology. But as France and others have observed, in reality, there is no highly developed ecclesiological structure or character in Matthew.[47] Matthew's use of ἐκκλησία, like many of his other terms, alludes to the Septuagint—specifically, the assembly or people of God in the Old Covenant (around 75x including Deut 4:10; 1 Kg 8:14; Ezra 2:64). Boldly, Jesus now calls this assembly/people of God *his* ἐκκλησία (16:18), which "surely intends to indicate that the Christian church now fills the role of the Old Testament congregation of God's people."[48]

In fact, Matthew employs several themes and texts to suggest that his disciples are the new people of God. As Jesus is himself depicted as the typological fulfillment of Israel, so his people are the chosen ones of

---

[46] John Meier, *The Vision of Matthew: Christ, Church and Morality in the First Gospel* (New York: Paulist Press, 1979), 216.
[47] France, *Matthew: Evangelist and Teacher*, 243.
[48] France, *Matthew: Evangelist and Teacher*, 211.

God, the descendants of Abraham (prefigured in the warning of 3:9). God himself has revealed Jesus' sonship to these true children (3:17; 11:25–27; 16:17; 17:5). With Peter as their representative head, Jesus' disciples are given heavenly-sanctioned authority on earth (16:18–19; 18:18–19). The kingdom is being transferred from the disobedient sons to the followers of Jesus (8:11–12; 15:12–13; 21:43). And Jesus' disciples will sit with authority on twelve thrones from which they will judge the twelve tribes of Israel (19:28). Thus, many students of Matthew have recognized that the theme of Jesus' church as the new people of God is very important and strong in the First Gospel. Stanton summarizes his assorted studies on Matthew with the title "A Gospel for a New People" and concludes that Matthew is a "foundation document" which "contains a whole series of 'legitimating answers' for the 'new people'" of Jesus' disciples.[49]

Again, we may inquire as to how the heaven and earth theme identified in the present study relates to Matthew's ecclesiological emphasis. At the most basic verbal level, as in the case of kingdom and Father language, there is an obvious and strong connection of heaven and earth with the church. The two famous teachings on ἐκκλησία in Matthew both define the church (and/or its leaders) as having an authority that transcends the merely earthly to the heavenly (16:18–19; 18:17–20). Moreover, both of these passages have a high concentration of other key heaven terms, such as Father in heaven and kingdom of heaven. It is very clear that in these "hot-spot" passages, Matthew piles up references to heaven and heaven and earth, thereby stoking up the theological heat of the term ἐκκλησία.

On a broader conceptual level, Matthew's emphasis on Jesus' coming as a New Genesis also connects intimately with his ecclesiology. I have suggested above (see also Chapter Eight below) that the New Genesis theme is supported by Matthew's frequent heaven and earth language. The observation that the Gospel of Matthew initiates a New Genesis is yet another strand of evidence that Jesus' community of disciples is depicted as the typological fulfillment of Israel/the people of God. All of this is strengthened by use of the strongly allusive heaven and earth theme. Additionally, as Filson points out, the church in Matthew is very much defined in terms of its mission.[50] It is no accident that the

---

[49] Stanton, *A Gospel for a New People*, 378.
[50] F. V. Filson, *A Commentary on the Gospel according to St Matthew* (London: A&C Black, 1960), 44.

commissioning of the church's calling is undergirded by the authority Jesus now has—an authority defined as both "in heaven and on earth" (28:18).

Eschatology and Apocalyptic

The two earliest advocates of an (apocalyptic) eschatological interpretation of the NT were Johannes Weiss and Albert Schweitzer. Since then, with scholarly ebb and flow, many have emphasized the importance of an apocalyptic and/or eschatological framework for understanding the literature of the NT.[51] The Gospel of Matthew is no exception, with numerous interpreters seeing the First Gospel as thoroughly apocalyptic-eschatological.[52]

This development in NT studies has been fed by an explosion of research into apocalyptic and eschatology in the Second Temple period.[53] One of the foundational blocks in this scholarly edifice was the Apocalypse Group of the SBL Genres Project. They provided an oft-repeated definition of an "apocalypse":

---

[51] A most helpful survey of the history of interpretation on this matter can be found in M. C. de Boer, "Paul and Apocalyptic Eschatology," in *The Encyclopedia of Apocalypticism, Volume 1: The Origins of Apocalypticism in Judaism and Christianity* (ed. J. J. Collins; New York: Continuum, 2000): 345–383.

[52] One of the most specific studies on this matter is David C. Sim, *Apocalyptic Eschatology in the Gospel of Matthew* (Cambridge: Cambridge University Press, 1996). Sim provides a helpful survey of the field on pages 2–14. Other works on apocalyptic in Matthew include G. Bornkamm, "End-Expectation and Church in Matthew," in *Tradition and Interpretation in Matthew*: 15–51; O. Lamar Cope, "'To the close of the age': The Role of Apocalyptic Thought in the Gospel of Matthew," in *Apocalyptic and the New Testament: Essays in Honor of J. Louis Martyn* (ed. Joel Marcus and Marion L. Soards; Sheffield: Sheffield Academic, 1989): 113–124; D. A. Hagner, "Apocalyptic Motifs in the Gospel of Matthew: Continuity and Discontinuity," *HBT* 7 (1985): 53–82; L. Sabourin, "Traits Apocalyptiques dan L'Évangile de Matthieu," *Science et Esprit* 33.3 (1981): 357–372; Christopher Rowland, "Apocalyptic, The Poor, and the Gospel of Matthew," *JTS* 45 (1994): 504–518; Kenneth L. Waters, "Matthew 27:52–53 as Apocalyptic Apostrophe: Temporal-Spatial Collapse in the Gospel of Matthew," *JBL* 122, no. 3 (2003): 489–515; Paul Trudinger, "The 'Our Father' in Matthew as Apocalyptic Eschatology," *Downside Review* 107 (1989): 49–54. John P. Meier understands Matthew's purpose as using "apocalyptic motifs to reinterpret the traditional Christian message of the death and resurrection of Jesus." Meier, *The Vision of Matthew*, 38.

[53] Standard discussions of apocalyptic include J. J. Collins, ed., *Apocalypse: The Morphology of a Genre*; D. Hellholm, ed., *Apocalypticism in the Mediterranean World and the Near East*; Paul D. Hanson, ed., *Visionaries and Their Apocalypses* (Philadelphia: Fortress, 1983); J. J. Collins, *The Apocalyptic Imagination*; and Christopher Rowland, *The Open Heaven*.

"Apocalypse" is a genre of revelatory literature with a narrative framework, in which a revelation is mediated by an otherworldly being to a human recipient, disclosing a transcendent reality which is both temporal, insofar as it envisages eschatological salvation, and spatial insofar as it involves another, supernatural world.[54]

Beyond defining the genre of an "apocalypse," scholarship has also more closely noted that there is a difference between an apocalypse as a type of writing, apocalypticism as a social ideology, and apocalyptic eschatology as a set of ideas or motifs.[55] A body of literature (such as Qumran or the NT) might reveal an apocalyptic worldview without producing apocalypses. As Collins writes, "A movement might reasonably be called apocalyptic if it shared the conceptual framework of the genre, endorsing a worldview in which supernatural revelation, the heavenly world, and eschatological judgment played essential parts."[56] This demarcation of the differences and overlap of the genre of apocalypse versus an apocalyptic viewpoint or worldview is an important step forward.

This discussion, however, only scratches the surface of what has become a massive area of study. Not surprisingly, there has been considerable debate on many points and a comprehensive survey of this field is beyond the purpose of this section. Instead, we may distill a few traits or motifs generally identified as part of an apocalyptic worldview and evaluate Matthew's heaven language against this grid. Although Matthew is clearly not an apocalypse in the sense of genre, it is not difficult to understand the First Gospel, along with the rest of the NT, as sharing an apocalyptic worldview, however broadly that may be defined (see below). Donald Hagner goes so far as to say, "From beginning to end, and throughout, the Gospel makes such frequent use of apocalyptic motifs and the apocalyptic viewpoint that it deserves to be called *the apocalyptic Gospel.*"[57]

---

[54] J. J. Collins, "Introduction: Towards the Morphology of a Genre," in *Apocalypse: The Morphology of a Genre*, 9.

[55] Collins, *Apocalyptic Imagination*, 2. This approach was most clearly set forth first by P. D. Hanson in *The Dawn of Apocalyptic: The Historical and Sociological Roots of Jewish Apocalyptic Eschatology* (rev. ed.; Philadelphia: Fortress, 1979); cf. idem, "Apocalypticism," in *IDB Supplement* 28–34.

[56] Collins, *Apocalyptic Imagination*, 13.

[57] D. A. Hagner, "Apocalyptic Motifs," 60. He also states that an apocalyptic perspective "holds a much more prominent place than in any of the other Gospels" (53). Instead of "apocalyptic worldview," Hagner uses the expressions "apocalyptic viewpoint" and "apocalyptic perspective" with apparently the same meaning.

Various scholars have evaluated the essential elements of an apocalyptic worldview differently. For J. J. Collins and the SBL Apocalypse Group, three aspects are central: (1) a temporal axis; (2) a spatial axis; and (3) concern with revelation. David Sim, focusing specifically on apocalyptic eschatology, sees dualism as the fundamental and pervasive element in the classical period of apocalypticism. There are also other motifs such as determinism, eschatological woes, and judgment, but the distinctive view of reality in apocalyptic eschatology is thoroughly dualistic. This dualism consists of three aspects: temporal, cosmic, and human dualism.[58] For E. P. Sanders, essential apocalyptic can be summed up with the ideas of revelation and reversal.[59] Many others, beginning with Weiss and Schweitzer, see the emphasis on the imminent kingdom of God as a tell-tale sign of apocalyptic eschatology.

These definitions obviously have much overlap. For the present inquiry, I will take a maximalist view rather than trying to negotiate the various proposals.[60] On any account we can see that for each element, Matthew's use of heaven language and the heaven and earth theme reflects an apocalyptic viewpoint and anticipates an eschaton initiated by the Christ.

The easiest place to discern this viewpoint is in the expressly eschatological discourse in chapters 24–25. The apocalyptic elements of these chapters are well recognized, but I may also point out that heaven language appears several times there. In addition to its predominance in the rich tapestry of 24:29–31 (5x), οὐρανός is referred to in 24:35–36 and 25:1 (and again in a similar sense in 26:64). Other crucial passages in Matthew that have been interpreted as apocalyptic likewise manifest the use of heaven language. The Beatitudes (5:3–10), which promise a reversal of the present order, are framed into a unit by references to the kingdom of heaven. Similarly, the opening invocation and the first half of the Lord's Prayer (6:9–10) also focus on heaven and the heaven and earth theme. Indeed, throughout the entire Sermon on the Mount, all of which can be understood as reflecting apocalyptic

---

[58] David Sim, *Apocalyptic Eschatology*, 35–53. A careful interaction with and critique of Sim on this point can be found in John Riches, *Conflicting Mythologies: Identity Formation in the Gospels of Mark and Matthew* (Edinburgh: T&T Clark, 2000), 264–269.

[59] See the review and critique of Sanders' view in Collins, *Apocalyptic Imagination*, 9–10.

[60] For example, I do not think it necessary to make a sharp distinction (cf. Hanson) between "apocalypticism" and "apocalyptic eschatology" for my purposes here.

eschatology,[61] language about the Father, kingdom, and rewards of heaven is frequent. The theme of apocalyptic revelation also connects with οὐρανός in Matthew. In three crucial revelatory texts, Matthew emphasizes the heavenly aspect: the baptism of Jesus and the open heavens and heavenly voice (3:16–17); Peter's Caesarean confession, revealed by the Father in heaven and followed by the promise of the keys of the kingdom of heaven (16:13–19); and the commissioning of the disciples by the post-resurrection Jesus who now has authority in heaven and on earth (28:16–20).

Broadly throughout the gospel, heaven and earth are used as counterposed ideas and realities. This too reflects an apocalyptic viewpoint, specifically, a "cosmic dualism" leading to a "human dualism" of the sort identified by Sim, and in line with the spatial axis of the SBL Group. Surprisingly, in his forceful case for dualism in Matthew, Sim does not even mention the heaven and earth theme.[62] The frequency of the heaven and earth contrasts throughout Matthew greatly strengthens the dualistic interpretation.

Finally, we may mention the obvious but overlooked fact that Matthew regularly modifies the idea of God's imminent kingdom with the phrase τῶν οὐρανῶν. Once we get beyond the mistaken notion of dismissing οὐρανός here as a reverential circumlocution, we can see that this modifying phrase emphasizes the universality of God's sovereignty (an eschatological theme in itself) as well the heavenly origin and (temporal) location of Jesus' kingdom in contrast to earthly kingdoms. Additionally, the way Matthew portrays this heavenly kingdom as radically different than the way of the world is reminiscent of the hope-giving function of an apocalyptic orientation toward the future age.

In sum, this brief survey shows that Matthew's varied use of οὐρανός confirms and strengthens the view that the First Gospel shares an apocalyptic viewpoint or worldview and looks forward to Christ's eschatological kingdom. Remarkably, the important role of heaven language (including the heaven and earth theme) has not been pointed out in the literature discussing apocalyptic motifs in Matthew.

---

[61] Cf. Hagner, "Apocalyptic Motifs," 64.
[62] Sim, *Apocalyptic Eschatology*, 75–87. For reasons that will be explained in the Conclusion, I think "oppositional duality" is better terminology than "dualism."

Conclusion

In this chapter I have tried to show how the theme of heaven and earth informs and relates to seven key topics in Matthean studies. This chapter situates the heaven and earth theme in the context of current Matthean studies and thereby shows its relevance. However, throughout this chapter I have had to assume the centrality of the heaven and earth theme in Matthew—something I have not yet proven to be the case.

Part One of this study has cleared the ground from misinterpretations of Matthew's heaven language and has presented a brief survey of how important heaven language is in the First Gospel. The subsequent chapters in Part Two will go further to explore Matthew's idiolectic use of heaven language in detail, and show how this contributes in a four-fold way to his literary and theological emphasis on the contrast of heaven and earth.

PART TWO

MATTHEW'S IDIOLECTIC USE OF
HEAVEN LANGUAGE
AND THE THEME OF HEAVEN AND EARTH

CHAPTER FIVE

ΟΥΡΑΝΟΣ AND ΟΥΡΑΝΟΙ IN THE SEPTUAGINT AND SECOND TEMPLE LITERATURE

One of the four elements of Matthew's idiolectic use of heaven language is his preference for the uncommon plural forms of οὐρανός. This chapter explores the possible precedents for this important aspect of Matthew's linguistic style through an examination of the plural forms of οὐρανός in the Septuagint and the Second Temple literature.

SINGULAR AND PLURAL Οὐρανός IN THE SEPTUAGINT[1]

As was observed in the preceding survey of heaven in the OT, one of the unique things about heaven in the Hebrew Bible is that the corresponding Hebrew and Aramaic words occur exclusively in plural form. No singular forms of שָׁמַיִם (Hebrew) or שְׁמַיִן (Aramaic) exist. It was also observed that the meaning of heaven in the Hebrew Bible and the LXX is nearly identical. The semantic domains of שָׁמַיִם and οὐρανός are virtually the same, and there is little variance in the use of heaven between the Hebrew and Greek Old Testaments. Unlike many other words when crossing languages, we have a particularly happy match and standardized translation equivalent with שָׁמַיִם and οὐρανός.

The nearly complete overlap of שָׁמַיִם and οὐρανός highlights, then, a very unexpected incongruity between the two words. In light of the universally-plural morphology of שָׁמַיִם, one might expect the LXX to typically translate this word with a Greek plural, οὐρανοί. However, just the opposite is the case. Plural forms of οὐρανός make up only around 9% of the uses of οὐρανός in the LXX. This is true for the Hebrew-canonical as well as apocryphal sections of the LXX.[2] Moreover, the

---

[1] The argument in this section can be found in substantially the same form in my article, "'Heaven' and 'Heavens' in the LXX".
[2] In the sections of the LXX which correspond to the Hebrew Bible, plurals occur 41 or 42 times (with one variance between OG and Th Daniel) out of 502 total uses (= 8.4%). In the non-MT LXX writings (excluding Odes but including Prayer of Manasseh and the Additions to Daniel) there are 11 instances out of approximately

plurals occur predominately in the Psalms (29 of 51–52 instances), and the remainder of the LXX has surprisingly few occurrences.[3]

In fact, the *singular* οὐρανός for *plural* שָׁמַיִם is such a standard in Septuagintal translation that even in the phrase, "the heaven of heavens" and "heaven and the heaven of heavens" where one might expect plural forms, instead we find the singular (ὁ οὐρανὸς τοῦ οὐρανοῦ).[4] As a result of this standard practice, the plural only appears once in the Pentateuch (Deut 32:43)[5] and inconsistently elsewhere in the LXX.[6]

It is striking that more plural forms were not used in the LXX, especially in the Pentateuch where the LXX typically shows close dependence on the Hebrew *Vorlage*. One recent writer has described the LXX Pentateuch this way: it "mimics in Greek many formal aspects of its Hebrew source text, which results in a translation that has at times been called everything from awkward to stilted to simply bad."[7] Yet

---

114 occurrences (= 9.6%). In the Greek Pseudepigrapha, the percentage is slightly higher: approximately 17%. However, most of these plurals are found in documents whose translations into Greek were later and/or contain later Christian interpolations such as *1 Enoch* and the *Testament of the Twelve Patriarchs*. See below. In the Qumran literature, a handful of forms of οὐρανός are found in the Greek manuscripts, but all are singular in form.

[3] The complete list of plurals is as follows:
"Canonical" LXX—Deut 32:43; 1 Rgns 2:10; 2 Rgns 22:10; 2 Chr 28:9; 2 Esd 19:6; Ps 2:4; 8:2, 4; 18:2; 32:6; 49:6; 56:6, 11, 12; 67:9; 68:35; 88:3, 6, 12; 95:5, 11; 96:6; 101:26; 106:26; 107:5, 6; 112:4; 113:11; 135:5; 143:5; 148:1, 4 (3x); Prov 3:19; Job 16:19; Hab 3:3; Isa 44:23; 49:13; Ezek 1:1; Dan (OG) 3:17.
"Apocryphal" LXX—Jdt 9:12; 13:18; Tob 8:5; 2 Macc 15:23; 3 Macc 2:2; Pr Man 15 [Ode 12:15]; Wis 9:10, 16; 18:15; Pss Sol 2:30; Dan (OG and Th) 3:59 [Hymn of the Three].

[4] Peter Katz, *Philo's Bible*, 6. More precisely, in the three-fold expression "heaven and the heaven of heavens," singular forms of οὐρανός *always* occur (Deut 10:14; 3 Rgns 8:27; 2 Chr 2:5; 6:18; 2 Esd 19:6), but the plural does occur once in the two-fold phrase, "heaven of heavens" (Ps 148:4). However, the other occurrences of "heaven of heavens" (Ps 113:24 [MT 115:16]; 3 Macc 2:15) also use the singular.

[5] There is no reference to heaven in the MT of Deut 32:43, though there is in the LXX and 4QDeutq, the latter of which represents in part the parent text of the LXX. Cf. J. W. Wevers, *Notes on the Greek Text of Deuteronomy* (Atlanta: Scholars Press, 1995), 533–35. In light of the rarity of plural forms in the LXX in general and especially in the Pentateuch, the plural form in Deut 32:43 may suggest that this reading is part of a later recension. Indeed, Katz argues that the plural here must be result of borrowing from elsewhere in the LXX (Katz, *Philo's Bible*, 144).

[6] Katz states that in contrast, plurals are a distinctive feature of the "Three." My examination of the Hexapla, however, does not reveal any significant difference in the occasion or use of plural forms.

[7] Benjamin G. Wright III, "Access to the Source: Cicero, Ben Sira, the Septuagint and their Audiences," *JSJ* 34 (2003), 4.

notwithstanding this mimicking, the singular οὐρανός still predominates, despite the plural שָׁמַיִם.

In the predominance of the singular forms, however, the LXX aligns very closely with the Greek of antiquity. In fact, outside of the LXX, one is hard-pressed to find more than a handful of plural forms of οὐρανός in all of Classical or Hellenistic Greek well into the Christian era.[8] It is not until the writings of the New Testament that plural forms of οὐρανός appear alongside the singular with any frequency. Yet, even there they remain in the minority.[9] The notable exceptions are Matthew, Hebrews, and 2 Peter, each of which has more plural forms than singular, while many of the NT books have few or no plurals of οὐρανός at all. After the time of the NT, plural forms begin to appear with slightly more regularity in several of the early Christian writings.[10]

The relevance of this discussion is especially heightened for our purposes because of Matthew's notable preference for plural forms (55 plural; 27 singular) and his predominant use of them in the NT (61% of plurals in the NT are in Matthew). This emphasis in Matthew calls for a closer examination of singular and plural forms of οὐρανός in the preceding literature, beginning with the LXX.

Previous Attempts at Understanding Plurals in the LXX

With the LXX use of οὐρανός we have on our hands a mystery, one that can be described with two related questions: (1) In light of the rarity of

---

[8] According to a search of TLG, there are a few occurrences in Anaximander (ca. 6th century BCE) and Aristotle and one each in Eratosthenes and Aesop. In the Greek Pseudepigrapha, plurals crop up occasionally but the dating on the documents is notoriously difficult and in many instances the Greek manuscripts we have are translations from other languages and evidence later (Christian) interpolation. Hence, it is difficult to determine how early some of these plural forms were. Regardless, the plural forms are still a small minority and show the later development of the plural. The Greek non-literary papyri likewise manifest a dearth of the plural forms: a search of the Duke Databank of Documentary Papyri reveals only one plural form, coming from a 4th century CE document (P.Erl. 107 r,1 1).

[9] There are 90 plurals in the NT out of 273 total occurrences of οὐρανός (= 33%). Matthew alone accounts for 55 of these 90 (61%). Apart from Matthew, the rest of the NT uses plural forms less than 13% of the time. Thus, when Matthew is removed from the reckoning, this percentage is only slightly higher than the frequency of usage in the LXX.

[10] In addition to Christian interpolations in the Greek Pseudepigrapha, occasional plural forms can be found in Irenaeus, Clement, Hermas, and some of the NT Apocrypha. Dependence on NT usage, especially that of Matthew, is the most likely explanation for this development.

plural οὐρανοί in the Greek language, why did the LXX begin to use this form at all? The typical answer, as we will see, is that the Septuagint translators are being influenced by the plural morphology of the Semitic words. However, if this is the case, we can ask a second question: (2) If the plurality of the Semitic words was the cause of the plural οὐρανοί in the LXX, why then do we find so *few* plurals there (less than 1 out of 10)? Previous scholarly discussions of שָׁמַיִם and οὐρανός offer a number of explanations for the plural forms in the LXX.

1. *Belief in Multiple Heavens*
One typical explanation is that the plural forms, at least in the later Septuagintal literature, are the result of a burgeoning belief in multiple heavens. The apocalyptic speculations about the various levels and furniture of heaven are well known to us today. In this theory, the plurals are "true plurals" in that they refer to several heavens in distinction. Typically, the argument starts from the phrase "the heaven(s) of the heavens" which is understood as referring to at least two or three distinct heavenly realms. Versions of this phrase occur some seven times in the MT and corresponding LXX passages. Von Rad and others saw in the post-exilic writings suggestive echoes of the Babylonian ideas of multiple heavens.[11] Traub, writing in the same *TDNT* article, says that this phrase "presupposes the idea of several heavens...a plurality."[12] These occurrences in Scripture are then connected with the well-known development of belief in multiple heavens in other later second temple literature and rabbinic materials.[13]

However, there is a marked difference between the use of heaven in the LXX (including the latest books) and the apocalyptic literature. In the LXX we have no heavenly journeys nor speculations about the levels of the heavens like we find in the later apocalyptic and rabbinic traditions. Any "levels" of heaven that may be discerned in the MT or LXX are quite vague and refer only to perceived differences of height in the created realm.[14] This is a quite different sense of "levels of heaven"

---

[11] Gerhard von Rad, "οὐρανός," *TDNT*, 5:503.
[12] Helmut Traub, "οὐρανός," *TDNT*, 5:511.
[13] Following Traub and Bietenhard, this is the approach of Adela Y. Collins in "The Seven Heavens in Jewish and Christian Apocalypses," 59–93.
[14] As Stadelmann observes: "The few references to different kinds of heaven are either so generic in their scope or metaphorical in their significance that an exact determination of the stages of the heavenly dome is impossible....this space was not conceived as a structured complex of clearly distinguishable levels." Stadelmann, *The Hebrew Conception of the World*, 41.

than the apocalyptic usage. J. Edward Wright concludes the same: "One looks in vain for clear references to a multiple heaven schema in the books traditionally identified as the Old Testament Apocrypha."[15] Moreover, those apocalyptic documents which manifest a clear notion of multiple heavens date from the Christian era and beyond.[16] They could not be the source of the plural innovation in the LXX (even granting occasional Christian interpolations into LXX texts).

Additionally, the phrase "heaven and the heaven of heavens" (which uses singular forms despite the plural *Vorlage*)[17] need be nothing more than hyperbolic, poetic language intended to communicate the vast greatness and exaltedness of God.[18] This phrase would have been the perfect opportunity to exploit a plurality of heavens. Yet we still find singular forms of οὐρανός there. Therefore, no direct causal connection can be made between a belief in multiple heavens and the development of the plural forms of οὐρανός. Von Rad himself concludes by concurring that connections with multiple-heavens views are at best "general connections" and not direct borrowing.[19]

Indeed, any partial causal connection that may exist probably goes the opposite way: the occasional use of plural forms of οὐρανός in the LXX lent credence and opportunity for apocalyptic writers to develop the idea of multiple heavens.[20] While later writers may have found in such phrases the "proof" for multiple heavens, this in no way argues that such a belief was in fact widespread and effective in pre- or post-exilic Judaism, nor the cause of the origin of plural forms. Even in the latest LXX apocryphal books, there is no evidence for a plurality of

---

[15] Wright, *The Early History of Heaven*, 130.
[16] J. J. Collins, "A Throne in the Heavens," 46. Himmelfarb, *Ascent to Heaven*, 127, n. 14.
[17] The only instance of plural forms of οὐρανός in the "heaven of heavens" phrase is Ps 148:4. As noted above, the others, as well as the fuller "heaven and heaven of heavens," all use singular forms.
[18] Koehler and Baumgartner state that this construction "probably does not mean a number of different heavens but is an expression of the superlative," *HALOT* 4:1561. Cf. Joüon, *A Grammar of Biblical Hebrew*, §141 l.
[19] Von Rad, "οὐρανός," *TDNT* 5:503.
[20] Traub argues that the Septuagint "contributed to the Greek word the *status constructus* form and the plural use" thereby giving Hellenistic thought "the possibility of expressing more easily and quickly" ideas about a plurality of heavens. H. Traub, *TDNT*, 5:511. D. F. Torm remarks that over time there was likely an interplay between the use of the plural and the growing concept of multiple heavens: "...der Gebrauch des Pluralis der Vorstellung einer Mehrheit von Himmeln förderlich sein musste, und...andereseits diese Vorstellung einen häufigen Gebrauch des Pluralis verursachen konnte." D. F. Torm, "Der Pluralis οὐρανοί" *ZAW* 33 (1934), 49.

heavens. Moreover, very few plural forms are found even in the Jewish apocalyptic documents which manifest multiple heavens schemes.[21]

2. Οὐρανοί *as a Semitism*

By far the most common explanation for plural forms of οὐρανός in the LXX and the NT is an apparently obvious solution: the plurals come about through the influence of the plural forms of שָׁמַיִם and שְׁמַיִן. Thus, the plural οὐρανοί is a Semitism. This explanation is frequently offered by scholars writing from the perspective of the plural forms in the NT and looking back on their origins (though not exclusively by such scholars). For example, one regularly finds comments that Matthew's frequent use of the plurals is "in accordance with the Semitic idiom."[22] Likewise, this argument from the Hebrew/Aramaic to the Greek is often used to explain Matthew's kingdom of heaven, as Davies and Allison state: "βασιλεία τῶν οὐρανῶν... is to be judged a Semitism in view of rabbinic usage, *malkūt šāmayim*."[23] In addition to the commentaries, this line of reasoning is found in nearly all of the standard dictionary[24] and grammar[25] discussions of οὐρανός.

A fuller (but still brief) version of the argument is found in E. C. Maloney's volume, *Semitic Interference in Marcan Syntax*.[26] Leaning on the work of A. Hilhorst and others, Maloney presents the argument this way: Only a few occurrences of plural οὐρανός exist in Classical Greek. With the exception of the Septuagint, the situation is similar for Hellenistic Greek. Yet in biblical Hebrew, Qumran Hebrew, biblical Aramaic, and Middle Aramaic, the word for heaven or sky (שָׁמַיִם / שְׁמַיִן) is always plural. The Septuagint nearly always translates this word with

---

[21] Indeed, most of the apocalyptic texts which have multiple-heavens journeys continue to use the singular primarily or exclusively. See below on singular and plural forms in the Pseudepigrapha.

[22] Beare, *Matthew* (Oxford: Basil Blackwell, 1981), 356. Almost verbatim is Davies and Allison, *Matthew*, 1:328.

[23] Davies and Allison, *Matthew*, 1:81.

[24] For example, *NIDOTTE, TDNT, NIDNTT*, and *New Dictionary of Biblical Theology*, s.v. heaven/οὐρανός. Interestingly, *BDAG* does not mention this widespread assumption, but instead leans toward seeing the plurals as reflective of multiple heavens.

[25] For example, Nigel Turner, *A Grammar of New Testament Greek, Vol. III: Syntax* (Edinburgh: T&T Clark, 1963), 25, and BDF §4.2, 141.1. Turner also discusses singular and plural forms in *Christian Words* (Edinburgh: T&T Clark, 1980), 202–205, and asserts the typical Hebrew plural argument on 203.

[26] Elliot C. Maloney, *Semitic Interference in Marcan Syntax* (SBLDS 51; Chico, Calif.: Scholars Press, 1981), 190–192.

οὐρανός. While most of these instances have a singular form, about 10% of the time οὐρανός is translated in the plural (mostly in poetic texts, unlike the Classical and Hellenistic plurals which are truly plural in number). Therefore, the plural forms in the Septuagint evidence Semitic influence. (From this Maloney infers that the plural forms in the NT show this same influence.)

This seems straightforward enough. But is this a sound interpretation regarding the development of the plural forms in the Septuagint?

Before answering this, we must clarify the terms at hand. What exactly is a "Semitism"? Stanley Porter distinguishes three possible levels of Semitic influence on the Greek of the NT: a) direct translation; b) intervention, "when a form that cannot reasonably be formed or paralleled in Greek must be attributed to the influence of a Semitic construction"; and c) enhancement, "when a rare construction that can be paralleled in Greek has its frequency of occurrence greatly increased due to associations with Semitic literature."[27] These distinctions between different levels of Semitic influence on Greek are very astute and are applicable to Septuagintal Greek as well. He observes that only an element of Greek that occurs at the level of an *incursion* by a Semitic language can be classified as a Semitism. In the cases when "a rare construction that can be paralleled in Greek has its frequency of occurrence greatly increased due to associations with Semitic literature," this should instead be called a "Semitic enhancement." This is an important clarification of terms. This nuanced difference between a "Semitic enhancement" and a "Semitism" enables us to reconsider whether an apparent linguistic anomaly in Greek (such as plural οὐρανοί) is truly a "Semitism" and not merely an "enhancement."

It should be clear from the preceding discussion that the plural forms of οὐρανός cannot rightly be classified as a "Semitism" but at best as evidence of a "Semitic enhancement" of biblical Greek: plural forms of οὐρανός are not morphologically irregular in Greek, but only uncommon. Is Semitic enhancement, then, the way to describe the development of the plural forms in the Septuagint? The answer is yes, but only in a qualified and careful way—*not* in the morphological way typically assumed.

---

[27] Stanley E. Porter, "The Language of the Apocalypse in Recent Discussion," *NTS* 35 (1989), 587.

Because plural forms of οὐρανός appear to have been almost non-existent in Greek literature before the time of the Septuagint translation (and even subsequently they are found almost exclusively in Jewish Greek literature for some centuries), it *is* reasonable to view those 51 (or 52) Septuagint occurrences as evidence of Semitic enhancement. However, this is different from arguing that the plural forms came about as a direct result of the *morphological plurality* of שָׁמַיִם. This needs to be proven, not just assumed, especially in light of the fact that in most cases (over 90%), the *singular* forms are found despite the universally-plural Hebrew counterpart. The plurality of שָׁמַיִם and שְׁמַיִן likely made the use of plural forms of οὐρανός a quite easy and a reasonable step when a translator chose to do this. However, it must be emphasized that the plurality of the Hebrew and Aramaic does not appear to be the *cause* of the plural οὐρανοί, either in the Hebrew-canonical LXX or the Apocrypha (most of which likely had Semitic *Vorlagen* as well). If indeed the morphology of the Semitic *Vorlagen* was the contributing factor in the plurals, we might expect to find that plurals occur less often in LXX documents which do *not* have a Semitic original. However, just the opposite is often the case: In Wisdom of Solomon (composed in Greek), half of the occurrences are plural, while none are in 1 Esdras or 1 Maccabees (translations of Semitic originals). Clearly, factors other than morphology are at work. Indeed, other identifiable causes led to the development of the plurals in the LXX.[28] To these we can now turn.

3. *Poetic and Syntactical Reasons (D. F. Torm and P. Katz)*

D. F. Torm was one of the first scholars to examine the oddity of the plural οὐρανοί in the LXX and to argue for an explanation other than a plurality of heavens or Semitic influence.[29] He was also the first to point out that plurals in secular Greek were not completely unknown. He disputes the Hebrew plural explanation by first pointing out that in the instances of ὁ οὐρανὸς τοῦ οὐρανοῦ, where the plural would be expected, it does not appear. He goes on to observe that of the 51

---

[28] In light of the literalizing tendency of the recensions of the LXX, one might argue that this is the source of the plural οὐρανοί. However, in Theodotion Daniel, we do not find an increase in plural forms (in fact, one less than in OG). Similarly, of the 23 occurences of οὐρανός in the *kaige* portion of Samuel and Kings, only one plural is found (2 Rgs 22:10).

[29] D. F. Torm, "Der Pluralis Ouranoi," 48–50.

plural occurrences in the LXX, more than half occur in the Psalms and most others, similarly, in elevated prophetic speech or prayers.[30] He concludes, therefore, that the plurals pertain to the category of poetical and ceremonial speech, and are not the result of Semitic influence.[31] Nor should the plurals be understood to indicate a difference in meaning than the singulars. Instead, they should be classified as examples of the poetic technique of *pluralis majesticus*[32] whereby the poet uses the plural to amplify or extend the expression.[33]

Some years later, the Septuagintal scholar Peter Katz dedicated an appendix to the question of plural οὐρανοί in the LXX.[34] He begins by reviewing Torm's argument, but concludes that his case is inconclusive. Katz argues that the important question is different than Torm's. The real question for Katz is: how did it come about that שָׁמַיִם could be expressed by both οὐρανός (sg.) and οὐρανοί (pl.)?

Similar to Torm, Katz observes that the singular οὐρανός in the complex phrases, "the heaven of heavens," shows that there was a consistent translation technique of שָׁמַיִם to singular οὐρανός at work for this word. The plural occurrences then call for explanation. Katz finds the solution in observing *syntactical* considerations in addition to poetic ones, specifically, where the Hebrew verb governing the phrase is plural and/or there are other plural nouns in a parallel stichus. Thus, in the latter case, many of the plural οὐρανοί can be understood as having been attracted by a parallel noun which is plural: e.g., οὐρανῶν—ἀβύσσων (Ps 106:26), οὐρανῶν—νεφελῶν (Ps 56:11; 107:5), ἐκ τῶν οὐρανῶν—ἐν τοῖς ὑψίστοις (Ps 148:1), ἐν οὐρανοῖς—ἐν ὑψίστοις (Job 16:19).[35]

---

[30] There are 29 plurals in the Psalms, though Torm does not make this number entirely clear. When we limit the reckoning to the canonical LXX books, the predominance of the Psalms is even stronger: 29 of 41 (or 42) uses. The variance between 41 and 42 depends on which version of Daniel one uses in the counting. At 3:17 the OG has a plural where the Theodotion lacks a reference to heaven. Typically, reference works refer to the 51 plural occurrences in the LXX, thereby (knowingly or unknowingly) following the Theodotion.

[31] G. Mussies' survey of the data of the Septuagint concurs with this conclusion, "the Hebrew equivalent...probably did not influence the use of the plural in Greek." G. Mussies, *The Morphology of Koine Greek as Used in the Apocalypse of St. John* (SNTS 27; Leiden: Brill, 1971), 84.

[32] Joüon, *Grammar*, prefers to classify the plural שָׁמַיִם under the category of "plural of extension" (§136c) and "plurale tantum" (§90f), and reserves "plural of excellence or majesty" for the sacred and divine (§136d–e).

[33] "Die Dichter brauchen den Plural oft, um den Ausdruck zu amplifizieren." Torm, "Der Pluralis," 49.

[34] Peter Katz, *Philo's Bible*, 141–146.

[35] Katz, *Philo's Bible*, 143–144. Katz gives other examples including a case such as

But even more strongly, Katz highlights the role that the Hebrew verbs in the *Vorlage* played in the Septuagint's plural οὐρανοί. That is, there are eleven cases in the Psalms where in the Hebrew, שָׁמַיִם governs a plural verb, thus, the translator had "either to transform the whole sentence into the singular or to use Hebraizing Greek."[36] In cases where the plural verb had more than one subject, οὐρανός, as only one of them, could remain singular (e.g., Gen 2:1). However, when plural שָׁמַיִם stood alone with a plural verb, the temptation to pluralize οὐρανός was strong (though not irresistible, it should be added), especially in cases of personification, such as εὐφράνθητε οὐρανοί (Isa 44:23) or εὐλογεῖτε οὐρανοί (Dan (Th) 3:59, Prayer).[37] Stated simply, "the choice of οὐρανοί in some parts of the LXX is caused by the fact that שָׁמַיִם was introduced by a plural verb."[38]

Therefore, Katz concludes by concurring with Torm that the plurals are elements of poetical and solemn language. But he disagrees with Torm's deduction that this means there is no Semitic influence. Indeed, the Semitic influence can be seen in the fact that plural שָׁמַיִם required a plural verb, which in turn often effected a plural οὐρανοί. The *pluralis majesticus* explanation is true as far as it goes, but the additional Hebrew *syntactical* considerations are required to explain the phenomenon of plural οὐρανοί.

Evaluation of Torm and Katz

Both Torm and Katz offer far better explanations of the phenomenon of plural οὐρανοί than the typical dictionary and commentary accounts that simply assume a morphological connection. Unfortunately, most such accounts acknowledge Torm's *ZAW* article in a footnote (and Katz less often), but then go straight on with the Semitic-morphology explanation.

Prov 3:19 where οὐρανούς is in direct parallel with (sg.) τὴν γῆν yet it is still embedded in a series of poetical plurals, hence its plurality.

[36] Katz, *Philo's Bible*, 145.

[37] The solitary occurrence of plural οὐρανοί in the Pentateuch (Deut 32:43), though it contains the phrase εὐφράνθητε οὐρανοί and could be explained that way, is instead explained by Katz as being unoriginal, a later borrowing from elsewhere in the LXX (p. 144). The portion of 32:43 containing heaven is indeed a Septuagintal plus as compared to the MT. However, it is found in the Qumran text, 4QDeut 9.

[38] Katz, *Philo's Bible*, 145. Katz points out that this rule does not generally apply in cases where the plural verb follows at the end of the sentence.

In comparing the two, Katz's treatment is a real improvement over Torm's and provides a persuasive explanation for most of the plurals in the LXX. And again, both are far superior to the standard reference works and scholarly assumption on this question. However, while Katz is basically right in his analysis, at times he gives a list of verses with only a cursory and less than satisfactory explanation. Moreover, there are a few troubling passages in earlier sections outside of the Psalms that he rather quickly dismisses as being not from the hand of the original translator (1 Rgns 2:10; 2 Rgns 22:10). This may be the case, but at times it seems a little too convenient and circular an explanation. Additionally, there are also a number of passages from the Psalms and other portions which Katz does not mention at all. Further, Katz does not deal with the eleven plurals which occur in the LXX Apocrypha.

Further Insights on Singular and Plural Οὑρανός in the LXX

While acknowledging the crucial insights of Torm and Katz, we may offer some additional explanations and observations. In the case of the nine canonical plurals which Katz did not mention in his treatment,[39] little can be said other than he judiciously chose not to include them. In each case except one there is no clear reason why the plural form appears. The rules put forth by both Torm and Katz fail to explain these instances. In 2 Chronicles, 2 Esdras, Psalms, and Daniel, the plural instance not mentioned is one among a vast majority of singular forms throughout the book with no apparent difference in meaning.[40] There are no recorded textual variants in any of these cases and no definitive explanation for the solitary plurals can be found. They remain an anomaly. In one instance which Katz neglects, however, his suggestion of plural Hebrew verb syntax influencing the LXX form proves right. In Ezekiel 1:1, heaven is the subject of a passive verb: "The heavens were opened." Thus, the Hebrew verb is naturally plural because of the plural שָׁמַיִם, and consequently, the plural οὐρανοί is not surprising. This instance, then, strengthens Katz's argument for syntactical considerations resulting in plural forms. Regarding the other plurals,

---

[39] 2 Chr 28:9; 2 Esd 19:6; Ps 2:4; 88:3; 95:5; 135:5; Hab 3:3; Ezek 1:1; Dan (OG) 3:17.

[40] In the case of Habakkuk 3:3, the plural is the only instance of heaven throughout the book, and interestingly, the only plural form of the word that exists in all of the Book of the Twelve Prophets.

however, it should be stated that the remaining anomalies in no way discredit the explanations of Torm and Katz. For such cases, we do well to remind ourselves of Katz's comments about the necessarily uncertain nature of our existing LXX text(s): "Amongst our evidence [of the LXX] there is hardly one MS which does not disclose some influence from [the] later stages of transmission."[41] This may very well be the best explanation of these odd plurals.

But one glaring deficiency in Katz's treatment is his failure to examine the eleven plurals which occur in the LXX Apocrypha. While these instances are not much more relatively frequent than plurals in the rest of the LXX,[42] in several cases they prove interesting. The eleven plurals are found in only eight of the seventeen apocryphal books and no book contains plurals exclusively.[43] In most instances, we find one plural occurrence in a book in the midst of many singular occurrences. We shall briefly examine the books containing these eleven occurrences, seeking to discern any patterns or development in the use of the plural.

Examination of the Plural Forms in the LXX Apocrypha

The use of οὐρανός in both manuscript traditions of Tobit is quite frequent, but especially in the version preserved in Codex Sinaiticus (א).[44] Both traditions share uses of heaven to describe God, as is quite common in the second temple literature. For example, God is the "God who dwells in heaven" (5:17), the "Lord of heaven (and earth)" (7:17), the "God of heaven" (10:13), and the "King of heaven" (13:13).[45] In

---

[41] Katz, *Philo's Bible*, 4.

[42] As mentioned above, the percentage of plural forms to the total in the canonical LXX is 8.4% (41 or 42 of 502). The percentage for the apocryphal LXX is only slightly higher: 9.6% (11 of 114).

[43] The plurals are Jdt 9:12; 13:18; Tob 8:5; 2 Macc 15:23; 3 Macc 2:2; Pr Man 15 [Ode 12:15]; Wis 9:10, 16; 18:15; Pss Sol 2:30; Dan (OG and Th) 3:59 [Hymn of the Three].

[44] This longer version is now generally considered the older, more reliable version as dozens of fragments of five separate manuscripts of Tobit have appeared from Qumran. These generally support the longer version over that found in codices A and B. Cf. Peter W. Flint, "Noncanonical Writings in the Dead Sea Scrolls: Apocrypha, Other Previously Known Writings, Pseudepigrapha," in *The Bible at Qumran: Text, Shape and Interpretation* (ed. Peter W. Flint; Grand Rapids: Eerdmans, 2001), 90. More recently, one may consult the commentary by Joseph Fitzmyer, *Tobit* (CEJL; Berlin: de Gruyter, 2003), whose judgment is the same.

[45] The greater number of occurrences in the Sinaiticus version are mainly due to multiple uses of these same epithets.

every case except one, however, the forms of οὐρανός are singular. The sole plural example is found in both manuscript traditions at 8:5 when the heavens and all creation are called upon to bless God (εὐλογησάτωσάν σε οἱ οὐρανοὶ καὶ πᾶσα ἡ κτίσις σου). This use of the plural is immediately recognizable as the typical formulation when the heavens are personified and addressed, as Katz argued for the Psalms.

The book of Judith has two instances of the plural out of a total of seven occurrences of οὐρανός. Here the usage is markedly inconsistent. We have two very common instances of the singular: the heaven and earth pair (7:28) and "the birds of heaven" (τὰ πετεινὰ τοῦ οὐρανοῦ) paired with "the beasts of the field" (11:7). Yet in 13:18, the heaven and earth pair appears again but this time with a plural form of οὐρανός. God is said to be the creator of τοὺς οὐρανοὺς καὶ τὴν γῆν. Similarly, in 9:12 in a list of appellations of God, he is described as the "Lord of heaven and earth" (δέσποτα τῶν οὐρανῶν καὶ τῆς γῆς), again using a plural form.[46] Yet this usage is somewhat inconsistent with the three times in which the singular appears in the common second temple moniker, "God of heaven" (5:8; 6:19; 11:17).

A similar inconsistency of usage is found in 2 and 3 Maccabees, the Psalms of Solomon, and the Prayer of Manasseh. In both 2 and 3 Maccabees we find many instances of οὐρανός (20 and 9, respectively)[47] in a variety of phrases, but only one plural each. In 2 Macc 15:23 God is called the "Sovereign of the heavens" (δυνάστα τῶν οὐρανῶν), though in 15:4 the singular is used in a very similar expression, "the living Lord himself, the Sovereign in heaven" (ὁ κύριος ζῶν αὐτὸς ἐν οὐρανῷ δυνάστης). Similarly, in 3 Macc 2:2 God is described as the "King of the heavens" (βασιλεῦ τῶν οὐρανῶν), yet throughout the rest of the book only singular forms appear, even when usage evidently refers to God at least in a metonymic sense. In the Psalms of Solomon, we find several instances of the heaven and earth pair, explicitly (8:7) and thematically (2:9; 2:33; 17:18), each using the singular. Yet in 2:30, God is the "King over the heavens" (βασιλεὺς ἐπὶ τῶν οὐρανῶν), which is contrasted thematically with the proud man who says he will be "lord of earth and sea" (2:29). The Prayer of Manasseh likewise fails to

---

[46] The combination of plural οὐρανοί with γῆ in the phrase "heaven and earth" is uncommon. Instead, singular οὐρανός plus γῆ is the standard throughout the LXX and NT. Notable exceptions are Ps 69:34 and 2 Peter 3: 7, 13.

[47] There are an additional three occurrences of an adjectival form of οὐρανός in 3 Macc: οὐράνιος in 6:18 and ἐπουράνιος in 6:28 and 7:6.

indicate any clear pattern of singular and plural usage. In verses 2 and 9 we find singular forms in the phrases "heaven and earth" and the "height of heaven" (τὸ ὕψος τοῦ οὐρανοῦ). Yet the prayer ends with a plural reference to the "host of the heavens" (ἡ δύναμις τῶν οὐρανῶν) (v. 15).[48]

Thus, none of these books manifests a clear and consistent reason for the mix of singular and plural forms. The only thing that can be said about these plurals is that they have one thing in common: they are all in words of praise and prayer addressed to God. In Judith 9:12 and 13:18, 2 Macc 15:23, 3 Macc 2:2, *Ps Sol* 2:30, and *Pr Man* 12, God is exalted as the Ruler, Lord, and King of the heavens (τῶν οὐρανῶν). In each of these phrases, a plural form of heaven is used. Most interesting, in these epithets for God with the plural we do not find the typical word for God (θεός) or even Lord (κύριος) but instead terms that emphasize God's ruling lordship: δυνάστα τῶν οὐρανῶν (2 Macc 15:23); δέσποτα τῶν οὐρανῶν (Jdt 9:12); βασιλεῦ τῶν οὐρανῶν (3 Macc 2:2). Conversely, in no instance does the frequent Second Temple phrase, "God of heaven" use a plural form. This appears to be a stereotyped expression that remains unaltered, while in a few instances, plural οὐρανός is used in similar expressions to enhance God's majestic lordship. Thus, while there does not seem to be a *consistent* pattern of singular and plural forms within each book, we do find that when God is addressed and his reigning lordship is emphasized, plural forms do sometimes appear.[49]

A Singular Versus Plural Pattern: Wisdom of Solomon

So far we have not been able to discern any consistent reason why plural forms occur in these apocryphal books. In one book, however, there appears to be an intentional contrast *in meaning* between the singular form of οὐρανός and the plural. The use of the plurals in the Wisdom of Solomon is best understood not as a Semitism nor a further example

---

[48] This combination of δύναμις plus a plural form of οὐρανός occurs elsewhere only in Matt 24:29; Mark 13:25; and Luke 21:26, though the similar στρατιαὶ τῶν οὐρανῶν is found in 2 Esd 19:6.

[49] It must be acknowledged that this pattern is not entirely consistent or developed, however. For example, in 2 Macc 15:3–4, God is referred to as the ἐν οὐρανῷ (sg.) δυνάστης. However, in this case, the difference may reflect that God is not being addressed but is being spoken about. In 1 Esdras, which has no plural forms, we find "the king of heaven" (βασιλεὺς τοῦ οὐρανοῦ) with the singular form (4:36). Likewise, the Sinaiticus reading of Tobit has βασιλεὺς τοῦ οὐρανοῦ (1:18; 13:13, 17).

of Katz's patterns, *but as part of an intentional singular versus plural usage coming from the author's literary style and serving a theological purpose.*

Of all the apocryphal LXX books, Wisdom uses plural forms most often. This work, known for its combination of Greek philosophical concepts and language with the biblical teachings, speaks much about the world, creation, and the elements of nature.[50] As a result, one might expect to find even more instances of οὐρανός than six.[51] Despite this low number, however, it is noteworthy that of these six occurrences, half are plural. Within these occurrences, the author of Wisdom apparently uses plural forms to refer to God's dwelling place and the singular to refer to the created realm. In 9:10, 9:16, and 18:15 "wisdom" or "the word" is said to search out and come forth from heaven, i.e., from the place of God's throne. In contrast, the singular occurrences in 13:2, 16:20, and 18:16 each refer to the sky. Thus, in Wisdom, which manifests no multiple-heavens speculation, the singular and plural forms are used to clearly distinguish between the two common semantic poles of οὐρανός: the sky (singular) and the abode of God (plural).[52]

In the plural category, 9:10 and 18:15 are put into clear apposition with God's royal or glorious throne as the place of his dwelling. In 9:16, we find a thematic heaven and earth pair: "We can hardly guess at what is on earth... but who has traced out what is in the heavens (ἐν οὐρανοῖς)?" (RSV). This might at first appear to be a reference to the entire universe, with ἐν οὐρανοῖς as the starry realm as compared to the earth. However, the context makes clear that this familiar phrasing is a sharp, Platonic distinction between two realms, the lower earthly realm contrasted with the place where wisdom dwells, with God.[53] Thus,

---

[50] Cf. James M. Reese, *Hellenistic Influence of the Book of Wisdom and its Consequences* (Rome: Biblical Institute Press, 1970). See also Michael Kolarcik, "Creation and Salvation in the Book of Wisdom," in *Creation in the Biblical Traditions* (ed. Richard J. Clifford and John J. Collins; Washington: Catholic Biblical Association, 1992), 97–107.

[51] Although the heaven and earth pair does occur explicitly (18:15) and thematically (9:16), the book's later date and Hellenistic origins shine forth through the more common use of κόσμος to refer to the world/universe (15x) rather than "heaven and earth." Thus, there are not as many occurrences of heaven as there would be without the use of κόσμος.

[52] My examination of commentaries on Wisdom unearths no mention of singular and plural οὐρανός nor a pattern thereof, even in a detailed phrase by phrase study such as A. T. S. Goodrick, *The Book of Wisdom* (London: Rivingtons, 1913).

[53] Cf. 9:15, "For a perishable body weighs down the soul, and this earthly tent burdens the thoughtful mind." The influence of Platonism on Wisdom and the similarities with Philo are well known, cf. David Winston, *The Wisdom of Solomon* (AB; Garden City, NY: Doubleday, 1979), especially 59–63.

Wisdom uses the OT language and contrastive sense of the heaven and earth pair, but uses it differently both philosophically and morphologically. The emphasis in this context is that humanity cannot understand the counsel of God (v.13) without God sending wisdom from heaven through the Holy Spirit (v.17).

The three singular occurrences of οὐρανός, conversely, are limited in reference to the phenomena of the created realm below the dwelling of God and wisdom. In 13:1–2 the foolishness of humanity is derided for failing to understand God as the creator despite the obvious craftsmanship of creation. Instead, foolish humans supposed that the created things like the fire, wind, the circle of the stars, and the luminaries of heaven (φωστῆρας οὐρανοῦ, i.e., the sun and moon) were gods (13:2). The polemic emphasizes the created nature of all these things. In 16:20, which alludes strongly to Ps 78:23–28, food is provided for the Israelites "from heaven" (ἀπ' οὐρανοῦ). Again, the context makes clear that the created realm ("the sky") is the emphasis. The third singular reference (18:16) also has a biblical precedent. Even as David sees the angel of death standing "between earth and heaven," i.e., the sky, so the stern warrior of Wisdom 18:16 stands and fills all things with death in the earthly realm. In fact, the two uses of οὐρανός together in 18:15–16 show the singular and plural distinction at work. The "all-powerful word" leaps from God's throne, from heaven (ἀπ' οὐρανῶν), onto the earth and stands, filling the earthly realm (οὐρανοῦ μὲν ἥπτετο βεβήκει δ' ἐπὶ γῆς, "it touched heaven while standing on the earth").

This pattern of singular versus plural usage appears to be part of the author's own idiolect, or stylistic mode. No precedents for such a developed pattern have been found from my examination of οὐρανός throughout the extant Greek literature. Of course, the occasional plural forms which do appear throughout the LXX and Pseudepigrapha provided raw materials with which the author of Wisdom could build this theological contrast between God in his abode and the inferior created realm. On occasion, other second temple texts come close to such a singular versus plural contrast, but none so consistently as Wisdom.[54]

Summary and Conclusion

The purpose of this section has been two-fold. First, I have sought to highlight the problem with the typical understanding of plural οὐρανοί

---

[54] See below on singular and plural in the Pseudepigrapha.

in the LXX and bring to bear upon it the overlooked insights of Torm and Katz. These scholars have provided a much more thoughtful and convincing explanation than the widespread assumption found in reference works on the matter. Second, I have examined the plural forms of οὐρανός which Torm and Katz did not discuss and have offered observations and suggestions which go beyond theirs.

In sum, there is little evidence that the occasional plurals in the LXX came about as a result of a belief in multiple heavens. On the other hand, they may be called Semitic enhancement, but not in the directly morphological way that is usually assumed (plural Hebrew to plural Greek). As a result, this common assumption in scholarship (especially at the reference-work level) needs to be qualified. Instead, there is often, though not always, an indirect Semitic influence stemming from the influence of the syntax of the Hebrew verbs. Additionally, poetic factors played a significant role, both attraction of words through parallelism and the use of hyperbolic and expansive speech. This poetic and syntactical combination is the best explanation for most but not all of the occurrences of οὐρανοί in the LXX, particularly in the canonical portions. The LXX Apocrypha provides other interesting uses of οὐρανός which deserve examination. There we find inconsistency even as in the other portions of the LXX, yet there is a development among some authors of using plural forms when addressing God as ruler. Moreover, the Wisdom of Solomon provides a well-crafted use of singular and plural forms in a pattern designed to distinguish the divine realm from the created. This last insight will prove particularly relevant for our examination of Matthew.

Singular and Plural Οὐρανός in the Second Temple Literature

Much like the LXX, the Greek literature of the Second Temple period has relatively few occurrences of the plural οὐρανοί. No plural forms are extant in Philo, Josephus, nor in the Greek manuscripts from Qumran. Only in the Greek Pseudepigrapha are occasional plurals found. A count based on the *Concordance Grecque des Pseudépigraphes D'Ancien Testament* reveals a maximum of 17% (47 of 282) of the occurrences of οὐρανός are plural. However, even this number is misleading in that the dating of many of these instances is certainly post-Christian. Moreover, many of the plurals are found in Greek manuscripts which are later translations from other languages, and many evidence later

Christian interpolation. For example, nine of the plurals are found in the two recensions of the *Testament of Abraham* (1st century CE plus interpolations), and eight plurals occur in the section of the *Testament of Levi* which is almost certainly a later redaction and not part of the earlier Aramaic form.[55] Additionally, there are several books within the Pseudepigrapha which have no plural forms at all (e.g., *Life of Adam and Eve*, *Sibylline Oracles*, *4 Baruch*, and *Greek Apocalypse of Moses*). Thus, the Second Temple Greek texts align rather closely with the LXX and other Greek of the period in using plural οὐρανοί only occasionally.[56] This pattern heightens the significance of Matthew's frequent usage of the plural relative to his literary predecessors and contemporaries. Before examining Matthew's usage in the next chapter, we will survey the plural forms which do occur in the Pseudepigrapha, and query whether any patterns can be discerned.

Occasional Plurals in the Greek Pseudepigrapha

1. *The Book of 1 Enoch*
Although the full corpus exists only in later Ethiopic manuscripts, scholarly consensus is that portions of *1 Enoch* provide us with the earliest Jewish apocalypses.[57] *1 Enoch* is a composite work, consisting of five major books as well as identifiable subsections within them, dating from the middle of the third century BCE (Book of the Watchers; Book of the Luminaries), the second century BCE (Epistle; Book of Dreams), and possibly as late as the third century CE (Similitudes).[58] In addition

---

[55] See M. de Jonge, "Testament of Levi and Aramaic Levi," in *Jewish Eschatology, Early Christian Christology, and the Testaments of the Twelve Patriarchs* (Leiden, 1991), 244–62; and J. J. Collins, "A Throne in the Heavens," 56 n. 11.

[56] The *Sibylline Oracles* which date from the Second Temple period (Books 3–5 and 11) show many affinities with secular Koine Greek usage and provide a good example of the use of οὐρανός there: of the 25 occurrences of heaven, not one is plural.

[57] See J. J. Collins, *The Apocalyptic Imagination*, 43–84; George W. E. Nickelsburg, *1 Enoch 1* (Minneapolis: Augsburg Fortress, 2001); James C. VanderKam, *Enoch and the Growth of an Apocalyptic Tradition* (Washington, D.C.: Catholic Biblical Association of America, 1984); M. A. Knibb, *The Ethiopic Book of Enoch* (2 vols.; Oxford: Clarendon, 1978); Matthew Black, *The Book of Enoch or 1 Enoch: a New English Edition* (Leiden: Brill, 1985).

[58] Regarding the dating of the Similitudes, Nickelsburg, *1 Enoch*, 7, suggests the earlier date of late first century BCE, while Milik provides the most radical and late reconstruction. Most of Milik's theory, upon which this late date was based, however, has been severely criticized. See Collins, *Apocalyptic Imagination*, 177, and D. W. Suter, "Weighed in the Balance: The Similitudes of Enoch in Recent Discussion," *RelStudRev* 7 (1981), 217–21. The current consensus is that it is comes from around the turn of the era and probably before the destruction of the temple in 70 CE, Collins, *Apocalyptic Imagination*, 178.

to the Ethiopic manuscripts, substantial portions of the first and fifth books and a passage from the fourth are extant in Greek.[59]

Because about one-third of *1 Enoch* is extant in Greek manuscripts, we are able to make some inquiry into the question of singular versus plural forms of οὐρανός. The convoluted relationship of the textual traditions for *1 Enoch* necessarily makes any firm conclusions based on the Greek manuscripts tenuous. Nonetheless, if Nickelsburg is right that the Greek translation, at least of the Watchers, was in place by the end of the first century CE, then Greek *1 Enoch* gives us a good sample of the use of οὐρανός relative to the LXX and Matthew.[60] Interestingly, like the LXX (and most of the NT except Matthew), there are relatively few plural forms (3–4x) of οὐρανός in *1 Enoch*, despite the widespread use of this term (about 60x in the Greek portions). Each of the Greek plurals occurs in the Book of the Watchers, and none in the other extant Greek portions (segments of Luminaries and most of the Epistle).[61] In addition to one of these being textually uncertain,[62] two of the four are lacking in some or all of the Ethiopic manuscripts.[63] This discrepancy does not prove that the plurals were later additions, but it does raise some doubts and corresponds with the infrequency of the plurals throughout the Greek manuscripts.

---

[59] Collins, *Apocalyptic Imagination*, 44. Nickelsburg, *1 Enoch*, 12, calculates the percentage of extant Greek at 28% of the total Ethiopic corpus. The standard critical edition of the Greek text is edited by Matthew Black in *Apocalypsis Henochi Graece* (Leiden: Brill, 1970). In the year following the publication of this edition, a few more previously published Greek portions were identified as belonging to *1 Enoch*. These can be found in the published *Oxyrhynchus Papyri* 2069 (vol. 17). Also, Aramaic fragments of all of the books except the Similitudes have been found at Qumran. Cf. J. T. Milik, *The Books of Enoch: Aramaic Fragments from Qumran Cave 4* (Oxford: Clarendon, 1976). Black, *The Book of Enoch, 1*, reports the percentage of Aramaic fragments to the Ethiopic as no more than 5%.

[60] Nickelsburg, *1 Enoch*, 14, states that "parallels in the Wisdom of Solomon suggest that the Greek is the product of a Jewish translator who worked before the turn of era."

[61] These calculations are based on the Greek manuscripts as collated in Black's *Apocalypsis Henochi Graece*. The later-discovered Enochic Greek fragments in the Oxyrhyncus Papyrus 2069 also contain four instances of οὐρανός (in 86:1 and 87:2), all of which are singular.

[62] In 8:4, Codex Panopolitanus reads the plural οὐρανούς, but both versions 1 and 2 of the Syncellus fragments have a singular form here.

[63] In the phrase ἀπὸ τοῦ οὐρανοῦ τῶν οὐρανῶν in 1:4, the second (plural) heaven is lacking in the Ethiopic mss, though Black deems that the Greek is likely original here. In 18:10, where the heavens come to an end, some Ethiopic mss read *mayat* (waters) instead of οἱ οὐρανοί.

Even taking each of the four plurals as original, it is difficult to discern any pattern for the plurals as opposed to the very common singular forms. They appear to be random and accidental. In 8:4, the cry of perishing mankind goes up to heaven (εἰς οὐρανούς) to the Most High God. But in 13:4 and 22:5–6 humans also look up to and lament to heaven, each time using the singular. Similarly, in 18:4 and 18:10, two plurals are found, but in the midst of many other singular occurrences of heaven, all referring the same multitude of meteorological phenomena. The only potentially significant use of the plural is the reference to the "heaven of heavens" (τοῦ οὐρανοῦ τῶν οὐρανῶν) in 1:4, a loaded phrase coming from the Hebrew Bible and LXX (cf. Deut 10:14; 1 Kg 8:27; 2 Chr 6:18).[64] However, this phrase does not prove to be a recurrent idea or theme in *1 Enoch*, occurring only two other times (60:1; 71:5), nor does it seem to imply a multiplicity of heavens. Unfortunately, we do not have Greek manuscripts for either 60:1 or 71:5, thus we cannot discern if the plural in "heaven of heavens" was an intentional, repeated pattern.

In sum, the few plurals in *1 Enoch* are of little significance. If some scribe did have a reason for inserting plural forms into the Greek translation, it was not done consistently or with a clear purpose. The plurals that do remain are likely accidental. Regardless, the Greek of *1 Enoch* is consistent with that of the LXX and other Koine Greek in regularly using singular οὐρανός, regardless of the topic or *Vorlage*.

2. *The Testaments of the Twelve Patriarchs*

The situation is slightly different in the *Testaments of the Twelve Patriarchs*. There are 36 occurrences of heaven in this collection with 14 plurals.[65] However, half of the 36 instances are found in the *Testament of Levi* alone, and a majority of the plurals (8 of 14) stem from *Levi* as well. Thus, it is especially in *Levi* that heaven plays a significant part and only there where the plurals are noteworthy.[66]

---

[64] As discussed previously, in the phrase "heaven of heaven" in the LXX, singular οὐρανός is used exclusively except in the case of Ps 148:4.

[65] The figure of 36 includes 3 textual variants in assorted manuscript traditions listed in the concordance but not in de Jonge's critical text. All 3 of these variants are among the 18 occurrences in the *Testament of Levi*.

[66] Regarding the frequency in other portions, the *Testament of Benjamin* has 5 occurrences and the *Testament of Judah* 6 instances, while a few of the testaments have none at all. The other plurals are found in the *Testament of Judah* 21:3 (2x); *Testament of Issachar* 5:13; *Testament of Asher* 2:10; 7:5; *Testament of Benjamin* 10:7.

The dating and origin of the whole collection have been hotly disputed. Against the older view of the Jewish origin of the *Testaments*, de Jonge has argued that the *Testaments* are essentially Christian compositions (c. 190–225 CE) which borrowed Jewish patterns, though admittedly they went through a long compositional and redactional history including Jewish influences.[67]

Even if one does not follow de Jonge's view, there is no doubt that the *Testaments* are full of later Christian interpolations. As stated above, this is especially clear in *Levi*.[68] The late date and heavily Christian influence on the *Testaments* does much to explain the greater frequency of plural forms. For example, the phrase "king of heaven" (βασιλέα τῶν οὐρανῶν) in *Benjamin* 10:7 is clearly a Christian interpolation, probably influenced by Matthew and with strong Christian messianic overtones and allusions to John. The striking frequency of plurals in *Levi* (14 of 18) is a result of its later apocalyptic emphasis on multiple heavens and reveals its Christian origins. Some of the plurals in *Levi* refer specifically to numbered heavens (2:9; 3:1), and once the earthly realm is contrasted with the divine heavens (13:5). Beyond this, however, there does not appear to be any particular pattern to the plurals nor an explanation other than apocalyptic reflections.[69]

Singular and Plural Patterns in the Greek Pseudepigrapha

Most of the occasional plurals in the Pseudepigrapha are like those in *1 Enoch*: they can be classified as little more than random. This is true for the plurals which appear in the *Testament of Job, Joseph and Asenath*, and the Greek fragments of *Jubilees*.[70] In a few texts, however, something of a singular and plural pattern begins to appear. In the *Greek*

---

[67] Robert A. Kugler, *The Testaments of the Twelve Patriarchs* (Sheffield: Sheffield Academic Press, 2001), 35–36.

[68] The *Testament of Levi* is textually uncertain and may even have a different *Vorlage*. Cf. de Jonge, "Testament of Levi and Aramaic Levi," 244–62, and Collins, "A Throne in the Heavens," 56 n. 11.

[69] It should be noted that in this *The Testaments* is unique. In most other multiple heavens apocalypses, singular forms are still predominant. That is, even developed multiple heavens views did not result in a greater number of plural forms in most texts. Instead, ordinal numbers were often used, "fourth heaven (sg)," "sixth heaven (sg)," etc.

[70] There are 10 occurrences of heaven in the *Testament of Job* with four plurals; 22 occurrences in *Joseph and Asenath* with three plurals; and three of the four occurrences in the Greek fragments of *Jubilees* are plural. In the case of *Jubilees*, there is too little data to make any conclusions except for the probable late dating of these fragments.

Apocalypse of Ezra, the three plural forms (of 13 occurrences) are used in reference to ascending to the divine realm, while the singulars are primarily used in cosmological references. However, the usage is not entirely consistent. Moreover, the late date and obvious textual corruption of this work limit its usefulness.[71] Similar is the *Apocalypse of Sedrach* which shows some hint of a pattern but is not uniform in its usage. In both texts there are inexplicable exceptions.

The *Testament of Abraham*, however, reveals a singular and plural pattern very similar to that found in the Wisdom of Solomon. The *Testament of Abraham* is the oldest of a set of three works which can be classified together as the "Testaments of the Three Patriarchs."[72] As with many other pseudepigraphal works, we have two distinct recensions of *Abraham*, each witnessed to by a variety of manuscripts. Also like many other multi-recension works, it is very difficult to determine which, if either, was original, and likewise difficult to disentangle the Jewish and Christian elements found in both.[73] The original language of both recensions was likely Greek, though with some differences: the shorter recension (B) is simpler while at points the language of the longer recension (A) has been clearly mediaevalised; yet at the same time, the language of A is more closely aligned with other Jewish literature of ancient Egyptian provenance, including LXX Genesis and 2–4 Maccabees.[74] The *Testament of Abraham* in its original form is roughly contemporary with the Gospel of Matthew (last quarter of the first century CE), though *Abraham* is likely younger. Most interestingly, *Abraham* (at least in its extant recensions) shows knowledge of Matthew, most strongly Mt 7:13 in *Abraham* 11:3.[75]

The use of heaven in *Abraham* is frequent: There are 21 occurrences in Recension A and 11 in Recension B. Despite the dependence on Genesis for the story's content and other evidence of Septuagintal lan-

---

[71] For dating and textual issues, see M. E. Stone in *OTP* 1:561–570.
[72] They are classified as such and discussed by E. P. Sanders and W. F. Stinespring in *OTP* 1:869–918.
[73] On the complicated matter of the relationship of the recensions, more up to date than *OTP* is Dale Allison's commentary, *Testament of Abraham* (Berlin: de Gruyter, 2003), 12–27.
[74] *OTP* 1:873; Allison, *Testament*, 12.
[75] Cf. Sanders' comments: "The compact and balanced form of Mt could hardly have been derived from T Ab; and in view of other evidence of verbatim agreement between T Ab A and the NT, the dependence of the former on the latter here seems indisputable" (*OTP* 1:888, n. 11b). See also Allison, *Testament*, 238–245.

guage, the use of heaven in *Abraham* is much more similar to broader and later Second Temple literature than it is to the LXX.

Although the Greek style of the two recensions varies at several points, both recensions reveal an apparently intentional distinction between singular and plural οὐρανός. The consistency of the pattern across both recensions with little textual variance argues that this distinction is likely original and not a product of later redaction.[76]

Of the twenty-one occurrences of οὐρανός in Recension A, four are plural (4:5; 7:4; 8:1; 15:11). Even more frequently, five of the eleven instances in Recension B are plural (4:4; 7:14, 16; 8:1; 14:6). Most of these are exact parallels in both recensions. Recension A has an occurrence in 15:11 which has no parallel text in B. Conversely, Recension B has an additional instance inserted into the context of 7:16, and the plural in B 14:6 has a singular parallel in A 20:12.

The patterned use of plural οὐρανοί across both recensions is very clear: every occurrence of the plural is found in the phrase εἰς τοὺς οὐρανούς, referring to ascending into heaven, specifically into the presence of God.[77] For example, in 4:5 (A; 4:4 in B) the archangel Michael, pretending to relieve himself, steps outside Abraham's tent and ascends εἰς τοὺς οὐρανούς to stand before God. Identical is 8:1 and 15:11 in A and 8:1 in B. The other plurals are similar and clearly refer to entering the presence of God. By contrast, the much more frequent singular forms are used in a variety of ways that are distinct from this reference to God's presence. The singular forms instead all refer to creation or the entrance of God's presence into this world. Thus, the focus is on the created, visible world. Even in the cases where reference is made to the divine entering this world ("in the skies" or "from heaven"), the reference centers on the earthly realm. In these kinds of references, while the origin is clearly divine, the emphasis is on the physical manifestation

---

[76] In fact, the textual variants which have singular instances where the others have plural are consistently found to be inferior according to the critical editions. Additionally, the tendency to correct toward the more common singular argues for the superiority of the plurals on internal grounds.

[77] The only exception is that a few manuscripts of Recension B have the archangel Michael ascending ἐν τοῖς οὐρανοῖς at 8:1. This reading is judged inferior, however, according to the critical edition as found in Francis Schmidt, *Le Testament grec d'Abraham* (Tübingen: Mohr Siebeck, 1986). On this point it is worth noting that the earlier edition produced by Michael Stone for the SBL Texts and Translations series presents inferior readings of οὐρανός at several points as it has simply followed the earlier 1892 edition of M. R. James.

to humans in the created realm. While there is inevitably some overlap of the divine and human spheres here, the visible, created realm is the focus, hence the singular forms.

The multiple occurrences of οὐρανός in chapters 7–10 (Recension A) show this singular-plural contrast at work, including the ambiguity found when referring to God's activity breaking into the human realm. In *Abraham*, these latter references are consistently singular and the plural is reserved for entering the presence of God:

> 7:3a—while looking at the sun and moon, Isaac sees the skies/heaven (sg) opened
> 7:3b—a light-bearing man comes down out of heaven (sg)
> 7:4—the sunlike man takes the sun and goes up into the heavens (pl)
> 7:5—the same angel-man again comes down out of heaven (sg)
> 7:8—the same angel-man is explained as an angel who came down from heaven (sg)
> 8:1—Michael becomes invisible (ἀναφής) and goes up into the heavens (pl) and stands before God
> 8:5—reference to the stars of heaven (sg), quoting Gen LXX
> 9:8 and 10:1—Abraham is taken on a cloud-level tour of the world from which he can view activities all over the earth; two times this place is called "the air of heaven" (sg) (εἰς τὸν αἰθέρα τοῦ οὐρανοῦ); it is clear this is not an ascent into the presence of God, but only to a plane above the earth
> 10:11 (2x)—fire comes down out of heaven (sg)
> 10:12—the voice of God comes down out of heaven (sg); while this is clearly divine activity, the emphasis is on the manifestation of this voice in the human realm
> 10:15 and 11:1—Abraham is taken to "the first gate of heaven" (sg)[78]

This closely repeated and consistent pattern must be more than coincidental, especially in comparison with so much other literature we have surveyed where it is very difficult to find any explanation for the occasional appearance of a plural. Here the consistency of alternation stands out, even if we might at first be a bit put off by the "out of heaven" being singular compared to "going to heaven" being plural. The fact that this distinction is upheld is one of the strongest proofs that an intentional singular-plural distinction is at play. The emphasis on coming down out of heaven seems to be on the visible appearing, while

---

[78] The "first gate of heaven" probably refers to the lowest sphere just above the earth through which the meteorological and divine elements pass, and is not a reference to the divine presence. Cf. Allison, *Testament*, 234. Thus, the singular is appropriate here.

the going up into heaven equates with the *disappearance* of the angel.[79] This pattern is found throughout the work and not only in chapters 7–10. In 15:11–12 the distinction is again found side by side. In verse 11 Michael ascends to the heavens (pl), to the presence of God, and in verse 12 complains that although he has shown Abraham "the entire earth under heaven (sg) as well as the sea," Abraham still refuses to die. The same pattern of contrast is found throughout Recension B as well, though there are fewer occurrences of οὐρανός overall and thus not as many examples for comparison.

The only potential exception to this striking pattern of singular and plural contrast is found in the last occurrence of οὐρανός in Recension A. In 20:12 the singing angels take Abraham's departed soul and ascend into (sg) heaven (εἰς τόν οὐρανόν). This is the only instance in either recension where a singular form appears with reference to ascending beyond the earthly realm. In every other case, the plural alone is used for this arrangement. This text thus proves inconsistent with the rest of A. Interestingly, the shorter Recension B does have the expected plural in the parallel passage, thus preserving the consistent pattern throughout. The singular in A 20:12 may simply be unoriginal. There are a couple of manuscripts which omit the phrase altogether, though none which have a plural instead. The strong pattern identified here plus the plural reading in B casts some doubt on the originality of A. Nonetheless, the current critical text includes the singular. Regardless, the pattern of singular versus plural stands throughout both recensions, and the reason for the seeming exception in 20:12 is unclear.

The similarity of pattern with Wisdom of Solomon is striking. Even more conspicuous is a comparable pattern that can be discerned in Matthew (see the next chapter). If indeed the pattern is more than coincidental, the question is whether the author(s) of *Testament of Abraham* were following Matthew in this sort of singular-plural distinction, or whether they both represent some first-century parlance of singular and plural usage. While there is clear evidence for dependence of *Abraham* on Matthew at certain points, it is not clear at what point in the evolution of the work such influence came to be. Likewise here, the similarity with Matthew's usage that we will see subsequently is likely more than

---

[79] 8:1 especially emphasizes this contrast, where becoming invisible and entering the presence of God are equated.

coincidence. But whether it was later Christian editors, influenced by Matthew, who altered the forms of οὐρανός to fit Matthew's pattern, or whether Matthew himself was following a pattern found in works such as Wisdom of Solomon and *Testament of Abraham*, is not clear.

Conclusion

The purpose of this chapter has been to explore what historical and literary precedents there might be for Matthew's odd preference for plural forms of οὐρανός. It has been shown that Matthew's frequent use of οὐρανοί stands out not only relative to the rest of the NT documents, but also to nearly all of the preceding literature. A close examination of the LXX as well as the other Greek Second Temple literature reveals that plural forms of οὐρανός were quite uncommon. When they do appear, the reason is neither because of a belief in multiple heavens nor because of the morphological influence of plural heaven in Hebrew and Aramaic. Instead, in the case of the LXX, the syntax of Hebrew verbs and poetic factors give rise to occasional plural forms of οὐρανός. In the case of the other Second Temple literature, relatively few plural forms of οὐρανός can be found and they exhibit no specific usage. However, in two books from this period—the Wisdom of Solomon and the *Testament of Abraham*—an intentional singular and plural pattern of οὐρανός can be discovered. This pattern parallels a similar but more developed pattern in Matthew, as the following chapter will show.

CHAPTER SIX

ΟΥΡΑΝΟΣ AND ΟΥΡΑΝΟΙ IN MATTHEW

This chapter builds on the previous survey of singular and plural forms of οὐρανός and seeks to show how Matthew intentionally uses both forms as part of his heaven and earth contrast theme.

Our examination of the plural forms of οὐρανός in the Septuagint and Second Temple documents makes clear that such forms were not very common in the literature preceding and even contemporary with Matthew. Indeed, it is not until the writings of the New Testament that plural forms of οὐρανός appear alongside the singular with any notable frequency. Yet even there they remain in the minority. Forms of οὐρανός occur some 273 times (depending on variants) in the NA^{27}. Ninety, or about a third of these, occur in the plural and two-thirds (183) in the singular. As can be seen from Table 6.1, the NT authors vary significantly in their usage.

Table 6.1 Occurrences of Οὐρανός in the NT by Singular and Plural Forms

	Singular	Plural	Total
Matthew	27	55	82
Mark	13[a]	5	18
Luke	31[b]	4	35
John	18	0	18
Acts	24	2	26
Pauline Epistles	11	10[c]	21
Hebrews	3	7[d]	10
Catholic Epistles	5	6[e]	11
Revelation	51	1[f]	52
Total	183	90	273

Notes

a – Includes one occurrence from the textually-weak longer ending to Mark.

b – Includes one occurrence from the textually-uncertain 22:43.

c – Seven of these ten plurals are found in Ephesians (4x) and Colossians (3x).

d – Heb 1:10 is a quote from Septuagint Ps 101:26 [MT 102:25] which contains a plural form.

e – All of the plurals in the Catholic Epistles occur in 2 Peter with the exception of one plural occurrence in 1 Peter 1:4 (though ℵ reads the singular there as well).

f – The only plural occurrence in Revelation (or any Johannine writings) is found in a quote from the Septuagint Isaiah 44:23.

Interestingly, a full 30% of all the occurrences of οὐρανός in the NT are found in Matthew. Even more striking is the fact that 61% of all the *plural* uses in the NT (55 of 90) occur there. If one were to remove Matthew's 82 occurrences of οὐρανός, the rest of the NT would have plural occurrences less than 13% of the time, which is comparable in frequency to the preceding literature. In addition to Matthew, only in Hebrews and 2 Peter do plural forms appear more frequently than singular. The point is that clearly, Matthew has a multitude of references to οὐρανός and stands out in plural usage.

An examination of the Synoptic tradition reveals more of Matthew's preference for and usage of plural forms in contrast to the singular. As noted in the preceding table, Mark contains οὐρανός eighteen times and Luke thirty-five times. All of these found in both Mark and Luke are subsumed into Matthew's account except Mark 7:35 and the Lukan occurrences which are either L material or insertions into triple-tradition passages. In the majority of instances (14 of 22) where Matthew has adopted an existing occurrence of οὐρανός, whether from Mark or Q or both, he has retained the same form in number (singular or plural). In fact, in all of these cases except Matt 24:29c (//Mark 13:25//Luke 21:26) that form is singular. This might be expected in light of the predominant preference for singular usage among Mark (13 of 18) and Luke (31 of 35). However, there are eight instances where Matthew apparently changed the number-form of οὐρανός from the sources he received.[1] In only two instances (Matt 22:30//Mark 12:25; Matt 6:20//Luke 12:33) does Matthew have a singular where Mark or Luke has a plural. Meanwhile, in six cases, a plural form is found in Matthew in comparison to a singular in Mark and Luke: three times in contrast to Mark (Mark 10:21//Matt 19:21; Mark 13:27//Matt 24:31; Mark 13:32//Matt 24:36), and three times in Lukan parallels (Luke 3:21//Matt 3:16; Luke 3:22//Matt 3:17; Luke 6:23//Matt 5:12). This kind of Synoptic comparison reveals that in Matthew's use and editing of his sources he was likely conscious of the singular and plural forms of οὐρανός.

---

[1] I am adopting the Marcan priority two-source theory as a working hypothesis for this analysis. But even if this theory proved inaccurate, my argument would not be lessened. Whether Matthew is using Mark and Q or just Mark or an Aramaic *logia* or some combination thereof, the point is that his idiolectic use of οὐρανός reveals an intentional crafting in this regard.

Οὐρανοί AS A SEMITISM?

Few scholars make much mention of the plural forms of οὐρανός in Matthew, but whenever the oddity of his predominant use of the plural is raised, the typical explanation is that this is evidence of Semitic interference on his Greek style. The argument is the same as is typically assumed for the LXX (as was discussed in the previous chapter): because the Hebrew and Aramaic words for heaven are plural, when οὐρανός is plural, it must be through the influence of these Semitic lexemes. Thus, one regularly finds comments such as that the plural is "in accordance with the Semitic idiom."[2] Similarly, Ulrich Luz classifies the vocable οὐρανοί as evidence of "Hellenistic Jewish and rabbinical material" in Matthew.[3] Likewise, this argument from the Hebrew/Aramaic to the Greek is often used to explain Matthew's kingdom of heaven. As Davies and Allison state: "βασιλεία τῶν οὐρανῶν... is to be judged a Semitism in view of rabbinic usage, *malkūt šāmayim*."[4] In addition to the commentaries, this understanding is found in nearly all of the standard dictionary and grammar discussions of οὐρανός, as was discussed in the previous chapter.

But as we have shown in the case of the LXX, the Semitic morphology argument is inadequate. There were at times *Vorlage*-influenced syntactical and poetical reasons why plurals were occasionally used in the LXX, but the direct morphological connection typically assumed cannot be sustained. Similarly, in the Second Temple literature, with the exception of intentional patterns in Wisdom and *Testament of Abraham*, the plurals are infrequent and random. Again, the Semitic morphology argument does not hold, even for texts which translate a Semitic *Vorlage*.

But what about Matthew? It is nothing new to recognize some degree of Semitic influence in the content and style of Matthew.[5] From earliest times, Papias' famous statement about the *logia* in the Hebrew/Aramaic

---

[2] Beare, *Matthew*, 356. Almost verbatim is Davies and Allison, *Matthew*, 1:328.

[3] Luz, *Matthew 1–7*, 64. When commenting on the language of Matthew, Luz states, "Matthew writes a Greek which is influenced by Jewish, occasionally rabbinic features" (49–50).

[4] Davies and Allison, *Matthew*, 1:81. Similar is David Hill, *Matthew*, 90, who says that kingdom of heaven "indicat[es] faithfulness to the Aramaic."

[5] For example, W. C. Allen and Adolf Schlatter both speak of the "Jewish colouring" or "palästinische Färbung" of Matthew's language. This less-specific phraseology is perhaps better than "Semitisms." Allen, *Matthew*, 180; Adolf Schlatter, *Der Evangelist Matthäus: seine Sprache, sein Ziel, seine Selbständigkeit* (Stuttgart: Calwer Verlag, 1957), 57.

language from Matthew has spawned assorted views on how to understand Matthew's sources, style of Greek, and audience.[6] Could it be that Matthew's frequent use of the plural reveals Semitic enhancement *on his own style* through his familiarity with Hebrew/Aramaic and/or by his own translation of an Aramaic sayings source?

While this is certainly possible, it fails to explain why Semitic morphology would particularly affect Matthew in this way when it did not do the same for his contemporaries (e.g., Josephus—no plurals) nor for the LXX, most of which was translated directly from Semitic sources.[7] But even more importantly, there is one crucial fact that makes this explanation doubtful: Matthew's use of οὐρανός does not just consist of *plural* forms, but of many *singular* forms as well, and apparently, with an intentional difference in referent (see below). If one wants to argue that Semitic morphology has led to Matthew's use of the plural, then one must also explain why Matthew continues to use many *singular* forms: he does not consistently use the plural, but only 66% of the time. Some twenty-seven singular forms still appear. Moreover, in the sayings of Jesus (which, according to the theory, should especially reflect the plural οὐρανός coming from the Aramaic original) we find both plural and singular forms throughout the Gospel. Similarly, we find that in some instances, Matthew has apparently changed a plural form in his source into a singular.[8] Certainly, this is difficult to square with a view that it is morphological Semitic influence causing Matthew's use of the plural. A different explanation is required.

Οὐρανοί as Evidence of Multiple Heavens?

The awakening of scholarly interest in apocalyptic literature has unearthed a diverse tradition of documents in which seers undertake heavenly journeys. Within this tradition, the notion of multiple layers of heaven develops. As a result, another possible interpretation is that

---

[6] For a concise overview of interpretations, see Carson, *Matthew*, 11–13. Or more recently, Scot McKnight, "Matthew, Gospel of," in *Dictionary of Jesus and the Gospels* (ed. Joel Green, Scot McKnight, and I. Howard Marshall; Downers Grove, Ill.: Intervarsity, 1992), 526–28. Fuller discussions can be found in Davies and Allison, *Matthew*, 1:7ff. See also the bibliography in Donald Hagner, *Matthew 1–13*, xliii.

[7] Indeed, translation Greek such as is found in the LXX would more likely show Semitic enhancement than works composed in Greek, such as Matthew.

[8] Matt 22:30//Mark 12:25 and Matt 6:20//Luke 12:33.

Matthew's preference for plural οὐρανός reflects his own apocalyptic belief in a multiple heavens cosmology.

As discussed previously, a few scholars have assumed this development is the explanation for the plural forms of οὐρανός which appear throughout the LXX, and especially those in the later, apocryphal books. For example, Adela Yarbro Collins states: "In the phrase 'who created the heavens and the earth,' which occurs in Judith, the Psalms, and Proverbs, οὐρανοί is probably a true plural, reflecting the idea of a plurality of heavens."[9] I have argued in the previous chapter, however, that this explanation is untenable for the LXX (canonical and apocryphal).

The case of plural οὐρανοί and multiple heavens in the Second Temple apocalyptic literature is more difficult to navigate. It appears that some multiple heavens views were extant in the first-century CE, though how developed and widespread these were is unclear. Most notable is Paul's reference to the "third heaven" in 2 Corinthians 12:2, one of the few indications of a multiple-heavens cosmology that we can confidently date to the first-century CE.[10] The more highly-developed seven-heavens views familiar to us from texts such as *2 Enoch* and the rabbinic materials *may* be contemporary with the latest writings of the NT, though most of these likely come from a later period as these views developed.[11] Therefore, it *is* possible that the slight increase of plural forms of οὐρανός in the Second Temple literature (including the NT) reflects the influence of developing multiple-heavens views. This is not clearly the case, however. Most notably, even those later texts which

---

[9] A. Y. Collins, *Cosmology and Eschatology in Jewish and Christian Apocalypticism* (Leiden: Brill, 1996), 24. In another essay she states the same and proposes that although plural οὐρανοί in the earlier Septuagintal writings should be understood as a "translation plural," in the later writings, it is likely a "true plural." A. Y. Collins, "The Seven Heavens," 62.

[10] Cf. J. J. Collins, "A Throne in the Heavens," 46: "The familiar pattern of ascent through a numbered series of heavens, usually seven, is not attested in Judaism before the Christian era...for a Jewish writer who claims to have ascended to heaven (apart from 4QM), we must wait until St Paul." On the meaning of 2 Corinthians 12 and the theme of heavenly ascent see now Paula Gooder, *Only the Third Heaven? 2 Corinthians 12.1–10 and Heavenly Ascent* (London: T&T Clark, 2006). Gooder acknowledges that the dating difficulties of all the ascent texts make it difficult to state with confidence whether Paul was influenced by them, though there does seem to be some similar tradition behind Paul's experience.

[11] M. Himmelfarb, *Ascent to Heaven*, 127, n. 14: "These apocalypses are by no means easy to date, but the works that contain seven heavens...all seem to date from the first century CE or later."

clearly manifest multiple heavens journeys continue to use singular forms of οὐρανός primarily or exclusively. For example, no plurals are found in the *Greek Apocalypse of Moses* or *3 Baruch* and very few in *1 Enoch*.[12] The *Testament of Levi* has the most plural forms and these may be connected with a multiple-heavens schema, but as observed in the previous chapter, the heavenly journeys section is almost certainly a later redaction and not part of the earlier Aramaic form.

The question at hand concerns whether a multiple-heavens view stands behind Matthew's preference for plural forms of οὐρανός. Although this understanding of the rise of the plurals has been given occasionally for the LXX, it has not typically been argued for Matthew. Instead, the Semitic morphology explanation is standard. In light of the trend toward an apocalyptic interpretation of Matthew, it is surprising that this argument is not more often made. Regardless, is it a valid option?

Below I will offer an alternative and comprehensive explanation for Matthew's frequent use of the plurals which eliminates the need to posit a multiple heavens cosmology for Matthew. However, this explanation does not necessarily preclude the possibility of such a cosmological worldview. The question must be answered based on other evidence within Matthew itself.

In short, there are no compelling reasons in Matthew to believe that his worldview, broadly apocalyptic though it was, contained a belief in specific, clearly defined levels of heaven. We may note first that this type of apocalyptic cosmology is nearly always found in connection with revelatory, angel-led journeys into the heavens, something which is noticeably lacking in Matthew's story. Additionally, even though Paul's reference in 2 Corinthians indicates the currency of some multiple-heavens view, it is difficult to find much textual evidence for such views in the literature which pre-dates Matthew. Such views were certainly developing in the time in which Matthew wrote, but they should not be assumed as widespread unless an author evinces such a perspective. In the NT, despite reports of much angelic activity and many references to heaven, reference to multiple heavens in 2 Corinthians 12:1–5 is the

---

[12] *2 Enoch* has one of the clearest seven-level schemes. However, we have no extant Greek manuscripts and thus we cannot be definitive about how this might have affected singular and plural forms of οὐρανός. Regardless, it is important to note that despite a developed heaven scheme, this does not result in many references to "the heavens." Instead, the various levels are referred to with ordinal numbers: the first heaven, second heaven, etc.

exception that proves the rule; this is simply not a clearly-held view in the NT documents. It is telling, for example, that even in John's Revelation, which does include a visionary journey to heaven, stratified levels of heaven are absent (as are plural forms of οὐρανός). Revelation is not only likely close in dating to Matthew, but also shares many similarities in outlook, as my thesis will show on several occasions. In the same vein, plural forms of οὐρανός in Matthew cannot be assumed as sufficient evidence for discerning in Matthew a multiple-heavens belief. The strength of this conclusion will be buttressed by the more compelling alternative solution offered below.

Instead of referring to multiple levels of heaven, Matthew's use of plural forms when referring to the divine and invisible realm (see below) likely reflects a more generalized and generic understanding of God's dwelling in the heights above (cf. also the plurals in Wisdom of Solomon and the *Testament of Abraham*). In this, Matthew aligns with the view of his OT heritage and most of the preceding Second Temple literature. In the OT, the plural שָׁמַיִם and occasional references to God in the "heaven of heavens" communicate the Jewish people's transcendent and exalted view of God, not specific (apocalyptic) levels of heaven. As Solomon prayed, "O Lord, God of Israel, there is no God like Thee in heaven above or on earth beneath...But will God indeed dwell on earth? Behold, heaven and the heaven of heavens cannot contain Thee!" (1 Kgs 8:23, 27).[13]

A DIFFERENT SOLUTION:
SINGULAR VERSUS PLURAL DISTINCTION

While the preceding Jewish literature's occasional use of plural forms likely made the plurals a possible option for Matthew, his predominant use of plural οὐρανός (55 plurals; 27 singulars) cannot be explained by the example of the preceding literature—either via Semitic influence on his style or apocalyptic views of multiple heavens. Instead, a different solution can be put forward.

---

[13] Dalman concludes the same. He says that the plural form has nothing whatsoever to do with the notion of seven heavens: "A Hellenist might *possibly*, indeed attach some such notion to the Greek οἱ οὐρανοί, but that is not a sufficient reason for imputing the idea to Matthew, who makes no allusion of the kind." Dalman, *Words of Jesus*, 93.

A close examination of the use of οὐρανός in the First Gospel reveals that there is in Matthew's idiolect an intentional distinction of meaning between the singular and the plural: *Matthew generally uses οὐρανός in the singular to refer to the visible (earthly) world and in "heaven and earth" pairs, and he uses the plural to refer to the invisible (divine) realm.* The categories of visible/earthly realm versus invisible/divine realm provide a comprehensive framework for understanding Matthew's frequent and varied use of οὐρανός. This intentional pattern is very similar to the one already discussed in both the Wisdom of Solomon and the *Testament of Abraham*. It is, however, far more developed, widespread, and important in Matthew.

That there is a distinction in meaning between the singular and plural forms of οὐρανός in the NT has been suggested previously by only a few reference works. While most scholars conclude that there is *no* difference in meaning between singular and plural forms (e.g., Louw and Nida, *NIDNTT, TDNT, ABD*, and Cremer's *Biblico-Theological Lexicon*),[14] a few studies have argued for the possibility of some pattern. For example, BDAG acknowledges that in most NT books "the singular and plural are interchanged for no apparent reason."[15] Yet shortly after this, they state that the plural is preferred for the meaning of "transcendent above." This remark concurs with Nigel Turner's view: "In the material sense of the *sky* the singular predominates... In the less common figurative sense of *heaven* as God's abode the plural predominates."[16] Similar is BDF, which argues that most authors use the plural for the abode of God, "while the singular predominates in the literal sense, except for those instances where, according to the Jewish conception, several heavens were to be distinguished."[17]

But when it comes to Matthew in particular, relatively few commentators have even mentioned the singular and plural use of οὐρανός. The general assumption appears to be that there is no discernible distinction in meaning between the forms, and thus it is not worth noting. As noted above, the seemingly easy solution of labeling the plurals a "Semitism" ends the discussion. Nevertheless, a few commentators have made at least passing remarks.

---

[14] Cremer, *Lexicon*, 465.
[15] *BDAG*, 738.
[16] Turner, *A Grammar of New Testament Greek, Vol. III*, 25. Similar remarks can be found in Turner, *Christian Words*, 203–205.
[17] BDF §141.

Probably the oldest exegete to infer a difference in meaning is Origen. In Book XIII, §31 of his commentary on Matthew, Origen highlights the superiority of Peter over the other apostles by comparing the forms of οὐρανός in the binding and loosing passages of 16:19 and 18:18. Chapter 16, spoken to Peter, promises a binding and loosing ἐν τοῖς οὐρανοῖς, while 18:18 gives this same authority to all of the disciples ἐν οὐρανῷ. According to Origen, Peter is superior "for it is no small difference that Peter received the keys not of one heaven but of more, and in order that whatsoever things he binds on the earth may be bound not in one heaven but in them all."[18] Many centuries later the great biblical scholar, Johann Albrecht Bengel, commenting on Matt 6:9, offers a different explanation: "οὐρανός (in the singular number), signifies here that place, in which the will of the Father is performed by all who wait upon Him; οὐρανοί (in the plural) signifies the whole Heavens which surround and contain that one, as it were, lower and smaller Heaven."[19]

But in the modern era, commentators on Matthew have not taken up any such position. For example, Alfred Plummer dismisses Origen's idea without argument by stating: "It is not likely that there was any difference in the words used by Christ."[20] No other commentators even mention Origen's idea, nor do they interact with Bengel. Occasionally scholars will make isolated comments but with no further development or recognition of a consistent pattern. For example, Davies and Allison, writing on 6:20, state: "Matthew, who is more fond of the plural, has here chosen the singular to underline the parallel with 'on the earth' (cf. 6.10)."[21] Similarly, Leon Morris, in two separate footnotes reports that Matthew "mostly uses the word in the plural, except when he refers to 'heaven and earth',"[22] and "usually has οὐρανός in the plural, but in the

---

[18] Origen, *Commentary on Matthew* XIII.31. This apparently reflects a later, developed view of the multiple heavens idea. It also shows Origen's careful attention to the details of the Greek text, as there is indeed a shift from a plural to a singular form from 16:19 to 18:18, as will be discussed below. In my survey of Patristic writings I was not able to find anyone else who argues the same or makes mention of the singular and plural distinction.

[19] J. A. Bengel, *Gnomon of the New Testament, Vol. 1, Matthew-Mark* (trans. A. R. Fausset and J. Bandinel; Edinburgh: T&T Clark, 1857), 189.

[20] Plummer, *Matthew*, 227. We will have opportunity to examine Origen's claim below in the analysis of 16:19 and 18:18.

[21] Davies and Allison, *Matthew*, 1:631. Similar is Gundry, *Matthew*, 106.

[22] Morris, *Matthew*, 52–53, n. 11.

expression 'heaven and earth' he prefers the singular."[23] Nevertheless, Morris follows this up by commenting that there is no apparent difference in meaning between the singular and plural forms.[24] In John Nolland's commentary on Matthew, he too makes brief mention of the possibility of a singular/plural distinction when discussing 6:10. He rightly observes that the plural regularly refers to the dwelling place of God, but confesses that "the meaning of the singular is more varied and harder to tie down."[25]

The outstanding exception to this trend in interpretation is Hans Betz in his massive Hermeneia commentary on the Sermon on the Mount.[26] In several passing comments and footnotes, Betz states that in the Sermon (but not necessarily in the rest of Matthew), the singular heaven is used in the sense of "sky" in conjunction with earth, while God's realm is spoken of with the plural.[27] Betz returns to this formulation several times throughout the volume and it impacts his interpretation of the meaning of heaven particularly in 6:10.[28] In this sense, Betz has done more towards recognizing a consistent pattern in Matthew than any other scholar. Yet even his work is only cursory on this matter. There are several occurrences of heaven in the Sermon that he does not mention, and he is not able to provide a convincing explanation for the apparent exception to his rule in 6:20. Moreover, his observations are necessarily limited to the Sermon on the Mount. The evidence from the rest of Matthew needs to be considered on this question as well. Interestingly, I have found no mention of Betz's theory in other commentators or discussions of Matthew's language.

Another German scholar, Ernst Lohmeyer, made similar observations some years before Betz. In his insightful volume on the Lord's Prayer, Lohmeyer also suggests in passing a singular-plural distinction with many similarities to what I have articulated above. He postulates that the plural is used in relationship with God and the singular with creation:

---

[23] Morris, *Matthew*, 109, n. 65.
[24] Morris, *Matthew*, 609.
[25] Nolland, *Matthew*, 288.
[26] Betz, *Sermon on the Mount*.
[27] This is stated on the following pages: 119; 152, n. 504; 184, n. 116; 379; 395; 434, n. 93; 474, n. 399.
[28] Betz, 379, argues that the singular οὐρανός in 6:10 ("on earth as it is in heaven") must, due to the Sermon's singular-plural pattern, refer "to the supramundane world of astral entities and not the higher spheres in which God exists." This may be correct but not for the reason Betz sets forth. For my own interpretation of this text, see below.

"In short, the singular is used wherever heaven and earth are combined in the unity of creation, the plural where 'heaven' means God's world away from all the bustle and distraction of earth."[29]

It is unclear whether Lohmeyer is suggesting this distinction holds for Matthew alone or for the entire NT. Traub understands him to imply the whole NT and therefore rejects this notion.[30] It does seem clear that there is no consistent pattern of usage across the entire NT. As we have observed, οὐρανός was a widespread and flexible term. It stands to reason that different authors with varying backgrounds and literary skills (such as we find in the NT) would use the term with more or less precision and/or intention. Only a brief amount of time in a concordance bears this out. To take but one example, the phrase "heaven and earth" is found in several places in the NT, yet in strikingly different forms. In Matthew this phrase is nearly always singular. Yet, in 2 Peter and Paul when the heaven and earth conjunction is used, οὐρανός is invariably plural. However, at the same time 2 Peter is *more* like Matthew than Paul in that plural forms of οὐρανός are preferred to singular. Thus, it is clear that each author uses οὐρανός in a somewhat distinct, or idiolectic way.[31]

However, agreeing that no consistent pattern of usage across the NT exists in no way eliminates the possibility that Matthew (or any author) makes a distinction between singular and plural forms. In fact, as shown from the example above, this expectation is quite reasonable. If Lohmeyer intends only to suggest a singular-plural distinction for Matthew, then I believe his overlooked comments, as well as Betz's, with some modifications, can now be substantiated from the present study.

In our survey of heaven we observed that שָׁמַיִם / οὐρανός has a semantic domain consisting of two main poles or foci: (1) heaven as the space of the created order; and (2) heaven as the dwelling place of God. There are also occasions where the use of heaven involves a semantic ambiguity, one that exists in instances where the edges of the two meanings overlap, as in promises and judgments coming "from heaven." The

---

[29] Ernst Lohmeyer, *The Lord's Prayer* (trans. J. Bowden; London: William Collins Sons, 1965), 114–115. Betz refers to Lohmeyer's works five times but does not make mention of the latter's comments about a singular-plural distinction.

[30] *TDNT*, s.v. "Οὐρανός," 534, n. 322.

[31] For Paul, A. T. Lincoln concludes that, except in Eph 4:10, his use of singular and plural is simply a stylistic matter, *Paradise Now and Not Yet* (London: Cambridge University Press, 1981; repr., Grand Rapids: Baker Book House, 1991), 184.

"bread from heaven" and the "brimstones from heaven" are in the sky, yet their origin is clearly divine. We also observed that one of the most important uses of heaven in the OT and Second Temple literature is in conjunction with earth. *Matthew's employment of a singular versus plural pattern of οὐρανός, with its own intricacies, aligns closely with each of these aspects of heaven usage in the preceding literature.* He almost exclusively uses the singular in accordance with the first semantic pole. Also, the singular is regularly utilized in the stock word pairing of heaven and earth, which in the LXX nearly always uses the singular as well.[32] On the other hand, Matthew uses the plural to refer to the invisible and divine realm, or the second semantic pole. Finally, there are a few instances in Matthew where the referent is ambiguous and in these cases, either the singular or plural can be used, depending on other factors. Thus, Matthew builds closely upon the foundation of the preceding literature, yet he creates a much more elaborate and developed use of οὐρανός in an idiolectic pattern.

In the following sections, I will provide examples of uses of οὐρανός in each of these categories as well as an examination of the few cases which remain anomalous. First, we may get an overview of the pattern by viewing the assorted referents used with οὐρανός in graphic form (Table 6.2).

1. *Singular οὐρανός as reference to the visible world/earthly realm*

As has been observed, singular forms of οὐρανός predominate throughout the LXX, Second Temple literature, and the NT—almost everywhere except in Matthew. Matthew does not abandon the singular, however, but often uses it in accordance with the most basic sense of heaven: as a reference to the visible realm above the earth. Ten times singular οὐρανός is used to refer to the weather, clouds or skies, the stars, and the birds flying in the sky. For example, in 16:2–3 Jesus discusses the red appearance of the οὐρανός as an indication of weather to come. Similarly, in 24:30a,c Jesus refers to the eschatological appearance of the Son of Man in the sky and his coming to earth on clouds in the sky (τοῦ οὐρανοῦ). The clouds of the sky are also mentioned in 26:64. In

---

[32] Beginning with the paradigmatic οὐρανός καὶ γῆ of Gen 1:1, the vast majority of heaven and earth occurrences in the Septuagint use the singular forms of οὐρανός. Only occasionally does one find the plural in conjunction with γῆ, e.g., Ps 69:34; Jdt 9:13; 13:18. This less common construction is found also in 2 Peter.

Table 6.2 Various Referents Used with Οὐρανός in Matthew

Referent	Singular	Plural
In conjunction with γῆ	15	2
In conjunction with ἄνθρωπος	2	
In conjunction with ᾅδης	1	
Birds	3	
Weather, sky, clouds	4	
Sign located in	2	
Swearing by	2	
Lifting up eyes unto	1	
Stars	1	
Angels	2	2
Kingdom of		32
Father in		13
What is bound/loosed	2	2
Reward/Treasure	1	2
Place of the Spirit's descending		1
Place of the voice of God		1
(Four) ends of		1
"The powers" of/in		1
Total	27	55

Note: The totals for singular and plural will not necessarily reflect the sum of each column as some references are necessarily listed under more than one category. For example, the singular form connected with "treasure" is also used in conjunction with γῆ (as at 6:19–20).

24:29c the trio of astral bodies which govern the earth (cf. Gen 1:16) will all fail cataclysmically: the sun will darken, the moon will cease to glow, and the stars will fall ἀπὸ τοῦ οὐρανοῦ, i.e., from the sky to the earth. Following a very frequent OT pattern, Matthew also uses singular οὐρανός to describe flying birds: τὰ πετεινὰ τοῦ οὐρανοῦ (6:26; 8:20; 13:32).[33] This stock phrase, which finds as many as 50 parallels

---

[33] πετεινά also occurs in Matthew 13:4 but without the additional description τοῦ οὐρανοῦ. In this instance, the birds devour the sower's seed which has fallen along the path. It is understandable in light of the close connection of heaven with God that to call the seed-snatching culprits (translated in 13:19 as "the evil one") the "birds of heaven" might put the reader off a bit. Therefore, this otherwise stock phrase is shortened to simply πετεινά. Interestingly, Mark agrees with Matthew here, but Luke (8:5) has the regular, fuller phrase, though in his account the birds may play a secondary role in the crop failure: the seed has been trampled and *subsequently* the birds eat it up.

in the OT, was used to distinguish wild birds which fly in the sky from domestic fowl, such as chickens.³⁴

2. *Singular οὐρανός in heaven and earth pairings*³⁵

The other major usage of singular forms of οὐρανός in Matthew occurs when heaven is put in conjunction with earth. The heaven and earth combination is one of the most recurrent and important uses of heaven throughout the OT and beyond (as well as in Matthew). As noted above, in the LXX only occasionally does one find plural οὐρανός in connection with earth, and *only* in Judith is οὐρανοί put directly in a copulative pair with γῆ (9:12; 13:18; cf. 2 Peter 3:7,13). Instead, from Gen 1:1 on, the stock expression is singular οὐρανός plus γῆ. This is true regardless of the semantic sense of heaven as a reference to the created world or to God and regardless of how the words heaven and earth are combined (i.e., in a simple copulative pair or thematically).³⁶ Both when heaven and earth are combined merismatically (heaven and earth) and when they are contrasted (heaven versus earth), the singular is the standard. When discussing the plurals in the LXX, Peter Katz observes that there are some "stock phrases which never admit a plural." These include τὰ πετεινὰ τοῦ οὐρανοῦ and οὐρανός closely connected with γῆ or as its parallel.³⁷ Similarly, E. Lohmeyer states that "it is the almost invariable Septuagint usage, which is followed by the New Testament, that the word 'heaven' is always put in the singular where it is associated expressly, or by implication, with 'the earth'."³⁸

Following standard usage and the LXX's pattern,³⁹ Matthew like-

---

³⁴ Louw and Nida, *Lexicon* (s.v. οὐρανός, 1.5).
³⁵ An explication and analysis of these 17 heaven and earth combinations will be found in Chapter Eight.
³⁶ For a fuller discussion of the idea of copulative and thematic pairings, see the next two chapters on heaven and earth. In short, copulative pairs occur where "heaven and earth" appears as one unit, not separated by prepositions or other words. Thematic pairs use heaven and earth but with some separation of intervening words or phrases, such as "the dew of heaven and the fatness of the earth."
³⁷ Katz, *Philo's Bible*, 143.
³⁸ Lohmeyer, *The Lord's Prayer*, 114.
³⁹ Matthew's dependence on the LXX (consciously and unconsciously) has been observed by many commentators. Ulrich Luz describes it this way: "Matthew is strongly influenced by the Septuagint...the language of Matthew is throughout stamped by biblical Greek." Luz, *Matthew 1–7*, 49–50. More generally on the influence of OT language on Matthew, Gundry states: "We will quickly learn that [Matthew] delights in conforming phraseology to the OT, as well as in quoting the OT explicitly, and that he likes to put his materials in parallelistic form, often by tightening the parallelism that already characterizes the tradition." Gundry, *Matthew*, 2.

wise typically employs singular forms of οὐρανός when combined with earth.⁴⁰ Thus, in Matthew we find the common OT phrase οὐρανὸς καὶ γῆ (referring to the entire created world) in 5:18, 11:25, and 24:35. Even more frequently, singular οὐρανός and γῆ are closely connected with prepositional phrases (usually ἐν and ἐπι) in several Matthean texts: 5:34–35; 6:10; 6:19–20; 18:18 (2x); and 28:18. Although these latter heaven and earth pairs are contrastive not merismatic, Matthew continues to follow the LXX pattern of singular οὐρανός plus γῆ.⁴¹

In a similar vein, throughout the OT, heaven is also often combined with other words closely connected with earth to form heaven and earth pairings of an implied sort. As will be discussed subsequently, these implied heaven and earth pairs use heaven plus other words closely associated with earth, such as תְּהוֹם / ἄβυσσος and שְׁאוֹל / ᾅδης. These form a less explicit pairing with the same purpose and sense.⁴² Katz observes that in the LXX, singular οὐρανός is used in parallel with γῆ-associated words such as θάλασσα and ᾅδης, with the result that some passages have singular and plural οὐρανός side by side.⁴³ In the same way, Matthew also occasionally employs implied heaven and earth pairs, and as in the case of explicit pairs, singular οὐρανός is utilized. In 11:23 οὐρανός is contrasted with ᾅδης, and twice in 21:25–26 οὐρανός is compared to earthly humanity (ἄνθρωπος).

The heaven and earth combination in Matthew is a very important theme and one of the key uses of οὐρανός there. The pairing of heaven and earth (both explicit and implicit) comprise the majority of instances of singular οὐρανός in Matthew. This usage is so standard that in a sense it stands alone as a separate category from the visible (sg) versus invisible (pl) pattern. Yet at the same time, it forms an important part of Matthew's intentional use of οὐρανός. Matthew closely and intentionally follows the pattern of the LXX here.

---

⁴⁰ The only exception is 16:19 (2x) on which, see below.

⁴¹ Guelich, who does not otherwise recognize a singular-plural pattern, comments that the singular in Matthew 6:10, "rather than the more typically Matthean and Semitic plural (e.g., 6:9) stems from the LXX use of the singular in the phrase *heaven and earth*, with the latter perhaps attracting the plural into the singular and together they stand for the world (e.g., Ps 134:6, LXX). The function of *as* (ὡς) and *so* (καί) forms a comparison rather than a coordination, since God's rule is to be effected on *earth* as it is already in *heaven*." Robert Guelich, *The Sermon on the Mount*, 291.

⁴² Another kind of implied pair which could be included consists of the use of earth in conjunction with a word closely related to heaven, such as "the heights." For example, "In his hand are the depths of the earth; the heights of the mountains are his also" (Ps 95:4).

⁴³ Katz, *Philo's Bible*, 143.

3. Plural οὐρανός as reference to the invisible world/divine realm

More than twice as often as the singular, Matthew makes use of plural forms of οὐρανός (55 plural; 27 singular). In contrast with the singulars used in heaven and earth pairs and in reference to the visible world, the plural forms in Matthew refer to the invisible realm, usually explicitly God's realm or speaking of God indirectly through metonymy.

The majority of the plurals (32 of 55) occur in the uniquely Matthean expression ἡ βασιλεία τῶν οὐρανῶν, "kingdom/reign of heaven." This is clearly a reference to God's kingdom or rule, whether heaven is understood as the source or nature.[44] The first occurrence of οὐρανός in Matthew appears in John the Baptist's announcement of the kingdom of heaven (3:2), and this kingdom is central to Jesus' proclamation from the beginning (4:17) and throughout the Sermon on the Mount (5:3, 10, 19, 20; 7:21) and Jesus' other teachings (8:11; 11:11, 12; 13:11, 24, 31, 33, 44, 45, 47, 52; 16:19; 18:1–4; 18:23; 19:12, 14; 19:23; 20:1; 22:2; 23:13; 25:1). It is also the message Jesus commissions to the twelve disciples when they are sent out on their own for the first time (10:7). As was previously discussed, this use of οὐρανός is not a reverential circumlocution nor can it be explained merely as a Semitism. Instead, ἡ βασιλεία τῶν οὐρανῶν is plural because it serves to contrast with the visible and created connotations of the singular in Matthew's idiolect.[45]

Similarly, thirteen times on the lips of Jesus Matthew uses the plural to refer to my or your Father who is in heaven (5:16, 45; 6:1, 9; 7:11, 21; 10:32, 33; 12:50; 16:17; 18:10b, 14, 19).[46] The use of Father in

---

[44] In twelve instances, Matthew's kingdom of heaven is in direct parallel with Mark and Luke's "kingdom of God" and it is clear that Matthew's phrase refers to the same thing as the other Evangelists, as well as other NT authors. For full discussion of the meaning of ἡ βασιλεία τῶν οὐρανῶν and various scholarly interpretations of it, see Chapter Twelve.

[45] Whether Matthew was influenced by the occasional use of the plurals in similar phrases in the LXX is unclear. Cf. δυνάστα τῶν οὐρανῶν (2 Macc 15:23); δέσποτα τῶν οὐρανῶν (Jdt 9:12); βασιλεῦ τῶν οὐρανῶν (3 Macc 2:2); βασιλεὺς ἐπί τῶν οὐρανῶν (Ps Sol 2:30). As with the other plurals in the LXX, these phrases likely made Matthew's use of the plural more possible and plausible, though they are not a sufficient explanation for how and why he uses the plurals so frequently. Also, as observed above, in the combination of heaven with terms for ruling in the Apocrypha, both singular and plural forms appear; there is no thoroughly consistent pattern.

[46] Related to these are Matthew's seven uses (5:48; 6:14, 26, 32; 15:13; 18:35; 23:9) of οὐράνιος ("heavenly") to refer to the Father. This adjectival form is singular because it could not be otherwise to agree with ὁ πατήρ.

heaven is woven throughout the Gospel even as kingdom of heaven is, though it finds special focus in the Sermon on the Mount.

The singular and plural contrast is particularly strong in these instances, as in no case does Matthew ever connect the Father or the kingdom with heaven and not use the plural. Additionally, the plural is utilized to refer to other invisible and divinely-related objects and beings. For example, in 3:17 the voice of God comes ἐκ τῶν οὐρανῶν at Jesus' baptism.[47] The plural is also used to refer to αἱ δυνάμεις τῶν οὐρανῶν, "the powers of the heavens" in 24:29. Though some have understood this as a reference to the stars and/or planets, the best evidence shows this to be a reference to angelic beings in the spiritual realm.[48] Thus, it accords with the expected plural.

Four other references to angels in connection with heaven appear in Matthew (18:10; 22:30; 24:36; 28:2).[49] Two of these (18:10; 24:36) use plural οὐρανός as the location of the angels, both of which explicitly connect these angels with the Father.[50] In contrast, 28:2 describes an angel of the Lord who, upon descending ἐξ οὐρανοῦ (sg), rolls back Jesus' tombstone and sits upon it. At first this may appear to be an exception until one recognizes that we have here a shift from the invisible realm to that of the visible. It is precisely the *appearing* of the angel in the earthly realm that is being emphasized, as contrasted with the invisible angels surrounding God's throne. The angel's appearing is described as a descent from the skies (singular οὐρανός), comparable to the coming of the Son of Man ἐπὶ τῶν νεφελῶν τοῦ οὐρανοῦ (24:30; 26:64).

---

[47] There are two occurrences of the plural in 3:16-17 where the heavens are opened and the voice of God speaks. While these are both clearly reference to the divine, 3:16 could also be classified as an ambiguous use, and will be discussed briefly below.

[48] See Morris, *Matthew*, 609. Davies and Allison, *Matthew*, 3:358, acknowledge the reference could be to the sun, moon, and stars, but point out that "the ancients identified the heavenly lights with living beings; so we could here think of the fall of evil beings, 'the spiritual forces of wickedness in the heavenly places' (Eph 6:12) or, alternatively, of the heavenly hosts who come down to do battle against evil (cf. T. Levi 3:1-3)."

[49] Matthew has a total of twenty uses of ἄγγελος, but only these four are paired explicitly with οὐρανός. The references in 18:10 and 28:2 are uniquely Matthean, while both 22:30 and 24:36 are found in Mark as well.

[50] Matt 24:35-36 provides a good example of the pattern consciously worked out in close proximity: Matthew uses the singular in a copulative heaven and earth pair in 24:35 and this is followed by a switch to the plural in reference to the angels in the heavens in 24:36. Similar is 13:31-32 where kingdom of heaven (pl) in 13:31 is followed by "birds of heaven" (sg) in 13:32. Apart from recognizing an idiolectic pattern, it is impossible to explain why he regularly switches between singular and plural forms in such close proximity.

This again points to an intentional distinction in meaning for Matthew between the singular and plural. Interestingly, this same usage of the singular for the appearance of an angelic being in the skies is found in *Testament of Abraham*. The fourth angel reference (22:30) also uses the singular in a somewhat anomalous way and will be dealt with below.

A similar outworking of the singular and plural pattern can be seen in Matthew's references to heavenly treasure or reward. Three times Jesus speaks of promised reward (μίσθος or θησαυρός) in heaven for his disciples (5:12; 6:19; 19:21). That this reward is of a divine/heavenly nature is made even more explicit in 6:1 where reference is made to receiving reward from "your Father in heaven." In 5:12, in the Beatitudes addressed to the disciples of the kingdom of heaven, reward for the persecuted is promised ἐν τοῖς οὐρανοῖς, presumably in the kingdom of heaven to come. Similarly, in 19:2, the rich young man is offered θησαυρὸν ἐν οὐρανοῖς if he is willing to give up all to follow Jesus. Both of these use the expected plural form to refer to the invisible (and future) divine heaven where the reward is.[51] By way of comparison, however, in 6:19–20 Jesus exhorts his hearers to get lasting reward by contrasting two kinds of treasures, those ἐπὶ τῆς γῆς versus the true treasure ἐν οὐρανῷ. The singular form of οὐρανός in 6:20, though potentially unexpected in light of the divine realm of the reward, accords with the idiolectic pattern observed so far: when used in heaven and earth pairings, Matthew continues to utilize singular forms of οὐρανός, even when the reference is to the divine.[52] In this sense, as stated above, the heaven and earth pairs stand apart from and complement the rest of the singular and plural pattern.[53]

---

[51] Cf. the notion of 1 Peter 1:4: "to obtain an inheritance which is imperishable and undefiled and will not fade away, reserved in heaven for you."

[52] This fuller understanding of Matthew's idiolectic pattern explains what would otherwise be an exception at 6:20 in Betz's theory. Betz saw only the singular-created/plural-divine usage and not the importance of the singular in the heaven and earth pairs, thus he was not able to explain the apparently inconsistent singular in 6:20.

[53] This interpretation is strengthened by comparison with Luke 12:33. In this parallel saying, Luke uses the plural (ἐν τοῖς οὐρανοῖς), one of only four instances throughout his gospel. If Matthew and Luke did indeed share a source (such as Q), it seems reasonable that this source likely had the plural, which would explain Luke's rare plural usage. Therefore, evidence of Matthew's intentional crafting can be seen in his uncommon change of a plural into a singular to accord with his singular heaven and earth pairing.

4. *Ambiguous uses of* οὐρανός

Due to the fluid and ambiguous nature of the concept of heaven, there are a few instances where the two meanings overlap so significantly that the forms of οὐρανός can vary. As in the OT, this occurs in cases where reference to heaven involves a visible manifestation coming from the invisible divine source, such as "bread from heaven." In Matthew there are three such uses, yet even in these cases, the singular and plural forms align reasonably well with the rest of Matthew's pattern.

In 14:19 Jesus looks up εἰς τὸν οὐρανὸν as he blesses the loaves and fish. This expression, very common in the LXX, is ambiguous in its reference—God is certainly the one to whom blessing is directed, but the lifting of one's eyes, hands and head also refers to an earthly physical activity. Why would Matthew utilize the singular here? Assuming he was intentional in his singular and plural usage, his choice was reasonable in that it would be somewhat odd to say Jesus looked up into the invisible heavens. The looking up for blessing, a very common practice, by its nature involves a physical seeing.

Similar is 16:1: καὶ προσελθόντες οἱ Φαρισαῖοι καὶ Σαδδουκαῖοι πειράζοντες ἐπηρώτησαν αὐτὸν σημεῖον ἐκ τοῦ οὐρανοῦ ἐπιδεῖξαι αὐτοῖς ("And the Pharisees and Sadducees came, and to test him they asked him to show them a sign from heaven."). The phrase, ἐκ τοῦ οὐρανοῦ is usually understood as meaning a sign "out of heaven," thus, a sign "from God."[54] To nuance this, however, the parallel in 12:38-39 helps us see that the request for a sign here is a request for a (visible) attesting miracle of some sort, likely in the skies. Davies and Allison reason this way and argue that ἐκ τοῦ οὐρανοῦ is *not* a periphrasis for God in this context, but "the object sought is rather some kind of sign in or from the heavens...as opposed to all the earthly signs Jesus has until now reportedly worked"—an unambiguous, eschatological sign such as a visible bloody sun and darkened moon.[55] We see that indeed, Jesus responds to them (16:2-3) by reference to interpreting the color of the skies (sg. οὐρανός). Regardless, a sign in the heavens certainly falls into the category of ambiguous uses of οὐρανός and could reasonably use either a singular or a plural form.

---

[54] Comparison can be made to 21:25 where ἐξ οὐρανοῦ is contrasted with ἐξ ἀνθρώπων, the contrast being between the source of John's teaching: either from God or merely from humanity. ἐκ + οὐρανός is a common construction in the fourth Gospel and Revelation and often has this sense.

[55] Davies and Allison, *Matthew*, 2:580.

Finally, at Jesus' baptism we find two plural uses of οὐρανός (3:16–17). Both Mark and Matthew record that the heavens (pl) were opened and that a voice speaks ἐκ τῶν οὐρανῶν, while Luke employs singular forms.[56] Mark, who shows no evidence of a conscious use of οὐρανός, may have been influenced by an apocalyptic notion of God's residence in the uppermost heavens, whereas Luke follows the more typical Hellenistic use of singular οὐρανός. The notion of the heavens being opened falls into the category of ambiguous usage because while obviously of divine origin, there may have also been a visible parting of the clouds in the sky. However, this pericope is highly significant for the Christology of each of the Gospels and it is not surprising that Matthew uses the plural here to emphasize the divine origin of the claim that "This is my beloved Son in whom I am well pleased" (3:17).

5. *Possible Anomalies*

The formulation of Matthew's idiolectic pattern above accounts for all but four instances of Matthew's manifold use of οὐρανός. These four instances occur in three passages which present somewhat anomalous uses in light of the observed pattern. Yet even in these cases, some explanation can be given.

(1) In the first instance, 22:30 has an unexpected singular in the phrase ἄγγελοι ἐν τῷ οὐρανῷ. As was discussed above, the other references to angels *in heaven* in Matthew (18:10; 24:36) use a plural form.[57] The reference in 22:30 comes near the end of a section of conflict between Jesus and the Jewish leaders (21:23–23:39). The Sadducees confront Jesus with an argument "designed to ridicule belief in the resurrection by a *reductio ad absurdum*."[58] He responds by rebuking their ignorance of the Scriptures and the power of God. Instead, he says, in the deathless state people will not marry but be like ἄγγελοι ἐν τῷ οὐρανῷ. Some manuscripts do record the plural οὐρανοῖς, but they are weak compared to the text.[59] Interestingly, the parallel in Mark 12:25 has what we might expect in Matthew, ἐν τοῖς οὐρανοῖς. Luke's paral-

---

[56] Matthew makes οἱ οὐρανοί the subject of the passive verb, ἠνεῴχθησαν, while Mark uses a different construction with the participial phrase, σχιζομένους τοὺς οὐρανούς.

[57] As shown above, the fourth reference to an angel coming from heaven (28:2) is singular due to the emphasis on its appearance in the earthly realm.

[58] France, *Matthew*, 316f.

[59] Θ r¹ sa^mss mae read the dative plural. The text is supported by ℵ B L 0161 f^{1.13} 33. 892. 1424 *al* sa^mss bo.

lel (20:36) is significantly different in wording and construction with no reference to heaven. In light of Matthew's singular-plural pattern, we might expect a plural form here.

There are two possible explanations for the singular form here. First, Davies and Allison suggest that the prepositional phrase ἐν τῷ οὐρανῷ is in direct (grammatical) parallel with the preceding ἐν τῇ ἀναστάσει,[60] thus explaining the singular (dative) form. According to our observations on the form of heaven and earth pairs above, then, this could be understood as another form of an implicit contrast pair (like heaven-humanity), albeit a temporal one, and thus the singular is used. That is, οὐρανός is singular here because it is in a contrast pair of two different states (in heaven versus in the resurrection age), comparable to the heaven and earth pairs. A second possible explanation comes from the observations by Robert Mowery on Jesus' varied language for different audiences.[61] Mowery demonstrates that Matthew's Jesus uses distinctly different terms when addressing two different audiences: the crowds and disciples on the one hand, and the opposed religious leaders on the other. In Matthew, Jesus reserves the phrase kingdom of heaven for the crowds and disciples, while using the more common kingdom of God in dialogue with the Jewish leaders.[62] Similarly, Jesus tends to use "Father" only with his followers, as opposed to "God" with his opponents.[63] There is a strong case here for the idea of special, "insider" language being reserved for the true followers of Jesus. By analogy, this same logic may apply to the use of οὐρανός outside of kingdom of heaven as well. An examination of the 82 occurrences of οὐρανός reveals that in no case does Jesus ever use a plural form when addressing his opponents (with the same possible exception of the mixed crowd in 22:2). Thus, it may be that in 22:30, which takes place in a sharp conflict between Jesus and the Sadducees, the reference to the angels is singular in accordance with the pattern of "disciples versus opponents" language. Thus, in Matthew's varied uses of οὐρανός

---

[60] Davies and Allison, *Matthew*, 3:227.
[61] Mowery, "The Matthean References to the Kingdom."
[62] The only potential exception out of the thirty-two occurrences of kingdom of heaven is 22:2. There Jesus does use the expression in the presence of the religious leaders, but as Mowery points out, Jesus is teaching the crowds and disciples in the Temple when a contingent of the religious leaders arrive, thus resulting in a mixed audience.
[63] See also, Mowery, "God, Lord and Father." Foster, "Why on Earth Use 'Kingdom of Heaven'?," 494–495, confirms Mowery's thesis and adds to it the observation that in Matthew only Jesus' opponents call him "Teacher" while his disciples call him "Lord."

and other words, at times his patterns irreconcilably conflict with one another. In this instance, the "outsiders" language forces the otherwise-expected plural form of οὐρανός to become a singular.

(2) A second possible anomaly occurs in 23:22: καὶ ὁ ὀμόσας ἐν τῷ οὐρανῷ ὀμνύει ἐν τῷ θρόνῳ τοῦ θεοῦ καὶ ἐν τῷ καθημένῳ ἐπάνω αὐτοῦ ("and he who swears by heaven, swears by the throne of God and by him who sits upon it"). This text is closely parallel to 5:34–35. In chapter 23 Jesus is rebuking the Pharisees for making arbitrary distinctions between what made oaths binding or not, thereby encouraging evasive oaths and lying.[64] This debate was not uncommon in rabbinic literature.[65] Jesus corrects them with a threefold statement explaining that such fine nuances do not hold up. "Therefore he who swears by the altar swears both by the altar and by everything on it. And he who swears by the temple swears both by the temple and by Him who dwells within it. And he who swears by heaven swears both by the throne of God and by Him who sits upon it." The third phrase refers to the (invisible) throne of God, and therefore, according to the observed pattern, we would expect the plural rather than ἐν τῷ οὐρανῷ. The parallel in 5:34–35 is also singular, but there we find an explicit heaven and earth contrast pair: μήτε ἐν τῷ οὐρανῷ...μήτε ἐν τῇ γῇ. Such an explicit pairing is not found in 23:22.

However, the two texts are strikingly parallel in the rhetorical concatenation of building images—heaven-earth-Jerusalem and altar-temple-throne. The singular usage in 23:22 may best be explained by seeing it as yet another "non-explicit" heaven and earth pair, analogous to 5:34–35. Both have the heaven and earth contrast in view: explicitly in chapter 5, and only slightly less so in 23, where heaven is contrasted with the (earthly) temple and the altar. Another possible explanation comes from referring again to Mowery's observations about "insider" and "outsider" language. This comes in the form of a "Woe to you, scribes and Pharisees" saying. It is reasonable to understand Matthew's unexpected use of the singular as part of his separation of the true disciples from the false.[66]

---

[64] Carson, *Matthew*, 479.
[65] See the discussion in Kenneth G. C. Newport, *The Sources and Sitz im Leben of Matthew 23* (Sheffield: Sheffield Academic Press, 1995), 138–140.
[66] This explanation is less certain than in the case of 22:30 because it is not entirely clear whether Jesus is speaking directly to the Pharisees or using this language rhetorically. 23:1 states that Jesus shifted away from answering the Sadducees to speak to

(3) Certainly the most puzzling exception to the singular and plural pattern is found in 16:19. Here, in one of the two famous Matthean passages about the authority to bind and loose "on earth and in heaven," we have the plural phrase, ἐν τοῖς οὐρανοῖς, twice in conjunction with the familiar ἐπὶ τῆς γῆς.

The reasons this passage is difficult to interpret are manifold:[67] there is debate over how to understand the rare future periphrastics,[68] the meaning of the "binding and loosing,"[69] and the objects of the binding and loosing. The most pointed problem, however, is that the closely parallel passage in 18:18, which uses the same language formula, has singular forms of οὐρανός, albeit with several difficult textual variants.[70]

In 16:17–19 there are four occurrences of οὐρανός, all of them in the plural (one in the common "my Father in heaven," one in kingdom of heaven, and the two in question in conjunction with earth). The first two occurrences accord with the pattern and the normal plural usage in Matthew. The second two are the *only* instances in Matthew where a plural form of οὐρανός is put in conjunction with earth. Even in the closely parallel passage in chapter 18 we find the expected pattern of singular οὐρανός with γῆ.

We observed above that Origen commented on these passages by arguing that Peter has some superiority over the other Apostles by the fact

---

his followers, and the mention of the heavenly Father (23:9) and kingdom of heaven (23:13) confirms this. Yet, the direct language of "Woe to you, scribes and Pharisees" makes the other argument possible as well.

[67] One clear discussion of the many difficulties can be found in Carson, *Matthew*, 364ff.

[68] See Stanley E. Porter, "Vague Verbs, Periphrastics, and Matt 16:19," *Filologia Neotestamentaria* 2 (1988): 155–173.

[69] In addition to Bornkamm's well-known essay, "The Authority to 'Bind' and 'Loose' in the Church in Matthew's Gospel" (in Stanton, ed., *The Interpretation of Matthew*), there are a number of essays which promote various views. For example, J. D. M. Derrett, "Binding and Loosing (Matt 16:19; 18:18; John 20:23)," *JBL* 102 (1983): 112–117; and R. H. Hiers, "'Binding' and 'Loosing': The Matthean Authorizations," *JBL* 104 (1985): 233–250. See also, Marcus, "The Gates of Hades and the Keys of the Kingdom (Matt 16:18–19)."

[70] The variants in 18:18 are quite tricky to work out. In 18b singular ἐν οὐρανῷ is witnessed by B Θ f[13] pc. This same phrase is read in 18c by these witnesses in addition to ℵ. However, 18b has ἐν τοῖς οὐρανοῖς in ℵ D² L 0281. 33. et al., while 18c has the same except ℵ which has shifted to the singular. The Majority Text and others read the singular form plus the article in both cases. It seems the singular is a slightly stronger reading. This is what one would expect according to the proposed rule. But regardless, it does not help solve the dilemma in 16:19. On a related note, I have observed that manuscript D has a tendency to pluralize οὐρανός as compared to the rest of the tradition. 18:18b in D is but one example of this later reading (cf. 24:30).

that what he binds and looses will occur in the plural "heavens" (16:18), while Jesus' words to the gathered apostles promise binding and loosing only in the singular heaven (18:18).[71] This interpretation is unlikely because in Matthew the plural form of οὐρανός does not function to communicate more than one numeric heaven in contrast to a single heaven denoted by singular οὐρανός. It is certainly possible that Matthew believed in multiple heavens, but there is no clear evidence of this in his Gospel; in fact, such apocalyptic speculations are noticeably absent relative to the Second Temple literature. Instead, as I have shown, the plural forms serve a literary and theological purpose: to distinguish the created/visible world from God's realm.

While Origen's argument is less than convincing, it does raise the question of whether there might indeed be a difference in meaning between the two passages. The two texts certainly overlap in meaning, but many have argued that the contexts of chapters 16 and 18 lead to distinct interpretations. Bornkamm's conclusion about the relationship between 16:19 and 18:18 points to this view: "Teaching authority [16:19] and disciplinary authority [18:18] are inseparably intertwined in this Jewish scholastic phrase about 'binding' and 'loosing,' but this does not rule out... that here one, there the other, meaning is emphasized."[72] The difference in forms of οὐρανός, then, would be but one indicator of this intended distinction, a clue that something different is meant in these passages rather than a mere anomaly.

However, there is another possible explanation. It seems likely that Matthew used the plural in 16:19 so as to not add confusion to the weight of Jesus' promises regarding the kingdom of heaven (which invariably uses plural forms) just mentioned. That is, in the sentences immediately preceding this binding/loosing promise to Peter, the (plural) heavenly source of Peter's confession is revealed. Even more significantly, the promise of the keys τῆς βασιλείας τῶν οὐρανῶν is juxtaposed right up against the phrase, ὃ ἐὰν δήσῃς ἐπὶ τῆς γῆς ἔσται δεδεμένον ἐν τοῖς οὐρανοῖς, καὶ ὃ ἐὰν λύσῃς ἐπὶ τῆς γῆς ἔσται λελυμένον ἐν τοῖς οὐρανοῖς, which is obviously connected conceptually (appositionally?). If Matthew were to follow ἡ βασιλεία τῶν οὐρανῶν (plural) with the statement about binding and loosing ἐν τῷ οὐρανῷ (singular), this

---

[71] I am not aware whether this argument was picked up in subsequent Roman Catholic theology. Regardless, even in Origen's own writings we find comments that mitigate Peter's superiority vis-à-vis the other apostles (cf. *On Mt.*, Bk. xii §11).

[72] Bornkamm, "The Authority to 'Bind' and 'Loose'," 93.

could misleadingly suggest a contrast between the terms and confuse the teaching. Thus, in this direct juxtaposition of kingdom of heaven with heaven and earth—the only occurrence of such in Matthew—the normal form of the heaven and earth pair is overridden. The context of chapter 18, where the normal heaven and earth pair does occur, is a bit different. The immediately preceding sentences do not contain kingdom of heaven, thus the normal singular οὐρανός plus γῆ stands without confusion. While there are a few occurrences of Father in heaven in the broader context of chapter 18 (including one in the *following* verse), there is nothing like the marriage of kingdom with heaven and earth as in 16:19. Thus, while it is possible that Matthew intended some difference in meaning between 16:19 and 18:18, most likely the exigencies of the direct combination of kingdom of heaven with heaven and earth resulted in a slight derivation from his typical pattern.

Summary

The preceding argument has sought to show that Matthew's frequent use of the plural forms of οὐρανός does not stem from the influence of Semitic morphology nor from a multiple heavens cosmology, but instead, he has intentionally used both singular and plural forms in an idiolectic pattern. Matthew inherited a linguistic world where singular forms of οὐρανός were by far the most common and were used in two different senses (for the visible world and the invisible/divine), and where heaven (sg) and earth was a stock phrase. He used the semantic flexibility of οὐρανός and formed an idiolectic way of speaking in which he typically uses the singular forms for the one semantic pole of οὐρανός (the visible, earthly realm) and the plural for the other (invisible, divine realm), all the while retaining the traditional singular heaven and earth phraseology. While there are a few anomalies in this formulation, in most instances, other overriding factors can be seen to explain the aberrations. Even the three texts which appear anomalous make up only four of the eighty-two occurrences of οὐρανός, the rest of which all accord with the pattern. Whether Matthew borrowed this pattern from other literature such as Wisdom of Solomon or shared a common source with *Testament of Abraham* is unclear. Either way, the usage is far more developed and thematic in Matthew than anywhere else. Most importantly, without exception, Matthew *never* uses singular forms of οὐρανός in connection with the Father or the kingdom. This uncommon use of the plural to refer to the divine would likely catch the ear of the hearers and highlight and heighten the distinction between

God and the world that the Evangelist is attempting to communicate.⁷³ Matthew's use of the uncommon plural forms reflects not a linguistic nor a cosmological source, but a rhetorical purpose. He develops this idiolectic use of singular and plural forms for a literary and theological purpose: to contrast the heavenly realm with the earthly. This last point will be developed in the subsequent chapters.

Exegetical Insights Stemming from the Singular and Plural Use of Οὐρανός

In light of the preceding arguments, I may now offer some specific exegetical insights into two key passages in Matthew 6:9–10 and 24:29–31.

1. *Matthew 6:9–10*

⁹ οὕτως οὖν προσεύχεσθε ὑμεῖς· Πάτερ ἡμῶν ὁ ἐν τοῖς οὐρανοῖς· ἁγιασθήτω τὸ ὄνομά σου· ¹⁰ ἐλθέτω ἡ βασιλεία σου· γενηθήτω τὸ θέλημά σου, ὡς ἐν οὐρανῷ καὶ ἐπὶ γῆς·

⁹ Pray then like this: Our Father who art in heaven, Hallowed be thy name. ¹⁰ Thy kingdom come. Thy will be done, On earth as it is in heaven. (RSV)

The Lord's Prayer has for centuries held a central place in Christian liturgy and practice. Some have also seen it as the centerpiece of the Sermon on the Mount⁷⁴ or even of the whole Gospel.⁷⁵ Considered structurally, Matthew 6:7–15 is a somewhat intrusive excursus within a series of three instructions about living to please the heavenly Father rather than earthly humans (6:1–21).⁷⁶ After an initial heading (6:1),

---

⁷³ Scott and Dean in their article on sound patterns in the Sermon on the Mount show how frequent and outstanding references to ὁ πατήρ ἐν τοῖς οὐρανοῖς and ἡ βασιλεία τῶν οὐρανῶν are throughout the Sermon. They serve as chiastic centers, indicators of an *inclusio*, and repeated epithets. I would add to their observations that the plural forms, infrequent outside of Matthew, cast these references in greater relief for Matthew's hearers. B. B. Scott and M. E. Dean, "A Sound Map of the Sermon on the Mount": 311–378.

⁷⁴ H. Benedict Green uses the term "centerpiece" to describe the Prayer's relationship to the Sermon. H. Benedict Green, *Matthew, Poet of the Beatitudes* (Sheffield: Sheffield Academic, 2001), 77.

⁷⁵ According to Betz, *Sermon on the Mount*, 378, Tertullian called the Lord's Prayer a *breviarium totius evangelii*.

⁷⁶ Commentators typically consider 6:1–18 a structural unit and 6:19–7:12 as a

these three admonitions concern (1) almsgiving (6:2–4); (2) prayer (6:5–6); and (3) fasting (6:16–18), with the famous Lord's Prayer expanding the second section.[77]

The Lord's Prayer proper (6:9–13) is introduced in verses 7–8, and similar to the Beatitudes, has an addendum tagged on at the end (6:14–15; cp. 5:11–12). The Prayer consists of an invocation ("Our Father who art in heaven") followed by two sets of three petitions, the first of which comprises verses 9b–10.[78] These first three petitions are often understood to share a common thrust and meaning. Davies and Allison state: "The coming of the kingdom, the hallowing of God's name, and the doing of God's will on earth as in heaven are in essence all one: each looks at the *telos* of history, each refers to the fitting culmination of God's salvific work."[79] Scholars have also noted that verses 9–10 are demarcated by an inclusio of references to οὐρανός.[80] Moreover, the majority of commentators understand the final phrase, "as in heaven so also on earth," as referring to all three of the preceding petitions together.[81]

The Lord's Prayer as found in Matthew is one of three related recensions we have from the earliest Christian documents. The other two are found in Luke 11:2–4 and Didache 8:2. The version in the Didache is very close to Matthew and is probably dependent thereupon. Luke's record of the prayer is considerably shorter, containing only five of the petitions and without qualifying phrases. There has been scholarly

---

separate section. However, as I will argue in a subsequent chapter, the heaven and earth contrast theme of 6:19–21 can be seen as a summary statement of the teaching in 6:1–18. 6:19–21 serves as hinge text with associations and connections with what follows as well as what precedes it.

[77] On the structure of the Prayer, see among others, Birger Gerhardsson, "The Matthean Version of the Lord's Prayer (Matt 6:9b–13): Some Observations," 207–220.

[78] Betz, *Sermon on the Mount*, 375.

[79] Davies and Allison, *Matthew*, 1:603. Similarly, Guelich, *Sermon on the Mount*, 289, observes that the first three petitions "are not only formally parallel but also materially interrelated." Craig S. Keener, *A Commentary on the Gospel of Matthew* (Grand Rapids: Eerdmans, 1999), 220, says they "are all variant versions of the same end-time promise: everything will be set right someday."

[80] Davies and Allison, *Matthew*, 1:606; Green, *Matthew, Poet of the Beatitudes*, 79; Gundry, *Matthew*, 106; John P. Meier, *Matthew* (Wilmington, Delaware: Michael Glazier, 1980), 61.

[81] This is explicitly the view of France, *Matthew*, 134–135; Filson, *Matthew*, 96; Green, *Matthew, Poet of the Beatitudes*, 86; Plummer, *Matthew*, 99. Gundry, *Matthew*, 107, is the only one to verbalize disagreement with this interpretation, though no reason is given. Neither Davies and Allison, Morris, or Guelich give an opinion on this question.

discussion about the various source critical options for these differences and about which is more likely original. Regardless, it is clear that the elements in Matthew's longer version align with typical Matthean phraseology, most notably reference to the Father in heaven and the expression "in heaven...on earth."[82]

Regarding the use of οὐρανός in 6:9–10, three matters will be discussed here. First, it is a worthwhile question to ask what is meant by saying God's will is done *in heaven*. The thrust of the petition is clear: followers of Jesus are to ask God to consummate his promised plan for the world—that his Name would be revered, his reign manifested, and his purposes completely fulfilled.[83] All of this should be done, "as it is heaven, so also on earth." But we may ask, In what sense is heaven being used here? To what does it refer? There are three options discernible in scholarly interpretation. (1) A few scholars[84] have understood the heaven and earth pair here as merismatic, i.e., referring to the cosmos. Thus, the meaning of the phrase is simply "Thy will be done universally."[85] (2) Betz has argued that the reference to heaven in 6:10 must mean the astral entities of the sun, moon and stars. His argument is based upon the fact that οὐρανός is singular here and for Betz, every singular occurrence must refer to the created realm according to the pattern he has suggested for Matthew. Heaven here in combination with earth refers to the whole world, but contrastively not merismatically. The point is that the other half of creation (the sun, moon, and stars) is obedient to God's will, and the prayer is that the only rebellious element, earthly humanity, will also come into submission.[86] (3) Several scholars have suggested that heaven here refers to God's realm, with some interpreters suggesting angelic beings in particular.[87] A subspecies of this view

---

[82] This has been recognized by several commentators including Davies and Allison, *Matthew*, 1:591; Guelich, *Sermon on the Mount*, 290; and Gundry, *Matthew*, 106. Graham Stanton, *A Gospel for a New People*, 334, cites these as an example of Matthew's expansion of Q according to his own emphases. Interestingly, most contemporary and comparable Jewish prayers (such as the Qaddish) use the term "world" where Matthew has "heaven and earth." This subtle difference highlights the emphasis that Matthew placed on this phraseology.

[83] Betz emphasizes that the first three petitions focus on reminding God to fulfill his promised obligations. *Sermon on the Mount*, 375, 378.

[84] Allen, *Matthew*, 58; Beare, *Matthew*, 174.

[85] Some manuscripts (D* a b c k bo^{mss}) omit the ὡς, thus giving this sense explicitly.

[86] Betz, *Sermon on the Mount*, 379, 395.

[87] As a general reference to God's realm, most commentators concur. As a specific reference to angelic beings, see Schnackenburg, *Matthew*, 67, and especially, Plummer, *Matthew*, 99. Plummer says that understanding heaven as the sun, moon, and stars is not necessarily wrong, but is inadequate; angelic beings is the primary sense.

interprets the angels as the rebellious creatures in the heavenly realm.[88] Most forceful in this last category is the provocative argument by G. H. P. Thompson.[89] On the basis of grammatical structure, Thompson argued that we have mistranslated the entire phrase. Instead, the request is for God's will to be done "*both* in heaven and on earth." The need is for rebellion in both the heavenly realm and on earth to be squelched by God's coming kingdom.

How are we to evaluate these interpretations? In the first instance, the meaning of heaven and earth here is not likely merismatic.[90] While on occasion in Matthew the heaven and earth pair means the entire cosmos (5:18; 11:25; 24:35), this is not the typical sense and never so in the ἐν...ἐπι clauses (e.g., 6:19–20; 16:19). Regarding the third option, heaven very well may refer to angelic beings here, but probably not to rebellious angels in the heavenly realm. To understand 6:10 as rebellious angels misses the point in that the presumption is that the heavens *do* obey and that it is the earth which is in disobedience by comparison. One could argue that this problem is mitigated if Thompson's new translation is accepted. However, Thompson's argument is not conclusive, especially because in Matthew heaven is regularly portrayed in a positive light (as the realm of God, his kingdom, and his rewards) and in Matthew we rarely find any indication of rebellious creatures in the heavenly realm as in other parts of the NT.[91] Therefore, οὐρανός does not refer to rebellious angels here. On the other hand, Betz's argument that heaven here must be the sun, moon, and stars is too forced. His argument is dependent on the singular οὐρανός pattern, but he fails to see that in heaven and earth pairs, οὐρανός will be singular, regardless of its sense (cf. discussion of 6:19–20 above). Thus, it is certainly possible that heaven in 6:10 means the astral bodies, but it is not necessitated by the singular form.[92] Overall, it is difficult and maybe impossible to

---

[88] Beare, *Matthew*, 174, begins with the merismatic interpretation but then connects Matt 6:10 with other NT passages about rebellion in heaven.

[89] G. H. P. Thompson, "Thy Will be Done in Earth, as it is in Heaven (Matthew vi.11): A Suggested Re-interpretation," *The Expository Times* 70 (1959): 379–381.

[90] Both Schnackenburg and Guelich argue explicitly against the merismatic interpretation.

[91] Davies and Allison, *Matthew*, 1:606, make a similar judgment regarding Thompson's argument. Matt 24:29d provides the only instance of heaven used in reference to rebellious creatures: αἱ δυνάμεις τῶν οὐρανῶν.

[92] Betz, *Sermon on the Mount*, 391, depends on the singular-plural distinction so strongly that he even sees a tension between the Lord's Prayer and the rest of the Sermon on the Mount regarding the kingdom of the heavens (pl.) elsewhere compared with 6:10!

decide the interpretation between (obedient) angelic beings and the astral bodies in light of the close identification in the Second Temple period between angels and the stars/planets.[93]

The second observation to make regarding οὐρανός in 6:9–10 is simply that this text manifests the three key themes in Matthew's use of οὐρανός and provides a good example of the intentional pattern of singular and plural usage. In these pithy lines of prayer we see in microcosm the themes of the Father in heaven, the kingdom, and contrast of heaven and earth, all the while distinguishing singular and plural uses of οὐρανός.

The invocatory address to the Father is expanded by Matthew to "*Our Father who art in heaven.*" Luke records only the simpler πάτερ, which most commentators assume as the original. The modifying phrase ὁ ἐν τοῖς οὐρανοῖς is certainly in line with Matthew's way of referring to the God of his disciples; in fact, as Chapter Ten will show, this is a particularly Matthean way of referring to God. Interestingly, the Didache follows Matthew though with this difference: the Father is referred to with the singular, ὁ ἐν τῷ οὐρανῷ. The exact nature of the Didache's relation to Matthew here is unclear.[94] It is clear that this difference highlights Matthew's idiolect and his uncommon use of the plural. The fact that the Didache does not agree here even though it so closely follows Matthew's wording everywhere else shows how unique and particular Matthew's use of plural οὐρανός is.

Matthew 6:10 also brings in the idea of the kingdom, one of the most important themes throughout Matthew and one often connected with heaven. Here we have the simpler "kingdom" without the frequent modifying phrase τῶν οὐρανῶν, though the same kingdom is clearly in view. The shorter phrase does occur in other places in the Gospel,[95] and the τῶν οὐρανῶν is likely omitted here for the sake of parallelism (the three consecutive lines each end with σου), rhythm and concision.[96]

---

[93] Davies and Allison, *Matthew*, 1:606.

[94] See the discussion in Kurt Niederwimmer, *The Didache: A Commentary* (Minneapolis: Augsburg Fortress, 1998), 135–137. Niederwimmer, 136, remarks without explanation that the difference is meaningless and footnotes different opinions on whether the singular or plural was original (136, n. 12).

[95] "The kingdom" occurs in 4:23; 8:12; 9:35; 13:19, 38; 24:14. There are also occasional references to the kingdom of the Son of Man (13:41; 16:28), Jesus' kingdom (20:21), Satan's kingdom (12:26), and the kingdom of God (12:28; 19:24; 21:31, 43).

[96] In this phrase (ἐλθέτω ἡ βασιλεία σου), Matthew, Luke, and the Didache all agree verbatim. In both Matthew 6:10 and the Didache 8:2, all three strophes in this verse have a nine-syllable rhythm. The latter two strophes are lacking in Luke.

This opening set of petitions in the Lord's Prayer concludes with one of Matthew's many conjunctions of heaven and earth. As will be shown in subsequent chapters, this comparison of God's way in heaven over against sinful humanity on earth is foundational to Matthew's use of οὐρανός throughout. For now we may note how this text conforms to Matthew's idiolectic singular and plural usage. We have observed above that the stock phrase heaven and earth regularly uses the singular of οὐρανός as it does here. Matthew 6:9–10 then, provides a rather textbook example of the alternation of the singular and plural according to the pattern: "Our Father who art in the heavens (pl)... as in heaven (sg) so also on earth." When referring to the divine/invisible realm, οὐρανός is found in the plural; when combined with earth, Matthew follows the typical OT phraseology of singular οὐρανός plus γῆ.

The third and final matter to discuss regarding this text concerns how exactly heaven and earth relate to each other in 6:9–10. This discussion is necessarily brief as it depends on the following two chapters which will more fully explore the word pair heaven and earth. Nevertheless, it is worthwhile raising the subject here proleptically. The point of this chapter has been that there is an intentional distinction in Matthew between singular and plural forms of οὐρανός. This chapter serves as part of a series of chapters which form a sustained argument that Matthew intends (in a four-fold way) to emphasize a *contrast* or *tension* between the two realms of heaven and earth or God and humanity. Matthew 6:9–10 is a very important text that manifests this contrast or tension while also providing important information about the nature of this contrast. Specifically, 6:9–10 shows that for Matthew, the current tension or contrast between heaven and earth is *not* part of God's creative and redemptive plans. The great Christian prayer is that the disjuncture between the two realms will *cease* to be: God's Name will be hallowed, his will done, and his kingdom manifested *not only in the heavenly realm but also in the earthly*. This is important because when emphasizing the contrast between heaven and earth it would be a mistake to understand this as a permanent and divinely designed state. The contrast between heaven and earth is a result of the sinfulness of the world and is thus unnatural. The eschatological goal, according to 6:9–10, is that this unnatural tension will be resolved into the unity of God's reign over heaven and earth. As the entire Gospel seeks to show, it is in Jesus Christ that the eschatological reuniting of heaven and earth has begun (cf. especially 28:18), and it will be consummated at his Parousia.

2. Matthew 24:29–31, 35

²⁹ Εὐθέως δὲ μετὰ τὴν θλῖψιν τῶν ἡμερῶν ἐκείνων
ὁ ἥλιος σκοτισθήσεται,
καὶ ἡ σελήνη οὐ δώσει τὸ φέγγος αὐτῆς,
καὶ οἱ ἀστέρες πεσοῦνται ἀπὸ τοῦ οὐρανοῦ,
καὶ αἱ δυνάμεις τῶν οὐρανῶν σαλευθήσονται.
³⁰ καὶ τότε φανήσεται τὸ σημεῖον τοῦ υἱοῦ τοῦ ἀνθρώπου ἐν οὐρανῷ, καὶ τότε κόψονται πᾶσαι αἱ φυλαὶ τῆς γῆς καὶ ὄψονται τὸν υἱὸν τοῦ ἀνθρώπου ἐρχόμενον ἐπὶ τῶν νεφελῶν τοῦ οὐρανοῦ μετὰ δυνάμεως καὶ δόξης πολλῆς·
³¹ καὶ ἀποστελεῖ τοὺς ἀγγέλους αὐτοῦ μετὰ σάλπιγγος μεγάλης, καὶ ἐπισυνάξουσιν τοὺς ἐκλεκτοὺς αὐτοῦ ἐκ τῶν τεσσάρων ἀνέμων ἀπ' ἄκρων οὐρανῶν ἕως [τῶν] ἄκρων αὐτῶν....
³⁵ ὁ οὐρανὸς καὶ ἡ γῆ παρελεύσεται, οἱ δὲ λόγοι μου οὐ μὴ παρέλθωσιν.

²⁹ Immediately after the tribulation of those days the sun will be darkened, and the moon will not give its light, and the stars will fall from heaven, and the powers of the heavens will be shaken; ³⁰ then will appear the sign of the Son of man in heaven, and then all the tribes of the earth will mourn, and they will see the Son of man coming on the clouds of heaven with power and great glory; ³¹ and he will send out his angels with a loud trumpet call, and they will gather his elect from the four winds, from one end of heaven to the other.... Heaven and earth will pass away, but my words will not pass away. (RSV)

A second text worth examining in light of our discussion of singular and plural οὐρανός is 24:29–35.[97] In this small subsection of the Olivet Discourse there is an intense concentration of references to heaven. In these verses οὐρανός occurs six times, with a variety of senses and alternating between singular and plural forms. This text provides a good example of Matthew's idiolectic pattern at work, and the recognition of this pattern sheds light on the meaning of several phrases in the discourse.

---

[97] Generally, 24:29–31 and 24:32–35 are understood as two separate units within the Olivet Discourse. Heil suggests that instead we should see verses 29–35 as one unit, demarcated by an inclusio of references to heaven in verses 29 and 35. I do not find it necessary to see these verses as one unit because a simple repeat of οὐρανός, very frequent throughout Matthew, is not sufficient to indicate a structural unit in and of itself. Nonetheless, for the purposes of examining singular and plural forms of οὐρανός in close proximity, it is worthwhile to handle these two related pericopae together. John Paul Heil in Warren Carter and J. P. Heil, *Matthew's Parables: Audience-Oriented Perspectives* (Washington: Catholic Biblical Association of America, 1998), 179.

The first occurrence of οὐρανός (v. 29c) in this passage refers to endtime cataclysmic events including the stars falling ἀπὸ τοῦ οὐρανοῦ.[98] The break up of the heavenly firmament (the sky) upon which the stars were fixed (Gen 1:14) forebodes calamitous times, an undoing of creation itself. This apocalyptic language about the end of the regular function of the heavenly bodies has several allusive predecessors including Isaiah 13:10, 34:4; and Joel 2:10, 3:4, 4:15. This use of heaven clearly refers to the created realm and the singular form corresponds with the rule as a visible part of the cosmos.

In contrast, the following versette (v. 29d) uses a plural in the phrase αἱ δυνάμεις τῶν οὐρανῶν ("the powers of the heavens").[99] In addition to the disturbance of the astral bodies, the spiritual elements of the world will also be shaken (σαλευθήσονται). We have observed above that the categories of the astral bodies and the astral deities are not always entirely distinct in the Second Temple period. Nonetheless, though there is certainly overlap, the two categories are not coextensive. In this highly apocalyptic text, as in other parts of the NT, the powers of the heavens are best understood "to denote the [angelic] powers which are connected with the stars or the heavens."[100] This interpretation is strengthened by the fact that in the following verses Jesus will come on the clouds of heaven μετὰ δυνάμεως ("with power") and send forth his ἄγγελοι. This creates a parallel contrast with the powers of the heavens (αἱ δυνάμεις τῶν οὐρανῶν). The use of οὐρανός here is plural in accord with the visible-invisible or earthly-divine realm distinction. Although the powers are created beings, they are invisible and part of the spiritual world, not the earthly, hence Matthew's use of the plural. Matthew's abrupt shift to the plural for this phrase and then back to the singular manifests the idiolect at work.[101]

---

[98] Mark 13:25 has ἐκ τοῦ οὐρανοῦ which is also read in Matthew by ℵ D 0281 pc. Luke 21:25 is less colorful: "there will be signs in sun and moon and stars."

[99] Matthew, Mark (13:25) and Luke (21:26) are all identical on this phrase with the exception that Mark uses an attributive construction with the repetition of the article, αἱ δυνάμεις αἱ ἐν τοῖς οὐρανοῖς. Although "stars" or "host of heaven" generally uses singular οὐρανός in the LXX (e.g. Isa 13:10), a variant reading at Isa 34:4 has αἱ δυνάμεις τῶν οὐρανῶν. Could this be the source of all three Evangelists' reading?

[100] Cremer, *Lexicon*, 219. Beare, *Matthew*, 471, concurs, stating that "'Powers' is probably to be taken in the sense of the astral divinities, regarded as inhabiting the stars...—the 'elemental spirits' of the Pauline letters." Cf. Schoonhoven, *TDNT*, s.v. "Heaven," 655. In agreement are Davies and Allison, *Matthew* 3:358, and Gundry, *Matthew*, 487; contra Hagner, *Matthew 14–28*, 713.

[101] It is interesting to note that the parallel Mark 13:25 also uses the singular in reference to the stars and then shifts to the plural for αἱ δυνάμεις αἱ ἐν τοῖς οὐρανοῖς.

The next two occurrences (neither of which are found in Mark or Luke) are both singular because they emphasize the visible appearing of the Son of Man in the human/earthly realm. In verse 30a, the glorious sign of the Son of Man[102] will appear in the sky (sg), now darkened by the loss of sun, moon, and stars. The addition of τοῦ οὐρανοῦ as compared to Mark also makes a thematic connection with αἱ φυλαὶ τῆς γῆς.[103] The Son will then arrive in the earthly realm on the clouds of heaven (sg).[104] Jesus' appearance on the clouds relies on multiple OT texts which connect divine activity with clouds (e.g., Dan 7; Exod 13:21–22; 40:35–38). As Davies and Allison state, "a cloud is the visible sign of the invisible presence of God."[105]

The fifth use of οὐρανός in this passage proves interesting (v. 31b). At the time of the coming of the Son of Man, the angels will be sent to gather the elect ἐκ τῶν τεσσάρων ἀνέμων ἀπ' ἄκρων οὐρανῶν ἕως [τῶν] ἄκρων αὐτῶν ("from the four winds, from one end of the heavens to the other").[106] In several places in the OT, "the four winds of heaven" (οἵ τέσσαρες ἄνεμοι τοῦ οὐρανοῦ) refer to the four points of the compass, a reference to the extremities of the earth.[107] In many of these

---

Luke 21:26 has no reference to falling stars but still uses the plural for αἱ δυνάμεις τῶν οὐρανῶν. For Mark, this is one of only five plural uses of οὐρανός while for Luke it is one of only four. This concurrence strongly suggests that the plural must have been original (and again, maybe stemming from one Greek manuscript tradition of LXX Isa 34:4). Additionally, the use of the uncommon plural by these other evangelists lends credence to the idea that something other than a normal "sky" reference is meant by αἱ δυνάμεις τῶν οὐρανῶν, especially for Mark who otherwise inexplicably shifts from singular to plural. Matthew's agreement with Mark and Luke here in no way argues against his idiolect pattern, but only that he had no need to modify his source in this instance. In light of other ample instances of redactional activity, we can safely assume that Matthew would have adjusted the form of οὐρανός here if needed (e.g. compare 6:20 with Lk 12:33).

[102] There has been considerable speculation about what exactly this sign is: Is it the appearance of the Son himself, or maybe the appearance of a military ensign, maybe even a cross? Cf. the survey of options in Sim, *Apocalyptic Eschatology in the Gospel of Matthew*, 104–105; Davies and Allison, *Matthew*, 3:359–360. Regardless, the visibility of the sign to all the world is emphasized. Cf. also Didache 16:6–8.

[103] Gundry, *Matthew*, 488, observes: "Matthew's adding 'of the sky' extends the allusion to Dan 7:13 and revives the contrast between heaven and earth."

[104] Matthew differs from Mark here in using the preposition ἐπί in connection with the clouds rather than Mark's ἐν. In this as well as the addition of τοῦ οὐρανοῦ, Matthew is closely following the Greek of Dan 7:13.

[105] Davies and Allison, *Matthew*, 3:362.

[106] Luke is lacking a parallel for this verse. Mark's wording is very similar except the concluding phrase for which he has ἀπ' ἄκρου γῆς ἕως ἄκρου οὐρανοῦ.

[107] For example, Jer 25:16 Septuagint [MT 49:36]; Zech 6:5; Dan 7:2, 8:8, 11:4.

OT passages, as here in Matthew, there is also a strongly eschatological connotation. The context in these places reveals a connection between this phrase and the gathering together of God's remnant people (by God or by his angels). This is true in the passage closest in language to Matthew, Deut 30:4: "Even if your dispersion be from one end of heaven to the other, from there the Lord your God will gather you..." (ἐὰν ᾖ ἡ διασπορά σου ἀπ' ἄκρου τοῦ οὐρανοῦ ἕως ἄκρου τοῦ οὐρανοῦ...).[108] So too in Matthew, and elsewhere in the Gospel, angels are involved in the eschatological gathering of people (13:41; 16:27; 25:31–32).

The question at hand is the meaning of heaven here and whether the plural form of οὐρανός corresponds with the proposed visible-invisible rule. As the meaning of "from one end of the heaven to the other" appears to refer idiomatically to the ends of the earth, one might expect the singular. There are several possible reasons why Matthew uses the plural form here. First, if indeed this phrase does refer to the created realm (as Mark's version makes explicit with his heaven and earth pair), then Matthew's inconsistent plural could be explained simply as a matter of grammatical and poetic attraction. The preceding phrase contains four words ending in -ων. Matthew, who is not oblivious to such assonance, may have used οὐρανῶν to agree with the preceding clause as well as the two words following, ἄκρων αὐτῶν. The result is a notable seven-word string of the same sound.

Secondly, there is reason to connect Matthew's whole phrase with the angelic host of God, hence the plural form here. Increasing throughout the OT and into the Second Temple literature, angels were associated with the natural elements such as the wind and were used by God to sovereignly control all of nature.[109] One such striking example which connects with Matt 24:31 is Zech 6:5. There the four winds of heaven are equated with four chariots pulled by differently-colored horses

---

[108] According to Gundry, *The Use of the Old Testament in St. Matthew's Gospel*, 54–55, Matthew's wording agrees with the Targums and Peshitta for Deut 30:4.

[109] See, among others, Harold B. Kuhn, "The Angelology of the Non-Canonical Jewish Apocalypses," *JBL* 67 (1948): 217–232. The overlap of the terms רוח, πνεῦμα, and ἄνεμος also contributed to a close connection between these concepts. See W. R. Schoemaker, "The Use of RUAH in the Old Testament, and of pneuma in the New Testament," *JBL* 23 (1904): 13–67. Outside of the biblical literature, one also finds connections between the winds and the angels in the Greek magical papyri, e.g., *PGM* XV, 14–16, as documented in H. D. Betz, *The Greek Magical Papyri in Translation* (2d ed.; Chicago: University of Chicago Press, 1992), 251.

which are sent out from the presence of the Lord to patrol the whole earth. The identification of these chariots with angelic beings is not difficult to perceive. In addition to several similar OT references, we see the same thought in texts such as Rev 7:1. In Matt 24:31 we also see a close connection between the angels and the four winds. Thus, in the fifth occurrence of οὐρανός in this brief passage, we find a plural form because of the close association of the winds of heaven with the (positive) angelic powers in the heavenly realm.

Alternatively, the collecting of the ἐκλεκτοί from the four winds of heaven may very well refer to the angels bringing the faithful dead *from God's presence*, hence the plural form. There are several Christian texts which indicate an eschatological view that entailed an angelic trumpet sound followed by the reappearance and transformation of the faithful dead (1 Cor 15:52; 1 Thes 4:16; Rev 8:2 + 11:15), who are presumably awaiting their vindication in heaven with God (e.g., Rev 6:9). The trumpet is found here in Matthew as well (24:31) and this eschatological view makes sense of the reference of Matthew's phrase.

The sixth and final occurrence of οὐρανός in this passage follows a few verses later in 24:35. This pericope (24:32–35) is an addendum to the previous one, commenting on when "all these things" will take place (24:34). This text ends with the statement that even though "heaven and earth will pass away," Jesus' words will not. Here we have one of the many explicit heaven and earth pairs found throughout Matthew (see Chapter Eight). In line with the pattern argued for in this chapter, the form of οὐρανός here, combined with earth, is indeed singular (ὁ οὐρανὸς καὶ ἡ γῆ).[110] Thus, in the final occurrence of οὐρανός in this short passage, we have another example of Matthew's developed idiolectic use of singular and plural forms of οὐρανός.[111]

---

[110] Interestingly, the verb "will pass away," which is governed here by the subject clause "heaven and earth," is singular in form (παρελεύσεται) rather than the plural which would be expected with a plural subject (cf. 5:18; see also discussion in Chapter Eight under merismatic uses of the heaven and earth pair).

[111] Although it falls outside this pericope, we may also observe that in the following verse (24:36) we have a plural use of heaven (οἱ ἄγγελοι τῶν οὐρανῶν). This "angels of heaven" reference serves a nice example of the difference between the singular and plural uses in these two juxtaposed verses.

Conclusion

In this chapter I have offered a new and different explanation for the plural uses of οὐρανός in Matthew. I have argued that Matthew intentionally uses singular and plural forms of οὐρανός in an idiolectic pattern. This pattern is part of a broader usage of heaven language throughout the Gospel and is one of the four elements of Matthew's stylized use of οὐρανός—all of which contribute to the overall theme of the contrast of heaven and earth.

CHAPTER SEVEN

HEAVEN AND EARTH IN THE OLD TESTAMENT AND SECOND TEMPLE LITERATURE

In addition to his frequent use of the plural forms of οὐρανός, Matthew's idiolectic style is also reflected in his emphasis on the word pair, heaven and earth. This chapter surveys the Jewish literary context for the meaning of this important phrase, tracing this central theme in the OT and Second Temple literature as a backdrop to examine how Matthew adapts and employs this word pair.

Heaven and Earth in the Old Testament

Frequency and Classification

When examining heaven in the OT, the observant reader will soon notice that the word very frequently stands in close connection with earth. This is true in the first verse of Genesis and throughout the OT. Cornelis Houtman, in his comprehensive study of heaven in the OT, begins by stating that when attempting to investigate heaven in the OT, one cannot speak of heaven without also giving consideration to earth.[1] In fact, heaven and earth cannot be understood in Scripture separately from one another. The structure of Houtman's wide-ranging volume matches this conviction. The entire middle part of the book (approximately 175 of its 370 pages) is dedicated to various aspects of "Himmel und Erde."

The pairing of heaven and earth in the OT occurs at least 185 times, depending on how broadly one considers the context.[2] This pairing

---

[1] Cornelis Houtman, *Der Himmel im Alten Testament*, 2.

[2] As mentioned previously when discussing the LXX pluses, there are several instances where the LXX has a heaven and earth pair where none existed in the Hebrew (at least in the MT tradition), e.g., Ex 10:13; Ps 113:11; Isa 8:21–22. In light of the frequency and importance of this word pair, it is likely that LXX translators occasionally added a reference to earth when heaven alone was found, thus granting the sense of completion provided by the heaven and earth phrase.

is but one example of many "fixed pairs" which occurred in ancient near eastern languages.³ Houtman classifies the occurrences into two main categories: those which are bound together with a copulative *waw* (around 65x), and those which are not (around 120x).⁴ Within these two categories there exists a wide variety of forms of expression. These include heaven and earth in a simple nominative form, with and without the article, with and without the Hebrew direct object marker את, and in prepositional phrases such as in heaven and on earth.⁵

My own examination of the heaven and earth pairs in the OT has led me to classify this conjunction in a different way, into a threefold system of copulative pairs, thematic pairs, and implied pairs. Copulative pairs are examples where "heaven and earth" appears as one unit, not separated by prepositions or other words. For example, "God created the heavens and the earth" (Gen 1:1). This type of pair occurs around 31 times in the canonical OT, nearly all of which are in reference to God's creation of both heaven and earth, that is, the entire cosmos.

Thematic pairs use the expression heaven and earth but with some separation of intervening words or phrases (or even sometimes whole sentences). These may be simple conjunctions, such as, "may God give you of the dew of heaven and of the fatness of the earth" (Gen 27:28), or with the use of paired prepositional phrases: "what god is there *in heaven* or *on earth*" (Deut 3:24), or a pair which spans across a brief discourse, such as "Whom have I in heaven but thee? And there is nothing upon earth that I desire besides thee" (Ps 73:25). Another common example is when "birds of the heavens" is put in conjunction with "beasts of the earth," thus forming a thematic heaven and earth pair (e.g. Deut 28:26; Ps 79:2; Ezek 29:5; Jer 7:33). Thematic pairs occur repeatedly in poetic language, though not exclusively. Often heaven is used and then its use draws out the mention of earth, as it were, and vice versa.⁶ Ezra Melamed has shown that OT prophetic

---

³ Cf. Stanley Gevirtz, *Patterns in the Early Poetry of Israel* (Chicago: University of Chicago Press, 1963); Yitzhak Avishur, *Stylistic Studies of Word-Pairs in Biblical and Ancient Semitic Literatures* (Neukirchen-Vluyn: Butzon & Bercker Kevelaer, 1984); Jože Krašovec, *Antithetic Structure in Biblical Hebrew Poetry* (Leiden: Brill, 1984).
⁴ Houtman, *Der Himmel im AT*, 26–49.
⁵ Houtman provides charts of these uses on pages 27 and 33–34.
⁶ Houtman, *Der Himmel im AT*, 33. Gervitz speaks of the effect of certain "fixed pairs" such as heaven and earth on the process of composition for the poet: "once he had set forth a line or two, three or four words or phrases, the formation of the parallel line was virtually at hand since the parallel terms, which would complete the thought, were already determined." Quoted in Houtman, *Der Himmel im AT*, 45.

and poetic literature had a propensity to take fixed word pairs (such as heaven and earth) and break them into parallel sentences.[7] This literary habit explains why so many occurrences of heaven and earth occur in this "thematic" form rather than the more simple "heaven and earth" structure. The grouping of thematic pairs comprises the most frequent use of heaven and earth in the OT.

The third category, implied pairs, comprises instances where heaven is used in conjunction with a word other than earth but one closely associated with it, thus making a less explicit pairing with the same purpose and sense.[8] For example, heaven is paired with the deep/depths (תְּהוֹם) in Deut 33:13, Ps 107:26 and others, and with Sheol (שְׁאוֹל) in Job 11:8, Ps 139:8, Amos 9:2 and others.

In either Houtman's schema or my alternative one, these assorted combinations result in an amazingly high number of references to heaven and earth in the OT. Additionally, as we will see, the pairing of earth with heaven also colors the semantic meaning of heaven in various ways. Houtman's contention that we cannot speak meaningfully about heaven without referring to earth proves true.

Word Order

Although the combination of heaven and earth usually occurs with heaven preceding earth, there are several instances where the order is reversed. Of the approximately 185 pairings of heaven and earth, less than one third (around 50x) occur with earth preceding heaven. Yet among the more strictly defined pairings which are bound with a copulative *waw*, only eight occur in the reverse order earth and heaven. While some have tried to argue that the order of earth and heaven was actually more original,[9] it can be observed that in many instances the normal order of heaven and earth is reversed for poetic-chiastic

---

[7] Ezra Zion Melamed, "The Break-Up of Stereotypical Phrases as an Artistic Device in Biblical Poetry," *Scripta Hierosolymitana* 8 (1961): 115–153.

[8] Another kind of implied pair which could be included consists of the use of earth in conjunction with a word closely related to heaven, such as "the heights." For example, "In his hand are the depths of the earth; the heights of the mountains are his also" (Ps 95:4).

[9] Houtman, *Der Himmel im AT*, 49–51, reviews the arguments of B. Hartmann who suggests that earth-heaven was the original sequence but was switched in the time of the kings or Babylonian exile, perhaps because of the connection of YHWH with heaven.

reasons. For example: "These are the generations of the heavens and the earth when they were created, in the day that the LORD God made the earth and the heavens" (Gen 2:4),[10] and "Thus shall you say to them: "The gods who did not make the heavens and the earth shall perish from the earth and from under the heavens" (Jer 10:11). In sum, regardless of which order of the phrase is original, heaven and earth came to predominate. It is such a widespread and frequently used pair that we should not be surprised at occasional variances in its appearance, especially in poetic usage.

The Meaning of the Heaven and Earth Pairs

As mentioned, the combination of heaven and earth can be understood as an example of the many "fixed word pairs" in the ancient near eastern languages. In addition to Hebrew, the heaven and earth pair is found in Phoenician, Ugaritic, Aramaic, and Akkadian.[11] Avishur describes such word pairs as "one of the more important building stones in the construction of the poetic parallelism so characteristic of ancient Semitic literature."[12] Indeed, as Tsumura points out, the phenomenon of word pairs is very much related to the nature of poetic parallelism.[13] Berlin asserts that it is the use of parallelism that activates or leads into word pair formation.[14] Melamed, mentioned above, observes that many such stereotypical word pairs are broken up across parallel lines but still serve as a unit together. The occurrence of word pairs in the OT is manifold; there is a habit and disposition toward this mode of speech throughout the biblical writings.

There are a number of ways in which the two elements of a word pair can relate to one another, e.g., as synonymous, antonymous, or hyponymous. Krašovec dedicated a volume each to two such relationships: antithesis and merismus.[15] Both of these ideas share in common the

---

[10] The dominance of the heaven and earth ordering can be seen in the fact the LXX, Peshitta, and Samaritan Pentateuch all retain the "heaven and earth" order in both parts of the verse.
[11] Avishur, *Stylistic Studies*, 603–604.
[12] Avishur, *Stylistic Studies*, 1.
[13] Tsumura, "A 'Hyponymous' Word Pair," 258.
[14] A. Berlin, "Parallel Word Pairs: A Linguistic Explanation," *UF* 15 (1983), 16.
[15] Jože Krašovec, *Der Merismus im Biblisch-Hebräischen und Nordwestsemitischen* (Rome: Biblical Institute Press, 1977); *Antithetic Structure in Biblical Hebrew Poetry* (Leiden: Brill, 1984).

sense of the "contraposition" of the two words; the concepts behind each word are opposites in some sense. However, antithesis and merismus describe different ways in which these opposites relate to each other: "The fundamental trait of the antithesis is that two opposing elements exclude each other in relation to a common idea" while in a merismus, "the opposite concepts do not serve to create a contrast of thought but a unity of thought—totality."[16]

One of the most interesting observations is that word pairs do not function in one way only; at times the same word pair can be used antithetically or merismatically. For example, the word pair צַדִּיק ("the righteous") and רָשָׁע ("the wicked") is merismatic in Eccl 3:17: "God will judge the righteous and the wicked"; but is antithetic in Ps 1:6: "The Lord knows the way of the righteous, but the way of the wicked will perish."[17] The word pair heaven and earth likewise functions in these two distinct ways.

1. *Merismatic Usage*

It is common knowledge that the phrase heaven and earth in the OT is the Israelites' ordinary way to refer to the cosmos or the entire created world. This is a classic example of a merism (or merismus), where a unity or totality is communicated by juxtaposing the extremities. Many texts use the phrase in this way. For example:

"In the beginning God created the heavens and the earth." (Gen 1:1)
"God Most High, Maker of heaven and earth..." (Gen 14:22)
"I will break the pride of your power, and I will make your heavens like iron and your earth like bronze." (Lev 26:19)
"I call heaven and earth to witness against you today." (Deut 4:26)
"Let the heavens be glad, and let the earth rejoice." (1 Chron 16:31)

Note that sometimes the phrase is used with a simple reference to creation (e.g., Gen 1:1; 14:22) and at other times there is a more general sense of "all things" or "all places" (e.g., Deut 4:26; 1 Chron 16:31).

While the OT does at times use כֹּל ("the whole, all"),[18] it appears too infrequently to qualify as a *terminus technicus* in any sense.[19] Most commonly, the cosmos is spoken of with the trope, heaven and earth.

---

[16] Krašovec, *Antithetic Structure*, 5.
[17] Krašovec, *Antithetic Structure*, 6, n. 26.
[18] Isa 44:24; 1 Chron 29:12; Ps 145:9.
[19] Houtman, *Der Himmel im AT*, 76.

The LXX typically translates the Hebrew phrase with the equivalent, οὐρανός καὶ γῆ. Classic Greek and Greek cosmology instead often used κόσμος ("world, universe") to speak of the entire realm of matter. In the LXX this word is not typically used with the sense of "world" until the later writings, particularly those composed in Greek such as Wisdom of Solomon and 2 and 4 Maccabees.[20] Another Greek word, κτίσις ("creation, created thing"), is used even less frequently. Again, when it does appear, it is usually in the apocryphal books.[21]

One rare example where heaven, earth and "the world" (Heb., תֵּבֵל;[22] Greek, οἰκουμένη) are put together is Ps 89:11 [LXX 88:12]: "The heavens are yours; the earth also is yours; the world and all that is in it, you have founded them." The parallel of heaven and earth combined with "the world" shows the typical merismatic function of this word pair.

2. *Antithetic Usage*

While the expression heaven and earth most often refers in the OT to the cosmos in a merismatic sense, very frequently the word pair is used with an antithetical or contrastive tone. That is, the two elements of heaven and earth are not being used together to speak of the cosmos, but some distinction is being made between the two. For example:

> "The heavens are the LORD's heavens, but the earth he has given to the sons of men." (Ps 115:16)
> "He looked down from his holy height, from heaven the LORD looked at the earth." (Ps 102:19)
> "Be not rash with your mouth, nor let your heart be hasty to utter a word before God, for God is in heaven, and you upon earth." (Eccl 5:2)
> "Thus says the LORD: Heaven is my throne and the earth is my footstool." (Isa 66:1)

The exact nature of the distinction in these types of uses of heaven and earth varies by context. Indeed, it is difficult to construct a rubric which covers well the various nuanced uses of this pair. There are in fact some passages which seem to fall in between the two general categories of

---

[20] Edward Adams, *Constructing the World: A Study in Paul's Cosmological Language* (Edinburgh: T&T Clark, 2000), 75. κόσμος does occur in earlier portions of the LXX but with its other semantic sense of "ornament" or "adornment." This is the term sometimes used to refer to the "host of heaven" (Dt 4:19; 17:3; cf. Gen 2:1).

[21] Adams, *Constructing the World*, 77–78.

[22] תֵּבֵל (46x in MT) is generally used as a poetic synonym for אֶרֶץ, hence the LXX's οἰκουμένη rather than κόσμος, though here the sense is apparently broader.

merismatic and antithetic,[23] but overall, the examples given above show that at times the typical merismatic usage of heaven and earth is not at work. In these instances, heaven is functioning metonymically for God and his realm while earth corresponds to all of humanity. Thus, this same word pair is being used to exploit a difference between God and humanity. The antithetic usage of heaven and earth still has the fundamental notion of God as the creator of all things (both heaven and earth), but functions as a way of communicating the elementary distinction between God and his creatures.

3. *Discerning Merismatic and Antithetic Uses*
The potential for heaven and earth to be used in such different ways as merismatic and antithetic stems from the flexibility in the semantic range of heaven. We have observed previously that the semantic domain of heaven in the OT contains two main poles: (1) the sky, atmosphere, and space of the created order; and (2) the dwelling place or presence of God. These two distinct poles of meaning prove to be the key to distinguishing between the two main uses of the heaven and earth pair. In a very real sense the two different uses of heaven and earth (merismatic and antithetic) can be understood as the outcome of earth being combined at times with one sense of שָׁמַיִם/οὐρανός, and other times with the other sense. That is, when heaven is functioning with reference to the above (skies, etc.) of the created order, a combination with earth naturally results in a reference to the entire created order, the cosmos depicted in a dualistic way (merismus). Conversely, when heaven is used with reference to God (e.g., as specifying his dwelling place), the occurrence of earth understandably serves as a point of contrast (antithetic).

Heaven and Earth as the Fundamental Weltbild *and* Weltanschauung *of the OT* [24]

In addition to the standard heaven and earth pairings throughout the OT, we also find occasional expansions of the expression to include

---

[23] For example, in Ps 76:8 ("From the heavens thou didst utter judgment; the earth feared and was still"), it is not clear whether this heaven refers to God's dwelling place (thus, contrastive) or some audible or visible sign/destruction coming from the sky (thus merismatic). Maybe the ambiguity is intentional and both are meant.

[24] Much of the argument in this section can be found in a different form in my article, "Dualism in Old Testament Cosmology: *Weltbild* and *Weltanschauung*," SJOT 18/2 (2004): 260–277.

other terms as well, such as the sea, the waters, the deeps, and the dry land.

For example:

> "For in six days the LORD made heaven and earth, the sea, and all that is in them" (Ex 20:11; cf. Ps 146:6, Jer 51:48)
> "Thus the heavens and the earth were finished, and all the host of them." (Gen 2:1)
> "You shall not make for yourself a graven image, or any likeness of anything that is in heaven above, or that is on the earth beneath, or that is in the water under the earth." (Deuteronomy 5:8)
> "Whatever the LORD pleases he does, in heaven and on earth, in the seas and all deeps." (Psalm 135:6)
> "Thou art the LORD, thou alone; thou hast made heaven, the heaven of heavens, with all their host, the earth and all that is on it, the seas and all that is in them." (Nehemiah 9:6)
> "Once again, in a little while, I will shake the heavens and the earth and the sea and the dry land." (Haggai 2:6)

These various descriptions have led many to assume that the ancient Hebrew people conceived the structure of the world as consisting of more than the heaven and earth scheme. The majority of scholars, relying heavily on ancient near eastern parallels, understand OT cosmology as tripartite.[25] Luis Stadelmann's volume, *The Hebrew Conception of the World*, typifies this approach. He observes that "heaven and earth" is a common phrase that the Hebrew Bible uses to describe the world, but that there are also "more comprehensive" descriptions that use multiple terms such as "heaven and earth and the seas or deeps." He states:

> The three-leveled structure of the world, attested in several passages throughout the Bible, accounts for a better understanding of the expression "heaven and earth," clarifying this less explicit concept of the universe by adding a new dimension.[26]

Specifically, the "new dimension" is contained in terms such as תהום (the deeps), בור (pit, cistern), and שאול (Sheol), which refer to a third tier, the lower level of the world. Stadelmann assumes a triple-decker cosmology because of the Bible's discussion of a place of postmortem existence,

---

[25] Representative examples from reference works are the entries on Cosmology in *ABD* 1:1167–68 and the *Dictionary of the OT: Pentateuch* (eds. T. Desmond Alexander and David W. Baker; Downers Grove, Ill.: IVP, 2003).

[26] Stadelmann, *Hebrew Conception of the World* (Rome: Pontifical Biblical Institute, 1970), 9.

often described as being accessed by going down.[27] He concludes by stating that the Hebrews conceived of the world under God as "a structure composed of three layers: the heavens above, the earth and sea in the middle, and the underworld beneath."[28]

In a recent book, J. Edward Wright follows this same line of thought. He surveys the ancient Egyptian, Mesopotamian, and Israelite cosmogonic and cosmological traditions and concludes that "the ancient Israelites, like their Near Eastern neighbors, imagined the cosmos as a tripartite structure: heaven, earth, netherworld."[29] Wright interprets the Babylonian myth of creation and flood as depicting a three-fold cosmos. Following this, he lists a handful of biblical texts which are understood as indications that the ancient Israelites held to the same tripartite cosmological view as their neighbors.

Few scholars have disagreed with this understanding, but one notable exception is Cornelis Houtman. Houtman concludes his volume with a chapter entitled, "Israels Weltbild und Weltanschauung."[30] His thesis is provocative. Quite simply, Houtman argues that the Israelites did not hold to a single, unifying view of the cosmos—tripartite or otherwise—but indeed, they simultaneously retained several images of the heavenly realm which contrast and even conflict with one another. Our modern attempts at nailing down the specifics of the biblical cosmology, especially with various pictorial depictions, have foisted upon the biblical texts a mistaken grid; we are trying to recreate the ancients' *one* logically consistent image of the cosmos when no such thing existed, at least not by modern "scientific" standards. Israel had no *Weltbild*. However, we do find in the Bible a clear and consistent *Weltanschauung*, namely, a uniform ascription to Yahweh of the creation and sustenance of the world. This *Weltanschauung*, which is expressed through the OT's declarations about the cosmos, reveals God as the sole creator and ruler of the universe.

Contrary to the standard scholarly assumption, it is better to see that the OT conception of the universe is indeed bipartite ("heaven and earth"), not tripartite, and that all other OT descriptions of the world can be subsumed under the two realms of heavenly and earthly. While Houtman is right that this cosmology is not as technical and precise as our

---

[27] Stadelmann, *Hebrew Conception of the World*, 169–170.
[28] Stadelmann, *Hebrew Conception of the World*, 177.
[29] Wright, *Early History of Heaven*, 96.
[30] Houtman, *Der Himmel im AT*, 283–317.

modern sensibilities might desire, we can still discern a consistent OT *Weltbild*, one that is fundamentally dualistic. This dualistic *Weltbild*, in turn, undergirds a dualistic *Weltanschauung* or worldview. The basic duality of the physical structure of the world matches the ontological dualism between God in the heavenly realm and humanity in the earthly, all the while playing on a beautiful ambiguity in the use of the term "heaven."

1. *Old Testament Cosmology—Bipartite Weltbild*

There is no question that the bipolar word pair, "heaven and earth," is the dominant picture of the world used in the OT. We have already observed the frequency of this conjunction and its multiple functions. Repeating the foundational revelation of Genesis 1:1, we find the "heaven and earth" refrain echoed in various forms throughout the Jewish scriptures.

The occasional lengthier descriptions of the world, including terms such as the sea and the deeps, at first glance, may appear to confirm a tripartite view rather than bipartite. This is especially true when one comes to the text armed with a tripartite assumption from ANE parallels. This has been the approach of Stadelmann, Wright, and many others.

However, such arguments suffer from two fundamental problems: (1) despite the quoting of biblical passages, they fail to present a clear case for anything other than a bipartite cosmology; and (2) they confuse the categories of the argument by slipping between descriptions of the earth and Sheol when the biblical record supports no clearly distinct third realm.

The first problem can be found in J. Edward Wright's presentation in *The Early History of Heaven*. He begins by quoting the *Atra-Hasis* Babylonian flood epic and concludes that "from this Babylonian text we learn that the gods divided the cosmos into heaven, earth, and netherworld."[31] Wright follows this by quoting a number of biblical passages which supposedly confirm this tripartite view for the Israelites. But in each instance, his arguments fall short. First, likely following Stadelmann, he quotes Ps 115:16: "The heavens are the LORD's heavens, but the earth he has given to the sons of men."[32] But this text actually

---

[31] Wright, *Early History of Heaven*, 54.
[32] Stadelmann, *Hebrew Conception of the World*, 9, quotes Ps 115:16–17 as one of his few examples of a tripartite structure presented in one passage. While verse 16 speaks of the duality of heaven and earth, verse 17 mentions the dead and those who go down

supports a two-fold view, not three. Second, Wright mentions Gen 49:25 and interprets this as an allusion to the tripartite universe. However, this questionable conclusion depends on the unlikely interpretation of "breasts and the womb" as a reference to the earth.[33] Next, Wright quotes the Ten Commandments injunction against idols: "You shall not make for yourself an idol, whether in the form of anything that is in heaven above, or that is on the earth beneath, or that is in the water under the earth" (Exod 20:4; cf. Deut 5:8). Here the tripartite view is supposedly being supported by the heaven-earth-waters under the earth grouping. However, as I will show below, it is not possible to clearly distinguish "waters under the earth" from the earthly realm; it is still part of the earthly structure, as Stadelmann himself agrees. Thus, no three distinct cosmological elements can be found in this text.

Wright's final offering of evidence for a tripartite cosmology at first appears to be his strongest, quoting Amos 9:2–3. Here for the first time we have what may appear as the three-fold structure all in one place: Sheol in conjunction with heaven and Mt Carmel. However, this example proves to be the weakest of all. Wright quotes Amos 9:2–3a, "Though they dig down to Sheol, from there shall my hand take them; and though they ascend to heaven, from there I will bring them down; and if they should hide on the top of Carmel, from there I will seek them and take them..." and states that the prophet "mentions three levels of the cosmos. " He concludes, "the ancient Israelite image of the cosmos, then, was that the cosmos is divided into three realms—heaven, earth, underworld."[34] However, not only does Sheol-heaven-Mount Carmel fall short of the heaven-earth-Sheol pattern, Wright's quoting of only the first half of Amos 9:3 belies his case. In fact, the full discourse of Amos 9:2–3 has *four* terms, broken into two merismatic pairs in chiasm:

---

in silence. From this he infers a three-fold view. However, there is no syntactical or conceptual reason to connect verses 16 and 17 together in this way. Just the opposite, verse 17 couples with verse 18: "[17]The dead do not praise the LORD, nor do any that go down into silence. [18]But *we* will bless the LORD from this time forth and for evermore." Thus, there are two sets of paired words: "heaven and earth" in verse 17 and "the dead and the living ('we')" in verses 17 and 18, not a tripartite structure.

[33] At least one ancient witness, the LXX, did not interpret the phrase this way. In this verse the heaven and deeps are understood as a contrast of heaven and earth, and the latter phrase ("breasts and womb") as a subset of the earthly blessings.

[34] Wright, *Early History of Heaven*, 54.

Though they dig into *Sheol* [A], from there shall my hand take them; though they climb up to *heaven* [B], from there I will bring them down. Though they hide themselves on *the top of Carmel* [B`], from there I will search out and take them; and though they hide from my sight at *the bottom of the sea* [A`], there I will command the serpent, and it shall bite them.

Rather than three distinct realms, here we have two bipolar pairs linked together: Sheol-heaven and top of Carmel-bottom of the sea. So rather than being evidence of a tripartite structure, Amos 9:2–3 is either support for a four-part cosmos, or clearly, confirmation of a basic concept of duality, using two pairs of terms. The basic duality consists of the heights and the depths, with Sheol and the bottom of the sea as comparable, and heaven and the mountaintop likewise. As a result, the arguments for a tripartite structure in the OT, argued more extensively by Wright than anyone else, prove quite unfounded.

Underneath Wright's tripartite arguments is the more fundamental problem of all such discussions: a slippery confusion of categories. Those who see the OT cosmology as three-fold uniformly understand the distinct elements as (1) heaven, (2) earth, and (3) Sheol (or the underworld place of the dead). However, quite simply, there are no biblical passages which present the universe in this way. The expanded expressions that go beyond the standard heaven and earth pair are read as proof of an expanded cosmological structure, but examination of these phrases shows that they always include other elements which are understood as constituent parts of the earth, never a separate third category of Sheol. The discussion of what Sheol is (and especially how views of the afterlife develop in the Second Temple period) gets overlaid with these expanded expression phrases and a confusion of categories results. Reference to "heaven and earth and sea" (Ex 20:11; Hag 2:6; *et al.*) does not constitute the necessary tripartite structure (heaven-earth-Sheol) that tripartite advocates hold to, although these are the passages which are universally quoted as evidence of something beyond a bipartite arrangement.

In other words, a tripartite cosmology depends on a clearly-defined third category, Sheol and/or the deeps/oceans (תהום), that is distinct from the earth. However, this proves impossible for the OT literature. David Tsumura's detailed study of the relationship between earth (ארץ) and the deeps/oceans (תהום) in Hebrew and Ugaritic provides conclusive evidence that we cannot separate the latter from the former.[35] Tsumura

---

[35] Tsumura, "A 'Hyponymous' Word Pair," 258–269.

shows that אֶרֶץ and תְּהוֹם in both Ugaritic and Hebrew have a hyponymic relationship. That is, תְּהוֹם is understood as part of what אֶרֶץ is. Likewise, a variety of scholars have shown that in Hebrew as well as cognate languages, "earth" and "water" often overlap in semantic meaning with Sheol or the underworld, and cannot be clearly distinguished.[36]

Interestingly, Stadelmann agrees that earth is often used to denote the underworld,[37] and that Sheol can serve as a substitute for earth in the common merism of heaven and earth.[38] Moreover, Stadelmann is very clear that the seas, oceans, rivers are all part of the "earth" category.[39] Note again his original delineation of the tripartite structure: "the heavens above, the earth and sea in the middle, and the underworld beneath."[40] Yet, he fails to see how this renders a three-tiered view impossible. He slips back into a confusion of categories, seeing the expanded expressions (using "the sea" or "deeps") as evidence of a tripartite view, yet failing to show that the third element, Sheol, is a distinct category.

One of the few scholars to reject the tripartite view is Othmar Keel. Keel, leader of the so-called Fribourg School, has spearheaded an approach to biblical studies which interacts deeply with ancient Near Eastern iconography. His volume on the Psalms seeks to clarify the meaning of various words, phrases, and concepts in the OT by reference to actual images from the ancient world.[41] He observes that in Mesopotamian and Egyptian understandings, while a three-fold structure can be found, the merism heaven and earth is older and predominant over a threefold view. Keel rejects the argument that the appearance

---

[36] For example, C. F. Barth writes, "the ocean below figures formally among underworld names." C. F. Barth, *Die Errettung vom Tode: Leben und Tod in den Klage- und Dankliedern des Alten Testaments* (3d ed.; ed., B. Janowski.; Stuttgart: Kohlhammer, 1997), 67. Many of these arguments are reviewed in Philip S. Johnston, *Shades of Sheol: Death and Afterlife in the Old Testament* (Leicester: Apollos, 2002), 99–119.

[37] Stadelmann, *Hebrew Conception of the World*, 167, gives at least twenty-five examples from the OT alone.

[38] Stadelmann, *Hebrew Conception of the World*, 169. For example, "Ask a sign of the LORD your God; let it be as deep as Sheol or high as heaven" (Isa 7:11). This substitution of Sheol in a normal heaven-earth pair shows the heavy semantic overlap of earth and Sheol and the fundamental duality of OT cosmology.

[39] Stadelmann, *Hebrew Conception of the World*, 154–164.

[40] Stadelmann, *Hebrew Conception of the World*, 177.

[41] Keel, *Symbolism of the Biblical World*. He explains the iconographic approach on pages 8–11. See also Keel's later discussion of this methodology (and its application to the question of Jewish monotheism) in Othmar Keel and Christoph Uehlinger, *Gods, Goddesses, and Images of God in Ancient Israel* (trans. Thomas H. Trapp; Minneapolis: Fortress, 1998), 1–18, 393–396.

of the tripartite formula (heaven, earth, and sea or the place of the dead) indicates a threefold cosmological view. He observes that these less frequent formulae are inconsistent and that the additional terms (the sea or the place of the dead) are a "far less necessary and independent" element in the structure. Instead, neither the sea nor the netherworld emerge as distinct regions but are associated with one pole or the other, most often the earth.[42] The netherworld "possesses a degree of reality essentially inferior to that of other regions."[43] The biblical view, like its ancient Near Eastern neighbors, is therefore essentially dualistic. God is the one "who made heaven and earth" (Ps 115:15; 121:2; 124:8; 134:3) and who has reserved the heavens for himself but leaves the earth (and the netherworld) to humanity (Ps 115:16–17). The bipartite formula of heaven and earth "illuminates very well the conception and perception of the world in the ancient Near East and in the OT."[44] See Figure 7.1 below. When discussing Genesis 1, Tsumura concludes likewise: "In other words, the cosmology in vv. 1–2 is bipartite, rather than tripartite, describing the entire world in terms of 'heavens and earth'."[45] And too, when discussing the cosmology of the Psalter: "The Psalmist's understanding of the world is bipartite, rather than tripartite."[46]

The traditional tripartite view is based not on how the OT presents itself cosmologically but on recognition of the heaven and earth pattern plus a desire to fit in the occasional data about the question of existence after death, the idea of the netherworld. However, this is an anachronistic reading stemming from the later, more developed ideas of the afterlife from the Second Temple period. A much simpler solution is to understand Sheol in the OT, like the seas and the ocean deeps, as part of the earthly realm. Thus, rather than a tripartite structure (Figure 7.2), we have a basic bipolarity (Figure 7.3).

---

[42] Keel, *Symbolism of the Biblical World*, 30. In the older Egyptian traditions, the earth is the region of the humanity and the common dead while the heavens are associated with the gods and dead kings.

[43] Keel, *Symbolism of the Biblical World*, 30. Annette Krüger makes a similar comment regarding Job 38: "the underworld here does not have its own weight, but is reckoned with the earth." A. Krüger, "Himmel—Erde—Unterwelt: Kosmologische Entwürfe in der poetischen Literatur Israels," in *Das biblische Weltbild und seine altorientalischen Kontexte* (ed. Bernd Janowski and Beate Ego; Tübingen: Mohr Siebeck, 2001), 79 (my translation).

[44] Keel, *Symbolism of the Biblical World*, 30.

[45] Tsumura, "A 'Hyponymous' Word Pair," 269.

[46] Tsumura, "A 'Hyponymous' Word Pair," 265.

HEAVEN AND EARTH IN THE OLD TESTAMENT 177

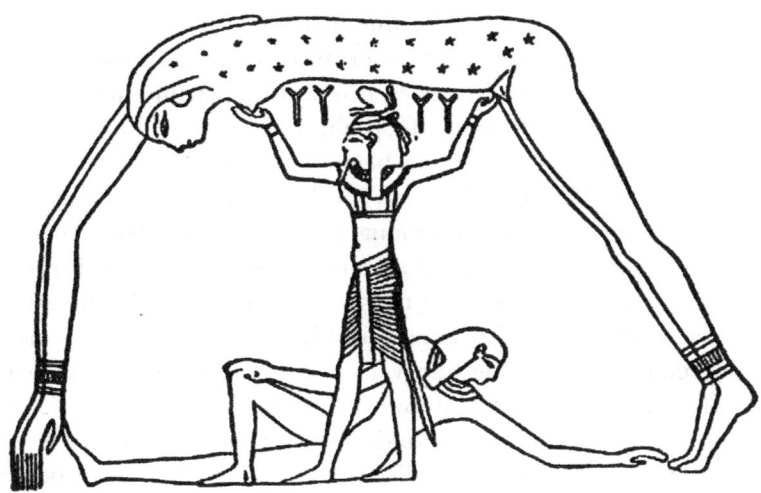

This image shows the two parts of the Egyptian universe (Nut and Geb) that have been separated by the god Shu. Keel offers an assortment of images which show the essentially two-part conception of the world. The caption under a picture very similar to this one reads: "This picture dramatically illustrates the manner in which earth and sky formerly constituted the universe (the "all"). The world in which the ancient Egyptian lived and moved came into being by the separation of the two (cf. Gen 1:7: "God...separated the waters")."[47]

Figure 7.1[48]

Heavens
Earth
Sheol/Netherworld

Figure 7.2

Heavenly Realm Astral, Meteorological, Angelic
Earthly Realm Land of the Living // Sheol/Depths

Figure 7.3

---

[47] Keel, *Symbolism of the Biblical World*, 31.
[48] This common image was accessed via <www.images.google.com> on 12 March 2007.

A good example of the fundamentally bipartite structure is found in Psalm 148. This psalm is broken into two parts under the rubric of heavenly phenomena in verses 1–6 and the earthly in verses 7–14. The fundamental structure of the psalm is thereby built on the heaven and earth theme.[49] Each section begins with an exhortation to praise Yahweh: verse 1 "from the heavens" and verse 7 "from the earth." The meaning of these paired prepositional phrases is explicated by the verses following each. The sense is "let praise redound to Yahweh from the arena of the heavens and from the arena of the earth." The arena of the heavens consists of his angels and host (v.2), the sun, moon, and shining stars (v.3), the highest heavens and the waters above the heavens (v.4). These are commanded to praise God because they are all created objects (v.5) and remain forever under his sovereign rule (v.6). The arena of the earthly realm is likewise filled out with sweeping illustrations: the sea monsters and deeps [תהמות] (v.7), storm phenomena (v.8), mountains and trees (v.9), domestic and wild animals and birds (v.10), and all ranks of humanity (vv.11–12). In both halves of the psalm the key word, either heaven or earth, is repeated. The heaven and earth compositional structure is then drawn together in verse 13. Here heaven and earth are brought together in the declaration that Yahweh's praise and glory are alone exalted over all creation—heaven and earth. In addition to the overall structural bipolarity, this psalm shows the hyponymous relationship of the sea and the deeps (v.7) with the earth.

Psalm 148 is but one example of the pervasive heaven and earth theme in the OT.[50] The other occasional expanded descriptions of the world are merely poetic expansions of this fundamental heaven and earth pair. They will not bear any additional technological-cosmological weight pressed upon them. Forcing a precise cosmological view on such descriptions is analogous to older attempts to construct a tripartite biblical anthropology of heart-soul-body on Deut 6:5: "and you shall love the LORD your God with all your heart, and with all your soul,

---

[49] Psalm 8, similarly, uses a heaven and earth theme for its structure. The heavenly bodies are termed the "work of your fingers" (v.3) followed by the earthly, paralleled as the "work of your hands" (v.6). The human being is put in the middle of this structure, serving as a fulcrum point (vv.4–5). In fact, Psalm 8 consists of a chiasm that hinges on the heaven and earth pair with humanity being the central point.

[50] Keel, *Symbolism of the Biblical World*, 57–58, points out that comparable catalogs of heavenly and earthly contents can be found in Ps 104, Sirach 43, and the Song of the Three Young Men, in addition to similar lists in Sumerian and Egyptian literature and iconography.

and with all your might." At first this may seem reasonable and may even accord with some human experience. However, when we encounter this same description in other places we find that heart, soul, and strength are not *termini technici*. Matthew 22:37 renders the verse with heart, soul, and mind, while Mark 12:30 and Luke 10:27 use heart, soul, strength, and mind. In the same way, as Houtman rightly points out, the cosmological language of the OT is symbolic, not technical.[51]

So is there a consistent OT *Weltbild*? Houtman is certainly right that we should not press our modern desires for a unified, comprehensive picture upon the variety of biblical cosmological images. Yet Wright is right that Houtman is probably too pessimistic about our ability to reconstruct Israel's *Weltbild*.[52] Rather than giving up the quest in the face of the variegated images, the best solution is to see that there is a fundamental bipolar structure of heavenly and earthly realms with an array of poetic expressions and embellishments used within it. This fundamental bipolarity is fed by and feeds into a deep-seated dualistic *Weltanschauung*, to which we now turn.

2. *Heaven and Earth in the Old Testament's* Weltanschauung

It would be a mistake and a linguistic fallacy to assume because the ancient Israelites spoke of the cosmos with the pair heaven and earth rather than with a single word comparable to κόσμος that this reflects their inability to conceptualize the world abstractly as a whole. In the earliest stages of reflection on the cosmos this may have been the case, but the retention of this fixed word pair in the biblical writings is no proof that the Hebrews could not conceptualize otherwise. Honeyman points out that a merism evolves over time from "the primitive inability to subsume particulars under the universal" to become a fossil of speech, "employed as a stylistic survival for the sake of emphasis and vividness after the use of the universal has been achieved and the inability which brought the usage into being has been transcended."[53] Such is the case

---

[51] "Am besten werden wir die alttestamentlichen Aussagen über den Kosmos als *symbolische* Ausdrücke charakterisieren können." Houtman, *Der Himmel im AT*, 302.

[52] Wright, *Early History of Heaven*, 88–89. Similar remarks are made in his article, "Biblical Versus Israelite Images of the Heavenly Realm," *JSOT* 93 (2001), 60–61.

[53] A. M. Honeyman, "Merismus in Biblical Hebrew," *JBL* 71 (1952), 17. Avishur, *Stylistic Studies of Word Pairs*, 91, is similar: "It would seem, that the primary linguistic function of these phenomena diminished as the language evolved and hendiadys and permerismum were used to serve as figures of speech."

for heaven and earth. The use of heaven and earth for the cosmos does not indicate a poverty in the Hebrew language.

Instead, its common usage can be explained for two reasons. First, as is well known, there is a propensity in Hebrew writing to converse in parallelisms. This proclivity promotes and preserves the use of heaven and earth as a fixed pair, even as its meaning expands beyond the merismatic sense to include an antithetic notion.

But the second factor is even more important. There is in the Israelites' *Weltanschauung* a fundamental duality in tension.[54] This too is preserved and promoted by the heaven and earth pair. Houtman sums it up well:

> Our opinion is that there is a relationship between the manner and the way in which the Israelite practiced reality and the fact that he used a word-pair to signify the 'cosmos': for the Israelites the cosmos was taken precisely not as a unity—only God is one—but a duality, a complementary duality and as such a harmony of two opposite poles in balance of the whole contents...the use of 'heaven and earth' for the 'cosmos' brings consciousness to the Israelite that the world, and also life, is ruled through polar powers.[55]

But contrary to Houtman, who sees only the *Weltanschauung* as dualistic, it is crucial to see that both the *Weltbild* and the *Weltanschauung* of the OT are organically related: Both flow from and are manifested through the pervasive heaven and earth pair. When heaven is used with its "direct meaning" of the astral and atmospheric world, "heaven and earth" refers to the *Weltbild*, the physical cosmology of the world. Conversely, when heaven is used in its "symbolic" sense of the place of God's dwelling, "heaven and earth" refers to the *Weltanschauung*, or what we may term its "ontological cosmology."[56] Thus, both the *Weltbild* and

---

[54] Many scholars have argued that the message of the Primal History of Gen 2–11 is about "the divinely ordained separation of heaven and earth as two distinct realms and the enforcement of distinct limits upon the human race." This deep-seated distinction in the first book of the Pentateuch weaves its way through much of the OT writings. P. D. Hanson, "Rebellion in Heaven, Azael, and Euhemeristic Heroes in 1 Enoch 6–11," *JBL* 96 (1977), 214, quoted in Robert A. Di Vito, "The Demarcation of Divine and Human Realms in Genesis 2–11," in *Creation in the Biblical Traditions* (ed. Richard J. Clifford and John J. Collins; Washington, D.C.: Catholic Biblical Association, 1992), 40. According to Di Vito, other scholars who hold to this distinction view (which Di Vito opposes) include R. A. Oden, Jr. and W. M. Clark.

[55] Houtman, *Der Himmel im AT*, 77 (my translation).

[56] This terminology is similar to that employed by G. W. E. Nickelsburg in his discussion of the spatial and ontological dualism of *1 Enoch*. See Nickelsburg, *1 Enoch 1: A Commentary on the Book of* 1 Enoch, *Chapters 1–36; 81–108* (Hermeneia; Minneapolis: Fortress, 2001), 40–41.

Heavenly Realm
Astral, Meteorological, Angelic
Earthly Realm
Land of the Living // Sheol/Depths

Figure 7.3
Physical Cosmology
"Weltbild"

Heavenly Realm (God)
Earthly Realm (Created World)
Heavens / Earth

Figure 7.4
Ontological Cosmology
"Weltanschauung"

the *Weltanschauung* of the OT are fundamentally bipolar and dualistic, playing on the semantic flexibility of heaven in the pairing of heaven and earth.

Thus, we may provide an additional diagram in tandem with Figure 7.3 already given above.

Figure 7.3 represents the created order or physical cosmology, expressed in the dualistic poles of heaven and earth. Figure 7.4 represents a similar dualism, but this time the two poles stand for God on the one hand and all of creation on the other. This ontological dualism is likewise expressed through the heaven and earth pair. The fundamental distinction here hinges on God as uncreated and all else as part of his creation. Therefore, Figure 7.3 in its entirety as the created world (heaven and earth) makes up the "Earthly Realm" element in Figure 7.4.[57]

3. *Summary*

In sum, the OT embodies a dualistic or bipolar idea in the phrase "heaven and earth." This word-pair forms the substructure of a bipartite cosmology which is manifested continually throughout the OT documents. The occasional descriptions of the world which use terms beyond heaven and earth should be understood as poetic subspecies of the broad dualism of heaven and earth. This includes the place of the dead, Sheol, or the deeps, which is an undeveloped thought in the OT, fundamentally a part of the earth.

This bipartite physical cosmology (*Weltbild*) in turn feeds and undergirds a symbolic ontological dualism (*Weltanschauung*) wherein God's being

---

[57] One example of this comes from Psalm 8. This psalm opens and closes with the refrain "How excellent is your name in all the earth!" Inside this inclusio we find the earth (or earthly realm) described, from the moon and stars of the heavens to the fish in the sea. All of the created world, heaven and earth, is in a very real sense "the earth."

and ways are contrasted with humanity's. "For as the heavens are higher than the earth, so are my ways higher than your ways and my thoughts than your thoughts" (Isa 55:9). This ontological cosmology (Figure 7.4) is organically related to the physical cosmological (Figure 7.3). That is, the basic duality of the physical cosmology is likewise reflected in the duality of the theological diagram. In the latter case, however, the emphasis is on the distinction between the uncreated, eternal God and all created things, including the heavenly bodies. Both the *Weltbild* and *Weltanschauung* of the OT are manifested through the heaven and earth pair, though the meaning of this pair varies in each, based on the powerful flexibility of the semantic range of heaven.

APOCRYPHA, PSEUDEPIGRAPHA, AND OTHER SECOND TEMPLE LITERATURE

We may now move beyond the canonical OT into subsequent Jewish literature. Here too, not surprisingly, the combination of heaven and earth is very frequent. While the wider chronological and geographical diversity of this literature makes it impossible to maintain a single *Weltbild* throughout these texts, a fundamental heaven and earth contrastive *Weltanschauung* remains and is even strengthened in much of this literature.

Heaven and Earth in the Septuagintal Apocrypha

The heaven and earth pair appears nearly thirty times in the texts which comprise the Apocrypha. We find several instances of copulative, thematic and implied pairs.[58] Most of the copulative pairs are in reference to God as the Creator or Lord "of heaven and earth." Although we find many such references in the canonical OT as well, the apocryphal references particularly emphasize the theme of God as the creator of all things, specifically all things not only on earth but also in the heavens. This polemical focus reflects the religious situation of early

---

[58] The copulative pairs are: Jdt 7:28; 9:12; 13:18; Add Esth C 4:17c; Sirach 1:3; 16:18; Ep Jer 6:54; 1 Macc 2:37; 2 Macc 7:28; 1 Esdras 4:34; 6:13; Ps Sol 8:7; Pr Man 1:2. The thematic pairs include: Wis 9:16; 18:16; Jdt 11:7; Sir 17:32; Baruch 1:11; Dan 3:80–81; Bel 1:5; 1 Macc 4:40; 2 Macc 15:4–8; 3 Macc 2:14–15; 1 Esdras 4:36; Ps Sol 2:9; 17:18. We also find a number of places where the heavenly and earthly realms are contrasted though a different word is substituted for earth. These implicit pairs include Ps Sol 2:29–30 and chapters 24 and 43 of Sirach.

Judaism. As a result, we find that the copulative heaven and earth pairs are frequently narrowed into declarations about God rather than the more general usage as the way of speaking about the created world as in the rest of the OT. The influence of the Greek concept of κόσμος often displaced heaven and earth as the general way of referring to the world.[59] This, combined with the felt-need to emphasize the uniqueness and supremacy of the Jewish God, affected the use of the copulative heaven and earth pair in this constricted way.

We also find that several of the apocryphal books reveal an underlying heaven and earth contrast theme. In the canonical OT, this is most prominent in Daniel (especially chapters 2–7).[60] In the Apocrypha we find many localized examples of this theme in places such as Wisdom 18:15–16, Sirach 17:32, 2 Macc 15:3–5, and 3 Macc 2:14–15. But aside from Daniel, it is especially in the book of Judith that an extended heaven and earth contrast motif appears. As in Daniel, this theme is interwoven with kingdom language as the heavenly God is shown to be superior to a king who rules over all the earth.

The powerful, realistic narrative of Judith is designed to encourage Jewish people of the first- or second-century BCE to be faithful to God and his commandments. Judith is a heroine of stellar piety and purity, even more positive, scrupulous, and faithful than Esther. The story describes how she outwits and defeats the powerful general Holofernes, thereby saving her people from destruction. The plot of the story is rich with literary pointers to the heaven and earth theme. We find in 2:4 that Nebuchadnezzar is described as "the great king, the lord of the whole earth." Nebuchadnezzar swears vengeance on the western nations with threats which are filled with geographic superlatives: "I will cover the whole face of the earth with the feet of my armies...and I will lead them away captive to the ends of the whole earth" (2:7–9).[61] The exaltation of Nebuchadnezzar continues in chapter 6 where Holofernes rebukes Achior with the shocking question: "Who is God except Nebuchadnezzar?" (6:2). King Nebuchadnezzar, "lord of the

---

[59] The use of κόσμος instead of heaven and earth is most noticeable in 2 Macc, 4 Macc, and Wisdom. The word also appears a number of times in other books, though usually with the older and broader Greek meaning of adornment or decoration.

[60] For a detailed exposition of the themes of heaven and earth and kingdom in Daniel 2–7, see Chapter Eleven.

[61] In fact, superlative terms such as "entire," "whole," "every," and "all" strikingly fill the early chapters of Judith, giving a sense of intensity to the narrative.

whole earth" (6:4) will destroy the Jews "from the face of the earth" (6:3). Again in chapter 11, as if this theme were not clear enough already, we find the same grandiose claims made of Nebuchadnezzar. Holofernes calls Nebuchadnezzar "the king of all the earth" (11:1). Judith, her speech dripping with irony, repeats this assertion and even heightens it beyond belief with the biblical dominion language: "not only do men serve him [Nebuchadnezzar]...but also the beasts of the field and the birds of the air will live by your power" (11:7). Holofernes is so enthralled with Judith that he garnishes her with accolades: there is not such a woman "from one end of the earth to the other" (11:21) and she will become renown "throughout the whole world" (11:23).

Throughout this repetitive language, we also find the refrain of the heavenly God. In 5:8, 6:19, and 11:17 the God of the Jews is referred to as the "God of heaven." Likewise, in 9:12 Judith calls God the "Lord of heaven and earth" (δέσποτα τῶν οὐρανῶν καί τῆς γῆς) and the "king of all thy creation." After Judith's successful return to her city (with Holofernes' head in her sack), Uzziah proclaims that she is "blessed by the Most High God above all women on earth; and blessed be the Lord God, who created the heavens and the earth..." (13:18).

Thus, we can see a contrast of heaven and earth theme woven into the story with skillful literary technique. This motif contrasts God the king of all creation (heaven and earth) with any human, even one who appears to have power over all the earth. This pattern in Judith is quite similar to what we find in Daniel, though in the latter book it is even more focused. In fact, in Judith, it is probable that the blatantly ahistorical use of Nebuchadnezzar serves to connect Judith with the well-known Daniel stories.[62] The descriptions of Nebuchadnezzar in both stories are quite similar and the rhetorical effect is the same: the God of heaven has the power to deliver those who are faithful to him, power even over the greatest king over all the earth. Thus, we see in Judith, along with many other Apocryphal texts, the working out of a dualistic theological worldview, expressed as a contrast of heaven and earth.

---

[62] On the idea of Judith as "ludic" or playful history, see Philip Esler, "Ludic History in the Book of Judith: The Reinvention of Israelite Identity?" *Biblical Interpretation* 10/2 (2002): 107–143, especially 115–122.

Heaven and Earth in the Pseudepigrapha and Apocalyptic Literature

1. *1 Enoch*

The theme of heaven and earth is very important in 1 Enoch. At the level of basic usage, about half of the occurrences of heaven (93 of 191) in the complete Ethiopic form of 1 Enoch are joined with a reference to the earth, forming the familiar word-pair. Unlike the Hebrew Bible and Septuagint, however, this is rarely in the form of a direct dyad "heaven and earth" (only 4x). Instead, 1 Enoch is loaded with closely contextual thematic pairings of heaven and earth. For example:

> Consider the works in heaven [the luminaries]...Consider the earth... (2:1–2)
> ...as men perished from the earth, their voice went up to heaven... (8:4)
> ...a storm-wind snatched me up from the face of the earth and set me down at the ends of heaven (39:3)
> ...all the heavens are thy throne forever and the whole earth thy footstool forever and ever (84:2)
> ...and heaven and all the heavenly luminaries shall shake and tremble in great alarm...and the whole earth shall shake and tremble and be disturbed (102:3b,d)

While the heaven and earth theme is frequent throughout all of 1 Enoch, it is particularly dominant in the Book of Dreams and the Similitudes, where the majority of heaven references are linked with earth. Additionally, in the Book of Watchers there are several extended passages which focus on the theme of heaven and earth. For example, in chapter 1 the opening of the whole book focuses on Enoch's revelation of the Holy One in heaven (1:2,4) and the judgment he will bring upon the whole earth. Chapters 2–4 use heaven in the meteorological/astronomical sense and give an extended reflection on the whole cosmos: the elements in both heaven and on earth (cf. Ps 148). Most significantly, the crucial chapters 15–16 are based on the motif of the heavenly versus earthly realms. The great sin and cause of evil on the earth is the heavenly watchers who have unlawfully mixed the heavenly realm with the earthly, the angelic with the human. Instead of obediently remaining in their place (even as the heavenly bodies do), these heavenly creatures have forsaken the high heaven, the holy sanctuary and acted like children of the earth (15:3), even though the habitation of the spirits of heaven should be in heaven (15:7,10).

These examples and the frequent recurrence of heaven and earth throughout 1 Enoch highlight the heaven and earth dualism that forms the substructure of the entire book. According to Nickelsburg, running through all the "consciously shaped compilation of traditions" in 1 Enoch is "a dualistic view of reality."[63] The worldview or construct of reality in 1 Enoch consists of two related dualisms: "a spatial dualism between this world and heaven and a temporal dualism between this age and the age to come."[64] In 1 Enoch there is a sharp dualism between heaven, the realm of the divine, and earth, the habitation of humans. Related to this spatial dualism is an ontological one: "the absolute distinction between divine beings and humans."[65] This dualistic worldview is found not only in 1 Enoch but likewise provides the framework for other important Second Temple books such as Daniel 7–12 and Wisdom of Solomon. In fact, the parallels of 1 Enoch with these other key works shows the predominance and importance of the heaven and earth theme to the apocalyptic construct of reality.

2. *Other Pseudepigrapha*

Other pseudepigraphal works show a wide variety of practice on the combination of heaven and earth. Some books rarely conjoin the two terms (*Testament of Abraham; Joseph and Aseneth; Ascension of Isaiah*),[66] while most use this pairing between one-third and one-half of the time that heaven language is employed (*3 Baruch; Apocalypse of Sedrach; Greek Apocalypse of Ezra; Jubilees*). The most notable works in this vein are *2 Enoch* and *Testament of Job*.

In line with the tradition of *1 Enoch*, the text called *2 Enoch* also shows a predilection toward using heaven and earth pairs. Of the 80 occurrences of heaven in the J recension, 36 times heaven and earth are conjoined in various ways (copulative and thematic pairs). Similarly, of the 45 instances in recension A, 16 are heaven and earth conjunctions. In both recensions, several of the heaven and earth pairs involve

---

[63] Nickelsburg, *1 Enoch*, 37.
[64] Nickelsburg, *1 Enoch*, 5.
[65] Nickelsburg, *1 Enoch*, 40. I find the idea of an ontological dualism along the lines of heaven and earth helpful, though I would prefer to think in terms of the distinction between God and creation rather than between all "divine beings" (including created angels) and humanity. The subtle difference between these two conceptions of the heaven and earth distinction is important.
[66] In the case of the *Ascension of Isaiah*, even though the word pair heaven and earth is not very frequent, a recent article suggests that the contrast of earthly times and heavenly times is foundational to the exhortational purpose of the book. Robert G. Hall, "Disjunction of Heavenly and Earthly Times in the *Ascension of Isaiah*," *Journal for the Study of Judaism* 35/1 (2004): 17–26.

expanded descriptions such as heaven, earth, and sea or the depths. Whether this reflects a different cosmological structure or is simply a pattern of speech such as in the OT, it is difficult to be certain. Most importantly, unlike *1 Enoch*, the heaven and earth pairs do not typically function to contrast earth/humanity with God. Instead, the sense of the heaven and earth pairs in *2 Enoch* is usually merismatic, referring to the whole world. This corresponds with the observation that *2 Enoch* is not particularly dualistic in its worldview. As Anderson states: "There are ingredients suspected of being Iranian in origin; but in spite of claim sometimes made, the work is totally devoid of dualistic thinking, except for a passing belief that man is free to choose good or evil."[67]

The *Testament of Job* is similar in frequency but with a different emphasis. This work draws from and is interlaced with LXX Job, and dates from somewhere in the first century BCE to first century CE.[68] Although heaven is only used ten times in the book, four of these occurrences are in direct heaven and earth combinations. Additionally, *Testament of Job* uses the adjectives οὐράνιος and ἐπουράνιος in contrast with earthly things (36:3; 38:2, 5). These uses reflect a strong theme of heavenly and earthly contrast throughout the book. Spittler's reflections on the theological outlook of the book state that a distinct emphasis throughout this testament is "a cosmological dualism that inculcates a certain otherworldliness."[69] In this way, *Testament of Job* aligns with the *1 Enoch* tradition. This does not indicate any particular connections between these documents, however, as a spatial dualistic worldview is one of the hallmarks of apocalyptic literature in general.[70]

Qumran

As was discussed in Chapter Two, the use of heaven throughout the Dead Sea Scrolls in many ways follows the tradition of the OT literature. Thus, most often heaven refers to astronomical and meteorological phenomena, and very frequently heaven is combined with earth. The heaven and earth pairing is probably the most frequent use of heaven in this mixed corpus of literature. This pairing, however, is almost entirely

---
[67] Anderson, *OTP* 1:96.
[68] Spittler, *OTP* 1:833.
[69] Spittler, *OTP* 1:835.
[70] A helpful overview of the emphases of "apocalyptic" and "apocalyptic eschatology" including dualism can be found in M. C. de Boer, "Paul and Apocalyptic Eschatology," 345–383.

restricted to merismatic uses, referring to all of creation. Surprisingly in light of the dualistic emphasis at Qumran, "heaven and earth" is rarely used in a contrastive sense.

The Qumran document that manifests the clearest heavenly and earthly connection is the Songs of the Sabbath Sacrifice. This text, however, does not emphasize this theme through the use of heaven and earth pairs, as heaven only occurs twice in the whole book. Instead, the heavenly and earthly realms are connected thematically in a particular way: as archetype and type. The Songs of the Sabbath Sacrifice portrays the heavenly sanctuary (in "the heights") as the model and origin of the earthly temple. This way of portraying the relationship of heaven and earth also appears in both biblical and postbiblical literature (e.g., Exod 25:9; 26:30; Heb 8:5; *1 Enoch* 14–15 and *2 Apoc. Bar.* 4:5–6; 59:4).

At first glance this appears to be of the same nature as the Middle-Platonic heaven and earth connection in Philo. However, this connection is only superficial and accidental. In fact, "the belief that the human world is a microcosm of the heavenly or ideal realm...is far more ancient than Plato."[71] Even more so for Middle-Platonism and Philo. In the ancient near east the heaven-earth, archetype-type idea was known (cf. Marduk's temple in *Enuma Elish*). Moreover, the relationship between heaven and earth in Songs of the Sabbath Sacrifice has a different tone than that in Philo. In Philo and Neo-Platonic thought, the emphasis is on a negative contrast of the superior (heaven) over the inferior (earth). In the Songs, however, while the heavenly is certainly perfect in comparison to the earthly, the emphasis is on the close organic connection between the earthly and the heavenly. Again, however, this use of heaven and earth in Qumran is the exception compared to the more common merismatic usage.

Mishnah

We have already described in Chapter Two how the use of heaven in the Mishnah is very restricted. Nearly every instance of heaven refers to God metonymically, using a variety of expressions such as the "fear of heaven" and "at the hands of heaven." Quite unexpectedly, the use of heaven in the Mishnah is noticeably unlike other Second Temple literature or the OT. The most noteworthy instance of this difference is

---

[71] Davila, *Liturgical Works*, 83.

how *infrequently* earth is combined with heaven, either merismatically or contrastively. Rare instances include *m. Ta'an.* 4:3 (which is a direct quote from Gen 1), *m. Sebu.* 4:13, and the looser implied conjunctions in *m. Nedarim* ii, 4 and *m. Yoma* viii, 9.[72] In later Rabbinic literature beyond the Mishnah, we do find occasional expressions such as that in *Berakot T* 3:7 (6): "Do Thy will in the heavens above and give tranquility of spirit to those who fear Thee on earth"[73] or "the honour of heaven" contrasted to "the honour of man" (*Tosefta Yoma* ii, 8). Nevertheless, in the Mishnah this theme is much less frequent than expected in light of how important the word pair is in the OT literature.

Certainly the definitive work on the use of heaven and earth in the Rabbinic literature is Beate Ego's monograph, *Im Himmel wie auf Erden*.[74] This volume concentrates on the later Rabbinic literature's way of speaking about the relationship of heaven and earth, especially on the *Urbild* (prefiguration) and *Abbild* (image) of these two realities. She concludes that early Judaism described the relationship of the heavenly and earthly worlds with a variety of categories, each with their own corresponding theological concepts.[75] For our purposes, it is noteworthy that the development that does occur on this matter is found only in the literature much later than the beginnings of the Christian era and the time of the writing of Matthew. The strong and developed interest in contrasting heaven with earth that we will observe subsequently in Matthew apparently did not stem from a contemporary widespread view in (pre-)Rabbinic Judaism.

CONCLUSION

Beginning with Genesis 1:1, heaven and earth is a very important expression and concept throughout the OT. This weighty phrase can function both merismatically and antithetically, depending on the sense

---

[72] This data comes from my examination of all the occurrences of heaven-related words in the Mishnah based on C. Y. Kasovsky, *Thesaurus Mishnae: Concordantiae Verborum quae in Sex Mishnae Ordinibus Reperiuntur* (Jerusalem: Massadah Publishing, 1960). There are also four heaven and earth combinations in chapter 6 of *m. 'Abot*, but this chapter stems from a much later recension of the Mishnah (11th-century CE or later).

[73] Morton Smith gives this text as a Tannaitic parallel to Matt 6:1. M. Smith, *Tannaitic Parallels to the Gospels* (Philadelphia: SBL, 1951), 137.

[74] Beate Ego, *Im Himmel wie auf Erden: Studien zum Verhältnis von himmlischer und irdischer Welt in Rabbinischen Judentum*.

[75] Ego, *Im Himmel wie auf Erden*, 169.

in which heaven is being employed. Heaven and earth is important not only because of its great frequency but also because it is fundamental to the *Weltbild* and *Weltanschauung* of the OT.

The use of heaven and earth is also quite common in many parts of the Second Temple literature. This is not surprising in light of how indebted this literature is (in various degrees) to the weighty traditions of the Hebrew Bible, where heaven and earth is a very important theme. It *is* surprising, however, that this theme does not play a larger role in the Qumran and Mishnaic corpuses. The apocalyptic literature, on the other hand, provides ample opportunity for the heaven and earth theme to multiply, with its emphasis on the heavenly realm in distinction from the earthly. Regarding cosmological views in the Second Temple period, it is difficult to make generalizations across the diversity of this literature. J. Edward Wright may be correct in asserting that there were a variety of cosmological views in this period due to the varying levels of influence of Hellenism among different Jewish groups.[76] Regardless, I do not see evidence in this corpus for a clearly defined tripartite cosmological view (as I have also argued against for the OT). When texts in this era do manifest cosmological interest, the fundamental dualistic elements of heaven and earth remain dominant, even though occasional expanded expressions including the sea and the deeps are found. There may have been evolution from a bipartite to a tripartite understanding in this period, but if so, it is not strongly emphasized and certainly not consistent. On the other hand, the influence of Greco-Roman views of the cosmos could push Jewish cosmology into a more bipartite structure in which the earth was the center and the rest of the world consisted of several concentric heavenly spheres.[77] There is no doubt that views of the afterlife expanded during this time, but it is important to remember that the descriptions are mixed concerning the location of postmortem existence, both paradise and punishment. In many instances, the place of punishment was not located below the earth in a new part of the cosmos, but was found in one section of the heavens.[78] Thus, even in

---

[76] Wright, *Early History of Heaven*, 185–186.
[77] Ulrich Mauser, "'Heaven' in the World View of the New Testament," *HBT* 9/2 (1987), 33. Cf. Wright, *Early History of Heaven*, ix–x, 139.
[78] Mauser, "'Heaven'," 33. Richard J. Bauckham, *The Fate of the Dead: Studies on the Jewish and Christian Apocalypses* (Leiden: Brill, 1998), 9, 33–34. Examples of hell being located in the heavens include *2 Enoch* 8–10; *Testament of Isaac* 5; *3 Baruch* (Greek Apocalypse) 4:3–6; 5:3; 10:5; *Greek Apocalypse of Ezra* 1:7; the *Apocalypse of the Seven Heavens* (cf. Bauckham, Fate of the Dead, 318).

these apocalyptic developments, there is not much clear evidence for a tripartite *Weltbild* any more than for the OT documents.

Regardless of whether cosmological views are indeed evolving, it is clear that a dualistic worldview remains widespread and even more important in the Second Temple period. This worldview is related to and propagates the use of heaven and earth combinations.

CHAPTER EIGHT

HEAVEN AND EARTH IN MATTHEW

Having observed the importance of the heaven and earth theme in the OT and Second Temple literature, we may now turn to Matthew. Here we find that the combination of heaven and earth is strikingly frequent and forms the second part of his idiolectic use of heaven language. In regularly employing the heaven and earth word pair Matthew follows the heritage of the OT texts. Yet, we will see that he especially highlights the contrastive or antithetical sense of the expression. Matthew emphasizes the (currently temporal) contrast between God and humanity and employs this theme as a rubric for his explanation of Jesus' radical kerygma. Following the fundamental bipartite structure found in the OT—both its physical and ontological senses—Matthew capitalizes upon this distinction as a structural clue to his theological purpose.

In this chapter I will catalogue and analyze the many heaven and earth pairs in Matthew. I will then discuss the *Weltbild* and *Weltanschauung* found throughout this Gospel and the connection of Matthew with Genesis.

HEAVEN AND EARTH PAIRS IN MATTHEW

Copulative, Thematic, and Implied Heaven and Earth Pairs

We have seen thus far that the combination of heaven and earth is very common throughout the OT and Second Temple literature. In the NT, it is in Matthew particularly that this stock phrase occurs more than any other. There are over twenty times where heaven and earth are connected in some form in Matthew. In comparison, Mark has only two instances of the heaven and earth pair and Luke five.[1] The only other book which regularly combines heaven and earth is Revelation (16x). Moreover, Matthew is the only Gospel writer to use the prepositional

---

[1] Mk 13:27, 31; Luke 4:25; 10:21; 12:56; 16:17; 21:33. Acts has five more occurrences, though four of them are direct quotations from the OT.

phrase, ἐν (τῷ) οὐρανῷ...ἐπὶ (τῆς) γῆς.² "In heaven...on earth" does occur occasionally in other parts of the NT, but nowhere else in the Gospels.³ Matthew's preference for this phrase (with the prepositions) is all the more noticeable in that it is not particularly common in the OT (only 12x), but occurs in very important texts in Matthew.

We have already observed that the heaven and earth word pair can take a number of forms. I have classified these in the OT as copulative, thematic, and implied. As discussed previously, copulative pairs are examples where "heaven and earth" appears as one unit, not separated by prepositions or other words. Thematic pairs use a combination of heaven and earth but with some separation of intervening words or phrases. Often instances in this category use a combination of prepositions such as "in heaven...on earth." Implied pairs occur when heaven is used in conjunction with a word other than earth but one closely associated with it, thus communicating the same idea. In Matthew, all three types of the heaven and earth word pair are found.

In the category of copulative pairs there are three instances in Matthew: 5:18, 11:25, and 24:35. In 5:18 and 24:35 Jesus speaks of the future passing away of heaven and earth. This use evokes the sense of an eschatological end comparable to its beginning in Gen 1:1. It is also interesting to note that these two of the three copulative pairs occur in the first and last of Matthew's five major discourses, serving in effect as bookends. In 11:25, Jesus addresses the Father as "Lord of heaven and earth." This phrase is reminiscent of many such monikers for God in the Second Temple literature, though surprisingly, God is rarely referred to in this way in the NT (cf. Acts 17:24).

There are also several instances in Matthew of implied pairs. In 11:23 and 16:18, heaven is put into conjunction with Hades (ᾅδης). This uncommon NT word serves in the LXX and the NT as the semantic equivalent of Sheol, or the place of the dead.⁴ In 11:23 (par. Lk 10:15), Capernaum is condemned for its pride: rather than being exalted to heaven, it will be cast down to Hades (cf. Isa 14:13; Amos 9:2). As

---

² This observation comes from Gerhard Schneider, "'Im Himmel—auf Erden'," 293. In four parallel instances (16:19b,c; 18:18b,c) the phrase is reversed, ἐπὶ (τῆς) γῆς...ἐν (τῷ) οὐρανῷ. In 16:19 the forms of οὐρανός are plural, as was discussed in Chapter Six.

³ Acts 2:19; 1 Cor 8:5; Eph 1:10; 3:15; Col 1:16, 20; Rev 5:3, 13.

⁴ ᾅδης occurs ten times in the NT: Matt (2x); Lk (2x); Acts (2x, both OT quotations); Rev (4x). In Revelation it is consistently put into apposition with Death.

Davies and Allison observe, this combination is not to be taken literally but serves as a powerful figure of speech for judgment.[5] The meaning of the πύλαι ᾅδου ("gates of Hades") in 16:18 has a wide variety of interpretations.[6] Regardless of its exact meaning, it is clear that the gates of Hades serve in this text as a counterpoint to the keys of the kingdom of heaven (16:19).

In several other texts heaven is put into conjunction with humanity, thereby providing another version of the implied pairs. Twice in 10:32–33 we find humanity (ἄνθρωπος) put into contrast with the Father in heaven. Everyone who confesses or denies Jesus ἔμπροσθεν τῶν ἀνθρώπων will receive the same from Jesus ἔμπροσθεν τοῦ πατρός μου τοῦ ἐν [τοῖς] οὐρανοῖς. This kind of parallel construction is found also in 5:16 and 6:1. In 5:16 Jesus' disciples are taught to let their light shine ἔμπροσθεν τῶν ἀνθρώπων so that they will bring glory to the Father ἐν τοῖς οὐρανοῖς. Using the same pattern, in 6:1 the disciples are warned not to practice their righteousness ἔμπροσθεν τῶν ἀνθρώπων to be seen by them, else they will have no reward with their Father who is ἐν τοῖς οὐρανοῖς. Similarly, twice in 21:25–26 Jesus asks his opponents about the source of John's baptism: Was it from heaven (metonymically for God) or of human origin (ἐξ ἀνθρώπων)? Closely related to these heaven-humanity contrasts is the pair in 16:17. In this text Jesus proclaims that the source of Peter's revelational confession was not "flesh and blood" but "my Father in heaven." "Flesh and blood" here is virtually synonymous with humanity and stands as the counterpoint to the heavenly Father.[7] In all of these implied pairs, it is clear that the alternate words for earth still communicate the same idea. There is a contrast between the earthly and heavenly realms.[8]

---

[5] Davies and Allison, *Matthew*, 2:269.

[6] A helpful survey of twelve interpretive options is found in Davies and Allison, *Matthew* 2:630–634.

[7] Davies and Allison observe that "flesh and blood" came to be a technical term meaning human agency in contrast to divine agency (*Matthew*, 2:623). Similarly, E. Schweizer observes that the phrase "describes man as being subject to sickness and death, always limited in strength and knowledge, while 'heaven' is the realm of God, not subject to limits" (*Matthew*, 340).

[8] There is one additional text which could potentially be classified as an implied-thematic pair. In 6:26–30 Jesus gives two examples of creatures which do not worry yet God provides for them: the birds τοῦ οὐρανοῦ (v. 26) and the κρίνα τοῦ ἀγροῦ ("lilies of the field"). The heaven-field pair is a looser connection but has some overlap with the other implied pairs. However, it is different in that it functions thematically in a merismatic way rather than with a contrast between the two poles of heaven and earth.

By far the most common (and the most important) type of heaven and earth combination in Matthew is the thematic kind. Heaven and earth are combined thematically fourteen times in close context.[9] The first occurrence is found in 5:13–16. We have just noted that 5:16 itself contains an implied pair which combines Father in heaven with humanity (ἄνθρωπος). Beyond this we can also observe that this whole pericope is framed by reference to the earth in 5:13 ("you are the salt of the earth") and heaven in 5:16 ("Father in heaven"). Shortly following, in 5:34–35 Jesus commands his disciples to swear neither by heaven (μήτε ἐν τῷ οὐρανῷ) nor by earth (μήτε ἐν τῇ γῇ). The next instance is found in the first set of petitions in the Lord's Prayer (6:10): "Thy kingdom come, thy will be done ὡς ἐν οὐρανῷ καὶ ἐπὶ γῆς." Following close by, Jesus exhorts his hearers not to treasure up treasures ἐπὶ τῆς γῆς but instead ἐν οὐρανῷ (6:19–20). These last two occurrences are actually part of a broader heavenly and earthly contrast theme that extends throughout 6:1–21.[10] In 10:33–34 there is a looser thematic connection between the Father in heaven and Jesus' non-peaceful mission on earth. Five more incidents of the heaven and earth combination are related and clustered together in 16:19, 18:18, and 18:19. Two times each in 16:19 and 18:18 heaven and earth are conjoined in sayings about binding and loosing. 18:19 reiterates this teaching by stating that anything the disciples agree about ἐπὶ τῆς γῆς will be done by Jesus' Father who is ἐν οὐρανοῖς. In the midst of these related texts, the kings of the earth (οἱ βασιλεῖς τῆς γῆς) are contrasted thematically with the kingdom of heaven (17:25+18:1). This topical connection is looser than the others and does not fall into the same structural patterns, but it is too striking to be only coincidental.[11] In 23:9 we have another instance (as in 10:33–34 and 18:19) where earth is connected with the Father in heaven. Jesus teaches that his disciples are not to call anyone ἐπὶ τῆς γῆς their father

---

[9] The passages which use thematic heaven and earth pairs are: 5:13–16, 34–35; 6:1–21 (including specifically 6:10 and 19–20); 10:33–34; 16:19 (2x); 18:18 (2x), 19; 17:25–18:1; 23:9; 24:30; and 28:18.

[10] As I will argue in Chapter Ten, 6:1–21 is structured on the contrast between pleasing the Father in heaven rather than humanity on earth. 6:19–21 sums up this teaching with the command regarding heavenly versus earthly treasure.

[11] Another example of a loose but not accidental thematic contrast is found in 4:8. Here in Satan's final temptation of Jesus, Jesus is offered "all the kingdoms of the world (τὰς βασιλείας τοῦ κόσμου) and their glory." This interesting phrase is sandwiched in between two references to the ἡ βασιλεία τῶν οὐρανῶν (3:2 and 4:17), which delimit this entire section which introduces Jesus' ministry (3:1–4:17). The contrast between the κόσμος and the οὐρανός is almost certainly intentional. See also Chapter Twelve.

but only the heavenly Father (ὁ πατὴρ ὁ οὐράνιος).[12] Then in 24:30, part of a text rich with heaven language, the sign of the Son of Man appears ἐν οὐρανῷ and all the tribes of the earth (πᾶσαι αἱ φυλαὶ τῆς γῆς) mourn in response. And finally, in the conclusion to the Gospel, Jesus claims that he has received all authority ἐν οὐρανῷ καὶ ἐπὶ [τῆς] γῆς (28:18). Thus, we can see that these assorted thematic heaven and earth pairs occur regularly throughout Matthew.

A number of comments are in order. First, the predominance of these word pairs accords with the rest of Matthew's highly skilled poetic style. M. Goulder analyzes Matthew's diction and finds that he has more "poetic" sayings than Mark and Luke—that is, sayings which manifest a balanced structure such as "many are called but few are chosen" or "be wise as serpents and harmless as doves."[13] Along the same lines, C. H. Lohr provided a lengthy analysis of "oral techniques" used by Matthew including poetic devices such as inclusio and refrain.[14] Heaven and earth is another example of this type of rhythmic, repeated, and balanced way of speaking. Similarly, Gundry observes that Matthew "delights in conforming phraseology to the OT, as well as in quoting the OT explicitly, and that he likes to put his materials in parallelistic form, often by tightening the parallelism that already characterizes the tradition."[15] Hagner remarks that "to a very large extent, the shape of the sayings of Jesus in the Gospel of Matthew reflects the parallelism and mnemonic devices of material designed for easy memorization"—maybe 80 percent of Jesus' sayings.[16] Again, Matthew's frequent pairing of heaven and earth provides another example of such stylistic devices.

Another observation is that most of the thematic pairs occur in a rather standardized Matthean form of ἐπὶ [τῆς] γῆς...ἐν οὐρανοῦ. This is the form for two-thirds of the pairs, with the slight variation of order ἐν οὐρανῷ καὶ ἐπὶ [τῆς] γῆς in 28:18.[17] The occurrence of

---

[12] The manuscript witnesses are mixed on whether the text should read ἐν οὐρανοῖς or the adjectival οὐράνιος. The latter reading (as the NA27 has) is likely original. Unfortunately, most English translations gloss over the difference between the noun and the adjective by translating the phrase as "who is in heaven." Regardless, the sense is the same here where the heavenly Father is being compared to earthly fathers.

[13] Michael D. Goulder, *Midrash and Lection in Matthew* (London: SPCK, 1974), 70–94.

[14] C. H. Lohr, "Oral Techniques in the Gospel of Matthew," *CBQ* 23/4 (1961): 403–435.

[15] Gundry, *Matthew*, 2.

[16] Hagner, *Matthew* 1–13, xlviii.

[17] The phrase in 5:34–35 is very close—ἐν τῷ οὐρανῷ...ἐν τῇ γῇ—with both phrases

γῆς before οὐρανός is atypical in the OT and Second Temple literature, though it is occasionally found there. Interestingly, in contrast to the thematic pairs, the copulative pairs in Matthew always follow the standard οὐρανός καὶ γῆ form.

Also noteworthy, *all* of the thematic pairs are unique to Matthew, while the copulative pairs are found in the other gospel traditions (either Q or triple-tradition).[18] The thematic pairs come from either distinctly M material or are clear redactional additions to his sources. In the latter category there are five texts where he has apparently added a thematic heaven and earth pair (5:13–16; 6:10; 19–20; 10:33–34; 24:30). In 5:13–16, similar sayings about the salt of the earth are found in Mark and Luke, but neither connect this with Father in heaven. In 6:10, the heaven and earth phrase is completely missing from the Lukan parallel (11:2), and likewise, no heaven and earth pairing is in view in the Lukan parallel (12:33) to Matt 6:19–20 or to Matt 10:33–34 (Lk 12:51). In 24:30, Matthew alone includes the references both to ἐν οὐρανῷ and the tribes τῆς γῆς (cp. Mk 13:26; Lk 21:27). Conversely, the copulative pairs in 5:18 and 11:25 are also found in Luke, and 24:35 is in all three gospels. This comparison again highlights Matthew's intentionality regarding the heaven and earth pairs and his focus on the thematic type.[19]

Finally, we may also note that the different types of heaven and earth pairs in Matthew may provide yet another example of "different terms for different audiences." As was discussed previously, Robert Mowery has suggested that Matthew's Jesus uses different terms when addressing the crowds and disciples versus his antagonists.[20] Jesus reserves "kingdom of heaven" for his followers and uses "kingdom of God" in dialogue with the Jewish leaders. Similarly, Jesus tends to use "Father" only with his followers but refers to "God" in the presence of his opponents. I

---

being used as instrumental datives. In 23:9 ἐπὶ τῆς γῆς still appears but the use of the adjective οὐράνιος disrupts the normal prepositional pairing. Similarly, in 24:30 the typical ἐν οὐρανῷ is found but its combination with γῆ in the subject of the next clause prevents the normal structure.

[18] Some of the implied pairs, which are obviously less explicit, are paralleled in Luke and Mark, but not all.

[19] Schneider, "Im Himmel—auf Erden," 292–293, understands the prepositional phrases "in heaven...on earth" as particularly characteristic of Matthew's thought regarding heaven.

[20] Mowery, "The Matthean References to the Kingdom," and idem, "God, Lord and Father."

observed that the singular and plural uses of οὐρανός have the same tendency: Jesus does not use the plural with his disputants, but only the more common-place singular forms. A similar distinction applies to the heaven and earth pairs. All of the copulative and thematic pairs—the most explicit way of speaking of heaven and earth—occur in Jesus' discourse with his disciples and the crowds. However, with the exception of one text, the implied pairs are spoken *to* those or *about* those opposed to Jesus.[21] In other words, Matthew generally preserves direct heaven and earth language for the followers, and uses less explicit, implied pairs for others. The point is that Matthew's literary fingerprints are evident once again in his crafted use of the heaven and earth pairs. One of the ways that this crafting functions is to distinguish insiders from outsiders.

The Meaning of the Heaven and Earth Pairs

Just as in the OT and other literature, the heaven and earth pairs in Matthew can function in two distinct ways: as merismatic or antithetic. This dual usage of the heaven and earth pair can be found in other parts of the NT as well.[22] Overall, the rest of the NT corresponds with the OT: the merismatic sense of heaven and earth is much more common than the antithetic. In Matthew the heaven and earth word pair not only occurs more frequently, but the contrastive sense dominates.

1. *Merismatic Uses*

The merismatic use of the heaven and earth word pair is the common OT way of describing all the cosmos; the creation is known as heaven and earth. Despite the widespread usage of this expression in the OT and beyond, Matthew only uses heaven and earth in a merismatic way three times:

---

[21] 11:23 and 21:25–26 (2x) refer to unbelieving Capernaum and the chief priests and elders, respectively; 10:32–33 (2x) refers to those who deny Jesus "before men." Similar are the ones (outside) observing the good works of the disciples in 5:16, and the ones who do not get a reward from the Father in 6:1. The only exceptions are found together in 16:17–19 where Jesus exclaims that "flesh and blood" did not reveal the truth to Peter but the Father in heaven (16:17) and counterpoises the gates of Hades with the kingdom of heaven (16:18–19).

[22] Schneider gives eight instances, most of which are merismatic (Acts 2:19; 1 Cor 8:5; Col 1:16; Eph 3:15; Rev 5:3), and the others, similarly, concern a new unity of things in heaven and on earth created through Christ's work (Col 1:20; Eph 1:10; Rev 5:13). On the other hand, one can discern a heaven and earth contrastive theme in other books, especially John and Revelation, though the specific phrase is not very common.

5:18 ἀμὴν γὰρ λέγω ὑμῖν· ἕως ἂν παρέλθῃ ὁ οὐρανὸς καὶ ἡ γῆ, ἰῶτα ἓν ἢ μία κεραία οὐ μὴ παρέλθῃ ἀπὸ τοῦ νόμου, ἕως ἂν πάντα γένηται.

For truly, I say to you, till heaven and earth pass away, not an iota, not a dot, will pass from the law until all is accomplished. (RSV)

11:25 Ἐν ἐκείνῳ τῷ καιρῷ ἀποκριθεὶς ὁ Ἰησοῦς εἶπεν· ἐξομολογοῦμαί σοι, πάτερ, κύριε τοῦ οὐρανοῦ καὶ τῆς γῆς, ὅτι ἔκρυψας ταῦτα ἀπὸ σοφῶν καὶ συνετῶν καὶ ἀπεκάλυψας αὐτὰ νηπίοις.

At that time Jesus declared, "I thank thee, Father, Lord of heaven and earth, that thou hast hidden these things from the wise and understanding and revealed them to babes." (RSV)

24:35 ὁ οὐρανὸς καὶ ἡ γῆ παρελεύσεται, οἱ δὲ λόγοι μου οὐ μὴ παρέλθωσιν.

Heaven and earth will pass away, but my words will not pass away. (RSV)

In each of these instances it is clear that the phrase refers to all of creation, following the common Jewish usage. Most interesting, these three merismatic pairs are also the only copulative uses of the word pair in Matthew. That is, Matthew demarcates these rather mundane merismatic uses of the word pair by always putting them—and only these—into a set structure of article-heaven-καὶ-article-earth. Further evidence of Matthew's intentional editing here can be seen in that each of these instances stands as the subject (or qualifying the subject, as in 11:25), and where "heaven and earth" is the grammatical subject (5:18; 24:35) it is followed by a *singular* verb.[23] The two parts are to be seen as one. The parallels in Mark 13:31 and Luke 21:33 instead both have the expected *plural* verb.[24] This synoptic difference is a strong indication of Matthew's intentional shaping and attention to the heaven and earth pair, and that he intends "heaven and earth" to be seen as one thing here: the cosmos.

2. *Antithetic Uses*

In contrast, the remainder of the heaven and earth pairs in Matthew can be classified as antithetic. The antithetic combination of many word pairs is common throughout Matthew, not only the heaven and

---

[23] In 24:35 many of the manuscripts, though of weaker weight, have changed the singular παρελεύσεται to the plural παρελεύσονται in an effort to make grammatical agreement. However, not only is the external evidence weak in 24:35, the singular verb in the parallel 5:18 is undisputed, and the shift to the expected plural is an understandable scribal error. These factors significantly strengthen the case for the original singular verb in 24:35, as the NA27 reads. In the LXX I find only two instances where "heaven and earth" is the subject of a singular verb: 1 Macc 2:37 and Joel 4:16.

[24] Luke 16:17 is also parallel but the verb form is an infinitive, which cannot communicate number.

earth conjunction.²⁵ The antithetic heaven and earth pairs in Matthew include the fourteen thematic combinations and the nine implied pairs. Examples of the antithetic thematic combinations are:

6:19–20 Μὴ θησαυρίζετε ὑμῖν θησαυροὺς ἐπὶ τῆς γῆς...θησαυρίζετε δὲ ὑμῖν θησαυροὺς ἐν οὐρανῷ

Do not lay up for yourselves treasures on earth... but lay up for yourselves treasures in heaven. (RSV)

18:18 Ἀμὴν λέγω ὑμῖν· ὅσα ἐὰν δήσητε ἐπὶ τῆς γῆς ἔσται δεδεμένα ἐν οὐρανῷ, καὶ ὅσα ἐὰν λύσητε ἐπὶ τῆς γῆς ἔσται λελυμένα ἐν οὐρανῷ.

Truly, I say to you, whatever you bind on earth shall be bound in heaven, and whatever you loose on earth shall be loosed in heaven. (RSV)

23:9 καὶ πατέρα μὴ καλέσητε ὑμῶν ἐπὶ τῆς γῆς, εἷς γάρ ἐστιν ὑμῶν ὁ πατὴρ ὁ οὐράνιος.²⁶

And call no man your father on earth, for you have one Father, who is in heaven. (RSV)

And the antithetic implied pairs include:

11:23 καὶ σύ, Καφαρναούμ, μὴ ἕως οὐρανοῦ ὑψωθήσῃ; ἕως ᾅδου καταβήσῃ

And you, Capernaum, will you be exalted to heaven? You shall be brought down to Hades. (RSV)

21:25 τὸ βάπτισμα τὸ Ἰωάννου πόθεν ἦν; ἐξ οὐρανοῦ ἢ ἐξ ἀνθρώπων

The baptism of John, whence was it? From heaven or from men? (RSV)

One can see that in each of these cases, some antithesis, comparison, tension or contrast is present in the conjunction of the two terms. The exact nature of this antithesis and the degree of distinction can vary somewhat depending on context. For example, in 11:23 the combination of heaven and Hades is idiomatic and hyperbolic more than a reference to two specific places, but the usage is not merismatic; the two poles are contrasted. Similarly, 5:34–35 compares heaven as God's throne and the earth as his footstool. In this expression from Isaiah 66:1 there is a close connection between heaven and earth, but the usage is not a

---

²⁵ Hagner, *Matthew 1–13*, xlviii, notes that "It is estimated that 80 percent of Jesus' sayings are in the form of *parallelismus membrorum* (Reisner), often of the antithetical variety."

²⁶ Notice that here the adjective οὐράνιος is used instead of οὐρανός, but the sense is the same. Interestingly, most of the English translations render this expression as "Father, who is in heaven," rather than "heavenly Father," probably stemming from a sense of the contrast apparent here with "father on earth."

simple merism; a contrast between God's dwelling place and the lower place of the earth is communicated, even though God's rulership over both is declared. Similarly, in 18:18, although heaven and earth are obviously organically related, the two different realms of heaven and earth are in view here. Most of the antithetic pairs, however, have a much stronger sense of contrast. Whether the text concerns where to lay up treasures (6:19–20), the source of John the Baptist's teachings (21:25), or the prayer for the consummation of God's kingdom (6:10), a contrast of the two realms of heaven and earth is present.[27]

We can also observe that the antithetic pairs stand out from the merismatic by their structure. Apart from 17:25+18:1 and 16:17—the loosest of the heaven and earth combinations—each occurrence of the antithetic word pair is rendered in Matthew using prepositional phrases, most often in the form of ἐν (τῷ) οὐρανῷ... ἐπὶ (τῆς) γῆς, but also with other words. As Schneider notes, this prepositional form of the heaven and earth pair does not refer to the created sphere, "but to the heavenly world and the angels on the one hand, and the earthly world of men on the other."[28]

We also observed above that all of the thematic pairs are unique to Matthew. The fact that the thematic pairs are consistently antithetic and often put into a particular grammatical structure shows Matthew's emphasis on the contrastive relationship of heaven and earth. Commenting on the heaven and earth pair in 24:30, Gundry states, "the phrase also sets up a contrast between heaven, where the sign of the Son of Man will appear, and earth, where all the tribes will mourn. This contrast typifies Matthew's composition."[29] Kari Syreeni's view of heaven and earth throughout Matthew is similar: "The emphasis [of heaven and earth] is primarily not on the total universe with its two parts, but on the dichotomy, the innate separateness of the heavenly and mundane spheres."[30]

---

[27] W. G. Thompson briefly observes the heaven and earth pairs in his monograph, *Matthew's Advice to a Divided Community: Matt 17:22–18:35* (Analecta Biblica 44; Rome: Biblical Institute Press, 1970). He states that heaven and earth at times signifies totality, but "in expressions of place the nouns are separated, and some contrast is always implied" (189). N. T. Wright remarks that in mainline Jewish thought the heavenly and earthly realms are "distinct but closely intertwined" as contrasted to their total separation in Epicureanism or their fusion in pantheism. N. T. Wright, *The New Testament and the People of God* (London: SPCK, 1992), 290.

[28] Schneider, "Im Himmel—auf Erden," 294.

[29] Gundry, *Matthew*, 488. Unfortunately, these insightful remarks are not developed.

[30] Kari Syreeni, "Between Heaven and Earth: On the Structure of Matthew's Symbolic Universe," *JSNT* 40 (1990), 3.

3. A Fitting Climax—28:18

Rudolf Schnackenburg is one of the few commentators to make mention of the two different senses of the heaven and earth pairs in Matthew. Commenting on the phrase "on earth as it is in heaven" (6:10), he writes, "'Heaven and earth' can stand for the whole world (5:18; 11:25; 24:35; 28:18), but it can also counterpoise the divine and human realms (5:34–35; 16:19; 18:18; 23:9)."[31]

These uses correspond with what I am terming the merismatic and antithetic categories in Matthew. But Schnackenburg classifies *four* of Matthew's occurrences as merismatic ("stand[ing] for the whole world") rather than three as I have listed above. He agrees in identifying 5:18, 11:25, and 24:35 in this category, but he also includes 28:18: "All authority in heaven and on earth has been given to me." Most, if not all, commentators would agree, even though few put it in those terms. That is, while most scholars do not even consider the difference between the merismatic and antithetic senses, nearly all understand 28:18 to be a reference to Jesus' *universal* authority. However, this standard interpretation is in need of re-examination.

In fact, it is difficult to decide whether to place the statement ἐδόθη μοι πᾶσα ἐξουσία ἐν οὐρανῷ καὶ ἐπὶ [τῆς] γῆς into the merismatic or antithetic group. It evinces elements of both categories. Like the other merismatic occurrences, οὐρανός precedes γῆ and they are closely connected with καί. Additionally, the heaven and earth phrase is obviously connected to the universal statement "all authority." On the other hand, the phrase occurs in Matthew's standard antithetic form using ἐν οὐρανῷ in comparison with ἐπὶ [τῆς] γῆς. Thus, how are we to classify this final occurrence of the heaven and earth pair?

It is best to categorize 28:18 as primarily antithetic, all the while acknowledging that this does not eliminate the aspect of the universality of Jesus' authority communicated by the phrase. That is, because the two different realms of heaven and earth are being spoken of (see on Schneider below), it is best to classify this text as primarily antithetic. Yet, at the same time, as observed above, the exact nature of this antithesis varies by text: sometimes the tension or contrast is stronger than at other times, even while the close relationship between heaven and earth is not denied. Such is the case in 28:18. Also, the recurrence of the standardized prepositional phrase usage as well as the frequency of the contrastive pairs throughout Matthew makes the antithetic usage most likely.

---

[31] Schnackenburg, *Matthew*, 67.

Corroborative evidence of this interpretation comes from BDAG. Under the entry for οὐρανός, two classes of the combination of heaven and earth are given: a) forming a unity as the totality of creation; and b) standing independently beside the earth or contrasted with it. Notably, 28:18 is listed under the second category.³²

But the most compelling piece of evidence that 28:18 is antithetic rather than merismatic comes from Gerhard Schneider. Schneider makes perceptive remarks about how 28:18 fits in with the rest of Matthew.³³ He observes that this verse completes Jesus' earlier assertions about having authority "on earth." For example, at the healing of the paralytic, Jesus uses this miracle to testify that "the Son of Man has authority *on earth* to forgive sins" (9:6). Also, Jesus, the preacher of the kingdom of heaven, is contrasted with the (earthly) scribes as being a teacher who manifests such great *authority* (7:29). Likewise, the source of Jesus' authority, exercised on earth, was challenged by the chief priests and elders (21:23–27). The implication of the dialogue is that Jesus' power, like John's, comes ἐξ οὐρανοῦ. Thus, when we come to 28:18, which picks up on the authority of Jesus theme, the emphasis of the phrase ἐν οὐρανῷ καὶ ἐπὶ [τῆς] γῆς lies on the "in heaven," not on the totality per se. The Son of Man had authority on earth; the resurrected Christ has been given *all* authority, both "in heaven and on earth."³⁴

Again, this is not to deny that a universal, cosmic-wide authority has been granted to Jesus.³⁵ While heaven in 28:18 refers to the divine realm and not merely as part of a merismatic heaven and earth statement, the fact that Jesus has been given authority in *both* of these realms

---

³² *BDAG*, s.v. οὐρανός.

³³ Schneider, "Im Himmel—auf Erden," 294–295. Oscar S. Brooks, Sr also observes some of these connections, though less pointedly, in his article, "Matthew xxviii 16–20 and the Design of the First Gospel," *JSNT* 10 (1981), 8–10.

³⁴ This phrase brings to mind the similarities in the opposite declaration found in *Sifre* §313 on Deut 32:10: "Before our father Abraham came into the world, God was, as it were, only the king of heaven...but when Abraham came into the world, he made him [God] king over heaven and earth" (Friedmann, 134 *b*). The similarities are highlighted when one considers the Abraham-all nations connection here in Matthew 28.

³⁵ Davies and Allison, *Matthew* 3:683, comment on the connection between 28:18 and 6:10. They observe that "Jesus' authority, gained by his comprehensive triumph, does imply that, in the words of the Lord's Prayer, he can guarantee that God's will will be done on earth as in heaven." They go on to say, "28:18 implies the same conviction that is expressed in several of the NT christological hymns, namely, that through the resurrection Jesus is exalted and made Lord of the cosmos. In other words, God hands to him all authority."

(heavenly and earthly) still results in a universal power. However, there is a distinction of realms intended by the phrase "in heaven and on earth." This is not just the merismatic idiom; κόσμος would *not* have served just as well here. The point is that Jesus' earthly authority—easily discernible by all who witnessed his ministry—has now been completed with the addition of his authority in the divine realm by nature of his righteous death and vindicating resurrection.[36] At the same time, his earthly authority has been expanded, hence the commissioning of the disciples. Now, Jesus has initiated the possibility for the fundamental Christian prayer of 6:10 to be fulfilled: "Thy will be done on earth as it is in heaven." He has achieved authority in both realms and his followers can now live in hope for his heavenly authority to one day be manifested throughout the earth. The tension that currently stands between the heavenly and earthly realms (cf. 6:9–10) will be resolved eschatologically. This has been inaugurated by Jesus' resurrection and will be consummated at his Parousia. Additionally, Jesus' authority in both the heavenly and earthly realms now transforms the disciples' mission. Originally, Jesus endowed his disciples with his authority and sent them to preach the kingdom of heaven only to the true people of the land of Israel (10:5–7). After the resurrection, they are re-commissioned to preach to all the nations. "The 'horizontal' universality of the sending out results from the 'vertical' totality of the power of the resurrection"—"in heaven and on earth."[37] As Meier observes in comparing 10:5–6 and 15:24 with 28:18–20, Jesus' previous ministry "was subject to geographical and ethnic restrictions which fall away after the death and resurrection."[38] Finally, we may also observe that the authority given to Jesus in 28:18 likely echoes and grounds the authority given to the church by Jesus as found in 16:19 and 18:18, texts which famously uses the same type of heaven and earth language.[39]

---

[36] This same motif of Jesus' heavenly authority and the disciples' mission is communicated in Luke (Lk 24:50–53; Acts 1:9–11) and the longer ending of Mark (Mk 16:19–20) with the narrative of Jesus' ascension, a story noticeably absent in Matthew. Luke emphasizes that only the exalted Jesus can bestow the Spirit, for which the disciples must wait before embarking on their mission. Similarly, Jesus' ascension into heaven in Mark 16:19 precedes the disciples' sign-attending preaching. Cf. also Paul's statement in Romans 1:4 that Jesus was declared the Son of God through his resurrection.
[37] Schneider, "Im Himmel—auf Erden," 295.
[38] Meier, *The Vision of Matthew*, 31.
[39] This insight comes from Nolland, *Matthew*, 1265.

It is not merely coincidental that Matthew concludes his Gospel with such a statement that exalts Christ and ties together the heaven and earth theme he has peppered throughout the narrative. In fact, many scholars have seen 28:16–20 as a summarizing statement of the entire Gospel.[40] The repetition of the heaven and earth theme in this crucial closing pericope highlights the importance of this rubric.

Weltbild and *Weltanschauung* in Matthew

We may now move from this analysis of the heaven and earth pairs to consider how this theme in Matthew relates to his cosmological framework (*Weltbild*) and theological worldview (*Weltanschauung*). We have already observed the fundamentally bipartite structure of the *Weltbild* and *Weltanschauung* of the OT and how these continue largely intact in the Second Temple literature. When examining Matthew we find the author of the First Gospel continues in this trajectory. His *Weltbild* is still fundamentally two-fold though with some developments, while his *Weltanschauung* consists of a clear oppositional duality.

Regarding Matthew's picture of the physical world, it is difficult to be definitive; the data is limited. There are few clear cosmological statements in Matthew, as with the rest of the NT.[41] Earth (γῆ) occurs forty-three times in this Gospel, sixteen of which are in combination with οὐρανός (37%). As in the OT, γῆ in Matthew reflects the wide semantic flexibility of this term. It can refer to specific peoples' areas such as the land of Israel, Judah and Zebulun (2:6, 20; 4:15; 11:24), more generally to geographic space (9:26, 31; 14:24), or to the ground or soil (10:29; 13:5, 8). Earth can also refer to the physical world (5:18;

---

[40] Especially Otto Michel, "The Conclusion of Matthew's Gospel: A Contribution to the History of the Easter Message," in *The Interpretation of Matthew* (ed. G. Stanton): 30–41. See also below on Genesis and Matthew.

[41] Bietenhard, *Die himmlische Welt*, 257, says that it is impossible to speak of a cosmological worldview of the NT. Mauser, "'Heaven'," 34, observes that "New Testament books exhibit, in contrast to some Jewish and non-Jewish Hellenistic works, a striking disinterest in details of a concept of heaven which are essential to providing a [cosmological] world view." For a discussion of the cosmological views of some NT books in light of Greco-Roman cosmology, see George H. van Kooten, *Cosmic Christology in Paul and the Pauline School: Colossians and Ephesians in the Context of Graeco-Roman Cosmology, with a New Synopsis of the Greek Texts* (Tübingen: Mohr Siebeck, 2003). See also the forthcoming volume which attempts to analyze the cosmological views of each of the NT writers: Jonathan T. Pennington and Sean M. McDonough, eds., *Cosmology and New Testament Theology* (London: T&T Clark, forthcoming 2007).

12:40, 42; 27:45, 51) as well as to the inhabitants and systems of the earth (5:13; 6:10; 17:25), and many times it is difficult to discern between these two. Matthew also occasionally employs the term κόσμος (8–9x), which for him apparently serves as a synonym for earth. It is found either in idiomatic phrases about the "foundation of the world" (13:35; 24:21; 25:34) or most often referring to the inhabited earth (4:8; 5:14; 13:38; 16:26; 26:13).[42]

We also find several references to Hades (2x) and Gehenna (7x). Hades is the Greek equivalent of the general place of the dead, Sheol. Its two occurrences in Matthew are strongly symbolic, both being used as hyperbolic counterpoints to heaven (11:23; 16:18). They do not appear to constitute a distinct cosmological element.[43] This heaven-Hades pairing confirms the semantic overlap of Hades/Sheol and earth, as was argued in the OT section. It is more difficult to analyze the meaning of Gehenna. This word occurs only twelve times in the NT, seven of which are in Matthew. Four of Matthew's occurrences find parallels in the other Gospel traditions. All of them refer to fire and judgment. Additionally, six times Matthew refers to a place of outer darkness and gnashing of teeth (8:12; 13:42, 50; 22:13; 24:51; 25:30). It is not clear whether this refers to the same thing as Gehenna or not, but it seems likely. The language of the fire and sentence of hell/Gehenna certainly reflects a Second Temple period development as compared to the OT. Moreover, their frequency in Matthew bespeaks their importance. However, it is less certain whether Gehenna and these other references should be considered a third part of the cosmological structure. The point of these images is to communicate a future judgment and condemnation. "Outer darkness," "gnashing of teeth," and Gehenna are "symbolic Jewish descriptions of the fate of the ungodly."[44] Nearly every one of the references to Gehenna and the place of gnashing of teeth connect this idea with raging fire. The emphasis is not on a place but on the eschatological judgment to come upon those who do not align themselves with the kingdom of heaven. Thus, it is difficult to know whether Matthew's references to Gehenna are evidence of a different cosmological view or not, but it seems unlikely.

---

[42] There is also one instance of the term οἰκουμένη in 24:14 which appears to be synonymous with κόσμος in 26:13.
[43] The same can be said for the four occurrences of Hades in Revelation. In each case they are put into apposition with and mean simply "death" or the angel of death.
[44] France, *Matthew*, 156. Cf. Filson, *Matthew*, 100; Schnackenburg, Matthew, 83.

Regardless, when Matthew does refer to the created world with anything close to a cosmological statement, he invariably uses the word pair heaven and earth. This occurs three times (5:18; 11:25; 24:35), as has been noted. Moreover, unlike the OT and parts of the NT, Matthew never uses any of the expanded expressions of heaven and earth plus some third element.[45] Even with his proliferation of heaven language and his preference for joining heaven and earth, in no case is this pair expanded to include other cosmological aspects. Notably, references to Gehenna and a place of punishment are in no way connected with his occasional cosmological references. It must be stated that Matthew's purpose, like the rest of the biblical literature, is not to provide information for or speculation upon the physical structure of the world. Even in Genesis 1, the purpose of the cosmological discussion is theological and polemical: the God of Israel, not the Ancient Near Eastern gods, is the creator and master of the world. The biblical writers' understanding of the makeup of the world is rarely stated clearly. Nevertheless, to the extent that we can discern a cosmological view in Matthew, a bipartite structure is most likely. We can tentatively represent this graphically with a chart very similar to that of the OT (see Figure 7.3 above):

| Heavenly Realm |
Astral and Meteorological
Earthly Realm
Land of the Living // Hades/Gehenna

Figure 8.1
Matthew's Physical Cosmology
"Weltbild"

Matthew's ontological/theological cosmology or *Weltanschauung*, on the other hand, is much clearer and much more important. This is not

---

[45] In the NT these expanded expressions occur in varied forms, though still not with great frequency. In Rev 5:3 the threefold description consists of heaven, earth, and under the earth, while 5:13 has a fourfold expression—heaven, earth, under the earth, and on the sea—as does 14:7 with slight variation—heaven, earth, sea, and fountains of water. Phil 2:10 uses the three-fold heaven, earth and under the earth, but with the later and more nuanced terms ἐπουράνιος, ἐπίγειος, and καταχθόνιος. Examples of the more common heaven and earth pairing include Acts 2:19; 1 Cor 8:5; 15:47; Eph 1:10; 3:15; Col 1:16, 20; Heb 1:10; Jms 5:12; 2 Pet 3:5, 7, 10, 13.

surprising in light of the biblical (and human) tendency to articulate one's worldview more clearly than one's cosmological view. The two are interrelated, though rarely do the biblical writers clearly spell out the latter.[46] We have seen how central the pairing of heaven and earth is throughout Matthew. We have also observed that this combination of words is used nearly always with a contrastive sense. Matthew is not merely leaning unconsciously on a Jewish way of referring to the world with "heaven and earth." He is crafting a sharp distinction between two realms: one represented by the earthly world and its unrighteous inhabitants and the other by God.[47] We can portray this with another figure similar to that of the OT (see Figure 7.4 above):

Heavenly Realm (God) Kingdom / Father / Rewards
Earthly Realm (Humanity)

Figure 8.2
Matthew's Ontological/Theological Cosmology
"Weltanschauung"

Those who encounter Jesus face a path which forks in two opposite directions: the upward way of the Father in heaven or the path of this world with its fading and temporary rewards (6:1–21), the world which will in some sense pass away (24:35), and whose people will be judged (cf. judgment parables of chs. 24–25). The ones who practice the radical kingdom ethics of the Sermon on the Mount are those who wisely build their house upon the rock, not on shifting sands (7:24–27). Such drastic dichotomies are frequent throughout the First Gospel. Even as he uses singular and plural οὐρανός to distinguish the earthly and divine realms, *Matthew uses the heaven and earth pair as a rubric to organize and explain this kind of dualistic thinking which is widespread throughout his Gospel.* In this he is not alone, as the preceding literature shows (e.g., Daniel, *1 Enoch*). However, Matthew alone develops and expands this

---

[46] E. C. Lucas, "Cosmology," in *Dictionary of the Old Testament: Pentateuch*, 131.

[47] U. Mauser states it this way: "in some sayings of Jesus the word 'heaven' assumes a strongly antithetical, if not polemical, note since it is directed against deep-seated human convictions and habits which defy the rule of heaven over the earth." Mauser, "'Heaven'," 44.

approach to include how he describes God (as "the Father in heaven"), the kingdom (as "of heaven"), and the relationship between this world and its creator (as "in heaven and on earth"). The proclamation of God's coming is not just the kingdom of God, it is the kingdom of *heaven* (3:2; 4:17; 13:11). The follower of Jesus does not just have God as Father, but as his or her Father *in heaven* (5:16; 6:1; 10:32). The way to practice righteousness (6:1) is described in terms of laying up *heavenly* treasures rather than fading *earthly* rewards (6:19–20). The follower of Jesus should call no one *on earth* his father, but only the *heavenly* Father (23:9). The Christian prayer is for the kingdom of the Father *in heaven* to manifest itself *on earth* (6:9–10). And as the church awaits the kingdom, they are given doctrinal and ecclesial authority *on earth* that receives sanction *from heaven* (16:19; 18:18–19). Over and over again, Jesus' message in Matthew is put into terms of a dualistic heaven and earth contrast.[48] While the heaven and earth theme is certainly not the only one emphasized in this highly skilled and polyvalent narrative, it proves to be both pervasive and foundational for Matthew.[49]

Yet while recognizing the tension that Matthew is regularly emphasizing with the heaven and earth theme, we must not forget that for Matthew, this tension has an eschatological resolution; heaven and earth will not always stand in contrast. Matthew 6:9–10 and 28:18–20 are especially important in showing that the goal of God's redemptive plan in Jesus is not the removal of the earth in the sense of being replaced with a kingdom *in* heaven, but is instead the eschatological reuniting of the heavenly and earthly realms according to the heavenly pattern (6:9–10). While Jesus does say somewhat cryptically that "heaven and earth will pass away" (24:35), he also speaks of the new genesis (παλιγγενεσία) to come at the end of God's redemptive work (19:28). These two statements can be related together by understanding that there will be some type of purging of the earthly realm (cf. 24:29) with the goal of a new creation, *not* a non-earthly, heavenly kingdom. In this way, the current contrast between heaven and earth will cease. Significantly, it is through Jesus' resurrection that he stands as the One

---

[48] For the use of such patterns of repetition, particularly strong in Matthew, see Lohr, "Oral Techniques," and Janice C. Anderson, *Matthew's Narrative Web: Over, and Over, and Over Again* (Sheffield: Sheffield Academic Press, 1994).

[49] We may also mention several texts in which Matthew directly contrasts God with humanity without using any form of the heaven and earth pairs. For example, 16:23; 19:26; 22:21.

now with authority in heaven and on earth (28:18) who will, at his Second Coming, consummate the heaven and earth relationship: the kingdom of heaven will come to earth.

MATTHEW AND GENESIS: A "BIBLICAL-THEOLOGICAL" FUNCTION OF THE HEAVEN AND EARTH THEME

The preceding study which highlights the prominence and importance of the heaven and earth pairs enables us to see that Matthew also uses these couplets for a biblical-theological purpose: to clearly connect his Gospel with the book of Genesis, showing Jesus to be the culmination of God's redemptive purposes.

Matthew did not write a second volume as Luke apparently felt the need to do. There is a comprehensiveness and finality to the feel of the Gospel of Matthew. From the opening genealogy to the universal mandate of the closing, and with large blocks of teaching on the law, the nature of the kingdom, and the eschaton, Matthew proffers an all-inclusive memorandum about Jesus. It has long been recognized that the Prologue to the Gospel of John sets the Fourth Gospel up as a complementary counterpart to the OT and Genesis in particular. A similar argument can be made for Mark's opening Ἀρχὴ τοῦ εὐαγγελίου Ἰησοῦ Χριστοῦ. In light of Matthew's apparently grand plan for his Gospel and the centrality of the book of Genesis in the Jewish mind, it is very probable that Matthew likewise intended his book to serve as a bookend or *inclusio* with the first book of the Hebrew Bible.[50] The importance of Matt 1:1 as an indicator of the "New Genesis" theme in Matthew has been argued by a number of students dating as far back as Jerome and including major scholars such as Theodore Zahn and Davies and Allison. However, scholars have not recognized that the heaven and earth theme so prominent in Matthew likewise provides strong evidence for an intentional Genesis connection throughout Matthew.

---

[50] Gundry, *Matthew*, 13, states that by Matthew's borrowing and tweaking of the language of Genesis 1:1, 2:4, and 5:1, he "portray[s] Jesus as the goal and fulfillment of the OT." We may also observe that in addition to the connections with Genesis (in contrast with John), Matthew goes on to use the genealogy to review the whole OT history from Abraham onwards, thereby making an inclusio with not only Genesis but also the entire OT.

Matthew's use of the OT in general is recognized as being "more thoroughgoing than that of the other Synoptic Gospels," with well over sixty explicit and implicit quotations and allusions.[51] Compared to the Synoptics, Matthew includes all of the OT citations from parallel passages in Mark and Q and expands upon them. Numerous studies on Matthew's frequent "formula quotations" have been undertaken, in addition to investigations into the influence of specific OT books and motifs on Matthew.[52] The importance of the OT for Matthew cannot be overstated. Graham Stanton sums it up this way: "The OT is woven into the warp and woof of this gospel; the evangelist uses Scripture to underline some of his most prominent and distinctive theological concerns."[53]

Many of the studies of the OT's influence on Matthew have unearthed the importance of the prophetic literature on the First Gospel,[54] but not a great deal has been done on Matthew's connection with Genesis. The suggestion that Matthew's form mimics the Pentateuch as a whole was famously argued by Bacon, but has been much disputed since. A few other studies have uncovered typological connections between Genesis-Exodus and Matthew.[55] But the importance of Genesis in particular has not attracted much attention apart from the discussion of the connection of Matthew 1:1 with the opening of Genesis. On this note, Davies and Allison make a lengthy and compelling argument for understanding the opening verse of Matthew as a preface to the whole book—one which communicates a complement to the Genesis story, a "new creation."[56] Matthew begins with the words βίβλος γενέσεως "in

---

[51] Richard Beaton, *Isaiah's Christ in Matthew's Gospel* (Cambridge: Cambridge University Press, 2002), 17, referring to the works of M. D. Goulder and D. Senior.

[52] Examples include Stendahl, *The School of St Matthew*; Gundry, *The Use of the Old Testament in St Matthew's Gospel*; Goulder, *Midrash and Lexicon*; Beaton, *Isaiah's Christ*; Michael Knowles, *Jeremiah in Matthew's Gospel: The Rejected Prophet Motif in Matthaean Redaction* (Sheffield: Sheffield Academic, 1993).

[53] Stanton, *A Gospel for a New People*, 346.

[54] In addition to several of the works already cited, a number of articles can be consulted, including Adrian Leske, "Isaiah and Matthew: The Prophetic Influence in the First Gospel; A Report on Current Research," in *Jesus and the Suffering Servant: Isaiah 53 and Christian Origins* (ed. W. H. Bellinger, Jr and W. R. Farmer; Harrisburg, Penn.: Trinity Press, 1998): 152–169.

[55] Dale Allison's *The New Moses*, provides a full-length treatment of this theme. Additionally, Michael Goulder uses the Genesis and Exodus allusions in Matthew 1–5 as an example of justified typological interpretation: Michael D. Goulder, *Type and History in Acts* (London: SPCK, 1964), 1–13. A helpful review and interaction with Goulder can be found in one of the appendices to Allison's *The New Moses*: 307–311.

[56] Davies and Allison, *Matthew* 1:150–154. They list several other scholars who likewise interpret Matt 1:1 this way: Zahn, Klostermann, Schniewind, Bonnard, Gaechter, Grundmann, Frankemölle, and Waetjen.

order to draw a parallel between one beginning and another beginning, between the creation of the cosmos and Adam and Eve on the one hand and the new creation brought by the Messiah on the other."[57] The reasons given for this interpretation are very persuasive.[58]

More recently, the Matthean scholar Warren Carter has similarly argued that the phrase βίβλος γενέσεως in Matthew 1:1 evokes for the reader not just the name of the Book of Genesis in the LXX and the references in Gen 2:4 and 5:1, but also "the larger Genesis accounts of which they are a part."[59] Leaning on John Foley's work on "traditional referentiality" and how a partial citation evokes a well-known larger text,[60] Carter suggests that Matthew intentionally alludes to Genesis to call to mind "the story of God's creative and sovereign purposes for the whole world as the initial context for hearing the story of Jesus."[61] Although Carter does not use this term, this could also be called typology.[62]

Matthean scholars have also recognized a few other connections with Genesis. There are the obvious quotations in Matthew 19:4-5 and 22:24. Additionally, the work of the Holy Spirit in 1:18-20 and 3:16 harkens back to the Spirit's activity at creation. Reference to the beloved son in 3:17 recalls Isaac, the son Abraham loves in Gen 22. References to Abraham also appear several times in Matthew (1:1-2; 3:9; 8:11;

---

[57] Davies and Allison, *Matthew*, 1:150. More recently, Dale Allison has revisited this issue in a short essay "Matthew's First Two Words" in his collection of essays, *Studies in Matthew: Interpretation Past and Present* (Grand Rapids: Baker, 2005): 157-162. In addition to citing many sources who understand Matt 1:1 as referring to Genesis, Allison points out that Ulrich Luz himself has changed his mind in this regard between the first and second editions of his commentary. Instead of translating Matthew's opening words as "Urkunde des Ursprungs' Jesu Christi," Luz now glosses the phrase as "Buch der 'Genesis' Jesu Christi."

[58] In a newly revised commentary, Frederick Dale Bruner also finds Davies and Allison's interpretation here persuasive, yet goes on to suggest that Matthew may have intended the reference to "genesis" to be multivalent—referring both to the first book of the Pentateuch as well as the genealogy, the first few chapters of Matthew, and the whole Gospel. F. D. Bruner, *Matthew 1-12: The Christbook* (rev. ed.; Grand Rapids: Eerdmans, 2004), 4.

[59] Warren Carter, "Matthew and the Gentiles: Individual Conversion and/or Systemic Transformation," *JSNT* 26.3 (2004), 262.

[60] John M. Foley, *Immanent Art: From Structure to Meaning in Traditional Oral Epic* (Bloomington: Indiana University Press, 1991). See also Warren Carter, "Evoking Isaiah: Matthean Soteriology and an Intertextual Reading of Isaiah 7-9 in Matthew 1:23 and 4:15-16," *JBL* 119 (2000): 503-520.

[61] Carter, "Matthew and the Gentiles," 262.

[62] See Goulder, *Type and History in Acts*, 1-13.

22:32) as do Sodom (10:15) and "the days of Noah" (24:37). Also significant is the three-fold allusion to the Cain and Abel story (Gen 4:1–16) in Matthew (5:21–25; 18:21–22; 23:34–36).[63] The uncommon word παλιγγενεσία in 19:28 connects with Genesis and affirms a new creation eschatological outlook. One may also see a probable allusion to the pre-creation darkness of Gen 1:2 in Matt 27:54, where the whole earth/land is covered with darkness at Jesus' death.[64] There is also a strong link in 28:18–19, completing the mention of Abraham in 1:1—now "all the nations" shall be blessed in him (see below).[65] The NA27 appendix of references lists four quotations and 23 allusions, the latter of which vary in strength. Thus, we can see that from Matthew 1:1 on, Genesis is referred to and alluded to throughout the First Gospel.

My point is that in the same way that these assorted quotes and allusions would trigger "Genesis" in the mind of the first-century readers, so too would Matthew's frequent heaven and earth refrain. Stanton rejects Davies and Allison's "new genesis" interpretation of Matthew 1:1 because he does not see sufficient evidence for this theme in Matthew (though he acknowledges this theological connection in Paul and John).[66] However, recognition of the frequent Genesis-evoking heaven and earth language throughout Matthew provides additional, strong support for this view. In other words, one of the important purposes of Matthew's developed heaven and earth theme is to make a close intertextual connection between his Gospel and the book of Genesis.

The closing and climactic pericope of Matthew (28:16–20) serves as a capstone for this intentional connection with Genesis.[67] Many schol-

---

[63] The words "the blood of Abel the just" in Matt 23:35 make this connection explicit. The other two passages in Matthew are thick allusions to Gen 4:1–16 as Dale Allison ably points out in his essay, "Murder and Anger, Cain and Abel (Matt. 5:21–25)," in *Studies in Matthew*: 65–78.

[64] W. D. Davies, *The Setting of the Sermon on the Mount*, 84. See also Allison's essay "Darkness at Noon," in his *Studies in Matthew*, 83–84.

[65] Davies and Allison, *Matthew*, 1:154; 3:683.

[66] Stanton, *A Gospel for a New People*, 13.

[67] This important text in Matthew likely serves several intertextual purposes. In addition to connecting to Genesis, it is widely recognized that Matt 28:16–20 also refers to Dan 7:13. Additionally, a good argument can also be made for a connection between Matt 28:16–20 and 2 Chron 36:23 (canonically, the last verse of the Hebrew Bible): "Thus says Cyrus king of Persia, 'The LORD, the God of heaven, has given me all the kingdoms of the earth, and he has charged me to build him a house at Jerusalem, which is in Judah. Whoever is among you of all his people, may the LORD his God be with him. Let him go up.'" Cf. B. J. Malina, "The Literary Structure and Form of Matt. 28:16–20," *NTS* 17 (1970): 87–103; Schnackenburg, *Matthew* 297.

ars have recognized that the final pericope in Matthew sums up and restates the purpose of his Gospel.[68] I have suggested above that this passage also provides a fitting culmination for the heaven and earth theme throughout Matthew. Combining these insights, we can observe a number of ways in which this passage highlights the intertextual connection with Genesis, forming an *inclusio* with Genesis at the beginning and Matthew at the end. As shown above, Matthew 1:1 makes an explicit reference to Genesis with its opening words, βίβλος γενέσεως. The prominence of heaven and earth in Genesis 1:1 (and beyond) connects with the heaven and earth theme throughout Matthew, with its climax in 28:18. In this way, an *inclusio* is formed between Genesis 1:1 and Matthew 28:16–20, with a strong pointer of this as Matthew's intention in Matthew 1:1.[69] It is also very significant that the final five words of Matthew (ἕως τῆς συντελείας τοῦ αἰῶνος) likewise show his book-ending intentions. Reference to the "the end of the age" seems clearly to form an *inclusio* with both Matt 1:1 and Gen 1:1, spanning from the creation to the end.

Matthew 1:1 also highlights the role of Abraham, as does 28:19 with its reference to the Gospel going forth to "all nations."[70] This clearly alludes to Genesis 11–12 and the introduction of Abraham as the one through whom God will bless "all the nations of the earth" (12:2–3). This connection is very significant because in Genesis God's authority as creator over heaven and earth (Gen 1–2) is the basis for his redemptive purpose for all the nations, worked out through the person of Abraham (Gen 12 and beyond). Matthew's structure shows sensitivity to this redemptive narrative, with its strong theme of heaven and earth

---

[68] For example, Davies and Allison, *Matthew*, 1:154, call 28:16–20 "a fitting capstone to the entire gospel, containing within itself the message of Matthew in miniature." Hagner, *Matthew*, 881, says that these words "distill the outlook and various emphases of the Gospel." Schnackenburg, *Matthew*, 297, calls the text "the climax of the Matthean conception of salvation history." Luz, *The Theology of the Gospel of Matthew*, 5, likens this passage to "a large terminal railway station in which many lines converge" (p. 5). Others with similar sentiments include O. Michel, W. Trilling, P. F. Ellis, B. J. Malina, and O. S. Brooks.

[69] The probable connection between Matt 28:16–20 and 2 Chron 36:23 provides further evidence for Matthew's intentional connection here. Canonically, 2 Chron 36:23, with its conjoining of heaven and earth—"God of heaven...kingdoms of the earth"—itself forms an inclusio with Gen 1:1 that spans the entire Hebrew Bible. I suggest that Matthew parallels this structure by alluding to Gen 1:1 in its opening verse and 2 Chron 36:23 (as well as Genesis) in its closing verses.

[70] Abraham appears in several important passages in Matthew, including 1:17; 3:9; 8:11; and 22:32.

throughout, culminating in Jesus' own authority over heaven and earth (God's prerogative in Gen 1:1) *with the result that* his disciples may go and bring the blessings of the gospel to all nations—the purpose and zenith of the process begun in Genesis 1–12.

Therefore, in light of all the previous discussion, there is good reason to believe that Matthew interwove his Gospel with the heaven and earth theme and structured his narrative in such a way as to show the consummation of God's redemptive work in Christ. He uses the familiar and foundational language of heaven and earth found in Genesis 1:1 and beyond to connect his own Gospel with the larger narrative of Genesis, thereby proclaiming that Jesus is the One in whom God's foundational purposes are consummated.[71]

Summary and Conclusion

In the previous chapter we examined heaven and earth in the OT and proceeded to argue for a fundamentally bipartite cosmological and theological worldview there. This worldview, expressed so often with the heaven and earth word pair, continues into the Second Temple literature. Consequently, it provides fertile soil for Jesus' and Matthew's message. In Jesus' teaching as presented by Matthew, the language of heaven and earth is very frequent and often serves to point out the contrast or tension that now exists between the realms of heaven and earth.

The bipartite *Weltbild* and *Weltanschauung* of the OT and Second Temple literature continue by and large intact in Matthew. The strong connection Matthew makes with Genesis through the recurrent use of heaven and earth language manifests his indebtedness to the OT traditions, while at the same time, his emphasis on the antithesis between God and humanity in a dualistic way shows his focus on the tension between the two realms as well as the eschatological goal of their reunification (cf. 6:9–10; 28:18).

There are yet two more aspects of Matthew's idiolectic use of heaven language through which he continues to express this fundamental heaven and earth contrast. In the following chapters we will examine both of these: the Father in heaven and the kingdom of heaven.

---

[71] Note again the discussion in Chapter Four about how the heaven and earth theme in Matthew serves his high Christological view: Jesus is regularly identified on the heaven side of the heaven-earth equation and participates in the uniquely divine prerogative of heavenly and earthly authority.

CHAPTER NINE

GOD AS FATHER IN THE OLD TESTAMENT AND SECOND TEMPLE LITERATURE

Continuing to examine the varied ways in which Matthew emphasizes the heaven and earth theme, we may now turn to a discussion of God as heavenly Father, which constitutes the third element in Matthew's idiolectic use of heaven. Before observing how this subject is fleshed out in the First Gospel, it will be helpful to survey the Jewish literary context for the idea of God as Father and specifically as a heavenly Father. This chapter serves this purpose, seeking to discover literary precedents and potential contemporary usage for Matthew's terminology.

After surveying the relevant Jewish literature from the OT through the Mishnah, we will also consider the question of whether Jesus' usage of God as Father is in continuity or discontinuity with his own tradition and setting. This will then set the stage in the subsequent chapter for the more specific study of the use of heavenly Father in Matthew.

GOD AS FATHER IN JEWISH LITERATURE

Old Testament

As is typical when analyzing many OT lexemes, we find that the common Hebrew word for father, אָב, is widespread not only in the OT, but also in cognate forms in a variety of Ancient Near Eastern languages.[1] As in these other languages, the usage of אָב in the OT is variegated; the term is used in different contexts with a variety of meanings including biological father or grandfather, the founder of a certain tribe or tradition, a respected elder or counselor, or more generally, ancestors. Across its semantic range, the father in ancient Israelite culture was a person in whom kinship and authority were centralized.

Compared to its frequency in early Judaism and Christianity, the application of the term father to God in the OT is quite rare.[2] Examples

---

[1] Cf. H. Ringren, "אָב" in *TDOT*, 1:1–7.
[2] Note that this fact does not necessitate the older, common view that there is therefore

include Deut 32:4–6, Isa 63:16, 64:8, Jer 31:9, and the LXX rendering of 1 Chron 29:10,³ each of which refers to Yahweh as the Father of Israel.⁴ In a few other instances God is compared to a father, as in Ps 103:13 and Prov 3:12. But of course, the word father does not have to appear explicitly to communicate the idea of the fatherhood of God. This concept is also conveyed in a number of implicit ways, such as the notion that God has begotten the people of Israel (Deut 32:18), that Israel is God's Son (Exod 4:22–23; Jer 3:19; Hos 11:1, 3), and that God will give to Israel a first-born son type of inheritance (Exod 32:13; Deut 1:38; 1 Kgs 8:36; Isa 61:7–9)—in fact, at times Israel is itself described as God's inheritance (1 Sam 10:1; 1 Kgs 8:53; Zech 2:12).⁵ Another way that the fatherhood of God is expressed in the OT is through the notion that the king of Israel is directly God's son. Comparable to other Ancient Near Eastern views, God promises in 2 Samuel 7:12–14 to relate to the line of Davidic kings as a father relates to a son. As Thompson describes it: "There is a mutuality between God and the king of Israel which can be expressed in terms of the father/son dyad."⁶

Apocryphal, Pseudepigraphal and Other Second Temple Literature

When we move from the canonical OT documents into the apocryphal and pseudepigraphal literature, we can observe that references to God

---

a great gulf in the conception of God between the Old and New Testaments. As Marianne Meye Thompson rightly observes: "The scarcity of the term as over against the New Testament does not signal radical discontinuity with the presentation of God in the Old Testament." M. M. Thompson, *The Promise of the Father: Jesus and God in the New Testament* (Louisville: Westminster John Knox, 2000), 39. On the question of continuity and discontinuity of the idea of God as Father, see the final section of this chapter.

³ In 1 Chron 29:10, the MT reads "O Lord God of Israel our father." In the LXX this appears in the slightly altered "O Lord God of Israel, our Father." Whether this was an intentional change (cf. some Targumic material), a misreading, or represents a different *Vorlage* is uncertain, but the first option seems most likely.

⁴ Hamerton-Kelly lists eleven places in the OT where God is designated "Father." Robert Hamerton-Kelly, *God the Father: Theology and Patriarchy in the Teaching of Jesus* (Philadelphia: Fortress, 1979), 20. Jeremias offers fifteen instances. Joachim Jeremias, *The Prayers of Jesus* (London: SCM Press, 1967), 12. For a more recent discussion of the OT background to God as father see Diane G. Chen, *God as Father in Luke-Acts* (New York: Peter Lang, 2006), 73–111.

⁵ Thompson, *The Promise of the Father*, 40–44. See also the discussion of various metaphors related to God's fatherhood in Willem VanGemeren, "Abba in the Old Testament?" *JETS* 31/4 (1988), 390–398.

⁶ Thompson, *The Promise of the Father*, 80.

as father seem to appear with greater regularity,[7] though this appellation still cannot be described as frequent. Of course, we are dealing here with a sundry collection of documents from a wide variety of provenances, and it is likely that a range of concepts of divine fatherhood existed. Nevertheless, it is beneficial to comment on the occurrences and meaning of these references in this corpus.

The designation of God as Father can be found in a number of apocryphal and pseudepigraphal texts as well as in a few documents from Qumran.[8] God is called Father and called upon as Father, often emphasizing his lordship/authority as well as his mercy as the great Father.[9] Often this address is used in cries for help and prayers of repentance. So, for example, Aseneth as a convert to Judaism asks God to be her father: "you, Lord, are a sweet and good and gentle Father" (*Joseph and Aseneth* 12:14-15) and Tobit announces with gratitude that "he is our God and Lord, he is our Father forever" (Tobit 13:4). These are but a few examples of many such intimate declarations. Father is never the primary way that God is addressed in these documents, but in at least one text, the *Testament of Job*, it plays an important role.[10]

We can observe in these texts that at times God is spoken of as the Father of an individual, but at other times the uses instead refer to God as the Father of the nation of Israel. These latter, corporate uses are more in line with the OT occurrences than the former, individual ones. Older scholars such as Dalman and Jeremias made a sharp distinction between these references as to whether they were found in "Palestinian" or "Hellenistic" sources. Thus, Dalman suggests that in the Hellenistic literature God is often referred to as one's individual Father, while in the Palestinian documents the Israelites as a whole are in view, "an idea which implies the love that God bears, in a special sense, to His own people in distinction from other peoples."[11] Similarly, Jeremias contrasts

---

[7] Contra Jeremias, *Prayers*, 15, who finds "amazingly few" instances before the NT period. But Jeremias has needlessly made a sharp distinction between "Palestinian" and "Hellenistic" texts and thereby disregarded several documents.

[8] Tob 13:4; Wis 2:16; 11:10; 14:3; Sir 23:1, 4; 51:10; *3 Macc.* 2:21; 5:7; 6:3, 8; 7:6; *Jub.* 1:25, 28; 19:29; *Jos. Asen.* 12:8-15; *Test. Job* 33:3, 9; 40:2; *Test. Abr.* 6:6; 20:12; *Apocr. Ezek.* fragment 2; 1QH 9, 35; 4Q379 6 1,1-7; 4Q382 55 2,1-9; 4Q460 5 1,5.

[9] Thompson, *The Promise of the Father*, 49.

[10] See Bruce Chilton, "God as 'Father' in the Targumim, in Non-Canonical Literatures of Early Judaism and Primitive Christianity, and in Matthew," in Charlesworth and Evans, eds., *The Pseudepigrapha and Early Biblical Interpretation*, 160-162.

[11] Dalman, *Words of Jesus*, 185.

the Hellenistic view with the Palestinian by saying the former tends to be "subjective" and "sentimental"—not apparently a positive thing as far as Jeremias is concerned.[12] It is accurate to observe that there are different senses of God as Father in the various documents, but making a distinction based on the supposed discrete provenances and viewpoints of these documents does not prove valid. For example, *both* senses are found in several texts, including Wisdom of Solomon, *Jubilees*, and *3 Maccabees*. This corporate versus individual distinction will play an important role in the question of whether or not Jesus' view was continuous with his contemporaries', as will be discussed below.

One very important observation to make about all the texts being discussed here is that when they do refer to God as Father (whether corporately or individually), this generally applies only to the people of Israel and not to all of creation. Even in documents which emphasize God's creation of all the world, such as Sirach, we do not find a corresponding universalizing of God's fatherhood to all peoples.[13] This corresponds with OT usage, but stands in noticeable contrast to the concept of divine fatherhood in both Josephus and Philo. In these two writers, God's fatherhood is expressed in terms very similar to those of Greek literature, where Zeus is characterized as the father of all gods and humans. God's fatherhood is linked directly with him as creator. For Josephus, God is the "father and source of the universe...creator of things human and divine" (*Ant.* 7.380). Similarly, Philo depicts God as the sole uncreated being who is often described as the father of all humans.[14] These emphases are not surprising in light of long-recognized correlations between Philo and Josephus and Hellenistic philosophical views, but again, they stand in distinction from the OT and most other Second Temple usage.

Targumic and Rabbinic Materials

An examination of the Targumic and rabbinic literature reveals yet another level of increased reference to God as Father. Thus, G. F. Moore states that "in the rabbinical literature the paternal-filial relation between

---

[12] Jeremias, *Prayers*, 23.
[13] Gottlob Schrenk, *TDNT*, s.v., πατήρ, 5:978–979; Thompson, *The Promise of the Father*, 51. Cf. also Alon Goshen-Gottstein, "God the Father in Rabbinic Judaism and Christianity: Transformed Background or Common Ground?," *Journal of Ecumenical Studies* 38/4 (2001), 475.
[14] E.g., *Spec.* 2.197; *Opif.* 74–77; *Mut.* 29; *Cher.* 49.

God and man is a common theme,"[15] and according to Bruce Chilton, "the Targumim reflect a rich conceptual development of God as 'father'."[16]

Regarding the Targums, Chilton focuses his analysis on the Pentateuch, and specifically on the *Neofiti*, *Fragmentary*, and *Pseudo-Jonathan* recensions rather than the *Onqelos*, the latter of which is most literal and therefore gives the least insights into theological developments.[17] He does not do more than mention the Targums of the Prophets because, he states, the fatherhood of God theme is much less evident there.[18] Martin McNamara is stronger in his judgment, observing that while there is clearly a tendency toward divine fatherhood in the Palestinian Targums of the Pentateuch, in the Targums to the Prophets there is in fact an intentional avoidance of this designation.[19]

In either judgment, there is at least evidence in the Pentateuch for the trend toward viewing God as the Father of Israel.[20] For example, in *Neofiti* Exodus 1:19, the Jewish midwives are said to "pray before their father in heaven." Similarly, *Neofiti* Numbers 20:21 says that the Israelites "were ordered by their father in heaven" not to attack the Edomites. Chilton is careful to point that in several instances, the readings cited are disputed or marginal notes. Nevertheless, there is still enough evidence to posit "a rich conceptual development of God as 'father'" in the Targums.[21]

Moving beyond the Targums into the rabbinic literature, we find a much greater proliferation of the term Father as applied to God. Scholars such as Moore and Dalman amassed many of these references to God as Father in the assorted documents of rabbinica from the Tannaitic period.[22] Their collections reveal how widespread this way of

---

[15] George Foot Moore, *Judaism in the First Centuries of the Christian Era: The Age of the Tannaim* (2 vols.; Cambridge: Harvard University Press, 1927), 2:203.

[16] Chilton, "God as 'Father'," 160.

[17] Chilton, "God as 'Father'," 155–156.

[18] Chilton, "God as 'Father'," 155, n. 14. Chilton comments that there appears to be a more circumspect approach to God's fatherhood in the prophetic Targums, at least in the Targumim to Isaiah.

[19] McNamara, *Targum and Testament: Aramaic Paraphrases of the Hebrew Bible: A Light on the New Testament* (Shannon: Irish University Press, 1972), 115–116.

[20] McNamara counts around eighteen such references across the various versions of the Pentateuch.

[21] Chilton, "God as 'Father'," 158, 160.

[22] Moore, *Judaism in the First Centuries*, 2:203–211. Dalman, *Words*, 184–189. More recent is the lengthy evalution by Goshen-Gottstein, "God the Father in Rabbinic Judaism and Christianity."

conceiving God became, attested first in rabbinic sayings of the first-century CE and increasing throughout the subsequent literature.[23] We also find its use in liturgical language such as the well-known prayer, the *Qaddish*: "may the prayers and tears of all Israel be accepted before their heavenly Father!"[24] Most commonly, the rabbinic literature attaches to God's fatherhood the adjective "heavenly." This development and its significance will be noted below.

The Meaning of the Fatherhood of God

One of the well-recognized dangers of reading ancient texts is the importing of assumptions that the modern reader brings to the documents regarding the meaning of particular words and concepts. The fatherhood of God is no exception. Modern readers inevitably have their own preconceived notions as to what "fatherhood" entails and these are often unconsciously applied to the idea of God as Father in Scripture. But these impressions do not necessarily align with the use and function of divine fatherhood language in the Jewish literature. It is imperative that we attempt to derive our notion of divine fatherhood from a close reading of the primary texts.

Various scholars who have analyzed these texts offer their own analysis of what exactly is being communicated when the Jewish people refer to God as their Father. Thompson, for example, demarcates three aspects which, she argues, would have been assumptions about a father in Israelite society and therefore shed light on the OT references to God as Father. These are that a father (1) is the source or origin of a family or clan, who provides an inheritance to his children; (2) protects and provides for his children; and (3) is due obedience and honor, and children who disobey are corrected or disciplined.[25] Each of these aspects is then identified in the texts which refer to God as Father. Mary D'Angelo also attempts to sum up the varied uses and identifies three ways in which these texts use divine fatherhood language: (1) to designate God as the refuge of the afflicted and persecuted; (2) to accompany a petition for or an assurance of forgiveness; and (3) to evoke the power and

---

[23] Representative examples include *m. Ber.* 5:1; *m. Sot.* 9:15; *m. Abot* 3:14; *b. Sot.* 49b; *b. Pes.* 112a; *Mek.* Beshallah 4; *Sifre* Deut 48.

[24] Translation from Dalman, *Words*, 187.

[25] Thompson, *The Promise of the Father*, 39. Thompson argues that these three aspects continue largely intact throughout the Second Temple literature and into Jesus' usage.

providence that govern the world.[26] Jeremias identifies only two convictions which stand behind the divine fatherhood idea.[27] Bruce Chilton proffers a total of five uses for God as Father in the Pseudepigrapha and Targums, many of which overlap with D'Angelo's.[28]

These helpful but mixed interpretations show that there is in fact a wide range of uses of divine fatherhood language and the assorted nuances defy airtight categorization. Inevitably, each scholar highlights certain texts which correspond with his or her proposed emphases to the neglect of others. None of the categorizations proves conclusive or comprehensive.

From these studies, however, we can make a few confident observations. There is in the Jewish appropriation of God as Father a primary focus on God as the Father of the Jews, not of all humanity as in Philo and Josephus, nor the universal Fatherhood of God which was popularized by 19th-century liberalism. Secondly, within this notion, God is the Father not only of the Israelites as a corporate people, but also as the father of individual, pious Jews; God's fatherhood is both corporate and individual. And finally, we do find that God as Father is frequently and increasingly connected with the idea of God as king. The rabbinic and liturgical writings are full of examples of this close connection, such as in the ancient prayer, Ahabah Rabbah: "Our Father, our King."[29] This common concatenation of images, which to the modern reader may seem disjointed, is informative of the Jewish notion of both divine fatherhood and divine kingship. As Thompson observes, these images reinforce each other. "Both are figures of authority; and both are figures of grace."[30] This combination is also obviously very relevant for our understanding of Jesus' own usage, such as in the Lord's Prayer.

The Father in Heaven in Jewish Literature

We have noted that in the rabbinic literature in particular God is often referred to not only as Father, but specifically as a heavenly Father or

---

[26] Mary Rose D'Angelo, "*Abba* and 'Father': Imperial Theology and the Jesus Traditions," *JBL* 111/4 (1992), 621.
[27] Jeremias, *Prayers*, 18–19.
[28] Chilton, "God as 'Father'," 166.
[29] Moore, *Judaism in the First Centuries*, 2:209–210, gives an impressive two pages of examples. Cf. also 3 Macc 6:2–4; Geza Vermes, *Jesus in His Jewish Context* (Minneapolis: Fortress, 2003), 29; Goshen-Gottstein, "God the Father in Rabbinic Judaism and Christianity," 489–490.
[30] Thompson, *The Promise of the Father*, 76.

the Father in heaven. Alon Goshen-Gottstein states that this epithet for God occurs around 100 times throughout the entire rabbinic corpus.[31] This way of referring to God deserves special note because of its great frequency in Matthew (20x) as well as the literature nearly contemporaneous with him.

The connecting of the notion of heaven specifically with God as Father apparently developed in the first-century CE and became especially prominent in mainstream rabbinic usage.[32] In fact, no occurrences of heavenly Father or Father in heaven are found in the OT nor in the Apocrypha or pre-Christian apocalyptic or pseudepigraphal literature. Even in the NT, apart from Matthew, God is only rarely referred to this way.[33] From textual evidence such as Matthew and the Targums, this way of referring to God was apparently current sometime in the first century CE. Frequent recurrence in the rabbinic literature shows that it became quite common in the second- through fourth-centuries. In addition to addressing God as heavenly Father in prayer, we also regularly find expressions such as "before the Father in heaven" and "the will of the heavenly Father."

The Targumic literature provides several examples of this way of referring to God. McNamara's analysis, referred to above, finds a total of thirteen occurrences of Father in heaven in the Palestinian Targums of the Pentateuch.[34] These amount to most of the eighteen or so references to God as Father in general in these documents. In the rabbinic materials, the situation is similar if not even more weighted toward Father in heaven references. Thus, in both the rabbinic literature and the Targums, when God is referred to as Father it is most often with the added description of "in heaven." In the Targum of Pseudo-Jonathan to Leviticus 22:28 we find the most direct parallel to Jesus' words: "My people, children of Israel, as our Father is merciful in heaven so shall you be merciful on earth" (cp. Mt 5:48; Lk 6:36).[35]

---

[31] Goshen-Gottstein, "God the Father in Rabbinic Judaism and Christianity," 477.

[32] For example, *Mek.* Exod. 12:2; *b. Sanh.* 42a; *m. Sot.* 9:15; *Sifre* Deut 48. For fuller lists, see *inter alia*, Dalman, *Words*, 186–189. See also discussion in Chen, *God as Father in Luke-Acts*: 113–143.

[33] On the two similar expressions in Mark 11:25 and Luke 11:13, see Chapter Three.

[34] McNamara, *Targum and Testament*, 118.

[35] Quoted in McNamara, *Targum and Testament*, 118. Yet McNamara is careful to point out the textual variances and uncertainties of this reading in the Targums. Nevertheless, he concludes it is a helpful parallel.

It is also noteworthy that in both the Targums and the rabbinic materials, the expression Father in heaven is always prefaced with a personal pronoun, whether it be "our," "your," "his," etc. and never simply as "*the* Father in heaven."[36]

In light of its great frequency, we may inquire what the meaning of this description was. What was added or emphasized by calling God a Father *in heaven* and not merely a Father?

While no one to my knowledge has dealt in depth with this question, a number of scholars have made passing suggestions. For example, G. F. Moore states that in the addition of heaven to Father there is no suggestion of remoteness, but instead it "remove[s] the ambiguity of the bare word 'father' by thus distinguishing between God and an earthly father."[37] This explicit heavenly versus earthly father contrast can be seen in several texts, including *Sifre* Deuteronomy 48, which declares that a wise son not only makes his earthly father glad but also his heavenly Father.[38] Additionally, Moore suggests that the use of "my heavenly Father" and "our heavenly Father" rather than "*the* heavenly Father" was intentional because the latter might be read to express God's fatherly relation to the entire universe (cf. Philo) rather than particularly to the Jews.[39]

G. Schrenk follows both of these observations but adds to them the suggestion that the use of heaven, which comes into usage particularly after 70 CE, is well suited to emphasize that "what is in heaven can now serve as a true substitute for what is destroyed on earth [i.e., the Temple]."[40] He acknowledges that this emphasis is not found consistently, but that in a situation of political bondage on earth, this expression would certainly provide consolation as the persecuted look to their Father in the heavenly world.

All of these suggestions seem sound. In support of Schrenk's final suggestion, we may also observe that it was common in contemporary Greco-Roman practice to refer to the Roman emperor as the *pater* of the empire, the *pater patriae*.[41] This adds credence to the idea that the Jewish people (and the early Christians) would use this terminology to

---

[36] Moore, *Judaism in the First Centuries*, 2:204.
[37] Moore, *Judaism in the First Centuries*, 2:205.
[38] This is also the understanding of Ephraim Urbach, *The Sages*, 1:61.
[39] Moore, *Judaism in the First Centuries*, 2:204.
[40] *TDNT*, 5:980.
[41] Cf. the brief but helpful discussion in D'Angelo, "*Abba* and 'Father'," 623.

posit an alternative, *true* Father—their God—in heaven, in the stead of the emperor on the earth.[42] To refer to God as the heavenly Father highlights this distinction.

However, we must not look only to the Roman Empire situation to understand this kind of conceptual usage. I would suggest that we find a comparable development in the earlier, post-Exilic situation with the phrase "God of heaven." As has been observed, this expression served at least in part to highlight the Jewish God's universal sovereignty—he is the God who is up above in the heavens, above all other gods. It very well may be that Father in heaven is a later adaptation for the same purpose. Here, in its later manifestation, the favorite contemporary appellation "Father" is used in the stead of "God" but with the same rhetorical effect; the God of heaven becomes the Father in heaven. And the "in heaven" element highlights God's universal sovereignty over against all earthly authorities.

One final, brief comment may be made on the preceding discussion. In light of the thesis of this entire work it is noteworthy to see how often the pairing of heaven and earth occurs when God is referred to as the Father in heaven. It cannot be claimed that this is a uniform theme with this expression, but it does occur frequently enough to stand out as yet another example of the pervasiveness of the heaven and earth theme which I have argued for in previous chapters. References to God as a heavenly Father often cannot resist the pull toward employing this language in the well-used heaven and earth contrast theme.

Jesus and Father God:
Continuity or Discontinuity with Jewish Usage?

Before moving on to Matthew's employment of divine fatherhood language and specifically the phrase Father in heaven, it will be beneficial to examine the question of whether the historical Jesus' frequent use of God as Father language stands in basic continuity or discontinuity with his own Jewish heritage and contemporary usage. This is important because it will help us evaluate how relatively important Matthew's emphasis on heavenly Father language is.

---

[42] A very important text of Roman propaganda along these lines was *Res Gestae Divi Augusti*, "The Deeds of the Divine Augustus."

A common assumption today—especially at the popular level—is that Jesus' language about God as Father was a new and decisive shift away from his own Jewish heritage, and that in fact divine fatherhood is one of the hallmarks of Christianity over against Judaism. The modern origins of this can be traced to the likes of Wilhelm Bousset and much of late 19th- and early 20th-century German scholarship. For example, Bousset writes:

> What is most completely original and truly creative in the preaching of Jesus comes out most strongly and purely when he proclaims God the heavenly Father.
> ...The [Judaism of Jesus' time] had neither in name nor in fact the faith of the Father-God; it could not possibly rise to it.[43]

Similarly, Gerhard Kittel comments that the term *abba* shows Jesus' Father-child relationship to God that "far surpasses any possibilities of intimacy assumed in Judaism, introducing indeed something which is wholly new."[44] This stance became widely assumed in 20th-century scholarship, and can be found in Bultmann, T. F. Torrance, G. B. Caird, and others.[45] Because of its homiletical power, it can also be found quite readily in popular books and preaching.

Nearly always, the strongest argument for this theological position is attributed to Joachim Jeremias and his analysis of the Aramaic term *abba*. Jeremias famously argued that Jesus' use of *abba* reveals a special intimacy between Jesus and God, and that before Jesus' usage, individuals did not address God as Father.[46] This emphasis, and especially the popularized understanding that *abba* is the intimate cry of "daddy," has led to a widespread assumption of the discontinuity between Judaism and Christianity on this point.

However, this position, which had the notorious title of "a scholarly consensus" throughout the 1970's, 80's, and 90's, was not without its critics then nor is it now. Several scholars revisited Jeremias' arguments

---

[43] Wilhelm Bousset, *Jesu Predigt in ihrem Gegansatz zum Judentum: Ein religionsgeschichtlicher Vergleich* (Gottingen: Vandenhoeck und Ruprecht, 1892), quoted in Thompson, *The Promise of the Father*, 14.
[44] Gerhard Kittel, "ἀββᾶ," *TDNT* 1:6.
[45] See the collection of quotations from these scholars and others in Thompson, *The Promise of the Father*, 10–11, 21–23.
[46] Jeremias, *Prayers*, 53–65. See also the shorter but more nuanced discussion in Jeremias, *New Testament Theology* (trans., John Bowden; 2 vols.; London: SCM Press, 1971), 1:61–67.

concerning *abba* and found them wanting.⁴⁷ Most helpful is Marianne Meye Thompson's more recent reevaluation of Jeremias' position.⁴⁸ She reviews the widespread influence of Jeremias as well as several of his critics, and then goes on to show that while Jeremias was indeed wrong at several points, quite often his position was misrepresented, both by his followers and critics. Jeremias is often quoted as claiming that Jesus' address to God as an individual Father and his use of the familiar *abba* for this purpose were completely new developments: that there were no precedents for this. This is patently not true, especially in the former instance, as has been shown above. God *was* addressed as Father by individuals. However, Thompson points out that Jeremias used a particular set of criteria that limited his survey to texts from Palestinian Judaism, disregarding the Diaspora literature as unduly influenced by Greek practices.⁴⁹ With this self-imposed limit, his case is stronger, though most today would not regard this as a valid methodological stance. Additionally, Jeremias also retracted his earlier view that *abba* was intimate baby-talk, even though this is what is typically remembered and reported as his position.⁵⁰ Most importantly, Thompson observes that in fact Jeremias did *not* support the view that Jesus' use of Father was entirely different from Judaism:

> Jeremias did not argue that Jesus' address to God as *abba* embodied a radically new conception of God.... [He] more modestly suggested only that there were new elements in the way Jesus spoke of God's Fatherhood.⁵¹

---

⁴⁷ For example, James Barr, "'Abba Isn't Daddy," *JTS* ns 39/1 (1988): 28–47, which attacked the "daddy" idea on linguistic grounds, and Mary D'Angelo, "*Abba* and 'Father'," which attempts to argue that not only is the "daddy" notion mistaken, but that Jesus did not even use the term *abba* himself. In his article "God as Father: Two Popular Theories Reconsidered," *JETS* 31.2 (1988), 181–190, Allen Mawhinney rejects Jeremias' claims for the uniqueness of Jesus' use of *abba* and suggests a serious revision of the notion that divine fatherhood primarily communicates a view of intimacy with God. Similarly, the OT scholar Willem VanGemeren rejects Jeremias' position in his article, "*Abba* in the Old Testament?," 385–390. Critique of Jeremias is also found in Geza Vermes' *Jesus and the World of Judaism* (London: SCM, 1983), 41f., and idem, *Jesus in His Jewish Context*, 37–38. A rejection of Jeremias' position is also one of the key conclusions to the lengthy study by Goshen-Gottstein, "God the Father in Rabbinic Judaism and Christianity," 493–494.

⁴⁸ Thompson, *The Promise of the Father*, 21–34. Also thorough is the lengthy discussion in Scot McKnight, *A New Vision for Israel: The Teachings of Jesus in National Context* (Grand Rapids: Eerdmans, 1999), 49–65.

⁴⁹ Thompson, *The Promise of the Father*, 26.

⁵⁰ Thompson, *The Promise of the Father*, 27. Cf. Jeremias, *New Testament Theology*, 1:67.

⁵¹ Thompson, *The Promise of the Father*, 32.

Unfortunately for Jeremias and for clear thinking on this matter, Jeremias is almost universally enrolled as the advocate of this radical discontinuity view which became the dominant view for some time. But in fact his position was much more nuanced.

When one looks outside of the earlier "scholarly consensus" it becomes clear that even before Jeremias (inadvertently) popularized a view of discontinuity between Jesus and Judaism, many scholars rejected this notion. So, for example, G. F. Moore, when discussing the Father references in the Second Temple literature concludes that these do "not indicate that the age had a new conception of God."[52] Similarly, another scholar of Judaism, conscious of the arguments of Bousset, concludes: "We deny that the Fatherhood of God is expounded by Jesus with more depth and intensity than by the great prophets and teachers of Israel who lived before the age of Jesus."[53] T. W. Manson is similar: "When Jesus spoke of God as Father he was not presenting a new and revolutionary doctrine for men's acceptance; but rather taking up into his teaching something that had been part of the faith of prophets, psalmists, and sages for centuries before."[54]

It seems that a major shift has now occurred and that these latter sentiments are on the way to becoming a new scholarly consensus, consciously opposed to the former discontinuity view.[55] Scot McKnight is representative of a position that sees radical *continuity* between Jesus' message and that of contemporary Judaism:

> What Jesus said about God was consistent with what he learned in public religious gatherings and from his parents. Jesus taught no new thing about God, and his experience of God was consonant with what other Jews, in Israel's past and present, had already experienced or were experiencing.... To argue that Jesus' experience of God was either unique or more intimate than that of other Israelites is to argue something that can't be shown.[56]

---

[52] Moore, *Judaism in the First Centuries*, 2:211.

[53] Gerald Friedlander, *The Jewish Sources of the Sermon on the Mount* (New York: Ktav, 1969), 126–127.

[54] T. W. Manson, *The Teaching of Jesus: Studies of its Form and Content* (Cambridge: Cambridge University Press, 1955), 93.

[55] Goshen-Gottstein's detailed analysis argues for a basic continuity between rabbinic and Jesus' usage on God as Father, though he acknowledges that "the unique and particular teachings of Jesus introduce new uses to the epithet." Yet Goshen-Gottstein is careful to restate that these "new uses" of the epithet are not in opposition to the rabbinic usage, "nor do they revolutionize theological understanding." Goshen-Gottstein, "God the Father in Rabbinic Judaism and Early Christianity," 495.

[56] McKnight, *A New Vision for Israel*, 21.

For various reasons and from various quarters, this view of a primary continuity between Jesus' understanding and his contemporary Judaism is now increasingly accepted. So too on the issue of divine fatherhood in Jesus' language.

How are we to evaluate this shift in consensus? I would tentatively suggest that the newer view is probably right to see greater continuity between the Christian view and the Jewish/rabbinic view of divine fatherhood than previous generations did. At the same time, however, it remains to be said that Jesus' usage does stand out in how exclusively Jesus referred to God as his Father, especially regularly using expressions such as "my Father." That is, the continuity view does not recognize the significance of the fact that what *is* unique about Jesus' Father language is that (at least according to the Gospel witnesses) this is virtually the *only* way that Jesus refers to God (especially in personal address). There do not appear to be any precedents for this level of exclusive usage, and thus Jesus' language does evidence some discontinuity, even though the fact that Jesus referred to God as his (heavenly) Father is not unique to him.[57]

Conclusion

From the data surveyed in this chapter we may conclude that the language of divine fatherhood, which was quite uncommon in ancient Israel, became increasingly important in early Judaism and potentially provided contemporary precedent for Jesus' usage. The conjunction of God as Father with the description of heavenly/in heaven, so common in Matthew, is not found very frequently before the second century CE, unless one considers the Targumic usage as earlier. In this regard, Matthew shows affinity with much of the later, rabbinic literature. Matthew's frequent use of this language, however, stands in marked contrast with the rest of the New Testament. In the following chapter we will turn to a close examination of Matthew's particular use of divine fatherhood language and how it functions as a part of his heaven and earth discourse.

---

[57] This important qualification to the new consensus view comes from personal conversation with Richard Bauckham.

CHAPTER TEN

THE FATHER IN HEAVEN IN MATTHEW

We have observed in the previous chapter that divine fatherhood language was increasingly important in Early Judaism and was therefore current in Jesus' linguistic milieu. There has been some debate in the realm of "Historical Jesus" studies about how much and in what form Jesus addressed God as Father—or if he even did at all.[1] The consensus among scholars, however, is that Jesus certainly did refer to God as Father and that this emphasis was important for Jesus' teaching. This can be seen most clearly in Matthew and in John. The historical Jesus question helps inform our understanding of the importance of divine Fatherhood language in the Jesus traditions. But for my purposes in this chapter, more important than the historical Jesus question is discerning how the image and language of God as Father *functions* in Matthew's narrative, particularly as it relates to the theme of heaven and earth. The current chapter focuses on this question, surveying Matthew's image of God as a heavenly Father and showing how this contributes to the broader heaven and earth contrast theme.

GOD AS FATHER IN MATTHEW: FREQUENCY AND FORMS

The Gospels record Jesus referring to God as Father (πατήρ) over 170 times. A closer examination reveals that these references are not evenly spread across the accounts but instead are found especially in Matthew (44x) and John (109x), and only occasionally in Mark (4x) and Luke (17x). The First and Fourth Gospels both emphasize divine fatherhood as a theme in Jesus' teaching, a topic that is also intimately related to Jesus as the Son of God, and therefore Christology.[2]

---

[1] Most radical (and unconvincing) is D'Angelo's view that Jesus did not refer to God as Father at all: Mary Rose D'Angelo, "*Abba* and 'Father'": 611–630. For the opposite view, see *inter alia* John P. Meier, *A Marginal Jew: Rethinking the Historical Jesus, Volume 2* (New York: Doubleday, 1994), 358–359; Dale C. Allison, *Jesus of Nazareth: Millenarian Prophet* (Minneapolis: Fortress, 1998), 47–50.

[2] Kingsbury observes this connection while arguing for Son of God as the central

Matthew employs the term πατήρ a total of sixty-three times in his Gospel, forty-four of which refer to God and nineteen times in reference to a human father. Here Matthew stands in contrast to Mark and Luke, both of which regularly refer to human fathers (Mk 14x; Lk 39x) more often than God as Father (Mk 4x; Lk 17x). The largest concentration of God as Father references in Matthew is found in the Sermon on the Mount. There πατήρ occurs seventeen times, all of which refer to God and none to human fathers. In fact, the first instance of God as Father in all of Matthew is found near the beginning of the Sermon (5:16); this theme then reappears throughout as a refrain.[3] In contrast, on either side of the Sermon, occurrences of πατήρ refer simply to a human father (4:21,22; 8:21). Strikingly, in every instance but one of Father in the Sermon, Jesus speaks of him to the disciples as *"your* Father (in heaven/heavenly)."[4] Throughout the rest of Matthew's narrative he makes frequent reference to both human fathers and God as a Father, especially in the words of Jesus as "my Father" (e.g., 12:50; 16:27; 26:53).

An important and unique aspect of Matthew's divine fatherhood theme is his connection of references to God as πατήρ with οὐρανός and οὐράνιος. Father in heaven (ὁ πατὴρ ὁ ἐν[τοῖς]οὐρανοῖς) and heavenly Father (ὁ πατὴρ ὁ οὐράνιος) occur thirteen[5] and seven times[6] respectively. The expression ὁ πατὴρ ὁ ἐν τοῖς οὐρανοῖς occurs nowhere else in the preceding literature and only one other time in the NT, in Mark 11:25.[7] As we saw in the last chapter, the Targums and rabbinic

---

Christological category of Matthew. Kingsbury believes that Jesus' frequent addressing of God as Father stems from the emphasis on the Son of God theme in Matthew. See Jack Dean Kingsbury, *Matthew: Structure, Christology, and Kingdom*. See also Donald J. Verseput, "The Role and Meaning of the 'Son of God' Title in Matthew's Gospel," *NTS* 33 (1987): 532–556.

[3] Father in reference to God in the Sermon on the Mount is found in 5:16, 45, 48; 6:1, 4, 6 (2x), 8, 9, 14, 15, 18 (2x), 26, 32; 7:11, 21.

[4] The only exception is 7:21 where Jesus says that only those who do "the will of *my* Father who is in heaven" will enter the kingdom of heaven. In 6:9 Jesus tells the disciples to refer to their heavenly Father when praying as "*Our* Father who art in heaven."

[5] Not *twelve* times as listed in Luz, *Matthew 1–7*, 65. The occurrences are: 5:16, 45; 6:1, 9; 7:11, 21c; 10:32, 33; 12:50; 16:17; 18:10c, 14, 19. These thirteen occurrences always have οὐρανός in the plural but vary quite a bit as to whether the article is present. As the NA27 stands, eight instances are articular and five anarthrous. However, three of the articular instances are extremely uncertain in light of mixed manuscript witnesses.

[6] Mt 5:48; 6:14, 26, 32; 15:13; 18:35; 23:9.

[7] Mark 11:25 is parallel with one of Matthew's occurrences of ὁ πατὴρ ὑμῶν ὁ

literature do regularly refer to the Father in heaven (in Hebrew and Aramaic), while the Greek phrase ὁ πατὴρ ὁ οὐράνιος is extant in no other Second Temple or NT literature.

In Matthew, both ὁ πατὴρ ὁ ἐν [τοῖς] οὐρανοῖς and ὁ πατὴρ ὁ οὐράνιος appear throughout without any difference in meaning or emphasis. It appears that the reason Matthew sometimes used one expression and sometimes the other stems simply from grammatical construction. That is, Matthew employs ὁ πατὴρ ὁ οὐράνιος when the reference serves as the grammatical subject, while he usually uses the more laborious ὁ πατὴρ ὁ ἐν [τοῖς] οὐρανοῖς as the object of a verb or prepositional phrase or in a genitive description.[8] Thus, the two ways of referring to the heavenly Father are synonymous in meaning.

We may conclude this section by briefly analyzing Matthew's divine Father references from the perspective of synoptic comparison.[9] Of the twenty-four occurrences of Father which do not use heaven or heavenly, twelve have no parallels in Mark or Luke, nearly all of which are in passages unique to Matthew.[10] In several other instances, Matthew refers to God as Father where either Mark or Luke or both have some other word, such as Holy Spirit or God.[11] In only five passages do either Mark or Luke or both have a parallel reference to Matthew's Father.[12] Thus, we can see that Matthew clearly emphasizes divine fatherhood, retaining occurrences found in Mark and Q, and adding many others from his own special material. The twenty occurrences of Father in heaven and heavenly Father in Matthew show even stronger redactional markings. Six of the occurrences are from M material and there is

---

οὐράνιος: Mt 6:14. Luke 11:13 has the unique expression ὁ πατὴρ ὁ ἐξ οὐρανοῦ, which is typically translated into English as "the heavenly Father," though this rendering is somewhat dubious. See discussion under "Synoptic Analysis" in Chapter Three.

[8] ὁ πατὴρ ὁ οὐράνιος serves as the grammatical subject in 5:48; 6:14, 26, 32; 15:13; 18:35, and is the construction *ad sensum* in 23:9. Conversely, ὁ πατὴρ ὁ ἐν [τοῖς] οὐρανοῖς serves as a grammatical object or genitive description in 5:16, 45; 6:1; 7:21; 10:32, 33; 12:50; 18:10, 14, 19. This phrase does appear as the grammatical subject in 7:11 and 16:17 and as a title of address is 6:9.

[9] Other analyses of synoptic comparisons on this point can be found in Sparks, "The Doctrine of Divine Fatherhood in the Gospels," 243–258; Manson, *The Teaching of Jesus*, 95–102; Jeremias, *The Prayers of Jesus*, 29–35; and Mowery, "The Matthean References to the Kingdom," 404.

[10] Matt 6:4, 6 (2x), 8, 18 (2x); 13:43; 20:23; 25:34; 26:42, 53; 28:19.

[11] Matt 10:20 // Mk 13:11 // Lk 12:12; Matt 10:29 // Lk 12:6; Matt 26:29 // Mk 14:25.

[12] Matt 6:15 // Mk 11:25; Matt 11:25–27 // Lk 10:21–22; Matt 16:27 // Mk 8:38 // Lk 9:26; Matt 24:36 // Mk 13:32; Matt 26:39 // Mk 14:36 // Lk 22:42.

only one exact parallel (Mk 11:25). The remainder of the instances come from Q or Triple Tradition material but in no case do the other Evangelists refer to God in this unique Matthean way.

The preceding analysis makes it clear that for Matthew in particular the theme of God as Father was very important. Only John refers to God this way more often than Matthew, and in Matthew God is referred to as Father almost as often as θεός is used for this purpose. Various scholars have observed this emphasis. For example, in a pair of articles, Robert Mowery discusses Father in Matthew and concludes that compared to God (θεός) and Lord (κύριος), Father (πατήρ) is the "special" appellation, used only in the words of Jesus addressed to God and crowds of his disciples.[13] He also suggests that the first seven chapters of Matthew "successively introduce the Deity as the Lord, as God, and as Father."[14] Ulrich Luz, commenting on key words in Matthew, states that together the words "righteousness" and "Father" indicate well the subject-matter of the whole Sermon on the Mount.[15] Likewise he observes that Father in heaven is the "guiding word" of the entire Sermon.[16] Similarly, H. F. D. Sparks concludes that Matthew "had a special interest in the Divine Fatherhood,"[17] and Armin Wouters argues that "the will of the Father" is a central idea in the whole proclamation of Matthew.[18]

The Meaning of God as a Heavenly Father

Despite the obvious significance of God as Father in Matthew and the fact that nearly half of the occurrences refer to God as a *heavenly* Father, relatively few scholars have focused on what significance there is in the phrases heavenly Father and Father in heaven. When it is discussed, the most common view, found in several commentaries, is that the "in heaven" added to Father results in a depiction of God that

---

[13] Mowery, "God, Lord and Father," 24; idem, "From Lord to Father in Matthew 1–7," 655–656.
[14] Mowery, "From Lord to Father," 654.
[15] Luz, *The Theology of the Gospel of Matthew*, 3.
[16] Luz, *Matthew 1–7*, 352. Similar is R. T. France who states that the Sermon is about the life and values of the followers of Jesus and "who recognise God as their Father in heaven." France, *Matthew: Evangelist and Teacher*, 254.
[17] Sparks, "The Doctrine of Divine Fatherhood in the Gospels," 251.
[18] Armin Wouters, "*...wer den Willen meines Vaters Tut*": *Eine Untersuchung zum Verständnis vom Handeln in Matthäusevangelium*.

combines transcendence with intimacy. Donald Hagner expresses the opinion of many commentators when he remarks that the expression Father in heaven "combines the personal, or immanent, element of fatherhood with the transcendental element of God's otherness, 'in heaven'."[19] Thus, the "heaven" element and the "Father" element are seen as complements or even contrasting aspects of the phrase. In contrast to this understanding, a few scholars have emphasized that the "in heaven" does *not* in fact communicate transcendence nor a spatial location, but instead the limitlessness of God,[20] or simply to contrast God with human (earthly) fathers.[21] A handful of other views can be found throughout the history of interpretation.[22] Hans Dieter Betz takes the heavenly aspect in yet a different way. He argues that the kingdom of heaven is the principal concept of the Sermon on the Mount and that the rule of this kingdom is expressed through the idea of a cosmic ("heavenly") Father. The heavenly fatherhood of God in the Sermon, says Betz, expresses both God's cosmic character as it relates to the *creatio continua* and his special relationship with the disciples.[23] Whether this unique view proves completely convincing or not, Betz is astute to observe the connection between the kingdom of heaven and the Father in heaven.

---

[19] Hagner, *Matthew 1–13*, 101. See also similar comments on 135–136, 147 and comparable sentiments in Robert H. Gundry, *Matthew* 2, 106; France, *Matthew*, 134; and Morris, *Matthew*, 144.

[20] Alfred Plummer sees heaven as a symbol that expresses God's unlimited perfections as compared to human imperfections, while Balz and Schneider suggest that heaven communicates the fact that God is not bound by any geographical limitations. Similar to the latter view is Ernst Lohmeyer: Calling God the Father *in heaven* clarifies for Jesus' hearers where exactly God now dwells, no longer in Zion or Sinai; these places are replaced with the immensity of heaven. E. Schweizer says the "in heaven" recalls the "miraculous aspect" of this title, though it is not clear what precisely is meant by this. Plummer, *Matthew*, 97; H. R. Balz and G. Schneider, *Exegetical Dictionary of the New Testament* (3 vols.; Grand Rapids: Eerdmans, 1990), 2:544; Lohmeyer, *The Lord's Prayer*, 60; Schweizer, *Matthew*, 95.

[21] Luz, *Matthew 1–7*, 377; Margaret Davies, *Matthew* (Sheffield: Sheffield Academic, 1993), 27. This view, mentioned only by Luz and Davies, is probably closest to the truth in light of the observations of G. F. Moore and G. Schrenk, as shown in the previous chapter: cf. *TDNT*, 5:980; Moore, *Judaism in the First Centuries*, 2:205. See also below on how Father in heaven fits into the broader heaven and earth discourse in Matthew.

[22] For example, Irenaeus argued that Matthew's expression Father in heaven shows that the God of Jesus was the sole and true creator of the world and the Lord over heaven and earth. See Jeffrey Bingham, *Irenaeus' Use of Matthew's Gospel in* Adversus Haereses (Louven: Peeters, 1998), 173–177.

[23] Hans D. Betz, "Cosmogony and Ethics in the Sermon on the Mount," in Betz, *Essays on the Sermon on the Mount* (Philadelphia: Fortress, 1985), 120.

Some of the most insightful observations concerning the function of Father in heaven in Matthew are found in Robert Foster's essay which revisits the Matthean phrase kingdom of heaven.[24] Foster rightly notes that Father in heaven does not stand alone in Matthew but is part of a larger heavenly language discourse. This heaven theme is found throughout Matthew, but nowhere more than in chapters 5–7 where "the heavenly language guides the whole structure of the sermon."[25] Together with kingdom of heaven, Father in heaven serves an important rhetorical and social purpose: to encourage the disciples in their allegiance to Jesus while undermining the temptation "to revert or convert to formative Judaism."[26] Foster's treatment is a real contribution to our understanding because he alone carefully observes how Father in heaven functions in conjunction with related themes and terms in Matthew, particularly other aspects of heaven language. But none of the above suggestions offers a comprehensive understanding of Father in heaven in Matthew.

The Father in Secret

One of the most intriguing aspects of Matthew's references to God as a heavenly Father/Father in heaven is how this notion intersects with the idea that God is a Father who sees in secret and is in secret (6:4, 6, 18), a depiction that is unique to Matthew. We have already observed that the greatest concentration of references to God as Father is found in the Sermon on the Mount (17x). Many of these call God a heavenly Father (5:16, 45, 48; 6:1, 9, 14, 15, 26, 32; 7:11, 21). Within the Sermon, most of these references to God as Father are found in the highly-structured section of 6:1–21 (see also below). This section starts with the heading of 6:1 which refers to the Father in heaven. Then following, repeated three times—once in each subsection of 6:1–21—we have the claim that God is the one who sees in secret—ὁ βλέπων ἐν τῷ κρυπτῷ (with the slight variation ἐν τῷ κρυφαίῳ in 6:18).[27] In verses

---

[24] Foster, "Why on Earth Use 'Kingdom of Heaven'?".
[25] Foster, "Why on Earth Use 'Kingdom of Heaven'?," 499.
[26] Foster, "Why on Earth Use 'Kingdom of Heaven'?," 490.
[27] The common Greek word κρυπτός is found five times in Matthew: two times each in 6:4 and 6:6 and one additional time in 10:26. The similar term κρυφαῖος is found in the NT only in Matt 6:18 (2x). It obviously serves as the third parallel in the highly-structured section of Matt 6:1–21 and is likely synonymous. Very possibly Matthew chose this less common word in the third part for climactic emphasis. On

6 and 18, just before the statement that God is the one who sees in secret, we also find this similar phrase, τῷ πατρί σου τῷ ἐν τῷ κρυπτῷ (again with the slight variation τῷ κρυφαίῳ in v. 18). Most translations understand this phrase as a statement about God—he is the Father who not only sees in secret, but he is himself also *in secret* or hidden.[28] A few commentators, however, have suggested that instead this phrase contains an ellipsis: we should insert the verb "sees" from verse 4 into verses 6 and 18. Thus, we have a statement not about God being *in secret* but again a repetition of the declaration that he sees things done in secret.[29] This latter view is an unnecessary conjecture and makes little sense of the passages. In both verses 6 and 18 the longer phrase about God seeing in secret appears immediately following, and there is no reason to think Matthew felt obliged to shorten the expression just before. Moreover, this interpretation would result in meaningless redundancy. Instead, verses 6 and 18 affirm two related truths: the Father God is in secret/hidden (even as his kingdom is) and at the same time, he sees and rewards the righteousness that his children do in secret.[30] Most importantly, we can see that stating that God is in secret is closely parallel with calling him the heavenly Father or Father in heaven. By its nature that which is in heaven is hidden, unless of course it is divinely revealed (cf. Matt 3:16–17). The Father in heaven, then, is virtually synonymous with the Father ἐν τῷ κρυπτῷ.[31]

This discussion leads directly into the most important insight regarding the heavenly Father references in Matthew: namely, that they form a part of Matthew's broader heaven and earth discourse.

---

the ear this uncommon word is striking and draws attention to itself, although there is likely no difference in meaning intended.

[28] Cf. *Gospel of Thomas* 5–6.

[29] This is the view of Gundry, *Matthew*, 103. Davies and Allison, *Matthew* 1:587, offer the possibility of an ellipsis and conclude only that it is unclear whether this is the correct understanding.

[30] Betz, *Sermon on the Mount*, 339, suggests that these ideas come from the two older, established doctrines that God is all-seeing (cf. Ps 33:13–15; 139:1–17) and that he is hidden or not able to be seen.

[31] Ulrich Mauser observes that heavenly Father and Father in heaven speak of the way that God carries out his care of his children and serve almost as a definition of God in these texts: "The word heaven has, in these contexts in Matthew's gospel, assumed the role of describing the manner in which God cares for his people...God is father in heaven, because from heaven he sees the truth in that which is hidden, and cares for those who dare to live in the power of the hiddenness of truth." Mauser, "Heaven in the Worldview of the New Testament," 39.

The Father in Heaven as Part of Matthew's Heaven and Earth Discourse

The thesis that I have been developing throughout this work is that heaven and earth is a key theological and literary theme in the First Gospel. This theme particularly emphasizes a contrast between the two realms, with humanity and earth on one side of the divide and God in heaven (with his kingdom, rewards, angels, etc.) on the other. It is not difficult to see that Matthew's frequent references to a Father in heaven form an important part of this same theme.[32] We may observe in the first instance that all such references to the Father in heaven invariably use the plural form of οὐρανός,[33] as according to the pattern observed above in Chapter Six. It was argued there that the singular versus plural pattern of οὐρανός in Matthew is one of the ways in which he regularly contrasts the two realms of heaven and earth. We can see that referring to the Father as ἐν τοῖς οὐρανοῖς accords precisely with describing his kingdom as τῶν οὐρανῶν—both referring to a locale (of sorts) or sphere that is distinct from the human and earthly realm.

There is another important way in which Matthew subtly implies a contrast between the Father in heaven and humanity on earth: human fathers throughout Matthew—in contrast to the heavenly Father—are portrayed in a primarily negative light, often being the ones that must be left behind to follow the commands of the kingdom of heaven message. For example, in 4:21–22 it is stated twice that the fishermen disciples leave their father in the midst of their joint work to follow Jesus, literally leaving their father holding the unmended nets. The opposite occurs in 8:21 where a would-be disciple's loyalty to his earthly father, expressed in the disciple's desire to remain behind to bury him, receives a sharp rebuke and rejection from Jesus. Later on, Jesus promises his somewhat worried disciples that because they have indeed left their fathers and other kin, they will be rewarded in kind as well as with eternal life (19:29). Even more explicitly, Jesus states in 10:21 that suffering and

---

[32] As noted above and in previous chapters, Robert Foster's essay on the function of kingdom of heaven and Father in heaven in Matthew is very insightful as far as it goes. His observation that kingdom of heaven and Father in heaven are part of a larger "heavenly discourse" is an accurate starting point, but he does not see that this "heavenly discourse" is itself part of a larger and more elaborate heaven and earth theme.

[33] Thirteen times, always in the form of ἐν [τοῖς] οὐρανοῖς. Of course the seven related occurrences of the adjective οὐράνιος are singular in form as they must be to agree grammatically with ὁ πατήρ.

persecution will come upon the disciples because of betrayal by their kin, even to the point that a father will hand over his own son. They are told not to worry in that hour, however, because the Spirit of their (true) Father God will give them words to speak (10:20). In the same discourse, Jesus goes on to say that he has not come to bring peace on the earth, but indeed conflict: he will even set a man against his father (10:34–35). And then he warns that those who love their father or mother more than Jesus are not worthy of him (10:37). Most strongly stated is the text in 23:29–32. In the series of stoutly-worded woes against the scribes and Pharisees, Jesus condemns them for hypocritically honoring the prophets of old and claiming that they would not have killed them had they been alive during the time of their fathers (23:29–30). Jesus picks up on their claim and condemns them as the guilt-sharing sons of these murderous fathers (23:31) and orders them to "fill up the measure of *your fathers*" (23:32). This likely alludes to John the Baptist's condemnation that these hypocrites claim Abraham as their father (3:9; cf. also 23:9), as well as serving as a contrast to the disciples, who throughout have been called the ones who have the Father (in heaven) as their God. Thus, throughout Matthew's narrative, the majority of his references to human fathers portray them in a primarily negative light.[34] This serves as a point of contrast with the disciples who have a heavenly Father (cf. 6:9) and who are defined as the ones who do with the will of the Father in heaven and therefore participate in the kingdom of heaven (7:21).[35]

Thus far we have discerned two ways in which divine Fatherhood forms part of the heaven and earth contrast theme. Even more explicit than the singular and plural distinction and the negative portrayal of earthly fathers, we also find that in a series of passages, Matthew clearly employs the Father in heaven and heavenly Father expressions as part

---

[34] It seems that the only positive connotations of human fathers in Matthew are found in quotations from the OT Law (15:4–6; 19:5, 19). Note also that nearly every one of the passages discussed above comes from either Triple Tradition or Q, thus this theme is not uniquely Matthean. However, as with many such themes, Matthew has taken up this notion and appropriated it as part of his extended heaven and earth contrast theme.

[35] Though not using 'father' language, another passage that communicates the same idea as observed above is 12:46–50. When Jesus' biological mother and brothers are seeking him, he turns to the crowd and redefines his kin as his disciples, "for whoever does the will of my Father who is in heaven, he is my brother and sister and mother" (12:50).

of contrasting, thematic heaven and earth pairs. While this stands out in Matthew as nowhere else, it does find parallel in a number of the Father of heaven references in the rabbinic literature. As was observed in the previous chapter, both G. F. Moore and G. Schrenk noted how often the Father in heaven phrases are found in conjunction with mention of the earth.[36] In Matthew, the frequent placement of Father in heaven in heaven and earth pairs is striking.

Seven of Matthew's references to the Father in heaven or heavenly Father are structured in such a way that they form a clear contrast between God and humanity, using some form of a heaven and earth pair.[37] The first instance is found in the very first occurrence of Father in heaven, in 5:16. The pericope of 5:13–16 uses several key cosmological terms including heaven, earth, and world. In fact, the pericope is book-ended with references to earth ("you are the salt of the earth") and heaven ("Father in heaven"), with κόσμος, a synonym for earth in Matthew, appearing in verse 14.[38] Most clearly, 5:16 contains a structured implied pair with ἄνθρωποι serving as the point of comparison with the Father ἐν τοῖς οὐρανοῖς: "Let your light so shine before men, that they may see your good works and give glory to your Father who is in heaven" (RSV). The logic is that the disciples' role as the salt of the earth (5:13) and light of the world (5:14) is like a light shining "before men" (ἔμπροσθεν τῶν ἀνθρώπων) which results in glory to the Father "in heaven" (5:16).[39]

The same kind of implied pair can also be found two times in 10:32–33. In these verses Jesus promises and warns that those who confess him ἔμπροσθεν τῶν ἀνθρώπων or fail to do so will receive Jesus' testimony (ὁμολογήσω) or denial (ἀρνήσομαι) before (ἔμπροσθεν) the Father in heaven. This structural conjoining of ἄνθρωπος and the Father ἐν

---

[36] *TDNT*, 5:980; Moore, *Judaism in the First Centuries*, 2:205.
[37] Recall from Chapter Eight that I have identified three types of heaven and earth pairs: copulative ("heaven and earth"), thematic ("heaven" and "earth" put together in context), and implied ("heaven" put into conjunction with a word closely associated with the earthly realm, such as ἄνθρωπος or ᾅδης).
[38] As observed in Chapter Eight, κόσμος appears 8 or 9 times in Matthew, usually in idiomatic phrases about the "foundation of the world" (13:35; 24:21; 25:34) or referring to the inhabited earth (4:8; 5:14; 13:38; 16:26; 26:13).
[39] It is worthwhile noting that, as was discussed in Chapter Eight, there are a variety of ways in which heaven and earth contrast with each other in the many heaven and earth contrast pairs in Matthew. That is, at times a sharp contrast is intended, while at other times, a tension or comparison is in view while not denying the intimate connection between the two poles. This passage lies somewhere on the softer end of the contrast spectrum.

τοῖς οὐρανοῖς is clearly one of a comparative contrast. As in 5:16 and 6:1 (cf. 21:25–26), "before men" (on earth) and "before the Father" (in heaven) serve as counterpoints.[40] Similar is the reference in 16:17. In this text Jesus proclaims that the source of Peter's revelational confession was not "flesh and blood" but my Father in heaven. "Flesh and blood" here is another way of saying humanity, and again stands as the counterpoint to the heavenly Father.

The last two such pairings are very explicit thematic pairs, using earth (γῆ), not just humanity (ἄνθρωπος), in closely structured parallelism. In 18:19 the disciples are promised that whenever two of them agree ἐπὶ τῆς γῆς it shall be done for them by the Father in heaven (παρὰ τοῦ πατρός μου τοῦ ἐν οὐρανοῖς). This statement is a reiteration of that which precedes immediately in 18:18: "whatever you bind on earth shall be bound in heaven, and whatever you loose on earth shall be loosed in heaven," which itself is a repeat of the promise to Peter concerning the keys of the kingdom of heaven in 16:19. In all of these verses, the same type of comparative relationship between heaven and earth (ἐπὶ τῆς γῆς...ἐν οὐρανοῖς) is being communicated. In 23:9 we find the last occurrence of heavenly Father (or Father in heaven) in Matthew and as a climax, it provides one of the most explicit contrasts between the Father in heaven and humanity on earth. Jesus makes the radical claim that the disciples should call no one on earth (ἐπὶ τῆς γῆς) father because for them there is only one true Father, the heavenly one (ὁ πατὴρ ὁ οὐράνιος).[41] This statement comes in the midst of a number of pronouncements against exalted human titles including "rabbi" and "teacher" (23:8, 10). The preceding verses (23:2–7) show the close connection between this passage and 6:1–21, where the self-exalting practices of the scribes and Pharisees are equally condemned. In fact, the only passage which makes a stronger Father in heaven versus earth contrast than 23:9 is the extended discourse of 6:1–21. This passage proves to be very significant and is worthy of a separate treatment.

---

[40] Notice also that in the following verse the word earth conspicuously appears in its regular heaven and earth contrast form: ἐπὶ τὴν γῆν. This appears to be an example of looser, thematic heaven and earth pair, in conjunction with the Father in heaven in 10:33. Note also that 10:35 is one of the strong negative portrayals of earthly fathers which form part of this theme in Matthew.

[41] Cf. the Shema; Mal 2:10. Davies and Allison, *Matthew* 3:277, point out that some interpreters have taken this verse to be comparable to the warnings not to claim Abraham as one's father (Matt 3:9; Lk 3:8), that is, to rely upon one's religious heritage. Along these lines, cf. also 23:29–36.

Matthew 6:1–21—An Extended Heaven and Earth Discourse

We have observed above that Father in heaven and heavenly Father are not mere throw-away phrases but are used by Matthew as part of his heaven and earth contrast theme. This is found nowhere more prominently than in 6:1–21, the very heart of the Sermon on the Mount, and the place where we find the greatest concentration of God as Father language.

Of the seventeen occurrences of God as Father in the Sermon, ten are found in this passage alone. Three of these ten refer specifically to the heavenly Father or Father in heaven (6:1, 9, 14) and most of the remainder speak of God as the one who sees in secret and is in secret, expressions which are closely analogous to the idea of the Father in heaven (see above). The opening verse of this passage serves as a heading over all,[42] and in it we find a clear heaven and earth contrast. As in 5:16 and 10:32–33, in 6:1 Father in heaven functions as a counterpoint to humanity, each of these verses using the expression ἔμπροσθεν τῶν ἀνθρώπων in parallel with your Father ἐν τοῖς οὐρανοῖς.

But at an even more profound level, *the entire structure* of 6:1–21 serves as an extended heaven and earth discourse, the longest one in the Gospel. Verse 1 establishes the point with its contrastive exhortation for the disciples not to please ἄνθρωποι (on earth) but instead their Father in heaven. The remainder of the passage fleshes out this foundational point, with a concluding exhortation to the same point in 6:19–21.

The Structure of 6:1–21

Jesus' instructions in 6:1–21 are closely connected with the preceding sections of the Sermon. In 6:2–18 the disciples are given more concrete examples (cf. 5:21–48) of how one's righteousness needs to surpass that of the scribes and Pharisees to enter the kingdom of heaven (5:20). The promise of reward with the Father in heaven also picks up the opening theme of heavenly reward from the Beatitudes (5:3–12). Participation in the kingdom of heaven is the repeated promise in 5:3 and 5:10, reiterated again in 5:12 as reward in heaven. There are here many conceptual and verbal connections with 6:1–21.

---

[42] This is sometimes called a *kelal* sentence. Cf. Hagner, *Matthew 1–13*, 137.

6:1 serves as a summative heading for the section—"Beware of practicing your piety before others [ἔμπροσθεν τῶν ἀνθρώπων] in order to be seen by them; for then you have no reward from your Father in heaven." (NRSV). This warning is the negative counterpart to the promises of the Beatitudes and is apparently very important for Matthew, as the point is reiterated in 23:2–7. While the children of the heavenly Father await their promised rewards, the hypocrites of 6:2ff. already have their reward in full (6:2, 5, 16). That is, because they are seeking the praise of others, this is the only honor or reward they will receive. The disciples should instead practice their righteousness "in secret" (6:4, 6, 18), not seeking the praise of others but instead pleasing their Father who sees in secret (6:4, 6, 18) and is in secret (6:6, 18). This Father God will repay them (6:4, 6, 18).

This entire section is tightly structured and crafted, with each of these key phrases repeated three times: ἀμὴν λέγω ὑμῖν ἀπέχουσιν τὸν μισθὸν αὐτῶν ("Truly I tell you, they have received their reward"); ὁ πατήρ σου...ἀποδώσει σοι ("Your father will repay you"); and ἐν τῷ κρυπτῷ...ἐν τῷ κρυπτῷ ("in secret"), two times plus the slight derivation ἐν τῷ κρυφαίῳ...ἐν τῷ κρυφαίῳ ("in secret") in the climax of verse 18.

Scholars have long recognized that this passage comprises a well-balanced tripartite structure.[43] Jesus is teaching his disciples how to practice their righteousness on three practical matters: the giving of alms (6:2–4); prayer (6:5–15); and fasting (6:16–18). The famous Lord's Prayer section (6:7–15) is an excursus inserted into the otherwise perfectly symmetric structure.[44] Yet even the excursus follows a very similar pattern:

I. 6:1 Introductory Heading: Pleasing the Father in heaven, not humans
II. 6:2–18 Three Areas of Piety
    A. 6:2–4 Almsgiving
        1. Negative instruction and statement of reward
        2. Positive instruction and statement of reward

---

[43] Most commentators recognize this structure. See Luz, *Matthew 1–7*, 352; Davies and Allison, *Matthew*, 1:572–573; Hagner, *Matthew 1–13*, 136–138; Betz, *Sermon on the Mount*, 330–331; Warren Carter, *Matthew and the Margins: A Socio-Political and Religious Reading* (Sheffield: Sheffield Academic, 2000), 158–171; Guelich, *Sermon on the Mount*, 272–274; Bruner, *Matthew*, 1:281–282.

[44] In addition to the discussion on the broader structural issues here, specific comments on how the Lord's Prayer fits into the structure of the rest can be found in Davies and Allison, *Matthew*, 1:592–593; Birger Gerhardsson, "The Matthaean Version of the Lord's Prayer (Matt 6:9–13b): Some Observations": 207–220.

B. 6:5–6 Prayer
      1. Negative instruction and statement of reward
      2. Positive instruction and statement of reward
   Excursus. 6:7–15 On Prayer
      1. Negative instruction
      2. Positive instruction
      3. Promise and warning
   C. 6:16–18 Fasting
      1. Negative instruction and statement of reward
      2. Positive instruction and statement of reward

This structural analysis (as far as it goes) is very sound and is clearly not merely a construction of later scholarly readers, but apparently existed in this form at some early stage in the tradition.[45]

However, there is one significant problem with the typical understanding of this passage. A survey of commentaries and scholarly literature reveals that almost without exception the pericope is understood to conclude at 6:18, as the structure above suggests. The following unit is said to consist of 6:19–34, and most often the two sections are said to be quite distinct.[46] However, this common view fails to see that in reality the 6:1–18 unit extends through verse 21. 6:1–21 hangs together as a structural unit with a consistent theme of heavenly versus earthly rewards. The command to lay up treasures in heaven, not on earth, in 6:19–21 is the concluding restatement of the same instruction through out 6:1–18 to practice righteousness to gain heavenly reward rather than the mere praise of earthly people. Thus, we must add a third and logical point to the outline given above:

---

[45] Not surprisingly, scholars are divided on whether this construction is a creation of Matthew's, dominical, or a received tradition. A review and evaluation can be found in Davies and Allison, *Matthew*, 1:573–575. See also H. D. Betz, "A Jewish-Christian Cultic *Didache* in Matt. 6:1–18: Reflections on Questions on the Historical Jesus," in Betz, *Essays on the Sermon on the Mount*: 55–69; Guelich, *Sermon on the Mount*, 316–320.

[46] Every commentary that I have surveyed begins a new section at 6:19, usually with no comment on how this section relates at all to what precedes it. France, *Matthew*, 138, comments that the contrast in 6:1–18 leads naturally into 6:19–20, but he still sees 6:19 as beginning a new section. The most negative (and completely unfounded) statement comes from Stephenson Humphries-Brooks who says of 6:19–21, "The paragraph bears no immediate syntactical connection to Mt. 6.1–18. Nor does its subject matter directly refer to the issues treated in the preceding verses." Humphries-Brooks, "Apocalyptic Paraenesis in Matthew 6.19–34," in Marcus and Soards, eds., *Apocalyptic and the New Testament*, 100.

I. 6:1   Introductory Heading: Pleasing the Father in heaven, not humans
II. 6:2–18   Three Areas of Piety
III. 6:19–21 Concluding Exhortation: Rewards in Heaven not on Earth

Though this structural breakdown is not the one found in most of the literature, it does find concurring support in the essay by Birger Gerhardsson, "Geistiger Opferdienst nach Matth 6,1–6.16–21".[47] His overall analysis of the passage is very astute and he depicts the threefold structure in the same way that I have above.

The reasons we should understand the structure as concluding with 6:19–21 rather than verse 18 are manifold. First, we may observe that 6:19–21 clearly provides a verbal *inclusio* with verse 1 at several points: the word heaven appears in both as a frame, both contain a type of heaven and earth pair, and both have as their subject reward with God (μισθός in 6:1, the closely related θησαυρός in 6:19–21). Also, simply, 6:19–21 provides a needed conclusion to this highly-structured passage. With a clear heading (*kelal*) in 6:1 and three tightly-arranged sub-sections, ending the pericope at verse 18 feels very inconclusive; a concluding exhortation on par with verse 1 is expected and even needed.[48] Along these same lines, we may observe that the positive promise of verses 19–21 balances out the negative statement in verse 1. Gerhardsson observes that verse 1 has only a negative declaration and that the positive-negative balance that is found throughout the pericope therefore finds its completion only in 19–21.[49] Finally, we may observe that the verbal and conceptual notions in 6:19–21 have much stronger connections with 6:1–18 than they do with 6:22–34. For example, the relatively uncommon word ἀφανίζω (to ruin, destroy; disfigure)[50] appears in 6:16 in reference to what the hypocrites do to

---

[47] Birger Gerhardsson, "Geistiger Opferdienst nach Matth 6,1–6.16–21," in *Neues Testament und Geschichte: Historisches Geschehen und Deutung im Neuen Testament*, FS for Oscar Cullmann (ed. Heinrich Baltensweiler and Bo Reicke; Tübingen: Mohr Siebeck, 1972): 69–77.

[48] We may observe also that seeing 6:19–21 as the conclusion to 6:1–21 makes it parallel the other two sections (or 'pillars') of the main section of the Sermon: 5:48 provides a conclusion to 5:17–48 and 7:12 provides a conclusion to 6:22 (or 6:19)–7:12. That is, it stands to reason that Matthew would provide 6:1–18 with a conclusion even as he has for the other sections.

[49] Gerhardsson, "Geistiger Opferdienst," 70–71.

[50] ἀφανίζω is found approximately 92 times in the LXX, primarily with the meaning

their faces when fasting, and then is found immediately after in 6:19 and 20 to describe the destruction which comes upon earthly treasures.[51] Such a powerful word-play is no accident of the pen with a master such as Matthew. In contrast, the varied attempts at seeing 6:19–34 as a coherent unit are often quite contorted and inconclusive.[52] But for all the reasons just given, it is not difficult to see how 19–21 completes 1–18 in many ways.[53]

Recognizing the structural break at verse 21 does not mean, however, that there are no connections with the verses that follow (6:22–34); indeed, there are some.[54] Verses 19–21 likely serve as a linking passage, though primarily going with 6:1–18. As one writer has observed, 6:19–21 is a "bridge" passage that connects the preceding and following texts, and thus has somewhat of a dual referent.[55] This is correct and finds precedent in other Matthean passages, as Gaechter, Nolland, and Allison have all observed.[56] It very well may be, then, that the θησαυρός of 6:19–21 alludes both to the μισθός of 6:1–18 as well as the mammon of 6:24. However, 6:22 does introduce a new idea and pericope,

---

of "destroy" or "perish." It appears only five times in the NT, three of which are in Matthew 6, once in Acts 13:41 (a quote from Hab 1:5), and once in James 4:14.

[51] Luz, who recognizes verbal connections between verses 1–18 and 19–21, still breaks the pericope at verse 18 with little comment. Luz, *Matthew 1–7*, 353.

[52] Guelich, *Sermon on the Mount*, 322ff., deals with 6:19–7:12 as a unit but admits that it consists of six "apparently disjointed units of tradition" which do not "exhibit any visible interrelationship with each other."

[53] Some time after I completed this section, Dale Allison's excellent essay on the structure of the Sermon appeared. Although he still breaks the text at 6:18 he sagaciously comments that despite the plethora of works on the structure of the Sermon, "the discussion has not yet run its course" and "some interesting and important observations have been missed." My novel suggestion assumes this same truth. Allison, "The Configuration of the Sermon on the Mount and Its Meaning," in *Studies in Matthew*, 173.

[54] See, e.g., Davies and Allison, *Matthew*, 1:625–626.

[55] Charette, *The Theme of Recompense in Matthew's Gospel*, 100.

[56] In Paul Gaechter's well-known work, *Die literarische Kunst im Matthäus-Evangelium* (Stuttgart: Katholisches Bibelwerk, 1965), 54–59, he has a discussion of such passages under the title of "Doppelfunktionen." In Nolland's commentary on Matthew, p. 28, he refers to Matthew's literary technique of "sectional overlaps," which "function as both the end of one piece and the beginning of a new piece." Davies and Allison, when discussing the multiple functions of βίβλος γενέσεως in Matt 1:1, observe that 7:1–12 and 28:1–20 similarly serve more than one structural purpose in this carefully-crafted narrative (*Matthew*, 1:154). I suggest the same could be said for 6:19–21—it looks both forward and back as a hinge text, although its primary connection is with what precedes. In his work on the structure of the Sermon, Allison points out that "many Matthean verses both end one section and introduce another. They are doors not walls." (Allison, *Studies in Matthew*, 176). He sees 5:11–12 as one such section, though primarily going with the preceding Beatitudes. I would argue the same is true for 6:19–21.

and the notional and structural connections are much stronger with 1–18. Thus, while we can acknowledge some links with 6:22–34, it is best to understand 6:1–21 as the primary structural unit.[57]

Thus, once again, when we tune in our antennae to hear Matthew's heaven and earth symphony, we gain new insight into the structure and purpose of this part of the Sermon. What lies before all people is the choice between God's ways (the kingdom of heaven, the Father in heaven, rewards in heaven) and humanity's ways (temporary and earthly reward, loss of the kingdom, future judgment). The exhortational point is patently clear. There are two ways to live: one will result in nothing more than the praise of humans ("they have their reward in full"), while the other promises staggering results, rewards from the heavenly Father. The failure of the ὑποκριταί is that their hearts value the temporary reward of appearance (cf. ὅπως φανῶσιν) and honor (cf. ὅπως δοξασθῶσιν) before others (ἔμπροσθεν τῶν ἀνθρώπων), rather than the eschatological rewards of the kingdom of heaven with the Father in heaven.

In sum, we can see that in addition to the pervasive heaven and earth theme throughout the Gospel, as well as the frequent use of Father in heaven in heaven and earth pairs, right here at the heart of the Sermon (6:1–21), we find an extended and well-crafted heaven and earth discourse.

The Lord's Prayer Revisited

In light of the preceding discussion, we may once again make mention of how the heavenly Father and heaven and earth themes relate to the Lord's Prayer. As was discussed in Chapter Six, the Lord's Prayer discourse (6:7–15) is a crucial Matthean passage at the heart of the Sermon on the Mount. As discussed above, it is a related but distinct subunit within the highly-structured instruction of 6:1–21. It serves as a discrete excursus on Jesus' teaching concerning prayer that pleases the

---

[57] As an interesting aside, in Ephraem the Syriac's commentary on the Diatessaron, he discusses the topic of almsgiving in Matthew 6 by referring to 6:21 and 6:23, apparently seeing these verses as related to what precedes, although he does not make this statement explicitly. In his comments on this section, Martin Hogan observes this but cannot make sense of it in light of his (standard) assumption that 6:1–18 is one unit and 6:19–7:12 as another. Martin Hogan, *The Sermon on the Mount in St. Ephrem's Commentary on the Diatessaron* (Bern: Peter Lang, 1999), 120–123.

heavenly Father (6:5–6), yet it is parallel to the rest of 6:1–21 in many ways. We have also observed previously that the Lord's Prayer is indeed one of the "hot spots" of the First Gospel and that it is ripe with key terms related to Matthew's heaven and earth theme: οὐρανός (2x), ἐν οὐρανῷ...ἐπὶ γῆς, βασιλεία, πάτηρ ὁ ἐν τοῖς οὐρανοῖς, and ὁ πατὴρ ὁ οὐράνιος.

My analysis of the use of πατήρ throughout Matthew heightens the already great importance of the Lord's Prayer and its opening line, "Our Father who art in heaven." In fact, not only does the prayer begin with the Father, but the prefatory remarks also speak of the Father (6:8) and Father appears twice at the conclusion of the instruction (6:14–15), thereby forming an inclusio. This emphasis on God as Father in the Prayer proves to serve an important social function for the disciples. Their identity is being clearly defined as association with their Father in heaven: they are even instructed to call him "*Our* Father."[58] As Jerome Neyrey points out, in ancient Jewish culture "one's identity and honour derive in large part from membership in a family or clan."[59] Therefore, a change of identity from one's natural father to the heavenly Father is of no small import for Matthew's readers. This new identification in 6:9 is surrounded by contrasting identifications, both in the immediate context and in the larger narrative. The preface to the Prayer sets up the disciples' kind of praying in contrast to that of "the Gentiles" (οἱ ἐθνικοί),[60] a term that clearly serves as a negative identity here as

---

[58] This idea has been most clearly articulated by Robert Foster in his article, "Why on Earth Use 'Kingdom of Heaven'?," 490. He argues that Father in heaven "reinforces the community's devotion to Jesus while simultaneously undermining the temptation of the disciples to revert or convert to formative Judaism."

[59] Jerome H. Neyrey, "Loss of Wealth, Loss of Family and Loss of Honour: The cultural context of the original makarisms in Q," in *Modelling Early Christianity: Social-scientific Studies of the New Testament in its Context* (ed. Philip F. Esler; London: Routledge, 1995), 142. Neyrey explores the economic and social implications of the loss of one's family identification. In the same volume, the social context of sonship is also explored by Richard Rohrbaugh in "Legitimating Sonship—A Test of Honour: A social-scientific study of Luke 4:1–30": 183–197.

[60] In 6:7 Matthew uses the rare term ἐθνικός, which is a derivation of the more common ἔθνος. ἐθνικός occurs not at all in the LXX and only four times in the NT, three of which are in Matthew (Matt 5:47; 6:7; 18:17; 3 John 1:7). *BDAG* states that this word has a particular focus on the morality or belief of a foreigner, offering glosses of "unbelieving, worldly, polytheistic." My own analysis in Matthew suggests that instead ἐθνικός is basically synonymous with ἔθνος, but is used when the focus is on individuals rather than "the Gentiles"/"the nations" in a corporate sense. ἔθνος occurs 15 times in Matthew, usually in a negative sense.

well as in other passages (e.g., 10:5; 20:25). Instead, the disciples have a Father who knows their needs before they ask (6:8). Therefore, they are to address him as "Our Father." Not far away is a similar contrast where the disciples are told not to be anxious about their daily needs as the Gentiles are because their heavenly Father knows their needs (6:32). More broadly in context, we see that Matthew's negative portrayal of human fathers proves very important in light of the divine Father in the Prayer. As I have shown above, throughout Matthew we find many texts where Jesus calls his disciples to make a decisive choice between their fathers and his heavenly Father (8:21; 10:34–37; 23:29–32). Earthly fathers are portrayed in a primarily negative light, in contrast with the heavenly Father who offers rewards and life. Recognizing this pattern throughout Matthew makes sense of the emphasis on the Father in the Lord's Prayer. Moreover, it is worthwhile noting again that all of this serves as part of the broader heaven and earth contrast theme. Not only does the Prayer manifest this theme on the surface (6:9–10), but the disciples' identification with the heavenly Father over against earthly fathers serves as an enlightening subtext to the Prayer. Additionally, the entire Prayer fits within the broader text of 6:1–21, which, as I have shown, proves to be the most extended application of the heaven and earth theme in Matthew.

Conclusion

When commenting on the Father in heaven and heavenly Father in Matthew, H. F. D. Sparks concludes that analysis of these expressions "sheds no light either on the problem of [their] immediate origin, or on any possible special significance [they] may have had for the evangelist."[61] This statement is commendable for its frank admission. However, in light of the heaven and earth theme that my study is highlighting, we may now see that there is indeed a "special significance" for Matthew when he uses Father in heaven and heavenly Father. Referring to God in these ways forms one part of Matthew's elaborate and highly-structured heaven and earth contrast theme. Through his always-plural use of οὐρανός with Father, his generally negative portrayal of human fathers, and his use of heavenly Father/Father in

---

[61] Sparks, "The Doctrine of Divine Fatherhood," 254.

heaven in specific heaven and earth contrast pairs (especially in 6:1–21), Matthew subtly yet powerfully makes clear the current tension between heaven/God and the earth/sinful humanity. Jesus regularly speaks to his disciples about God as *his* Father and *their* Father. This is special "insider" language that distinguishes the new people of God—Jesus' disciples—from all others, especially the scribes and Pharisees.[62] The disciples' Father God is the one who is ἐν τοῖς οὐρανοῖς. He resides in this secret or hidden place and from there will reward faithfulness and righteousness.

As to the origin of these favorite Matthean expressions, it is clear that he did not coin the references to Father in heaven; they were likely contemporary turns of phrase, if the later textual witnesses of the Targums and rabbinic literature do reflect earlier practices. It is also possible that Matthew found this dominical way of speaking in the Jesus tradition sources. Regardless, Matthew adopted, adapted and expanded this newer and relatively infrequent way of speaking about God, and employed it skillfully within the rest of his elaborate heaven and earth schema.

Additionally, the connection between Father in heaven and kingdom of heaven should not be overlooked. It provides a crucial clue to Matthew's theological point. These two phrases have significant overlap in Matthew's narrative. In several passages Father and kingdom are connected,[63] and both consistently use the ear-striking plural οὐρανοί attached to them as a descriptor. In light of the close connection between God as King and as Father in Jewish literature,[64] we can see that it made perfect sense for Matthew to emphasize the heavenly nature of the one when stating the same for the other. That is, as Matthew emphasizes that God's kingdom is a heavenly one/from heaven, so too it is appropriate for him to emphasize that God the Father is likewise heavenly/in heaven. Which came first into his mind is impossible to tell, but the connection of heaven with both Father and kingdom is a completely understandable correlation in light of the intimate connection of Father and King in contemporary Jewish thought. As I will

---

[62] Cf. the discussion in Chapter Six of Robert Mowery's insider language: "different terms for different audiences." See also Foster, "Why on Earth Use 'Kingdom of Heaven'?," 494–495.

[63] E.g., 7:21; 13:43; 18:23+35; 25:34; 26:29.

[64] Cf. Moore, *Judaism in the First Centuries*, 2:209–210; Geza Vermes, *Jesus in His Jewish Context*, 29.

argue in the following chapters, Matthew's kingdom of heaven is an expression that he significantly developed by combining the Second Temple phrase "God of Heaven" with the contrast of God's kingdom with earthly kingdoms from Daniel 2–7. In the same way, Father in heaven stems from contemporary usage and likely serves several of the same purposes that kingdom of heaven does for Matthew—namely, to emphasize the uniqueness and universal sovereignty of God in the Roman Imperial context,[65] as well as the exclusiveness of God as the Father of the disciples in its Jewish context. That is, the "in heaven" element indicates that God rules over all and is distinct from the earth, while at the same time Matthew distinguishes between the disciples and others by showing their alignment with the heavenly Father. For Matthew, Father in heaven, like kingdom of heaven, is an important tool for communicating his own theological and polemical purposes.

---

[65] As Marianne Meye Thompson observes concerning Father language in 3 Maccabees: "God is 'first Father,' implying that he is the source or origin 'of all,' and he 'oversees all,' implying his universal sovereignty. The emphasis on 'all' and on God as 'first Father' gives some clue to the polemical edge of these claims. The emphasis on the universal scope of God's Fatherhood and sovereignty are features of Jewish monotheistic polemic. Inasmuch as Zeus is routinely referred to as 'father of gods and mortals,' the reference to Israel's God as the 'first Father of all' scores a point for the uniqueness of Israel's God." M. M. Thompson, *The Promise of the Father: Jesus and God in the New Testament*, 49.

CHAPTER ELEVEN

THE KINGDOM OF GOD IN THE OLD TESTAMENT AND SECOND TEMPLE LITERATURE

In the final two chapters, we will examine the fourth and last element in Matthew's idiolectic use of heaven language, his unique expression kingdom of heaven. As before, we will begin by examining the literary and historical precedents for this notion before proceeding to study its function in Matthew's Gospel.

The amount of secondary literature that has been produced on the topic of the kingdom of God is so vast[1] that nearly every scholar who ventures into this subject feels it is necessary to begin with a disclaimer. The present writer is no exception: To comprehensively analyze the various views and debates concerning the kingdom of God would be a massive task that goes beyond the constraints on this project. Moreover, this kind of secondary literature analysis is not necessary for the development of my thesis.

Nevertheless, because of the great importance of the kingdom in Jesus' proclamation, some understanding of contemporary notions of God's kingdom is essential for interpreting Matthew. It is a fair question to ask, What would preaching about the kingdom of God have meant to Jesus' hearers? To Matthew's? Therefore, what follows is a stream-lined examination of the relevant concepts and texts related to the kingdom of God in the literature preceding and contemporary with Jesus' ministry. We will begin by examining the issue of the translation of מלכות and βασιλεία and then proceed with a roughly chronological treatment, tracing the kingdom of God from the Old Testament through the various corpora of the Second Temple literature. This chapter will conclude with a study of how the themes of kingdom and heaven and earth are interwoven in the stories of Daniel 2–7.

---

[1] Roy Harrisville cleverly describes the study of the kingdom of God theme as a well-worn path that has evolved to the ultimate point of a concrete thoroughfare, on which nothing truly new can be said, "only a perpetual tinkering for purposes of employment or repair." Roy A. Harrisville, "In Search of the Meaning of 'The Reign of God'," *Interpretation* 47/2 (1993), 140.

Preliminary Issue:
The Translation of מלכות and βασιλεία

Although "kingdom" is the common English translation for βασιλεία and מלכות, the majority of scholars have long accepted that words such as "reign" and "sovereignty" better communicate the typical usage of these words. It was Gustaf Dalman's late 19th-century study that effected the consensus view that the Hebrew root מלכות and its Greek counterpart βασιλεία are best understood to mean sovereignty rather than a territorial or spatial kingdom. Dalman writes: "No doubt can be entertained that both in the Old Testament and in Jewish literature מַלְכוּת, when applied to God, means always the 'kingly rule,' never the 'kingdom,' as if it were meant to suggest the territory governed by Him."[2] Most scholars have been convinced by Dalman's argumentation and his view is regularly cited, though some have offered assorted critiques.[3] One important qualification was made by S. Aalen in his 1962 article on kingdom of God in the Gospels.[4] In this lengthy and reasonable treatment, Aalen generally agrees with Dalman's view, but shows that on a few occasions in the OT and often in the Gospels, the idea of God's kingdom does indeed have the sense of a sphere or territory.[5] Brevard Childs also follows Dalman but offers a different kind of modifying critique. Childs points out that our understanding of the kingdom should not be determined so strictly by the rabbinic tradition (as Dalman does) because this tradition was rather suspicious of and ultimately rejected the views of kingdom found in the apocalyptic literature. Instead, we must also take into account the usage of kingdom in the apocalyptic literature.[6] In a series of articles from the perspective of translation theory, the linguist Rick Brown offers yet another correction to Dalman's widespread view.[7] Brown convincingly shows that

---

[2] Dalman, *Words of Jesus*, 94.

[3] J. C. O'Neill in "The Kingdom of God," *NovTest* 35 (1993), 130, calls Dalman's statement "perhaps the most influential sentence ever written" in New Testament studies. While being certainly an overstatement, this remark does reveal how widespread Dalman's view has become.

[4] Aalen, "'Reign' and 'House' in the Kingdom of God in the Gospels": 215–240.

[5] In a 1988 article Joel Marcus revisits the question of the sense of kingdom and offers a critique of Aalen while supporting a view that basically aligns with Dalman. Joel Marcus, "Entering Into the Kingly Power of God": 663–675.

[6] Childs, *Biblical Theology of the Old and New Testaments*, 632.

[7] Rick Brown, "Translating the Whole Concept of the Kingdom," *Notes on Translation* 14/2 (2000): 1–48; idem, "A Brief History of Interpretations of 'The Kingdom of God' and Some Consequences for Translation," *Notes on Translation* 15/2 (2001): 3–23.

rather than always referring to rule, "the Jews had a more complicated kingdom expectation with several components of meaning."[8] It simply will not do to attempt to contort the diverse kingdom sayings into a singular meaning of rule or reign.

In this work I will continue to use the English gloss "kingdom" while acknowledging that there are indeed a variety of meanings associated with this word, including at times an emphasis on the rule or sovereignty of God while also at other times a locative kingdom is the meaning.[9] In the subsequent chapter we will revisit this issue briefly when examining how assorted Matthean scholars have understood the expression ἡ βασιλεία τῶν οὐρανῶν.

The Kingdom of God in the Old Testament

For some scholars, the kingdom of God is understood as one of the fundamental and foundational realities of ancient Israelite religion and belief. For others, the notion of God's kingdom was a later development that is not fully manifested until the latest writings of the OT.[10] One's allegiance to either view is dependent on a number of other decisions based on the dating of various texts, one's understanding of the editing that went into the OT canon as we have it, and other hermeneutical

---

[8] Brown, "A Brief History of Interpretations," 9.

[9] A brief but helpful discussion of how to translate βασιλεία is also found in an appendix to Rudolf Schnackenburg's *God's Rule and Kingdom* (trans., John Murray; Freiburg: Herder, 1963): 354–357. Schnackenburg argues that while "reign" and "rule" are preferable to "kingdom," the latter should not be abandoned because eschatologically, it will be appropriate to speak of the kingdom of God. He concludes that there is simply no single term (in English or German) that can successfully be employed in all contexts.

[10] The former category includes A. Alt, Martin Buber, John Bright, Walther Eichrodt, J. Jeremias, G. R. Beasley-Murray, and the authors of "kingdom" entries in many Bible and theological dictionaries. Those who reject the kingdom of God as a comprehensive OT notion include Gerhard von Rad, Michael Lattke, and probably the majority of scholars writing since the second half of the 20th-century. Martin Buber, *Königtum Gottes* (Heidelberg: L. Schneider, 1956); John Bright, *The Kingdom of God* (Nashville: Abingdon, 1953); Walther Eichrodt, *Theology of the Old Testament* (2 vols.; London: SCM, 1961–1967); Gerhard von Rad, *TDNT*, s.v. *mlkt*; Michael Lattke, "On the Jewish Background of the Synoptic Concept 'The Kingdom of God'," in Chilton, ed., *The Kingdom of God*: 72–91; G. R. Beasley-Murray, *Jesus and the Kingdom of God* (Grand Rapids: Eerdmans, 1986), 17–25. Other discussions of the evidence can be found in Rudolf Schnackenburg, *God's Rule and Kingdom*, 11–40; John Gray, *The Biblical Doctrine of the Reign of God* (Edinburgh: T&T Clark, 1979); Dale Patrick, "The Kingdom of God in the Old Testament," in Willis, ed., *The Kingdom of God in 20th-Century Interpretation*: 67–79.

judgments. Regardless, it is clear that the idea of God's kingdom does find witness throughout many OT texts as they stand in their final form, and that this belief grew quantifiably and in importance throughout the subsequent Jewish history.

The Hebrew root מלכות occurs around 91 times in the MT, with an additional 57 occurrences of the Aramaic equivalent מלכותא. The Hebrew word is found especially in later documents such as Chronicles, Ezra, Esther, and Daniel, while nearly every occurrence of the Aramaic form comes from Daniel 2–7. As has been discussed, these terms generally have the sense of royal power, dominion, or reign, though sometimes the more traditional kingdom is the best translation. The Hebrew and Aramaic root מלך ("king") occurs well over 2500 times and can refer to a wide variety of offices, as well as its appearance in the verbal form which means "to reign." This root occurs throughout the OT corpus, but especially in Samuel, Kings, Chronicles, Jeremiah, Ezra, and Daniel. King is used as a epithet for God some fifty times in the OT.

Eichrodt, Bright, and others trace the beginnings of the notion of the kingdom of God to Mt Sinai in Exodus 19–20. There, as Bright explains, we find that God has called a people to himself to live under his rule. Thus, although the phrase kingdom of God does not appear there, we have the first expression of God's kingdom.[11] Schnackenburg finds the first allusion to God's kingship just before this event in the song of Moses on the far side of the Red Sea. The celebrating Israelites sing that "the Lord shall reign for ever and ever" (Exod 15:18).[12] Beasley-Murray, similarly, finds the idea of God's kingship in the earliest stages of Israel's history. Following Buber, he understands the covenant with the wandering tribes as a "theo-political act" which defined Israel's existence as a people under a king.[13]

By all accounts, the establishment of the Davidic monarchy obviously heightens and increases the idea of God's kingship on earth, especially when one considers the notion of the filial relationship between God and the Davidic kings (2 Samuel 7:12–14).[14] God's kingship is also

---

[11] John Bright, *The Kingdom of God*, 28.
[12] Schnackenburg, *God's Rule and Kingdom*, 12.
[13] Beasley-Murray, *Jesus and the Kingdom*, 18.
[14] Robert Rowe calls this the "two-tier" kingship of the OT, "with God as King over all, and King David and his successors supposed to act under God's authority." Robert D. Rowe, *God's Kingdom and God's Son: The Background to Mark's Christology from Concepts of Kingship in the Psalms* (Leiden: Brill, 2002), 1.

exalted in the prayer of David's son, Solomon (1 Chron 29:11), while the Chronicler provides two of the most explicit references to God's kingdom (1 Chron 28:5; 2 Chron 13:8). No OT book addresses the kingdom more often than the Psalms.[15] We find many Psalms which speak of God's kingship (Ps 29; 65; 84; 93),[16] refer to him specifically as a king (e.g., Ps 5:2; 10:16; 24:7; 44:4; 47:2; 68:24; 95:3; 145:1), and speak of his kingdom (Ps 103:19; 145:11–13). In connection with several of these Psalms there has been no small debate about the so-called "Enthronement Psalms." In the opinion of some scholars, these psalms were part of an ancient near eastern ritual in which the divine-human king re-enacted a death and resurrection myth. This view in various forms still finds some adherents while others reject it in part or entirely.[17] In the Psalms we also find many references to God's throne (Ps 11:4; 45:6; 89:14; 103:19) as well as the description of God as the Lord of hosts or of the heavenly council (Ps 24:10; 46:7; 82:1; 84:3). Both of these expressions clearly communicate the notion of God's kingship (usually in a universe-wide sense) without using the מלך root.[18] These types of reference to God's kingdom are also found in the prophetic literature. For example, God's throne is found in several texts including Isaiah 6:1, 66:1, Jeremiah 3:17, 49:38, Ezekiel 1, and Daniel 7. God is called the Lord of hosts—a designation which communicates the idea of a king sitting amidst his court—at least fifty times in Isaiah, over seventy times in Jeremiah, and many other times in the minor prophets. Beyond these references, God is explicitly called king throughout the prophetic literature.[19] Despite the disruption of the great Davidic dynasty, the prophets offer post-exilic hope for the restoration of the kingdom of God.[20]

This very brief survey of references to God as king and his kingdom shows that the theme of God's kingdom which we find often in the

---

[15] J. L. Mays, in discussing the importance of kingdom language in the Psalms, remarks "The Psalms are the liturgy of the kingdom of God.... The Psalter as a whole composes a language world in which God and world and human life are understood in terms of the reign of the Lord." James Luther Mays, "The Language of the Reign of God," *Interpretation* 47/2 (1993), 121.

[16] On these Psalms and others, see especially, John Gray, *The Biblical Doctrine of the Reign of God*, 39–116.

[17] Schnackenburg, *God's Rule and Kingdom*, 15–16, reviews and rejects this notion. A most thorough treatment is found in Gray, *The Biblical Doctrine of the Reign of God*, 7–38. See also, more recently, Rowe, *God's Kingdom and God's Son*, 13–62.

[18] See the discussion in Schnackenburg, *God's Rule and Kingdom*, 17–19.

[19] For example, Isa 6:5; 33:22; 43:15; 44:6; Jer 8:19; 10:10; 46:18; 48:15; 51:57; Ezek 20:33; Dan 2:47; 4:37; Mic 2:13; Zeph 3:15; Zech 14:9, 16–17; Mal 1:14.

[20] See especially John Bright, *The Kingdom of God*, 71–155.

post-biblical literature and Jesus' ministry was born out of the importance of God as king in the Old Testament. Beasley-Murray is right to observe that although "kingdom" per se is found little, there is a consistent emphasis in the OT writers on the ruling activity of God.[21] Dale Patrick concludes: "the expression 'kingdom of God' has sufficient antecedents in the OT to justify Jesus' use of it. In other words, the antecedents are sufficiently frequent, widely distributed, and prominent to constitute precedents for the use of this expression as a comprehensive, synthetic theologumenon."[22]

As to what exactly the conception of God's kingdom was in the OT, we can observe that, not surprisingly, there is no single, monolithic notion. Instead, God's kingship is at times portrayed as an eternal and universal one, or as primarily kingship over his people Israel, while in the later writings the emphasis falls on the eschatological expectation of the coming kingdom.[23] The assorted OT texts which speak of the kingdom of God can be summarized into three categories of meaning: 1) God as the king of all nations and the world by virtue of being the creator. 2) God as the king of Israel, his people. 3) God as the king whose dominion is yet to be realized in the future.[24] This diversity of concepts continues and even increases in the subsequent literature.

THE KINGDOM OF GOD IN THE APOCRYPHA, PSEUDEPIGRAPHA, AND QUMRAN

The various bodies of literature that stem from the Second Temple period reveal that the kingdom of God theme was increasingly important for Jewish people living during this era. Nevertheless, it still cannot be described as a major theme. As is true in the OT literature, we find an assortment of views across the broad range of texts that come from this period.

---

[21] Beasley-Murray, *Jesus and the Kingdom*, 17.
[22] Patrick, "The Kingdom of God in the Old Testament," 73. Dennis C. Duling provides a similar conclusion, stating that although the exact phrase is missing [which is not entirely accurate], "the *idea* of the kingdom of God is present, indeed even widespread, in the Hebrew Scriptures." Duling, "Kingdom of God, Kingdom of Heaven," *ABD* 4:50.
[23] Gerhard von Rad in *Bible Key Words from Gerhard Kittel's* Theologsiches Wörterbuch zum Neuen Testament: *Basileia* (London: A&C Black, 1957), 10–12.
[24] Conveniently summarized as such in Martin Hengel, *The Zealots: Investigations into the Jewish Freedom Movement in the Period from Herod I until 70 A.D.* (trans. D. Smith; Edinburgh: T&T Clark, 1989), 91–92.

The Apocrypha and Pseudepigrapha[25]

The exact expression "kingdom of God" is found several times throughout this literature, but our survey should not be limited to this phrase alone. In fact, more common than this phrase, the same idea is communicated quite frequently by referring to God as king. It is helpful to begin by mentioning several such texts. God is addressed as king many times in the Second Temple literature, very often in the context of prayer and worship. For example, *Judith* 9:2 calls God the king of creation while *Sirach* 50:15 terms God "the Most High, the King of all" (cf. also 51:1ff.). Likewise, *Tobit* describes God as king multiple times in the prayer of chapter 13 (verses 6, 7, 10, 11, 15), in addition to referring to his kingdom in 13:1. In the *Additions to Esther* both Mordecai and Esther speak of God as king in their prayers (13:9, 15; 14:3, 12). And in the Song of the Three Children in Greek Daniel we read "Blessed art Thou upon the throne of Thy kingdom" (3:54). Moving into apocalyptic literature we also find God addressed as king by his creatures. For example, each of the five subsections which together comprise *1 Enoch* call God king. In 9:4 the angels call God "the Lord of lords, and the God of gods, and the King of kings." Enoch and the angels call him "the king of the universe" and "the eternal king" in several places (12:3; 25:3, 5, 7; 27:3) as well as other ascriptions such as "the king of glory" and "the great king" (81:3; 84:2–3, 5; cf. 91:13; 103:1; 63:4). Similar expressions can be found also in the *Assumption* (or *Testament*) *of Moses* (4:2; 10:1–10), *Jubilees* (1:28; 50:9 [Eth.]), the *Testament of Benjamin* (9:1), and the *Testament of Job* (39:11–12). The *Psalms of Solomon* also speak of God's kingship in several instances (2:29–32; 5:18; 17:1, 32, 34, 46). When we examine the literature that stems from the Diaspora, the same kind of language is often found. This is especially true in Book 3 of the Sibylline Oracles, where God is very frequently described with

---

[25] Helpful overviews of the kingdom theme in this literature can be found in Jacques Schlosser, *Le Règne de Dieu dans les dits de Jésus* (2 vols.; Paris: Gabalda, 1980); Odo Camponovo, *Königtum, Königsherrschaft und Reich Gottes in den frühjüdischen Schriften* (Göttingen: Vandenhoeck & Ruprecht, 1984); M. Lattke, "On the Jewish Background of the Synoptic Concept 'The Kingdom of God'," in Chilton, *The Kingdom of God*: 72–91; J. J. Collins, "The Kingdom of God in the Apocrypha and Pseudepigrapha," in Willis, *The Kingdom of God in 20th-Century Interpretation*: 81–95; assorted essays in Martin Hengel and Anna Maria Schwemer, eds., *Königsherrschaft Gottes und Himmlischer Kult im Judentum, Urchristentum und in der Hellenistischen Welt* (Tübingen: Mohr-Siebeck, 1991); and R. Rowe, *God's Kingdom and God's Son*, 87–114. Much of the survey below follows the work of Rowe and Collins.

expressions such as "the great king" and "the immortal king" (verses 48, 56, 499, 560, 617, 717, 808; cf. 1–2, 11, 19, 46–50, 780). Thus we can observe that the idea of God's kingship is widespread across a variety of genres and locales.

In addition to these references, we also find several instances of the expression "kingdom of God." Many of these come from the same texts mentioned above and are understandably connected. For example, the bulk of Book 3 of the *Sibylline Oracles* is taken up with the theme of the kingdoms of the world with the polemical point that God's sovereignty rules over all of them (cf. Daniel 1–7).[26] Reference to God's kingdom can also be found in other Diaspora texts such as Wisdom of Solomon (6:4, 20; 10:10), and 4 Maccabees (2:23). We observed above that God as king is found several times in the Enochic literature. However, it does not appear that the kingdom as such is a prominent motif in Enoch. This phrase itself does not appear, possibly because the emphasis on the kingship of God here is primarily negative, focusing on the destruction of the kings of the earth.[27] The same could be said for 4 Ezra and 2 Baruch, both of which draw upon the traditional four-kingdom schema (cf. Daniel), but do not explicitly use the phrase "kingdom of God." We also observed that the reign of God is emphasized at several points in the *Psalms of Solomon*. This is especially so in psalm 17 (the most prolonged messianic text before the time of Christ), which speaks explicitly of the kingdom of God in verse 3.

In light of the great frequency of "kingdom of God" in the Gospels, we might expect to find this specific phrase more often than we do in the preceding literature. However, the notion of God's kingship is nevertheless found throughout, being spoken of sometimes with the specific phrase, but more often via reference to God as king and his rule and throne.[28]

As to the meaning and emphasis of the theme of God's kingship, scholars have noted that the diverse literature from this period presents of a variety of perspectives. In one strand of the Second Temple tradition, especially that of the Hellenistic Diaspora, the kingdom of God

---

[26] Cf. J. J. Collins, "The Kingdom of God in the Apocrypha and Pseudepigrapha," 84–85.

[27] J. J. Collins, "The Kingdom of God in the Apocrypha and Pseudepigrapha," 88–89.

[28] Schnackenburg, *God's Rule and Kingdom*, 41.

is understood primarily in a moral or spiritual way.²⁹ The same could be said for Philo and Josephus as well.³⁰ Yet in the bulk of the Second Temple literature, the kingdom of God was understood eschatologically and emphasized the destruction of the kingdoms of this world. But even within an eschatological understanding, there was a diversity of views. Some traditions envision an apocalyptic kingdom that is otherworldly, such as in Daniel 7–12, the *Testament of Moses* 10, and the Enochic literature. In comparison, other texts anticipate a messianic kingdom that will come upon the earth, with God acting decisively in history, such as in the *Psalms of Solomon* 17, the *Assumption of Moses*, and the *Sibylline Oracles* 3. However, it is important to note that these two traditions are not always distinct. Some texts manifest an intertwining of the earthly messianic kingdom with apocalyptic elements like the resurrection of the dead (e.g., 4 Ezra, 2 Baruch).³¹ Overall, the literature of the Apocrypha and Pseudepigrapha is unified in emphasizing that God's kingship is eternal and is over all. The historical context of Jews living under (often-hostile) foreign rule both in the Diaspora and in Palestine explains why God's ultimate kingship was such an important and hope-giving motif. The variety of ways in which God's kingdom is presented in this literature shows that, as Camponovo has observed, the kingship of God functions "as a symbol, not as a precisely defined concept."³²

Qumran³³

An examination of the theme of God's kingdom/kingship in the Qumran documents reveals a similar situation to other Second Temple literature: the theme is certainly found and in some texts is very important, but

---

²⁹ J. J. Collins, "The Kingdom of God in the Apocrypha and Pseudepigrapha," 95.
³⁰ See K. L. Schmidt in *Bible Key Words: Basileia*, 25–26.
³¹ Schnackenburg, *God's Rule and Kingdom*, 41, 63; J. J. Collins, "The Kingdom of God in the Apocrypha and Pseudepigrapha," 95; Rowe, *God's Kingdom and God's Son*, 113.
³² Camponovo, *Königtum, Königsherrschaft und Reich Gottes*, 437–438, quoted in James D. G. Dunn, *Jesus Remembered* (Grand Rapids: Eerdmans, 2003), 385, n. 13.
³³ Surveys of the kingdom theme at Qumran can be found in M. Lattke, "On the Jewish Background of the Synoptic Concept," 81–83; B. T. Viviano, "The Kingdom of God in the Qumran Literature," in Willis, ed., *The Kingdom of God in 20th-Century Interpretation*: 97–107; R. D. Rowe, *God's Kingdom and God's Son*, 97–103; Craig Evans, "Jesus and the Dead Sea Scrolls," in *The Dead Sea Scrolls After Fifty Years: A Comprehensive Assessment* (ed. Peter W. Flint and James C. Vanderkam), 2:575–585; A. M. Schwemer, "Gott als König und seine Königsherrschaft in den Sabbatliedern aus Qumran," in Hengel and Schwemer, *Königsherrschaft*: 45–118.

overall it is still not as prevalent as in the Jesus traditions. Additionally, a diversity of perspectives on the kingdom of God can be detected.

It is difficult to provide exact statistics for the occurrences of the *mlk* word-group because of the number of textual uncertainties involved in reconstructing the texts. Moreover, some of the best detailed studies on this issue as well as the concordances were produced before all of the scrolls received full publication. Nonetheless, we can mention several of the texts where the kingship of God is found. The kingdom is mentioned in an assortment of texts including the Rule of the Blessing (1QSb 3:5 4:25–26; 5:21), 4Q286 (1 2:2), 4Q301 (5 i.2), 4Q448, 4Q521, 11QT^a (59:17), and others. God is called king in several places such as the Genesis Apocryphon (1QapGenar 2:4ff.; 20:13), 1QH^a (3:5; 18:8), 4Q299 (i.3), 4Q381 (76–77, 7), and 4Q427 (7, 1:13, 15). And God or his people are spoken of as having dominion or reigning or sitting on a throne in a number of texts, including 1QH^a (5:17), 4Q174 (1:3), 4QDibHam^a (4:7–8), as well as many others.

By far the two most important scrolls for the theme of God's kingdom are the War Scroll (1QM) and the series of texts that make up the Songs of the Sabbath Sacrifice (4Q400–407; 11Q17). The War Scroll is based upon a number of OT texts that speak of war and conquest by God's people. The influence of Daniel and the contrast of righteous and wicked kingdoms is evident in some places (17:6–7), and several other passages likewise contrast the dominion of Israel and the saints with those of Belial (10:12; 14:9–10; 17:7; 18:1, 11). God's kingdom is explicitly mentioned in 6:6. Additionally, God's kingship is particularly highlighted in the three-part hymn of 12:7–15. References to God's kingdom and sovereignty form an inclusio around the texts and the hymn "gathers together many threads which make up the kingdom theme."[34]

The most detailed analysis of the kingship theme in the Songs of the Sabbath Sacrifice has been done by Anna Maria Schwemer.[35] She contends that this text, which likely dates from the first century BCE, is the most important pre-Christian document concerning the kingdom of God theme. Indeed, the Songs speaks of the kingdom over twenty times, although the exact phrase "kingdom of God" does not appear.

---

[34] Viviano, "The Kingdom of God in the Qumran Literature," 105. The analysis given above comes from Viviano, 104–107.

[35] Schwemer, "Gott als König und seine Königsherrschaft in den Sabbatliedern aus Qumran."

Reference is made several times to "his/your lofty kingdom," "his kingdom," and "your glorious kingdom." Additionally, God is several times called the "king of princes," "king of holiness," "king of truth and majesty," the "king of kings," and many other similar titles. The theme of the kingship of God is clearly at the forefront of the Songs. The vision of the kingdom in the Songs is similar to the traditions of Chronicles and Daniel "in which the kingdom of God is portrayed as a universal kingdom that encompasses the heavens as well as the earth and all its nations."[36] The emphasis on the kingdom theme in the Songs is especially noteworthy in that these texts also display a great interest in the heaven and earth theme, as was discussed above in Chapter Seven.

As to the function of the kingdom theme at Qumran, we can find a diversity of meanings in the different texts. Some scrolls closely connect God's kingship with the Davidic line (4Q174; 4Q504), some texts focus especially on the eschatological hope of the coming kingdom (e.g., 4Q521), and the War Scroll is particularly more militaristic and vindictive than many other kingdom texts.

Summary

Overall, we may observe that the kingdom of God theme is certainly a familiar one throughout the Second Temple literature. For many texts and apparently for many strands of the Jewish tradition, it was a very important idea. The OT itself revealed a variety of uses of the kingdom theme and we are not surprised to find this diversity continues and increases in the subsequent literature, especially with the development of stronger eschatological notions. Common to all the kingdom traditions is the idea that God is sovereign not only over Israel, but also over the whole world, his creation. The great future orientation of the kingdom hinged on the hope that God's *de facto* sovereignty over Israel would eventually extend to the whole world, whether through the rise of the earthly messiah or through a heaven-sent irruption into this world. Very clearly, all of the kingdom traditions in the Second Temple period were consciously opposed to the foreign rule which resided over them. In fact, this could be said to be the consistent element of the kingdom idea throughout the literature. We will see in the next chapter

---

[36] *NIDOTTE*, 2:960.

that this idea proves very relevant for Jesus' own kingdom proclamation and especially Matthew's emphasis on the kingdom of heaven, which stands in opposition to all earthly kingdoms.

THE KINGDOM OF GOD IN THE TARGUMS AND RABBINIC LITERATURE

The Targums

An examination of the Targumic material on the question of the kingdom of God provides additional insights into the development of this idea in early Judaism and Christianity. Although the dating of the various Targums is notoriously difficult, many scholars believe that at least some of the exegetical traditions can be traced back to ordinary Aramaic usage and understanding around the time of Jesus.[37] The theme of the kingdom of God may be one such tradition. It is striking that the expressions "kingdom of God" and "kingdom of the Lord" appear to be used in the Targums (especially the Prophets) in a set and standard way.[38] This is in noticeable contrast with the other Second Temple literature in which we have found the idea of the kingship of God regularly, but relatively few examples of the exact phrase "kingdom of God." Reference to God's kingdom can be found regularly throughout the Targums, especially in the Targum to the Prophets (e.g., *Tg. Isa.* 24:23; 40:9; *Tg. Ezek.* 7:7; *Tg. Mic.* 4:7; *Tg. Zech.* 4:9; also *Tg. Onk. Exod* 15:18). My own examination of many references to the kingdom in the Targums reveals that various forms including "kingdom of the Lord," "kingdom of (your) God" and the simple "kingdom" all occur regularly. Sometimes the fuller phrases are expansions upon a plain reference to the kingdom or to reigning, while in some instances, as Chilton has pointed out, they are substituted for a reference to God himself (e.g., *Tg. Isa.* 31:4). For the purposes of this study, it is important to note than I have found no instance of the Rabbinic and Matthean

---

[37] This has been most strongly argued in a number of works by Bruce Chilton, though his voice is not alone in this view. Geza Vermes summarizes it this way: "the main body of Targumic exegesis reflects the ordinary, non-technical understanding of the message of the Bible current among Aramaic-speaking Jews in the first two or three centuries of the Christian era." Vermes, *IDB* Supplement (1976), 443. See also notes on the relevance of the Targums in Chapter Two of this work.

[38] J. J. Collins, "The Kingdom of God in the Apocrypha and Pseudepigrapha," 94.

phrase "kingdom of heaven" despite many references to God's kingdom in the Targums.

As to the meaning and function of the kingdom in the Targums, Bruce Chilton has led the charge in arguing for the close similarities between the Targumic usage and that of Jesus. In several works, Chilton has suggested that "the Targumic kingdom passages are substantively, as well as linguistically, coherent with Jesus' preaching of the kingdom."[39]

What do the Targums and Jesus mean by the kingdom of God? According to Chilton, the kingdom of God is not a distinct entity that arrives from God in the future, but is "the LORD's assertion of [his] sovereignty";[40] the announcement of the kingdom affirms "vividly but simply that God was acting and would act in strength on behalf of his people."[41] Chilton is consciously seeking to correct the predominant apocalyptic and eschatological interpretations with their specific temporal and spatial understandings of the kingdom. Chilton's work is generally careful and insightful, though not all scholars have followed his interpretation. John Collins offers critiques at several points, specifically in interpreting the Targumic references in a more 'apocalyptic' way, which do indeed look for a Jewish restoration and the resurrection of the dead (*Tg. Isa.* 26:19). In these ways Collins sees the Targumic use of the kingdom as basically "compatible with that of the Psalms of Solomon or perhaps (but less clearly) of 4 Ezra and 2 Baruch."[42] I would suggest that Chilton's view, though helpful at points, suffers in part from the same problem that Dalman's does—an overly narrow restricting of βασιλεία to the sense of "rule" or "reign."[43]

The Rabbinic Literature and Early Jewish Prayers

We may conclude our survey by examining the theme of the kingdom in the Rabbinic literature, especially the Mishnah, as well as extant forms of prayers that were used in synagogues in the first few centuries. In the latter category we find many ancient prayers which substantiate the

---

[39] Chilton, *Targumic Approaches to the Gospels*, 102. See also his *God in Strength: Jesus' Announcement of the Kingdom* (Freistadt: Plochl, 1979); idem, *The Glory of Israel: The Theology and Provenience of the Isaiah Targum* (Sheffield: JSOT, 1983); and idem, *Pure Kingdom: Jesus' Vision of God*.
[40] Chilton, *Targumic Approaches*, 103.
[41] Chilton, "Introduction," in *The Kingdom of God in the Teaching of Jesus*, 23.
[42] J. J. Collins, "The Kingdom of God in the Apocrypha and Pseudepigrapha," 94.
[43] See my critique of Dalman above in the first part of this chapter as well as the lengthier discussion in Chapter Twelve.

importance of the kingdom idea in early Judaism. For example, the eleventh petition of the Eighteen Benedictions (*Shemoneh 'Esreh*) asks God to "reign over" his people. The well-known Aramaic prayer, the *Qaddish*, which shows clear affinities to the Lord's Prayer, includes the line "May he let his kingdom rule."[44] Another prayer records that God's people "shall delight in Thy sovereignty."[45] And sometime later we have the pronouncement that "every benediction to be valid must contain not only the name of God, but must refer also to God's Kingdom" (*b. Ber.* 40b).[46] These practices in the synagogue reveal the close connection between the life and prayers of synagogue experience and the Targums, which likewise show an emphasis on the kingdom motif.

The codified Rabbinic literature, however, even its earliest manifestation in the Mishnah, shows a somewhat different appropriation of the kingdom of God.[47] In the first instance, we may note that rather than the expression "kingdom of God," we find for the first time (outside of Matthew) the phrase "the kingdom of heaven." As has been noted several times in the preceding chapters, this phrase is typically understood as equivalent to kingdom of God, except with heaven substituted for God as a reverential circumlocution. I have argued previously that there is little ground for this widespread assumption.[48] But regardless, it is important to note that even though the impression is often given that kingdom of heaven is widespread in the rabbinic literature, it is patently not. In all of the Mishnah it occurs only twice, both together in *m. Ber.* 2:2 and 2:5.[49] In fact, as Kuhn has observed in his *TDNT* study, "the

---

[44] This is the rendering of Jeremias. Dalman, *Words of Jesus*, 99, translates it as "and may He set up His sovereignty."

[45] Seder Rab Amram, i. 29b, quoted in Dalman, *Words of Jesus*, 98.

[46] Quoted in Friedlander, *The Jewish Sources of the Sermon on the Mount*, 137.

[47] Listings of kingdom references in the Mishnah and subsequent rabbinic literature can be found in several places including Dalman, *Words of Jesus*, 96–101, and Strack and Billerbeck, *Kommentar zum Neuen Testament aus Talmud und Midrasch*, 1:172–184.

[48] Recall especially Urbach's insightful study which suggests that the varied uses of Heaven as a name for God throughout the rabbinic literature (including kingdom of heaven) is used to stress the difference between God (in heaven) and humanity (on earth). E. E. Urbach, *The Sages*, 70–71.

[49] As to the dating of the expression, both instances are attributed specifically to Rabbis of the later generations (Joshua b. Karha, fourth gen., ca. 140–165; and Gamaliel, sixth gen., ca. 200–220), thus, while the dates of this phrase might indeed be later than the second century, they are likely not much earlier than these Rabbis. On the dating of sayings and Rabbis' names, see G. Stemberger, *Introduction to the Talmud and Midrash*, 56–62.

first point to notice is that the expression is rare in the rabbinic literature and not nearly as important as, e.g. in the preaching of Jesus."[50]

So we may note that the theme of the kingdom is not nearly as predominant in the rabbinic literature as we might suppose. But what is the theological use of this motif in this corpus? Scholars have observed that in the rabbinic literature the idea of the kingdom of heaven is closely identified with the rule of God's Law. The one who "takes upon himself the yoke of the kingdom of heaven" (*m. Ber.* 2:2) is obliging himself to love God and keep his commandments. The one who ceases to cite the Shema daily would cast off "the yoke of the kingdom of heaven" (*m. Ber.* 2:5). Even the proselyte, as Simeon ben Lakish (c. 260 CE) says, who adopts the law thereby "takes upon himself the sovereignty of heaven."[51] As Ladd summarizes it, "obedience to the Law is thus equivalent to the experience of God's kingdom or rule."[52] Beyond this personal and individualistic focus on the kingdom of God,[53] the assorted rabbinic traditions also at times speak of the kingdom in an eschatological way, looking forward to the coming of the Messiah. At this point God's sovereignty will be manifest to all.[54] Overall, however, there does not seem to be a very developed use of or great theological significance to the use of kingdom of heaven in the early rabbinic literature. Recently, Jacob Neusner has queried whether kingdom of heaven functions as a heavy "category-formation" idea in the Aggadic and Halakic literature like it obviously does in the Gospels. He concludes in the negative. For the early Jewish literature, unlike the Gospels, kingdom of heaven "forms no more than an inert category-formation, one that figures as part of the background of ideas that everywhere inhere but nowhere take an active, generative role."[55]

---

[50] Kuhn in *Bible Key Words: Basileia*, 17, which is a reproduction of his *TDNT* article.

[51] Dalman, *Words of Jesus*, 97. Dalman gives other similar examples.

[52] G. E. Ladd, *A Theology of the New Testament* (rev. ed.; Grand Rapids: Eerdmans, 1993), 59.

[53] Louis Jacobs defines the kingdom of heaven as "the Rabbinic expression for the sovereignty of God as acknowledged by human beings." Louis Jacobs, "Kingdom of Heaven," *A Concise Companion to the Jewish Religion* (Oxford University Press, 1999), cited at *Oxford Reference Online*.

[54] Kuhn in *Bible Key Words: Basileia*, 18–19.

[55] Jacob Neusner, "The Kingdom of Heaven in Kindred Systems, Judaic and Christian," *BBR* 15.2 (2005), 281.

Conclusion

The preceding discussion of the idea of God's kingship throughout the Second Temple period establishes that although this motif was nowhere as predominant as it became in Jesus' teaching, it was not an uncommon nor unintelligible theme. The question remains open as to which strand or strands of the diverse Jewish tradition most informed Jesus' understanding of the kingdom. But a more significant question for this project concerns the origin of Matthew's unique phrase kingdom of heaven, which, as we have seen, finds no chronological literary precedents and only two instances in the Mishnah. To conclude this chapter we will examine a number of texts which combine language about God's kingship with heaven and earth. The most important of these will prove to be the highly-structured stories of Daniel 2–7, which very likely relate closely to Matthew's phrase.

THE KINGDOMS OF HEAVEN AND EARTH AND DANIEL 2–7

Throughout this work I have been highlighting various texts and traditions which combine the two ideas of heaven and earth. We have observed that at times these words are conjoined as a merismatic expression of the universe, while frequently this relationship is instead inverted so that the two terms (still conjoined) communicate a contrast, antithesis, or comparison between the two poles of heaven and earth. For the purposes of this chapter and the next, it is worthwhile to highlight an assortment of texts which in some way combine the notion of God's kingdom with either heaven or both heaven and earth.

In the first instance, we can note several occasions where God is described in the Second Temple literature as the Sovereign, King, or Lord of heaven. For example, the Jewish God is called the "King of heaven" three times in Tobit,[56] as well as once each in 3 Maccabees (2:2), Psalms of Solomon (2:30), and 1 Esdras (4:36).[57] 2 Maccabees gives us three

---

[56] 13:13 plus twice more in the Sinaiticus manuscript of Tobit at 1:18 and 13:17. This longer version (from Codex Sinaiticus) is now considered the older, more reliable version, based on manuscript finds of Tobit at Qumran. See Peter W. Flint, "Noncanonical Writings in the Dead Sea Scrolls: Apocrypha, Other Previously Known Writings, Pseudepigrapha," in *The Bible at Qumran: Text, Shape and Interpretation* (ed. Peter Flint), 90.

[57] "King of heaven" also appears in *Test Benj* 10:7, but this text is clearly a Christian interpolation, most likely influenced by Matthew. See discussion in Chapter Five.

occurrences of the similar phrase "Sovereign (δυνάστα) of heaven/the heavens" in 15:3, 4, and 22. We also find a couple of instances of "Lord of heaven and earth" in Tobit (7:17) and Judith (9:12). These ways of referring to God cannot be said to form a consistent pattern or trend.[58] They are certainly not widespread expressions and likely arose as a specific derivation from the more popular Second Temple expression "God of heaven." Moreover, most of these do not appear to be consciously connected with the heaven and earth theme.

There is an assortment of texts, however, which do in some measure combine the idea of God's kingship with the heaven and earth word pair. In the OT this theme crops up on occasion, primarily (but not exclusively) in the latest writings. A good example is found in Psalm 2. This psalm, which has played an important part in Jewish and Christian interpretive history, has at its core a contrast between the Lord in heaven on the one hand and the soon-to-be judged kings and rulers of the earth on the other. Throughout the psalm this contrast uses the familiar language of the heaven and earth disjunction. In verses 2–3 the kings *of the earth* (also in v. 10) take counsel against the Lord and his anointed one, but the Lord laughs and scoffs at their foolishness from his throne *in heaven* (v. 4). He sets his Son-King upon Mount Zion (vv. 6–7) and will give possession "of the ends of the earth" to him (v. 8).

Similarly, several times in Isaiah and Jeremiah we find a comparable contrast, though usually more subtly delivered. Often these books use the regal expression "Lord of Hosts" to describe God. At the same time, both Isaiah and Jeremiah many times refer to Gentile rulers as the kings and kingdoms of the earth, nearly always in a negative way (e.g., Isa 14:19; 23:17; 37:16; Jer 15:4; 29:18; 50:41). In several texts we also have an explicit connection of the heaven and earth and kingdom themes. For example, Isaiah 37:16 states "O LORD of hosts, God of Israel, who art enthroned above the cherubim, thou art the God, thou alone, of all the kingdoms of the *earth*; thou hast made *heaven and earth*" (RSV).

In the latest OT writings as well as in the Apocrypha, we find several texts where kingdom, heaven and earth are combined. In 2 Chronicles 36:23 (repeated in Ezra 1:2) we read, "Thus says Cyrus king of Persia,

---

[58] Though, as I have suggested in Chapter Five, there appears to have been some trend toward using plural forms of οὐρανός when referring to God with a term such as δυνάστα. Nevertheless, calling God the Ruler or King of heaven was not a common practice in the Second Temple period.

'The LORD, the God of *heaven*, has given me all the kingdoms of the *earth*, and he has charged me to build him a house at Jerusalem, which is in Judah'."[59] In *Psalms of Solomon* 2:30 the expression "king over the *heavens*" (βασιλεὺς ἐπὶ τῶν οὐρανῶν) is explicitly contrasted with the proud man in 2:29 who claims he will be "lord of *earth and sea*." In 2 Maccabees 15:1–5 we find an interplay between God as the "Sovereign in *heaven*" (ἐν οὐρανῷ δυνάστης) and the wicked Nicanor who proclaims himself "sovereign on *earth*" (δυνάστης ἐπὶ τῆς γῆς). Nicanor plans to attack Judas and his followers on the Sabbath, and the Jews with Nicanor beg him not to because it violates a command given by "the Living Lord himself, the Sovereign in *heaven*" (15:4). He responds that he is a "sovereign on *earth*" and so they must obey him.

This same kind of contrast can be found in a more extended way in the book of Judith, which is roughly contemporary with 2 Maccabees. As was discussed in Chapter Seven above, the story of Judith is rich with literary pointers to the heaven and earth theme. Throughout the book, the God of heaven is posited as the Lord of heaven and earth, over against Nebuchadnezzar who depicts himself as the king of all the earth (see the full discussion in Chapter Seven). As was mentioned previously, it is probable that the blatantly ahistorical use of Nebuchadnezzar in Judith serves to connect this book with the well-known and related stories of Daniel. To these we now turn.

Daniel 2–7 and the Themes of Heaven, Earth and Kingdom

So far we have seen that on occasion throughout the Jewish literature the themes of heaven, earth, and kingdom are woven together. But no text combines and appropriates these themes to the extent and degree that we find in Daniel 2–7.

The importance of the book of Daniel in the apocalyptic tradition is widely recognized and cannot be overestimated. Because of this, chapters seven through twelve—concerning a series of "apocalyptic" visions—typically receive the bulk of scholarly treatment. However, the first six chapters of stories are equally important. As John Goldingay writes, Daniel is "as much a series of short stories to which visions are attached as a series of visions prefaced by some stories."[60] Moreover,

---

[59] It appears to be no accident canonically that the closing words of the MT have "God of heaven" and "kingdoms of the earth" affixed together. This likely reflects in part the importance of the heaven and earth theme in the Jewish literary tradition.

[60] John Goldingay, *Daniel*, 321.

while the book of Daniel can be broken into two parts (chapters 1–6 and chapters 7–12), it is important to recognize that in fact chapters 2–7 also form a coherent unit. It is not without significance that 2:4–7:28 comes to us in Aramaic and not Hebrew like the rest of the book. This unit of the book has some degree of independent status by virtue of its separate language and the fact that it very well may have circulated as an independent Aramaic work.[61] Additionally, many scholars have observed that chapters 2–7 form a structured unit consisting of a chiastic arrangement of stories: chapters 2 and 7 are related by the four-kingdom schema; 3 and 6 are both tales of deliverance; and 4 and 5 present stories of two kings' different responses to God.[62] While there are also other ways to structure the material and its relationship to the rest of the book, there is sufficient evidence to support this basic arrangement.[63]

All of this leads to the conclusion that examining chapters 2–7 as a separate unit is a reasonable exercise. Few studies have been done on this subsection of Daniel,[64] and none has uncovered what I consider to be the most striking point: that this important section of Daniel provides the most extensive and elaborate development of the heaven, earth, and kingdom themes found anywhere in the Jewish literature.[65] Both

---

[61] See John J. Collins, *Daniel: With an Introduction to Apocalyptic Literature* (Grand Rapids: Eerdmans, 1984), 30; idem, *Daniel* (Hermeneia), 33–35. In light of the linguistic difference and the way these chapters hang together, this is certainly possible.

[62] This was first observed by A. Lenglet, "La structure littéraire de Daniel 2–7," *Bib* 53 (1972): 169–190, and followed by many scholars since, such as Jürgen C. H. Lebram, *Das Buch Daniel* (Zürich: Theologische Verlag, 1984).

[63] Seeing chapters 2–7 as a coherent unit is not to deny that there is also a structural distinction between chapters 1–6 (the stories) and 7–12 (the visions). In an elaborate work of literature such as Daniel, more than one structure can often be discerned. In the case of Daniel the rare bilingual nature of the extant MT gives credence to some distinct structure along these lines although a genre distinction can still be made between 1–6 and 7–12. Goldingay, *Daniel*, 324–326, reviews several different ways in which the structure of Daniel can be analyzed, each of which "enables us to perceive aspects of the book" (p. 324).

[64] The fullest I have found is Meadowcroft, *Aramaic Daniel and Greek Daniel*, which analyzes not only literary differences, but also theological *Tendenz* of the Aramaic and Hebrew sections. For chapters 4–6 one may also consult R. Albertz, *Der Gott des Daniel: Untersuchungen zu Dan 4–6 in der Septuagintafassung sowie zu Komposition und Theologie des aramäischen Danielsbuches* (SBS 131; Stuttgart: Katholisches Bibelwerk, 1988).

[65] Goldingay's discussion of Daniel comes the closest to recognizing the centrality of these three combined themes. He notes that chapter four introduces the key antithetical pair of terms, heaven and earth, and that the significance of "King of heaven" in 4:37 brings together at the climax the chapter's two key motifs, kingship and heaven. But he does not note the juxtaposition of these three themes nor develop the idea. Goldingay, *Daniel*, 85, 90.

the Aramaic and the Greek traditions of Daniel 2–7 go to great lengths to describe God as the Most High, heavenly God in contrast to and reigning over all the kingdoms and potentates of the human and earthly realm. This, as we will see, proves to be a key idea in Daniel 2–7 and points forward to a similar focus in the Gospel of Matthew.

The centrality of the heaven and earth theme in Dan 2–7 is seen in the first instance by the sheer frequency of the pair lexically. Thirteen times in the Aramaic MT, heaven and earth are paired together, and the OG has two additional occurrences (4:17, 37).[66] An even more dominant lexical theme, as is widely recognized in scholarship, is that of kingdom. Aramaic מלכות ("kingdom") appears some 53 times in the MT and the Greek equivalent only slightly less frequently in the Theodotion (52x) and OG (47x) versions. The crucial point here is how closely connected these two themes are in the narrative of chapters 2–7.

The most lengthy and weighty of the stories in chapters 2 to 7 is found right in the middle of the chiastic structure in chapter 4.[67] The themes of heaven and earth and kingdom occur throughout all the stories, but are found in their most developed form in this central story. In the following analysis, I will follow the chiastic structure of chapters 2–7, beginning with the outer ring in chapter 2.

In chapter 2 the God of heaven appears as the one who alone can reveal dreams and their interpretations (2:19–23, 27–28). The unsuccessful and fretting wise men defend their inability by claiming that "no person on earth" could do what the king is asking (2:10). In contrast, before Daniel proves the hero, he assures the king that instead, "there is a God in heaven who reveals mysteries" (2:28). Chapter 2 then culminates with the introduction of the kingdom theme. The interpretation of Nebuchadnezzar's dream predicts a downward progression of four earthly kingdoms, each typified by a different metal—gold, silver, bronze, and iron. Each kingdom "will rule over all the earth" (2:39) though the last will be brittle in parts. Following these kingdoms,

---

[66] In a more recent article Tim Meadowcroft has argued for "an apocalyptic cosmology of permeability between earth and heaven" in the latter half of Daniel, although he does not comment on the centrality of heaven and earth pairs throughout. Tim Meadowcroft, "Who are the Princes of Persia and Greece (Daniel 10)? Pointers Towards the Danielic Vision of Earth and Heaven," *JSOT* 29/1 (2004): 99–113.

[67] Matthias Henze concurs with Lenglet's analysis and observes that while chapters 4 and 5 together form a unit in the middle of the chiasm, Daniel 4 is the center and most important story. Henze, *The Madness of King Nebuchadnezzar: The Ancient Near Eastern Origins and Early History of Interpretation of Daniel 4* (JSJS 61; Leiden: Brill, 1999), 13–14.

however, God himself will establish his kingdom, which will crush all other kingdoms and, unlike them, will be everlasting (2:44). Throughout this description, woven in is the heaven and earth theme. Daniel tells Nebuchadnezzar that he is the epitome of kingship, the "king of kings" who rules over all the realm of beasts of the field and the birds of the heavens (2:37-38; cf. Gen 1-2 language). But Daniel also makes very clear that it is the God of heaven who has given all this to him (2:37). Moreover, in contrast to the four earth-reigning kingdoms, it is the God of heaven who will establish the everlasting kingdom (2:44), and the rock of his kingdom will consequently "become a great mountain and fill the whole earth" (2:35). Thus, all that is earthly is shown to be ultimately limited and contingent upon the heavenly God.

Chiastically, chapter 7 parallels the vision of chapter 2, though using much more symbolic and apocalyptic language.[68] Here Daniel has a dream in which four beasts arise and reign until the Ancient of Days appears (7:9-12), followed by the Son of Man to whom is given all dominion forever (7:13-14). This dream is interpreted for Daniel, like chapter 2, as a picture of four kingdoms to come. These kingdoms rule over the earth and the fourth, most vicious kingdom "devours the whole earth" (7:23). However, the one like a Son of Man, who appears on the clouds of heaven, will destroy the evil leaders of this fourth kingdom on behalf of "the saints of the Most High" (7:18, 22, 27). The vision concludes with a benedictory word that these saints will receive a kingdom greater than all the kingdoms which are under heaven:

> And the kingdom and the dominion and the greatness of the kingdoms under the whole heaven shall be given to the people of the saints of the Most High; their kingdom shall be an everlasting kingdom, and all dominions shall serve and obey them. (7:27 RSV)

Thus, in both chapters 2 and 7, the outer ring of the chiasm, we find a predominance of the kingdom idea, interwoven with the contrastive theme of heaven and earth.[69] The number of times that heaven,

---

[68] The connections between chapters 2 and 7 have been observed by several scholars. For example, Towner states that the dream of Nebuchadnezzar in chapter 2 "is in many ways recapitulated in the animal allegory of Daniel 7." W. Sibley Towner, *Daniel* (Atlanta: John Knox, 1984), 6.

[69] In an interesting essay, Robert Wilson has suggested that behind the imagery of Daniel 7 lies the creation myth of Genesis. His argument could be strengthened by the observation that heaven and earth is a key theme in Daniel 2-7, as it obviously is in Genesis as well. Robert W. Wilson, "Creation and New Creation: The Role of

earth, and kingdom occur in these stories is striking and more than coincidental.

The next pair of chapters, 3 and 6, will not require as much comment as neither the heaven and earth theme nor the kingdom motif finds the same breadth of expression in this duo of deliverance stories, though the idea is still present. Both tales extol the virtue of Jewish fidelity to God even when it requires breaking the laws of an all-powerful earthly potentate. Both focus on the superiority of the God of the Jews over any earthly king as seen in God's ability to protect his faithful servants even in the midst of gruesome kingly punishments—the furnace and the lions' den. The earthly kings have the authority and ability to inflict death upon those on the earth, but the ones who trust in the God of heaven are delivered (cf. Judith). Both stories end with the pagan king confessing and decreeing worship of the God of the Jews because he is the true god. In fact, the chapter divisions in the MT make this parallelism much stronger than is reflected in the English and Greek versions. In the MT, chapter 3 concludes with the kingly speech of 4:1–3 and for reasons of parallelism, they are better considered as the conclusion to chapter 3. The content and wording of these verses closely parallel Darius' decree in 6:25–28 [MT 6:26–29]. In both speeches, the signs and wonders of God are exalted (MT 3:32; 6:28) and most interesting, the kingdom theme materializes out of nowhere. That is, although neither of the stories in chapters 3 and 6 focus on a contrast of kingdoms as in chapters 2 and 7, an inclusio is formed (in the MT at least) by a closing note on the everlasting nature of God's kingdom (MT 3:33; 6:27).

The verses in question really form an overlapping transition between chapters 3 and 4. As just seen, they form clear bookends for the parallel stories in chapters 3 and 6, but they also naturally align with chapter 4 with its strong emphasis on the kingdom of God.

We now come to the key middle section of the cycle of stories in Daniel 2–7: chapters 4 and 5. These chapters parallel one another as stories of a pagan king's response to God,[70] but there is no doubt that

---

Creation Imagery in the Book of Daniel," in *God Who Creates: Essays in Honor of W. Sibley Towner* (ed. William P. Brown and S. Dean McBride; Grand Rapids: Eerdmans, 2000): 190–203.

[70] Towner observes that Nebuchadnezzar's success at learning the sovereignty of God will be contrasted by the failure of his 'son' Belshazzar to learn the same in chapter 5. Towner, *Daniel*, 65.

chapter 4 is the lengthier and weightier of the two. The centrality of the heaven and earth and kingdom themes in Dan 2–7 is highlighted by the fact that in this crucial fourth chapter, these themes are the predominant focus. Chapter 4 is the epicenter from which the heaven and earth plus kingdom motif emanates throughout Daniel 2–7.

As stated above, MT 3:31–33 [Engl 4:1–3] serves to conclude the cycle of stories in chapters 3 and 6, and Nebuchadnezzar's speech also introduces the main theme of chapter 4. Throughout, we find the language of heaven and earth and kingdom. It is noteworthy that Nebuchadnezzar's declaration is addressed in universal terms, to all peoples and nations "that live in all the earth" with a message of God's universal kingdom. We learn from the subsequent dream and its interpretation that Nebuchadnezzar's kingdom is described as spanning the entire earthly realm. It is the tree whose height reaches to heaven/the sky and is visible to the end of the whole earth (4:11 [MT 4:8]).[71] The foliage and fruit of the tree provides sustenance for the beasts of the field and the birds of the heavens (4:11). Daniel explicates this imagery by telling Nebuchadnezzar that he has "grown and become strong. Your greatness has grown and reaches to heaven, and your dominion to the ends of the earth" (4:22 [MT 4:19]). This point is made three times with the original vision, Daniel's retelling of it, and finally his interpretation. There could be no fuller description of the greatness of a human and earthly king, and the emphasis on Nebuchadnezzar's magnitude is clear.[72]

Just as the greatness of Nebuchadnezzar's kingdom is described with heaven and earth language, so is the humiliating punishment which his hubris brings about. The same beasts and birds will scatter, and the tree/king will be drenched with the dew of heaven and share with the beasts the grass of the earth. Again, this Genesis creation imagery and language is repeated multiple times (4:14–15, 23, 25, 32, 33).

All of this culminates with the very clear point of the entire story: "in order that the living may know that the Most High rules over the kingdom/realm of humanity, and gives it to whom he will, and sets over

---

[71] The OG has a slightly different poetic description, still utilizing the heaven and earth pair: "Its crown drew near to heaven and its trunk to the clouds, filling everything under heaven. The sun and moon dwelt in it and it lit all the earth." (Meadowcroft's translation from *Aramaic Daniel and Greek Daniel*.)

[72] Again, the OG makes this claim even more explicit: "all the birds of heaven nesting in [the tree] are the might of the earth and of the nations and of all tongues unto the ends of the earth. And all regions serve you" (4:21, Meadowcroft's translation).

it the lowliest of men" (4:17, my translation).[73] This point first appears in the dream in the words of the angelic watchers from heaven (4:17) and is then paraphrased repeatedly throughout the narrative:

> "until you know that the Most High is ruler over the kingdom/realm of humanity and bestows it on whomever he wishes..." (4:25)

> "your kingdom will be assured to you after you recognize that heaven [or, the heavenly power] rules..." (4:26)

> "until you recognize that the Most High is ruler over the kingdom/realm of humanity and bestows it on whomever he wishes..." (4:32)

And finally, Nebuchadnezzar's post-beast declaration is a confession of this same point, full of kingdom and heaven and earth language:

> At the end of the days I, Nebuchadnezzar, lifted my eyes to heaven, and my reason returned to me, and I blessed the Most High, and praised and honored him who lives for ever; for his dominion is an everlasting dominion, and his kingdom endures from generation to generation; all the inhabitants of the earth are accounted as nothing; and he does according to his will in the host of heaven and among the inhabitants of the earth; and none can stay his hand or say to him, "What doest thou?" (4:34–35 RSV)

The powerful story of chapter 4 ends with Nebuchadnezzar's words: "Now I praise, exalt, and honor the King of heaven" (4:37), thereby combining the two themes into one phrase. This expression is unique in the canonical OT, though as mentioned above, it does occur a few times in other literature (1 Esd 4:46, 58; Tobit 13:7, 11; cf. similar expression in Dan 5:23). Goldingay confirms my thesis that these two themes are central to chapter 4 and points out that phrase "King of heaven" "brings together at the climax of the chapter its two key motifs, kingship and heaven."[74]

Although the OG of chapter 4 varies significantly in wording and expanded material, the same main point of the story is emphasized in OG 4:17 and following.[75]

---

[73] Many commentators understand this to be the focus of the story, such as Porteous, *Daniel*, 65. On the contrast of kingdoms in chapter 4, see also K. Koch, "Gottes Herrschaft über das Reich des Menschen: Daniel 4 im Licht neuer Funde," in *The Book of Daniel in the Light of New Findings* (ed. A. S. van der Woude; Leuven: Leuven University Press, 1993): 77–119.

[74] Goldingay, *Daniel*, 90.

[75] The following translations come from Meadowcroft.

> "until he knows the Lord of heaven has authority over everything in heaven and on earth, and whatever he wants he does among them…" (4:17)
>
> "the Lord lives in heaven and his authority is over all the earth…" (4:27; cp. 4:26)
>
> "so that you might find out that the God of heaven has authority in the kingdom of men…" (4:31)
>
> "For it has pleased me to bring before you and your wise men that God exists and his marvels are great, his kingdom is a kingdom forever…" (4:37c)

The point of the chapter 4 story is clear: the God of heaven's everlasting kingdom rules over all and even the greatest human king on earth is nothing in comparison (4:35). In fact, all human-earthly kings have their authority from this heavenly God and can likewise lose all authority according to his sovereign plan. This tension between God's and humanity's kingdoms is described in terms of a heaven and earth contrast. It is the God of heaven (or Most High; cf. the semantic connection of the heights and heaven) whose kingdom reigns forever, while all earthly kingdoms are shown to be dependent and fragile. This same point is made throughout the cycle of stories in chapters 2 and 7 as well.

Thus, woven into the story of Daniel 2–7 we find God's kingdom contrasted with the empires of humankind, all the while overlapping with a similar contrast of heaven and earth. This rich tapestry matches other furnishings in Jewish literature, though in Daniel 2–7 it is more compact and tightly woven. It is not only in these chapters of Daniel that these themes appear, although they are brightest there. John Collins observes that "throughout the book [of Daniel] the kingdom of God provides the frame for human history."[76] Goldingay concurs: "The theme that is central to Daniel as it is to no other book in the OT is the kingdom of God."[77] These sentiments are widely acknowledged. Goldingay also goes further and discerns the importance of the heaven theme. He concludes: "the whole book looks for the realization of the reign of [the heavenly] God on earth" and "the purpose of God is to be realized on earth…by the power of heaven."[78]

---

[76] J. J. Collins, *Daniel: With an Introduction to Apocalyptic Literature*, 38.
[77] Goldingay, *Daniel*, 330.
[78] Goldingay, *Daniel*, 330.

My point is that in the narrative of Daniel 2–7, the author is addressing the crucial Second Temple question concerning the kingdom of God—how does the God of heaven rule in light of the apparent superior power of the oppressive earthly kings? Daniel 2–7 offers the consoling answer that God the King does indeed rule in heaven and from there will protect those who trust in him. But even more, as the God of heaven/Most High, he is the one who has placed earthly rulers in their places and can easily depose them as he did Nebuchadnezzar. This indeed he will do when his eternal kingdom comes from heaven upon the earth. Thus, with great literary skill and theological sensitivity, Daniel 2–7 handles the important question of theodicy through juxtaposing the themes of kingdom and heaven and earth. As we will see in the next chapter, this literary device and social context likely provide the background for Matthew's unique expression, kingdom of heaven.

CHAPTER TWELVE

MATTHEW'S "KINGDOM OF HEAVEN"

The fourth and final aspect of Matthew's idiolectic use of heaven can be found in his frequently-used expression kingdom of heaven. It is appropriate to save until last the discussion of this important phrase because of the centrality of the kingdom message in Jesus' ministry and because in many ways, the heaven and earth theme in Matthew finds its consummation in these words.

This chapter will cover several important topics related to the kingdom of heaven in Matthew. First we will observe how central the kingdom message is in the First Gospel and review the semantic issues of how to understand and translate βασιλεία. We will then turn to the origin and meaning of kingdom of heaven in Matthew, offering a new understanding for its development in Matthew. Also to be examined is the important question of whether there is a difference in Matthew between kingdom of heaven and kingdom of God. Finally, we will examine how Matthew's kingdom of heaven functions as part of his broader heaven and earth theme.

Jesus' Kerygma and the Kingdom

Centrality and Forms

Regardless of whether one is approaching the Gospels from a narrative perspective or one is engaging in some form of historical Jesus study, there is undoubtedly a scholarly consensus that the kingdom or reign of God is the central message of Jesus' ministry. Substantiation of this claim can easily be found in even the most cursory treatments of the kingdom of God theme.[1]

---

[1] Virtually every book on Jesus' kingdom message begins with this understanding. James Dunn's recent *Jesus Remembered*, which could certainly not be called a cursory treatment, summarizes the issue this way: "In short, the evidence we have points to one and only one clear conclusion: that Jesus was remembered as preaching about the kingdom of God and that this was central to his message and mission." Dunn, *Jesus Remembered*, 387.

Each of the Synoptic accounts readily shows the centrality of the kingdom, but Matthew above all highlights this theme. For example, at the basic level of vocabulary frequency, Matthew uses both βασιλεία and βασιλεύς significantly more often than the other Evangelists.[2] More telling, we find that the kingdom is emphasized at crucial points in Matthew's narrative. At the beginning of John the Baptist's ministry (3:2), at the beginning of Jesus' shortly after (4:17), and then again in 10:7 when Jesus commissions his own followers to go out, we find the same announcement: "The kingdom of heaven is near." Likewise, at the structural seams of Matthew in 4:23, 9:35, and 24:14, we find the thrice-repeated phrase "the gospel of the kingdom."[3] Additionally, through the weight of simple repetition, Matthew makes the kingdom focus clear: the Beatitudes are framed with reference to the kingdom of heaven (5:3, 10); entering the kingdom is what Jesus regularly exhorts people to do (5:19–20; 7:21; 18:3; 21:31; 23:13); the great Christian prayer—the Lord's Prayer—has at its heart the request for God's kingdom to come to earth (6:10); the entire Sermon on the Mount is rife with the language of the kingdom[4]; the series of parables in chapter 13—which chiastically form the center of Matthew—describe in manifold ways what the kingdom is like,[5] and later the kingdom is compared to laborers in a vineyard (20:1), a king throwing a wedding feast for his son (22:2), and virgins who keep their lamps lit (25:1). At crucial places and through constant repetition, Matthew particularly makes his hearers aware of the centrality of the message of the coming kingdom of God. In agreement with the sentiments of many commentators, Donald Hagner calls the kingdom in Matthew the "controlling theme."[6]

---

[2] βασιλεία occurs 55 times in Matthew in a variety of phrases, including kingdom of heaven (32x) and kingdom of God (4x). This is more often than any other Gospel and more frequent than the rest of the NT combined. The same is true for βασιλεύς ("king") which occurs 22 times in Matthew, 16 in John, 12 in Mark and 11 in Luke.

[3] See Jack Dean Kingsbury, *Matthew: Structure, Christology, and Kingdom*, 128–131. Hagner, *Matthew 1–13*, li ff.

[4] Betz states that "the principal theological concept in the Sermon on the Mount is that of 'the kingdom of heaven'." Betz, "Cosmogony and Ethics in the Sermon on the Mount," 120.

[5] R. T. France observes that kingdom of heaven "functions (especially in chapter 13) virtually as a slogan for the whole scope of the ministry of Jesus." France, *Matthew: Evangelist and Teacher*, 262.

[6] Hagner, *Matthew 1–13*, lx.

It is well recognized that unique to Matthew is the expression kingdom of heaven. Much more will be said about this phrase in subsequent sections. For now, it is important to note that although this expression is the predominant one, it is not the only way to which the kingdom is referred in Matthew. We also find four occurrences of the traditional kingdom of God (12:28; 19:24; 21:31, 43), five references to the Father's kingdom (6:10, 33; 13:43; 25:34; 26:29), two occurrences of the kingdom of the Son of Man (13:41; 16:28), one reference to Jesus' kingdom (20:21), as well as six instances of the simple kingdom (4:23; 8:12; 9:35; 13:19, 38; 24:14).[7] These frequent and manifold expressions have led many scholars to understand the kingdom as "the single most comprehensive concept in the first Gospel."[8]

Semantic Matters

There are two related semantic matters concerning the kingdom to discuss. The first concerns how to understand the intended sense of βασιλεία. In the previous chapter we observed that Gustaf Dalman's view (that the Hebrew/Aramaic words for kingdom mean *always* kingly rule and never the kingdom) has become a widely held position. This "rule/reign-only" view has been applied not only to OT and Jewish studies, but also to the analysis of Jesus' proclamation. However, as helpful and correcting as Dalman's view may be to an older view of the kingdom as territory only, we are not required to swing to the opposite arc point of the pendulum in our understanding. There have been several sympathetic but reasoned critiques of Dalman which manifest a more balanced view.[9] A close reading of the Gospels reveals that in

---

[7] There are also a few instances where kingdom occurs but not in reference to God's kingdom, such as Satan's kingdom (12:26) and kingdoms of the earthly world (4:8; 12:25; 24:7 [2x]).

[8] Kingsbury, *Matthew: Structure, Christology, and Kingdom*, 128.

[9] A well-known example is Aalen, "'Reign' and 'House' in the Kingdom of God in the Gospels": 215–240. Less well-known are the number of articles written by and for Bible translators. In a couple of specialized translation journals, several linguists working "on the ground" in foreign language Bible translation have wrestled repeatedly with how to understand and faithfully render the NT's use of βασιλεία into an assortment of world languages. Many (but not all) of these scholars argue that there are a variety of meanings that vary according to context and these contextual factors must be taken into consideration. βασιλεία cannot always be translated as "rule" or "reign." This stands in noticeable contrast with Dalman's advocacy for the single meaning of "rule." Notable essays include Barclay Newman, Jr. "Translating 'The Kingdom of God' and 'The Kingdom of Heaven' in the New Testament," *Bible Translator* 25/4 (1974): 401–404; idem, "The Kingdom of God/Heaven in the Gospel of Matthew,"

fact, the uses of kingdom language are too variegated and nuanced to force upon all of them the monolithic conception of kingly rule.[10] In the Gospels βασιλεία is a multivalent term whose semantic range at times includes spatial notions.[11] While the idea of reign or rule may indeed be the most frequent usage, it is a naïve linguistic understanding to operate as if this "core idea" excludes all other areas on the map of meaning. It is far more reasonable to speak of the different ways in which βασιλεία is used in different contexts.[12] We will revisit this idea one more time below when discussing Matthew's kingdom of heaven.

Bible Translator 27/4 (1976): 427–434; idem, "Translating 'The Kingdom of God' Outside the Gospels," *Bible Translator* 29/2 (1978): 225–231; Warren Glover, "'The Kingdom of God' in Luke," *Bible Translator* 29/2 (1978): 231–237; Willis Ott, "A New Look at the Concept of the Kingdom of God," *Notes on Translation* special edition 2 (1984): 2–81; Tony Pope and Randall Buth, "Kingdom of God, Kingdom of Heaven," *Notes on Translation* 119 (1987): 1–31; Rick Brown, "Translating the Whole Concept of the Kingdom," *Notes on Translation* 14/2 (2000): 1–48; idem, "A Brief History of Interpretations of 'The Kingdom of God' and Some Consequences for Translation," *Notes on Translation* 15/2 (2001): 3–23.

[10] A most recent survey of this discussion is found in Hans Kvalbein's essay on the meaning of kingdom language in the *Gospel of Thomas*. He argues that the spatial sense may indeed be the best starting point for understanding βασιλεία τοῦ θεοῦ in all four Gospels. He mentions several scholars who have expressed similar sentiments and he concludes that "there is no reason to replace the well-established translation 'kingdom of God' with a *nomen actionis* like 'rule' or 'reign of God' in presentations of the message of Jesus." Hans Kvalbein, "The Kingdom of the Father in the Gospel of Thomas," in John Fotopoulos, ed., *The New Testament and Early Christian Literature in Greco-Roman Context: Studies in Honor of David E. Aune* (Leiden: Brill, 2006), 206.

[11] This is the understanding expressed by a number of scholars including *BDAG*, U. Luz, J. C. O'Neill, F. W. Beare, S. Aalen, Norman Perrin, Mark Saucy, Herman Ridderbos, J. P. Meier, and others. Saucy observes that "while the emphasis of the term may be on the reign, one can hardly imagine a reign that has no realm." He goes on to quote Ridderbos to the same effect: "In the nature of the case a dominion to be effective must create or maintain a territory where it can operate. So the absence of any idea of a spatial Kingdom would be very strange." H. Norman Perrin, *The Kingdom of God in the Teaching of Jesus*, 168–185; Mark Saucy, "The Kingdom-of-God Sayings in Matthew," *Bibliotheca Sacra* 151 (April–June 1994), 182, n.21; Herman Ridderbos, *The Coming of the Kingdom* (Philadelphia: Presbyterian and Reformed, 1962), 26, 343–344. Beare, *Matthew*, 35. Ulrich Luz, "βασιλεία" in Balz and Schneider, *Exegetical Dictionary of the New Testament*, 1:201. J. C. O'Neill, "The Kingdom of God": 130–141. J. P. Meier, *A Marginal Jew, Volume 2*, 240.

[12] This is the view convincingly argued by Rick Brown in his essay, "A Brief History of Interpretations of 'The Kingdom of God'." Brown traces the history of interpretation and shows how Dalman's novel views fit into late nineteenth-century thoughts. Now, however, as Brown points out (concurring with O'Neill), commentators who follow Dalman's "one meaning only" view must go to unbelievable lengths of contorting assorted texts to fit their one meaning. This over-simplified approach "can blind the translator to the breadth of meaning that the kingdom terms have in their many different contexts" (p. 18). Again, it is unfortunate

Intimately related to discerning the semantic meaning of βασιλεία is the question of how to translate the term into English. This is obviously the counterpart to the previous discussion, but of late it has taken on some new hues because of political and social concerns related to the term "kingdom." While Dalman's view has been known and heeded for some time, it has only been in the last few decades that scholars have actually begun using a different term when translating βασιλεία. Old habits die hard, and the medium of print (especially when it comes to Bible translations) is a conservative enterprise. Nevertheless, with increasing frequency in recent years, one finds works in both English and German which use some form of "rule" or "reign" as a conscious substitute for "kingdom." Footnotes testify that this is due to the influence of Dalman. In the last ten years particularly, however, another translation option has come to the table: "empire." This latter term has arisen because of new readings of the NT in light of its Roman imperial context. Several scholars have begun translating βασιλεία with "empire," stating that the use of this term in the NT was in conscious opposition to Caesar and the injustices of the Roman Empire. Most notable in this regard is the prolific Matthean scholar Warren Carter. In fact, a chronological reading of Carter's works over the last decade reveals a conscious concern about how to translate βασιλεία and a shift in emphasis. In his 1997 *JSNT* article, Carter acknowledges the difficulty of translating the word and recognizes that while "reign" is the primary meaning, at times spatial and temporal aspects *are* present.[13] He goes on to point out a trend in some quarters to use even more non-traditional translations. Several feminist scholars prefer to avoid the supposed patriarchy in "kingdom" and instead use "household" or "kin-dom."[14] As another example, W. J. Everett wants instead to retranslate the kingdom of God as "God's Federal Republic" for the contemporary church in the United States.[15] In his 1997 article Carter

---

that Brown's excellent articles fall outside the radar screen of most NT scholars because of their appearance in translation-specific journals.

[13] Warren Carter, "Narrative/Literary Approaches to Matthean Theology: The 'Reign of the Heavens' as an Example (Mt. 4.17–5.12)," *JSNT* 67 (1997), 15, n. 46.

[14] Letty M. Russell, *Household of Freedom: Authority in Feminist Theology* (Philadelphia: Westminster Press, 1987); A. M. Isasi-Diaz, "Solidarity: Love of Neighbor in the 1980's," in S. B. Thistlethwaite and M. P. Engels (eds.), *Lift Every Voice: Constructing Christian Theologies from the Underside* (New York: Harper & Row, 1990).

[15] W. J. Everett, *God's Federal Republic: Reconstructing our Governing Symbol* (New York: Paulist Press, 1988).

only acknowledges these alternatives and states that they "are not without difficulty." He chooses instead to employ "reign of the heavens" for Matthew's phrase.[16] In subsequent years, however, Carter has moved away from "reign" more toward the term "empire." He is sensitive to the injustices perpetrated in the colonial period and does not want to suggest God's reign is of a similarly oppressive nature.[17] Nevertheless, he is now preferring the term "empire" "to highlight God's empire as resistance to and as an alternative to Rome's empire."[18]

How are we to evaluate these various translation options for βασιλεία? Because the notion of βασιλεία occurs in so many different contexts and with apparently nuanced meanings, there is simply no single translation equivalent that will work in all instances (*contra* Dalman).[19] The option of choosing not to translate the term at all, but instead just transcribing *basileia* is a less than helpful solution because it fails to communicate anything to the modern reader.[20] The more radical alternatives such as "kin-dom" and "household" are too disconnected from the Jewish tradition of the kingdom, not to mention the eschatological vision of many NT texts which maintain a hierarchy with Jesus as King (cf. 1 Cor 15:23–28; Rev 19:11–20:4). The development of using the term "empire" is helpful in highlighting the reality of the Roman Imperial context to the Gospels, but I fear too narrowly construes the idea along those lines as if this is the only or even most important historical context of the NT. The long Jewish tradition of the notion of the kingdom must be at least as important for Jesus' kerygma as the situatedness of

---

[16] This expression continues to be used throughout the essays in Carter's 1998 book with John Paul Heil: *Matthew's Parables: Audience-Oriented Perspectives* (Washington: Catholic Biblical Association, 1998).

[17] Carter, "Narrative/Literary Approaches," 16.

[18] Carter, *Matthew and the Margins*, 372. Discussion can also be found on page 93. See also his book, *Matthew and Empire*. On page 5 of *Matthew and Empire* Carter writes, "the term *basileia*, which is usually translated with the quaint English term 'kingdom,' commonly refers to empires like Rome's... To speak of, to pray for God's Empire (Matt 6:10) in the midst of Rome's empire is to indicate profound dissatisfaction with Rome's empire."

[19] This is the conclusion of Schnackenburg, *God's Rule and Kingdom*, 354–357. Stegemann concludes likewise: depending on context, Jesus' expression "can mean *the Reign of God, the Rule of God*, or *the Realm of the Rule of God*... It is difficult, then, to find a single translation that will fit all cases." Hartmut Stegemann, *The Library of Qumran: On the Essenes, Qumran, John the Baptist, and Jesus* (Grand Rapids: Eerdmans, 1998), 235.

[20] This is the tack taken by Elaine Wainwright in her essay "The Gospel of Matthew," in *Searching the Scriptures: A Feminist Commentary* (ed. Elisabeth Schüssler Fiorenza; New York: Cross Road, 1994): 635–677.

the NT documents in the Roman Empire. This is the great danger inherent in the current spate of interest in reading the NT against the Roman Empire: in a faddish way it tends to overplay the Roman card and construe all texts through this lens.[21] Additionally it is also worth noting that, unwittingly, "empire" shifts the semantic sense back on to a primarily spatial concept rather than a focus on the "rule" or "reign." These latter two terms are acceptable and again, may even be a good translation for many of the instances of βασιλεία in the NT. They are not exclusively accurate, however. Retaining the traditional "kingdom," as I have done in this work, is also a valid option as at times this is the sense communicated by the word and, as has been observed, God's reign logically necessitates a spatial territory over which he reigns, at least eschatologically. Moreover, I will argue below that *in Matthew* the spatial sense is the predominant one.

The Origin and Meaning of Kingdom of Heaven

Daniel 2–7 as the Origin of Matthew's Kingdom of Heaven

In the last chapter we observed the development of the notion of God's kingship throughout the literature preceding the time of Jesus. We also observed that the expression kingdom of heaven is found in no texts before Matthew and only occasionally afterwards. Thus, there are no direct literary precedents for Matthew's phrase. Its great frequency in Matthew cries out for an historical explanation. We do find that in the later literature, a few texts begin to connect the notions of God's kingship/kingdom with his heavenly dwelling. This connection crops up in expressions like "King of Heaven" (Tobit 13:13; 3 Macc 2:2) and "Sovereign of heaven" (2 Macc 15:3–4, 22). Even more specifically, in the book of Judith in particular, God's reigning from heaven ("the God of heaven") is often contrasted with earthly potentates. Such trends are the primordial soup out of which Matthew's usage apparently evolved. However, we can discern an even more direct, genetic origin for Matthew's unique expression: Daniel 2–7.

---

[21] Also, as Philip Esler points out in personal conversation, first-century Jews and Christians were aware of many empires other than the Roman one, such as the Parthian/Persian, Indian, and even Chinese empires. Thus, it is too constricting to read βασιλεία as if the Roman Empire is the only connotation that this word would conjure up.

A study of the history of influence of the book of Daniel reveals that this work was very important throughout the Second Temple period and beyond.[22] One of the most important roles that Daniel played was in the stream of development from the pre-exilic prophets to the later "apocalyptic" literature (however broadly defined).[23] But beyond this connection, we also find that, in general, Daniel was a widely attested and an apparently well-known work. Several copies of the book have been discovered at Qumran, and mention of Daniel is found in 1 Maccabees, *Sibylline Oracles* 3, 3 Maccabees, and 4 Ezra, as well as frequently in many eras of the rabbinic traditions.[24] Additionally, Josephus calls Daniel "one of the greatest prophets" and devotes a portion of his *Antiquities* to a lengthy paraphrase of Daniel.

The marked influence of Daniel is also found in the NT. It is clear that Daniel formed an important conceptual context for Jesus and the authors of the NT.[25] The most obvious connection is the Gospels' frequent emphasis on the "Son of Man," apparently stemming from Daniel 7:13.[26] The other well-recognized connection between Daniel and the NT is the idea of the "abomination of desolation."[27] In addition to these specific links between Daniel and the NT, the index of citations and allusions in the Nestle-Aland *Novum Testamentum Graece* (27th ed.) also bespeaks Daniel's importance: listed are approximately 200 references to Daniel in the NT books. As Craig Evans points out, "proportionately, this puts Daniel in the same category as Isaiah and

---

[22] Recently a weighty, two volume analysis of Daniel's composition and reception has appeared as *The Book of Daniel: Composition and Reception* (ed. J. J. Collins and P. Flint).

[23] The exact relationship of Daniel to the origins of "apocalypticism" has been debated. Related to this, the connection of Daniel to the Enochic traditions has generated an assortment of views. Collins, against Plöger and Hanson, sees not a continuous strand of this tradition, but both similarities and differences which stem from a similar historical situation. J. J. Collins, *Daniel* (Hermeneia), 70–71.

[24] Collins, *Daniel* (Hermeneia), 72–89.

[25] See especially A. Y. Collins, "The Influence of Daniel on the NT." Other specific works include Greg Beale, *The Use of Daniel in Jewish Apocalyptic Literature and in the Revelation of St John* (Washington: University Press of America, 1984).

[26] The translation, meaning, and origin of this phrase has virtually spawned its own cottage industry of defenders and detractors. A list of relevant articles and monographs can be found in the footnotes of A. Y. Collins, "The Influence of Daniel," 90–91. More recently, on the history of the interpretation of "son of man," see Delbert Burkett, *The Son of Man Debate: A History and Evaluation* (SNTSMS 107; Cambridge: Cambridge University Press, 1999).

[27] Found in Dan 9:27; 11:31; 12:11; cf. Matt 24:15; Mark 13:14. See D. Ford, *The Abomination of Desolation in Biblical Eschatology* (Washington: University Press of America, 1979).

the Psalms, the books most frequently quoted and alluded to in the New Testament."²⁸

Even more directly relevant to our discussion, a few scholars have argued that Jesus' understanding of the kingdom was likely most influenced by the kingdom theme in Daniel. David Wenham observes that several scholars have mentioned the possible influence of Daniel on Jesus' kingdom teaching, but "the full significance of the Danielic background has not usually been recognized, and that in fact *the book of Daniel may be the primary background to the Gospels' teaching about the Kingdom.*"²⁹ Wenham identifies the key passages as Daniel 2 and 7, and argues that there are both linguistic and conceptual links with these texts and the Gospels. He acknowledges that there are other possible backdrops for the Gospels' usage (such as the Targums and rabbinic literature), but that the Daniel texts provide a more direct and obvious context.³⁰ Further, he points out that with the other obvious connections between Daniel and the Gospels (cf. the Son of Man), it is very reasonable to assume Danielic influence on the crucial matter of the kingdom as well. Craig Evans concurs with Wenham and develops this idea much more fully. He argues that Jesus' proclamation of the kingdom is consistent with other Second Temple texts but that it "bears important affinities to some of the distinctive elements that make up the Danielic vision."³¹ Evans highlights seven "telling indications" of Daniel's influence on Jesus' proclamation of the kingdom.³² Through an impressive array of linguistic links between the Gospels and Daniel, Evans presents a convincing case for the essential Danielic background to Jesus' proclamation of the kingdom. Neither Wenham nor Evans seems aware that the famous Gustaf Dalman much earlier had concluded that in fact the historical Jesus "borrowed the term 'sovereignty of God' as an eschatological designation from the Book of Daniel."³³

Drilling down one more level, we can find several bits of evidence of Daniel's influence on Matthew in particular. There are at least thirty

---

²⁸ Craig A. Evans, "Daniel in the New Testament: Visions of God's Kingdom," in *The Book of Daniel: Composition and Reception*, 2:490.
²⁹ D. Wenham, "The Kingdom of God and Daniel," *ExpTim* 98 (1987), 132. Emphasis mine.
³⁰ Wenham, "The Kingdom of God and Daniel," 133.
³¹ Evans, "Daniel in the New Testament," 509.
³² Evans, "Daniel in the New Testament," 510–523.
³³ Dalman, *Words of Jesus*, 136.

allusions to Daniel in the Gospel of Matthew.[34] For example, in the rationale given for the parabolic nature of Jesus' teaching (13:10–15), Jesus says that to the outsiders things are hidden, but the mysteries of the kingdom of heaven are granted to the disciples. This has close connections to Daniel 2:27–28 where Daniel proclaims that it is the God in heaven who will reveal mysteries to the king.[35] This Daniel passage also refracts its light onto Jesus' words in Matthew 11:25–27, where Jesus thanks the Lord of heaven and earth for hiding things from the wise but revealing them to babes (cp. Dan 2:21–23+28–29).[36] The parable of the mustard seed (13:31–32) likewise alludes strongly to a Danielic saying. Matthew's description of the birds of heaven dwelling in the branches of the seed-sprung tree is verbally almost a direct quote from Theodotion Daniel 4:21 (cf. 4:12). The correlation drawn between a tree and the kingdom that occurs in Matthew 13:31–32 clearly draws upon the image of Nebuchadnezzar's tree-kingdom dream in Daniel 4:10–27.[37] Also noteworthy is Matthew's eschatological discourse in chapters 24–25. These chapters reveal many references to Daniel,[38] including a direct connection in Matthew 24:15: "So when you see the desolating sacrilege *spoken of by the prophet Daniel*..." the last portion of which is absent in Mark and Luke.

Beyond these specific textual connections, there are also several conceptual links between Matthew and Daniel. As discussed above, Evans makes an extensive argument for the close relationship between Daniel's eschatological vision of the kingdom and Jesus' proclamation. This connection certainly applies to Matthew and is even highlighted by texts like Matthew 16:28 where the other Gospels read "kingdom of God" while Matthew refers to the kingdom of the Son of Man (cf. Dan 7:13–14). There are also the interesting conceptual connections

---

[34] Based in part on the listing of Daniel-Matthew connections in the index of the NA27 Greek text.

[35] Evans, "Daniel in the New Testament," 513; A. Y. Collins, "The Influence of Daniel," 106. Notice also that Matthew alone retains the plural μυστήρια that comes directly from the Greek of Daniel.

[36] Werner Grimm, *Jesus und das Danielbuch*, Band 1: *Jesu Einspruch gegen das Offenbarungsystem Daniels* (Frankfurt: Peter Lang, 1984), 1–66, has an extensive discussion of the connection of these two passages. See also Evans, "Daniel in the New Testament," 513.

[37] Hagner, *Matthew 1–13*, 386–387; A. Y. Collins, "The Influence of Daniel," 107.

[38] Examples include Matt 24:13–15 and Dan 9:24–27, 11:31, 12:1; Matt 24:30 and Dan 7:13; Matt 25:31–32 and Dan 7:9–14; Matt 25:46 and Dan 12:2. See also the insightful comments on how Daniel informs Matt 24–25 in Davies and Allison, *Matthew*, 3:332.

between Joseph, Daniel and Matthew. As has been observed, the stories of Daniel and the patriarch Joseph have many obvious parallels.[39] The significance of this is highlighted even more when one observes how Joseph the husband of Mary in Matthew 1–2 parallels both Daniel and the OT Joseph.[40] Related to this connection is the appearance of the "magi from the East," who were often associated with Daniel and the Babylonian Exile (cf. Dan 2:2, 10).[41] Not only at the beginning of Matthew (1–2), but also at its consummating end (28:16–20), we find conceptual connections with Daniel. Several scholars have argued that reflection on Daniel 7:13–14 forms the very structure of the formula at the end of Matthew.[42]

All of these rich connections between Daniel and the NT, the Gospels, and particularly Matthew—and especially the insight that Daniel's kingdom image was influential for Jesus—provide a solid foundation on which to propose a new explanation for Matthew's expression kingdom of heaven. *Matthew, drinking deeply at the waters of Daniel, has developed his kingdom of heaven language and theme from the same motif and similar language in Daniel 2–7.* I suggest that the theme, narrative, and theology of Daniel 2–7 provide the most likely historical and literary origin for Matthew's kingdom of heaven language and the heaven and earth theme.[43] This proposal builds upon the already-recognized connections between

---

[39] See Collins, *Daniel* (Hermeneia), 39–40.

[40] As Davies and Allison point out, the Matthean Joseph is like the OT Joseph in that "(1) he has a father named Jacob; (2) goes down to Egypt; (3) has dreams given to him about the future; (4) is chaste and godly; and (5) is long-suffering and disinclined to shame others or exhibit their faults." Several of these parallels could be made with Daniel as well. *Matthew*, 1:182.

[41] According to Davies and Allison, *Matthew*, 1:228, traditionally this was the view of Celsus, Jerome, and Augustine. Many modern commentators understand the reference to magi from the East as Danielic and Babylonian. For example, Hagner *Matthew 1–13*, 27; Gundry, *Matthew*, 26–27.

[42] Most strongly argued is J. Schaberg, *The Father, the Son and the Holy Spirit: The Triadic Phrase in Matthew 28:19b* (Chico, CA: Scholars Press, 1981). Reviews of this idea can be found in Hagner, *Matthew 14–28*, 881–883; Davies and Allison, *Matthew*, 3:676–678.

[43] After developing this understanding, I was pleased to find confirmation buried in the supplement to Cremer's *Lexicon*. He briefly suggests that rather than being a circumlocution, Matthew's ἡ βασιλεία τῶν οὐρανῶν likely comes from Daniel 2:44–45 with its contrast with the world kingdoms. Cremer does not develop this nor does he make mention of the theme in Daniel 2–7, but he does notice that both in Daniel 2 and Matthew, an antithesis of kingdoms is present. Cremer, *Lexicon*, 663. Similarly, Gundry in passing calls Daniel 4 the "seed-plot" for Matthew's use of the term. Gundry, *Matthew*, 43.

Daniel and Matthew, and shows that these connections are more than allusive and incidental, but are fundamental and vital. A. Y. Collins has observed that the book of Daniel as a whole (and especially chapters 7–12) "served as one of several models for the author of Revelation in shaping that work's form and content."[44] I suggest that in the same way Daniel as a whole (and especially chapters 2–7) shape much of Matthew's perspective, including especially his kingdom of heaven language.

Evidence for this proposal can be found in the first instance by noticing the similar emphasis on heaven language and the heaven and earth theme in both Daniel and Matthew. As discussed in Chapter Two and Chapter Eleven, the Hebrew and Aramaic words for heaven appear quite frequently in Daniel (33x), especially in chapters 2–7 (28x). The frequency of heaven in the Aramaic portion is very high relative to its length. One of the recurrent uses of heaven is in the phrase "God of heaven" (2:18, 19, 37, 44) and the related, "God in heaven" (2:28), "Lord of heaven" (5:23), and "King of heaven" (4:34). Additionally, it is noteworthy that thirteen of the twenty-eight Aramaic references are joined in context with a reference to the earth, thus forming thematic pairs. This last observation corresponds to the insight that Daniel 2–7 itself provides an elaborate and extended discourse which juxtaposes the themes of heaven, earth, and kingdom, as was argued in the previous chapter. These themes are woven into the chiastic structure of the stories of chapters 2–7, focusing especially on the central and lengthy narrative of Nebuchadnezzar (4:1–37). The theme of the God of heaven's kingdom over against the kingdoms of the earth is markedly apparent and strong throughout. Additionally, particular verses serve as concentrated lightning rods for these themes, such as Daniel 2:37 and 44, and 4:37 ("King of heaven"). The great frequency in Matthew of heaven language, kingdom language, and the heaven and earth theme have all now been demonstrated by the present work. It is not difficult to see, then, how strikingly similar the juxtaposition of these themes is in both Daniel and Matthew. The significance of this

---

[44] A. Y. Collins, "The Influence of Daniel," 90. As an interesting sidenote, it is worth mentioning how often the connections between Matthew and Revelation have been highlighted to me while researching for the present work. This has been most apparent in the use in both books of the heaven and earth motif. The broader connections between Matthew and Revelation as the canonical bookends of the NT deserve further study.

is highlighted by the fact that while other ancient Jewish and Christian works do occasionally manifest these themes, no two works do to the degree that Matthew and Daniel do. This fact, combined with the other demonstrable connections between Matthew and Daniel makes the postulation of a literary connection highly probable.

Specifically, it appears that Matthew (and/or Jesus, see below) takes up and adjusts Daniel's "God of heaven" and kingdom language and converts them into his own expression "kingdom of heaven."[45] In a similar way, God of heaven likely feeds into Matthew's Father in heaven.[46] At the same time, Matthew employs both kingdom of heaven and Father in heaven as important parts of the broader heaven and earth contrast theme—a theme that is also very apparent in Daniel 2–7. Diagrammatically, the linguistic connection can be pictured like this:

Daniel		*Matthew*
God of heaven + kingdom	→	kingdom of heaven
God of heaven	→	Father in heaven[47]
God of heaven in contrast with earthly kings	→	kingdom of heaven in contrast with earthly kingdoms

Not only the language, but also the flow of the narrative of Daniel 2–7 likewise provides clues for Matthew's own structure. As observed above, the opening chapters of Matthew 1–2 show many connections

---

[45] In a similar way to what I am suggesting, Timothy McLay has recently argued that Matthew picks up on the language and ideas of OG Jonah to weave a nascent "Descent into Hades" theme into his Gospel. McLay observes that Matthew's unique phrase, καρδία τῆς γῆς (Matt 12:40) is likely a Matthean creation combining the OG Jonah phrases εἰς βάθη καρδίας θαλάσσης ("into the depths of the heart of the sea") and κατέβην εἰς γῆν ("I descended into the earth"). R. Timothy McLay, *The Use of the Septuagint in New Testament Research* (Grand Rapids: Eerdmans, 2003), 161.

[46] Note again the close connection between God as Father and God as King in the Jewish literature (see Chapter Nine) and the fact that at times the kingdom is explicitly described as the (heavenly) Father's kingdom: Matt 13:43; 26:29; cf. 6:9–10, 33. Gerhard Schneider likewise suggests that "kingdom of heaven" and "Father in heaven" are closely related to each other and to "God in heaven," though he does not draw any connections to Daniel. Gerhard Schneider, "'Im Himmel—auf Erden'," 286–287.

[47] Notice that "God of heaven," a regular description of God in the Second Temple literature and especially Daniel, appears nowhere in Matthew, nor does Matthew ever speak explicitly about God (θεός) being in heaven, though certainly this is the implication of the Father in heaven and the fact that God's throne is there (5:34). This lends credence to the suggestion that "God in heaven" and his kingdom have been converted into "the kingdom of heaven" and "Father in heaven." Could the preference for the latter expression also reflect the emphasis on the "*Son* of Man"?

with Daniel 2–7. Both books feature important dreams as well as manifesting a contrast of two different kings (Nebuchadnezzar and God; Herod and Jesus). Also, both Daniel 2–7 and Matthew look forward to a similar eschatological ending: the consummation-coming of God's eternal kingdom by the heavenly coming ("on the clouds of heaven") of the Son of Man (Dan 7:13–14; Matt 24:30). Also noteworthy is the fact that the conclusion of Matthew (28:16–20) alludes strongly to the conclusion of the Daniel 2–7 cycle (especially 7:13–14). N. T. Wright has suggested that the Son of Man (cf. Adam) in Daniel 7 is in conscious contrast to the bestiality of Nebuchadnezzar, and also is understood by Jesus as a picture of restored creation and humanity.[48] If this is correct, it highlights the coherence of Daniel 2–7 and makes the connections between Daniel 7 and Matthew 28 even stronger (cf. the heaven and earth allusion to creation in 28:18).[49]

In sum, the accumulation of links between Daniel 2–7 and Matthew and the juxtaposition of the themes of God's kingdom and the heaven and earth contrast make it very likely that Matthew has developed his expression kingdom of heaven and its usage in the heaven and earth motif from reflection on Daniel 2–7. This is not necessarily suggesting that Matthew has uniquely coined the phrase kingdom of heaven, although he may well have. But I am arguing that he certainly creatively developed the phrase through reflection on the important text of Daniel. Though the actual genesis of the expression is forever covered by the mists of history, of course someone must have been the first person to put the words together in this way, and in terms of textual witnesses, Matthew is the earliest. It is not difficult to see how such a useful expression, especially one that draws richly on other similar phrases in the tradition, could quickly disseminate beyond the author's own realm and become adopted by other users of different persuasions (cf. later rabbinic literature). Therefore, it is certainly possible that Matthew was the creator, even though the expression is found later in textual traditions that are almost certainly not dependent on him.

---

[48] Wright discusses the importance of Daniel (including how Dan 2–7 hang together) in *The New Testament and the People of God*, 289–297, 312–318.

[49] Recall also from Chapter Eleven reference to Robert Wilson's argument that behind the imagery of Daniel 7 lies the creation myth of Genesis. Robert W. Wilson, "Creation and New Creation: The Role of Creation Imagery in the Book of Daniel," in *God Who Creates*, 190–203.

To return to the main point, Matthew's favorite expression kingdom of heaven is a shorthand-joining together of the two ideas of the universal "God of heaven" with this God's coming eschatological kingdom, all the while in conscious counterpoint to the rulers of the earth. Thus, we end up with this perfect and weighty phrase, the kingdom of heaven, which Matthew uses as one of his four idiolectic ways to speak of the heaven and earth contrast. Because of the centrality of the kingdom message and the importance of Daniel, this element of the four in many ways is the culminating one. The fuller significance of Matthew's evocation of Daniel will be discussed below in relation to the function of kingdom of heaven in Matthew's heaven and earth scheme.

The Basic Meaning of Kingdom of Heaven

Having offered an explanation for the origin of Matthew's important phrase kingdom of heaven, we can now consider its meaning. I will argue in the final section of this chapter that the ultimate meaning of kingdom of heaven in Matthew resides in its function in the heaven and earth theme. But before this, there are other aspects of the basic meaning of kingdom of heaven that need to be addressed.

(1) The Grammar and Semantics of ἡ βασιλεία τῶν οὐρανῶν

I argued above that the semantic range of βασιλεία in the Gospels has a variety of meanings; it cannot be limited only to "rule" or "reign," even though these at times may serve as the best glosses. When considering the meaning of ἡ βασιλεία τῶν οὐρανῶν in particular it is worthwhile to revisit these questions of semantics and translation. We must begin by examining the entire expression, ἡ βασιλεία τῶν οὐρανῶν. When discussing the meaning of kingdom in Matthew, scholars rarely if ever begin with what is obviously the most unique and most important way that Matthew speaks about the kingdom: ἡ βασιλεία τῶν οὐρανῶν. This is a consequence of too quickly assuming that heaven is merely a reverential circumlocution and therefore no more needs to be said. However, this crucial Matthean phrase must first be mined for its meaning.

So, to do justice to the question of whether ἡ βασιλεία τῶν οὐρανῶν has spatial or territorial connotations or only means rule or reign, we must first examine the grammatical relationship between βασιλεία and the following genitive phrase, τῶν οὐρανῶν. It is difficult to find much discussion on this question at all in the literature, again, because of the reverential circumlocution assumption. It appears that the unspoken (and probably unconsidered) understanding is that the τῶν οὐρανῶν is a subjective genitive, such that the "heavens" is the subject of the verbal idea inherent in βασιλεία; hence, in effect, "God rules."[50] It is apparent that this is based on two key assumptions: that βασιλεία exclusively means "rule" or "reign" (very verbal notions), and that heaven is merely a direct (circumlocutionary) reference to God. But regarding both assumptions, I have sought to show that there are better and fuller understandings; βασιλεία does not always mean "rule" or "reign," and οὐρανός is a metonymical reference to the realm of God above and only indirectly to God himself (and not for reverential circumlocution reasons).

The Greek genitive is an incredibly flexible case with a wide variety of potential meanings and there are other grammatical options for the relationship between βασιλεία and τῶν οὐρανῶν.[51] Of these the most viable options in this instance are a genitive of source/origin or an attributive genitive.[52] As a genitive of source or origin, the expression communicates that heaven is the source or origin of the kingdom that Jesus is proclaiming. This interpretation could conceivably be adopted whether one holds to heaven as a reverential circumlocution or not, and however one understands the semantic meaning of βασιλεία. This interpretation is in fact the one taken by a few scholars[53] and is an improvement over the subjective genitive assumption.

---

[50] The only scholar I have discovered to explicitly argue this is Kingsbury: "Since the genitive '(of) Heaven' (*ton ouranon*) is subjective in nuance and a metonym for 'God,' the purpose of the expression 'the kingdom of heaven' is to assert the truth that 'God rules (reigns).' Hence, 'the Rule of God' or 'the Reign of God' is a proper paraphrase of it." J. D. Kingsbury, *Matthew: Structure, Christology, and Kingdom*, 134.

[51] A most helpful and comprehensive delineation of the different possible meanings of the genitive in the Greek New Testament can be found in Daniel Wallace, *Greek Grammar Beyond the Basics: An Exegetical Syntax of the New Testament* (Grand Rapids: Zondervan, 1996), 72–136.

[52] One other potential option would be the basic genitive sense of possession. This is how R. C. H. Lenski, *Interpretation of St. Matthew's Gospel* (Columbus: Lutheran Book Concern, 1932), 91, takes the genitives in both kingdom of heaven and kingdom of God. Thus, "the kingdom which belongs to the heavens, belongs to God." But it seems a more specific and appropriate kind of genitive is more likely for this particular phrase. In fact, Lenski goes on to suggest that in addition to the possessive, the genitives in kingdom of heaven also function subjectively and qualitatively (p. 92).

[53] Gundry, *Matthew*, 43, says explicitly that kingdom of heaven is a genitive of source. Carter, *Matthew and the Margins*, 93, writes, "the genitive of the heavens points

Alternatively, the τῶν οὐρανῶν could validly be understood as an attributive genitive. An attributive genitive "specifies an *attribute* or innate quality of the head substantive."[54] Examples include ὁ κριτὴς τῆς ἀδικίας, "judge of unrighteousness" = "unrighteous judge" (Lk 18:6) and τὸ σῶμα τῆς ἁμαρτίας, "body of sin" = "sinful body" (Rom 6:6). As can be seen from these examples, the genitive phrase serves in effect as an attributive adjective, though it is more emphatic than a simple adjective. There are many uses of the attributive genitive throughout the NT, especially because of its similarity to Semitic style.[55] On rare occasions it is possible to understand a genitive reference to God (θεός) in an attributive sense. For example, 2 Corinthians 1:12 reads ἐν ἁπλότητι καὶ εἰλικρινείᾳ τοῦ θεοῦ, which is typically translated as "with holiness and *godly* sincerity." While this use of τοῦ θεοῦ would not work in explaining the phrase βασιλεία τοῦ θεοῦ (a "godly kingdom"), it is intriguing to consider how the change in Matthew to τῶν οὐρανῶν does in fact work very well as an attributive genitive. In this reading ἡ βασιλεία τῶν οὐρανῶν, the kingdom of heaven, has the sense of "the heavenly kingdom." This very possible rendering makes sense on its own, but is further enhanced by recognition of the broader heaven and earth contrast theme throughout Matthew. The heavenly kingdom—or the kingdom whose characteristic relates to the divine, heavenly realm (indicated by the plural)—stands in obvious contrast to the earth.[56]

---

to God as the origin of this empire." Thayer's *Lexicon*, 97, explains kingdom of heaven as "the kingdom which is of heavenly or divine origin and nature." This seems also to be the view of Zahn, *Das Evangelium des Matthäus* (repr.; Wuppertal: R. Brockhaus, 1984), 129, who says that kingdom of heaven indicates that the kingdom does not come from earth but heaven. It is difficult to discern exactly the view of Davies and Allison. They speak of the rule of God "whose creator is indicated by the genitive" (*Matthew* 1:389). This comes close to seeing the heaven as the origin. David Wenham, "The Kingdom of God and Daniel," 134, when speaking of the kingdom of God in Daniel, observes that it is possible that "the genitive in the phrase 'Kingdom *of God*' should be understood as a genitive of origin, i.e. as 'the kingdom established by God' rather than subjectively as 'the kingdom that God rules'." This is obviously comparable to kingdom of heaven.

[54] Wallace, *Greek Grammar*, 86.

[55] In fact, this type of genitive construction is sometimes called a "Hebrew Genitive" because of its similarity to the attributive Semitic construction. It is found most often in authors whose style in other ways also reflects Semitic influence. Wallace, *Greek Grammar*, 86–87.

[56] Further evidence of the possibility of this understanding is found in other NT texts which speak of the kingdom as being heavenly or other-worldly. For example, Jesus says in John 18:36 that his kingdom is "not of this world," and 2 Timothy 4:18 describes the kingdom as "heavenly" (τὴν βασιλείαν αὐτοῦ τὴν ἐπουράνιον). Additionally, in light of Semitic influences on Matthew's style, this type of genitive is very plausible.

These grammatical options open up new vistas of understanding upon Matthew's important way of speaking about the kingdom. But as with all such discussions, we must not begin to think of these helpful grammatical categories as entirely distinct and mutually exclusive. While I do not think that the subjective genitive is the best understanding of ἡ βασιλεία τῶν οὐρανῶν, we are not forced to make an either-or choice between the source genitive and the attributive genitive. The nature of language, especially in a highly literary work, is such that multiple senses are often conveyed. It is very possible that both the source and attributive genitive understandings of ἡ βασιλεία τῶν οὐρανῶν communicate important meanings for Matthew. Moreover, it is apparent that for this phrase, both the source genitive and attributive genitive overlap greatly in meaning. To speak about the kingdom as having its source or origin in heaven and also being characterized as heavenly are closely related; the one entails the other. Thus, while Matthew likely did not consciously consider what kind of genitive τῶν οὐρανῶν was, he would probably be very happy with either of these overlapping grammatical interpretations; both are true reflections of what he intended with the phrase kingdom of heaven.

Additionally, it is noteworthy that both the source genitive and attributive genitive understandings of ἡ βασιλεία τῶν οὐρανῶν retain some sense of territory and space. As a source genitive, the kingdom is one which comes *from heaven* and whose origin is *in heaven*. As an attributive genitive, the kingdom is one that is characterized as having a heavenly nature, referring to the realm of heaven in distinction to the earth. And this is the crucial point: the addition of τῶν οὐρανῶν to βασιλεία in Matthew makes it inevitable that some sense of a spatial understanding of the kingdom is communicated: understanding ἡ βασιλεία τῶν οὐρανῶν as meaning only the rule or reign of God in a non-spatial sense fails to account for the importance of Matthew's ascription of the kingdom as τῶν οὐρανῶν.

To flesh out this statement, we may observe that heaven does indeed regularly have a spatial sense in Matthew and therefore it is logical to see the same in his phrase ἡ βασιλεία τῶν οὐρανῶν. The ancient notion of heaven as a place is to modern, "enlightened" scholars either a source of embarrassment or derision.[57] In response, many prefer to

---

[57] For example, Alfred North Whitehead queried, "As for the Christian theology, can you imagine anything more appallingly idiotic than the Christian idea of heaven?" Quoted in Wilbur M. Smith, *The Biblical Doctrine of Heaven* (Chicago: Moody Press, 1968), 12.

construe the notion of heaven theologically as a symbol.[58] Regardless, it is undeniable that for most ancient peoples there was some real sense in which heaven was a place distinct from the earth. Hints of this can be seen in the strong semantic overlap between the invisible heavens (God's dwelling) and the visible heavens *above*. Additionally, the OT and Second Temple literature testify that heaven was understood as the place of God's throne (a symbol of his kingdom), the place of God's angels, and the place from which God spoke and issued help and judgment.[59] The NT evidently shares this worldview. Matthew is no exception. It is clear that when Matthew refers to the Father as ἐν τοῖς οὐρανοῖς, this must have some sense of a dwelling place distinct from the earth. In Matthew 6:1–21 this heaven-dwelling Father is also described as being "in secret"—i.e., not visible—but this does not make his dwelling less of a place. Heaven is also described in Matthew as the place of God's throne (5:34) and the place of God's angels (18:10; 22:30; 24:36; 28:2). To reiterate the point: to deny a spatial sense to ἡ βασιλεία τῶν οὐρανῶν would require interpreting οὐρανός in this phrase as bearing no relation to the rest of the spatial uses of οὐρανός throughout Matthew—especially the spatial sense of the many references to the Father in heaven. This last point is very important because of the close connection between God as Father and the kingdom in Matthew, both of which are described as τῶν οὐρανῶν/ἐν τοῖς οὐρανοῖς.[60] It made perfect sense for Matthew to emphasize the heavenly nature of the one when stating the same for the other. That is, as Matthew emphasizes that God the Father is heavenly/in heaven, so too it is appropriate to depict God's kingdom as a heavenly one/from heaven. We may also recall the fact that ἡ βασιλεία τῶν οὐρανῶν inevitably uses the plural form of οὐρανός. According to my findings in Chapter Six above, these forms point to a reference to the divine realm as distinct from the earth. Again, this corresponds exactly with the form of the Father in heaven occurrences (ἐν τοῖς οὐρανοῖς).[61]

---

[58] As but one example, see the discussion in Plummer, *Matthew*, 97.

[59] Guelich, *Sermon on the Mount*, 77, is on target when he states that heaven has a much broader function in Matthew than as a metonym for God. Instead, "it stands in continuity with the Old Testament concept of *heaven* as being God's realm where, enthroned, he rules over all the world."

[60] Note also that among the texts which show a close relationship between the Father and the kingdom, 6:10 and 6:33 in particular speak in close proximity of the heavenly Father and his kingdom. These texts show the close connection between God as heavenly Father and God's heavenly kingdom.

[61] Interestingly, Hermann Cremer observes that plural forms of οὐρανός never refer to God directly, but instead to his realm. Cremer, who seems to assume the idea that

There have indeed been a few scholars who have suggested that the kingdom of heaven in Matthew does relate some spatial or territorial notion, though none has pursued this line of thinking very far. Ulrich Mauser, reflecting on Matthew's kingdom of heaven, understands heaven as having "a spatial element" according to the ancient worldview.[62] Gerhard Schneider, whose essay manifests more reflection on heaven in Matthew than any other scholar, argues explicitly for a spatial understanding of kingdom of heaven in the First Gospel. He observes that the idea that the "kingdom of heaven has drawn near" (Matt 3:2) has a spatial sense, especially compared to Matthew's *Vorlage* in Mark 1:15 which has a temporal aspect missing in Matthew. He also notes that in 4:8 Matthew contrasts the kingdom of heaven with the kingdoms of the world, again implying a spatial sense.[63] Schneider also states the Matthew replaces Mark's "kingdom of God" with "kingdom of heaven" not to avoid the name of God, but to underline *the heavenly background* of the kingdom.[64] This last point corresponds with my suggestion above that one of the senses of the genitive τῶν οὐρανῶν is attributive: a heavenly kingdom.

To sum up the present argument: to understand Matthew's presentation of the kingdom we must begin with his most frequent and ear-catching description of it, ἡ βασιλεία τῶν οὐρανῶν. When examined closely, taking care to notice the significance of the genitive phrase, we find that Matthew likely intended to communicate by the grammatical structure that God's kingdom is *from heaven* and *heavenly*. This understanding necessarily entails a spatial notion of the kingdom, contrary to the common Dalman-influenced view of βασιλεία which insists that only "rule" or "reign" are intended by the word. This spatial sense does not *require* that "rule" and "reign" be excluded from the semantic range of βασιλεία in Matthew, but only that the sense of the kingdom as originating from a realm distinct from the earth be maintained. Additionally, the *from heaven* and *heavenly* senses of ἡ βασιλεία τῶν οὐρανῶν correspond precisely with the broader heaven and earth contrast theme throughout Matthew. Finally, the other, varied references to the kingdom

---

heaven could refer to God in a metonymical way, states that when οὐρανός is used in this way, it is always in the singular (presumably, Dan 4:23; 1 Maccabees). Cremer, *Lexicon*, 662–663.

[62] Ulrich Mauser, "Heaven in the World View of the New Testament," 40.
[63] Schneider, "'Im Himmel—auf Erden'," 289.
[64] Schneider, "'Im Himmel—auf Erden'," 287.

in Matthew—such as the Father's kingdom, the kingdom, the kingdom of the Son of Man, the kingdom of God—should be understood in the same line as the predominant form Matthew employs, ἡ βασιλεία τῶν οὐρανῶν. This predominant form sets the tone for the other, less-specific references, which in turn communicate some additional aspect of Jesus' kingdom proclamation.

(2) The Kingdom of Heaven and the Kingdom of God in Matthew

We have just mentioned again that in Matthew the kingdom is referred to in a variety of ways—including four times as the kingdom of God[65]—even though kingdom of heaven is clearly the predominant and formative expression. In light of Matthew's obvious preference for kingdom of heaven and the lack of this phrase in the other Gospels, a perennially perplexing question for scholars has been why these four instances of kingdom of God occur at all. The difficulty of this question is particularly acute because of the typical assumption that kingdom of heaven is simply Matthew's redactional version of the other Evangelists' kingdom of God, employed to avoid the name of God. Starting with this assumption, the four instances of kingdom of God then, are seen as anomalous and in need of explanation. If the purpose of kingdom of heaven in Matthew is to avoid saying kingdom of God, why are four occurrences of the latter still found? This dilemma for the traditional understanding of kingdom of heaven has resulted in a variety of explanations. A closely related question that arises when comparing Matthew with the other Gospels is which expression was original and which was redactional: did Jesus originally say (in Aramaic) "kingdom of heaven" hence Matthew's phrase, or did he say "kingdom of God" as the other Evangelists have it? These two questions will now be examined, beginning with the latter first.

---

[65] The four certain instances of kingdom of God in Matthew are: 12:28, 19:24; 21:31, 43. There is also a textually-uncertain occurrence at 6:33, which would bring the total to five. For this verse the NA27 reads βασιλεία but has the following τοῦ θεοῦ in brackets. This is because the two major witnesses, ℵ and B both omit the latter phrase. However, both Hagner (*Matthew 1–13*, 161) and Davies and Allison (*Matthew*, 1:660) offer some arguments in favor of the longer reading. Davies and Allison opt for taking the whole phrase as original, while Hagner apparently does the same (p. 161, 343), although in his Introduction (p. lx) he does not include it as one of the occurrences of kingdom of God. Both Hagner's and Davies and Allison's arguments have some merit but are ultimately not weighty enough to override the significant external manuscript witnesses against the longer reading. Cf. Gundry, *Matthew*, 119. Also note that *BDAG*, s.v. βασιλεία, has inaccurately listed the four occurrences of kingdom of God in Matthew as 6:33; 12:28; 21:31, 43, thereby including 6:33 and omitting 19:24.

When Jesus proclaimed the kingdom, what exactly did he say, kingdom of God or kingdom of heaven? There are three viable answers to this question: (1) Jesus said kingdom of God and Matthew has changed (most of) these into kingdom of heaven, while also adding several occurrences of the latter; (2) Jesus said kingdom of heaven and the Evangelists (except Matthew) and the rest of the NT systematically changed all of these to kingdom of God; or (3) Jesus used both expressions on occasion and different NT authors preserve different traditions.

A survey of scholarly discussion reveals that each view has its adherents. Several writers suggest that kingdom of God was original and that the unique Matthean expression was used by Matthew to avoid saying the name of God, revealing his own Jewish milieu.[66] Many commentators do not discuss this specifically, but it seems this view is the one most widely assumed because of how unique Matthew's expression is historically, and the typical explanation of why kingdom of heaven occurs in Matthew (out of his own Jewish sensibilities). On the other hand, there are a number of important scholars who have instead argued that kingdom of heaven must have been original and the other Evangelists changed what they found in their sources to kingdom of God. Often these scholars begin with arguments related to Jesus' use of Aramaic and the assumption that in that language he would have said a form of kingdom of heaven. In this view, it is usually argued that the reason the original kingdom of heaven was changed to kingdom of God was to accommodate the authors' Gentile readers for whom kingdom of heaven would have meant little.[67] Still fewer writers have

---

[66] Most strongly stated is W. Trilling in *Das Wahre Israel: Studien zur Theologie des Matthäus Evangeliums* (3d ed.; Munich: Kösel, 1964), 143, who claims "That the expression βασιλεία τῶν οὐρανῶν has been introduced for βασιλεία τοῦ θεοῦ by Matthew into the synoptic tradition belongs to the most assured results of Matthean exegesis." Quoted and translated in Saucy, "The Kingdom-of-God Sayings in Matthew," 176, n. 4. Jeremias wrestles with the question and decides that because kingdom of heaven appears nowhere before the last first-century CE, it is "highly improbable, if not completely inconceivable, that the expression 'kingdom of heaven' was already current language at the time of Jesus." Joachim Jeremias, *New Testament Theology*, 1:97. Others include E. Schweizer (it seems), *Matthew*, 338; Gundry, *Matthew*, 43; J. P. Meier, *A Marginal Jew, Vol. 2*, 240–241; and according to Dalman, *Words of Jesus*, 93, Weiss and Holtzmann.

[67] Supporting this view we find Dalman, *Words of Jesus*, 93, who says that it is most likely that Jesus spoke kingdom of heaven and then Mark and Luke "out of regard to heathen readers, avoided the specifically Jewish expression and followed the Greek Bible." Also in this camp are Plummer, *Matthew*, 25; and Beare, *Matthew*, 33; Vermes, *Jesus in his Jewish Context*, 37; G. Vos, *The Teaching of Jesus Concerning the Kingdom of God and the Church* (repr.; Eugene, Oregon: Wipf and Stock, 1998), 31–32; and though it

suggested that instead, Jesus at times used both expressions and this explains why both occasionally occur in Matthew and why the NT traditions are mixed.[68]

How are we to evaluate these interpretations? Option (2)—that kingdom of heaven (exclusively) was original—is almost certainly inaccurate for a number of reasons. First, beginning with Jesus' use of Aramaic proves inconclusive for their argument and even provides counter-evidence because in the corpus of literature that likely bears closest affinity to Jesus' usage—the Targums—*not a single occurrence of kingdom of heaven is found*, nor is heaven ever used in a circumlocutionary way. Instead, a variety of forms of kingdom of God are employed in the Targums. Only through viewing Jesus exclusively through the lens of much later rabbinic literature can one come to think that Jesus' expression must have been kingdom of heaven; according to the Targums, it was most likely kingdom of God. Also, it is difficult to sustain the argument that Mark and Luke and other authors felt it necessary to systematically expunge the Jesus traditions of kingdom of heaven because Gentile readers would not understand the phrase. This overlooks the fact that many of the early Christians were first Jewish proselytes who had some exposure to synagogue language, and that most of the early congregations were mixed with both Gentiles and Jews, the latter of whom could easily explain and expound more "Jewish" elements. Moreover, the expression kingdom of heaven is not so mysterious and abstract that it would baffle an intelligent person even outside the Jewish tradition.[69]

---

is difficult to tell with certainty, this seems to be the view of Luz, *Matthew 1–7*, 167. B. C. Butler in *The Originality of St Matthew: A Critique of the Two-Document Hypothesis* (Cambridge: Cambridge University Press, 1951), 148, says that Mark, copying Matthew, omits this "quite un-Greek expression which no New Testament writer except St Matthew himself will tolerate."

[68] Allen, *Matthew*, 135, says that both phrases were found in Matthew's sources. Similar is McNeile, *Matthew*, xxiii. Cremer, *Lexicon*, 663, says explicitly that kingdom of God and kingdom of heaven were used side by side by Jesus. G. E. Ladd observes that it may be possible that Matthew's usage reflects his own Jewish-Christian milieu and not that of Jesus, however, he goes on to suggest that "possibly he used both phrases, and the Gospels that were addressed to a Gentile audience omitted the Semitic idiom, which would be meaningless to their ears." Ladd, *Theology of the New Testament*, 61. Similar is Michaels who acknowledges the other two options and concludes that maybe Jesus' usage varied. J. Ramsey Michaels, "The Kingdom of God and the Historical Jesus," in *The Kingdom of God in 20th-Century Interpretation*, 111.

[69] It is not difficult to conceive the results of a modern, analogous experiment of gathering a group of completely secularized people and asking them the meaning of kingdom of heaven: they would almost certainly be able to make some sense of the

Further, this view cannot explain why Matthew does use kingdom of God four times. If the theory is that Jesus originally said kingdom of heaven and the other Evangelists removed it for their Gentile audiences, then it is nonsensical to say that Matthew did not do this (in retaining kingdom of heaven) yet he did change kingdom of heaven to kingdom of God four times. But most importantly, option (2) results in the highly implausible situation that *out of all* the oral and written traditions about Jesus and the great diversity of NT authors, *only* Matthew would retain the expression kingdom of heaven, even though Jesus likely said it thousands of times.[70] The weight of this fact is simply too heavy to be borne by the belief that only kingdom of heaven was original.

Option (3)—that Jesus used both expressions—is certainly more viable than option (2), mainly because it can explain why both kingdom of heaven and kingdom of God are found in the Gospels. However, it still shares in part the main problem with option (2): if Jesus did say kingdom of heaven, why does *only* Matthew out of all the NT authors retain this expression? It is not as if he is the only "Jewish" author. To say that this expression reflects Matthew's own synagogual milieu begs the question: evidence for the use of kingdom of heaven outside of Matthew in the first-century is almost non-existent (only 2 times in the Mishnah) and is quite late. It is certainly possible (in favor of both options (2) and (3)) that Jesus, reflecting on Daniel himself, developed the phrase kingdom of heaven and employed it alongside kingdom of God. Again, however, it is difficult to explain why *only* Matthew would retain this important phrase from the lips of Jesus.

This leaves us with the most likely explanation that option (1)—that Jesus said kingdom of God and Matthew has converted most of these occurrences into kingdom of heaven—corresponds with the historical Jesus. In the first instance, over against option (2), this view can accommodate the fact that Matthew contains both kingdom of God and kingdom of heaven. For whatever reason Matthew has chosen to retain kingdom of God at four points, though in the majority of cases, for his own purposes he has converted most of the sayings into kingdom

---

expression even if it lacked for them the rich overtones and subtle nuances that it contains for Jews and Christians.

[70] Cf. the sentiments of Jeremias above. Gundry, *Matthew*, 43, sums it up this way: "We may presume Jesus ordinarily spoke of the kingdom of God and Matthew paraphrased with τῶν οὐρανῶν. It seems unlikely that all the other evangelists [and I would add, "and the rest of the NT authors"] paraphrased in the opposite direction with absolute consistency."

of heaven.⁷¹ Also, if one wants to insist that Matthew's synagogual or Jewish milieu is determinative for his expression kingdom of heaven, option (1) is still a valid explanation. Both of these reasons could apply to option (3) as well, however, option (1) proves more likely because of the remaining question as to why, if kingdom of heaven was dominical, only Matthew retained it. The strongest reason to agree with option (1) stems from the thesis of the present work: kingdom of heaven does not stand alone in Matthew, but evinces stylistic and theological crafting which corresponds to Matthew's broader heaven and earth theme. In other words, because of the careful use and employment of kingdom of heaven in Matthew (combined with the fact that it is found in no other contemporary literature), it seems almost certain that he has developed this phrase for his own purposes.

Having wrestled with which form of the kingdom phrase was likely original, we can now turn to Matthew in particular and ask why the First Gospel continues to use kingdom of God in four instances when it is apparent that kingdom of heaven is the preferred and predominant expression. As I have stated, this problem is felt most keenly because of the assumption of reverential circumlocution. If Matthew was so worried about not offending his readers with the expression kingdom of God that he diligently massaged into his sources the odd phrase kingdom of heaven, then why would this highly-skilled literary artist fail to remove four instances of the offending phrase?⁷²

A number of proposals have been offered in scholarly discussion. These can be broken into two general categories: (1) explanations which see a difference in referent between kingdom of God and kingdom of heaven; and (2) explanations which see the two expressions as interchangeable and offer some other account as to why both occur.

---

[71] On the Synoptic relationship of kingdom of God and kingdom of heaven, see the Synoptic Analysis in Chapter Three above and the Appendix, "Data from a Synoptic Comparison of Οὐρανός." In brief, despite the impression one usually gets from commentaries, most of Matthew's occurrences of kingdom of heaven are *not* a change from a parallel kingdom of God in Mark and/or Luke. In only twelve instances is this the case, while the other 20 occurrences of kingdom of heaven in Matthew are either redactional insertions or come from distinct (M) material.

[72] When stated in its straightforward form like this, it becomes clear again how problematic the reverential circumlocution view is. Additionally, if kingdom *of God* was so offensive, why were not the 50 occurrences of θεός removed?

In the first category we find quite a variety of explanations offered throughout the last century of Matthean studies.[73] Common to all of these explanations is the view that Matthew is operating with two different notions of kingdom and that he intentionally uses kingdom of God and kingdom of heaven to communicate these respective senses. One such proponent is W. C. Allen. In his 1912 commentary on Matthew, Allen argues that kingdom of heaven was the message of the kingdom that Jesus announced as at hand and that will be inaugurated at the parousia.[74] In distinction, Allen understands "kingdom of God" as something different, as a general phrase used "to sum up that whole revelation of God to the Jewish people which was to be transferred to others."[75] He derives this distinction from suggesting that the four Matthean occurrences of kingdom of God have this common theme, in contrast to the kingdom of heaven passages. Allen's discussion is very brief and he does not offer a great deal of support. More fully argued, and in the same vein, is Margaret Pamment's 1981 article.[76] Pamment likewise argues that kingdom of God and kingdom of heaven have intentionally different referents in Matthew. Kingdom of heaven, she suggests, "refers to a wholly future reality which is imminent but otherworldly," while kingdom of God instead refers to "God's sovereignty, actualized and recognized in the past and present here on earth."[77] The most extended argument for a difference between kingdom of God and kingdom of heaven is found in Albright and Mann's Anchor Bible commentary. They argue for a temporal distinction between the two terms: "'Kingdom of God' in the Matthean tradition is applied to the Father's reign after the judgment of the End, and 'Kingdom of heaven' to the continuing community of The Man, lasting up to the time of the judgment."[78] Rather than focusing on the four problematic occurrences of kingdom of God, Albright and Mann cast their nets much more widely and argue for a consistent distinction in Matthew between the kingdom of the Father and the kingdom of the Son of

---

[73] J. C. Thomas gives a helpful overview of the various interpretations in his essay, "The Kingdom of God in the Gospel according to Matthew": 136–146. Thomas not only surveys the state of the question (at the time) but also offers his own interpretation, which we will review below.

[74] Allen, *Matthew*, lxvii.

[75] Allen, *Matthew*, lxviii.

[76] Margaret Pamment, "The Kingdom of Heaven according to the First Gospel."

[77] Pamment, "The Kingdom of Heaven," 232.

[78] Albright and Mann, *Matthew*, 155.

Man.[79] These two different kingdoms are spoken of with the two different expressions, kingdom of God and kingdom of heaven. Instead of a temporal difference, Daniel Patte offers a unique understanding. He suggests that kingdom of God refers to "an aggressive manifestation of the *power of God* which asserts itself against satanic and demonic powers," while kingdom of heaven "refers to the *authority of God*—an authority which, at present, is not imposed upon people through the use of power but which people (should) recognize and acknowledge in the meekness and mercy of the Father and the Son."[80] Another attempt at distinguishing kingdom of God and kingdom of heaven is found in Armin Kretzer's detailed study.[81] He argues that there is not just a formal distinction but also a material difference between the two terms. In particular, the unique expression kingdom of heaven emphasizes the in-breaking of God's rule from heaven to earth, while the narrower term kingdom of God refers to God's personal reign over his people.[82] Another interpretation is found in the unpublished dissertation of Harry Manhoff.[83] Manhoff has argued that the two expressions, which are found exclusively in either the Targums (kingdom of God) or the rabbinic literature (kingdom of heaven), are distinct in meaning: kingdom of God was "an Aramaic Jewish idiom for God's perfect eschatological world," while kingdom of heaven was "a different Hebrew idiom referring to the obligation to perform God's commandments."[84] Finally, we may mention the view held by many in the conservative theological strain called Dispensationalism. This theological view, especially in its classical form, "holds that 'kingdom of God' is a distinctively spiritual kingdom, a narrower category embracing only true believers, whereas 'kingdom of heaven' is the kingdom of millennial splendor, a broader

---

[79] They dedicate three entire sections (Parts VI–VIII) of the Introduction, over 25 pages, to developing this thesis. Albright and Mann, *Matthew*, lxxxi–cv.

[80] Daniel Patte, *The Gospel according to Matthew: A Structural Commentary on Matthew's Faith* (Philadelphia: Fortress, 1987), 177.

[81] Armin Kretzer, *Die Herrschaft der Himmel und die Söhne des Reiches: eine redaktionsgeschichtliche Untersuchung zum Basileiabegriff und Basileiaverständnis im Matthäusevangelium* (Würzburg: Echter, 1971), 167–172.

[82] See also the summaries of Kretzer in Kingsbury, *Matthew: Structure, Christology, and Kingdom*, 134, n. 19, and Saucy, "The Kingdom-of-God Sayings in Matthew," 176, n. 4.

[83] Harry A. Manhoff, "All of the Kingdoms: Semitic Idiom in the Synoptic Gospels and Related Jewish Literature" (Ph.D. diss., University of California, Santa Barbara, 2001).

[84] Manhoff, "All of the Kingdoms," vii.

category including both good and bad fish."[85] This difference is understood in temporal terms, with the kingdom of heaven as Christ's earthly manifestation of the fuller kingdom of God to come.

When the various opinions are collated together like this, it reveals what a difficult problem these four kingdom of God references have posed for understanding Matthew's kingdom language. However, despite these dissenting voices, the vast majority of scholars do *not* understand kingdom of God and kingdom of heaven as having different referents. Instead, they offer assorted explanations for why kingdom of God does appear even though the two expressions are interchangeable in referent. For some scholars the answer is simply that Matthew found kingdom of God in his source and for whatever reason failed to change it, maybe even as the result of editorial error or fatigue.[86] For others, the occurrences of kingdom of God simply reflect stylistic variation on Matthew's part.[87]

Quite a few commentators have instead suggested that the four instances of kingdom of God are intentional on Matthew's part and serve a literary and/or theological purpose. For example, many have argued that kingdom of God in 12:28 is used because it provides a clearer point of contrast with Satan's kingdom (12:26) and parallel to "the spirit of God" (12:28).[88] Similar types of arguments are made for the other kingdom of God passages, seeking to explain why in these

---

[85] This is the summary given by (the non-Dispensationalist) D. A. Carson in *Matthew*, s.v. 3:2. The "Classic Dispensational" view has gone through much revision in the last quarter of the 20th-century and there is now a group who call themselves "Progressive Dispensationalists." Even though their views are more nuanced and sophisticated than the older version, fundamental still is an eschatological-temporal difference between the kingdoms. Without using the term "Dispensational," this presupposition stands behind the arguments made by the Progressive Dispensationalist Mark Saucy in his essay, "The Kingdom-of-God Sayings in Matthew."

[86] Others who mention Matthew's source as the origin of kingdom of God include P. Gaechter, *Das Matthaus-Evangelium* (Innsbruck: Tyrolia, 1962); P. Bonnard, *L'Evangile selon Saint Matthieu* (Neuchatel: Delachaux et Niestlee, 1963); Hill, *Matthew*; E. Schweizer, *Matthew*; and McNeile, *Matthew*. Even Albright and Mann, *Matthew*, 155, offer this suggestion because 12:28 does not fit neatly into their proposal. The proposal of editorial fatigue comes from James D. G. Dunn, *Jesus and the Spirit* (Philadelphia: Westminster, 1975), 45.

[87] Davies and Allison, *Matthew*, 1:390–392.

[88] France, *Matthew*, 209; Gundry, *Matthew*, 235; Bengel, *Gnomon*, 2:272; Carson, *Matthew*, 289; Hagner, *Matthew 1–13*, 343; McNeile, *Matthew*, 176; Davies and Allison, *Matthew*, 2:339.

instances the rare form was retained.[89] Two noteworthy studies that examine the question at a broader level than just the individual passages are the essays by J. C. Thomas and Robert Mowery.[90] Thomas reviews the other options and suggests instead that "the most plausible explanation for the substitution of kingdom of God for kingdom of heaven...is that for Matthew kingdom of God is a literary device used to draw the reader's attention to passages of special significance."[91] Mowery analyzes the various occurrences of kingdom in Matthew and suggests that the reason kingdom of God occasionally occurs is because it is part of a pattern of different terms for different audiences: Matthew tends to use "God" (including kingdom of God) when Jesus is addressing his opponents, but reserves Father and kingdom of heaven for his disciples and the crowds.[92]

Evaluating these assorted options is not as difficult as it might seem. Quite simply, none of the proposals in the first category, novel as they are, is able to sustain a referential difference between kingdom of God and kingdom of heaven. W. C. Allen's suggestions are too thinly supported to be convincing. Pamment offers slightly more evidence, but must resort to a very contorted explanation of 19:23–24.[93] Albright and Mann provide the most extensive argumentation, but must acknowledge a probable exception (out of four!) at 12:28, with the result that it is blamed on Matthew accidentally overlooking this instance of kingdom

---

[89] For example, McNeile, Gundry, Lagrange, *ad loc.* Succinct and clear along these lines is also Goulder, *Midrash and Lection in Matthew*, 332, n. 64. A collection of such views can be found in J. C. Thomas, "The Kingdom of God," 139–140.

[90] J. C. Thomas, "The Kingdom of God," 141–146; Robert Mowery, "The Matthean References to the Kingdom," 398–405.

[91] J. C. Thomas, "The Kingdom of God," 141. Thomas goes on to propose that the reason Matthew highlights these particular texts is because the Matthean community was struggling with the issues these texts speak to.

[92] Mowery, "The Matthean References to the Kingdom," 403. I have utilized Mowery's insights earlier in the present work and found that his proposal generally holds true for heaven language overall.

[93] This is the most troubling text for any theory that distinguishes between kingdom of God and kingdom of heaven because the two expressions occur side-by-side in these verses: "And Jesus said to his disciples, 'Truly, I say to you, it will be hard for a rich man to enter the kingdom of heaven. Again I tell you, it is easier for a camel to go through the eye of a needle than for a rich man to enter the kingdom of God.'" (19:23–24, RSV). Pamment, 232, diligently following her theory, must see the two different terms in this text as having different referents. Also, it is surprising that Pamment fails to mention or interact with either Albright and Mann or Kretzer.

of God.⁹⁴ Likewise, Manhoff's conjecture that there is a consistent difference between the two phrases (based on Targumic versus rabbinic uses) founders when it comes to applying it to the NT documents.⁹⁵ Overall, it can be said that each of the proposed theories of a difference between kingdom of God and kingdom of heaven falters when having to explain particular instances of either phrase. In every case there prove to be disturbing exceptions. For example, the arguments about a temporal distinction between kingdom of God and kingdom of heaven run aground on several texts which speak of either expression in either way.⁹⁶ Also, if Matthew is intending to communicate a clear difference between the expressions, then the six occurrences of the plain βασιλεία make little sense for Matthew's readers.⁹⁷ As a result, each theory proves to be a square peg being forcefully jammed into a round hole. It is not surprising then, that these assorted proposals have been largely critiqued and rejected by other Matthean scholars.⁹⁸ Most telling, none of the theories has created a following. Instead, each proposal appears to be held only by the original proponent.

What about the proposals in category 2—that kingdom of God and kingdom of heaven have the same referent but occur for some other reason? In the first instance, explanations that state that Matthew simply overlooked the four kingdom of God references due to editorial error or fatigue simply strain credulity. Matthew's literary subtlety and prowess are easily demonstrable, and it is highly unlikely that on such a central matter as the depiction of the kingdom that Matthew would

---

[94] Albright and Mann, *Matthew*, 155.

[95] Specifically, Manhoff is forced by his theory to argue that Mark and Luke consistently refer to the kingdom with an eschatological meaning (hence, kingdom of God), while Matthew always uses the kingdom to mean obeying God's commands now (hence, kingdom of heaven). The varied uses of kingdom across the Synoptics and their obvious parallels at many points show this theory to be untenable.

[96] As Davies and Allison point out, while kingdom of heaven certainly can have a future aspect, "a present reference cannot be altogether omitted from 11:1 and especially 11:12. Moreover, only by special pleading can a future reference be eliminated from all the 'kingdom of God' sayings, 6:10 and 21:31 being decisive." Davies and Allison, *Matthew*, 1:391.

[97] Davies and Allison, *Matthew* 1:390.

[98] Review and critique of several proposals can be found in Davies and Allison, *Matthew*, 1:390–392; and Carson, *Matthew*, s.v. 3:2. Cf. also Kingsbury's critique of Kretzer in *Matthew: Structure, Christology, and Kingdom*, 134, n. 19, and Morris' dismissal of Patte in *Matthew*, 317, n. 65. W. O. Walker reviews the idea that there is a distinction between the kingdom of the Son of Man and the kingdom of the Father in Matthew (cf. Albright and Mann) and concludes that this distinction "simply cannot be substantiated." W. O. Walker, "The Kingdom of the Son of Man and the Kingdom of the Father in Matthew: An Exercise in *Redaktionsgeschichte*," *CBQ* 30 (1968): 573–579 (at 579).

lack careful attention. Therefore, the solution remains that there must be some theological and/or literary reason for the retention of the four kingdom of God references. In several cases the suggestions for why kingdom of God might have been retained in a particular context seem very reasonable. For example, there is a clear contrast between the kingdom of Satan and the kingdom of God in 12:26–28, as well as a parallel between the latter and the spirit of God. Such literary parallels certainly do not necessitate kingdom of God for Matthew, but they can help explain it.[99] John Christopher Thomas' analysis is interesting, but ultimately proves unconvincing when he suggests that the themes in the four kingdom of God passages must be particularly important issues for the Matthean community. The themes these texts highlight were certainly important but cannot be shown to be as or more important than several others in Matthew.[100] Robert Mowery's insights seem valid as far as they go; they do not provide a comprehensive solution but do point out the tendency for Matthew to use different terms for different audiences.

Ultimately, the solution to understanding why Matthew retains four instances of kingdom of God comes from recognizing that Matthew uses a full quiver of expressions when describing Jesus' proclamation of the kingdom. While kingdom of heaven is the preferred and predominant one, he uses a variety of phrases with differently-shaped points (to continue the archery metaphor) such as the kingdom of the Father, the kingdom of the Son of Man, and simply ἡ βασιλεία. These assorted expressions appear for stylistic variation as well as for particular contextual reasons (cf. 12:28). Davies and Allison concur and point out that the other Gospels also use a variety of expressions for the kingdom, all of which have the same referent.[101] It is best, therefore, to think in terms of denotation and connotation. Each of the many kingdom expressions in Matthew (including kingdom of God and kingdom of heaven) *denote* God's kingdom, having been inaugurated

---

[99] Another suggestion along literary lines is that of Robert Foster in "Why on Earth Use 'Kingdom of Heaven'?," 494–495. Foster states that the four instances of kingdom of God occur for "shock value" in the midst of the escalating conflict with the religious leaders.

[100] Mowery, "The Matthean References to the Kingdom," 398, n. 7, also questions Thomas' conclusions and points out that his view fails to explain why Matthew did not use kingdom of God more often.

[101] Davies and Allison, *Matthew*, 1:391–392.

and yet to come eschatologically, but the forms of the expressions have different *connotations*; they perform slightly different functions literarily and theologically.

The Kingdom of Heaven as Part of Matthew's Heaven and Earth Theme

Foundational Review

The opening chapter of this work offered a lengthy critique of the traditional view that before and around the time of Jesus heaven functioned as a reverential circumlocution. The critique focused on Dalman's original argument and the Second Temple evidence. I suggested also that there is contrary evidence in Matthew. Now, having analyzed the heaven and earth pattern throughout Matthew, and having explored various issues related to the meaning of kingdom of heaven, we are in a position to show more fully why Matthew employs the odd phrase kingdom of heaven: it is a crucial part of and consummates Matthew's heaven and earth theme.

To begin, it is worthwhile to recall two key items from the discussion above. First, I have argued that the most direct origin of Matthew's phrase can be traced to the cycle of stories in Daniel 2–7. In the previous chapter I offered an analysis of these chapters which showed in them the centrality of the heaven and earth contrast, juxtaposed with the kingdom theme. Above, I have suggested that reflection on these elements in particular has generated for Matthew the specific terminology of kingdom of heaven (and in part also Father in heaven). The heaven and earth theme manifest in Daniel 2–7 cannot be understood as the *sole* source behind the same theme in Matthew, but it is certainly influential. That is, a study of heaven in the Old Testament and Second Temple literature reveals that heaven and earth was a prominent and important theme *throughout* the Jewish literature. Beginning with the crucial prolegomenon of Genesis 1:1 and ending with the last verse of the Hebrew Bible (2 Chron 36:23), heaven and earth language permeates the textual traditions preceding and contemporary with Jesus. Matthew breathes this air deeply and speaks regularly with the language and concepts of heaven and earth. Daniel 2–7 likewise depends on the rich heaven and earth theme tradition and in many ways brings it to a climax in the Old Testament literature. The combination of this theme with the contrast of kingdoms (earthly and heavenly) marries together two important Second Temple motifs. Matthew, then, stands on the shoulders of the broader Old Testament heaven and earth tradition and particularly its manifestation in Daniel 2–7.

A second point worth reiterating from the previous discussion concerns the semantic sense of ἡ βασιλεία τῶν οὐρανῶν. The analysis presented above suggests that Matthew's phrase is likely intended to communicate both a spatial sense of God's kingdom in heaven and from heaven as well as a qualitative sense, that God's kingdom is heavenly. Both of these notions feed well into the heaven and earth theme. To depict God's kingdom as in heaven and heavenly naturally brings to mind the counterpoint of earthly kingdoms and earthly ways of operating a kingdom. In fact, as we will see below, a number of texts in Matthew reveal this type of contrast explicitly. Additionally, we may recall the fact that Matthew's consistent choice of plural τῶν οὐρανῶν in this phrase also reflects a distinction between the divine realm and the earthly, per his idiolectic use of singular and plural forms.

Hints of the Heaven and Earth Theme in Kingdom Discussions

The goal of this work overall has been to show the centrality and function of the heaven and earth theme in Matthew. As has been observed above, occasional notes of this theme have been sounded by a number of scholars. Likewise, scholarship has sporadically and briefly hinted that kingdom of heaven might do more than serve as a reverential circumlocution, but function as a part of a broader heaven and earth theme. For example, in the discussion of οὐρανός in Balz and Schneider's theological dictionary, they state that in the dynamic expression ἡ βασιλεία τῶν οὐρανῶν, "heaven is more and different than an embellishing adjective." The phrase refers to the βασιλεία τοῦ θεοῦ but does more because "it formulates *principles* (Matt 5:3ff.) *in opposition to a world that seeks its own autonomy*, i.e., confuses itself with God and heaven (cf. Matt 23:13)."[102] They do not go on to develop this, but the statement does hint at the idea that kingdom *of heaven* has some performative function vis-à-vis the world and its kingdoms. Another undeveloped hint is found in J. Gnilka's *Das Matthausevangelium*. Gnilka states that kingdom of heaven is not just a circumlocution for God's name; it refers to "the universal

---

[102] Balz and Schneider, *Exegetical Dictionary of the New Testament*, 2:544. Emphasis mine. In his recent commentary on Matthew, John Nolland makes a similar statement: "Running through the Gospel story is a major critique of how the world works: its typical values and priorities." Nolland, *Matthew*, 40.

and worldwide power" with which God will reveal himself.[103] Also brief but interesting are Ulrich Mauser's comments. Mauser argues that kingdom of heaven communicates "*the way* in which God from heaven governs the world." It is related to the depiction of God as a heavenly Father and (especially in the kingdom of heaven parables) describes what happens when heaven rules the earth.[104] In the case of these last two scholars, they both question the reverential circumlocution assumption because they sense that something more is going on with the expression ἡ βασιλεία τῶν οὐρανῶν. This same sense can be detected in a number of scholars who likewise have questioned heaven as a reverential circumlocution. I mentioned several such writers in Chapter One of the present work. For example, Joel Marcus argues that circumlocution is probably only a "partial truth" because, according to 6:10, the kingdom of heaven "is the projection of God's heavenly rule into the earthly sphere."[105] Similarly, David Garland suggests that kingdom of heaven is used to refer to "God's transcendent work and lordship that is coming down from heaven."[106] Gerhard Schneider, also mentioned above, proposes that kingdom of heaven communicates the "power which has come here from heaven and has entered this world."[107] Even more directly to the point, Geerhardus Vos wrote that "in view of the profound significance which Jesus throughout ascribed to the contrast between the heavenly and earthly world, it is hardly likely that heaven was to him a mere formal circumlocution for God. It meant not God in general, but God as known and revealed in those celestial regions which had been our Lord's eternal home."[108]

All of these comments can be called merely hints that there may be a connection between kingdom *of heaven* and the kingdoms *of the earth/world*. The clearest statements along these lines are found not in contemporary scholarship but in the much older works (now largely overlooked) of Albrecht Bengel and Hermann Cremer. Bengel suggests

---

[103] J. Gnilka, *Das Matthäusevangelium* (2 vols.; Freiburg: Herder, 1986), 1:66. His expression is "die Universalität und weltumspannende Macht." This overlaps with Gundry's suggestion that heaven in Matthew emphasizes the *universality* of God's reign.

[104] Mauser, "Heaven in the Worldview of the New Testament," 39–40. Emphasis mine.

[105] Joel Marcus, "The Gates of Hades and the Keys of the Kingdom (Matt 16:18–19)," 447.

[106] D. Garland, *Reading Matthew*, 47.

[107] Schneider, "'Im Himmel—auf Erden'," 289.

[108] Vos, *The Teaching of Jesus*, 37.

that kingdom of heaven is used by Matthew "who employed it that he might cure the Jews, for whom he was writing, of the notion of an *earthly* kingdom."[109] Later he states that the expression was used such that "the hope of an *earthly* kingdom was cut away, and all were invited to *Heavenly* things."[110] Cremer quotes Bengel and expounds upon the heaven and earth connection, taking it a step further. He sees in ἡ βασιλεία τῶν οὐρανῶν that "both the natural and moral antagonism between [God's kingdom] and this world is expressed and emphasized."[111] In a later Supplement he develops the idea even more. The use of kingdom of heaven

> tells against the so-called materialistic or worldly Messianic hopes entertained by the contemporaries of Jesus, and against the fashion of this world in its entirety... It is a kingdom which has not its origin in the present earthly order of things, but which comes down to earth from heaven as a new order, moulded not after the pattern of this present life; a kingdom wherein what hitherto was heavenly and beyond this world is manifested, and to which also the future belongs.[112]

My own study confirms the accuracy of these basic statements concerning Matthew's expression. But going beyond the scope of what Cremer was able to offer in his lexicon, we can also see that kingdom of heaven indeed functions in several Matthean texts as part of this antithetical heaven and earth theme.[113] To such texts we now turn.

The Contrast of Kingdoms in Matthean Texts

It was observed above in the first section of this chapter that βασιλεία and related cognate forms occur very frequently in Matthew (approximately 79x). Deeper digging into the kingdom references reveals that many occurrences of this root appear in structures which create a

---

[109] J. A. Bengel, *Gnomon*, 132. Emphasis mine.
[110] J. A. Bengel, *Gnomon*, 157–158. Emphasis mine.
[111] Cremer, *Lexicon*, 134.
[112] Cremer, *Lexicon*, 663.
[113] Lest there be misunderstanding, it is worth noting again that to speak of the antithesis of heaven and earth is not to suggest that there is no relationship between the two realms (as might be emphasized in Dialectical Theology), nor that the two realms will forever remain separated. Instead, the use of "antithesis," "contrast," and "tension" in my description highlights that, for Matthew, the two poles of heaven and earth currently represent the important *differences* between God's realm and humanity's realm, differences that will be obliterated when the kingdom of heaven comes to earth (6:9–10).

contrast between God's kingdom and other kingdoms and other people. These can be broken into two groups: (1) general kingdom contrasts;[114] and (2) explicit kingdom of heaven and earth contrasts.

An example from the first group is 8:11–12, where Jesus says that "many will come from east and west and sit at table with Abraham, Isaac, and Jacob in the kingdom of heaven, while the sons of the kingdom will be thrown into outer darkness." This saying, which is much less pointed in the Lukan parallel (Lk 13:28–29), juxtaposes the kingdom of heaven, a worldwide, Gentile-inclusive kingdom, with the unbelieving Jews' notion of a Jewish-only kingdom (referenced by "the sons of the kingdom"). The former notion of God's kingdom is broader than the latter and is the one proclaimed by Jesus. To call it the kingdom of heaven highlights the disjuncture between the two perceptions of the kingdom. "Sons of the kingdom" appears again but in an opposite, positive sense in 13:38. In this verse the sons of the kingdom are the good seed of the parable of the sower who are put into parallel contrast with "the sons of the evil one." The pairing of the "sons of the kingdom" (using the Semitic form "sons of") and the "sons of the evil one" creates an evident type of contrast of kingdoms.

In fact, this verse likely relates closely to the contrast of kingdoms that is emphasized in the previous chapter in 12:22–32 (cp. the implied "sons of Satan" in 12:27 and the kingdom of Satan with the "sons of the evil one" in 13:38). The extended conflict story of 12:22–32 has at its core the contrast of two different kingdoms, God's (12:28) and Satan's (12:26). The story opens with Jesus' healing of a blind and dumb man. In response, the crowds ask an unexpected question: "Can this be the Son of David?" (12:23; cf. 1:1). The point of this query, which is lacking in the Lukan parallel (Lk 11:14), is not immediately apparent to us—how does being the Son of David relate to performing a healing? But for first-century readers the connection is obvious: they are asking whether the Davidic Messiah, deliverer and king, has come.[115]

---

[114] In a very early application of narrative criticism to the biblical documents, Jan Wojcik argues that Matthew of all the Evangelists especially emphasizes the theme of two contrasting kingdoms through a series of juxtaposed scenes contrasting the kingdoms of this world with God's kingdom. The following arguments were originally stimulated by this essay but go far beyond the data presented there. Jan Wojcik, "The Two Kingdoms in Matthew's Gospel," in *Literary Interpretations of Biblical Narratives* (ed. Kenneth R. R. Gros Louis; Nashville: Abingdon, 1974): 283–295.

[115] Davies and Allison, *Matthew*, 2:335.

This allusion to God's kingdom does not stand on its own; the kingship element is worked out explicitly in the rest of the pericope. The Pharisees ascribe Jesus' healing power not to his Davidic Messiahship but to an opposite Ruler (ἄρχων), Beelzebul. Jesus follows their lead in this contrast and makes the claim explicit, saying that no kingdom which is divided against itself can stand (12:25–26). He then consummates the argument and simultaneously answers the crowd's question by claiming that indeed, the kingdom of God has come upon them through his ministry (12:28); he is the Davidic Messiah bringing the kingdom of God. This passage, then, serves as a good example of the theme in Matthew of a general conflict of kingdoms.

But certainly the most prominent text which highlights this theme is found right at the beginning of Matthew, in chapters one and two. Even a surface reading of Matthew 1–2 reveals that one of the points of this prologue to the Gospel is to portray Jesus as the true king of the Jews. But more than merely making this statement, these chapters manifest an explicit emphasis on the fact that Jesus as king stands in opposition to all other false kings and kingdoms. This contrast is woven frequently throughout these first two chapters of Matthew. It begins in 1:1, a verse whose eight words are full of many weighty allusions. One such allusion is the reference to Jesus as the "son of David." As noted above, this ascription, which is not terribly frequent in the OT (approx. 8x), is repeated again in Matthew 12:23, where the contrast of kingdoms is clear. But these are not the only occurrences of "son of David" in Matthew; it is found a total of nine times.[116] Compare this to only three occurrences in Mark and four in Luke. Davies and Allison observe that "of all the NT writers, Matthew lays the most stress on the Davidic ancestry of Jesus." They also note that this theme is especially prominent in chapters 1–2, with the repeated mention of David (1:6, 17), and the importance of Bethlehem, the city of David (2:1–8, 16). "Clearly Matthew's opening two chapters are intended to demonstrate that Jesus (through his father: 1:16) qualifies as the royal Messiah, the Davidic king (cf. 21.9, 15)."[117] The depiction of Jesus as the Davidic king found in the opening verse and thoughout the genealogy[118]

---

[116] Matt 1:1, 20; 9:27; 12:23; 15:22; 20:30, 31; 21:9, 15. Cf. also 22:42, 45.
[117] Davies and Allison, *Matthew*, 1:156–157.
[118] See especially 1:6 where David's kingship is emphasized. Comparison can also be made to Luke's genealogy of Jesus in Lk 3:23–38. There David is mentioned in passing, but does not serve as a focal point for Luke as he does for Matthew. Instead, the emphasis on Luke is tracing the genealogy from Jesus all the way back to Adam.

continues into chapter two. In 2:1–12 the story of the visit of the magi has as its subtext the ironic contrast between the mad Herod, who has (disputedly) taken upon himself the title "King of the Jews," and the helpless infant Jesus *who is in fact* the true King of the Jews (and the world). Verse 1 situates Jesus' birth "in the days of Herod the king," and is immediately followed in the same sentence by the magi's shocking question, "Where is he who has been born king of the Jews?" (2:2). The magi deftly avoid king Herod's wrath and schemes and find the Christ child before secretly returning to their own land. Before returning, they offer him gifts as tokens of his royal status (2:11).[119] The positing of two radically different kings in this short story is striking. Carter sees this whole section beginning with the genealogy through chapter two as dealing with the question, "To whom does the sovereignty of the world belong?"[120] The obvious answer is God in Christ. It should also be noted that the irony of this contrast of two kings is heightened by the fact that the Jewish people (at least those surrounding Herod in Jerusalem) do not acknowledge that the King of the Jews has been born, while the foreigners from the East do—in fact, they are the ones who ascribe to Jesus the title of king. Thus, in this narrative we have not only a clear contrast of kingdoms (God's and the Roman's/Jew's), but also foreshadowing of the Gentile inclusion and judgment upon the Jewish leaders. Both of these themes will reappear repeatedly throughout Matthew. In this regard it is noteworthy that specific references to Jesus as "the King of Jews" resurface and are concentrated in the penultimate chapter of Matthew. Four times in chapter 27 (27:11, 29, 37, 42), during the events of the Passion, Jesus is called the King of the Jews. These references themselves appear in contexts which contrast Jesus' kingship with others', as they take place on the backdrop of Roman Imperial power (cf. especially 27:11).[121] These references also form a clear inclusio with the same emphasis in chapter 2: in both his birth and death, the note of Jesus' other-worldly kingship is sounded,

---

[119] The exact meaning of these three gifts has attracted a variety of options over the church's history. Discussion can be found in Davies and Allison, *Matthew*, 1:249–251. Among the likely intended meanings is a typological connection between Jesus and Solomon, as well as the eschatological vision of the heathen nations coming with gifts in hand to the Son of David (see esp. Ps Sol 17:31).

[120] Carter, *Matthew and Empire*, 60–61.

[121] Note also that when Jesus is entering Jerusalem (the place of Herod in chapter 2) right before the Passion, he is hailed as Son of David and refers to himself as king (21:1–11).

while the narrative time in between seeks to evince and illustrate Jesus' kingship and his proclamation of the kingdom.

To sum up, there are several texts throughout Matthew which establish the general theme of a contrast of kingdoms. The veracity of this assertion finds its greatest support by observing how important the contrast of kingdoms is in the opening chapters of Matthew 1–2. A source-critical mindset has often led readers to think about Matthew 1–2 mainly in terms of special material distinct from the Gospel proper which begins at chapter 3 (where the Synoptics are unified). But this fails to see how crucially these chapters set the stage for the rest of the Gospel not only historically but also thematically. From this vantage point, the importance of the kingdom contrast theme *throughout* the First Gospel begins to come into sharper focus.

Matthew 1–2 forms a broadly-construed kingdom contrast theme and thereby corresponds nicely with the understanding of kingdom of heaven I have argued for above. However, it must be noted that this theme in Matthew 1–2 is not explicitly described as *a heaven and earth* contrast, though it is certainly not inconsistent with such a description. In fact, interestingly, the word heaven does not occur in Matthew at all in the first two chapters—a notable thing in light of the great recurrence of οὐρανός in Matthew—but is found first in the phrase ἡ βασιλεία τῶν οὐρανῶν in 3:2, immediately after the thirty year narrative gap between chapters 1–2 and the rest of the Gospel. For whatever reason, Matthew has chosen not to employ heaven and heaven and earth language in the prologue, even though this theme will obviously become very prominent throughout the rest of the Gospel. Nevertheless, I suggest that the contrast of kingdoms that is first set up in chapters 1–2 will become explicitly a "heaven and earth" contrast within the rest of the Gospel. Chapters 1–2 lay the groundwork for Matthew's theme of the contrast of God's kingdom with humanity's, highlighted by the conspicuous difference between the earthly-powerful Herod and the helpless infant Jesus. Although heaven and earth language is not used yet, it will become clear in the subsequent narrative that this is the contrast in view.

This observation leads to the second group of texts, those which *explicitly* contrast the kingdom of heaven with earth. In addition to passages throughout Matthew which connect the kingdom of heaven with the ubiquitous heaven and earth pairs (e.g. 16:18–19), we can focus attention on three passages in particular.

(1) The Lord's Prayer (6:9–10)

First, we can return once again to the key Matthean text of the Lord's Prayer. We have had occasion to examine this text in other parts of this work because it plays such a central role in Matthew while also providing several working examples of the heaven and earth theme. Specifically, 6:9–15 is sandwiched by references to the Father ἐν τοῖς οὐρανοῖς in addition to a classic heaven and earth pair in 6:10 (ἐν οὐρανῷ καὶ ἐπὶ γῆς), all of which also manifest the pattern of singular and plural forms of οὐρανός. In the present discussion, the relevance of this text comes from the fact that in the fundamental petitions of the Lord's Prayer we find a request for the kingdom of heaven to come to earth. *This crucial point is at the heart of the relationship between heaven and earth in Matthew.* Following the opening address to the Father in heaven, we have three related petitions which are all modified by the phrase, "as in heaven, so also on earth." Jesus' disciples are to pray for God's Name to be revered, his purposes to be accomplished, and his kingdom to come—all things which are realities in the heavenly realm but need yet to happen fully in the earthly realm. The reference to the kingdom in 6:10 is not explicitly given in the full form ἡ βασιλεία τῶν οὐρανῶν (probably for reasons of poetic meter), but the surrounding references to heaven and the Father in heaven make it clear that it is the heavenly kingdom in view. Additionally, the fact that the kingdom that is "in heaven" is being requested to come "on earth" makes this implicit reference to ἡ βασιλεία τῶν οὐρανῶν clear. All of this enables us to see that inherent in this text is a consciousness that the kingdom of heaven needs to and will come upon the earth. This idea entails the fact that the present earthly order, including its kingdoms, empires, and current social and political realities, will be superseded and replaced when God's heavenly kingdom comes to earth.[122] This is in fact the great Christian eschatological hope, the one Jesus proclaimed was "at hand" and the one which was inaugurated through Jesus' life, death and resurrection (cf. 28:16–20). Such a petition, being taught to the disciples as a matter of regular prayer, was not without religio-political consequences in the highly-charged, Roman Empire-dominated situation of first-century Palestine.[123] Matthew

---

[122] Note also that this text and this claim emphasizes again the spatial aspect of Matthew's depiction of the kingdom as *in heaven* waiting to come *to earth*.

[123] On this important point, in addition to Carter's *Matthew and Empire*, see now also the interesting series of essays in John Riches and David C. Sim, eds., *The Gospel of Matthew in its Roman Imperial Context* (London: T&T Clark, 2005).

depicts this as a heavenly kingdom coming to earth to highlight the radicality and difference of this kingdom from all earthly kingdoms.

(2) *The Two-Drachma Tax and the Kingdom (17:24–18:5)*

Another text which evinces a use of the kingdom of heaven in a contrastive way is 17:24–18:5. In 17:24–27 we have the story of the question about the payment of the two-drachma tax. In several ways this text parallels the pericope in 22:16–22, where the question of taxes to Caesar is raised. In fact, there has been debate about whether this tax in chapter 17 is indeed the Temple tax or instead a Roman civil or toll tax.[124] Regardless, Jesus takes the question about the tax and converts it into a teaching which contrasts the "kings of the earth" with the sons of God (17:25–26). This same type of general kingdoms contrast has been observed above in 12:22–32 and 13:38.

But more explicitly, immediately following this text, in 18:1–5, the topic flows into the question about status in the kingdom of heaven, with ἡ βασιλεία τῶν οὐρανῶν repeated three times in a very short space (18:1, 3, 4). We typically think of 18:1–5 as separate but the two pericopae are linked with the connecting sentence, "at the same time" (18:1). Moreover, there appears to be a subtle but real contrast in these verses between the "kings of the earth" (17:25) and the "kingdom of heaven" (18:1, 3, 4). In 17:25 the sons of the kings of the earth are in view, while in 18:1–5 children serve as the model for the very different kingdom of heaven.[125] Also, "kings of the earth" (οἱ βασιλεῖς τῆς γῆς) in 17:25 almost certainly alludes to Psalm 2, a classic Jewish text which contrasts the kings of the earth with God in heaven. The close proximity of the references to "kings of the earth" and "kingdom of heaven" is more than accidental, especially in light of the recognized theme throughout. The two are appearing as contrasting ways of living on earth.

---

[124] Cf. the review of the arguments and their ultimate siding with the Temple Tax interpretation in Davies and Allison, *Matthew*, 2:739–741. An enlightening discussion of 17:24–27 in light of the Roman Imperial context can be found in Carter, *Matthew and Empire*, 130–144.

[125] Richard Bauckham gives 18:1–4 as an example of how radically different Jesus' depiction of God's kingdom is from worldly notions of the kingdom, though he does not observe the close connection of "kings of the earth" in context. Richard J. Bauckham, "Kingdom and Church According to Jesus and Paul," *Horizons in Biblical Theology* 18/1 (1996), 12. More clearly, Carter, *Matthew and Empire*, 143–144, mentions briefly that 17:24–27 relates to the rest of chapter 18, though he also overlooks the explicit contrast between the kings of the earth and the kingdom of heaven.

(3) The Temptation Narrative (4:1–11)

One of the most explicit contrasts of the kingdom of heaven with earthly kingdoms is found in the passage which narrates Jesus' preparation for ministry, the temptations in the wilderness. In the devil's third and last-ditch attempt to nip Jesus' ministry in the bud before he goes public, he offers to Jesus πάσας τὰς βασιλείας τοῦ κόσμου καὶ τὴν δόξαν αὐτῶν, "all the kingdoms of the world and their glory." It is especially interesting that for Matthew, this temptation is emphasized by its placement as the final and presumably most tempting temptation (cp. Lk 4:1–13). Warren Carter has observed that we need to understand that Satan's claim here establishes Rome, the leading empire of the world, "as the devil's agent who shapes a world that enacts the devil's purposes, not God's."[126] This makes sense, and clearly, a contrast of God's kingdom with the kingdoms of the world is in view here, with Rome as the immediate example of a kingdom opposed to God. But for my purposes, notice specifically that this phrase "the kingdoms of the world" is intentionally framed or sandwiched by Matthew with the weighty, contrasting references to the kingdom of heaven in both 3:2 and 4:17. In fact, this entire section about the beginning of Jesus' ministry is book-ended with reference to the kingdom of heaven (3:2; 4:17); from John the Baptist up until the calling of the first disciples, the preparatory time of Jesus' ministry is demarcated by these references to the kingdom of heaven. And serving as a point of contrast in the midst of this is Satan's own offer of instead "the kingdoms of the world."[127]

Thus, we can see that again, the expression kingdom of heaven is used as part of the thematic contrast between God's kingdom and the kingdoms of the world, or the kingdom of heaven versus kingdoms of the earth. The "of heaven" part of kingdom of heaven here is not accidental or reverentially circumlocutionary, but serves a very powerful literary and rhetorical purpose: to contrast the world's kingdoms

---

[126] Warren Carter, "Matthew and the Gentiles: Individual Conversion and/or Systemic Transformation," 267. This is an accurate enough statement as far as it goes. It is misleading, however, if it communicates that the Roman Empire was the *only* context in the mind of first-century readers or if this is the only way in which we must understand the point of Matthew's contrasting the kingdoms of the world with the kingdom of heaven.

[127] Allusion to these ideas is made again in Matthew in 12:22–32 as well as in 28:16–20 where Jesus, having successfully weathered all storms of temptation, is now given not only authority over the kingdoms of the world, but "all authority in heaven and earth."

(offered by Satan) with God's (announced by Jesus). We may add to this observation the point emphasized several times already, that τῶν οὐρανῶν is always plural, which, according to Matthew's singular and plural pattern of οὐρανός, also communicates a distinction between the divine and human realms.

Conclusion: One Point and Two Applications of the Kingdom of Heaven Theme

We may conclude this many-pronged discussion by pinpointing the one primary point in Matthew's use of kingdom of heaven and its two particular applications for his own *Sitz im Leben*. The arguments above, in addition to the foundation laid in the previous chapters, leads to the following conclusion: *Matthew's choice to regularly depict the kingdom as τῶν οὐρανῶν is designed to emphasize that God's kingdom is not like earthly kingdoms, stands over against them, and will eschatologically replace them (on earth).* For Matthew, this point has two different applications: one relates to the Jewish expectations for a kingdom and Matthew's Jewish context; the other corresponds with the Roman Imperial context of early Christianity.

The Point: The Kingdom of Heaven is Unlike All Earthly Kingdoms

In a 1996 essay, Richard Bauckham examined the relationship between "kingdom" and "church" in the Gospels and Paul's letters. In his analysis of the kingdom of God theme in the Gospels, he observes that while "kingdom of God" is shown as the central theme in Jesus' preaching, the Gospels rarely depict God explicitly as King.[128] He concludes that the reason for this noticeable difference from the Jewish literature is that "Jesus was at pains to avoid the implication that God rules in the way that earthly kings rule. In fact, *much of Jesus' teaching seems designed precisely to show how God's rule differs from earthly rule.*"[129] Although Jesus' view of the kingdom does in many ways stand in continuity with the Jewish expectations, by avoiding the concrete image of God as king and using other depictions for God (especially Father), "he shifts the focus much more

---

[128] Bauckham, "Kingdom and Church," 4–5.
[129] Bauckham, "Kingdom and Church," 5. Emphasis mine. Bauckham's wording here is more judicious than that of Carter and others who emphasize (almost exclusively) the Roman imperial context, because the point is certainly a contrast of God's rule with *all* different manifestations of *earthly* rule, Roman included but not exclusively so.

to characterizing God's rule as radically different from that of earthly rulers."[130] Bauckham goes on to give several pages of examples of how Jesus portrays the kingdom in ways very much unlike contemporary kingdom and social relationships.

Bauckham's point and argument are persuasive. Jesus' teachings about the kingdom are indeed radical and "status quo"-overturning. At times, the best description is simply "topsy-turvy." As J. Ramsey Michaels observes, Jesus' teachings about the kingdom affirm traditional Jewish expectations, yet they contain "what Henry James would call a 'turn of the screw,' a new twist that shocks his hearers and in some respects call their behavior and world-view into question." The result of Jesus' proclamation about the kingdom is a restored Israel, but "a transformed, a topsy-turvy Israel."[131] This turn of the screw is especially felt in many of Jesus' parables. In fact, Jesus spends much of his time using parables to explain odd truths about what God's kingdom is really like. One of the most radical of these is the story of the Laborers in the Vineyard in Matthew 20:1–16. This uniquely Matthean parable is one of the many illustrations of Jesus' oft-used aphorism, "the first shall be last and the last shall be first" (20:16). In this case, the climactic point is unexpected even by Jesus' topsy-turvy standards: All the laborers receive the same wages even though they have worked different amounts. As Warren Carter describes it, this parable "upsets expectations about how life 'ought' to be ordered and measured. It disorientates and reorientates existence away from human merit and to divine presence and summons."[132] Notably, this unsettling teaching is prefaced, like many other parables, with the words, "the kingdom of heaven is like this".

And this sits directly on the main point. Building upon Bauckham's reflections and the insights of many scholars regarding the radical nature of Jesus' teachings, we may add the observation that *by describing this kingdom as heavenly or from heaven (including the consistent use of plural οὐρανός), Matthew highlights and heightens the tension between God's kingdom and all earthly kingdoms.* In other words, seeing that indeed "much of Jesus' teaching seems designed precisely to show how God's rule differs from earthly rule" (Bauckham), leads directly into understanding *why*

---

[130] Bauckham, "Kingdom and Church," 6.
[131] J. Ramsey Michaels, "The Kingdom of God and the Historical Jesus," in *The Kingdom of God in 20th-Century Interpretation*, 116.
[132] Warren Carter in Carter and Heil, *Matthew's Parables*, 143.

Matthew would choose to call the kingdom the kingdom *of heaven*: this weighty expression serves perfectly as the counterpoint to all earthly kingdoms, and thereby highlights the intended contrast. Additionally, it evokes the language and themes of Daniel while it also plays in perfectly to the broader heaven and earth theme in Matthew, which itself evokes Genesis 1:1 and beyond. Thus, it stands on and suggests the rich OT tradition while contrasting the nature and *modus operandi* of God's kingdom with all earthly kingdoms. The assorted oral and written traditions about Jesus clearly testified to the radical nature of Jesus' teaching, and Matthew follows these traditions and seeks to explain them in terms loaded with literary and theological allusions: "heaven and earth." God's kingdom, the kingdom of heaven, is indeed unlike all earthly kingdoms.

This assertion, which is powerful rhetoric by itself, also has specific content for Matthew. The First Gospel repeatedly shows that the social order of the kingdom of heaven is very unlike the present earthly order, and that the latter will eventually be replaced by the former (6:9–10). In addition to radical teachings such as the Laborers in the Vineyard (20:1–16), Matthew depicts the heavenly kingdom as one in which the mourning and poor in spirit are blessed (5:3, 4, 10–12), while those who are meek (πραΰς) stand to inherit the earth (5:5). Equally topsy-turvy, the nature of the kingdom of heaven is such that the one who is lowly like a child will be the greatest therein (18:1–4; cf. 19:13–15), while the leaders in God's community should be the slaves of all (20:25–28; cf. 23:11). Those who give up everything for the heavenly kingdom will gain all back and more (19:26–29)—the first shall be last, and the last first (19:30). In the kingdom of heaven, the Father King evaluates righteousness on the unexpected basis of one's ministry to the "least" ones, the outcasts of society—the stranger, the hungry, thirsty, naked, sick, and imprisoned ones (25:31–46). In these ways and more Matthew makes it clear that Jesus proclaimed a heavenly kingdom that is very unlike all societies of the earth. And all of these teachings entail a forward-looking hope. The fact that God's heavenly kingdom is in fact *so* different from the current earthly kingdoms creates (for some) and extends (for others) dissatisfaction with the present earthly schemes. This foments the eschatological hope that in Jesus, the kingdom of heaven will come to earth (6:9–10).

324   CHAPTER TWELVE

The Application: Jewish and Roman Contexts

This emphatic point—that God's kingdom is unlike earthly kingdoms and will replace them—has polemical and practical application for Matthew's first-century hearers. This application is two-fold, corresponding to the overlapping contexts which many of the early Christians found themselves in, both Jewish and Roman. In the first instance, Matthew's emphasis on the non-earthly kingdom of heaven critiques first-century Jewish expectations for a kingdom that focuses on the overthrow of Roman domination and the restoration of a Jewish-only, Palestine-exclusive Davidic state. Jesus is indeed the Davidic Messiah, as Matthew particularly is at pains to show, but not with a violently politically revolutionary purpose, nor in a way that benefits only the Jewish people. The memories of the Maccabeans and their violent, Gentile-expunging kingdom were still fresh and celebrated annually. Jesus' depiction of the kingdom stands in sharp contrast. It is not difficult to see how emphasizing the heavenly nature of the kingdom likely served to discourage earthly plots and schemes for the overthrow of Roman control. While Matthew emphasizes Jesus' true kingship, especially in the Passion narrative, he also shows its non-violent manner by rebuking the disciple who strikes the slave of the high priest with his sword in the garden of Gethsemane (12:52–53), and of course, ultimately, willingly dying even though he was king.[133] In view of the highly-charged revolutionary environment of first-century Palestine, one way to discourage Christian involvement was to emphasize the heavenly nature of the kingdom; change would come with God's irruption from heaven (in answer to prayer; cf. 6:9–10), not through reactionary or violent earthly actions (cf. the non-retaliation commands in the Sermon on the Mount).

Matthew's critique of the Jewish expectation of a kingdom also focused on the issue of Gentile-inclusion versus an ethnically Jewish state. Through Matthew's focus on Gentile-inclusiveness, he makes clear that in Jesus, the boundaries of the sacred are no longer ethnic, but the people of God are defined as whosoever does his will. Matthew from beginning (genealogy; magi) to end (the Great Commission) manifests the *prophetic* vision of eschatological Gentile inclusion into the people of God, an inclusion that will result in *all the nations* streaming to God

---

[133] Willard M. Swartley, *Israel's Scripture Traditions and the Synoptic Gospels: Story Shaping Story* (Peabody, Mass.: Hendrickson, 1994), 215–219, gives several other texts which highlight the nonmilitary nature of Jesus' kingship.

the King (cf. Ps 22:27–28; Isa 18:7; 60:3–16; Jer 3:17; Mic 4:1–7; Zech 14:16–17; *Pss. Sol.* 17:30–31; *Sib. Or.* 3:772–776).[134] The coming of the Davidic Messiah does inaugurate the Davidic kingdom, but in its prophetically-revealed form which is worldwide, universal, and Gentile-inclusive;[135] Jesus is not only the "son of David" but also the "son of Abraham" (1:1).[136] As John Riches points out, Matthew has distanced himself from the traditions of Jewish restorationist ideology and sacred space has been 'de-territorialized': "Sacred space is no longer defined simply in terms of the Land of Israel, in which the Davidic kingdom is to be inaugurated and the Temple restored to its former glory...the whole world is now a mission field...sacred space is wherever Jesus is present with his followers (Matt 28:20 [cf. 1:23])."[137] The emphasis

---

[134] As is well-known, there were a variety of conflicting views in Second Temple Jewish literature concerning the place of Gentiles in the eschatological kingdom. Dunn, *Jesus Remembered*, 393–396, offers fourteen aspects of the various strands of Second Temple traditions concerning the kingdom of God. These serve to fill out "the context of expectation within which Jesus' preaching about the kingdom of God would have been heard" (at 396). It is clear that from the earliest days Christians understood and aligned themselves with a view that included Gentiles into the one people of God.

[135] In a recent article, Mary Ann Beavis, following D. Mendels, has argued that "Jesus' interpretation of the kingdom stressed the *universality* of divine rule, almost to the exclusion of its particularity" and that Jesus spoke of the βασιλεία in a way "that downplayed explicitly nationalistic and particularistic overtones and aspirations." While concurring with these insights, I do not think it is necessary to interpret Jesus' vision of the kingdom in as starkly *anti*-political terms as Beavis does. That is, I think that Jesus was critiquing Jewish nationalistic hopes in favor of a Gentile-inclusive kingdom, but this does not make his message an anti-political one. Mary Ann Beavis, "The Kingdom of God, 'Utopia' and Theocracy," *Journal for the Study of the Historical Jesus* 2/1 (2004), 103–104. Another recent essay which argues for a Gentile-inclusive focus in Matthew is Warren Carter's, "Matthew and the Gentiles." Carter gives seven aspects of the Gospel which show that Matthew is concerned to engage the Gentile world with God's kingdom.

[136] Davies and Allison, *Matthew*, 1:156–160, reflecting on the many allusions of Matt 1:1, point out that "son of David" points to Jesus as the king of Israel and the rightful heir to the Davidic promises, while "son of Abraham," the "father of many nations," speaks to Matthew's interest in the salvation of the Gentiles. Donald Verseput has argued that the combination of the Son of David with the Son of God theme in Matthew communicates Jesus' universal mission. Jesus is presented not only as the Davidic Messiah but also the Son of God. "His was a gentile mission blessed by God to call men to himself, in stark contrast to the imperial and triumphal traits of Jewish Davidic expectation." Verseput, "The Role and Meaning of the 'Son of God' Title in Matthew's Gospel," 532–556, especially 541–549. Cf. also France, *Matthew: Evangelist and Teacher*, 285–286, and 232–235.

[137] John Riches, *Conflicting Mythologies: Identity Formation in the Gospels of Mark and Matthew*, 292–293. Riches argues similarly in his essay, "Matthew's Missionary Strategy in Colonial Perspective," in Riches and Sim, *The Gospel of Matthew in its Roman Imperial Context*, 140: there is an "expansion of sacred space to include no longer only the land but the whole world."

on the *heavenly* nature of the kingdom cuts to the heart of the Jewish dependence on the *land* of Israel as the sign of God's covenant with them. The Gospel proclaimed by Jesus is worldwide, encompassing the heavens and all the earth, including the Gentiles.[138] Christianity from its earliest days is not just a Palestine- and land-based religion, but a universal one including all the nations of the earth. In this way, Matthew's emphasis on the heavenly nature of the kingdom serves as part of his Gentile-inclusive focus. This is not to suggest that Matthew's vision for a Gentile-inclusive kingdom necessarily *excludes* the land of Israel and Jerusalem (though it does reject its leaders), but only that this is no longer the focus, as is emphasized by the heavenly language.[139]

My proposal that kingdom of heaven emphasizes the Gentile-inclusive vision of the eschaton has similarities to but is a much better understanding than that proposed by Bengel. Bengel, quoted above, saw in kingdom *of heaven* an attempt to cut off the Jewish hope for an *earthly* kingdom. I agree that there was resident in Matthew's expression a critique of the earthly Jewish kingdom hope, but not by being replaced with a heavenly kingdom *rather* than an earthly one. Instead, the critique concerns the *nature* of this coming kingdom in regards to its ethical practicalities, social relationships, and Gentile inclusion. After all, the great Christian prayer is that God's (heavenly) kingdom would come to earth (6:9–10); the Christian hope is *not* for an ethereal, heaven-situated existence, but the consummation of the heavenly realities coming into effect *on the earth*; not for a destruction of the earth

---

[138] Very little has been done on the connection between the heaven and earth theme and the question of the land of Israel in Matthew. An exception is Joon-Sik Kim, "'Your Kingdom Come on Earth': The Promise of the Land and the Kingdom of Heaven in the Gospel of Matthew" (Ph.D. diss., Princeton Theological Seminary, 2001). Kim rightly observes that Matthew's lack of focus on the land of Israel is due to his "preoccupation with legitimating the Gentile mission" (p. 1). Unfortunately, despite the promising title and subject matter, this dissertation primarily has only a negative conclusion: Matthew does not show evidence of interest in the loss of the Land after 70 CE. Kim does not see how important the kingdom *of heaven* is for the issue of a critique of Judaism, nor how it forms part of the broader heaven and earth theme. More generally on the theological theme of the land of Israel, see Walter Brueggemann, *The Land: Place as Gift, Promise, and Challenge in Biblical Faith* (2d ed.; Minneapolis: Fortress, 2002), and W. D. Davies, *The Gospel and the Land: Early Christianity and Jewish Territorial Doctrine* (Berkeley: University of California Press, 1974).

[139] Amidst the many eschatological visions current in the Second Temple period there was certainly a strand that remained Zion-centered yet also included the Gentiles (cf. Isa 2; Zech 14). I am not arguing that Matthew necessarily opposed this view, but only that his focus is on Gentile inclusion such that emphasizing the universal outreach of the Gospel was primary, hence the emphasis on heaven.

and a kingdom that exists only in heaven, but for a παλιγγενεσία, a new genesis (19:28).[140]

This understanding goes far in explaining Matthew's very pointed and at times harsh critiques of the Jewish leadership establishment. As Bauckham observes, "From the perspective of Jesus' understanding of the kingdom, the Jewish theocracy, i.e. the chief priests who ran the temple and claimed to represent God's rule over his people, grossly misrepresented the nature of God's rule. Instead of differing from the way the kings of the Gentiles ruled, they imitated it."[141] Thus, Matthew warns the Jewish leaders that the kingdom for which they are hoping (usually called "the kingdom of God" in Matthew as part of the insider-outsider language) will be taken away from them (8:11–12; 21:43); they will be judged and rejected (23:13–39). Yet God's true kingdom—ἡ βασιλεία τῶν οὐρανῶν—will be entered by all those (Jew or Gentile) who do the will of the Father in heaven (7:21; cf. 12:50). To reiterate, in light of Matthew's Jewish context, kingdom of heaven serves to critique the nature of the Jewish expectation for a kingdom, including the way God's people relate to one another, and especially in its lack of the prophetic vision for Gentile inclusion.

The powerful rhetorical expression kingdom of heaven also has an application to the Roman imperial context of Matthew's hearers and readers. In this context, kingdom of heaven critiques the Roman Empire, proclaims the superiority and universality of God's sovereignty, and provides solace for God's people. In the Second Temple literature, the notion of kingdom of God/God as king is clearly used in opposition

---

[140] Robert Foster has suggested that Matthew uses heavenly language as a rhetorical and social strategy which "defends Jesus as a Davidic messiah, showing that he came to establish a heavenly, not earthly kingdom." He goes on to state that in light of Messianic expectations in formative Judaism, "one would legitimately expect the Messiah to re-establish God's rule from Zion. The use of FH [Father in heaven] indicates that the leaders of formative Judaism fundamentally misunderstand Jesus because they likewise misunderstand how God exercises his reign from heaven in this world." Foster, "Why on Earth Use 'Kingdom of Heaven'?," 487, 493. Though the basic point about a critique of Jewish expectations is correct, the thesis as stated here could be construed as erroneous in the same way that Bengel's is. Again, in light of 6:9–10, clearly the *telos* of the heavenly kingdom will be its coming upon the earth. Therefore, it can be misleading to state that Jesus' message was about a heavenly kingdom *not* an earthly one. The distinction must be understood as one of nature not of ultimate, eschatological space.

[141] Bauckham, "Kingdom and Church," 13.

to other ruling governments. In fact, this could be said to be the most consistent usage of the kingdom of God idea throughout the literature. Jewish life under Roman rule was no exception, and opposition to Rome in literary and revolutionary form was not uncommon.[142] It is worth recalling that Jesus himself was crucified between two insurrectionists and with a mocking placard above his head which read "King of the Jews." Rome, like many empires before it, developed its own grandiose claims and rhetoric of universal rulership. They were the "lords of the world" (Virgil, *Aeneid* 1.282), and emperors such as Domitian were described as "lord of the earth," "ruler of the nations" (Statius, *Silvae* 3.4.20; 4.2.14–15), and "master of sea and land" (Philostratus, *Apollonius* 7.3).[143] Not only did Roman emperors claim such universal lordship, but even eternality and increasingly, divinity. Matthew in several texts posits God's sovereignty over against such audacious Roman claims: rather than Jupiter or any emperor, it is God who is the Father in heaven (6:9 et al.), who controls the sun and rain (5:45), and who is the "Lord of heaven and earth" (11:25).[144] Even the series of descriptors of Jesus in Matt 1:1 seem to present him as the one who "contests and relativizes Rome's claim to sovereignty and divine agency."[145]

However one dates the origin of the Daniel traditions, exilic or post-exilic, it is clear that the book of Daniel represents the same view of God's kingdom against contemporary kingdoms, as is found in the other Second Temple literature. The many connections between Daniel and Matthew have already been noted. In fact, Matthew and his audience were facing a situation strikingly similar to the Jewish people of the exilic and post-exilic times. They were a minority group under the power of the greatest earthly empire at the time. It is not difficult

---

[142] A helpful survey of this can be found in Philip F. Esler, "Rome in Apocalyptic and Rabbinic Literature," in Riches and Sim, *The Gospel of Matthew in its Roman Imperial Context*: 9–33. Interestingly for my own arguments about the influence of Daniel on Matthew's depiction of the kingdom, Esler points out that much of the discourse about Rome in Jewish literature is reliant upon the myth of the four beasts in Daniel 7.

[143] Carter, "Matthew and the Gentiles," 262.

[144] Carter, *Matthew and Empire*, 63.

[145] Carter, "Matthaean Christology in Roman Imperial Key: Matthew 1.1," in Riches and Sim, *The Gospel of Matthew in its Roman Imperial Context*, 143. It should be noted again that the Roman imperial context is not the only context for these polyvalent expressions, but it does highlight their significance vis-à-vis Roman claims. Discussion of the Roman imperial context of the Gospels can be found also in several works of Richard Horsley, including *Jesus and Empire: The Kingdom of God and the New World Disorder* (Minneapolis: Fortress, 2003).

to see that Matthew's emphasis on the kingdom of heaven performs the same functions as Daniel's narrative does. It may be that reflection on the similarity of social situations led Matthew to consciously employ Daniel's themes and language. Like Daniel, Matthew critiques the Roman Empire (and really all earthly kingdoms and societies) by positing an alternative kingdom that is superior in every way.[146] This kingdom, proclaimed by Jesus, is not only earthly, but heavenly. This speaks of its universality[147] and higher nature. In the same way that the Second Temple title "God of heaven" asserted the Jewish God's superiority over all pagan gods and rulers, Matthew's Father in heaven and kingdom of heaven likewise proclaim that the Roman Empire (with its *pater* emperors and numerous kings) is inferior and ultimately subservient to God's sovereignty.[148] Any Jewish person's hope in the kingdom *of God* inherently entails this critical view of the Roman Empire, but to call the kingdom the kingdom *of heaven* heightens and emphasizes the superiority of the kingdom which Jesus announced.

Additionally, in the same way that Daniel's stories and visions provided solace and hope for his Jewish readers, Matthew's emphasis on the kingdom of heaven over all earthly kingdoms gives Jesus' disciples the consolation that with the coming of God's kingdom all will be made right.[149] This hope and vision also enables Jesus' followers to live now, while awaiting the eschaton, with the radical ethics of the coming kingdom, especially as taught in the Sermon on the Mount. Matthew's expression kingdom of heaven and his stress on the heaven and earth

---

[146] Recall that Satan's offer to Jesus of "all the kingdoms of the world" (4:8) indicates that Satan stands as the "sponsoring" deity behind the Roman Empire. This in itself provides an obvious critique of the Roman Empire. See Carter, "Matthew and the Gentiles," 266–267.

[147] Robert Gundry has suggested that Matthew uses heaven in combination with Father and kingdom as a "means of stressing another of his favorite motifs, the majesty of God's universal dominion." Though he does not offer any additional discussion, this idea is undoubtedly based on the fact that in Hellenistic Greek (secular and Jewish uses), οὐρανός was often used to communicate the idea of universality. Gundry, *Matthew*, 43.

[148] Interestingly, Diane Chen also sees the Roman Imperial idea of the emperor as the *pater patriae* as informing Luke's use of God as Father language. However, she concludes that instead of being subversive to the Roman Empire, Luke's usage does not cast Rome in an entirely negative light, though God is clearly a superior father to any emperor. Chen, *God as Father in Luke-Acts*, 13.

[149] This idea is developed by David C. Sims in his essay, "Rome in Matthew's Eschatology," in Riches and Sim, *The Gospel of Matthew in its Roman Imperial Context*: 91–106.

theme evoke for his readers the Danielic witness and hope.[150] Looking backward, the evocation of Daniel ties in Matthew once again to the OT tradition. Looking forward, connecting with the narrative of Daniel also serves Matthew's readers' needs.[151] In sum, Matthew is skillfully re-appropriating the language and vision of Daniel for his own hearers' context. This simultaneously critiques the ruling and oppressive Roman Empire and gives eschatological hope.

In conclusion, the preceding analysis of Matthew's kingdom of heaven has shown that rather than existing as a reverential circumlocution for God, this important Matthean phrase serves one primary point: God's kingdom, which is in heaven and heavenly, is radically different from all earthly kingdoms and will eschatologically replace them (on the earth). It is the coming kingdom which is proclaimed by Jesus and is embodied in himself, the unexpected servant-leader.

---

[150] In an analogous argument, Warren Carter has suggested that the early portions of Matthew evoke particular Isaianic texts. This was done by Matthew because of a similar imperial context between Isaiah's readers and Matthew's. "Just as the eighth-century prophet countered and relativized imperialist claims, so does his word for the Matthean audience." "The Isaiah texts provide perspective on the imperial situation and give content to God's salvific promise." Warren Carter, "Evoking Isaiah," 513, 508. See also, idem, "Matthew and the Gentiles."

[151] Is it merely coincidence that many manuscripts of the Lord's Prayer add on the phrase from Daniel 2:37—"the kingdom, the power, the strength, and the glory"? Very possibly this shows that at least some early Christians made the connection between the Lord's Prayer and Jesus' kingdom and Daniel 2. Evans, "Daniel in the New Testament," 511, makes similar remarks.

CONCLUSION

HEAVEN AND EARTH IN THE GOSPEL OF MATTHEW

This concluding chapter of reflections will cover three areas. First, I will examine how the heaven and earth theme argued throughout this thesis relates to dualism and the symbolic universe of Matthew. Next, I will offer an interesting example of how Matthew's kingdom of heaven was appropriated in the second century. And finally, I will provide a brief summary of the overall findings of this work followed by a number of conclusions that can be drawn from it.

Dualism, Duality and the Symbolic Universe of Matthew

Dualism, Duality and Matthew's "Heaven and Earth"

"Dualism" is a term and concept that has been so widely appealed to in religious studies that inevitably, it has been abused and misapplied. For example, Second Temple apocalyptic literature, the Qumran community, and the Gospel of John have all been summarily labeled (and often vilified, especially John) as "dualistic."[1] The problem with this is not that these documents do not manifest any dualistic polarities—they do—but that the *label* "dualism" is too vague to be used so freely. The term is used to encompass such a wide variety of different views that it ceases to be reliable. Moreover, as Miroslav Wolf has observed, "dualism" often serves simply as a convenient term of opprobrium, applied derisively to "any duality deemed unacceptable" by the scholar using it.[2]

---

[1] Such a view can be found in countless standard discussions of apocalyptic literature, Qumran ideas, and John. An early article which propounds and compares "dualism" in Qumran and John is J. H. Charlesworth, "A Critical Comparison of the Dualism in 1QS III, 13–IV, 26 and the 'Dualism' Contained in the Fourth Gospel," *NTS* 15 (1969): 389–418. Charlesworth concludes that both documents share several types of modified dualistic views, and in fact that John borrowed some of his terminology and concepts from 1QS. Another essay which examines dualistic thought at Qumran is Jörg Frey, "Different Patterns of Dualistic Thought in the Qumran Library:" 275–s335. Like Charlesworth and Wright (see below), Frey lists ten different kinds of dualism.

[2] Miroslav Wolf, "Johannine Dualism and Contemporary Pluralism" (paper presented at the "Gospel of John and Christian Theology" conference, St Andrews, Scotland, July 2003), 2.

Charlesworth begins his discussion of dualism at Qumran and in John by noting that there are in fact "various types of dualism in the history of ideas: philosophical, anthropological, psychological, physical, metaphysical, cosmological, cosmic, ethical, eschatological, and soteriological."[3] In discussing the thought-world of first-century Judaism, N. T. Wright offers a similar categorization of ten types of duality: theological/ontological; theological/cosmological; moral; eschatological; theological/moral; cosmological; anthropological; epistemological; sectarian; psychological.[4] Wright also injects a very important distinction into this discussion. He points out that despite this great variety of "dualisms," the general term is regularly applied indiscriminately to any or all of them. Not only does this result in confusion, but it also causes many common Jewish ways of speaking and thinking to be shackled with associations of "dualism" broadly conceived and usually negative. In fact, many elements in Jewish and Christian literature that are labeled as "dualistic" are in reality "perfectly normal features of most if not all biblical theology" and do not indeed reflect Iranian Zoroastrianism or any other type of dualism.[5] Consequently, Wright wisely suggests that we refer instead to "dualities" and save the term "dualism" only for specific types of dualities, such as the moral dualism of classic Zoroastrianism and Gnosticism, the cosmological dualism of Plato, and the anthropological dualism which divides body and soul.[6] Bianchi's discussion of dualism comes to a similar conclusion: "Not every duality or polarity is dualistic, but only those that involve the duality or polarity of causal principles."[7] Thus, many basic Jewish and

---

[3] Charlesworth, "A Critical Comparison," 389, n. 1. Charlesworth goes on to give brief definitions of several of these types, and to state that he is concerned in this essay with a "modified dualism" which is not "a polarity between two equal, eternal forces or concepts."

[4] N. T. Wright, *The New Testament and the People of God*, 252–254. Wright references Charlesworth and notes that he worked out these ten categories independently before coming across Charlesworth's article.

[5] Wright, *New Testament and the People of God*, 252–253.

[6] Wolf does not show awareness of Wright's argument but comes to a similar conclusion. He quotes the standard definition of religious dualism as found in Ugo Bianchi's *Encyclopedia of Religion* article, and points out that by this definition (specifically, that opposite ontological principles are responsible for bringing the world into existence) the Gospel of John cannot be understood as dualistic. Instead, we should speak of "oppositional dualities" which are found in the text. These stable and firm dualities are important and widespread, but they do not in fact imply dualism. Wolf, "Johannine Dualism and Contemporary Pluralism," 3.

[7] Ugo Bianchi, quoted in Stephen Barton, "Johannine Dualism and Contemporary Pluralism" (paper presented at the "Gospel of John and Christian Theology" conference, St Andrews, Scotland, July 2003), 5.

Christian concepts such as God and the devil are not properly dualistic. This is a positive step forward for any discussion of dualism or dualities in ancient documents.

We may now inquire how Matthew's theme of heaven and earth relates to these ideas. I have repeatedly argued in this work that the motivation behind Matthew's highly developed heaven and earth theme is to highlight the tension or contrast that currently exist between God's realm and humanity's. This can be seen, then, as an example of one of many oppositional dualities in the Judeo-Christian literary tradition. In fact, it is interesting to see how similar this is to the "above-below" duality that is used pervasively throughout John, as well as the heaven and earth contrast in the book of Revelation. But the most important point to make is that, in line with Wright's observations, it would be a misnomer to label Matthew's heaven and earth theme as evidence of dualism proper.[8] "Heaven and earth," even used contrastively, is ancient biblical language that should not be confused with Zoroastrianism or Platonism; heaven and earth do not represent two original, opposing forces in the world, but biblically are seen as organically related realms all under the rule of God. It is also interesting to note that unlike some uses of the heaven and earth pair in Jewish and Christian literature, Matthew's employment of the motif does *not* particularly manifest the idea that earthly structures are copies of heavenly realities. In this sense, some distinction can be observed between Matthew's use of the heaven and earth theme and that of the book of Hebrews (e.g., Heb 8:5). In Matthew, heaven is used mainly as a foil for earth, as a means of critiquing what is wrong with the way humans live on the earth, by contrasting the two realms and by looking forward to the eschaton when the tension between the two realms will be resolved. The problem is that sinful earth currently is not in line with heavenly realities (6:9–10)—it is radically different—such that eschatologically, the former will be reinvented by the latter.

Related to this discussion, we may once more raise the topic of Matthew's *Weltbild* and *Weltanschauung*. I argued previously that in the OT as well as in Matthew, we find evidence of an essentially bipartite picture of the world. This cosmological view is organically related to

---

[8] In Chapter Four I discussed the relationship between Matthew's heaven and earth theme and apocalyptic motifs. There I suggested that heaven and earth provides further evidence for what David Sim sees as a foundational "dualism" in Matthew's apocalyptic eschatology. This point still stands, although it is unfortunate that Sim does not carefully distinguish between "dualism" and "oppositional dualities."

and undergirds the much more important matter which is the conceptual worldview. Both the *Weltbild* and *Weltanschauung* of Matthew hinge upon the oppositional duality of heaven and earth. Again, it is crucial that in observing this we do not fall into the error of calling either "dualism." For Matthew, the one God, Lord of heaven and earth (11:25), is the creator of all, both heaven and earth. This is a monotheistic cosmological duality, but not a cosmological dualism. Similarly, in Matthew's bipartite *Weltanschauung* we can discern moral duality (good versus evil) and an eschatological duality (this age and the age to come), but this should not be confused with a Zoroastrian or Gnostic dualism or anthropology, nor is the eschatological vision that of the total destruction of the inferior earthly realm—a preferencing of the spirit over the physical. Instead, the hope is for the establishment of God's kingdom upon the earth, a new genesis (παλιγγενεσία, 19:28).

Matthew's Symbolic Universe and the Heaven and Earth Theme

This discussion of Matthew's *Weltanschauung* relates also to another important and overlapping topic, Matthew's symbolic universe. The last twenty years have witnessed the rise of a variety of social scientific approaches to the NT. The Gospel of Matthew has been a particular focus of interest for the practitioners of these methods.[9] As was discussed in Chapter Four, the hottest debates in Matthean studies have centered on Matthew's community and its relationship to Judaism. Social scientific studies have largely contributed to and shaped this discussion.

One of the most important ways that social scientific research has affected the interpretation of Matthew comes from the subspecies of the discipline known as the sociology of knowledge. Stemming especially from the work of Peter Berger and Thomas Luckmann, many Matthean scholars have discussed Matthew's "symbolic universe." Berger and Luckmann define symbolic universes as "bodies of theoretical tradition that integrate different provinces of meaning and encompass the institutional order in a symbolic totality."[10] In less technical terms, a symbolic universe is the integrated system of beliefs, values, and symbols which

---

[9] For studies up through 1993, a helpful overview can be found in Janice Capel Anderson, "Life on the Mississippi: New Currents in Matthaean Scholarship 1983–1993," *Currents in Research: Biblical Studies* 3 (1995), 173–184. Other specific studies are referenced above in Chapter Four.

[10] Peter L. Berger and Thomas Luckmann, *The Social Construction of Reality: A Treatise in the Sociology of Knowledge* (London: Penguin, 1966; repr. 1991), 113.

are used by groups to legitimate their understanding of the world. The symbolic universe is understandably important for religious groups, especially ones which have broken away from another, "mother" group. Berger has called this a "sacred canopy."[11]

The cash value of this idea is immediately apparent to scholars attempting to reconstruct the first-century setting behind Matthew's Gospel. As a result, there have been many studies of how Matthew's symbolic universe functions for his community.[12] The point is frequently made that Matthew's goal is to consolidate and legitimate his community, to encourage them that they are the true people of God.[13] At this point we can make an important connection with Matthew's heaven and earth theme. As has been suggested above, many aspects of Matthew's use of this theme serve this same purpose: to provide encouragement and legitimization for his audience. At a subtle, narrative level, Matthew reserves certain key terms for his disciples—such as Father in heaven, kingdom of heaven, and plural forms of οὐρανός—while using more generic expressions such as God and kingdom of God for those "outside." At a more blatant level, he offers very pointed criticisms and judgments against Jesus' opponents, and uses the major theme of the kingdom of heaven as a way to emphasize that the kingdom Jesus is proclaiming is very different from those of the Jewish establishment. The true people of God are not ethnically-derived but are the ones who do the will of their heavenly Father by aligning themselves with Jesus and keeping his commandments. Jesus' followers are defined very much by their association with heaven (kingdom; Father; rewards) over

---

[11] Peter L. Berger, *The Sacred Canopy: Elements of a Sociological Theory of Religion* (New York: Anchor Books, 1990). See also the discussion in Philip Esler, *The First Christians in their Social Worlds: Social-Scientific Approaches to New Testament Interpretation* (London: Routledge, 1994), 8–10; and John Riches, Matthew, 68.

[12] For example, Anthony Saldarini, *Matthew's Christian-Jewish Community* (Chicago: University of Chicago Press, 1994); J. Andrew Overman, *Matthew's Gospel and Formative Judaism* (Minneapolis: Fortress, 1990); idem, *Church and Community in Crisis: The Gospel According to Matthew* (Valley Forge, Penn.: Trinity, 1996); John Riches, Conflicting Mythologies.

[13] For example, Saldarini writes that Matthew "seeks to legitimate his particular form of Judaism by utilizing the sources of authority in the Jewish community (see chaps. 5–6 on his use of Scripture generally) and by delegitimating the Jewish leaders (see esp. chap. 23)." Anthony Saldarini, "The Gospel of Matthew and Jewish-Christian Conflict," in *Social History of the Matthean Community: Cross-Disciplinary Approaches* (ed. David L. Balch; Minneapolis: Fortress, 1991), 41. John Riches states that "whether or not Matthew was writing from inside or outside the Jewish community, he was engaged in consolidating and legitimising his community." Riches, *Matthew*, 66–67.

against the earth. One can easily see then, how "heaven and earth" provides the parameters and content for Matthew's symbolic universe.[14] What is most striking is how this theme is able to serve this purpose so comprehensively and powerfully while also functioning as a *Weltbild* and *Weltanschauung* for the Gospel. That is, there are many other dualistic expressions that could be used as part of a community-legitimizing symbolic universe—such as sons of light and sons of darkness, above and below, righteous and sinners, etc.—but by consistently using the expression "heaven and earth" Matthew is able to provide a comprehensive symbolic universe while also indicating his understanding of the world physically and ontologically, all the while trafficking in the most foundational language of the biblical tradition and creation (cf. Gen 1). It is hard to imagine a richer linguistic and literary means by which Matthew could perform so many functions than the expression "heaven and earth."

A Foray into the Reception-History of Matthew's "Kingdom of Heaven"

Matthew's influence on the early church is so great and his unique expression kingdom of heaven is so important, that it is worthwhile to observe one important way that Matthew's linguistic idiom was re-appropriated in the late first- and early second-centuries. This foray into the reception-history of the phrase will also shed light on Matthew's own meaning.

I have argued above that for Matthew's original audience, kingdom of heaven had a polemical and very practical application in regards

---

[14] Hints of this understanding can be heard in Overman, who says that Matthew wants his community to see itself as a microcosm of a heavenly macrocosm (as summarized in Anderson, "Life on the Mississippi," 178), as well as in Riches, who briefly mentions the importance of the heaven language in 5:45, 48, and 6:10. According to its title, the most promising study of heaven and earth and Matthew's symbolic universe is Kari Syreeni's "Between Heaven and Earth: On the Structure of Matthew's Symbolic Universe," 3–13. However, while Syreeni, depending on Schneider, acknowledges that the polarized pair "heaven and earth" "indicates a deep-lying structure in his symbolic universe" (p. 9), this short essay focuses not on the contours or function of this symbolic universe, but instead on vague notions of Matthew's attempt to mediate assorted tensions in his Gospel—a work which Syreeni evaluates at points as quite "irrational" (pp. 7, 9). Thus, the article provides very little in the way of furthering our understanding of Matthew's symbolic universe.

to the Roman Empire. Building on the model of Daniel, Matthew's language provided a devastating and subversive critique of this great *earthly* empire, while providing solace and hope that God's kingdom would eventually come upon the earth.

We find that in the decades following Matthew's work, his "kingdom of heaven" terminology was appropriated somewhat differently by the immediately succeeding generation of Christians, people still living very conspicuously under Roman rule. As Matthew re-appropriated Daniel's language for his own situation, we can see that many late first-century and early second-century Christians likewise took up Matthew's "kingdom of heaven" terminology and used it for their own purposes as they sought to live peaceably under the often-hostile Roman Empire—something very important for these second-century Christians who often faced persecution.[15] They did this by emphasizing that Christ's kingdom was *heavenly*, not *earthly*, and thereby, not a threat to the Roman Empire.

A good example of this comes from Hegesippus' account of the grandsons of Jude (as recorded in Eusebius *HE* 3:19:1–3:20:7). According to Hegesippus, during the Emperor Domitian's rule, some people brought charge against Zoker and James, who were the grandsons of Jude, the brother of Jesus. The charge was that because these men were descendants of David, they were a potential threat to the Empire. Therefore, the story goes, Domitian called them to trial and examined them to see if they were a potential source of Jewish political uprising. When asked about Christ and his kingdom the grandsons of Jude responded that his kingdom "was not of the world nor earthly, but heavenly and angelic; and that it would appear at the end of the world" (20:5). After this, Zoker and James were dismissed and, miraculously, Domitian's persecution of the church ceased from that time. Apparently, their answer, which emphasized the *heavenly* nature of Christ's kingdom, succeeded in showing, as Richard Bauckham has suggested,

---

[15] According to Samson H. Levey (following Uri D. Herscher), many Jews followed a similar turn within their own tradition in the hostile post-70 environment. Rabbi Johanan b. Zakkai led his disciples into Merkabah Mysticism instead of Messianic activism to protect them from being charged with treason by the Romans. At the same time, because this mysticism placed the divine throne in heaven (cf. Ezekiel) and out of reach of the adversary, it could still "keep alive their faith in God and their hope for national restitution and restoration of their sovereignty, all symbolized by the Temple." Samson H. Levey, *The Targum of Ezekiel* (Edinburgh: T&T Clark, 1987), 4.

"that allegiance to Christ's kingdom does not make Christians political revolutionaries intent on overthrowing the Roman state."[16]

In fact, an examination of the many references to the kingdom in the second-century writings shows this same emphasis. For example, Justin stresses that Christians have been misunderstood if it is thought they are looking for a human kingdom (*1 Apol.* 11), and in the Martyrdom of Paul, Paul explains to two Roman officials that "we do not march, as you suppose, with a king who comes from the earth, but one from heaven, the living God" (4).[17] There are many such examples, and they likely reflect a perception among many Romans that Christians were potentially armed and dangerous. This perception likely came about because of a confused association of Christianity with the many revolutionary Jewish messianic movements in the first and second-centuries. As Bauckham explains, these texts reveal "an apologetic concern to make clear the real nature of the kingdom of Christ as heavenly rather than earthly."[18] And in so doing, these second-century Christians were able to protect themselves.

Everett Ferguson, in his interesting essay on the kingdom of God in Patristic literature provides several insights along these same lines. He observes that "neither Jews nor Christians in the second century were permitted a 'political' expression of their kingdom claims"[19] and that "the Apologists were particularly aware that the biblical word for "kingdom" was the ordinary word for the empire or any kingship."[20] Therefore, "in political contexts Christians emphasized that Christ's kingdom is otherworldly and heavenly."[21]

Thus, we can see that Matthew's recurrent phrase kingdom of heaven proved to be an important and helpful means by which later Christians could justify their peaceful existence within the Roman Empire. I suggest that this appropriation of Matthew's terminology, though not exactly what Matthew meant by the expression, is understandable for the early Christians living precariously in the Roman Empire. There are several other reasons for Matthew's employment of kingdom of heaven, all

---

[16] Richard J. Bauckham, *Jude and the Relatives of Jesus in the Early Church* (Edinburgh: T&T Clark, 1990), 101.
[17] Quoted in Bauckham, *Jude and the Relatives of Jesus*, 103.
[18] Bauckham, *Jude and the Relatives of Jesus*, 103.
[19] Everett Ferguson, "The Kingdom of God in Early Patristic Literature," in Wendell Willis, editor, *The Kingdom of God in 20th-Century Interpretation*, 193.
[20] Ferguson, "The Kingdom of God," 194.
[21] Ferguson, "The Kingdom of God," 200.

of which focus on the tension between heaven and earth (see below). One of these was likely to encourage Christians not to be involved in first-century revolutionary plots, but even this differs somewhat from the second-century appropriation as seen in the case of James and Zoker. The difference is this: these Christians gladly emphasized the heavenly nature of God's kingdom in such a way that they presented Christianity as a non-threat to Roman power; the heavenly and earthly realms of kingdoms are distinct. But for Matthew, the kingdom of heaven did critique and promise to overthrow the Roman Empire—but via God's irruption into the world from heaven.

Summary and Conclusions

In light of the length, number of details, and assorted conclusions of the preceding chapters, it will be beneficial to provide here a summary of the findings argued previously in the book. This will enable us to see how the arguments together form a broad and cohesive thesis. Following this, I will offer several conclusions regarding how the heaven and earth theme functions in Matthew.

Summary of Findings

In Part One I have argued that before being able to appreciate the elaborate and highly developed use of heaven language in the First Gospel, we must first be disabused of the assumption that heaven is merely functioning in Matthew as a reverential circumlocution for God. When we return *ad fontes* to Dalman's arguments in this regard we find that they are methodologically flawed and historically inaccurate. Unfortunately, the assumption that heaven functions in Matthew as a reverential circumlocution is so widespread that very few have thought to reconsider its basis. Instead, however, Matthew regularly employs οὐρανός in a metonymic way, referring indeed to the divine realm, but for literary, rhetorical, and polemic reasons, not out of reverential circumlocution.

Our general survey of heaven language from the OT through to Matthew reveals that heaven is a very common and important cosmological and theological concept throughout the Jewish and Christian literature. Somewhat unexpectedly, we find that of all the NT authors, Matthew ranks first in his employment and emphasis on heaven language. While Matthew stands in basic continuity with the Jewish literary tradition, his use of heaven language stands apart in four particular ways:

(1) in a preference for the plural οὐρανοί; (2) through the frequent use of the heaven and earth pair; (3) in the use of the phrases Father in heaven and heavenly Father; and (4) via the frequently repeated and historically unique expression, kingdom of heaven. We have also found that Matthew's regular use of heaven language and the heaven and earth theme relates to many other key theological issues in the First Gospel.

In Part Two, I have proceeded to analyze each of the four elements of Matthew's particular use of heaven language. Regarding singular and plural uses of οὐρανός we have found that neither in the LXX nor in Matthew do the standard explanations prove sufficient. Building on the work of Torm and Katz, I suggest that the occasional occurrences of the plural in the LXX are not morphological Semitisms nor evidence of a belief in multiple heavens, but the result of poetic and syntactical factors which can be described as a Semitic enhancement. Going beyond Torm and Katz, I also suggest that in the cases of Wisdom of Solomon and the *Testament of Abraham*, singular and plural forms are used in an intentionally patterned way, distinguishing between the two poles in the semantic range of οὐρανός: the singulars refer to the created realm and the plurals to the divine. These findings feed directly into the study of singular and plural forms in Matthew. Contrary to standard treatments, I argue that Matthew's preference for the plural is not a result of the Semitic influence of שָׁמַיִם nor a belief in multiple heavens. Instead, in a way similar to but much more developed than in Wisdom or *Testament of Abraham*, Matthew regularly uses οὐρανός in the singular to refer to the visible (earthly) realm and in heaven and earth pairs, while he always uses the plural forms to refer to the invisible (divine) realm.

Regarding the word-pair heaven and earth, I have traced this theme throughout the OT and Second Temple literature and into the NT. In addition to being a ubiquitous and theologically ripe expression, heaven and earth provides the fundamental framework for both the *Weltbild* and *Weltanschauung* of the Old Testament. These are organically related, and the fundamentally bipartite cosmological understanding of the world in the OT undergirds a symbolic ontological duality between God and humanity. A close reading of Matthew reveals that, like much of his literary tradition but in a more concentrated way, heaven and earth is a significant element in his Gospel presentation. Not only does Matthew rely upon the common OT phraseology and concept of heaven and earth, but he particularly emphasizes the contrastive or tensive use of the heaven and earth pair. Additionally, I argue that Matthew's worldview continues in the trajectory of the OT and Second Temple literature: his *Weltbild* is still fundamentally two-fold though with some developments, while his *Weltanschauung* is definitely comprised of the oppositional duality of heaven and earth. Even as he uses singular and plural οὐρανός to distinguish the earthly and divine realms, Matthew uses the heaven and earth pair as a rubric to organize and explain this kind of dualistic thinking which is widespread throughout his Gospel.

Chapters Nine and Ten proceed to study the third aspect of Matthew's use of heaven language: his many references to the Father in heaven and heavenly Father. Reference to God as Father was not particularly common in the OT or Second Temple period, though the idea is not absent. Jesus' regular use of divine fatherhood language was somewhat similar to that of his contemporaries, yet more frequent. In Matthew, most striking is the regular connection of Father with the language of heaven. This is best understood as part of Matthew's idiolectic use of heaven and the broader heaven and earth theme. Also, the close connection between the Father in heaven and the kingdom of heaven should not be overlooked (including the fact that they both also always use plural forms of οὐρανός).

Finally, we turn to the fourth element of Matthew's idiolectic use of heaven language: the kingdom of heaven. After tracing this notion through the preceding literature and discussing its meaning, I turn to the predominance of the kingdom theme in Matthew. While using a variety of kingdom expressions, Matthew especially employs the unique phrase, kingdom of heaven. Matthew likely develops this phrase through reflection on the themes of heaven, earth, and kingdom in Daniel 2–7. The consummate point of kingdom of heaven in Matthew is to emphasize that God's kingdom is not like earthly kingdoms, it stands over against them, and it will eschatologically replace them on earth. This point applies to Matthew's Jewish context as a critique of widespread kingdom expectations, especially those which failed to include the prophetic vision of Gentile inclusion. It applies to the Roman Imperial context as a critique of the Roman Empire (as well as all human empires), proclaiming the superiority and universality of God's sovereignty and providing solace for God's people living under oppressive rule.

Building upon all of these findings, the important point is this: these four aspects of Matthew's idiolectic use of heaven language all contribute to one key focus, *the tension that now exists between heaven and earth*, between God and humanity. In very similar ways, each of the four elements communicates this same emphasis: (1) The singular and plural distinction in Matthew's well-crafted use of οὐρανός hinges on the distinction between the divine realm and the human. The standard singular form is used to refer to the created realm (and following customary usage, in heaven and earth pairs), while the ear-striking plural is employed with reference to the divine realm, especially with its consistent attachment to the expressions ὁ πατὴρ ὁ ἐν τοῖς οὐρανοῖς and ἡ βασιλεία τῶν οὐρανῶν. Thus, the current disjuncture between the two is posited at this most basic level of vocabulary. (2) Less subtly, Matthew's regular employment of the word pair heaven and earth stands out as one of the unique features of his Gospel. Through repeated use and in crucial texts (e.g., 6:9–10, 19–21; 16:18; 28:16–20) the heaven and earth theme continues to rise to the surface of the narrative. But unlike much of the preceding literature, instead of primarily using heaven and earth in a merismatic way (only 3x), Matthew prefers to emphasize a distinction or tension between the two realms. In fact, this serves as a "turn of the screw" allusion to Genesis 1:1—while using the same phraseology, Matthew emphasizes the current *dis*junction rather than the *con*junction of heaven and earth, all the while looking forward to the future reuniting of the two realms (6:9–10; 19:28; 28:18). The repeated heaven and earth pair also serves as a telling indicator of Matthew's worldview which consists of a basic oppositional duality of heaven and earth (see above). It also functions as the preferred language to describe Matthew's symbolic universe. (3) The third element of Matthew's idiolect likewise supplies further emphasis on the existing tension between heaven and earth. In Matthew, not only is God the Father, but most importantly, he is the Father in heaven/heavenly Father. Through always using a plural form of οὐρανός in reference to the Father and generally portraying earthly fathers in a negative light, the "of heaven" element of this description of God becomes an important tool to communicate the heaven and earth contrast. Moreover, in several key passages in the Gospel, the Father in heaven is put into clear counterpoint with earthly fathers (e.g. 6:1–21; 23:9). (4) Finally, as has been observed, the ultimate point of the important expression kingdom of heaven is that God's kingdom is very unlike earthly kingdoms, both in their Jewish and Roman manifestations, and will eschatologically replace them.

Thus, by stepping back and analyzing Matthew's rich and varied use of heaven language we can see that behind it all is *an intentional focus on the theme of heaven and earth, specifically highlighting the current contrast or tensive relationship between the two realms, between God and humanity. Yet Matthew does not only emphasize the contrast, but also the fact that this contrast or tension will be resolved at eschaton when heaven and earth are reunited through Jesus (6:9–10; 28:18). In fact, only by recognizing the intensity of the tension that currently exists between heaven and earth can we fully appreciate the significance of the eschaton in which the kingdom of heaven will come to earth.*

This heaven and earth theme serves a dual role, both as a literary motif which connects several narrative threads and as a symbolic or theological point.[22] Also, as was argued in Chapter Four, the heaven and earth theme informs and strengthens a host of other theological themes in the Gospel. Matthew's Christology, ecclesiology, eschatology, and emphasis on the New Covenant are all interconnected and undergirded by the contrast that Matthew sets up between the divine and heavenly realms. Jesus' identity (Christology) as well as that of his people (ecclesiology; New Covenant) and their ultimate goal and hope (eschatology) can all be understood as part of the heaven and earth disjuncture; in each case, these realities are depicted as being on the "heaven" side of the heaven versus earth equation.

Conclusions: The Multiple Functions of the Heaven and Earth Theme

Having surveyed the above findings, we are now in a position to suggest more broadly some of the many functions that this theme of the tension between heaven and earth performs in Matthew. I have already argued that kingdom of heaven in particular operates as a critique of both Jewish expectations for the kingdom as well as all earthly kingdoms, including the Roman Empire. But we may also observe several functions of the heaven and earth theme overall, most of which have been hinted at already in this study. These functions can be described variously as theological, pastoral, and polemical.

In the first instance, the heaven and earth theme *emphasizes the universality of God's dominion*. We have observed on several occasions that in the exilic and post-exilic literature, calling God the "God of

---

[22] This way of describing the heaven and earth theme is analogous to the mountain theme as described in Terence Donaldson, *Jesus on the Mountain: A Study in Matthaean Theology* (Sheffield: JSOT, 1985). John Riches summarizes Donaldson's view this way: "the motif of the mountain has a dual role: on the one hand, it serves as a literary motif which draws together certain passages and focuses attention on them; on the other hand, it has a symbolic—theological—content which is related principally to contemporary Mount Zion ideologies." Riches, *Conflicting Mythologies*, 247, n. 33.

heaven" was a way of stating that he was above all gods, despite the daily oppressive realities of the Exile and the continuing problems with subsequent ruling empires. This is seen very clearly, for example, in the book of Daniel. For Matthew, the contrast of the two realms of heaven and earth strikes this same note, for the Father God and his kingdom are regularly described as *in heaven* as opposed to their corresponding realities *on earth*.[23] Even as "God of heaven" communicates that God's sovereignty is universal by virtue of it being above all earthly rulers, so do Matthew's expressions Father in heaven and kingdom of heaven. The Father and the kingdom are regularly put on the "heaven" side of the heaven-earth equation to communicate that the reality being proclaimed by Jesus is of a superior and universal nature. In this way the heaven and earth theme provides solace and hope for the disciples by emphasizing that in fact the world consists of two realities: the heavenly one and the earthly one, the first of which is universal and abiding, while the other is limited and temporal. This emphasis also looks forward to the eschaton when God's universal dominion, which is now *de jure*, will also be *de facto*.[24]

Another important use of the heaven and earth theme in Matthew is *to make a biblical-theological connection with the Old Testament*. In Chapter Four I suggested that the heaven and earth theme touches on the theological issue of the relationship of the Old and New Testaments, and closely related, on Jesus' disciples as the new people of God. Throughout the work, I have shown that Matthew is deeply indebted to the OT literary tradition. This corpus forms the starting point for his reflections. In Chapter Eight I offered a more substantial argument concerning the specific connection between Matthew and Genesis in particular. In agreement with Davies and Allison, Warren Carter, and others, I understand Matthew's opening words as a very direct allusion to Genesis 1 and following. Many other texts in Matthew likewise confirm the conceptual and intertextual connections with Genesis. This understanding of the bond between the two books is strengthened

---

[23] Following Stendahl, R.T. France observes how the many geographical references in Matt 2 show the Messiah's connection with the wider Gentile world as well as the places of Israel's exile and thereby indicate "the universality of his role as Messiah." France, "The Formula Quotations," 240. I would add that after the geographical emphasis of chapter 2, the immediately following proclamation of the kingdom *of heaven* by John and Jesus serves as a powerful example of the "above all," universal nature of God's kingdom.

[24] U. Mauser, "Heaven in the World View of the New Testament," 44.

greatly by recognizing how important the heaven and earth theme is in Matthew. This theme has obvious connections with Genesis, and suggests that Matthew is intentionally correlating his own account of the Christ with this foundational witness of the OT. An important text in this regard is the climax of Matthew 28:16–20. In this grand conclusion to the First Gospel, which is understood by many as a summary of the whole work, the heaven and earth theme is again highlighted, and the passage likely serves for Matthew as an inclusio with Genesis 1:1, the matching bookend of God's revelation. In Chapter Twelve I made a similar kind of argument for the connection between Matthew and the book of Daniel. Like Genesis, Daniel is noticeably a very important book for the early Christians and for Matthew in particular. I have suggested that central to Daniel 2–7 is the juxtaposition of the themes of heaven and earth (contrasted) and the kingdom of God versus earthly kingdoms. This combination of themes, found nowhere more strongly than in the stories and language of Daniel 2–7, provides a fertile seedbed for Matthew's own heaven and earth theme, including kingdom of heaven. But more than merely providing a literary source, Matthew's own employment of the same themes and language communicates to Matthew's readers the connection between Jesus' ministry and the revelation of God to Daniel. Together, these close intertextual connections between Genesis and Daniel and Matthew reveal that Matthew was very concerned to posit his own work as the culminating revelation in line with the Jewish Scriptures. Steeped in the rich tradition of heaven and earth language, Matthew uses this theme as one of the many tools for connecting his account with the Old Testament.

Thirdly, the heaven and earth theme *serves to strengthen the Christological claims of the Gospel.* As was observed in Chapter Four above, Matthew shows a great interest in emphasizing a high Christology of Jesus. This is certainly a goal of each of the Gospels, but many have discerned a particularly strong emphasis on Messiahship in Matthew. One important text that stands out in this regard is Peter's Caesarean confession (16:13–20). This Triple-Tradition passage is much fuller in Matthew than in Mark and Luke, and also incorporates a key ecclesiological teaching, promising the victory of the church and the authority of the church's actions in the heavenly realm (16:18–19). This important Christological passage is woven deeply with heaven and earth language, even as several other Christological passages are (e.g., 3:17; 28:16–20): Father in heaven (16:17), kingdom of heaven (16:19), heaven and earth pairs (16:19). Knowledge that Jesus is the Christ comes to Peter not through "flesh and blood," i.e., earthly humanity, but from the Father in heaven. The authority that Jesus gives is the authority of the kingdom *of heaven*, and the repercussions are not only earthly, but even heavenly. These are bold claims about Jesus' person and authority. Even more importantly for Matthew's Christology, throughout the Gospel the heaven and earth theme is used as a way to depict Jesus' identity. That is, Jesus is regularly and unmistakably associated with the divine; he is put on the divine side of the divine-human/heaven-earth equation. This is seen nowhere more clearly than in the climactic passage of 28:16–20, where Jesus is worshipped (28:17) and given authority not only on earth (sscf. 9:6), but even in heaven (28:18). The divine prerogative of universal rulership granted to Jesus in these words goes far beyond any claims that could be made of a prophet or angelic figure. In short, Jesus is the divine Christ.

A fourth function of the heaven and theme in Matthew is *to undergird the radical nature of the ethics and teachings of Jesus*. Jesus' teachings and parables have a clear ring about them of challenge, urgency, and world-overturning realities. This is true nowhere more than in Matthew's Sermon on the Mount. The followers of Jesus are called to live now with a God-hoping ethical standard that is counter-intuitive and counter-cultural. Mourners, the poor, the persecuted, and the meek are said to be blessed (5:3–5, 10–12). The standard of righteousness that Jesus requires must go beyond even the strictest interpretations of the scribes and Pharisees (5:20): it must cut to the level of the heart. Stated negatively, hating your brother is murder (5:21–26), and looking lustfully is adultery (5:27–30). Stated positively, instead of retaliation, the response should be gracious giving (5:38–42); instead of loving only one's neighbor, the disciples must love and pray for their enemies (5:43–47). The disciples' piety must be done from the heart and not from hypocrisy—as in the cases of almsgiving, prayer, and fasting (6:1–21). In short, God's standard of righteousness as proclaimed by Jesus is perfection, for single-heartedness in the very same way that the Father himself is perfect (5:48). The radical nature of all such teachings is clearly seen and felt by any hearer. I suggest that the pervasive heaven and earth theme (which is itself concentrated in the Sermon) undergirds these radical teachings by positing the ways of God against the ways of humanity. That is, Jesus is presented as calling disciples to align themselves with the kingdom *of heaven*, as calling them to be sons of the Father *in heaven* (5:44–45; 7:21; 12:50), as calling them to lay up treasures *in heaven* and not *on earth* (6:19–21), as calling them to pray and hope for the kingdom *of heaven* to come *to earth* (6:9–10). This constant refrain of the tension or current disjuncture between the two realms of heaven and earth provides a tangible vision for the kind of hope that transforms daily living. To use Bauckham and Hart's language, it provides resources for the Christian imagination which give God-ward hope.[25] This heaven and earth disjunction is reminiscent of the same point in several of Paul's exhortations to godly living.[26] In Matthew, this way of speaking provides the framework of a symbolic universe that encourages the disciples to align themselves within the world with a different vision and set of values.[27] Only this can sustain such a radical ethical call as Matthew presents. At the core of this vision is the heaven and earth theme.

Finally, and related to the previous ideas, we can also see that Matthew's heaven and earth theme serves *to legitimate and encourage Matthew's readers that they are the true people of God*.[28] This observation builds upon those already made above. By consciously connecting his Gospel with the OT witness, especially Genesis, Matthew gives great weight to the supposition that the followers of Jesus are the true people of God. There is a New Genesis beginning in Jesus (cf. Matt 1:1). In the παλιγγενεσία that Jesus is inaugurating, his disciples will sit on

---

[25] Bauckham and Hart give an excellent account of how a grand Christian vision (via imagination) re-sources the Christian life in Richard Bauckham and Trevor Hart, *Hope Against Hope: Christian Eschatology at the Turn of the Millennium* (Grand Rapids: Eerdmans, 1999). I suggest that Matthew's vision of the world now and in the eschaton, described regularly with reference to heaven and earth, provides the kind of imaginative vision Bauckham and Hart are describing.

[26] For example, Col 3:1–4 makes the basis for godliness the fact that the believer has been raised up with Christ, therefore his or her mind should be set on "things above, not on the things that are on the earth." This is followed by the exhortation: "Put to death therefore what is earthly in you: fornication, impurity, passion, evil desire, and covetousness, which is idolatry." (3:5). Cf. Eph 1:19–20; 2:5–6.

[27] Stanton argues that Matthew "has used several literary strategies in order both to press his case against the Jewish leaders and to convince his readers and listeners that as a 'new people' they are expected to carry out diligently the will of their Father in heaven." These strategies include repetition of his main points, narrative development of conflict with the religious leaders, and *synkrisis*. Stanton, *A Gospel for a New People*, 278. I would add to these the observation that the widespread heaven and earth theme emphasizes these same points.

[28] In addition to the many social-scientific studies which emphasize this idea (see above), Matthew's focus in this regard is ably argued throughout Stanton's *A Gospel for a New People*, especially 113–281 and 378–383. In an analogous way, David Pao has shown that the use of Isaiah in Acts serves in part to provide community identity for Christians as the true people of God. David W. Pao, *Acts and the Isaianic New Exodus* (Tübingen: Mohr-Siebeck, 2000; repr. Baker Academic, 2002).

the thrones of Israel (19:28). Even as Jesus himself is the fulfillment of Israel (son called out of Egypt; tempted in the wilderness), so too, Jesus' community of disciples is depicted as the typological fulfillment of Israel/the people of God. Jesus defines this people not by ethnic pedigree, including having Abraham as one's father (3:9–10; 8:11–12; 23:9), nor by positions of honor (23:2–11), but as those who do the will of the Father who is in heaven (7:21; 12:50), as those whose lives bear the fruit of following God's commands from the heart (3:7–10; 7:15–23; 12:33–38). How does the heaven and earth theme relate to this important motif in Matthew? First, most of these passages are full of references to heaven and the heaven and earth word pair. But more importantly, in the same way that the heaven and earth contrast theme gives a worldview vision that justifies the ethical calls of discipleship, this theme likewise creates a heaven-oriented *identity* for the disciples in the midst of a hostile earthly world. To quote Robert Foster again, Matthew's use of "heavenly language" affirms "the disciples' allegiance both to Jesus as the Christ and to his teaching which truly revealed the righteousness of God." It "reinforces the community's devotion to Jesus while simultaneously undermining the temptation of the disciples to revert or convert to formative Judaism" by reminding them that their identity is a heavenly one (yet awaiting the consummation of heaven and earth).[29] The world is depicted as bipartite—heaven and earth—and Jesus' disciples are the true people of God aligned with heaven, as opposed to the rulers (Roman and Jewish) on earth. In this way, Matthew's heaven and earth theme is an important part of his ecclesiology (see esp. 16:17–19; 18:14–20).

---

[29] Foster, "Why on Earth Use 'Kingdom of Heaven'?," 489, 490, 487.

APPENDIX

DATA FROM A SYNOPTIC COMPARISON OF ΟΥΡΑΝΟΣ

This comparative analysis of οὐρανός in the Synoptic tradition incorporates two distinct but overlapping models: the two-source theory of Marcan priority and Q, and Eusebius' Canon Tables. The following abbreviations are used:

Eusebius' Canon Tables (see NA27, pp. 79, 84–89)
I = 4 Gospels
II = 3 Gospels (Mt, Mk, Lk)
III = 3 Gospels (Mt, Lk, Jn)
IV = 3 Gospels (Mt, Mk, Jn)
V = 2 Gospels (Mt, Lk)
VI = 2 Gospels (Mt, Mk)
VII = 2 Gospels (Mt, Jn)
VIII = 2 Gospels (Lk, Mk)
IX = 2 Gospels (Lk, Jn)
X = special material per evangelist (Mt, Mk, Lk, Jn)

Q = Matt & Lk
  "Q" determinations based on James M. Robinson, Paul Hoffmann, and John S. Kloppenberg, *The Critical Edition of Q* (Minneapolis: Fortress, 2000).
M = Matthew
T = Triple Tradition

- Instances of οὐρανός occurring in all 3 Synoptics (II) (10 occurrences)
  Matt 3:16; 3:17; 13:32; 14:19; 16:1; 19:21; 21:25a; 21:25b; 24:29c; 24:35

- Instances of οὐρανός occurring in both Matt & Luke and not in Mark (V) (9 occurrences)
  Matt 5:12; 5:18; 6:20; 7:11; 8:20; 11:23; 11:25; 16:3b; 18:14 (rough parallel with Luke; not in critical edition of Q)

- Instances of οὐρανός occurring in both Matt & Mark and not in Luke (VI) (5 occurrences)
  Matt 22:30; 24:29b; 24:31; 24:36; 26:64

- Instances of οὐρανός occurring only in Matthew (X) (58 occurrences)
  Matt 3:2; 4:17; 5:3; 5:10; 5:16; 5:19a; 5:19b; 5:20; 5:34; 5:45; 6:1; 6:9; 6:10; 6:26; 7:21b; 7:21c; 8:11; 10:7; 10:32; 10:33; 11:11; 11:12; 12:50; 13:11; 13:24; 13:31; 13:33; 13:44; 13:45; 13:47; 13:52; 16:2; 16:3a; 16:17; 16:19a; 16:19b; 16:19c; 18:1; 18:3; 18:4; 18:10b; 18:10c; 18:18a; 18:18b; 18:19; 18:23; 19:12; 19:14; 19:23; 20:1; 22:2; 23:13; 23:22; 24:30a; 24:30b; 25:1; 28:2; 28:18

- Instances where kingdom of heaven occurs, paralleled with kingdom of God (12 occurrences)
  Matt 4:17; 5:3; 8:11; 10:7; 11:11; 11:12; 13:11; 13:31; 13:33; 19:14; 19:23; 22:2
  - Substituted when kingdom of God occurs in both Mark & Luke: Matt 13:11: 13:31; 19:14; 19:23
  - Substituted when kingdom of God occurs only in Mark: Matt 4:17
  - Substituted when kingdom of God occurs only in Luke: Matt 5:3; 8:11; 10:7; 11:11; 11:12; 13:33; 22:2 (rougher | |)

- Instances where kingdom of heaven occurs, *not* paralleled with kingdom of God (20 occurrences)
  Matt 3:2; 5:10; 5:19a; 5:19b; 5:20; 7:21b; 13:24; 13:44; 13:45; 13:47; 13:52; 16:19a; 18:1; 18:3; 18:4; 18:23; 19:12; 20:1; 23:13; 25:1
  - Of these in M: Matt 5:19a; 5:19b; 5:20; 13:24; 13:44; 13:45; 13:47; 13:52; 16:19a; 18:3; 18:4; 18:23; 19:12; 20:1; 25:1
  - Of these in Q: Matt 5:10; 7:21b; 23:13
  - Of these in T: Matt 3:2; 18:1

- Instances where "Father in heaven" occurs (13 occurrences)
  Matt 5:16; 5:45; 6:1; 6:9; 7:11; 7:21c; 10:32; 10:33; 12:50; 16:17; 18:10c; 18:14; 18:19
  - Of these in M (no parallel): Matt 6:1; 16:17; 18:10c; 18:19
  - Of these in Q: Matt 5:45(//ὕψιστος); 6:9 (//πατήρ); 7:11 (//ὁ πατὴρ [ὁ] ἐξ οὐρανοῦ); 7:21c (no //); 10:32 (//ἄγγελοι τοῦ θεοῦ); 10:33 (//ἄγγελοι τοῦ θεοῦ)
  - Of these in T: Matt 5:16 (no //); 12:50 (//God)

- Instances where "heavenly Father" occurs (7 occurrences)
  Matt 5:48; 6:14; 6:26; 6:32; 15:13; 18:35; 23:9
  - Of these in M (no parallel): Matt 15:13; 18:35; 23:9
  - Of these in Q: Matt 5:48 (//ὁ πατήρ); 6:26 (//θεός); 6:32 (//πατήρ)
  - Of these in Matt & Mk: Matt 6:14 (//ὁ πατὴρ ὑμῶν ὁ ἐν τοῖς οὐρανοῖς)

- Instances where either "Father in heaven" or "heavenly Father" occurs (combined) (20 occurrences)
  Matt 5:16; 5:45; 5:48; 6:1; 6:9; 6:14; 6:25; 6:32; 7:11; 7:21c; 10:32; 10:33; 12:50; 15:13; 16:17; 18:10c; 18:14; 18:19; 18:35; 23:9
  - Of these in M (no parallel): Matt 6:1; 15:13; 16:17; 18:10c; 18:19; 18:35; 23:9
  - Of these in Q: Matt 5:45(//ὕψιστος); 5:48 (//ὁ πατήρ); 6:9 (//πατὴρ); 6:26 (//θεός); 6:32 (//πατήρ); 7:11 (//ὁ πατὴρ [ὁ] ἐξ οὐρανοῦ); 7:21c (no //); 10:32 (//ἄγγελοι τοῦ θεοῦ); 10:33 (//ἄγγελοι τοῦ θεοῦ)
  - Of these in T: Matt 5:16 (no //); 12:50 (//God)
  - Of these in Matt & Mk: Matt 6:14 (//ὁ πατὴρ ὑμῶν ὁ ἐν τοῖς οὐρανοῖς)

BIBLIOGRAPHY

Aalen, Sverre. "'Reign' and 'House' in the Kingdom of God in the Gospels." *New Testament Studies* 8 (1962): 215–240.
Abbot, Edwin. *Johannine Grammar.* London: A&C Black, 1906.
Abel, E. L. "Who Wrote Matthew?" *New Testament Studies* 17, no. 2 (1971): 138–152.
Adams, Edward. *Constructing the World: A Study in Paul's Cosmological Language.* Edinburgh: T&T Clark, 2000.
Albertz, Rainer. *Der Gott des Daniel: Untersuchungen zu Dan 4–6 in der Septuagintafassung sowie zu Komposition und Theologie des aramäischen Danielsbuches.* Stuttgart: Katholisches Bibelwerk, 1988.
Albright, W. F., and C. S. Mann. *Matthew: Introduction, Translation, and Notes. The Anchor Bible.* Garden City, New York: Doubleday & Company, 1971.
Alexander, Philip. "Rabbinic Judaism and the New Testament." *Zeitschrift für die neutestamentliche Wissenschaft* 74 (1983): 237–246.
Alexander, T. Desmond, and David W. Baker, eds. *Dictionary of the OT: Pentateuch.* Downers Grove, Ill.: IVP, 2003.
Alfrink, Bernard. "L'expression 'šamain or š°mei Haššmaim' dans l'Ancien Testament." Pages 1–7 in *Mélanges Eugène Tisserant.* Edited by Paule Hennequin. Vatican City: Biblioteca Apostolica Vaticana, 1964.
Allen, W. C. *A Critical and Exegetical Commentary on the Gospel According to S. Matthew.* 3d ed, *The International Critical Commentary.* Edinburgh: T&T Clark, 1912.
Allison, Dale C., Jr. "A Millennial Kingdom in the Teaching of Jesus?" *Irish Biblical Studies* 7 (1985): 46–52.
———. *Jesus of Nazareth: Millenarian Prophet.* Minneapolis: Fortress, 1998.
———. *The New Moses: A Matthean Typology.* Edinburgh: T&T Clark, 1993.
———. *Studies in Matthew: Interpretation Past and Present* (Grand Rapids: Baker, 2005)
———. *Testament of Abraham.* Berlin: de Gruyter, 2003.
———. "Two Notes on a Key Text: Matt. XI.25–30." *Journal of Theological Studies* 39 (1988): 472–480.
———. "What Was the Star That Guided the Magi?" *Bible Review* 9, no. 6 (1993): 20–24, 63.
Anderson, Bernhard W. "Cosmic Dimensions of the Genesis Creation Account." *Drew Gateway* 56, no. 3 (1986): 1–13.
———. "The Role of the Messiah: The Terms 'Christ' and 'Messiah' Do Not Refer to a Divine Being but to the Function an Agent of God Plays in Bringing the Kingdom That Is to Come on Earth as in Heaven." *Bible Review* 11 (1995): 19, 48.
Anderson, Bernhard W., ed. *Creation in the Old Testament.* SPCK: London, 1984.
Anderson, Janice Capel. "Life on the Mississippi: New Currents in Matthaean Scholarship 1983–1993." *Currents in Research: Biblical Studies* 3 (1995): 169–218.
———. *Matthew's Narrative Web: Over, and over, and over Again.* Sheffield: JSOT Press, 1994.
Argyle, A. W. *The Gospel According to Matthew. The Cambridge Bible Commentary.* Cambridge: Cambridge University Press, 1963.
Auffret, Pierre. "Note on the Literary Structure of Psalm 134." *Journal for the Study of the Old Testament* 45 (1989): 87–89.
Aune, David E., ed. *The Gospel of Matthew in Current Study.* Grand Rapids: Eerdmans, 2001.
Avishur, Yitzhak. *Stylistic Studies of Word-Pairs in Biblical and Ancient Semitic Literatures.* Neukirchener-Vluyn: Butzon & Bercker Kevelaer, 1984.

Balch, David L., ed. *Social History of the Matthean Community: Cross-Disciplinary Approaches*. Minneapolis: Fortress Press, 1991.
Barag, D. "The Kingdom of Heaven in a Christian Epitaph of 474 CE from Gaza [title in Hebrew]." *Eretz-Israel* 19 (1987): 242–245.
Balz, H. R. and G. Schneider. *Exegetical Dictionary of the New Testament*. 3 vols. Grand Rapids: Eerdmans, 1990.
Barr, James. "'Abba' Isn't Daddy." *Journal of Theological Studies* 39, no. 1 (1988): 28–47.
Barrett, C. K. *The Holy Spirit and the Gospel Tradition*. London: SPCK, 1947.
Bartelmus, Rüdiger. "Šamajim-Himmel: semantische und traditionsgeschichtliche Aspekte." Pages 87–124 in *Biblische Weltbild und seine altorientalischen Kontexte*. Edited by Bernd Janowski and Beate Ego. Tübingen: Mohr-Siebeck, 2001.
Barth, C. F. *Die Errettung vom Tode: Leben und Tod in den Klage- und Dankliedern des Alten Testaments*. Edited by B. Janowski. 3d ed. Stuttgart: Kohlhammer, 1997.
Barton, Stephen. "Johannine Dualism and Contemporary Pluralism," Paper presented at the "Gospel of John and Christian Theology" conference. St Andrews, Scotland, July 2003.
Bauckham, Richard J. "The Apocalypses in the New Pseudepigrapha." *JSNT* (1986): 97–117.
———. "The Ascension of Isaiah: Genre, Unity and Date," In Bauckham, *The Fate of the Dead: Studies on the Jewish and Christian Apocalypses*. Leiden: Brill, 1998: 363–390.
———. "Early Jewish Visions of Hell." *Journal of Theological Studies* (NS) 41 (1990): 355–385.
———. *The Fate of the Dead: Studies on the Jewish and Christian Apocalypses*. Leiden: Brill, 1998.
———. *God Crucified: Monotheism and Christology in the New Testament*. Carlisle: Paternoster, 1998.
———, ed. *The Gospels for All Christians: Rethinking the Gospel Audiences*. Grand Rapids: Eerdmans, 1998.
———. *James: Wisdom of James, Disciple of Jesus the Sage*. London: Routledge, 1999.
———. *Jude and the Relatives of Jesus in the Early Church*. Edinburgh: T&T Clark, 1990.
———. "Kingdom and Church According to Jesus and Paul." *Horizons in Biblical Theology* 18, no. 1 (1996): 1–26.
———. "Life, Death, and the Afterlife in Second Temple Judaism." In *Life in the Face of Death: The Resurrection Message of the New Testament*, edited by Richard N. Longenecker, 80–95. Grand Rapids: Eerdmans, 1998.
———. "Visiting the Places of the Dead in the Extra-Canonical Apocalypses." *Proceedings of the Irish Biblical Association* 18 (1995): 78–93.
Bauckham, Richard J. and Trevor Hart. *Hope Against Hope: Christian Eschatology at the Turn of the Millennium*. Grand Rapids: Eerdmans, 1999.
Bauer, David R. *The Structure of Matthew's Gospel: A Study in Literary Design*. Sheffield: Sheffield Academic, 1988.
Beale, Greg. *The Use of Daniel in Jewish Apocalyptic Literature and in the Revelation of St John*. Washington: University Press of America, 1984.
Beare, Francis Wright. *The Gospel According to Matthew: A Commentary*. Oxford: Basil Blackwell, 1981.
Beasley-Murray, G. R. *Jesus and the Kingdom of God*. Grand Rapids: Eerdmans, 1986.
Beaton, Richard. *Isaiah's Christ in Matthew's Gospel*. Cambridge: Cambridge University Press, 2002.
Beavis, Mary Ann. "The Kingdom of God, 'Utopia' and Theocracy." *Journal for the Study of the Historical Jesus* 2, no. 1 (2004): 91–106.
Bellinger, William H., Jr. "Maker of Heaven and Earth: The Old Testament and Creation Theology." *Southwestern Journal of Theology* 32, no. 2 (1990): 27–35.

Bengel, Johann Albrecht. *Gnomon of the New Testament, Volume 1*. Edited by Andrew Robert Fausset. Translated by Andrew Robert Fausset and James Bandinel. 5 vols. Edinburgh: T&T Clark, 1857.

Berger, Peter L. and Thomas Luckmann. *The Social Construction of Reality: A Treatise in the Sociology of Knowledge*. London: Penguin, 1966. Repr. 1991.

Berger, Peter L. *The Sacred Canopy: Elements of a Sociological Theory of Religion*. New York: Anchor Books, 1990.

Berlin, A. "Parallel Word Pairs: A Linguistic Explanation." *Ugarit-Forschungen* 15 (1983): 17–24.

Betz, Hans Dieter. *Essays on the Sermon on the Mount*. Philadelphia: Fortress, 1985.

———. *The Greek Magical Papyri in Translation*. 2d ed. Chicago: University of Chicago Press, 1992.

———. *The Sermon on the Mount: A Commentary on the Sermon on the Mount, including the Sermon on the Plain (Matthew 5:3–7:27 and Luke 6:20–49*. Hermeneia. Minneapolis: Augsburg Fortress, 1995.

Bietenhard, H. *Die himmlische Welt im Urchristentum und Spätjudentum*. Tübingen: Mohr-Siebeck, 1951.

Bingham, Jeffrey. *Irenaeus' Use of Matthew's Gospel in* Adversus Haereses. Louven: Peeters, 1998.

Black, Matthew. *Apocalypsis Henochi Graece*. Leiden: Brill, 1970.

———. *An Aramaic Approach to the Gospels and Acts*. 3d ed. Peabody, MA: Hendrickson Publishers, 1998.

———. *The Book of Enoch or 1 Enoch: a New English Edition*. Leiden: Brill, 1985.

Blass, F., A. Debrunner, and Robert W. Funk. *A Greek Grammar of the New Testament and Other Early Christian Literature*. Translated from the 9th–10th German ed. by Robert W. Funk. Chicago: University of Chicago Press, 1961.

Blomberg, Craig L. "Degrees of Reward in the Kingdom of Heaven." *Journal of the Evangelical Theological Society* 35 (1992): 159–172.

Bonnard, Pierre. *L'évangile Selon Saint Matthieu. Commentaire Du Nouveau Testament*. Neuchatel (Suisse): Éditions Delachaux & Niestlé, 1963.

Borg, Marcus J. *Conflict, Holiness, and Politics in the Teachings of Jesus*. New York: Edwin Mellen Press, 1984.

Bornkamm, Günther. "The Authority to 'Bind' and 'Loose' in the Church in Matthew's Gospel." Pages 85–97 in *The Interpretation of Matthew*. Edited by Graham N. Stanton. Philadelphia: Fortress, 1983.

———. "Der Aufbau der Bergpredigt." *New Testament Studies* 24, no. 4 (1978): 419–432.

———. "End-Expectation and Church in Matthew." Pages 15–51 in *Tradition and Interpretation in Matthew*. Edited by Günther Bornkamm, Gerhard Barth, and Heinz Joachim Held. Philadelphia: Westminster Press, 1963.

Bornkamm, Günther, Gerhard Barth, and Heinz Joachim Held, eds. *Tradition and Interpretation in Matthew*. Philadelphia: Westminster Press, 1963.

Bousset, Wilhelm. *Jesu Predigt in ihrem Gegansatz zum Judentum: Ein religionsgeschichtlicher Vergleich*. Gottingen: Vandenhoeck and Ruprecht, 1892.

Bowker, John. *The Targums and Rabbinic Literature: An Introduction to Jewish Interpretations of Scripture*. Cambridge: Cambridge University Press, 1969.

Braun, Herbert. "Das himmlische Vaterland bei Philo und im Hebräerbrief." Pages 319–327 in *Verborum Veritas: Festschrift für Gustav Stählin*. Edited by Otto Böcher and Klaus Haacker. Wuppertal: R. Brockhaus, 1970.

Bright, John. *The Kingdom of God*. Nashville: Abingdon, 1953.

Brooks, Oscar S., Sr. "Matthew 28:16–20 and the Design of the First Gospel." *Journal for the Study of the New Testament* 10 (1981): 2–18.

Brooks, Stephenson H. *Matthew's Community: The Evidence of His Special Sayings Material*. Sheffield: JSOT Press, 1987.

Brown, Colin, ed. *New International Dictionary of New Testament Theology*. 4 vols. Grand Rapids: Zondervan, 1975–1985.
Brown, Raymond E. "The Pater Noster as an Eschatological Prayer." *Theological Studies* 22 (1961): 175–208.
Brown, Rick. "Translating the Whole Concept of the Kingdom." *Notes on Translation* 14, no. 2 (2000): 1–48.
———. "A Brief History of Interpretations of 'The Kingdom of God' and Some Consequences for Translation." *Notes on Translation* 15, no. 2 (2001): 3–23.
Bruce, F. F. "'to the Hebrews' or 'to the Essenes'?" *New Testament Studies* 9 (1963): 217–232.
Brueggemann, Walter. "The Hope of Heaven...On Earth." *Biblical Theology Bulletin* 29 (1999): 99–111.
———. *The Land: Place as Gift, Promise, and Challenge in Biblical Faith*. 2d ed. Minneapolis: Fortress, 2002.
Bruner, Frederick D. *Matthew 1–12: The Christbook*. Revised ed. Grand Rapids: Eerdmans, 2004.
Buber, Martin. *Königtum Gottes*. Heidelberg: L. Schneider, 1956.
Burnett, Fred W. *The Testament of Jesus-Sophia: A Redaction-Critical Study of the Eschatological Discourse in Matthew*. Washington: University Press of America, 1981.
Burnett, Fred W. "Exposing the Anti-Jewish Ideology of Matthew's Implied Author: The Characterization of God as Father." *Semeia* 59 (1992): 155–191.
Burnham, F. B., G. Green, D. H. Juel, P. Keifert, and Ben C. Ollenburger. Papers presented at the Consultation on Bible and Theology, Princeton, NJ 1990. *Horizons in Biblical Theology* 12 (1990): 1–96.
Butler, B. C. *The Originality of St Matthew: A Critique of the Two-Document Hypothesis*. Cambridge: Cambridge University Press, 1951.
Burkett, Delbert. *The Son of Man Debate: A History and Evaluation*. Cambridge: Cambridge University Press, 1999.
Byrskog, Samuel. *Story as History—History as Story: The Gospel Tradition in the Context of Ancient Oral History*. Tübingen: Mohr-Siebeck, 2000.
Caird, George Bradford. "On Deciphering the Book of Revelation (Part 1)." *Expository Times* 74 (1962): 13–15.
Camponovo, Odo. *Königtum, Königsherrschaft und Reich Gottes in den frühjüdischen Schriften*. Göttingen: Vandenhoeck & Ruprecht, 1984.
Caragounis, C. C. "Kingdom of God/Heaven." Pages 417–430 in *Dictionary of Jesus and the Gospels*. Edited by Joel B. Green, Scot McKnight and I. Howard Marshall. Downers Grove, Ill.: InterVarsity Press, 1992.
Carson, D. A. "The Homoios Word-Group as Introduction to Some Matthean Parables." *New Testament Studies* 31 (1985): 277–282.
———. *Matthew*. 2 vols. *The Expositor's Bible Commentary*. Grand Rapids: Zondervan, 1995.
Carter, Warren. "Evoking Isaiah: Matthean Soteriology and an Intertextual Reading of Isaiah 7–9 in Matthew 1:23 and 4:15–16." *Journal of Biblical Literature* 119 (2000): 503–520.
———. "Matthaean Christology in Roman Imperial Key: Matthew 1.1." Pages 143–165 *The Gospel of Matthew in its Roman Imperial Context*. Edited by John Riches and David C. Sim. London: T&T Clark, 2005.
———. *Matthew and Empire: Initial Explorations*. Harrisburg, Penn.: Trinity Press International, 2001.
———. "Matthew and the Gentiles: Individual Conversion and/or Systemic Transformation," *Journal for the Study of the New Testament* 26, no. 3 (2004): 259–282.
———. *Matthew and the Margins: A Socio-Political and Religious Reading*. Sheffield: Sheffield Academic, 2000.

———. "Narrative/Literary Approaches to Matthean Theology: The 'Reign of the Heavens' as an Example (Mt 4.17–5.12)." *Journal for the Study of the New Testament* 67 (1997): 3–27.
Carter, Warren, and J. P. Heil. *Matthew's Parables: Audience-Oriented Perspectives*. Washington: Catholic Biblical Association of America, 1998.
Casey, Maurice. *Aramaic Sources of Mark's Gospel*. Cambridge: Cambridge University Press, 1998.
Catchpole, David R. "The Poor on Earth and the Son of Man in Heaven: A Reappraisal of Matthew 25:31–46." *Bulletin of the John Rylands University Library of Manchester* 61, no. 2 (1979): 355–397.
Charette, Blaine. *The Theme of Recompense in Matthew's Gospel*. Sheffield: Sheffield University Press, 1992.
Charlesworth, J. H. "A Critical Comparison of the Dualism in 1QS III, 13–IV, 26 and the 'Dualism' Contained in the Fourth Gospel." *New Testament Studies* 15 (1969): 389–418.
———. *The Old Testament Pseudepigrapha and the New Testament: Prolegomena for the Study of Christian Origins*. Cambridge: Cambridge University Press, 1985.
———, ed. *The Old Testament Pseudepigrapha*. 2 volumes. Garden City, New Jersey: Doubleday, 1985.
Chen, Diane G. *God as Father in Luke-Acts*. New York: Peter Lang, 2006.
Childs, Brevard. *Biblical Theology of the Old and New Testaments: Theological Reflections on the Christian Bible*. London: SCM, 1992.
Chilton, Bruce D. *The Glory of Israel: The Theology and Provenience of the Isaiah Targum*. Sheffield: JSOT, 1983.
———. "God as 'Father' in the Targumim in Non-Canonical Literatures of Early Judaism and Primitive Christianity, and in Matthew." Pages 151–169 in *The Pseudepigrapha and Early Biblical Interpretation*. Edited by J. H. Charlesworth and Craig A. Evans. Sheffield: JSOT Press, 1993.
———. *God in Strength: Jesus' Announcement of the Kingdom*. Freistadt: Plochl, 1979.
———, ed. *The Kingdom of God in the Teaching of Jesus*. London: SPCK, 1984.
———. *Pure Kingdom: Jesus' Vision of God*. Grand Rapids: Eerdmans, 1996.
———. *Targumic Approaches to the Gospels: Essays in the Mutual Definition of Judaism and Christianity*. Lanham, Maryland: University Press of America, 1986.
Clark, David J. "Our Father in Heaven." *Bible Translator (Ap, O Practical Papers)* 30, no. 2 (1979): 210–213.
Clark, Kenneth W. "The Gentile Bias in Matthew." *Journal of Biblical Literature* 66 (1947): 165–172.
Cohen, Shaye J. D. *From the Maccabees to the Mishnah*. Philadelphia: Westminster, 1989.
Collins, Adela Yarbro. *Cosmology and Eschatology in Jewish and Christian Apocalypticism*. Leiden: Brill, 1996.
———. "The Influence of Daniel on the NT." Pages 90–123 in John J. Collins, *Daniel: A Commentary on the Book of Daniel. Hermeneia*. Minneapolis: Fortress, 1993.
———. "The Seven Heavens in Jewish and Christian Apocalypses." Pages 59–93 in *Death, Ecstasy, and Other Worldly Journeys*. Edited by John J. Collins and Michael Fishbane. Albany: SUNY Press, 1995.
Collins, John J. ed., *Apocalypse: The Morphology of a Genre*, Semeia 14. Missoula: Scholars Press, 1979.
———. *Apocalypticism in the Dead Sea Scrolls*. London: Routledge, 1997.
———. *The Apocalyptic Imagination*. 2d ed. Grand Rapids: Eerdmans, 1998.
———. *Between Athens and Jerusalem*. 2d ed. Grand Rapids: Eerdmans, 2000.
———. *Daniel: A Commentary on the Book of Daniel. Hermeneia*. Minneapolis: Fortress, 1993.

———. *Daniel: With an Introduction to Apocalyptic Literature*. Grand Rapids: Eerdmans, 1984.
———. "The Kingdom of God in the Apocrypha and Pseudepigrapha." Pages 81–95 in *The Kingdom of God in 20th-Century Interpretation*. Edited by Wendell L. Willis. Peabody, Mass.: Hendrickson, 1987.
———. "A Throne in the Heavens: Apotheosis in Pre-Christian Judaism." Pages 43–58 in *Death, Ecstasy, and Other Worldly Journeys*. Edited by John J. Collins and Michael Fishbane. Albany: SUNY Press, 1995.
Collins, John J. and Robert Kugler, eds. *Religion in the Dead Sea Scrolls*. Grand Rapids Eerdmans, 2000.
Colson, F. H. and G. H. Whitaker, *Philo*. 12 vols. Cambridge: Harvard University Press, 1927.
Cook, Johann. "Hope for the Earth in the Early Judaic Era (Jewish Apocalypticism)." *Scriptura* 66 (1998): 235–243.
Cope, O. Lamar. "'To the close of the age': The Role of Apocalyptic Thought in the Gospel of Matthew." Pages 113–124 in *Apocalyptic and the New Testament: Essays in Honor of J. Louis Martyn*. Edited by Joel Marcus and Marion L. Soards. Sheffield: Sheffield Academic, 1989.
Cremer, Herman. *Biblico-Theological Lexicon of New Testament Greek*. Translated by William Urwick. 4th English ed. Edinburgh: T&T Clark, 1895.
Crossan, John Dominic. *The Historical Jesus: The Life of a Mediterranean Jewish Peasant*. Edinburgh: T&T Clark, 1991.
Curtis, John B. "On Job's Witness in Heaven." *Journal of Biblical Literature* 102 (1983): 549–562.
Dacy, Marianne. "The Divine Name in Qumran Benedictions." *Australian Journal of Jewish Studies* 15 (2001): 6–16.
Dalman, Gustaf. *The Words of Jesus*. Translated by D. M. Kay. Edinburgh: T&T Clark, 1902.
D'Angelo, Mary Rose. "*Abba* and 'Father': Imperial Theology and the Jesus Traditions." *Journal of Biblical Literature* 111, no. 4 (1992): 611–630.
Daniels, Dwight R. "Is There a 'Prophetic Lawsuit' Genre?" *Zeitschrift für die alttestamentliche Wissenschaft* 99, no. 3 (1987): 339–360.
Danker, Frederick W. *A Greek-English Lexicon of the New Testament and Other Early Christian Literature (BDAG)*. 3d ed. Chicago: University of Chicago Press, 2000.
Davies, Margaret. *Matthew*. Sheffield: JSOT Press, 1993.
Davies, W. D. *The Gospel and the Land: Early Christianity and Jewish Territorial Doctrine*. Berkeley: University of California Press, 1974.
———. *The Setting of the Sermon on the Mount*. Cambridge: Cambridge University Press, 1966.
Davies, W. D., and Dale C. Allison. *A Critical and Exegetical Commentary on the Gospel According to St. Matthew. International Critical Commentary*. 3 vols. Vol. 1, Matthew 1–7. Edinburgh: T & T Clark, 1988.
———. *A Critical and Exegetical Commentary on the Gospel According to St. Matthew. International Critical Commentary*. 3 vols. Vol. 2, Matthew 8–18. Edinburgh: T&T Clark, 1991.
———. *A Critical and Exegetical Commentary on the Gospel According to St. Matthew. International Critical Commentary*. 3 vols. Vol. 3, Matthew 19–28. Edinburgh: T&T Clark, 1997.
Davila, James R. "Heavenly Ascents in the Dead Sea Scrolls." Pages 461–485 in *The Dead Sea Scrolls After Fifty Years: A Comprehensive Assessment, Volume 2*. Edited by Peter W. Flint and James C. VanderKam. 2 vols. Leiden: Brill, 1999.
———. *Liturgical Works*. Grand Rapids: Eerdmans, 2000.
———. "The Macrocosmic Temple, Scriptural Exegesis, and the Songs of the Sabbath Sacrifice." *Dead Sea Discoveries* 9, no. 1 (2002): 1–19.

de Boer, M. C. "Paul and Apocalyptic Eschatology." Pages 345–383 in *The Encyclopedia of Apocalypticism, Volume 1: The Origins of Apocalypticism in Judaism and Christianity*. Edited by J. J. Collins. New York: Continuum, 2000.
de Jonge, M. *Jewish Eschatology, Early Christian Christology, and the Testaments of the Twelve Patriarchs*. Leiden: Brill, 1991.
The Dead Sea Scrolls Electronic Reference Library 2. Leiden: Brill, 1999.
Derrett, J. Duncan M. "Binding and Loosing (Matt 16:19, Matt 18:18, John 20:23)." *Journal of Biblical Literature* 102 (1983): 112–117.
Di Lella, Alexander A. "The Textual History of Septuagint Daniel and Theodotion Daniel." Pages 586–607 in *The Book of Daniel: Composition and Reception, Volume 2*. Edited by J. J. Collins and Peter W. Flint. Leiden: Brill, 2001.
Di Vito, Robert A. "The Demarcation of Divine and Human Realms in Genesis 2–11." Pages 39–56 in *Creation in the Biblical Traditions*. Edited by Richard J. Clifford and J. J. Collins. Washington, D.C.: Catholic Biblical Association, 1992.
Dodd, C. H. *The Bible and the Greeks*. London: Hodder & Stoughton, 1935.
Donaldson, Terence. *Jesus on the Mountain: A Study in Matthaean Theology*. Sheffield: JSOT, 1985.
du Rand, Jan A. "Now the Salvation of Our God Has Come. . . A Narrative Perspective on the Hymns of Revelation 12–15." *Neotestamentica* 27, no. 2 (1993): 313–330.
———. "Your Kingdom Come 'on Earth as It Is in Heaven': The Theological Motif of the Apocalypse of John." *Neotestamentica* 31, no. 1 (1997): 59–75.
Dufort, Jean-Marc. "Coeleste Convivium dans la Symbolique Des Premiers Peres." *Sciences Ecclesiastiques* 14 (1962): 31–56.
Dumbrell, William J. "Daniel 7 and the Function of Old Testament Apocalyptic." *Reformed Theological Review* 34 (1975): 16–23.
Dunn, James D. G. *Jesus and the Spirit*. Philadelphia: Westminster, 1975.
———. *Jesus Remembered*. Grand Rapids: Eerdmans, 2003.
Ego, Beate. "Der Diener im Palast des Himmlischen Königs: zur Interpretation einer priesterlichen Tradition im rabbinischen Judentum." Pages 361–384 in *Königsherrschaft Gottes und himmlischer Kult im Judentum, Urchristentum und in der Hellenistischen Welt*. Edited by Martin Hengel and Anna Maria Schwemer. Tübingen: Mohr-Siebeck, 1991.
———. "Der Herr blickt herab von der Hohe seines Heiligtums: zur Vorstellung von Gottes himmlischem Thronen in exilisch-nachexilischer Zeit." *Zeitschrift für die alttestamentliche Wissenschaft* 110, no. 4 (1998): 556–569.
———. *Im Himmel wie auf Erden: Studien zum Verhältnis von himmlischer und irdischer Welt in rabbinischen Judentum*. Tübingen: Mohr-Siebeck, 1989.
Eichrodt, Walther. *Theology of the Old Testament*. 2 vols. London: SCM, 1961–1967.
Ellingworth, Paul. "Jesus and the Universe in Hebrews." *Evangelical Quarterly* 58, no. 4 (1986): 337–350.
Ellis, P. F. *Matthew: His Mind and His Message*. Collegeville: Liturgical Press, 1974.
Elmore, W. Emory. "Linguistic Approaches to the Kingdom: Amos Wilder and Norman Perrin." Pages 53–65 in *The Kingdom of God in 20th-Century Interpretation*. Edited by Wendell L. Willis. Peabody, Mass.: Hendrickson, 1987.
Epp, Eldon Jay. "Mediating Approaches to the Kingdom: Werner Georg Kümmel and George Eldon Ladd." Pages 35–52 in *The Kingdom of God in 20th-Century Interpretation*. Edited by Wendell L. Willis. Peabody, Mass.: Hendrickson, 1987.
Esler, Philip F. "Community and Gospel in Early Christianity: A Response to Richard Bauckham's Gospels for All Christians." *Scottish Journal of Theology* 51 (1998): 235–248.
———. *The First Christians in their Social Worlds: Social-Scientific Approaches to New Testament Interpretation*. London: Routledge, 1994.
———. "Ludic History in the Book of Judith: The Reinvention of Israelite Identity?" *Biblical Interpretation* 10, no. 2 (2002): 107–143.

———. "Rome in Apocalyptic and Rabbinic Literature." Pages 9–33 *The Gospel of Matthew in its Roman Imperial Context*. Edited by John Riches and David C. Sim. London: T&T Clark, 2005.

Evans, Craig A. "Daniel in the New Testament: Visions of God's Kingdom." Pages 490–527 in *The Book of Daniel: Composition and Reception, Volume 2*. Edited by John J. Collins and Peter W. Flint. Leiden: Brill, 2001.

———, ed. *The Interpretation of Scripture in Early Judaism and Christianity: Studies in Language and Tradition*. Sheffield: Sheffield Academic, 2000.

———. "Jesus and the Dead Sea Scrolls." Pages 575–585 in *The Dead Sea Scrolls After Fifty Years: A Comprehensive Assessment, Volume 2*. Edited by Peter W. Flint and James C. VanderKam. Leiden: Brill, 1999.

———. *Noncanonical Writings and New Testament Interpretation*. Peabody, Mass: Hendrickson, 1992.

Everett, W. J. *God's Federal Republic: Reconstructing our Governing Symbol*. New York: Paulist Press, 1988.

Farmer, Ron. "The Kingdom of God in the Gospel of Matthew." Pages 119–130 in *Kingdom of God in 20th-Century Interpretation*. Edited by Wendell L. Willis. Peabody, Mass: Hendrickson, 1987.

Fenton, J. C. "Inclusio and Chiasmus in Matthew." Pages 174–179 in *Studia Evangelica: Papers Presented to the International Congress Held at Christ Church*, Oxford. Edited by Kurt Aland and F. L. Cross. Berlin: Akademie-Verlag, 1959.

Ferguson, Everett. "The Kingdom of God in Early Patristic Literature." Pages 191–208 in *The Kingdom of God in 20th-Century Interpretation*. Edited by Wendell L. Willis. Peabody, Mass.: Hendrickson, 1987.

Filson, Floyd V. *The Gospel according to St Matthew. Black's New Testament Commentaries*. 2d ed. London: A. & C. Black, 1971.

Fischer, David H. *Historians' Fallacies: Toward a Logic of Historical Thought*. London: Routledge and Kegan Paul, 1971.

Fitzmyer, Joseph. *A Wandering Aramean*. Missoula, Montana: Scholars Press, 1979.

———. *Tobit*. Commentaries on Early Jewish Literature (CEJL). Berlin: de Gruyter, 2003.

Flint, Peter W. "Noncanonical Writings in the Dead Sea Scrolls: Apocrypha, Other Previously Known Writings, Pseudepigrapha." Pages 80–126 in *The Bible at Qumran: Text, Shape and Interpretation*. Edited by Peter W. Flint. Grand Rapids: Eerdmans, 2001.

Foley, John M. *Immanent Art: From Structure to Meaning in Traditional Oral Epic*. Bloomington: Indiana University Press, 1991.

Ford, D. *The Abomination of Desolation in Biblical Eschatology*. Washington: University Press of America, 1979.

Ford, J. Massyngberde. "Heaven." *Irish Theological Quarterly* 43, no. 2 (1976): 124–132.

Forestell, J. T. *Targumic Traditions and the New Testament*. Atlanta: Scholars Press, 1979.

Foster, Robert. "Why on Earth Use 'Kingdom of Heaven'?: Matthew's Terminology Revisited." *New Testament Studies* 48 (2002): 487–499.

France, R. T. "The Formula-Quotations of Matthew 2 and the Problem of Communication." *New Testament Studies* 27 (1981): 233–251.

———. *The Gospel According to Matthew: An Introduction and Commentary. The Tyndale New Testament Commentaries*. Grand Rapids: Eerdmans, 1985.

———. *Matthew: Evangelist and Teacher*. Downers Grove, Ill.: InterVarsity Press, 1989.

Freund, R. A. "From Kings to Archons." *Scandinavian Journal of the Old Testament* 2 (1990): 58–72.

Frey, Jörg. "Different Patterns of Dualistic Thought in the Qumran Library: Reflections on their Background and History." Pages 275–335 in *Legal Texts and Legal Issues*. Edited by M. Bernstein, F. Garcia Martinez, and J. Kampen. Leiden: Brill, 1997.

Friedlander, Gerald. *The Jewish Sources of the Sermon on the Mount.* New York: Ktav, 1969.
Furley, D. *The Greek Cosmologists.* Cambridge: Cambridge University Press, 1987.
Gaechter, Paul. *Die literarische Kunst im Matthäus-Evangelium*, Stuttgarter Bibelstudien, 7. Stuttgart: Katholisches Bibelwerk, 1965.
———. *Das Matthaus-Evangelium.* Innsbruck: Tyrolia, 1962.
Garcia Martinez, Florentino, and Eibert Tigchelaar. *The Dead Sea Scrolls Study Edition.* Leiden: Brill, 1998.
Garland, David E. *The Intention of Matthew 23.* Leiden: Brill, 1979.
———. *Reading Matthew: A Literary and Theological Commentary on the First Gospel.* New York: Crossroad, 1993.
Garrow, Alan. *The Gospel of Matthew's Dependence on the Didache.* London: T&T Clark International, 2004.
George, A. "Le Pére et le Fils dans les évangiles synoptiques." *Lumiére et Vie* 29 (1956): 603–616.
Gerhardsson, Birger. "Geistiger Opferdienst nach Matth 6,1–6.16–21." Pages 69–77 in *Neues Testament und Geschichte: Historisches Geschehen und Deutung im Neuen Testament*, FS for Oscar Cullmann. Edited by Heinrich Baltensweiler and Bo Reicke. Tübingen: Mohr-Siebeck, 1972.
———. "The Matthaean Version of the Lord's Prayer (Matt 6:9b–13): Some Observations." Pages 207–220 in *The New Testament Age: Essays in Honor of Bo Reicke, Volume 1.* Edited by W. C. Weinrich. Macon, Georgia: Mercer University Press, 1984.
Gesenius' Hebrew Grammar (GKC). Edited by E. Kautzsch. Translated by A. E. Cowley. 2d ed. Oxford, 1910.
Gevirtz, Stanley. *Patterns in the Early Poetry of Israel.* Chicago: University of Chicago Press, 1963.
Gilkey, Langdon. "Cosmology, Ontology, and the Travail of Biblical Language." *Journal of Religion* 41, no. 3 (1961): 194–205.
———. *Maker of Heaven and Earth: A Study of the Christian Doctrine of Creation.* Garden City, New Jersey: Anchor Books, 1965.
Glover, Warren W. "'The Kingdom of God' in Luke." *Bible Translator (Ap, O Practical Papers)* 29, no. 2 (1978): 231–237.
Gnilka, Joachim. *Das Matthäusevangelium, Erster Teil: 1,1–13,58.* Herders Theologischer Kommentar Zum Neuen Testament. Freiburg: Herder, 1986.
Goodacre, Mark. *The Case Against Q: Studies in Markan Priority and the Synoptic Problem.* Harrisburg, Penn.: Trinity Press Int., 2002.
Goldingay, John. *Daniel. Word Biblical Commentary.* Dallas: Word, 1989.
Gooder, Paula. *Only the Third Heaven? 2 Corinthians 12.1–10 and Heavenly Ascent.* London: T&T Clark, 2006.
Goodrick, A. T. S. *The Book of Wisdom.* London: Rivingtons, 1913.
Goshen-Gottstein, Alon. "God the Father in Rabbinic Judaism and Christianity: Transformed Background or Common Ground?" *Journal of Ecumenical Studies* 38, no. 4 (2001): 470–504.
Goulder, Michael D. *Midrash and Lection in Matthew.* London: SPCK, 1974.
———. *Type and History in Acts.* London: SPCK, 1964.
Gourgues, Michel. "The Thousand-Year Reign (Rev 20:1–6): Terrestrial or Celestial." *Catholic Biblical Quarterly* 47 (1985): 676–681.
Gray, John. *The Biblical Doctrine of the Reign of God.* Edinburgh: T&T Clark, 1979.
Gray, Martin. *A Dictionary of Literary Terms.* 2d ed. Essex: Pearson Education Limited, 1992.
Green, Dennis. "Divine Names: Rabbinic and Qumran Scribal Techniques." Pages 497–511 in *The Dead Sea Scrolls Fifty Years After Their Discovery.* Edited by L. Schiffman, E. Tov, and J. VanderKam. Jerusalem: Israel Exploration Society, 2000.

Green, H. Benedict. *The Gospel According to Matthew in the Revised Standard Version.* New Clarendon Bible. London: Oxford University Press, 1975.
———. *Matthew, Poet of the Beatitudes.* Sheffield: Sheffield Academic, 2001.
Grelot, Pierre. "L'arriere-Plan Arameen du 'Pater'." *Revue Biblique* 91, no. 4 (1984): 531–556.
Grimm, Werner. *Jesus und das Danielbuch,* Band 1: *Jesu Einspruch gegen das Offenbarungsystem Daniels.* Frankfurt: Peter Lang, 1984.
Guelich, Robert A. *The Sermon on the Mount: A Foundation for Understanding.* Dallas: Word, 1982.
Gundry, Robert H. *Matthew: A Commentary on His Handbook for a Mixed Church under Persecution.* 2d ed. Grand Rapids: Eerdmans, 1994.
———. *Matthew: A Commentary on His Literary and Theological Art.* Grand Rapids: Eerdmans, 1982.
———. *The Use of the Old Testament in St. Matthew's Gospel with Special Reference to the Messianic Hope.* Leiden: Brill, 1967.
Günther, Hartmut. "Die Gerechtigkeit des Himmelreiches in der Bergpredigt." *Kerygma und Dogma* 17, no. 2 (1971): 113–126.
Gunton, Colin E. *The Triune Creator: A Historical and Systematic Study.* Grand Rapids: Eerdmans, 1998.
Habel, Norman C. "Yahweh, Maker of Heaven and Earth: A Study in Tradition Criticism." *Journal of Biblical Literature* 91, no. 3 (1972): 321–337.
Hadot, Pierre. "Ouranos, Kronos and Zeus in Plotinus' Treatise against the Gnostics." Pages 124–137 in *Neoplatonism and Early Christian Thought: Essays in Honor of A. H. Armstrong.* Edited by H. J. Blumenthal and Robert A. Markus. London: Variorum Publications, 1981.
Hagner, Donald A. "Apocalyptic Motifs in the Gospel of Matthew: Continuity and Discontinuity." *Horizons of Biblical Theology* 7 (1985): 53–82.
———. *Matthew 1–13.* Vol. 33a, *Word Biblical Commentary.* Dallas: Word Books, 1993.
———. *Matthew 14–28.* Vol. 33b, *Word Biblical Commentary.* Dallas: Word Books, 1995.
———. "Matthew: Christian Judaism or Jewish Christianity?" Pages 263–282 in *The Face of New Testament Studies: A Survey of Recent Research.* Edited by Scot McKnight and Grant Osborne. Grand Rapids: Baker, 2004.
———. "The *Sitz im Leben* of the Gospel of Matthew." Pages 27–68 in *Treasures New and Old: Recent Contributions to Matthean Studies.* Edited by David R. Bauer and Mark Allan Powell. Atlanta: Scholars Press, 1996.
Hall, Robert G. "Disjunction of Heavenly and Earthly Times in the *Ascension of Isaiah.*" *Journal for the Study of Judaism* 35, no. 1 (2004): 17–26.
Hamerton-Kelly, Robert G. *God the Father: Theology and Patriarchy in the Teaching of Jesus.* Philadelphia: Fortress, 1979.
———. "The Temple and the Origins of Jewish Apocalyptic." *Vetus Testamentum* 20, no. 1 (1970): 1–15.
Hanson, Paul D. *The Dawn of Apocalyptic: The Historical and Sociological Roots of Jewish Apocalyptic Eschatology.* Revised ed. Philadelphia: Fortress, 1979.
———. "Rebellion in Heaven, Azazel, and Euhemeristic Heroes in 1 Enoch 6–11." *Journal of Biblical Literature* 96 (1977): 195–233.
———, ed. *Visionaries and Their Apocalypses.* Philadelphia: Fortress, 1983.
Hare, Douglas R. A. *The Theme of Jewish Persecution of Christians in the Gospel According to St. Matthew.* Cambridge: Cambridge University Press, 1967.
Harris, R. Laird. "The Bible and Cosmology." *Bulletin of the Evangelical Theological Society* 5, no. 1 (1962): 11–17.
Harris, W. Hall, III. "'The Heavenlies' Reconsidered: Ouranos and Epouranios in Ephesians." *Bibliotheca Sacra* 148 (1991): 72–89.

Harrisville, Roy A. "In Search of the Meaning of 'The Reign of God'." *Interpretation* 47, no. 2 (1993): 140–151.
Hartenstein, Friedhelm. "Wolkendunkel und Himmelsfeste: zur Genese und Kosmologie der Vorstellung des himmlischen Heiligtums Jhwhs." Pages 125–179 in *Biblische Weltbild und seine altorientalischen Kontexte*. Edited by Bernd Janowski and Beate Ego. Tübingen: Mohr-Siebeck, 2001.
Hartman, Lars. "Your Will Be Done on Earth as It Is in Heaven." *Africa Theological Journal* 11, no. 3 (1982): 209–218.
Held, H. J. "Matthew as Interpreter of the Miracle Stories." Pages 165–299 in *Tradition and Interpretation in Matthew*. Edited by G. Bornkamm, G. Barth, and H. J. Held. Philadelphia: Westminster Press, 1963.
Helfritz, H. "Hoi Ouranoi Th Dioikesei Autou Saleuomenoi En Eirhnh Upotassontai Autoi (1 Clem 20,1)." *Vigiliae Christianae* 22, no. 1 (1968): 1–7.
Hellholm, David. ed., *Apocalypticism in the Mediterranean World and the Near East: Proceedings of the International Colloquium on Apocalypticism, Uppsala, August 12–17, 1979*. Tübingen: Mohr-Siebeck, 1983.
———. "'Rejoice and Be Glad, for Your Reward Is Great in Heaven': An Attempt at Solving the Structural Problem of Matt 5:11–12." Pages 47–86 in *Festschrift Günter Wagner*. New York: Peter Lang, 1994.
Hengel, Martin. *The Zealots: Investigations into the Jewish Freedom Movement in the Period from Herod I until 70 AD*. Translated by D. Smith. Edinburgh: T&T Clark, 1989.
Hengel, Martin and Anna Maria Schwemer, eds., *Königsherrschaft Gottes und Himmlischer Kult im Judentum, Urchristentum und in der Hellenistischen Welt*. Tübingen: Mohr-Siebeck, 1991.
Henze, Matthias. *The Madness of King Nebuchadnezzar: The Ancient Near Eastern Origins and Early History of Interpretation of Daniel 4*. Leiden: Brill, 1999.
Hiers, R. H. "'Binding' and 'Loosing': The Matthean Authorizations." *Journal of Biblical Literature* 104 (1985): 233–250.
Hill, David. *The Gospel of Matthew, New Century Bible*. London: Oliphants, 1972.
———. "On the Use and Meaning of Hosea 6:6 in Matthew's Gospel." *New Testament Studies* 24 (1977): 107–119.
Himmelfarb, Martha. *Ascent to Heaven in Jewish and Christian Apocalypses*. Oxford: Oxford University Press, 1993.
Hogan, Martin. *The Sermon on the Mount in St. Ephrem's Commentary on the Diatessaron*. Bern: Peter Lang, 1999.
Honeyman, A. M. "Merismus in Biblical Hebrew." *Journal of Biblical Literature* 71, no. 1 (1952): 11–18.
Horsley, G. H. R. *New Documents Illustrating Early Christianity: A Review of the Greek Inscriptions and Papyri Published in 1978*. North Ryde, Australia: The Ancient History Documentary Research Centre, Macquarie University, 1983.
Horsley, Richard. *Jesus and Empire: The Kingdom of God and the New World Disorder*. Minneapolis: Fortress, 2003.
Houtman, Cornelis. *Der Himmel im Alten Testament: Israels Weltbild und Weltanschauung*. Leiden: Brill, 1993.
Howard, G. "The Tetragram and the New Testament." *Journal of Biblical Literature* 96 (1977): 63–83.
Howell, D. *Matthew's Inclusive Story: A Study in the Narrative Rhetoric of the First Gospel*. Sheffield: JSOT Press, 1990.
Iersel, Bastiaan Martinus Franciscus van, and Edward Schillebeeckx, eds. *Heaven*. Vol. 123, *Concilium*. New York: Seabury Press, 1979.
Innes, Donald Keith. "Heaven and Sky in the Old Testament." *Evangelical Quarterly* 43 (1971): 144–148.

Isasi-Diaz, A. M. "Solidarity: Love of Neighbor in the 1980's." Pages 31–40 in *Lift Every Voice: Constructing Christian Theologies from the Underside.* Edited by S. B. Thistlethwaite and M. P. Engels. New York: Harper & Row, 1990.
Jacobs, Louis. "Names of God" in *A Concise Companion to the Jewish Religion.* Oxford University Press, *Oxford Reference Online,* http://www.oxfordreference.com/views/.
———. *A Jewish Theology.* London: Dartmon, Longman & Todd, 1973.
Janowski, Bernd. "Der Himmel auf Erden: zur kosmologischen Bedeutung des Tempels in der Umwelt Israels." Pages 229–260 in *Biblische Weltbild und seine altorientalischen Kontexte.* Edited by Bernd Janowski and Beate Ego. Tübingen: Mohr-Siebeck, 2001.
Jellicoe, Sidney. *The Septuagint and Modern Study.* Oxford: Oxford University Press, 1968.
Jensen, Robin A. "Dining in Heaven: The Earliest Christian Visions of Paradise." *Bible Review* 14 (1998): 32–39, 48–49.
Jeremias, Joachim. *New Testament Theology, Volume 1: The Proclamation of Jesus.* Translated by John Bowden. London: SCM, 1975.
———. *The Prayers of Jesus.* London: SCM Press, 1967.
Johnson, Luke Timothy. *The Writings of the New Testament: An Interpretation.* Philadelphia: Fortress, 1986.
Johnston, Philip S. "Heaven." Pages 540–542 in *New Dictionary of Biblical Theology.* Edited by T. Desmond Alexander, Brian S. Rosner, D. A. Carson and Graeme Goldsworthy. Leicester, England: Inter-Varsity Press, 2000.
———. *Shades of Sheol: Death and Afterlife in the Old Testament.* Leicester: Apollos, 2002.
Joüon, Paul. *A Grammar of Biblical Hebrew.* Translated and revised by T. Muraoka. 2 vols. Rome: Pontifical Biblical Institute, 1991.
Kasovsky, C. Y. *Thesaurus Mishnae: Concordantiae Verborum quae in Sex Mishnae Ordinibus Reperiuntur.* Jerusalem: Massadah Publishing, 1960.
Katz, Peter. *Philo's Bible: The Aberrant Text of Bible Quotations in Some Philonic Writings and Its Place in the Textual History of the Greek Bible.* Cambridge: Cambridge University Press, 1950.
———. *The Text of the Septuagint: Its Corruptions and Their Emendation.* Edited by D. W. Gooding. Cambridge: Cambridge University Press, 1973.
Keel, Othmar. *The Symbolism of the Biblical World: Ancient near Eastern Iconography and the Book of Psalms.* Translated by Timothy J. Hallet. London: SPCK, 1978.
Keel, Othmar and Christoph Uehlinger. *Gods, Goddesses, and Images of God in Ancient Israel.* Translated by Thomas H. Trapp. Minneapolis: Fortress, 1998.
Keener, Craig S. *A Commentary on the Gospel of Matthew.* Grand Rapids: Eerdmans, 1999.
———. "Matthew 5:22 and the Heavenly Court." *Expository Times* 99, no. 2 (1987): 46.
Kilpatrick, George Dunbar. *The Origins of the Gospel According to St. Matthew.* Oxford: The Clarendon Press, 1946.
Kim, Joon-Sik. "'Your Kingdom Come on Earth': The Promise of the Land and the Kingdom of Heaven in the Gospel of Matthew." Ph.D. diss., Princeton Theological Seminary, 2001.
Kingsbury, Jack Dean. *Matthew: A Commentary for Preachers and Others.* London: SPCK, 1978.
———. *Matthew as Story.* Revised and enlarged ed. Philadelphia: Fortress, 1988.
———. *Matthew: Structure, Christology, Kingdom.* Minneapolis: Fortress Press, 1989.
———. "The Theology of St Matthew's Gospel According to the Griesbach Hypothesis." Pages 331–361 in *New Synoptic Studies: The Cambridge Gospel Conference and Beyond.* Edited by William R. Farmer. Macon: Mercer University Press, 1983.
Kline, Meredith G. "Space and Time in Genesis Cosmogony." *Perspectives on Science and Christian Faith* 48 (1996): 2–15.
Knibb, M. A. "Martyrdom and Ascension of Isaiah." Pages 143–176 in *The Old Testament Pseudepigrapha, Volume 2.* Edited by James H. Charlesworth. Garden City, New Jersey: Doubleday, 1985.

———. *The Ethiopic Book of Enoch*. 2 vols. Oxford: Clarendon, 1978.
Knowles, Michael. *Jeremiah in Matthew's Gospel: The Rejected Prophet Motif in Matthaean Redaction*. Sheffield: Sheffield Academic, 1993.
Koch, K. "Gottes Herrschaft über das Reich des Menschen: Daniel 4 im Licht neuer Funde." Pages 77–119 in *The Book of Daniel in the Light of New Findings*. Edited by A. S. van der Woude. Leuven: Leuven University Press, 1993.
Koehler, L., W. Baumgartner, and J. J. Stamm. *The Hebrew and Aramaic Lexicon of the Old Testament*. Translated and edited by M. E. J. Richardson. 4 vols. Leiden, 1994–1999.
Kolarcik, Michael. "Creation and Salvation in the Book of Wisdom." Pages 97–107 in *Creation in the Biblical Traditions*. Edited by Richard J. Clifford and John J. Collins. Washington: Catholic Biblical Association, 1992.
Korvin-Krasinsky, Cyrill von. "Himmel und Erde als Manifestationen des göttlichen Urgrundes in der Ältesten Mittelmeerkultur." Pages 65–81 in *Symbolon, Volume 2*. Cologne: Wienand Verlag, 1974.
Krašovec, Jože. *Antithetic Structure in Biblical Hebrew Poetry*. Leiden: Brill, 1984.
———. *Der Merismus im Biblisch-Hebräischen und Nordwestsemitischen*. Rome: Biblical Institute Press, 1977.
Kretzer, Armin. *Die Herrschaft der Himmel und die Söhne des Reiches: eine redaktionsgeschichtliche Untersuchung zum Basileiabegriff und Basileiaverständnis im Matthäusevangelium*. Würzburg: Echter, 1971.
Krüger, Annette. "Himmel—Erde—Unterwelt: Kosmologische Entwürfe in der poetischen Literatur Israels." Pages 65–83 in *Das biblische Weltbild und seine altorientalischen Kontexte*. Edited by Bernd Janowski and Beate Ego. Tübingen: Mohr-Siebeck, 2001.
Kugler, Robert A. *The Testaments of the Twelve Patriarchs*. Sheffield: Sheffield Academic Press, 2001.
Kuhn, Harold B. "The Angelology of the Non-Canonical Jewish Apocalypses." *Journal of Biblical Literature* 67 (1948): 217–232.
Kvalbein, Hans. "The Kingdom of the Father in the Gospel of Thomas." Pages 203–228 *The New Testament and Early Christian Literature in Greco-Roman Context: Studies in Honor of David E. Aune*. Edited by John Fotopoulos. Leiden: Brill, 2006.
Ladd, George Eldon. *The Presence of the Future*. Grand Rapids: Eerdmans, 1996.
———. *A Theology of the New Testament*, Revised Edition. Revised ed. by Donald A. Hagner. Grand Rapids: Eerdmans, 1993.
Lagrange, P. M.-J. *Évangile Selon Saint Matthieu*. Paris: J. Gabalda, 1941.
Landman, C. "Heaven and Its Relevance." *Acta Patristica et Byzantina* 10 (1999): 152–163.
Lang, Bernhard. "Afterlife: Ancient Israel's Changing Vision of the World Beyond." *Bible Review* 4 (1988): 12–23.
Lattke, Michael. "On the Jewish Background of the Synoptic Concept 'The Kingdom of God'." Pages 72–91 in *The Kingdom of God in the Teaching of Jesus*. Edited by Bruce Chilton. London: SPCK, 1984.
Lash, Christopher J. A. "Where Do Devils Live? A Problem in the Textual Criticism of Ephesians." *Vigiliae Christianae* 30, no. 3 (1976): 161–174.
Lebram, Jürgen C. H. *Das Buch Daniel*. Zürich: Theologische Verlag, 1984.
Lee, John. *A Lexical Study of the Septuagint Version of the Pentateuch*. Chico, California: Scholars Press, 1983.
Lenglet, A. "La structure littéraire de Daniel 2–7." *Biblica* 53 (1972): 169–190.
Lenski, R. C. H. *Interpretation of St. Matthew's Gospel*. Columbus: Lutheran Book Concern, 1932.
Leske, Adrian M. "The Prophetic Influence in the First Gospel: A Report on Current Research." Pages 152–169 in *Jesus and the Suffering Servant: Isaiah 53 and Christian Origins*.

Edited by William H. Bellinger, Jr. and William R. Farmer. Harrisburg, Pennsylvania: Trinity Press International, 1998.

Levey, Samson H. *The Targum of Ezekiel*. Edinburgh: T&T Clark, 1987.

Levine, Étan. "Distinguishing 'Air' from 'Heaven' in the Bible." *Zeitschrift für die alttestamentliche Wissenschaft* 99 (1976): 97–99.

———. *Heaven and Earth, Law and Love: Studies in Biblical Thought*. Berlin: Walter de Gruyter, 2000.

Liebenburg, Jacobus. *The Language of the Kingdom and Jesus: Parable, Aphorism, and Metaphor in the Sayings Material Common to the Synoptic Tradition and the Gospel of Thomas*. Berlin: Walter de Gruyter, 2001.

Lincoln, Andrew T. *Paradise Now and Not Yet: Studies in the Role of the Heavenly Dimension in Paul's Thought with Special Reference to His Eschatology*. Cambridge: Cambridge University Press, 1981.

———. "Re-Examination of 'the Heavenlies' in Ephesians." *New Testament Studies* 19 (1973): 468–484.

Linton, Olof. "Demand for a Sign from Heaven (Mk 8:11–12 and Parallels)." *Studia Theologica* 19, no. 1–2 (1965): 112–129.

Littleton, C. Scott. "The 'Kingship in Heaven' Theme." Pages 83–121 in *Myth & Law among the Indo-Europeans*. Edited by Jaan Puhvel. Berkeley: University of California Press, 1970.

Lohfink, Gerhard. "Die Korrelation von Reich Gottes und Volk Gottes bei Jesus." *Theologische Quartalschrift* 165, no. 3 (1985): 173–183.

Lohmeyer, Ernst, and Werner Schmauch. *Das Evangelium des Matthäus. Kritich-Eregetischer Kommentar über das Neue Testament*. Göttingen: Vandenhoeck & Ruprecht, 1958.

Lohmeyer, Ernst. *The Lord's Prayer*. Translated by John Bowden. London: William Collins Sons & Co., 1965.

Lohr, C. H. "Oral Techniques in the Gospel of Matthew." *Catholic Biblical Quarterly* 23, no. 4 (1961): 403–435.

Loisy, Alfred. *The Gospel and the Church*. Translated by Christopher Home. London: Isbister & Co, 1903.

Lotz, David W. "Heaven and Hell in the Christian Tradition." *Religion in Life* 48 (1979): 77–92.

Louw, J. P. and E. A. Nida. *Greek-English Lexicon of the New Testament: Based on Semantic Domains*. 2d ed. 2 vols. New York: United Bible Socities, 1989.

Luck, Ulrich. "Himmlisches und erdisches Geschehen im Hebraerbrief." *Novum Testamentum* 6, no. 2/3 (1963): 192–215.

Lunde, Jonathan. "Heaven and Hell." Pages 307–312 in *Dictionary of Jesus and the Gospels*. Edited by Joel B. Green, Scot McKnight and I. Howard Marshall. Downers Grove, Ill.: InterVarsity Press, 1992.

Luter, A. Boyd and Emily K. Hunter. "The 'Earth-Dwellers' and the 'Heaven Dwellers': An Overlooked Interpretative Key to the Apocalypse." Paper presented to the annual meeting of the Evangelical Theological Society, Toronto, 2002.

Luz, Ulrich. *Matthew 1–7: A Commentary*. Translated by Wilhelm C. Linss. Minneapolis: Augsburg, 1989.

———. *Matthew 8–20: A Commentary. Hermeneia*. Translated by James E. Crouch. Minneapolis: Augsburg Fortress, 2001.

———. *Matthew in History: Interpretation, Influence, and Effects*. Minneapolis: Fortress, 1994.

———. *The Theology of the Gospel of Matthew*. Translated by J. Bradford Robinson. Cambridge: Cambridge University Press, 1995.

Magonet, Jonathan. "Convention and Creativity: The Phrase 'Maker of Heaven and Earth' in the Psalms." Pages 139–152 in *"Open Thou Mine Eyes...."* Edited by H. J. Blumberg and B. Braude. Hoboken, NJ: Ktav Publishing House, 1992.

Maile, J. F. "Heaven, Heavenlies, Paradise." Pages 381–383 in *Dictionary of Paul and*

His Letters. Edited by Gerald F. Hawthorne, Ralph P. Martin and Daniel G. Reid. Downers Grove, Ill.: InterVarsity Press, 1993.

Malbon, Elizabeth Struthers. "Narrative Criticism: How Does the Story Mean?" Pages 23–49 in *Mark and Method: New Approaches in Biblical Studies*. Edited by J. C. Anderson and Stephen D. Moore. Minneapolis: Fortress, 1992.

Malina, Bruce J. "The Literary Structure and Form of Matt. 28:16–20." *New Testament Studies* 17 (1970): 87–103.

Maloney, Elliot C. *Semitic Interference in Markan Syntax*. Chico, California: Scholars Press, 1981.

Manhoff, Harry A. "All of the Kingdoms: Semitic Idiom in the Synoptic Gospels and Related Jewish Literature." Ph.D. dissertation, University of California, Santa Barbara, 2001.

Manson, T. W. *The Sayings of Jesus as Recorded in the Gospels According to St. Matthew and St. Luke Arranged with Introduction and Commentary*. London: SCM, 1949.

———. *The Teaching of Jesus: Studies of its Form and Content*. Cambridge: Cambridge University Press, 1955.

Marcus, Joel. "Entering into the Kingly Power of God." *Journal of Biblical Literature* 107 (1988): 663–675.

———. "The Gates of Hades and the Keys of the Kingdom (Matt 16:18–19)." *Catholic Biblical Quarterly* 50, no. 3 (1988): 443–455.

Mare, W. Harold. "The New Testament Concept Regarding the Regions of Heaven with Emphasis on 2 Corinthians 12:1–4." *Grace Journal* 11, no. 1 (1970): 3–12.

Marmorstein, Arthur. *The Old Rabbinic Doctrine of God*. 2 Vols. London: Oxford University Press, 1927.

Massaux, Édouard. *The Influence of the Gospel of Saint Matthew on Christian Literature before Saint Irenaeus*. Edited and translated by Norman J. Belval, Suzanne Hecht, and Arthur J. Bellinzoni. 3 vols. Macon: Mercer University Press, 1990.

Mauser, Ulrich W. "'Heaven' in the World View of the New Testament." *Horizons in Biblical Theology* 9, no. 2 (1987): 31–51.

Mauser, Ulrich W., C. B. Kaiser, P. D. Miller, Jr., and H. P. Nebelsick. "Biblical Theology and Biblical Cosmology." Papers presented at the 4th Biblical Colloquium, Pittsburgh 1987. *Horizons in Biblical Theology* 9: 1–103.

Mawhinney, Allen. "God as Father: Two Popular Theories Reconsidered." *Journal of the Evangelical Theological Society* 31, no. 2 (1988): 181–189.

Mayer, Günter. *Index Philoneus*. Berlin: de Gruyter, 1974.

Mays, James L. "The Language of the Reign of God." *Interpretation* 47, no. 2 (1993): 117–126.

———. "'Maker of Heaven and Earth': Creation in the Psalms." Pages 75–86 in *God Who Creates: Essays in Honor of W. Towner*. Edited by William P. Brown and S. Dean McBride. Grand Rapids: Eerdmans, 2000.

McDannell, Colleen, and Bernhard Lang. *Heaven: A History*. New Haven: Yale, 1988.

McDonough, Sean M. *YHWH at Patmos: Rev. 1:4 in its Hellenistic and Early Jewish Setting*. Tübingen: Mohr-Siebeck, 1999.

McIver, Robert K. "The Parable of the Weeds among the Wheat (Matt 13:24–30, 36–43) and the Relationship between the Kingdom and the Church as Portrayed in the Gospel of Matthew." *Journal of Biblical Literature* 114, no. 4 (1995): 643–659.

McKnight, Scot. "Matthew, Gospel of." Pages 526–541 in *Dictionary of Jesus and the Gospels*. Edited by Joel B. Green, Scot McKnight and I. Howard Marshall. Downers Grove, Ill.: InterVarsity Press, 1992.

———. *A New Vision for Israel: The Teachings of Jesus in National Context*. Grand Rapids: Eerdmans, 1999.

McLay, R. Timothy. *The OG and Th Versions of Daniel*. Atlanta: Scholars Press, 1996.

———. *The Use of the Septuagint in New Testament Research*. Grand Rapids: Eerdmans, 2003.
McNamara, Martin. *The New Testament and the Palestinian Targum to the Pentateuch*. Rome: Pontifical Biblical Institute, 1966.
———. *Targum and Testament: Aramaic Paraphrases of the Hebrew Bible: A Light on the New Testament*. Shannon: Irish University Press, 1972.
McNeile, Alan Hugh. *The Gospel According to St. Matthew*. London: MacMillan and Co., 1915.
Meadowcroft, Tim J. *Aramaic Daniel and Greek Daniel: A Literary Comparison*. Sheffield: Sheffield Academic Press, 1995.
———. "Who are the Princes of Persia and Greece (Daniel 10)? Pointers Towards the Danielic Vision of Earth and Heaven." *Journal for the Study of the Old Testament* 29, no. 1 (2004): 99–113.
Meier, John P. *A Marginal Jew: Rethinking the Historical Jesus, Volume 2: Mentor, Message, and Miracles*. New York: Doubleday, 1994.
———. *A Marginal Jew: Rethinking the Historical Jesus, Volume 3: Companions and Competitors*. New York: Doubleday, 2001.
———. *Matthew*. Wilmington, Delaware: Michael Glazier, 1980.
———. "Salvation History in Matthew: In Search of a Starting Point." *Catholic Biblical Quarterly* 37 (1975): 203–215.
———. *The Vision of Matthew: Christ, Church and Morality in the First Gospel*. New York: Paulist Press, 1979.
Melamed, Ezra Zion. "The Break-Up of Stereotypical Phrases as an Artistic Device in Biblical Poetry." *Scripta Hierosolymitana* 8 (1961): 115–153.
Metzger, Bruce M. *An Introduction to the Apocrypha*. New York: Oxford University Press, 1957.
———. *A Textual Commentary on the Greek New Testament*. 3d ed. New York: United Bible Societies, 1971.
Michaels, J. Ramsey. "The Kingdom of God and the Historical Jesus." Pages 109–118 in *The Kingdom of God in 20th-Century Interpretation*. Edited by Wendell L. Willis. Peabody, Mass.: Hendrickson, 1987.
Michel, Otto. "The Conclusion of Matthew's Gospel: A Contribution to the History of the Easter Message." Pages 30–41 in *The Interpretation of Matthew*. Edited by Graham N. Stanton. London: SPCK, 1983.
Migliore, Daniel L., ed. *The Lord's Prayer: Perspectives for Reclaiming Christian Prayer*. Grand Rapids: Eerdmans, 1993.
Milik, J. T. *The Books of Enoch: Aramaic Fragments from Qumran Cave 4*. Oxford: Clarendon, 1976.
Minear, Paul S. "Heavens." *Reformed World* 32 (1973): 250–256.
Mitchell, Margaret M. "Patristic Counter-evidence to the Claim that The Gospels were written for All Christians." *New Testament Studies* 51, no. 1 (2005): 36–79.
Moe, Olaf. "Das irdische und das himmlische Heiligtum: zur Auslegung von Hebr 9:4f." *Theologische Zeitschrift* 9 (1953): 23–29.
Moltmann, Jürgen. *God in Creation: An Ecological Doctrine of Creation*. Translated by Margaret Kohl. London: SCM Press, 1985.
Moody, Dale. "Matthew: Thy Kingdom Come." *Review & Expositor* 73 (1976): 81–82.
Moore, George Foot. *Judaism in the First Centuries of the Christian Era: The Age of the Tannaim*. 2 vols. Cambridge: Harvard University Press, 1927.
Moore, Stephen D. *Literary Criticism and the Gospels: The Theoretical Challenge*. New Haven: Yale University Press, 1989.
Morris, Leon. *The Gospel According to Matthew. The Pillar New Testament Commentary*. Grand Rapids: Eerdmans, 1992.
Moule, C. F. D. "St Matthew's Gospel: Some Neglected Features." Pages 67–74 in *Essays in New Testament Interpretation*. Edited by C. F. D. Moule. Cambridge: Cambridge University Press, 1982.

Mowery, Robert L. "From Lord to Father in Matthew 1–7." *Catholic Biblical Quarterly* 59, no. 4 (1997): 642–656.

———. "God, Lord, and Father: The Theology of the Gospel of Matthew." *Biblical Research* 33 (1988): 24–36.

———. "The Matthean References to the Kingdom: Different Terms for Different Audiences." *Ephemerides Theologicae Lovanienses* 70, no. 4 (1994): 398–405.

Mueller, Dieter. "Kingdom of Heaven or Kingdom of God." *Vigiliae Christianae* 27, no. 4 (1973): 266–276.

Mussies, G. *The Morphology of Koine Greek as Used in the Apocalypse of St. John.* Leiden: Brill, 1971.

Nelson, Diedrick A. "An Exposition of Matthew 20:1–16." *Interpretation* 29, no. 3 (1975): 288–292.

Neusner, Jacob. "The Kingdom of Heaven in Kindred Systems, Judaic and Christian." *Bulletin for Biblical Research* 15.2 (2005): 279–305.

Newman, Aryeh. "Linguistic Issues in a Talmudic Debate." *Tradition* 18, no. 3 (1980): 281–287.

Newman, Barclay M., Jr. "The Kingdom of God/Heaven in the Gospel of Matthew." *Bible Translator (Ap, O Practical Papers)* 27, no. 4 (1975): 427–434.

———. "Translating 'the Kingdom of God' and 'the Kingdom of Heaven' in the New Testament." *Bible Translator (Ap, O Practical Papers)* 25, no. 4 (1974): 401–404.

———. "Translating 'The Kingdom of God' Outside the Gospels," *Bible Translator* 29/2 (1978): 225–231

Newport, Kenneth G. C. *The Sources and Sitz im Leben of Matthew 23.* Sheffield: Sheffield Academic Press, 1995.

Newsom, Carol A. "The Development of 1 Enoch 6–19: Cosmology and Judgment." *Catholic Biblical Quarterly* 42, no. 3 (1980): 310–329.

———. "Heaven." Pages 338–340 in *Encyclopedia of the Dead Sea Scrolls, Volume 1.* Edited by Lawrence Schiffman and James VanderKam. Oxford: Oxford University Press, 2000.

———. *Songs of the Sabbath Sacrifice: A Critical Edition.* Atlanta: Scholars Press, 1985.

Neyrey, Jerome H. "Loss of Wealth, Loss of Family and Loss of Honour: The Cultural Context of the Original Makarisms in Q." Pages 139–158 in *Modelling Early Christianity: Social-scientific Studies of the New Testament in its Context.* London: Routledge, 1995.

Nickelsburg, George W. E. *1 Enoch 1: A Commentary on the Book of 1 Enoch, Chapters 1–36; 81–108. Hermeneia.* Minneapolis: Augsburg Fortress, 2001.

———. *Jewish Literature between the Bible and the Mishnah: A Historical and Literary Introduction.* London: SCM, 1981.

———. *Resurrection, Immortality, and Eternal Life in Intertestamental Judaism.* Cambridge, Mass: Harvard University Press, 1972.

Nida, Eugene A. "Meaning and Translation." *Bible Translator* 8 (1957): 97–108.

Niederwimmer, Kurt. *The Didache: A Commentary.* Minneapolis: Augsburg Fortress, 1998.

Nolland, John. *The Gospel of Matthew. The New International Greek Testament Commentary.* Grand Rapids: Eerdmans, 2005.

Notley, R. Steven. "The Kingdom of Heaven Forcefully Advances." Pages 279–311 in *The Interpretation of Scripture in Early Judaism and Christianity.* Edited by Craig A. Evans. Sheffield: Sheffield Academic Press, 2000.

Oesterley, William O. E. *An Introduction to the Books of the Apocrypha.* London: SPCK, 1953.

Ollenburger, Ben C. "We Believe in God…Maker of Heaven and Earth: Metaphor, Scripture, and Theology." *Horizons in Biblical Theology* 12 (1990): 64–96.

Olley, John W. "'The God of Heaven': A Look at Attitudes to Other Religions in the Old Testament." *Colloquium* 27 (1995): 76–94.

O'Malley, T. P. "The Opposition Caelestia:Terrena in Tertullian." Pages 190–194 in *Studia Patristica, Volume 10.* Edited by Frank L. Cross. Berlin: Akademie Verlag, 1970.

O'Neill, J. C. "The Kingdom of God." *Novum Testamentum* 35 (1993): 130–141.
Orlinsky, H. M. "Introductory Essay: On Anthropomorphisms and Anthropopathisms in the Septuagint and Targum." Pages xv–xxiv in *The Septuagint Translation of the Hebrew Terms in the Relation to God in the Book of Jeremiah*. Edited by B. M. Zlotowitz. New York: Ktav, 1987.
Ott, Willis. "A New Look at the Concept of the Kingdom of God." *Notes on Translation Vol. 2; Special Edition* (1984).
Overman, J. Andrew. *Church and Community in Crisis: The Gospel According to Matthew*. Valley Forge, Penn.: Trinity, 1996.
———. *Matthew's Gospel and Formative Judaism: The Social World of the Matthean Community*. Minneapolis: Fortress Press, 1990.
Paas, Stefan. "'He Who Builds His Stairs into Heaven...' (Amos 9:6a)." *Ugarit-Forschungen* 25 (1994): 319–325.
Painter, J. "World, Cosmology." Pages 979–982 in *Dictionary of Paul and His Letters*. Edited by Gerald F. Hawthorne, Ralph P. Martin and Daniel G. Reid. Downers Grove, Ill.: InterVarsity Press, 1993.
Pamment, Margaret. "The Kingdom of Heaven According to the First Gospel." *New Testament Studies* 27, no. 2 (1981): 211–232.
Pao, David W. *Acts and the Isaianic New Exodus*. Tübingen: Mohr-Siebeck, 2000; reprint, Baker Academic, 2002.
Parry, Donald W. "Notes on Divine Name Avoidance in Scriptural Units of the Legal Texts of Qumran." Pages 437–449 in *Legal Texts and Legal Issues*. Edited by M. Bernstein, F. Garcia Martinez, J. Kampen. Leiden: Brill, 1997.
Patrick, Dale. "The Kingdom of God in the Old Testament." Pages 67–79 in *The Kingdom of God in 20th-Century Interpretation*. Edited by Wendell L. Willis. Peabody, Mass.: Hendrickson, 1987.
Patte, Daniel. *The Gospel According to Matthew: A Structural Commentary on Matthew's Faith*. Philadelphia: Fortress Press, 1987.
Pennington, Jonathan T. "Dualism in Old Testament Cosmology: *Weltbild* and *Weltanschauung*." *Scandinavian Journal of the Old Testament* 18, no. 2 (2004): 260–277.
———. "'Heaven' and 'Heavens' in the LXX: Exploring the Relationship Between שָׁמַיִם and Οὐρανός." *Bulletin of the International Organization of Septuagint and Cognate Studies* 36 (2003): 39–59.
Perrin, Norman. *Jesus and the Language of the Kingdom: Symbol and Metaphor in New Testament Interpretation*. Philadelphia: Fortress, 1976.
Peters, F. E. *Greek Philosophical Terms: A Historical Lexicon*. New York: New York University Press, 1967.
Peterson, Erik. *'Eis Theos': Epigraphische, Formgeschichtliche und Religionsgeschichtliche Untersuchungen*. Göttingen: Vandenhoeck & Ruprecht, 1926.
Pietersma, Albert. "Kyrios or Tetragram: A Renewed Quest for the Original LXX." Pages 85–101 in *De Septuaginta: Studies in Honour of John William Wevers*. Edited by A. Pietersma and C. Cox. Mississauga, Ont., Canada: Benben Publications, 1984.
Plummer, Alfred. *An Exegetical Commentary on the Gospel According to S. Matthew*. London: Robert Scott, 1928.
Pope, T., and R. Buth. "Kingdom of God, Kingdom of Heaven." *Notes on Translation* 119 (1987): 1–31.
Porter, Stanley E. "The Language of the Apocalypse in Recent Discussion." *New Testament Studies* 35 1989: 582–603.
———. "Vague Verbs, Periphrastics, and Matt 16:19." *Filologia Neotestamentaria* 2 (1988): 155–173.
Porteous, Norman. *Daniel*. London: SCM Press, 1965.
Powell, Mark Allan. "Matthew's Beatitudes: Reversals and Rewards of the Kingdom." *Catholic Biblical Quarterly* 58 (1996): 460–479.
———. *What Is Narrative Criticism? A New Approach to the Bible*. London: SPCK, 1993.

Prockter, L. J. "The Blind Spot: New Testament Scholarship's Ignorance of Rabbinic Judaism." *Scriptura* 48 (1994): 1–12.
Puech, Emile. "Messianism, Resurrection, and Eschatology at Qumran and in the New Testament." Pages 235–256 in *The Community of the Renewed Covenant: The Notre Dame Symposium on the Dead Sea Scrolls*. Edited by Eugene Ulrich and James VanderKam. Notre Dame, Indiana: University of Notre Dame Press, 1994.
Reddish, Mitchell G. "Heaven." Pages 90–91 in *Anchor Bible Dictionary, Volume 3*. Edited by David Noel Freedman. New York: Doubleday, 1992.
Reese, James M. *Hellenistic Influence of the Book of Wisdom and its Consequences*. Rome: Biblical Institute Press, 1970.
———. "How Matthew Portrays the Communication of Christ's Authority." *Biblical Theology Bulletin* 7 (1977): 139–144.
Rengstorf, Karl H. *A Complete Concordance to Flavius Josephus*. Leiden: Brill, 1979.
Reventlow, Henning, ed. *Eschatology in the Bible and in Jewish and Christian Tradition, Journal for the Study of the Old Testament Supplement Series*. Sheffield, England: Sheffield Academic Press, 1997.
Riches, John. *Conflicting Mythologies: Identity Formation in the Gospels of Mark and Matthew*. Edinburgh: T&T Clark, 2000.
———. *Matthew. New Testament Guides*. Sheffield: Sheffield Academic Press, 1997.
Riches, John, and David C. Sim, eds. *The Gospel of Matthew in its Roman Imperial Context*. London: T&T Clark, 2005.
Ridderbos, Herman. *The Coming of the Kingdom*. Philadelphia: Presbyterian and Reformed, 1962.
Ringgren, Helmer. *The Faith of Qumran: Theology of the Dead Sea Scrolls*. Expanded ed. Translated by Emilie T. Sander. New York: Crossroad, 1995.
Robinson, James M., Paul Hoffmann, and John S. Kloppenberg, *The Critical Edition of Q* (Minneapolis: Fortress, 2000).
Rohrbaugh, Richard. "Legitimating Sonship—A Test of Honour: A social-scientific study of Luke 4:1–30." Pages 183–197 in *Modelling Early Christianity: Social-scientific Studies of the New Testament in its Context*. Edited by Philip F. Esler. London: Routledge, 1995.
Rothfuchs, W. *Die Erfüllungszitate des Matthäusevangeliums*. Stuttgart: Kohlhammer, 1969.
Rowe, Robert D. *God's Kingdom and God's Son: The Background to Mark's Christology from Concepts of Kingship in the Psalms*. Leiden: Brill, 2002.
Rowland, Christopher. *The Open Heaven: A Study of Apocalyptic in Judaism and Early Christianity*. London: SPCK, 1982.
———. "Apocalyptic, The Poor, and the Gospel of Matthew." *Journal of Theological Studies* 45 (1994): 504–518.
Russell, David S. "Earth and Heaven: Bridging the Gap." *Expository Times* 109, no. 1 (1997): 7–9.
Russell, Jeffrey Burton. *A History of Heaven: The Singing Silence*. Princeton: Princeton University Press, 1997.
Russell, Letty M. *Household of Freedom: Authority in Feminist Theology*. Philadelphia: Westminster Press, 1987.
Ryken, Leland, Tremper Longman, and James C. Wilhoit, eds., *Dictionary of Biblical Imagery*. Downers Grove, Ill: InterVarsity, 2000.
Sabourin, L. "Traits Apocalyptiques dan L'Évangile de Matthieu." *Science et Esprit* 33, no. 3 (1981): 357–372.
Sailhammer, John H. *The Translational Technique of the Greek Septuagint for the Hebrew Verbs and Participles in Psalms 3–41*. New York: Peter Lang, 1991.
Saldarini, Anthony J. *Matthew's Christian-Jewish Community*. Chicago: University of Chicago Press, 1994.
Salmond, S. D. F. "Heaven." Pages 320–324 in *Hastings Dictionary of the Bible*. Edinburgh: T&T Clark, 1903.

Sand, Alexander. *Das Evangelium nach Matthäus. Regensburger Neues Testament.* Regensburg: Friedrich Pustet, 1986.

———. *Das Gesetz und die Propheten: Untersuchungen zur Theologie des Evangeliums nach Matthäus.* Regensburg: Friedrich Pustet, 1974.

———. *Reich Gottes und Eheverzicht im Evangelium nach Matthäus.* Stuttgart: Katholisches Bibelwerk, 1983.

Sanders, James A. "Introduction: Why the Pseudepigrapha?" Pages 13–19 in *The Pseudepigrapha and Early Biblical Interpretation.* Edited by J. H. Charlesworth and Craig A. Evans. Sheffield: Sheffield Academic Press, 1993.

Sandmel, Samuel. "Parallelomania." *Journal of Biblical Literature* 81 (1962): 1–13.

Saucy, Mark. "The Kingdom-of-God Sayings in Matthew." *Bibliotheca Sacra* 151 (1994): 175–197.

Sawyer, John F. A. "'From Heaven Fought the Star' (Judges 5:20)." *Vetus Testamentum* 31, no. 1 (1981): 87–89.

Schaberg, J. *The Father, the Son and the Holy Spirit: The Triadic Phrase in Matthew 28:19b.* Chico, CA: Scholars Press, 1981.

Schenk, Wolfgang. *Die Sprache des Matthäus: Die Text-Konstituenten in ihren Makro- und Mikrostrukturellen Relationen.* Göttingen: Vandenhoeck & Ruprecht, 1987.

Schlatter, Adolf. *Der Evangelist Matthäus: seine Sprache, sein Ziel, seine Selbständigkeit.* Stuttgart: Calwer Verlag, 1957.

Schlosser, Jacques. *Le Règne de Dieu dans les dits de Jésus.* 2 vols. Paris: Gabalda, 1980.

Schmidt, Francis. *Le Testament grec d'Abraham.* Tübingen: Mohr-Siebeck, 1986.

Schmidt, Thomas E. "The Penetration of Barriers and the Revelation of Christ in the Gospels." *Novum Testamentum* 34 (1992): 229–246.

Schmidt, Thomas E., and Moisés Silva. *To Tell the Mystery: Essays on New Testament Eschatology in Honor of Robert H. Gundry.* Sheffield, England: JSOT Press, 1994.

Schnackenburg, Rudolf. *God's Rule and Kingdom.* Translated by John Murray. Freiburg: Herder, 1963.

———. *The Gospel of Matthew.* Translated by Robert R. Barr. Grand Rapids: Eerdmans, 2002.

Schneider, Gerhard. "'Im Himmel—auf Erden': eine Perspektive matthäischer Theologie." Pages 285–297 in *Studien zum Matthäusevangelium: Festschrift für Wilhelm Pesch.* Edited by Ludger Schenke. Stuttgart: Katholisches Bibelwerk, 1988.

Schoonhoven, C. R. "Heaven." Pages 654–655 in *International Standard Bible Encyclopedia (ISBE).* Edited by Geoffrey W. Bromiley. Grand Rapids: Eerdmans, 1982.

———. *The Wrath of Heaven.* Grand Rapids: Eerdmans, 1966.

Schwarz, G. "'Ihnen Gehort das Himmelreich' (Matthaus V.3)." *New Testament Studies* 23, no. 3 (1977): 341–343.

Schweizer, Eduard. *The Good News According to Matthew.* Translated by David E. Green. London: SPCK, 1976.

Scott, Bernard Brandon and Margaret E. Dean. "A Sound Map of the Sermon on the Mount." Pages 311–378 in *Treasures New and Old: Recent Contributions to Matthean Studies.* Edited by David R. Bauer and Mark Allan Powell. Atlanta: Scholars Press, 1996.

Scott, J. M. "Heavenly Ascent in Jewish and Pagan Traditions." Pages 447–452 in *Dictionary of New Testament Background.* Edited by Craig A. Evans and Stanley E. Porter. Downers Grove, Ill.: InterVarsity Press, 2000.

Schoemaker, W. R. "The Use of RUAH in the Old Testament, and of pneuma in the New Testament." *Journal of Biblical Literature* 23 (1904): 13–67.

Segal, Alan F. "Heavenly Ascent in Hellenistic Judaism, Early Christianity and Their Environment." Pages 1333–1394 in *Aufstieg und Niedergangder römischen Welt: Geschichte und Kultur Roms im Spiegel der neueren Forschung (ANRW), Volume 23/2.* Edited by H. Temporini and W. Haase. Berlin: De Gruyter, 1980.

---. *Two Powers in Heaven: Early Rabbinic Reports About Christianity and Gnosticism*. Leiden: Brill, 1977.
Shunary, Jonathon. "Avoidance of Anthropomorphism in the Targum of Psalms." *Textus* 5 (1966): 133–144.
Sim, David C. *Apocalyptic Eschatology in the Gospel of Matthew*. Cambridge: Cambridge University Press, 1996.
---. "The Gospels for all Christians? A Response to Richard Bauckham." *Journal for the Study of the New Testament* 84 (2001): 3–27.
---. "Rome in Matthew's Eschatology." Pages 91–106 in *The Gospel of Matthew in its Roman Imperial Context*. Edited by John Riches and David C. Sim. London: T&T Clark, 2005.
Simon, Ulrich E. *Heaven in the Christian Tradition*. London: Rockliff, 1958.
Skehan, P. W. "The Divine Name at Qumran, the Masada Scroll, and in the Septuagint." *Bulletin of the International Organization for Septuagint and Cognate Studies* 13 (1990): 14–44.
Smith, Morton. *Tannaitic Parallels to the Gospels*. Philadelphia: SBL, 1951.
Smith, Wilbur M. *The Biblical Doctrine of Heaven*. Chicago: Moody Press, 1968.
Sparks, H. F. D. "The Doctrine of the Divine Fatherhood in the Gospels." Pages 241–262 in *Studies in the Gospels: Essays in Memory of R. H. Lightfoot*. Edited by D. D. Nineham. Oxford: Basil Blackwell, 1955.
Stadelmann, Luis I. J. *The Hebrew Conception of the World: A Philological and Literary Study*. Rome: Pontifical Biblical Institute, 1970.
Stanley, D. M. "The Conception of Salvation in the Synoptic Gospels." *Catholic Biblical Quarterly* 18 (1956): 345–363.
Stanton, Graham N. "5 Ezra and Matthean Christianity." *Journal for the Study of the New Testament* 28 (1977): 67–83.
---, ed. *The Interpretation of Matthew*. London: SPCK, 1983.
---. *A Gospel for a New People: Studies in Matthew*. Louisville, Ky.: Westminster/John Knox Press, 1993.
---. "The Origin and Purpose of Matthew's Gospel: Matthean Scholarship from 1945 to 1980." Pages 1889–1951 in *Aufstieg und Niedergangder römischen Welt: Geschichte und Kultur Roms im Spiegel der neueren Forschung (ANRW), Volume 25/3*. Edited by H. Temporini and W. Haase. Berlin: De Gruyter, 1985.
Starbuck, Charles Casey. "As It Is in Heaven." *Andover Review* 16, no. 93 (1891): 317.
Starr, J. M. *Sharers in Divine Nature: 2 Peter 1:4 in Its Hellenistic Context*. Stockhohm: Almqvist & Wiksell, 2000.
Stegemann, Hartmut. *The Library of Qumran: On the Essenes, Qumran, John the Baptist, and Jesus*. Grand Rapids: Eerdmans, 1998.
Steiner, George. *After Babel: Aspects of Language and Translation*. 3d ed. New York: Oxford University Press, 1998.
Stemberger, Günter. *Introduction to the Talmud and Midrash*. 2d ed. Translated by Markus Bockmuehl. Edinburgh: T&T Clark, 1996.
Stendahl, Krister. *The School of St Matthew and Its Use of the Old Testament*. Lund: Gleerup, 1968.
---. "Your Kingdom Come." *Cross Currents* 32, no. 3 (1982): 257–266.
Strack, H. L., and P. Billerbeck. *Kommentar zum Neuen Testament aus Talmud und Midrasch*. 3d ed. 4 vols. Munich: Beck, 1951–1956.
Strecker, G. *Der Weg der Gerechtigkeit: Untersuchung zur Theologie des Matthäus*. Göttingen: Vandenhoeck & Ruprecht, 1962.
Suggs, M. Jack. *Wisdom, Christology and Law in Matthew's Gospel*. Cambridge: Harvard University Press, 1970.
Suter, David W. "Weighed in the Balance: The Similitudes of Enoch in Recent Discussion." *Religious Studies Review* 7 (1981): 217–221.

Swartley, Willard M. *Israel's Scripture Traditions and the Synoptic Gospels: Story Shaping Story.* Peabody, Mass.: Hendrickson, 1994.
Sykes, Stephen W. "Life after Death: The Christian Doctrine of Heaven." Pages 250–271 in *Creation, Christ and Culture.* Edinburgh: T&T Clark, 1976.
Syreeni, Kari. "Between Heaven and Earth: On the Structure of Matthew's Symbolic Universe." *Journal for the Study of the New Testament* 40 (1990): 3–13.
Tabor, James D. *Things Unutterable: Paul's Ascent to Paradise in Its Greco-Roman, Judaic, and Early Christian Contexts.* Lanham, Md.: University Press of America, 1986.
Tabor, James D., and Michael O. Wise. "The Messiah at Qumran." *Biblical Archaeology Review* 18, no. 6 (1992): 60–63, 65.
Talmon, S. "The Community of the Renewed Covenant: Between Judaism and Christianity." Pages 3–24 in *The Community of the Renewed Covenant: The Notre Dame Symposium on the Dead Sea Scrolls.* Edited by E. Ulrich and J. VanderKam. Notre Dame: University of Notre Dame Press, 1994.
Thomas, John Christopher. "The Kingdom of God in the Gospel According to Matthew." *New Testament Studies* 39 (1993): 136–146.
Thompson, G. H. P. "Thy Will Be Done in Earth, as It Is in Heaven." *Expository Times* 70 (1959): 379–381.
Thompson, Marianne Meye. *The Promise of the Father: Jesus and God in the New Testament.* Louisville: Westminster John Knox, 2000.
Thompson, W. G. *Matthew's Advice to a Divided Community: Matt 17:22–18:35.* Rome: Biblical Institute Press, 1970.
Torm, D. Frederik. "Der Pluralis Ouranoi." *Zeitschrift für die alttestamentliche Wissenschaft* 33 (1934): 48–50.
Towner, W. Sibley. *Daniel* (Interpretation). Atlanta: John Knox, 1984.
Traub, H. "Ouranos." Pages 497–525 in *Theological Dictionary of the New Testament (TDNT).* Edited by Gerhard Friedrich and Geoffrey W. Bromiley. Grand Rapids: Eerdmans, 1967.
Trilling, Wolfgang. *Das wahre Israel: Studien zur Theologie des Matthäus Evangeliums.* 3d. ed. München: Kösel, 1964.
Trudinger, Paul. "The 'Our Father' in Matthew as Apocalyptic Eschatology." *Downside Review* 107 (1989): 49–54.
Tsumura, David Toshio. "A 'Hyponymous' Word Pair: 'rs and thm(t) in Hebrew and Ugaritic." *Biblica* 69, no. 2 (1988): 258–269.
———. "rqi'." Page 1198 in *New International Dictionary of Old Testament Theology and Exegesis (NIDOTTE).* Edited by Willem VanGemeren. Grand Rapids: Zondervan, 1997.
———. "šamayim." Pages 160–166 in *New International Dictionary of Old Testament Theology and Exegesis (NIDOTTE).* Edited by Willem VanGemeren. Grand Rapids: Zondervan, 1997.
Tuckett, Christopher M. *Nag Hammadi and the Gospel Tradition: Synoptic Tradition in the Nag Hammadi Library.* Edinburgh: T&T Clark, 1986.
———. "Q, Prayer, and the Kingdom." *Journal of Theological Studies* 40 (1989): 367–376.
Turner, Nigel. *Christian Words.* Edinburgh: T&T Clark, 1980.
———. *A Grammar of New Testament Greek, Vol. III: Syntax.* Edinburgh: T&T Clark, 1963.
Ulansy, David. "Heaven Torn Open: Mark's Powerful Metaphor Explained." *Bible Review* 7, no. 4 (1991): 32–37.
Urbach, Ephraim E. *The Sages: Their Concepts and Beliefs.* Translated by Israel Abrahams. 2 vols. Jerusalem: Magnes Press, 1975.
van Kooten, George H. *Cosmic Christology in Paul and the Pauline School: Colossians and Ephesians in the Context of Graeco-Roman Cosmology, with a New Synopsis of the Greek Texts.* Tübingen: Mohr-Siebeck, 2003.
VanderKam, James C. *Enoch and the Growth of an Apocalyptic Tradition.* Washington, D.C.: Catholic Biblical Association of America, 1984.

———. *An Introduction to Early Judaism*. Grand Rapids: Eerdmans, 2001.
VanderKam, James and Peter Flint. *The Meaning of the Dead Sea Scrolls*. San Francisco: HarperCollins, 2002.
VanGemeren, Willem. "Abba in the Old Testament?" *Journal of the Evangelical Theological Society* 31 (1988): 385–398.
Vawter, Bruce. "Yahweh: Lord of the Heavens and the Earth." *Catholic Biblical Quarterly* 48, no. 3 (1986): 461–467.
Vermes, Geza. *Jesus and the World of Judaism*. Philadelphia: Fortress, 1984.
———. *Jesus in His Jewish Context*. Minneapolis: Fortress, 2003.
Verseput, Donald J. "The Role and Meaning of the 'Son of God' Title in Matthew's Gospel." *New Testament Studies* 33 (1987): 532–556.
Viviano, B. T. "The Kingdom of God in the Qumran Literature." Pages 97–107 in *The Kingdom of God in 20th-Century Interpretation*. Edited by Wendell L. Willis. Peabody, Mass.: Hendrickson, 1987.
von Rad, Gerhard. In *Bible Key Words from Gerhard Kittel's* Theologsiches Wörterbuch zum Neuen Testament: *Basileia*. London: A&C Black, 1957.
———. *Old Testament Theology*. Translated by D. M. G. Stalker. 2 vols. Edinburgh: Oliver and Boyd, 1962–1965.
Vos, Gerhardus. *The Teaching of Jesus Concerning the Kingdom of God and the Church*. Reprint. Eugene, Oregon: Wipf and Stock, 1998.
Wainwright, Elaine. "The Gospel of Matthew." Pages 635–677 in *Searching the Scriptures: A Feminist Commentary*. Edited by Elisabeth Schüssler Fiorenza. New York: Cross Road, 1994.
Walker, William O. "Kingdom of the Son of Man and the Kingdom of the Father in Matthew: An Exercise in *Redaktionsgeschichte*." *Catholic Biblical Quarterly* 30, no. 4 (1968): 573–579.
———. "The Lord's Prayer in Matthew and in John." *New Testament Studies* 28 (1982): 237–256.
Wallace, Daniel. *Greek Grammar Beyond the Basics: An Exegetical Syntax of the New Testament*. Grand Rapids: Zondervan, 1996.
Walser, Georg. *The Greek of the Ancient Synagogue: An Investigation on the Greek of the Septuagint, Pseudepigrapha and the New Testament*. Stockhom: Almqvist & Wiksell International, 2001.
Waltke, Bruce K. and M. O'Connor. *An Introduction to Biblical Hebrew Syntax*. Winona Lake, Ind.: Eisenbrauns, 1990.
Walvoord, Johh F. "The Kingdom of Heaven." *Bibliotheca Sacra* 124 (1967): 195–205.
Waters, Kenneth L. "Matthew 27:52–53 as Apocalyptic Apostrophe: Temporal-Spatial Collapse in the Gospel of Matthew." *Journal of Biblical Literature* 122, no. 3 (2003): 489–515.
Weder, Hans. "Die 'Rede der Reden': Beobachtungen zum Verständnis der Bergpredigt Jesu." *Evangelische Theologie* 45 (1985): 45–60.
Weinberg, Joel P. "Die Natur im Weltbild des Chronisten." *Vetus Testamentum* 31, no. 3 (1981): 324–345.
Wenham, David. "The Kingdom of God and Daniel." *Expository Times* 98, no. 5 (1987): 132–134.
Wevers, John William. *Notes on the Greek Text of Deuteronomy*. Atlanta: Scholars Press, 1995.
———. "The Rendering of the Tetragram in the Psalter and Pentateuch: A Comparative Study." Pages 21–35 in *The Old Greek Psalter: Studies in Honour of Albert Pietersma*. Edited by Robert J. V. Hiebert, Claude E. Cox, and Peter J. Gentry. Sheffield: Sheffield Academic Press, 2001.
Whitcomb, John C. "The Creation of the Heavens and the Earth." *Grace Journal* 8 (1967): 27–32.

Whitehouse, Walter A. "God's Heavenly Kingdom and His Servants, the Angels." *Scottish Journal of Theology* 4, no. 4 (1951): 376–382.
Wifall, Walter. "Models of God in the Old Testament." *Biblical Theology Bulletin* 9, no. 4 (1979): 179–186.
Willaert, B. "'Tu Es Petrus', Mt xvi, 17–19." *Collationes Brugenses et Gandavenses* 2 (1956): 452–465.
Willis, Wendell L. *The Kingdom of God in 20th-Century Interpretation*. Peabody, Mass.: Hendrickson Publishers, 1987.
Wilson, R. McL. "Did Jesus Speak Greek?" *Expository Times* 68 (1957): 121–122.
Wilson, Robert W. "Creation and New Creation: The Role of Creation Imagery in the Book of Daniel." Pages 190–203 in *God Who Creates: Essays in Honor of W. Sibley Towner*. Edited by William P. Brown and S. Dean McBride. Grand Rapids: Eerdmans, 2000.
Winden, J. C. M. van. "The Early Christian Exegesis of 'Heaven and Earth' in Genesis 1,1." Pages 371–382 in *Romanitas et Christianitas: Studia Iano Henrico Waszink*. Edited by W. Den Boer. Amsterdam: North-Holland Pub Co, 1973.
Winston, David. *The Wisdom of Solomon. Anchor Bible*. Garden City, NY: Doubleday, 1979.
Witherup, R. D. "Paradise and Heaven." *Bible Today* 33, no. 6 (1995): 337–341.
Wojcik, Jan. "The Two Kingdoms in Matthew's Gospel." Pages 283–295 in *Literary Interpretations of Biblical Narratives*. Edited by Kenneth R. R. Gros Louis, James S. Ackerman, and Thayer S. Warshaw. Nashville: Abingdon Press, 1974.
Wolf, Miroslav. "Johannine Dualism and Contemporary Pluralism." Paper presented at the "Gospel of John and Christian Theology" conference. St Andrews, Scotland, July 2003.
Wouters, Armin. "*... Wer den Willen meines Vaters Tut*": *Eine Untersuchung zum Verständnis vom Handeln in Matthäusevangelium*. Edited by Jost Eckert and Josef Hainz. Regensburg: Friedrich Pustet, 1992.
Wright III, Benjamin G. "Access to the Source: Cicero, Ben Sira, the Septuagint and their Audiences." *Journal for the Study of Judaism in the Persian, Hellenistic, and Roman Period* 34, no. 1 (2003): 1–27.
Wright, J. Edward. "Biblical Versus Israelite Images of the Heavenly Realm." *Journal for the Study of the Old Testament* 93 (2001): 59–75.
———. *The Early History of Heaven*. Oxford: Oxford University Press, 2000.
Wright, N. T. *Jesus and the Victory of God*. Minneapolis: Fortress, 1996.
———. *The New Testament and the People of God*. Minneapolis: Fortress, 1992.
Zahn, Theodor. *Das Evangelium des Matthäus. Nachdruck aus dem Kommentar zum Neuen Testament*. Wuppertal: R. Brockhaus, 1984. Reprint, Dei Theologische Verlagsgemeinschaft (TVG).
Zeitlin, Solomon. *The First Book of Maccabees*. New York: Harper & Bros., 1950.

INDEX OF TEXTS
(excludes *Appendix*)

Old Testament

Genesis
General	39, 81, 120, 212
1	176, 336
1–2	8, 9, 39, 215, 273
1:1	37, 84, 138, 164, 167, 172, 189, 194, 211, 215, 216, 310, 232, 342, 345
1:2	214
1:7–9	42
1:8	42
1:14	42, 157
1:16	137
2:1	108, 168, 170
2:4	166, 211, 213
4:1–16	214
4:10	47
4:20	47
4:28	47
5:1	211, 213
7:11	42
8:2	41
10–12	84
11–12	215
12	215
11:4	45
1–12	216
12:2–3	215
14:22	167
15:15	41
21:17	44, 45
22	213
22:11	45
27:28	47, 164
27:39	47
28:12	44
28:17	44
40:17	48
40:19	48

Exodus
4:22–23	218
10:13	49, 163
13:21–22	157
15:18	256
16:4	46
19–20	256
20:4	173
20:7	19
20:11	170, 174
25:9	188
26:30	188
32:13	218
40:35–38	157

Leviticus
22:28	224
26:19	167

Numbers
General	39

Deuteronomy
General	39
1:38	218
3:24	164
4:10	89
4:19	41, 44, 168
4:26	167
5:8	170, 173
6:5	178
10:14	43, 100, 118
13:33	165
17:3	44, 168
28:26	164
32:4–6	218
30:4	159
32:8	218
32:10	204
32:43	49, 100, 108
33:13	41

Joshua
10:11	41, 46

Ruth
General	39

INDEX OF TEXTS

1 Samuel		9:8–9	41
2:10	41, 100, 109	11:8	165
10:1	218	15:15	48
		16:19 (LXX)	100, 107
2 Samuel		22:12	44
7:12–14	218, 256	22:14	42
18:9	43	28:24	47
22:10	100, 109	Ch. 38	176
		38:29	41
1 Kings			
8:14	89	*Psalms*	
8:23	131	General	39, 47, 10, 109
8:27	43, 45, 118, 131	1:6	167
8:27	100	2	319
8:36	218	2:2–3	269
8:53	48 (LXX), 218	2:4	100, 109, 269
22:19–22	45	2:6–7	269
		2:8	269
2 Kings		2:10	269
17:16	44	5:2	257
		8	178, 181
1 Chronicles		8:2	100
16:31	167	8:3	41, 178
28:5	257	8:4–5	178
29:10 (LXX)	218	8:4	100
29:11	257	8:6	178
		8:9	43
2 Chronicles		10:16	257
General	47, 109	11:4	44, 257
2:5	43, 100	14:2	44
6:18	43, 100, 118	18:2	100
6:23	43	19:1	42
13:8	257	22:27–28	325
28:9 (LXX)	100, 109	24:7	257
36:23	44, 75, 214, 215, 269, 310	24:10	257
		29	257
		32:6 (LXX)	100
Ezra		33:13–15	237
General	47, 256	44:4	257
1:2	44, 269	45:6	257
2:64	89	46:7	257
9:6	24	47:2	257
		49:6 (LXX)	100
Nehemiah		56:6 (LXX)	100
General	47	56:11 (LXX)	100, 107
9:6	43, 170	56:12 (LXX)	100
		65	257
Esther		67:9 (LXX)	100
General	18, 27, 39	67:15 (LXX)	51
4:14	27	68:24	257
		68:35 (LXX)	100
Job		73:25	164
1–2	45	76:8	169
8:29	48	78:23–28	114

78:23	42	*Proverbs*	
79:2	164	3:12	218
82:1	257	3:19 (LXX)	100, 108
84	257	8:27	42
84:3	257		
88:3 (LXX)	100, 109	*Ecclesiastes*	
88:6 (LXX)	100	5:2	45, 168
88:12 (LXX)	100, 168	3:17	167
89:11	168		
89:14	257	*Song of Songs*	
93	257	General	39
95:3	257		
95:4	139, 165	*Isaiah*	
95:5 (LXX)	100, 109	General	39
95:11 (LXX)	100	2	326
96:6 (LXX)	100	6:1–2	45
101:26 (LXX)	100	6:1	257
102:19	168	6:5	257
103:13	218	7:11	175
103:19	44, 257	8:21–22	49, 163
103:20–21	45	13:10	157
104	178	14:13	194
106:26 (LXX)	100, 107	14:19	269
107:5 (LXX)	100, 107	18:6	48
107:6 (LXX)	100	18:7	325
107:26	165	23:17	269
112:4 (LXX)	100	33:22	257
113:11 (LXX)	49, 100, 163	34:4	157, 158
113:24 (LXX)	100	37:16	269
115:15	176	43:15	257
115:16	43, 168, 172	44:3	100
115:16–17	172, 176	44:6	257
115:16–18	173	44:23	108
121:2	176	44:24	167
124:8	176	49:13	100
127:4–128:4	xii	55:9–11	41
134:3	176	55:9	182
134:6 (LXX)	139	60:3–16	325
135:5 (LXX)	100	61:7–9	218
135:6	170	63:16	218
139:1–17	237	64:8	218
139:8	165	66:1	44, 168, 257
143:5 (LXX)	100		
145:1	257	*Jeremiah*	
145:11–13	257	General	39, 256
146:6	170	3:17	257, 325
147:8	41	3:19	218
148	185	7:33	164
148:1–6	178	8:19	257
148:1 (LXX)	100, 107	10:10	257
148:4	43, 100, 103, 118	10:11	166
		15:4	269
148:7–14	178	25:16 (LXX)	158
		28:9 (LXX)	24

29:18	269	3:31–4:34	9
31:9	218	3:31–33 (MT)	275
46:18	257	3:32	274
48:15	257	3:33	274
49:36	158	3:56	42
49:38	257	3:59 (OG and Th)	100, 108, 110
50:41	269	4	271, 272, 274, 275, 289
51:57	257	4:1–37	290
51:48	170	4:1–3	274
		4:2	29
Ezekiel		4:8	47, 329
General	337	4:9	43, 47
1	257	4:10–27	288
1:1 (LXX)	100, 109	4:10	47
20:33	257	4:11	275
29:5	164	4:12	47, 288
		4:14–15	275
Daniel		4:17	29, 47, 49, 272 (OG), 276, 277
General	9, 18, 81, 109, 183, 209, 256, 286	4:18	43, 47
1–6	271	4:19	47
1–7	260	4:20	47
2–7	8, 28, 46, 47, 251, 253, 256, 261, 268, 270, 271, 272, 274, 277, 278, 285, 289, 290, 291, 292, 310, 311, 341, 345	4:21	288
		4:22	47, 275
		4:23	27, 29, 30, 48, 50, 275, 298
		4:24	29
		4:25	29, 275, 276
2	273, 287	4:26 (LXX)	28, 50, 276 (MT)
2:2	289	4:27 (LXX)	49, 277
2:4–7:28	271	4:28	47
2:10	272, 289	4:30	47
2:18	29, 47, 290	4:31 (LXX)	49, 277
2:19–23	272	4:32	47, 275, 276
2:21–23	288	4:33	275
2:27–28	272, 288	4:34–35	276
2:19	29, 47, 290	4:34	47, 290
2:27–28	288	4:37	257, 272 (OG), 276, 277 (OG), 290
2:28	47, 272, 290		
2:35	273	5	271, 274
2:37–38	273	5:18	29
2:37	29, 47, 273, 290, 330	5:21	29, 47
		5:23	47, 290
2:38	42, 47	6	271, 274
2:39	272	6:25–28	273
2:44–45	289	6:27	274
2:44	29, 47, 273, 290	6:28	47, 274
2:47	257	7	84, 157, 257, 273, 287, 295, 328
3	271, 274		
3:17 (OG and Th)	49, 100, 109	7–12	186, 271, 290
3:26	29	7:2	158

7:9–14	288	*Obadiah*	
7:13–14	288, 289, 292	General	39
7:13	158, 214, 288		
7:18	273	*Jonah*	
7:22	273	General	47
7:23	273		
7:27	273	*Micah*	
8:8	47, 158	General	39
8:10	47	2:13	257
9:12	47	4:1–7	325
9:24–27	288		
9:27	286	*Habakkuk*	
11:4	47, 158	1:5	246
11:31	286, 288	3:3 (LXX)	100, 109
12:1	288		
12:2	288	*Zephaniah*	
12:7	47	3:15	257
12:11	286		
		Haggai	
Hosea		2:6	170, 174
11:1	218		
11:3	218	*Zechariah*	
		2:12	218
Joel		6:5	41, 157, 159
2:10	157	14	326
3:4	157	14:9	257
4:15	157	14:16–17	257, 325
4:16	200		
		Malachi	
Amos		1:14	257
9:2–3	173, 174	2:10	241
9:2	165, 194		

New Testament

Matthew		2:2	316
General	117, 119, 123,	2:5	89
	135, 193	2:6	206
1–2	289, 291, 315,	2:11	316
	317	2:15	89
1:1–2	213	2:16	315
1:1	84, 211, 212,	2:20	206
	213, 214, 215,	3:1–4:17	196
	246, 314, 315,	3:2	84, 140, 196,
	325, 328, 347		210, 280, 298,
1:6	315		317, 320
1:16	315	3:9	90, 213, 215,
1:17	215, 315		239, 241
1:18–20	213	3:7–10	348
1:20	315	3:9–10	348
1:22	89	3:16–17	94, 141, 144,
1:23	88, 325		237
2:1–8	315	3:16	2, 69, 126, 141,
2:1–12	316		213

3:17	2, 69, 83, 89, 126, 140, 144, 213, 345	5:45	140, 232, 233, 236, 328, 336
		5:47	248
4:1–11	320	5:48	74, 140, 224, 232, 233, 236, 336, 346
4:7–5:12	283		
4:8	207, 240, 281, 298	6:1–21	80, 87, 150, 196, 209, 236, 241, 242, 244, 245, 247, 248, 249, 250, 297, 342, 346
4:15	206		
4:17	83, 84, 140, 196, 210, 280, 320		
4:21–22	238		
4:21	232		
4:22	232	6:1–18	150, 244, 245, 246, 247
4:23	84, 154, 280, 281		
5–7	236	6:1	2, 69, 70, 74, 140, 150, 195, 199, 210, 232, 233, 236, 242, 243, 245
5:3–12	242		
5:3–10	93		
5:3–5	346		
5:3	74, 140, 242, 280, 311, 323		
		6:2–18	242, 245
5:4	323	6:2–4	151, 243
5:5	74	6:2	243
5:10	74, 140, 242, 280	6:4	232, 233, 236, 243
5:10–12	323, 346		
5:11–12	74, 151, 246	6:5–6	151, 244
5:12	2, 67, 69, 70, 126, 142, 242	6:5–15	243
		6:5–6	248
5:13–16	196, 198, 240	6:5	243
5:13	196, 207, 240	6:6	232, 233, 236, 237, 243
5:14	207, 240		
5:16	2, 69, 87, 140, 195, 196, 199, 210, 232, 233, 236, 240, 241, 242	6:7–15	150, 243, 244, 247
		6:7	248
		6:8	232, 233, 248, 249
5:17–48	245	6:9–15	318
5:17–18	89	6:9–10	7, 9, 93, 150, 152, 154, 155, 196, 205, 210, 215, 249, 291, 318, 323, 324, 326, 327, 333, 342, 343, 347
5:18	139, 153, 160, 195, 198, 200, 203, 206, 208		
5:19–20	280		
5:19	140		
5:20	74, 140, 242, 346	6:9	87, 133, 139, 140, 232, 233, 236, 239, 242, 328
5:21–48	242		
5:21–25	214		
5:27–30	346		
5:34–35	139, 146, 196, 197, 201, 203	6:10	33, 84, 133, 134, 139, 152, 153, 154, 196, 198, 202, 203, 204, 205, 207, 280, 281, 297, 308, 312, 318, 336
5:34	2, 67, 69, 291, 297		
5:38–42	346		
5:43–47	346		
5:44–45	346		

6:14–15	74, 151 248	9:26	206
6:14	87, 140, 232, 233, 236, 242	9:27	315
		9:31	206
6:15	232, 233, 236	9:35	84, 154, 280, 281
6:16–18	243, 244	10:5–7	205
6:16	243, 245	10:5–6	89, 205
6:18	232, 233, 231, 236, 237, 243, 244, 245	10:5	249
		10:7	84, 140, 280
		10:15	214
6:19–34	244, 246	10:20	233, 239
6:19–21	83, 242, 244, 245, 246, 342, 346	10:21	238
		10:26	236
		10:29	206, 233
6:19–20	139, 142, 153, 196, 198, 201, 202, 210	10:32–33	195, 199, 240, 242
		10:32	70, 140, 201, 231, 233
6:19–7:12	150, 246, 247		
6:19	142, 246	10:33–34	196, 198
6:20	2, 67, 69, 70, 74, 126, 128, 133, 134, 142, 157, 246	10:33	70, 140, 231, 233, 241
		10:34–37	249
		10:34–35	239
6:21	246, 247	10:35	241
6:22–34	246, 247	10:37	239
6:22	246	11:1	308
6:23	247	11:2	198
6:24	246	11:11	140
6:26–30	195	11:12	140, 308
6:26	2, 69, 137, 140, 232, 233, 236	11:23	139, 194, 199, 201, 207
6:32	140, 231, 233, 236, 249	11:24	206
		11:25–27	90, 233, 288
6:33	281, 291, 297, 299	11:25	139, 153, 194, 198, 200, 203, 208, 328, 334
7:1–12	246		
7:2	21	11:27	83
7:11	74, 140, 232, 236	12:22–32	314, 319, 320
7:12	245	12:23	314, 315, 315
7:13	120	12:25–26	315
7:15–23	348	12:25	281
7:21	9, 74, 87, 140, 232, 233, 239, 250, 280, 327, 346, 348	12:26–28	309
		12:26	154, 312
		12:28	299, 308, 314
		12:28	35, 69, 154, 281, 315
7:24–27	209		
7:28–29	75	12:33–38	348
7:29	204	12:38–39	143
8:11–12	90, 140, 314, 348	12:40	207
8:11	213, 215	12:42	207
8:12	154, 207, 281	12:46–50	239
8:20	2, 137	12:50	9, 87, 140, 232, 233, 239, 327, 346, 348
8:21	232, 236, 238, 249		
9:6	75, 204, 346	12:52–53	324

INDEX OF TEXTS

13	280	17:24–18:15	319
13:4	1	17:24–27	319
13:5	206	17:25–18:1	196, 202
13:8	206	17:25–26	319
13:10–15	288	17:25	196, 207, 319
13:11	140, 210	18	149
13:19	137, 154, 281	18:1–5	319
13:24	74, 140	18:1–4	140, 319, 323
13:31–32	141, 288	18:1	196, 319
13:31	74, 140, 141	18:3	71, 280, 319
13:32	2, 69, 137, 141	18:4	319
13:33	74, 140	18:10	2, 67, 69, 70, 140, 141, 144, 232, 233, 297
13:35	207, 240		
13:38	154, 207, 240, 281, 314, 319	18:11–12	327
13:41	154, 159, 281	18:14–20	348
13:42	207	18:14	140, 232, 233
13:43	233, 250, 281, 291	18:17–20	90
		18:17	89, 248
13:44	74, 140	18:18–20	x, 75, 83
13:45	74, 140	18:18–19	90, 210
13:47	74, 140	18:18	70, 133, 139, 147, 148, 149, 194, 196, 201, 202, 203, 205, 210, 241
13:50	207		
13:52	74, 89, 140		
14:19	143		
14:24	206		
15:4–6	239	18:19	2, 69, 140, 196, 232, 233, 241
15:12–13	90		
15:13	140, 232, 233	18:21–22	214
15:24	205	18:21	2, 69, 70, 126
16:1	143	18:23–35	250
16:2–3	2, 69, 136, 143	18:23	140
16:13–20	x, 345	18:35	140, 232, 233
16:13–19	94	19:2	142
16:17–19	75, 147, 199, 348	19:4–5	213
16:17	2, 69, 70, 85, 90, 140, 195, 199, 202, 232, 241, 345	19:5	239
		19:12	140
		19:13–15	323
		19:14	140
16:18–19	33, 90, 199, 317, 345	19:19	239
		19:21	142
16:18	89, 148, 195, 207, 342	19:23–24	307
		19:23	140
16:19	133, 139, 140, 147, 148, 149, 153, 194, 195, 196, 203, 205, 210, 241, 345	19:24	35, 71, 154, 281, 299
		19:26–29	323
		19:26	210
		19:29	238
16:23	210	19:28	7, 90, 214, 327, 334, 342, 348
16:26	207, 240		
16:27	159, 232, 233	20:1–16	322, 323
16:28	154, 281, 288	20:1	74, 140, 280
17	319	20:16	322
17:5	90	20:21	154

INDEX OF TEXTS

20:25–28	323	24:14	84, 154, 207, 280, 281
20:30	315		
20:31	315	24:15	286, 288
20:36	145	24:21	207, 240
21:1–11	316	24:29–35	156
21:9	315	24:29–31	75, 93, 15, 156
21:15	315	24:29	112, 126, 137, 141, 157, 210
21:23–23:39	144		
21:23–27	204	24:30	2, 69, 75, 136, 141, 147, 157, 196, 197, 198, 202, 288, 292
21:25–26	83, 139, 195, 199, 241		
21:25	36, 143, 201, 202, 249	24:31	67, 126, 157, 159, 160
21:31	35, 71, 154, 280, 281, 299, 308	24:32–35	156, 160
21:43	35, 71, 90, 154, 281, 299, 327	24:35–36	93, 141, 144
		24:35	75, 139, 141, 153, 156, 160, 194, 200, 203, 208, 209, 210
22:2	71, 140, 145		
22:13	207, 311		
22:16–22	319		
22:21	210	24:36	2, 69, 75, 126, 141, 160, 233, 297
22:24	213		
22:30	2, 69, 126, 128, 141, 142, 144, 145, 297	24:37	214
		24:51	207
22:32	214, 215	25:1	140, 280
22:37	179	25:30	207
22:42	315	25:31–46	323
22:45	315	25:31–32	159, 288
23	146	25:34	207, 233, 240, 250, 281
23:1	146		
23:2–11	348	25:46	288
23:2–7	241, 243	26:13	207, 240
23:8–9	87	26:29	233, 250, 291
23:8	241	26:39	233
23:9	83, 140, 196, 198, 201, 203, 210, 232, 239, 241, 342, 348	26:42	233
		26:53	232, 233
		26:64	2, 69, 93, 136, 141
23:10	241	26:29	281
23:11	323	27:11	316
23:13–19	327	27:29	316
23:13	140, 280	27:37	316
23:22	2, 69, 14	27:42	316
23:29–36	241	27:45	207
23:29–30	239	27:51	207
23:29–32	239, 249	27:54	214
23:31	239	28:1–20	246
23:32	231	28:2	2, 69, 141, 144, 297
23:34–36	214		
23:35	214	28:16–20	75, 94, 206, 214, 215, 289, 292, 318, 320, 342, 345, 346
24–25	93, 209, 288		
24:7	281		
24:13	288		

28:17	84, 346	11:13	72, 87, 224, 233
28:18–20	9, 84, 89, 205, 210	11:14	314
		12:6	233
28:18–19	214	12;12	233
28:18	83, 139, 196, 197, 203, 204, 205, 211, 215, 216, 292, 342, 343, 346	12:23	128, 157
		12:33	142, 198
		12:51	198
		12:56	193
		13:28–29	314
28:19	215, 233	15:18	23
28:20	88	15:21	23
		16:17	193, 200
Mark		18:6	295
General	2, 4, 71, 86	18:13	67
1:15	298	21:25	157
6:41	67	21:26	112, 126, 157, 158
7:35	126		
8:38	233	21:27	198
10:21	126	21:33	193, 200
11:25	71, 72, 87, 224, 232, 233, 234	22:42	233
		24:50–53	205
12:25	67, 126, 128, 144		
12:30	179	*John*	
13:14	286	General	2, 86, 119, 211, 331, 332, 333
13:11	233		
13:25	112, 126, 157	17:1	67
13:26	198	18:36	295
13:27	126, 193		
13:31	193, 200	*Acts*	
13:32	67, 126, 233	General	193
14:25	233	1:9–11	205
14:36	233	1:11	67
16:19–20	205	2:19	194, 199, 208
16:19	205	4:24	67
		7:49	67
Luke		7:55	67
General	2, 4, 71, 86	13:41	246
3:8	241	14:15	67
3:21	126	17:24	67, 194
3:22	126		
3:32–38	315	*Romans*	
4:1–30	248	1:4	205
4:1–13	320	6:6	295
4:25	193		
5:23	67	*1 Corinthians*	
6:23	126	8:5	194, 199, 208
6:36	224	15:23–28	284
8:5	137	15:47	208
9:26	233		
10:15	194	*2 Corinthians*	
10:21–22	233	1:12	295
10:21	193	12:1–5	130
10:27	179	12:2	129
11:2–4	151	15:52	160

INDEX OF TEXTS

Galatians		*1 Peter*	
4:26	67	1:4	67, 142
Ephesians		*2 Peter*	
1:10	194, 199, 208	General	101, 126, 135
1:19–20	347	3:5	208
2:5–6	347	3:7	138, 208
3:15	67, 194, 199, 208	3:10	208
4:10	135	3:13	138, 208
6:12	141		
		3 John	
Philippians		7	248
2:10	208		
3:20	67	*Jude*	
		General	67
Colossians			
1:16	208	*Revelation*	
1:20	194, 199	General	131, 193, 290, 333
1:26	194, 208		
3:1–4	347	3:12	67
		4	67
1 Thessalonians		5:3	194, 199, 208
4:16	67, 160	5:13	194, 199, 208
		6:9	160
2 Timothy		7:1	160
4:18	295	8:2	160
		10:6	67
Hebrews		11:15	160
General	101, 126	11:19	67
1:10	208	12:7	67
8:1	67	14:7	67, 208
8:5	188, 333	19:1	67
12:22	67	19:11–20:4	284
		19:11f	67
James		21:2–22	67
4:4	246		
5:12	208		

Texts From Qumran

1 QH		*1QSb*	
Col XI, 22	57	3:5	262
Col XXIII	57	4:25–26	262
Col XXVI	59, 219	5:21	262
35	219		
3:5	262	*4Q174*	
5:17	262	General	263
18:8	262	1:3	262
1QS		*4Q286*	
General	58, 331	12:2	262

4Q299		*4QDibHam*	
i.3	262	4:7–8	262
4Q301		*4Q Deut*	
5 i.2	262	32:43	100, 108
4Q379		*4QM*	
6 1–7	219	General	56
6 1	219		
		11QT	
4Q381		11:57	262
7	262		
76–77	262	*Genesis Apocryphon*	
		(1QapGenar)	
4Q382		2:4ff	262
55 2, 1–9	219	20:13	262
4Q427		*Songs of the Sabbath Sacrifice*	
7	262	General	58
1:13	262		
1:15	262	*War Scroll*	
		10:12	262
4Q448		12:7–15	262
General	262	14:9–10	262
		17:6–7	262
4Q460		17:7	262
5 1, 5	219	18:1	262
		18:11	262
4Q504			
General	263	*4Q Wisdom*	
		416	58
4Q521		418	58
General	262, 263	298	58
		521	58

PSEUDEPIGRAPHA, APOCRYPHA

Apocalypse of Abraham		*Apocalypse of Moses*	
General	52, 56	General	116, 130
2 Apocalypse of Baruch		*Apocalypse of Sedrach*	
4:5–6	188	General	120, 186
59:4	188		
		Apocalypse of the Seven Heavens	
Apocalypse of Elijah		General	190
General	52		
		Apocalypse of Zepheniah	
Apocalypse of Ezra		General	52, 56
General	120		
		Apocryphon of Ezekiel	
Apocalypse of Ezra (Greek)		General	52
General	186	Fragment 2	219
1:7	190		

INDEX OF TEXTS

Ascension of Isaiah
General — 186

Assumption of Moses
4:2 — 259, 261
10 — 261
10:1–10 — 259

Baruch
General — 50
1:11 — 182

2 Baruch
General — 52, 260, 261, 265

3 Baruch
General — 52, 56, 130, 186
4:3–6 — 190
5:3 — 190
10:5 — 190

4 Baruch
General — 116

Bel and the Dragon
General — 50
1:5 — 182

Daniel (With Additions)
3:54 — 259
3:59 (OG and Th) — 100, 108, 110
3:80–81 — 182

1 Enoch
General — 8, 52, 53, 54, 55, 56, 57, 58, 59, 100, 116, 117, 119, 130, 186, 187, 209
1;2,4 — 185
2–4 — 185
2:1–2 — 185
4:36 — 112
8:4 — 118, 185
9:4 — 259
12:3 — 259
13:4 — 118
14–15 — 188
15–16 — 185
15:3 — 185
15:7–10 — 185
18:4 — 118
18:10 — 117, 118
22:5–6 — 118
25:3 — 259
25:5 — 259
25:7 — 259
27:3 — 259
39:3 — 185
60:1 — 118
63:4 — 259
71:5 — 118
81:3 — 259
84:2–3 — 185, 259
84:5 — 259
91:13 — 259
102:3 — 185
103:1 — 259

2 Enoch
General — 52, 53, 55, 129, 130, 186, 187
8–10 — 190

Epistle of Jeremiah
General — 50
6:54 — 182

1 Esdras
General — 50, 106
4:34 — 182
4:36 — 182, 268
4:46 — 276
4:58 — 276
6:13 — 182

2 Esdras
General — 109
19:6 — 100, 109, 112

Esther (Additions)
General — 50
4:17 — 182
13:9 — 259
13:15 — 259
14:3 — 259
14:12 — 259

4 Ezra
General — 52, 260, 261, 265, 286

Joseph and Aseneth
General — 53, 119, 186
12:8–15 — 219
12:14–15 — 219
14:3 — 54
15:4 — 54

15:7	54	15:1–5	270
17:8–9	54	15:3–5	183
19:5	54	15:3	269
		15:3–4	285
Jubilees		15:4	111, 182, 269,
General	53, 119, 186, 220		270
1:25	219	15:22	269, 285
1:28	219, 259	15:23	100, 110, 111,
19:19	219		112, 140
50:19 (Eth.)	259		
		3 Maccabees	
Judith		General	50, 51, 111, 167,
General	50, 270, 274		219, 286
2:4	183	2:2	100, 110, 111,
2:7–9	183		112, 140, 268,
5:8	111, 184		285
6:2	183	2:14–15	182, 183
6:3	184	2:15	43, 100
6:4	184	2:21	219
6:19	111, 184	5:7	219
7:28	111, 182	6:2–4	223
9:2	259	6:3	219
9:12	100, 110, 111,	6:8	219
	112, 138, 182,	6:18	111
	184, 269	6:28	111
11:1	184	7:6	111, 219
11:7	111, 182, 184		
11:17	111, 184	*4 Maccabees*	
11:21	184	General	50, 51, 168, 183
11:23	184	2:23	260
13:18	100, 110, 111,		
	112, 138, 182,	*Martyrdom and Ascension of Isaiah*	
	184	6–11	55
Ladder of Jacob		*Odes*	
General	52	General	50
		12:15	100, 110
Life of Adam and Eve			
General	116	*Prayer of Manasseh*	
		General	50
1 Maccabees		1	112
General	18, 27, 30, 31,	9	112
	48, 50, 106, 298	15	112
2:27	182		
2:37	200	*Prayer of Azarias*	
4:24	30	General	50
4:40	182		
		Prayer of Manasses	
2 Maccabees		General	50
General	30, 31, 50, 51,	1:2	182
	111, 183	12	111
2:3–4	112	15	100, 110
7:28	182		

Psalms of Solomon

General	50, 260, 265
2:9	111, 182
2:29–32	259
2:29–30	182
2:29	111
2:30	100, 110, 111, 112, 140, 268, 270
2:33	111
5:18	259
8:7	111, 182
17	260, 261
17:1	259
17:3	260
17:18	111, 182
17:30–31	325
17:31	316
17:32	259
17:34	259
17:46	259

Sibylline Oracles

General	51, 116, 286
3–5	52, 53
3	261
3:1–2	260
3:11	260
3:19	260
3:46–50	260
3:48	260
3:56	260
3:499	260
3:560	260
3:617	260
3:717	2
3:772–776	325
3:780	260
3:808	260
11	52

Sirach

General	50, 220
1:3	182
16:18	43, 182
17:32	182, 183
23:1	219
23:4	219
24	182
43	178, 182
50:15	259
51:1ff	259
51:10	219

Susanna

General	50

Testament of Abraham

General	116, 120, 121, 124, 127, 131, 132, 142, 186, 340
4:4	121
4:5	54, 121
6:6	219
7–10	123
7:3	54, 122
7:4	54, 121, 122
7:5	54, 122
7:8	122
7:13	121
7:14	121
7:16	121
8:1	54, 121, 122
8:5	122
9:8	122
10:1	122
10:11–12	54
10:11	122
10:12	122
10:15	122
11:1	122
11:3	120
14:6	121
14:13	54
15:11–12	123
15:11	54, 121, 123
20:12	121, 123, 219

Testament of Asher

2:10	118
7:5	118

Testament of Benjamin

General	118
9:1	259
10:7	118, 119

Testament of Isaac

5:3	190

Testament of Issachar

5:13	118

Testament of Judah

21:3	118

Testament of Job

General	119, 186, 187, 219
33:3	219
33:9	219
36:3	187
38:2	187
38:5	187
39:11–12	259
40:2	219

Testament of Levi

General	56, 116, 118, 119, 130
2:9	119
3:1–3	141
3:1	119
13:5	119

Testament of the Twelve Patriarchs

General	53, 54, 100, 118, 119

Gospel of Thomas

General	3, 69
5–6	237

Tobit

1:18	112, 268
5:17	110
7:12	44, 50
7:17	110, 269
8:5	100, 110, 111
10:13	110
13:4	219
13:6	259
13:7	259, 276
13:10	259
13:11	259
13:13	110, 112, 268, 285
13:15	259
13:17	112, 268

Wisdom

General	50, 106, 112, 113, 120, 123, 124, 127, 131, 132, 168, 183, 186, 220, 340
2:16	219
6:4	260
6:20	260
10:10	260
9:10	100, 110, 113
9:13	114
9:15	113
9:16	100, 110, 113, 182
9:17	114
11:10	219
13:1–2	114
13:2	113, 114
14:3	219
16:20	113, 114
18:15–16	114, 183
18:15	100, 110, 113
18:16	182
18:19	114

Other Jewish, Christian and Classical Writings

CLEMENT

General	101

DIDACHE

General	154
8:2	151, 154
16:6–8	158

EUSEBIUS

HE 3:19:1–3:20:7	337

GREEK MAGICAL PAPYRI

XV, 14–16	159

IRENAEUS

General	101

JOSEPHUS

General	31, 61, 128, 261
Ant. 7.380	219

JUSTIN

1 Apol. 11	338

ORIGEN

On Matthew	133, 148–149

PHILO

General	31, 51, 219, 261
On Creation	60, 61
On Cherubim	60
Cher.	220
Mut.	220

INDEX OF TEXTS

Opt.	220	*m. Sanh*	
Special Laws	61, 220	11:1	26
Who is the Heir?	60	7:10	62

PHILOSTRATUS
Apollonius 7:3   328

b. Sanh
General   62
90a   26
42a   224
4:5   63

STATIUS
Silvae
3.4.20   328
4.2.14–15   328

b. Šebu
General   20, 63
4:13   189

VIRGIL
Aeneid 1.282   328

Sifre
Deut 48   222, 224, 225

m. 'Abot		*m. Soṭa*	
1:3	22	7:6	20
3:14	222	9:15	62, 222, 224
4:4	22		
4:11	22	*b. Soṭa*	
5:20	62	49b	222
6	63		

b. Ber
33b   22

m. Ta'an
4:3   63, 189

m. Ber		*m. Tamid*	
2:2	22, 62, 266, 267	7:2	20
2:5	62, 266, 267	3:8	20
5:1	222		
9:5	20, 26	*Tosefta Yoma*	
		ii, 9	189

b. Hag		*m. Yad*	
5b	22	4:3	63
16A	22		

m. Kil		*m. Yoma*	
9:8	62	6:2	20
		viii, 9	62, 189

Mekilta
Beshalla 4   222
Exod 12:2   224

Tg. Ezekiel
7:7   264

m. Ned		*Tg. Isaiah*	
General	62	24:23	264
ii, 4	189	26:19	265
		31:4	264
b. Pes		40:9	264
112a	222		

m. Roš Haš
3:8   62

Tg. Jeremiah
17:12   64

Tg. Micah
4:7 264
6:6 64

Tg. Neofiti
General 221
Numbers 20:21 221

Tg. Onqelos
General 221
Exod 15:18 264

Tg. Pseudo-Jonathan
General 221

Tg. 2 Samuel
22:13 64

Tg. Zephaniah
4:9 264

INDEX OF MODERN AUTHORS

Aalen, S. 85, 254, 281, 282
Abbott, E. 70
Adams, E. 168
Alexander, P. 25, 62
Albertz, R. 271
Albright, W. F
  with C. S. Mann 13, 14, 304, 305, 307, 308
Alfrink, B. 40
Allen, W. C. 127, 301, 304, 307
Allison, D. C. 1, 83, 120, 122, 212, 213, 214, 231, 246
  with W. D. Davies 5, 13, 104, 127, 128, 133, 141, 143, 145, 151, 152, 153, 154, 157, 158, 195, 204, 211, 212, 213, 214, 215, 237, 241, 243, 244, 246, 288, 289, 295, 299, 306, 308, 309, 314, 315, 316, 319, 325, 344
Alt, A. 255
Anderson, J. C. 210, 334, 336
Avishur, Y. 166, 179

Balch, D. L. 79
Balz, H. R.
  with Schneider, G. 235, 311
Barr, J. 228
Bartelmas, R. 40
Barth, C. F. 175
Barton, S. 332
Bauckham, R. 21, 52, 55, 56, 83, 190, 230, 319, 321, 322, 327, 338
  with T. Hart 347
Bauer, D. R.
  with M. A. Powell 78, 79
Beale, G. 286
Beare, F. W. 5, 13, 104, 127, 152, 153, 157, 282, 300
Beasley-Murray, G. R. 255, 256, 258
Beaton, R. 212
Beavis, M. A. 325
Bengel, J. A. 133, 306, 312, 313, 326, 327
Berger, P. L. 335
  with T. Luckman 334
Berlin, A. 166
Betz, H. D. 134, 142, 151, 152, 153, 159, 235, 237, 243, 244, 280

Bianchi, U. 332
Bietenhard, H. 206
Billerbeck P.
  with H. L. Strack 16, 17, 19, 24, 26, 266
Bingham, J. 235
Black, M. 116, 117
Bonnard, P. 306
Bornkamm, G. 91, 147, 148
Bousset, W. 227
Bright, J. 255, 256, 257
Brooks, O.S. 204, 215
Brooks, S. H. 80
Brown, R. 254, 255, 282
Brown, S. 80
Brueggemann, W. 326
Bruner, F. D. 213, 243
Buber, M. 255
Burnett, F. W. 83, 86
Bultmann, R. 227
Buth, R.
  with T. Pope 282
Butler, B. C. 301

Caird, G. B. 227
Camponovo 259, 261
Carson, D. A. 33, 128, 306, 308
Carter, W. 85, 213, 243, 283, 284, 294, 316, 318, 319, 320, 322, 325, 328, 329, 330, 344
Casey, M. 23, 24
Charette, B. 246
Charles, R. H. 29
Charlesworth, J. H. 331, 332
Chen, D. G. 218, 224, 329
Childs, B. 254
Chilton, B. 27, 219, 220, 221, 223, 264, 265
Clark, K. 5, 34
Clark, W. M. 180
Cohen, S. 25, 47
Collins, A. Y. 55, 102, 129, 286, 288, 290
Collins, J. J. 8, 41, 45, 54, 56, 57, 58, 60, 91, 92, 93, 103, 113, 116, 117, 119, 129, 259, 260, 261, 264, 265, 271, 277, 286, 289
  with R. Kugler 57

INDEX OF MODERN AUTHORS

Colson, F. H.
  with G. H. Whitaker 60
Cope, O. L. 91
Cremer, H. 33, 157, 289, 297, 298, 301, 312, 313

Dacy, M. 20, 26
Dalman, G. 7, 14, 16, 17, 18, 19, 23, 24, 25, 27, 29, 30, 31, 32, 33, 34, 36, 85, 131, 219, 221, 222, 224, 254, 266, 267, 281, 282, 283, 284, 287, 298, 300, 339
D'Angelo, M. R. 223, 225, 228, 231
Davies, M. 235
Davies, W. D. 79, 214, 326
  with D. C. Allison 5, 13, 104, 127, 128, 133, 141, 143, 145, 151, 152, 153, 154, 157, 158, 195, 204, 211, 212, 213, 214, 215, 237, 241, 243, 244, 246, 288, 289, 295, 299, 306, 308, 309, 314, 315, 316, 319, 325, 344
Davila, J. 54, 57, 59, 188
Dean, M. E.
  with B. B. Scott 74, 150
de Boer, M. C. 91, 187
de Jonge, M. 116, 119
DeMoor, J. C. 26
Di Lella, A. A. 29, 49
DiVito, R. A. 180
Derrett, J. D. M. 147
Donaldson, T. 343
Duling, D. C. 258
Dunn, J. D. G. 261, 279, 306, 325

Ego, B. 189
Eichrodt, W. 255, 256
Ellis, P. F. 215
Elmore, W. E. 85
Engels, M. P. 283
Esler, P. 184, 285, 328
Evans, C. 17, 60, 26, 286, 287, 288, 330
Everett, W. J. 283

Ferguson, E. 338
Filson, F. V. 90, 151, 207
Fitzmyer, J. 110
Flint, P. W. 110, 268
  with VanderKam, J. 57, 58
Ford, D. 286
Foster, R. 5, 6, 34, 35, 74, 81, 236, 238, 248, 250, 309, 327, 348

France, R. T. 82, 88, 89, 144, 151, 207, 234, 235, 244, 280, 306, 325, 344
Friedlander, G. 229, 266
Frey, J. 58, 331

Gaechter, P. 246, 306
Garland, D. 5, 33, 34, 79, 312
Gerhardsson, B. 72, 243, 245
Gevitz, S. 164
Glover, W. 282
Gnilka, J. 311, 312
Goldingay, J. 46, 270, 271, 276, 277
Gooder, P. 129
Goodrich, A. T. S. 113
Goshen-Gottstein, A. 220, 221, 223, 224, 228, 229
Goulder, M. D. 197, 212, 213, 307
Gray, J. 255, 257
Green, D. 20, 22, 151
Grimm, W. 288
Grossfield, B. 26
Guelich, R. 5, 34, 139, 151, 152, 153, 243, 246, 297
Gundry, R. H. 5, 6, 33, 79, 88, 138, 151, 152, 157, 158, 159, 197, 202, 211, 212, 235, 237, 289, 294, 299, 300, 302, 307, 329

Hagner, D. 13, 80, 81, 82, 84, 91, 92, 94, 128, 157, 197, 201, 215, 235, 242, 243, 280, 288, 289, 299, 306
Hall, R. G. 186
Hammerton-Kelly, R. 218
Hanson, P. D. 91, 92, 180
Hare, D. R. E. 79
Hart, T.
  with R. Bauckham 347
Harrisville, R. 253
Hartmann, B. 165
Heil, J. P. 156
Held, H. J. 83
Hellholm, D. 54, 91
Hengel, M. 258
Henry, M. 33
Henze, M. 272
Herscher, U. D. 337
Hiers, R. H. 147
Hill, D. 1, 127, 306
Himmelfarb, M. 54, 56, 103, 129
Hoffmann, P.
  with J. Robinson
  and J. Kloppenborg 70

Hogan, M. 247
Honeyman, A. M. 179
Horsley, G. H. R. 32, 328
Houtman, C. 39, 44, 163, 164, 165, 167, 171, 179, 180
Humphries-Brooks, S. 244

Innes, D. K. 45
Isasi-Diaz, A. M. 283

Jacobs, L. 19, 21, 32, 37, 267
James, M. R. 121
Jeremias, J. 218, 219, 220, 223, 227, 228, 229, 25, 266, 300, 302
Johnston, P. S. 175
Joüon, P. 43, 103, 107

Katz, P. 43, 45, 100, 107, 108, 109, 110, 111, 112, 115, 138, 139, 340
Keel, O. 44, 175, 176, 177, 178
Keener, C. S. 151
Kim, J.-K. 326
Kingsbury, J. D. 82, 84, 231, 232, 280, 281, 294, 305, 308
Kittel, G. 227
Kline, M. 46
Kloppenborg, J.
  with J. Robinson
  and P. Hoffmann 70
Knibb, M. A. 55, 116
Koch, K. 276
Knowles, M. 212
Kolarcik, M. 113
Kosovsky, C. Y. 62, 189
Krašovec, J. 166, 167
Kugler, R. 119
  with J. J. Collins 57
Kretzer, A. 305, 307, 308
Kruger, A. 176
Kuhn, H. B. 59, 267
Kvalbein, H. 282

Ladd, G. E. 267, 301
Lattke, M. 24, 255, 259, 261
Lebram, J. C. H. 271
Lenglet, A. 271
Lenske, R. C. H. 294
Leske, A. 212
Levey, S. H. 337
Levine, E. 42
Lincoln, A. T. 135
Lohmeyer, E. 134, 135, 138, 235
Lohr, C. H. 197, 210

Lucas, E. C. 209
Luckman, T.
  with P. L. Berger 333
Luz, U. 13, 86, 127, 138, 213, 215, 232, 234, 235, 243, 246, 282, 301

Malina, B. J. 214, 215
Maloney, E. C. 104, 105
Manhoff, H. A. 30, 308
Mann, C.S.
  with W. F. Albright 13, 14, 304, 305, 307, 308
Manson, T. W. 13, 229
Marcus, J. 5, 33, 85, 147, 254, 312
Marmorstein, A. 19, 22
Massaux, E. 1
Mauser, U. W. 190, 206, 209, 237, 298, 312, 344
Mawhinney, A. 228
Mayer, G. 60
Mays, J. L. 257
McDonough, S. M. 20, 26
McKnight, S. 128, 229
McLay, R.T. 291
McNamara, M 21, 221, 224
McNeile, A. H. 5, 33, 35, 301, 306
Meadowcroft, T. J. 29, 49, 271, 272, 275, 276
Meier, J. 24, 89, 91, 151, 205, 231, 282
Melamed, E. Z 165, 166
Mendels, D. 325
Metzger, B. M. 6
Michaels, J. R. 301, 322
Michil, O. 206, 215
Milik, J. T. 116, 117
Moltmann, J. 41
Montgomery, J. 47
Moore, G. F. 24, 220, 221, 223, 225, 229, 235, 240, 250
Morris, L. 5, 33, 133, 134, 141, 151, 235, 308
Mowery, R. 35, 71, 85, 86, 145, 146, 198, 234, 250, 307, 309
Mussies, G. 107

Neusner, J. 25, 62, 267
Newman, Lr., B. 281
Newport, K. G. C. 146
Newsome, C. 58, 59
Neyrey, J. H. 248
Nickelsburg, G. W. E 116, 117, 180, 186

INDEX OF MODERN AUTHORS

Niederwimmer, K. 154
Nolland, J. 13, 134, 205, 246

Oden, R. A. 180
Oesterly, W. 30
O'Neill, J. C. 254, 282
Orlinsky, H. M 21
Ott, W. 282
Overman J. A. 79, 335, 336

Pamment, M. 85, 304, 307
Pao, D. W. 347
Parry, D. W 19
Patrick, D. 255, 258
Patte, D. 305, 308
Pennington, J. T. 169
Perrin, N. 36, 85, 282
Pietersma, A. 20
Plummer, A. 13, 133, 151, 152, 235, 297, 300
Pope, T.
  with R. Buth 282
Porter, S. E. 105, 147
Powell, M. A.
  with D. R. Bauer 78, 79

Reddish, M. G. 45
Reese, J. M. 113
Riches, J. 78, 83, 93, 325, 335, 336, 343
  with D. C. Sim 318
Ridderbos, H. 282
Ringgren, H. 57, 217
Rengstorf, K. H. 60, 61
Robinson, J.
  with P. Hoffmann
  and J. Kloppenborg 70
Rohrbaugh, R. 248
Rothfuchs, W. 88
Rowe, R. D. 256, 257, 259, 261
Rowland, C 54, 91
Rudinger, P. 91
Russell, L. M. 283
Ryken, L. 32

Sabourin, L. 91
Sand, A. 81
Saldarini, A. 25, 79, 335
Sanders, E. P. 25, 93, 120
Sanders, J. A. 52
Sandmel, S. 25
Saucy, M. 282, 300, 305
Segal, A. F. 54
Schaberg, J. 289

Schlatter, A. 13, 127
Schlosser, J. 259
Schmidt, F. 121
Schmidt, K. F. 261
Schwimmer, A. M. 261
Schnackenburg, R. 6, 13, 82, 152, 153, 203, 207, 214, 215, 255, 256, 257, 260, 261, 284
Schneider, G. 5, 6, 34, 69, 194, 198, 199, 202, 203, 204, 205, 291, 298, 312
  with Balz, H. R. 235, 311
Schoemaker, W. R. 159
Schoonhoven C. R. 157
Schrenk, G. 220, 225, 235, 240
Schweitzer, E. 5, 32, 195, 235, 300
Schwemer, A. M. 262
Scott, B. B.
  with M. E. Dean 74, 150
Senior, D. 82, 212
Sim, D. C. 91, 93, 94, 158, 329, 333
Simon, U. 39, 47
  with J. Riches 318
Skehan, P. W. 20
Smelik, W. F. 26
Smith, M. 189
Sparks, H. F. D. 86, 87, 234, 249
Stadelman, L. I. J. 39, 40, 44, 102, 170, 171, 172, 175
Stanton, G. 77, 79, 80, 88, 90, 151, 212, 214, 347
Stegeman, H. 284
Steiner, G. 6
Stemberger, G. 16, 25, 26, 62, 266
Stendahl, K. 88, 212, 344
Stinespring, W. F. 120
Strack, H. L.
  with P. Billerbeck 16, 17, 19, 24, 26, 266
Stone, M. E. 120
Suggs, J. 83
Suter, D. W. 116
Swartley, W. M. 324
Syreeni, K. 6, 202, 336

Tabor, J. D. 54
Talmon, S. 57
Tawaga, K. 80
Thomas, J. C. 85, 304, 307, 309
Thompson, G. H. P. 153
Thompson, M. M. 218, 219, 220, 222, 223, 227, 228, 251
Thompson, W. G. 202

Torm, D. F.   103, 106, 107, 108, 109, 110, 115, 340
Torrance, T. F.   227
Towner, W. S.   273, 274
Traub, J.   102, 103
Trilling, W.   215, 300
Turner, N.   104, 132
Tsumura, D. T.   39, 42, 45, 166, 174, 176

Urbach, E.   19, 22, 26, 29, 30, 36, 37, 266

VanderKam, J.   116
  with P. Flint   57, 58
VanGemeren, W.   218, 228
van Kooten, G. H.   206
Vermes, G.   63, 223, 228, 264, 300
Verseput, D. J.   232, 325
Viviano, B. T.   80, 261, 262
von Rad, G.   42, 44, 45, 102, 103, 255, 258
Vos, G.   300, 312

Wainwright, E.   284
Walker, W. O.   308
Wallace, D.   294, 295
Waltke, B. K.
  with M. O'Connor   40
Waters, K. L.   91
Wenham, G.   287
Wevers, J. W.   20
Whitaker, G. H.
  with F. H. Colson   60
Whitehead, A. N.   296
Willis, W.   85, 338
Wilson, R. W.   273, 292
Winston, D.   113
Wojcik, J.   314
Wolf, M.   331, 332
Wouters, A.   87, 234
Wright, III, B. G.   100
Wright, J. E.   40, 42, 43, 44, 59, 103, 171, 172, 173, 174, 179, 190
Wright, N. T.   292, 332

Zahn, T.   211, 295
Zeitland, S.   31